ACCESS
PARIS

S0-AGZ-191

Paris

Rue Victor-Hugo

Blvd. Bessieres

Levallois-Perret

Ave. de Clichy

Rue de Villiers

Blvd. du Fort-Vaux

Rue Guy-Moquet

Blvd. Victor-Hugo

American Hospital

British Hospital

Blvd. de Reims

Cimetièr Montm

17e

Blvd. Bineau

Rue de Clichy

Neuilly-sur-Seine

Blvd. Gouvion-St-Cyr

Ave. de Villiers

Blvd. Malesherbes

Blvd. des Batignolles

Ave. Charles-de-Gaulle

Blvd. Pereire

Ave. Niel

Ave. de Wagram

Parc de Monceau

Gare St-Lazare

Jardin d'Acclimatation

Ave. des Ternes

Blvd. de Courcelles

Rue de Monceau

Rue de Courcelles

Rue St-Lazare

Ave. de la Grande-Armée

Ave. Hoche

Rue de Miromesnill

Blvd. Haussmann

L'Arc de Triomphe

8e

Opér Garni

Ave. de Malakoff

Ave. Foch

Ave. de Friedland

Rue du Faubourg-St-Honoré

Alleé de Longchamp

Bois de Boulogne

Ave. Victor-Hugo

Ave. d'Iéna

Ave. des Champs-Elysées

Blvd. de la Mad

Ave. de la Faisanderie

Rue de la Pompe

Rue Lauriston

Ave. Marceau

Ave. George-V

Rue St-Honoré

Royal Pavilion

Rue Kléber

Rue Boissière

Ave. Montaigne

Ave. F.-D.-Roosevelt

Rue de Rivoli

Blvd. Périphérique

Blvd. Lannes

Rue de Longchamps

Place de la Concorde

Jardin des Tuileries

Ave. Henri-Martin

Ave. G. Mandel

Ave. Raphaël

Palais de Chaillot

Ave. de New-York

Quai d'Orsay

Ave. W. Churchill

Quai des Tuileries

Ave. P.-Doumer

Rue de l'Université

Qu Vol

16e

Jardin du Ranelagh

Ave. de la Bourdonnais

Blvd. St-Germain

Musée d'Orsay

Ave. du Pres.-Kennedy

Tour Eiffel

Ave. Bosquet

Rue de Boulainvilliers

Ave. de Suffren

Parc du Champ-de-Mars

Ave. de la Motte-Picquet

Hôtel des Invalides

Ave. des Saints-Pères

Auteuil

Rue de Sèvres

Musée Rodin

6

Ave. Mozart

Ave. de Lowendal

Ave. de Tourville

Ave. Suchet

Rue St-Charles

Blvd. de Grenelle

Blvd. Garibaldi

7e

Blvd. des Invalides

Ave. de Versailles

Rue Linois

Ave. Émile-Zola

Rue de Rennes

Parc des Princes

Blvd. Exelmans

Rue Balard

Rue de la Convention

Rue du Commerce

Blvd. Montparnasse

Blvd. Raspail

Rue Michel-Ange

Quai André-Citroën

Blvd. du Gen. M Valin

Parc André Citroën

Ave. Félix-Fauré

Rue Lecourbe

15e

Blvd. Pasteur

Rue de Vaugirard

Rue de l'Arrivée

Rue du Départ

Blvd. Edgar Quinet

Gare Montparnasse

Cimetière du Montparnass

Blvd. Victor

Rue de Vaugirard

Rue de Vouillé

Parc Georges Brassens

Rue d'Alésia

Rue du Château

Ave. du Maine

Place Den Roche

Parc Suzanne Lenglen

Blvd. Lefebvre

Rue Brancion

14e

Ave. du Général-Leclei

Blvd. Gatillieri

Blvd. Périphérique

Blvd. Brune

Un

Ave. Victor-Cresson

Rue Jean-Bleuzen

Rue Pierre-Brossolette

Ave. Aristide-Briand

Blvd. Je

5e Arrondissement numbers

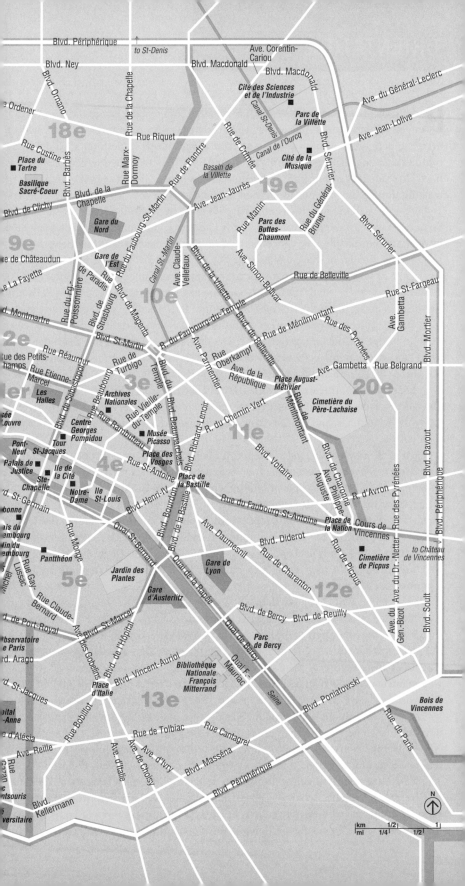

Paris is the greatest temple ever built to material joys and the lust of the eyes," wrote novelist Henry James. Indeed, the richness and variety of France's capital elevates even the necessities of life to works of art. Parisians seem to perform such everyday routines as eating and dressing with vitality and flair. The streets themselves are museums lined with splendid architecture and historic monuments, making even the simple act of walking through the city one of life's greatest pleasures.

Paris is located in the north-central part of France in the **Ile-de-France** region, in the **Seine** river valley. Covering only 105 square kilometers (40 square miles) and populated by over 2 million people, it is France's largest city and the densest of all European capitals. It is roughly circular in shape and bounded by the **Boulevard Périphérique**, a ring road on the site of mid–19th-century fortifications that once defined the city limits.

Cutting across the whole map is a 7-mile stretch of the Seine that separates Paris into two distinct areas, the northern **Rive Droite (Right Bank)** and the southern **Rive Gauche (Left Bank)**. The Seine unites rather than divides the city; Paris is linked by no fewer than 26 bridges in the city center alone. The quays are lined with fine apartment and town houses, *bouquinistes* (booksellers) and street artists, such world-class museums as the **Musée du Louvre** and the **Musée d'Orsay**, and dazzling monuments, including the **Tour Eiffel** and the **Cathédrale de Notre-Dame**. The Seine is alive with commercial barges and *bateaux mouches* (small passenger steamers) taking sightseers up- and downriver to enjoy the panoramas, and the riverbanks are animated with people promenading along their course.

Each of the city's 20 *arrondissements* (quarters) boasts its own distinct character, so Paris feels less like a monstrous metropolis and more like a score of small towns. Travel from the villagelike atmosphere of **Montmartre**, the **Latin Quarter**, or the **Marais** to the grandeur of the **Avenue des Champs-Elysées** and the **Hôtel des Invalides**; from the haute couture shopping areas along the **Rue du Faubourg-St-Honoré** and the **Boulevard St-Germain** to the trendy regions around the **Bastille** and **Les Halles**; and to the two islands that form the physical and spiritual heart of the city, the **Ile de la Cité** and the **Ile St-Louis**. In Paris, the past is ever present, and a stroll through the city of today is also a journey back in time.

Paris is an ancient city, more than 2,000 years old. Begun as a village named Lutetia and inhabited by a tribe called the Parisii, it was subsequently settled by the Romans and then became the capital city of the kingdom of the Franks. Under Charlemagne, the capital of France was moved to Aix-la-Chapelle, but Paris regained its capital status in 987 under Hughues Capet, the first of the Capetian line of kings. During the Middle Ages, the city was an intellectual and religious center, but it lapsed into chaos during the Hundred Years' War with England (1337-1453), a period that also saw outbreaks of the bubonic plague.

The city again flourished during the Renaissance and saw significant expansion and development under the Bourbon kings of the 17th and 18th centuries. Although Louis XIV moved the court to **Versailles** in the late 17th century, Paris enjoyed great wealth and power during his reign, known as *Le Grand Siècle* (the Great Century). Under Louis XV, Paris emerged as a center for culture and ideas, the arts flourished, and such intellectuals as Voltaire, Rousseau, Diderot, and Montesquieu were renowned throughout Europe. At the end of the 18th century, however, the extravagances of Louis XVI and his court led to the French Revolution and the bloodbath known as the Reign of Terror.

The instability following the revolution allowed General Napoléon Bonaparte to seize control of the French government, and by 1804 he had proclaimed himself emperor of France and set about making Paris the most magnificent city in the world. After Napoléon's defeat at Waterloo and subsequent exile, the Bourbon monarchy took one last gasp; then Napoléon's nephew assumed power, declaring himself Napoléon III in 1851. Like his uncle, he undertook a vast urbanization program. Unfortunately, however, he also embroiled the country in a succession of wars, culminating in the 1870 Franco-Prussian War, during which Paris suffered under siege and famine. The insurrection that followed France's capitulation to Prussia in 1871 saw violent massacres in Paris.

By the end of the 19th century, Paris had recovered and was once again a driving force in Western culture. This optimistic period, known as the Belle Epoque (Beautiful Age), was captured in the work of the Impressionist painters. In the early part of this century, Paris became a mecca for intellectuals, artists, and philosophers, including Henri Matisse, Pablo Picasso, Georges Braque, Man Ray, Marcel Duchamp, James Joyce, Gertrude Stein, Ernest Hemingway, F. Scott Fitzgerald, Samuel Beckett, Simone de Beauvoir, and Jean-Paul Sartre. After being occupied by the Germans, the city emerged from World War II with relatively little damage to its buildings and monuments. The 1950s, 1960s, and 1970s saw the construction of numerous modern buildings in Paris; more recently, there were the *grands projets* of the late Socialist president François Mitterrand.

Paris continues to evolve, in the 21st century, as one of Europe's most modern cities, yet it is at the same time an ancient city, with reminders of its remarkable history evident at every turn. The artistic and cultural capital of a unified Europe, the Paris of today offers a wealth of beauty and experiences. Few visitors fail to succumb to the splendor of this city, made even more appealing by the Parisian's love of grace, beauty, and fine living.

All numbers in the Paris area are preceded by the code 01. (Numbers in the northwest of France are preceded by 02; in the northeast, 03; in the southeast and Corsica, 04; and in the southwest, 05.) To call Paris from the US, dial 011.33.1, then the 8-digit phone number. To call Paris from elsewhere in France, dial 01, then the 8-digit number.

Getting to Paris

Airports

Roissy–Charles-de-Gaulle Airport

Twenty kilometers (12 miles) north of Paris, **Roissy–Charles-de-Gaulle Airport** is the busier of Paris's two airfields. It consists of two separate terminals: **Roissy I** handles most foreign carriers, and **Roissy II** services Air France and a few foreign carriers. Both have tourist information and money-exchange facilities, and a shuttle bus connects the two terminals.

AIRPORT SERVICES

General Information 01.48.62.12.12

Airport Emergencies/Security................01.48.62.31.22

Business Service Center 01.48.62.22.90

Currency Exchange 01.48.64.37.15

Customs 01.48.62.35.35

Immigration 01.48.62.31.22

Flight Information.................................01.48.62.22.80

Recorded Information 08.36.68.15.15

Lost and Found

Roissy I 01.48.62.13.34

Roissy II 01.48.64.25.94

Medical Emergencies

Roissy I 01.48.62.28.00

Roissy II 01.48.62.53.32

Parking 01.48.62.63.63

Traveler's Aid (for people with disabilities).....................
....01.48.16.45.24

AIRLINES

Air France 08.20.82.08.20, 800/237.2747

Air Tahiti 01.56.81.13.30, 877/824.4846

American...................08.10.87.28.72, 800/433.7300

British Airways 08.25.82.54.00, 800/AIRWAYS

Continental 01.42.99.09.09, 800/231.0856

How To Read This Guide

ACCESS® PARIS is arranged so you can see at a glance where you are and what is around you. The numbers next to the entries in the following chapters correspond to the numbers on the maps.

The text is color-coded according to the kind of place described:

Restaurants/Clubs: Red

Hotels: Purple | Shops: Orange

📍 **Parks/Outdoors: Green** | Sights/Culture: Blue

RATING THE RESTAURANTS AND HOTELS

The restaurant star ratings take into account the quality, service, atmosphere, and uniqueness of the restaurant. An expensive restaurant doesn't necessarily ensure an enjoyable evening; a small, relatively unknown spot could have good food, professional service, and a lovely atmosphere. Therefore, on a purely subjective basis, stars are used to judge the overall dining value (see the star ratings at right). Keep in mind that chefs and owners often change, which sometimes drastically affects the quality of a restaurant. The ratings in this guidebook are based on information available at press time.

The price ratings, as categorized at right, apply to restaurants and hotels. These figures describe general price-range relationships among other restaurants and hotels in the area. The restaurant price ratings are based on the average cost of a three-course meal for one person, excluding tax and tip. Hotel price ratings reflect the base price of a standard room for two people for one night during the peak season.

RESTAURANTS

★	Good
★★	Very Good
★★★	Excellent
★★★★	An Extraordinary Experience
$	The Price Is Right (less than $25)
$$	Reasonable ($25–$70)
$$$	Expensive ($70–$120)
$$$$	Big Bucks ($120 and up)

HOTELS

$	The Price Is Right (less than $75)
$$	Reasonable ($75–$150)
$$$	Expensive ($150–$300)
$$$$	Big Bucks ($300 and up)

At press time, the exchange rate was about 1.10 Euros to $1 US.

MAP KEY

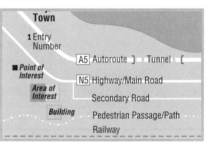

Town

1 Entry Number

■ Point of Interest

Area of Interest

Building

A5 Autoroute] Tunnel [

N5 Highway/Main Road

Secondary Road

Pedestrian Passage/Path

Railway

Delta	08.00.35.40.80, 800/221.1212
Lufthansa	08.02.02.00.30, 800/645.3880
Northwest	01.44.56.18.18, 800/447.4747
United	08.01.72.72.72, 800/241.6522
US Airways	08.01.63.22.22, 800/428.4322

Getting to and from Roissy–Charles-de-Gaulle Airport

Barring any major traffic snarls, the trip to **Roissy–Charles-de-Gaulle Airport** from the center of Paris by airport minibus, bus, car, or taxi should take about 45 minutes. The suburban **RER** (**Réseau Express Régional**) trains also provide 45-minute service, except during peak commuting hours, when there may be significant delays. To play it safe, allow twice that time to get to the airport.

BY AIRPORT MINIBUS

Several minibus services provide daily transportation to and from the airports. The fare is lower for two or more people traveling together. The shuttle services don't charge for baggage (as do taxis), and unlike on other

buses, passengers are delivered to their door. Some leading services are **Airport Shuttle** (01.45.38.55.72; fax 01.34.45.81.33; www.airportshuttle.fr), **ParisShuttle** (01.43.90.91.91; fax 01.43.90.91.10; www.Parisshuttle.com), and **Paris Airports Service** (01.49.62.78.78; fax 01.49.62.78.79; www.parisairportservice.com).

BY BUS

An **Air France** bus (01.41.56.89.00) travels between the airport and **Place Charles-de-Gaulle** (the **Arc de Triomphe**) at Avenue Carnot and **Place de la Porte Maillot** opposite the **Méridien Etoile Hotel** (both stops on the métro line **Grande Arche de La Défense/Château de Vincennes**). Buses leave daily every 15 minutes between 5:45AM and 11PM. Another **Air France** bus runs between the airport and the **Gare Montparnasse** train station, with a stop at **Gare de Lyon**. Buses leave daily every 30 minutes between 7AM and 9:30PM. The **Roissybus** (01.48.04.18.24) is operated by **Régie Autonome des Transports Parisiens** (www.ratp.fr) (**RATP**), the public mass transit system, and runs between the airport and the **Place de l'Opéra** opposite the **American Express office** at 5 Rue Scribe.

Buses leave daily every 15 minutes between 5:45AM and 11PM.

BY CAR

From the airport, take **Autoroute A1** south to **Porte de la Chapelle** in the north of Paris, or **Highway N17** south straight to **Porte de la Villette** in the north of Paris. From Paris, take Autroute A1 north from Porte de la Chapelle or Highway N17 north from Porte de la Villette to the airport. Shuttle service is offered from the parking lots to the terminals daily every 8 minutes between 4:30AM and 1AM.

RENTAL CARS

The following rental car companies have counters at **Roissy–Charles-de-Gaulle Airport**; all are open Monday through Friday between 6AM and midnight.

Avis

    Roissy I ....01.48.62.34.34; www.avis.com

    Roissy II..................01.48.62.59.59, 800/331.1084

Europcar

    Roissy I..............01.48.62.33.33; www.europcar.com

    Roissy II..............01.48.62.56.47, 800/CAR.EUROPE

Hertz

    Roissy I ....01.48.64.29.00; www.hertz.com

    Roissy II.................01.48.62.58.58, 800/654.3001

BY LIMOUSINE

To arrive in (or depart from) Paris in expensive style, hire a chauffeur-driven private car, minibus, or stretch limousine. The trip from the airport into town (or vice versa) costs 100 to 140 euros for a private car and 170 to 180 euros for a limo (rates are slightly higher for night service). The following limousine companies offer round-the-clock service to the airport:

American Limousines (stretch limos) 01.39.35.09.99

Avis Chauffeurs 01.45.54.33.65, 800/331.1084

Biribin et Guarniéri 01.43.48.65.65

Martin Didier 01.45.54.71.07

Massey 01.43.80.51.89

Prestige Limousines 01.42.50.81.81

BY TAXI

There are a number of taxi stands at the airport (look for the signs), and there are usually plenty of cabs. A ride downtown will cost between 38 and 53 euros, depending on traffic and destination. There is a baggage charge of 1.50 euros per suitcase. Rates increase by 30% between 7PM and 6AM.

BY TRAIN

The **RER B** (08.36.68.77.14) train runs between **Roissy–Charles-de-Gaulle Airport** and the **Gare du Nord**, **Châtelet-Les Halles**, and **Luxembourg** stations. Trains leave daily about every 15 minutes between 5:30AM and midnight; the trip from the airport to Châtelet-Les Halles takes about 45 minutes.

Orly Airport

Orly Airport, located 14 kilometers (9 miles) south of Paris, has two terminals: **Orly Sud** (south) handles both trans atlantic and European flights, and **Orly Ouest** (west) handles mostly domestic flights. Both terminals have tourist information and money-exchange facilities, and there is frequent transportation service into the city. A complimentary shuttle bus connects both terminals.

AIRPORT SERVICES

General Information 01.49.75.15.15

Airport Emergencies/Security 01.49.75.43.04

Currency Exchange 01.49.75.89.25

Customs..01.48.75.09.10

Immigration/Border Police 01.49.75.43.04

Information 01.49.75.15.15

Lost and Found

    Orly Sud..01.49.75.34.10

    Orly Ouest 01.49.75.42.34

Medical Emergencies 01.49.75.45.12

Parking...01.49.75.56.50

Louvre Pyramid

Traveler's Aid (for people with disabilities) ....
....01.49.75.30.70

Getting to and from Orly Airport

GROUND TRANSPORTATION

Like **Roissy–Charles-de-Gaulle Airport,** Orly is about a 45-minute trip from the center of Paris by bus, car, taxi, or train. But allow double that time in case there are traffic tie-ups or other delays, which are common during weekday rush hours.

BY AIRPORT MINIBUS

See **Roissy–Charles-de-Gaulle Airport** above (page 6) for a list of companies that provide door-to-door minibus service. The rates are the same for both airports.

BY BUS

The **Air France** bus service (01.41.56.89.00) provides transportation between **Orly** and the **Air France** offices in **Montparnasse** (25 Blvd de Vaugirard, between Pl Raoul-Dautry and Blvd Pasteur) or the **Air France Terminal at Invalides** (Esplanade des Invalides, between Rue de l'Université and Quai d'Orsay). Departures are daily every 12 minutes between 5:50AM and 11PM. **RATP**'s **Orlybus** (01.40.02.32.94; recorded information, 08.92.68.41.14) travels between the airport and **Place Denfert-Rochereau.** Buses leave daily about every 15 minutes between 6AM and 11PM. The trip takes 30 minutes.

BY CAR

From the airport, take **Highway N7** north to **Porte d'Italie** in the south of Paris. From Porte d'Italie, take N7 south to **Orly.** The **P1** parking lot is closest to the **Orly Sud** terminal and the **P0** lot is closest to **Orly Ouest.** Free shuttle service operates daily every 7 minutes between 5AM and 12:15AM from the **P4** through **P7** parking lots, which are farther away from the terminals.

RENTAL CARS

The following rental car companies have counters at **Orly Airport**; they usually are open Monday through Friday between 6AM and midnight.

Avis

Orly Sud   01.49.75.45.09, 800/331.1084; www.avis.com

James Baldwin called Paris "the city where everyone loses his head, and his morals, lives through at least one *histoire d'amour* (love story), ceases quite to arrive anywhere on time, and thumbs his nose at the puritans—the city, in brief, where all become drunken on the fine old air of freedom."

An astonishing number—16,000—of cafés and restaurants are allowed to place tables on the sidewalk.

Orly Ouest 01.49.75.44.91
Budget
Orly Sud   01.49.75.76.00, 800/527.0700, www.budget.com
Orly Ouest 01.49.75.76.00
Europcar
Orly Sud   01.49.75.47.40, 800/CAR.EUROPE, www.europcar.com
Orly Ouest 01.49.75.47.47
Hertz
Orly Sud   01.49.75.84.84, 800/654.3001; www.hertz.com
Orly Ouest 01.49.75.84.84

BY LIMOUSINE

See **Roissy–Charles-de-Gaulle Airport** above (page 7) for a list of companies that offer chauffeur-driven private-car and stretch-limousine service to and from both airports. The trip from **Orly** into town (or vice versa) will cost 90 to 120 euros for a private car or 140 to 180 euros for a limo (rates are slightly higher for night service).

BY TAXI

There are a number of taxi stands at **Orly**; look for signs. A ride into Paris will cost between 15 and 23 euros. Rates increase by 30% between 7PM and 6AM.

BY TRAIN

The **RER Orly C Line** (01.40.02.32.94; recorded information 08.36.68.77.14) is linked to **Orly Airport** by shuttle bus; it connects with the **Gare d'Austerlitz, St-Michel/Notre-Dame,** and **Invalides** stations. Trains leave approximately every 15 minutes between 5:30AM and 11PM. The trip takes 50 minutes.

Orly is also connected to the **RER B Line,** the métro, and train stations by the **Orlyval** monorail service from **Antony** station; the combined monorail–train trip takes about 30 to 45 minutes. The monorail operates M-Sa 6AM-10:30PM, Su 7AM-11PM.

BUS STATION (LONG-DISTANCE)

Buses arriving from other European cities disembark at the **Gare Routière Internationale** (Ave Général-de-Gaulle) in the eastern suburb of **Bagnolet.** The métro connection to the city center is via the **Galliéni** station. For bus information, call **Eurolines** (08.36.69.52.52).

TRAIN STATION (LONG-DISTANCE)

In Paris, you can't simply jump into a taxi and cry *"A la gare!"* ("To the station!"). Paris has six train stations, each offering service to different regions of France and Europe: **Gare d'Austerlitz** (53 Quai d'Austerlitz, between Pont de Bercy and Pl Valhubert), for southwest France, Spain, and Portugal; **Gare de l'Est** (Pl du 11-Novembre 1918, at Rue du 8-Mai 1945) for eastern France, Luxembourg, Switzerland, southern Germany, Austria, and Hungary; **Gare de Lyon** (Cour Diderot, off Blvd Diderot) for south and southeastern France, Switzerland, Italy, and

Greece; **Gare Montparnasse** (17 Blvd de Vaugirard, between Pl Raoul-Dautry and Blvd Pasteur) for western France (including Versailles), Chartres, and Brittany; **Gare St-Lazare** (20 Rue de Rome, between Pl Gabriel-Péri and Rue de Vienne) for northwest France, Normandy, and Le Havre; and **Gare du Nord** (15 Rue de Dunkerque, between Rue du Faubourg-St-Denis and Pl de Roubaix) for northern France, Belgium, the Netherlands, Scandinavia, Poland, Russia, northern Germany, and Britain, including the **Eurostar** trains, which travel between London and Paris via the **Channel Tunnel** in 3 hours.

Two types of train serve each station: *grandes lignes*, for long-distance travel, and *banlieue lignes*, for riding to the suburbs. Before boarding either type of train, you must *composter* (punch) your ticket in one of the orange machines in the station; if you fail to do this, the conductor might charge you the price of another ticket.

When reserving a ticket, be sure to request either a *fumeur* or *non-fumeur* (smoking or nonsmoking) car. Reserved seats are available in both first and second class. First-class tickets are approximately 40% more expensive; the extra bucks buy you a slightly more comfortable seat, a less crowded car, and a fancier dining car.

Trains are operated by **Société Nationale de Chemin de Fer (SNCF)**. For reservations and information, call 08.92.35.35.35 for the **Eurostar**, 08.92.35.35.39 for the *grandes lignes*, and 01.53.90.20.20 for the *banlieue lignes*. The web site is: www.sncf.fr.

Getting Around Paris

The quickest and easiest ways of getting around Paris are by métro, taxi, and often your own two feet.

BICYCLES

Two wheels can be more fun—albeit more hazardous—than four. Bicycle lanes are now a permanent fixture along a number of major arteries in central Paris, and the *quais* (embankments) along the Seine in the center of the city are closed to automobile traffic on Sunday morning and afternoon. From March through October.

The **RATP** (01.53.46.43.77; www.ratp.fr) rents bikes at seven **Roue Libre** (Free Wheel) centers at **Châtelet** (Avenue Victoria, Métro: Châtelet), **Bois de Boulogne** (Pl de la Porte d'Auteuil, métro: Porte d'Auteuil), **Bois de Vincennes** (Esplanade Saint-Louis, métro: Château de Vincennes), **Bassin de la Villette** (Quai de la Loire, métros: Jaurès, Stalingrad), **155 Blvd Vincent Auriol** (métro: Nationale), **Denfert-Rochereau** (Pl Denfert-Rochereau, métro: Denfert-Rochereau); and at their main office at **Forum des Halles** (95 *bis* Rue Rambuteau, métro: Châtelet-Les Halles).

Energetic and adventurous visitors can also rent bicycles from **Paris Vélo** (2 Rue du Fer-à-Moulin, at Rue Geoffroy-St-Hilaire, 01.43.37.59.22), **La Maison du Vélo** (11 Rue Fénelon, between Rue d'Abbeville and Rue de Belzunce, 01.42.81.24.72), or **Paris à Velo C'est Sympa** (37 Blvd Bourdon, between Rue de la Cerisaie and Blvd Henri IV; 01.48.87.60.01).

Paris is surrounded with beautiful, flat countryside that's perfect for bicycling. If you're planning day trips outside Paris—to **Chantilly**, **Fontainebleau**, or **Versailles**, for example—it might be a good idea to wait until you get to your destination and rent a bike for the day at the local train station. The **RER** stations in **Noisiel-le-Luzard**, **Vincennes**, **St-Germain-en-Laye**, **Courcelle Vallée de Chevreuse**, and **Vallée de la Marne** all have bikes for rent.

For general cycling information, contact the **Fédération Française de Cyclotourisme** (8 Rue Jean-Marie-Jégo, between Rues de la Butte-aux-Cailles and Samson; 01.44.16.88.88; fax 01.44.16.88.98; info@ffct.org; www.ffct.org).

BOAT

The **Batobus**, operated by **Compagnie des Batobus** (01.44.11.33.99), is a boat service that runs up and down the Seine between mid-April and mid-October. The circuit covers six stops: **Port de la Bourdonnais** (near the **Tour Eiffel**), **Porte de Solférino** (near the **Musée d'Orsay**), **Quai Malaquais** (opposite the **Louvre**), **Quai de Montebello** (near **Notre-Dame**), **Quai du Louvre** (near the **Louvre**), **Quai de l'Hôtel-de-Ville** (near the **Hôtel de Ville**).

BUS

Riding the métro may be the quickest and easiest way to get around town, but buses are a far more pleasant means of transportation in Paris. The tourist office on the **Champs-Elysées** has selected more than a dozen get-acquainted bus routes for tourists, and it provides maps and trilingual (English, German, and Italian) commentary on the sights along the way. The **No. 24** bus, for example, makes a marvelous circuit of Paris. It crosses the **Seine** four times; passes **Place de la Concorde**, the **Assemblée Nationale**, the **Louvre**, **Pont-Neuf**, **Notre-Dame**, **Ile St-Louis**, and **Place St-Michel**; goes down **Boulevard St-Germain**; and finally turns back past the **Jardin des Plantes** and the **Musée d'Orsay**—all for just a few francs. The **Nos. 30, 48, 69, 82**, and **95** routes are equally enjoyable. Maps of the bus system and schedules are posted on the walls of bus shelters.

Bus service is limited in the evening and on Sunday. The standard fare is one métro ticket; an additional ticket will be needed for transfers to another bus. Buy a bus ticket at any métro station or on the bus. Be sure to punch your ticket in the machine beside the driver when you board and hold onto your punched ticket throughout the trip; occasionally a *contrôleur* in a blue uniform boards the bus to check them. Those without punched tickets receive heavy fines. Travelers who have multiride public transport passes, such as *Le Paris Visite* or the *Carte Orange*, should show them to the driver but not have them punched. For discount ticket and pass information, see **Métro** below.

DRIVING

Those planning on driving in Paris stand forewarned: The most civilized Parisian becomes a homicidal maniac on the road. Rush-hour periods are Monday through Friday between 8 and 10AM and between 5 and 8PM. Conditions are also rough on Sunday nights between 5 and 9PM, when weekend travelers are heading back into the city.

If you dare to drive, the main car-rental agencies are **Avis** (5 Rue Bixio, at Ave de Ségur, 01.46.66.67.58; 60 Rue de Ponthieu, at Rue de Berri, 01.43.59.03.83), **Hertz** (92 Rue St-Lazare, at the Gare St-Lazare, 01.55.31.93.21; Esplanade des Invalides, 2 Rue Robert-Esnault-Pelterie, between Rue de l'Université and Quai d'Orsay, 01.45.51.20.37); and **Europcar** (48 Rue de Berri, between Rue du Faubourg-St-Honoré and Blvd Haussmann, 01.53.93.73.40). These companies also have offices at **Roissy–Charles-de-Gaulle** and **Orly Airports**. All these companies offer a nonresident discounts for visitors from outside the European Community, but you must make your reservations 24 hours before arriving in France, and there is a minimum rental period of 3 days and a maximum of 99 days. When renting a car, be sure to take the rental company's insurance if your auto insurance doesn't cover you. If your credit card company offers coverage, check before leaving home to be sure that it is valid in Europe.

Métro

It's one of the oldest—and best—subway systems in Europe. The first line, designed by engineer Fulgence Bienvenue, opened on 19 July 1900 between **Porte Maillot** and **Vincennes**. In the early 1900s, the station entrances were Art Nouveau masterpieces designed by Hector Guimard. These days, the symbol of the system is the aqua-and-brown ticket of the **RATP**.

The first new métro line since 1935 opened in October 1998. Called **Météor** (or **No. 14**), it runs from **Bibliothèque Nationale de France, Site François Mitterrand/Tolbiac** to the **Madeleine**.

Nearly 120 miles of rail snake beneath the streets of Paris, connecting about 300 stations. Aboveground, you're never very far away from a métro stop, and for the cost of a single ticket you can ride all day anywhere within the system, which operates between 5AM and about 12:45AM. (Each train pulls into its final destination at 1:15AM.) Hang onto your ticket: Occasionally a team of *contrôleurs* in olive brown uniforms boards the train to check them.

Getting lost in Paris takes some effort. Métro maps (see inside back cover) are everywhere—inside and outside the stations. Ask at the ticket booth for *un grand plan du métro* (a big métro map), because the small ones are hard to read. The métro lines are named for the stations at which they end. Simply follow the signs for the terminus in the direction you are headed. If, for example, you want to go from the **Bastille** to **Concorde**, take the line marked **Direction La Defense**. To transfer from one line to another, look for an orange-and-white *correspondance* sign on the station platform. Each station has a map of the neighborhood surrounding it, so you can get your bearings before you emerge aboveground.

To use the métro, slip the magnetized ticket into the slot by the turnstile, retrieve it when it pops up, and pass through. Remember that when getting on and off the métro you must open the car door yourself (except on the **No. 1** and **No. 14** lines, which are fully automatic); on all lines, the door closes automatically behind you.

When you're purchasing tickets, it's less expensive to buy a *carnet* (book) of 10, which cuts the price of a single ticket by a third. Also available are tourist passes, which are valid for both the métro and the bus. *Le Paris Visite* passes are usable for 1, 2, 3, and 5 days of unlimited travel in the metropolis of Paris and the suburbs (the price increases the farther you go) and include reductions on admission to numerous places of interest. The *Carte Orange* offers a week or month of travel privileges in Paris and the suburbs (again, the card costs more for longer distances) and requires a photograph.

A métro ticket also allows you to use the **RER** rail system (an express métro) within Paris, but study its route before you board, because it is primarily a suburban line, and the stops within the city are few and far between. Always hang onto your tickets; you may need them to get in and out of the station. Call 08.36.68.41.14 for métro information or check the RATP's web site at www.ratp/fr.

Parking

If you think driving in Paris is tough, wait until you try to park your car. If you are lucky enough to find a legal spot on the street, you can leave your car there as long as you keep feeding the meter, in effect Monday through Saturday between 9AM and 7PM, except holidays. (August is considered a holiday in certain quarters of Paris.) If your car is towed, be prepared to pay a very hefty fine and spend the better part of a day trying to resolve the problem and recover the vehicle. The easiest option is an underground parking lot. There are many throughout the city; look for the "Parking" signs or the big letter *P*.

Taxis

The best way to get one of Paris's 14,900 cabs is to go to one of Paris's many taxi stands, shelters marked with bold blue-and-white "Taxi" signs. If you're lucky, one will be one waiting for you at the *tête de station* (head of the line). If not, wait in line until one shows up. Hailing a cab in the street is not a very rewarding experience; if you try it, look for a taxi with a bright roof light. (A dim light means it's occupied.) Even then, drivers may not pick you up, because if you're not going in their direction, *tant pis* (tough luck). Either way, fake some knowledge of the city and tell the driver the main street or métro station closest to your destination; given that guidance, she or he is less likely to take you out of your way. Taxis usually aren't expensive, but the rates increase between 10PM and 6:30AM, on Sunday, and if you're picked up at a train station, hotel, or outside the city.

If you need to be somewhere at a specific time (including the airport), you can try calling call ahead for a taxi; the meter starts running the moment the driver receives the call, but the dispatcher will tell you how long it will take for the cab to arrive. It's usually less than 10 minutes once you get a commitment, but getting that commitment can be a problem. The radio-taxi companies favor their corporate clients, and individuals without credit accounts get short shrift. Cab companies include **Taxis Bleus** (08.25.16.10.10), **Taxis G-7** (01.47.39.47.39 for reservations in English), and **Alpha Taxis** (01.45.85.85.85). The most reliable company for trips to the airports is **Air Taxi** (01.43.90.91.91). Tip the driver 10% to 15%.

TOURS

To observe the city through the windows of a climate-controlled, double-decker tour bus, climb aboard one of the sleek coaches of **Cityrama** (4 Pl des Pyramides, between Rues de Rivoli and des Pyramides; 01.44.55.61.00) or **Paris Vision** (214 Rue de Rivoli, between Rues St-Roch and d'Alger; 01.42.60.31.25). Both companies offer tours (in several languages) past all the main attractions, as well as separate excursions to **Versailles, Giverny, Malmaison, Chantilly, Chartres, Fontainebleau** and **Barbizon,** the **Loire Valley, Mont St-Michel,** and the **Normandy landing beaches.** They also run Paris by Night tours to the **Moulin Rouge** and the **Lido** and to X-rated hot spots (for adults only).

The jaunty red double-deckers of **Les Cars Rouge** (01.53.95.39.53), with open upper decks in good weather, offer *Paris en toute liberté* (Paris at your leisure). They stop at nine main spots of tourist interest (**Notre-Dame, Tour Eiffel,** etc.), and passengers can get on and off as they please. Tickets are valid for 2 days, and the commentary is in French and English. **L'OpenTour** (13 rue Auber, between Rue Scribe and Blvd Haussmann; 01.42.66.56.56) offers essentially the same service, open top decks included, but with more than 40 hop-on/hop-off stops.

On a late summer afternoon, nothing could be better than spending an hour touring the Seine river in a *bateau mouche,* especially if you take along some creamy goat cheese, a fresh baguette, and a bottle of cool St-Joseph. Take a seat at the rear of the boat out of range of the irritating tape-recorded commentary, then put your feet up and watch the sun set over the City of Light. For a more luxurious trip, book one of the expensive candlelit dinner cruises. Tours lasting between 1 and 3 hours (the longer excursions feature lunch or dinner) are available from **Bateaux Mouches** (Pont de l'Alma, and Pl de l'Alma; 01.42.25.96.10), **Bateaux Parisiens** (Port de La Bourdonnais, just northeast of Pont d'Iena; 01.44.11.33.44), **Bateaux Vedettes de Paris** (Port de Suffren, between Ponts de Bir-Hakeim and d'Iena; 01.47.05.71.29), and **Vedettes du Pont-Neuf** (Sq du Vert-Galant, just west of Pl du Pont-Neuf, Ile de la Cité; 01.46.33.98.38). The boats operated by **Vedettes du Pont-Neuf** tend to be smaller and have live guides rather than recorded commentary.

Tours of the **Canal St-Martin** are offered by **Paris Canal** (01.42.39.15.00) daily between April and November and on Sunday January through March and December. The offbeat 3-hour cruises run between the **Musée d'Orsay** and the **Parc de la Villette,** passing through a mile-long subterranean tunnel under the **Place de la Bastille** and **Boulevard Richard Lenoir,** encountering nine locks and two turning bridges en route. Reservations are required.

Paris Walking Tours (01.48.09.21.40; fax 01.42.43.75.51; paris@paris-walks.com; www.pariswalkingtours.com) offers walks through virtually every district in Paris, with lively and informative commentary in English by Peter and Oriel Caine, a British couple who created this service in 1994. Some of the most popular of the 70 walks they have designed are the Historic Marais, Hemingway's Paris, the Opéra,

Montmartre, and the Sewers of Paris. There is at least one walk daily; each lasts about 2 hours. The Caines also lead coach tours to **Vaux-le-Vicomte** and **Auvers-sur-Oise.**

Former Ecole de Beaux Arts history of art professor Velma Bury (01.43.21.52.11; buryvelma@noos.fr), a Montparnasse resident since the 1960s, takes you on **Paris—Then and Now,** a personal and historical 2-hour walking tour of the haunts of the district's many artists and writers from the days of Picasso, Gertrude Stein, Kiki, and Man Ray to the present, ending at the final address of some of them (Sartre, de Beauvoir, Beckett, Duras), the astonishing Montparnasse Cemetery.

Journalist Ricki Stevenson's **Black Paris Tours** (01.46.37.03.96; 06.62.68.03.96; Rickis@club-internet.fr) explores the exciting history of African-Americans in Paris, from the days of Sally Hemings (who became Thomas Jefferson's mistress here), painter Henry Ossawa Tanner, W. E. B. DuBois, the World War I Harlem Hellfighters, Josephine Baker, Richard Wright, and James Baldwin to contemporary artist and writer Barbara Chase-Riboud, among many others. This is an all-day tour by foot, bus, and métro, with a stop for lunch.

Paris Contact (01.42.51.08.40; paris.contact@wanadoo.fr), Jill Daneels's multilingual guide service, offers 2-hour cultural walks between April and November in 15 corners of Paris, including "Bohemian Montmartre" in her own part of town. Her languages are English, French, Dutch, German, Russian, Hungarian, and Chinese. She also arranges custom tours for small groups, including jaunts to Versailles.

For serious shoppers who want the inside scoop on where and what to buy, **Shopping Plus** (99-103 Rue de Sevres, between Rues de L'Abbé Saint-Grégoire and Saint-Romain; 01.47.53.91.17; fax 01.44.18.96.68;

ireneadamian@minitel.net; www.parisgourmet.com)
offers half-day walking tours with bilingual guides
focusing on a theme and a place, such as haute couture
in the **Triangle d'Or** (bounded by the Champs-Elysées,
Avenue Montaigne, and Rue François Premier) on the
Right Bank, antiques in the Marais, or home decoration
in the Left Bank. In a daylong tour, French for a Day,
participants go to an outdoor food market and then to a
2-hour class at the **Toque d'Or** cooking school where
their culinary efforts are savored. The afternoon brings
visits to fashion boutiques, art galleries, antiques stores,
and home decoration shops of the Left Bank and a stop
for tea at a suitably chic spot. Lunch with wine and
afternoon tea are included. Tours can also be custom-
tailored for individuals or small groups.

For an exciting audiovisual tour of Paris, **Paris Story** (11
bis Rue Scribe, at Rue Auber, métro: Opéra or Havre-
Caumartin; 01.42.66.62.06; www.paris-story.com), right
next to American Express, presents a wide-screen journey
through space and time, covering Paris's 2-millennia-long
evolution from the pre-Roman settlement of Lutetia to
today's capital of glamour and grands projets. This
splendid show focuses on Paris's architecture and
lifestyle as they have developed over the ages—Roman,
Medieval, Renaissance, Enlightenment, Revolution and
Empire, Belle Epoque, and 20th century—with poetic,
informative commentary available in English and 11
other languages and magnificent music by Lully, Offenbach, Debussy, Ravel, Edith Piaf, and others. The 45-
minute program is a fine introduction to the many
architectural styles visitors will encounter as they explore
the city. The show is presented daily every hour on the
hour between 9AM and 8PM April through October and
daily between 9AM and 6PM November through March.

With her **Promenades Gourmandes** (01 48 04 56 84;
www.promenadesgourmandes.com), Paule Caillat offers
open market tours followed by a hands-on cooking class
and lunch in her custom-designed kitchen in the Marais
district (classes are limited to 6 people). Full-day
programs include an afternoon walking tour to gourmet
specialty shops.

The **Gourmet Concierge** (06.11.25.79.82;
www.thegourmetconcierge.com) is food consultant and
writer Wendy Lyn Whitehurst, who organizes personalized
half-day and full-day itineraries around culinary themes.
Taste your way through Paris in outdoor markets and
gourmet food shops, enjoy a classic French picnic, take
cooking lessons, or go behind the scenes to meet chefs,
bakers, wine experts, market vendors, cheese makers,
and chocolate creators in their shops and restaurants.
Whitehurst, who has produced specials in France for the
Food TV Network, organizes custom tours for 2-6 people.

WALKING

Whether by promenading along the broad boulevards or
threading your way through intimate medieval neighborhoods, the best way to discover Paris and its environs is
by foot. Strolling yields the joy of discovering the little
things—the grace notes, embellishments, and architectural details that define the feel and texture of Paris. But
walking can be a somewhat perilous proposition: On the
street you're fair game for distracted drivers and reckless
in-line skaters, and on the sidewalk you're likely to tread
on what dogs have left behind.

FYI

ACCOMMODATIONS

Hotel reservations are essential in Paris not only in the
summer months but also during the heavy convention
and trade-show months of March and October. Keep in
mind that hotel rates rise regularly and renovations often
prompt hotels to raise their prices, so it is always
sensible to call in advance to check rates. If you do
arrive without accommodations, contact the **Office de
Tourisme de Paris** (see "Visitors' Information Centers,"
page 17). The tourist office also offers a free brochure
charting room availability throughout the year.

For those looking for an alternative to the traditional
hotel room, the **Organisation pour le Tourisme Universitaire** (**OTU**; 01.40.29.12.12; otuvoyages@terranet.fr)
maintains more than 700 clean, safe, inexpensive beds
in youth centers throughout the Paris area. Reservations
must be made in person, and those 35 years of age and
under have priority. Rooms generally sleep one to eight
people, and bathrooms are shared. The centers in the
Marais quarter, housed in 17th-century mansions, are
the most desirable.

There are three **OTU** offices in central Paris: **OTU
Beaubourg** (119 Rue St-Martin, at Pl Georges-
Pompidou; 01.42.72.72.09), the largest; **OTU Port
Royal** (39 Ave Georges-Bernanos, between Blvds de
Port-Royal and St-Michel; 01.44.41.38.50); and **OTU
Jussieu** (2 Rue Malus, at Rue de la Clef;
01.43.36.80.27). To secure a room, get to one of the
offices by 9AM, when they open.

For information on youth hostels in Paris and elsewhere
in France, contact **Fédération Unies des Auberges de
Jeunesse** (**FUAJ**), 27 Rue Pajol, 75018 Paris
(01.44.89.87.27; fax 01.44.89.87.10; www.fuaj.org).
Try the web site first. It has all the information you need
in English.

Those wishing to rent an apartment can contact **France
Appartements** (97 Ave des Champs-Elysées, 75008
Paris; 01.56.89.31.00; fax 01.56.89.31.01;
www.apartments-of-france.com), which has first-rate
studios and apartments in the classy parts of Paris. Or
check listings in the free publication FUSAC (France
America Contacts) available at many English-language
bookstores and Anglo establishments in Paris. **Citadines**
(01.41.05.79.05; www.citadines.com) has 17 of its
modern Apart'Hotels scattered about Paris; they have
studios and one- or two-bedroom apartments with
kitchens and offer full hotel services as well (reception
desk, breakfast lounge, laundry, parking). **The French
Experience** (370 Lexington Ave, New York, NY 10017,
212/986-3800, 800/283-7262; fax 212/986-3808,
info@frenchexperience.com; www.frenchexperience.com)
also arranges bed-and-breakfast accommodations, as
well as apartment and country cottage rentals and hotel
reservations.

ADDRESSES

Parisian addresses include a street name and a number,
plus which of the 20 arrondissements the address is in.
For instance, an address in the Latin Quarter (fifth
arrondissement) might be "23 Quai St-Bernard, 5ᵉᵐᵉ," or
"75005 Paris" (the small ème is the French equivalent

of an English *th*), whereas an address in the Ile de la Cité (first arrondissement) would read "25 Place Dauphine, 1ᵉʳ," or "75001 Paris" (*er* standing in for the English *st*).

Cafés

As noble a French institution as the **Académie Française**, cafés serve sandwiches, simple meals, and a variety of beverages throughout the day. If *un café* (a demitasse of espresso) is too potent for you in the morning, try a *café crème* (a large cup of coffee with hot, frothy milk); in the afternoon you might switch to *vin rouge* (red wine), *un demi* (a 25-centiliter draft beer), or a *citron pressé* (fresh lemonade). Drinks are cheaper at the *zinc* (bar), and coffee can be more expensive after 10PM, but by then you'll probably have moved on to cognac, Armagnac, or perhaps Calvados.

Climate

Chances are that fabled Paris in the springtime will be soggy. The city logs more rainy days a year than London, so bring an umbrella or trench coat. Winters are cold and damp, and summers can be as cool and dry as the martinis at the **Ritz Bar**. The average temperature ranges from 38 degrees F in January to 75 degrees in July. August, when most Parisians leave the city, can be very hot, with temperatures rising well up into the 80s during a *canicule* (heat wave). May and September or October are generally the best times for finding decent weather and fewer tourists.

Months	Average Temperature (°F)
December–February	46
March–May	58
June–August	76
September–November	61

Drinking

The legal drinking age is 18. Bars typically stay open until 2 or 4AM. As in most cities, drunk driving is a serious problem, so police often stop erratic drivers for a breath test. For drivers who fail it, the penalties are severe: a heavy fine that must be paid on the spot, a possible stay in jail, and possible loss of a driver's license.

Embassies and Consulates

American Embassy: 2 Ave Gabriel, at Rue Boissy-d'Anglas, 01.43.12.23.47

American Consulate: 2 Rue St-Florentin, at Rue de Rivoli; 01.43.12.23.47

Australian Embassy: 4 Rue Jean Rey, between Ave de Suffren and Quai Branly; 01.40.59.33.00

British Embassy: 35 Rue du Faubourg-St-Honoré, between Rues Boissy-d'Anglas and de l'Elysée; 01.44.51.31.00

British Consulate: 18 *bis* Rue d'Anjou, between Rues de Surène and du Faubourg-St-Honoré; 01.44.51.31.00

Canadian Embassy/Consulate: 35 Ave Montaigne, at Rue François, 1ᵉʳ, 01.44.43.29.00

Entertainment

Paris is one of the world's greatest cities for all kinds of entertainment—opera, ballet, classical music in churches and concert halls, films, jazz and blues, theater and floor shows, and discotheques and rock clubs. For up-to-date listings on all musical and theatrical events, movies, and art exhibits, check out the publications *Pariscope* and *L'Officiel des Spectacles*, both of which come out every Wednesday.

Parisians are film fanatics. Each week more than 300 films are shown in the city, and all are listed along with their show times in *Pariscope* and *L'Officiel des Spectacles*. The *v.o.* (*version originale*) after a film title means the movie is being shown in its original language with French subtitles; *v.f.* (*version française*) means it's dubbed in French. If you arrive in time for the *séance* (showing), you'll see the ads, which are often risqué, usually silly, and sometimes brilliantly imaginative. Ticket prices for movies are uniformly reduced by 30% on Mondays.

Health and Medical Care

For round-the-clock medical house calls, call **SOS Médecins** (01.47.07.77.77). The **American Hospital** is just outside Paris (63 Blvd Victor-Hugo, between Blvds du Château and de la Saussaye, Neuilly-sur-Seine; switchboard, 01.46.41.25.25; hot line, 01.47.47.70.15); most of the physicians there speak English. An English-language crisis line (operated 3-11PM) can be reached by dialing 01.47.23.80.80.

In Paris, all pharmacies are marked by a neon green cross on the front of the building. When the cross is lit, it means the pharmacy is open for business. Many pharmacists speak English, and you can be sure of getting English prescriptions translated and filled with equivalent medicines at the following places: **British and American Pharmacy** (1 Rue Auber, at Pl de l'Opéra; 01.47.42.49.40), **Pharmacie Anglaise** (130 Rue La Boétie, at Ave des Champs-Elysées; 01.43.59.22.52), **Pharmacie Dhéry** (84 Champs-Elysées, between Rues La Boétie and de Berri; 01.45.62.02.41), and **Pharmacie Swann** (6 Rue de Castiglione, between Rues Rivoli and du Mont-Thabor; 01.42.60.72.96).

Holidays

On the following *jours feriés* (national holidays), most shops and businesses, including banks, are closed, whereas many museums and restaurants stay open. Buses don't run, but the métro remains operational.

Jour de l'An (New Year's Day), 1 January

Pâques (Easter), 31 March 2002, 20 April 2003

Lundi de Pâques (Easter Monday), 1 April 2002, 21 April 2003

Fête du Travail (Labor Day/May Day), 1 May

Fête de la Victoire (VE—Victory in Europe—Day), 8 May

Fête de l'Ascension (Ascension Day), 9 May 2002, 29 May 2003

Lundi de Pencôte (Pentecost Monday), mid- to late May

Fête Nationale/Jour de la Bastille (Bastille Day), 14 July

Fête de l'Assomption (Assumption Day), 15 August

Toussaint (All Saints' Day), 1 November

Armistice (Armistice Day), 11 November

Noël (Christmas), 25 December

HOURS

Shops are usually open Monday through Saturday between 10AM and 7PM, but many observe the tradition of closing on Monday, and some still close for lunch (noon-2PM). Some larger department stores stay open one night a week, usually Thursday; they also offer additional hours during busy holiday seasons. The **Virgin Megastore** on the Champs-Elysées and a number of boutiques in the Marais district have pioneered business hours on Sunday, but they are exceptions. Other than the morning food markets and the flea markets, Sunday shopping is not commonplace in Paris.

Most Parisian museums are open between 10AM and 6PM; many stay open until 10PM one night a week. Museums are open on Sunday, but many are *fermé* (closed) on either Monday or Tuesday. Restaurants generally are open between noon and 2PM and 7 and 10:30PM. Cafés open early in the morning and often stay open late in the evening.

Although August is still the *fermeture annuelle*, when many Parisians flee the city on vacation and leave countless shops and restaurants closed in their wake, more and more stores and restaurants are staying open during this time. Annual closing times may vary from one year to the next.

Opening and closing times for shops, attractions, cafés, and so on are listed by day(s) if the normal hours described above apply. In all other cases, specific hours will be given (e.g., 6AM-2PM, daily 24 hours, noon-5PM).

LAUNDRY

Almost 200 self-serve *laveries* (Laundromats) are peppered throughout the city. The best way to find one convenient to you is to check in the *Pages Jaunes* (Yellow Pages) of the Paris phone book, where they are listed by arrondissement under the heading of *laveries*. Even better, simply ask in your neighborhood. You're sure to find one nearby. A single wash costs around 3.50 euros.

MONEY

The Euro is the official money of France and 11 other members of the European Union (Germany, the Benelux countries, Spain, Portugal, Italy, Austria, Greece, Ireland, and Finland). Euro banknotes and coins came into circulation on 1 January 2002. The fixed Euro–French franc rate of exchange is 1 Euro = 6.55957 francs.

People who still had French francs after that date were to be allowed to exchange them for Euros at commercial banks until 30 June 2002. Branches of the Banque de France will continue to exchange French franc coins for Euros for 3 years (until 17 February 2005) and bills until 17 February 2012. There are seven bills (of 5, 10, 20, 50, 100, 200, and 500 Euros) and eight coins (of 1 and 2 Euros and of 1, 2, 5, 10, 20, and 50 cents). Each bill is a different color and size; the higher the value, the larger the bill. The bills are the same design in all the countries. Coins put into circulation in France bear the words *République Française* or *RF*, and the 1-, 2-, and 5-cent coins bear an image of France's symbolic figure Marianne on one side. The coins can be used in any of the 12 countries.

Banks are generally open Monday through Friday between 9AM and 4:30PM, but they close at midday the day before a holiday. They will display a sign reading "Change" if they exchange foreign currency. The exchange window of **American Express** (11 Rue Scribe, at Rue Auber; 01.47.77.77.58) is open on Saturday, and there are exchange booths open daily at **Beaubourg**, Les Halles, on the **Rue de Rivoli** opposite the **Tuileries** gardens, and other spots frequented by tourists. If you're stuck with dollars and the banks are closed, you can change money at these train stations: **Gare d'Austerlitz** (until 8PM), **Gare de l'Est** (until 7PM), **Gare St-Lazare** (until 7PM), and **Gare de Lyon** (until 11PM). (For train station locations, see pages 8-9.)

Credit cards (especially VISA) are in wider use here than elsewhere in Europe. Automatic teller machines (ATMs) are common; check with your bank or credit card company about using cash machines in Paris.

MUSEUMS

Most Parisian museums stay open late one night a week and are open on Sunday, but many are closed on either Monday or Tuesday. If you're planning on serious museum-hopping, buy a *Carte Musées*, a pass that allows admission to 70 Parisian museums and monuments without waiting in line. Available in 1-, 3-, and 5-day variations, they are sold in major métro stations, at most of the participating attractions, and at the **Office de Tourisme de Paris** (see page 17). Admission to the **Louvre**, the **Musée d'Orsay**, and the **Musée National d'Art Moderne** at the **Centre Georges Pompidou** is free the first Sunday of every month.

PERSONAL SAFETY

Paris is a fairly safe city, and visitors generally need to concern themselves only with pickpockets, who prey on tourists. Crowded cars on such large métro lines as **Grande Arche de La Défense/Château de Vincennes** are these thieves' natural habitat. In general, be aware of your surroundings. Watch your money pouch, keep the clasp of your purse against your body, and don't put your wallet in your back pocket, especially if it bulges. Beware of bands of children—sometimes they possess a sleight of hand Fagin would have envied. Don't wear jewelry in crowded places (like on the métro or at Montmartre) and don't leave possessions unattended.

France maintains a strong police and military presence at borders, airports, and railway stations after

---

The city offers 72,778 registered hotel rooms.

It's a good thing it almost never snows in Paris—the city has no snow-removal equipment.

experiencing some terrorist bombings in the not-too-distant past. Additionally, police officers and heavily armed soldiers patrol the main Paris subway stations and other potential targets, such as the **Arc de Triomphe** and the **Eiffel Tower**. Travelers are advised to carry their passports with them in the unlikely event of being stopped by police for an identity check. French law requires everyone to carry proof of identity.

POST OFFICES

Post offices are marked **PTT** and are open Monday through Friday between 8AM and 7PM and Saturday between 8AM and noon. The main post office (52 Rue du Louvre, at Rue Etienne-Marcel; 01.40.28.20.00) is open 24 hours a day. If you want to buy stamps, make sure you're in the correct line and not wasting your time queuing up at the window where Parisians pay their gas and telephone bills. Stamps are also sold at *tabacs* (tobacco shops), hotels, and some newsstands.

PUBLICATIONS

The English-language *International Herald Tribune* (a child of the *Washington Post* and the *New York Times*) will keep you abreast of world events and some Parisian happenings. It appears at newsstands every morning except Sunday. The main French dailies in Paris are *Libération* and *Le Figaro* in the morning and *Le Monde* in the afternoon.

For weekly listings of exhibitions, movies, concerts, plays, discos, and restaurants, pick up a copy of *Pariscope* or *L'Officiel des Spectacles*, which both come out on Wednesday. They are sold at newsstands, and although they're written in French, they are possible to decipher even if you do not speak the language. *Pariscope* includes a short guide in English edited by *Time Out*, highlighting restaurants and top arts and entertainment events for the week.

The *Paris Free Voice*, an English-language monthly, has brightly written, informative articles about current cultural goings-on, restaurant and wine bar reviews, and tips on living in Paris. It is distributed free in all English-language bookshops including the **American Church** (65 Quai d'Orsay, between Rue Henri Moissan and Rue Jean Nicot), the **American Cathedral** (23 Avenue George V, between Pl de l'Alma and Ave Pierre-1er-de-Serbie, and many other establishments that attract an English-speaking public. Their office is at 7 Rue Papillon (between Rues La Fayette and de Paradis; 01.47.70.45.05). The free magazines *e.m@le* and *illico* have extensive lists of bars, clubs, restaurants, businesses, organizations, and special events for gays and lesbians; they are in French but are easily decipherable and are available at the **Centre Gai et Lesbien** (3 Rue Keller, between Rues de Charonne and de la Roquette, métros: Ledru-Rollin, Bastille; 01.43.57.21.47) and at most gay bars and restaurants.

REST ROOMS

You can usually walk into any café and use the toilet. Such a facility may be a hole or a throne, with or without toilet paper. Your alternative is using the beige automatic toilets in the streets. For a $\in 0.40$ (two 20-cent coins), these clever contraptions automatically let you in and out and disinfect themselves between visits. Warning: Don't let young children into the automatic toilets alone; they may not be strong enough to push open the doors to get out.

RESTAURANTS

The French generally lunch between noon and 2PM and dine between 7:30 and 10PM. To eat at a particularly prestigious restaurant, such as **Taillevent**, **Le Grand Véfour**, **Lucas-Carton**, or **Alain Ducasse**, you may have to book reservations months in advance, but in most cases advance notice of 1 week, or even 1 or 2 days, should suffice. In less expensive restaurants, reservations are not usually necessary. In many dining spots you may either order à la carte or choose a less expensive prix-fixe menu, which often includes the day's special. The fancier restaurants usually offer a *dégustation* (sampler) of the chef's specialties. If the wine list puzzles you, ask the waiter or the sommelier for advice; remember, the quality of the wine does not necessarily increase with the price. A 15% service charge is always included in the bill. Restaurants are normally open only at lunchtime and dinnertime.

The term *bistro* (sometimes spelled *bistrot*) usually refers to small, quaint, family-run restaurants serving modestly priced traditional French cooking, though in recent years several top chefs have opened chic little bistro spinoffs of their famous and far more expensive restaurants. They are generally open for lunch and dinner. A brasserie is literally a brewery, and these lively Alsatian-style eateries feature draft beer, Riesling and Gewürztraminer wines, *choucroute* (sauerkraut with boiled ham, pork, and sausages), and other specialties of Alsace, along with a goodly array of traditional French dishes, and usually a fresh seafood bar. Brasseries serve meals all day long without interruption and generally stay open later than restaurants or bistros.

SHOPPING

Perhaps no other city in the world enjoys such a reputation as a shoppers' mecca. Haute couture, jewelry, perfume, and gourmet delights are all here. The biggest department stores are located on **Boulevard Haussmann** in the **Opéra** district. The most chic boutiques are located in the 1st, 6th, 7th, and 8th arrondissements and the most avant-garde ones in the 4th (the Marais) and the 11th (the Bastille district).

Big department stores include **Galeries Lafayette** (40 Blvd Haussmann, at Rue de Mogador; 01.42.82.34.56), **Printemps** (64 Blvd Haussmann, at Rue de Caumartin; 01.42.82.57.87), **La Samaritaine** (19 Rue de la Monnaie, between Quai du Louvre and Rue de Rivoli; 01.40.41.20.20), **Le Bazar de l'Hôtel de Ville** (BHV, 52 Rue de Rivoli, at Rue des Archives; 01.42.74.90.00), and **Au Bon Marché** (main store, 22 Rue de Sèvres, at Rue Velpeau; 01.44.39.80.00). Also worth a visit are such major shopping centers as **Forum des Halles** (at Rues Pierre-Lescot and Rambuteau; 01.44.76.96.56), the glass-roofed **Galerie Vivienne** (main entrance at 4 Rue des Petits-Champs, between Rues des Petits-Pères and Vivienne), the **Carrousel du Louvre** (beneath the Arc de Triomphe du Carrousel at the Louvre), and the posh **Passy Plaza** (53 Rue de Passy, at Pl de Passy; 01.40.50.09.07). **Maine Mont-**

parnasse (Pl du 18-Juin 1940, at Blvd du Montparnasse and Rue de Rennes) is a large shopping area with several big stores.

The most elegant designer boutiques for fashion, shoes, and leather goods are to be found along **Rue du Faubourg-St-Honoré**, in the **Triangle d'Or**, and, in recent years, **St-Germain-des-Prés** on the Left Bank. Many of the best (and most expensive) antiques dealers are located in **Le Carré Rive Gauche**, an association of more than 100 antiques shops in the area bordered by Quai Voltaire and Rues du Bac, de l'Université, and des Sts-Pères. Another important concentration of prestigious antiques dealers is at **Le Louvre des Antiquaires**, an association of 250 shops in a grand old building at 2 Place du Palais Royale, just across Rue de Rivoli from the Louvre.

Antiques and curio collectors also should explore such flea markets as **Puces de la Porte de Montreuil** (at Ave de la Porte-de-Montreuil), especially good for second-hand clothing; **Puces de la Porte de Vanves** (at Aves Georges-Lafenestre and Marc-Sangnier), for furniture and bric-a-brac; and the largest and best known, **Marché aux Puces de St-Ouen** (more commonly called the **Puces de Clignancourt**; Blvd Périphérique, at Porte de Clignancourt), which offers an admirable array of antiques. The **Marché Biron** is one of the best of the smaller markets that make up the **Puces de Clignancourt**; it is especially good for fine crystal, china, and furniture. Most of the flea markets are held on the weekend year-round, no matter the weather.

SMOKING

French law prohibits smoking in the métro and requires that all restaurants provide separate smoking and nonsmoking areas. However, most smokers still consider it only a politeness, certainly not a mandate, to refrain from smoking in no-smoking zones.

STREET PLAN

At first glance, Paris's broad expanse looks like one great tangle of medieval streets. Don't be dismayed, however, for there's logic in the layout that, once grasped, makes Paris as easy to navigate as the average college campus. The reference points provided by the major monuments (**Eiffel Tower**, **Panthéon**, **Arc de Triomphe**, etc.) and the **Seine** make locating yourself and your destination surprisingly easy. The series of axes that cut through the city also is a splendid means of orientation. The most obvious axis runs in a straight line from **La Défense** in the west, eastward through the **Arc de Triomphe**, and down the **Champs-Elysées** to the **Louvre** and along **Rue de Rivoli** to the **Bastille** and beyond. Part of the logic is that the city is subdivided into 20 arrondissements, or quarters. Starting from the first arrondissement (the area around the **Louvre**), they spiral outward like the compartments of a snail's shell to the city limits. Though this overall understanding of Paris's layout is helpful, it won't change the fact that the streets are labyrinthine. For navigating the city's streets, Parisians carry a map of the métro in their heads and a *Paris par Arrondissement* guide in their pockets. Sold at most Parisian newsstands and bookshops, and at some travel bookstores in the US, this little book lists every street in Paris, with indexed references to maps of each

of the city's 20 arrondissements (indicating the nearest métro station). Don't leave home without it.

TAXES

Included in the purchase price of many items is a 19.6% VAT (Value Added Tax). Non-EEC (European Economic Community) tourists are entitled to VAT refunds on items that they take out of France; a minimum purchase of 175 Euros per store is required. To get a refund, ask for the VAT refund forms when you make your purchase and be prepared to produce the items and the forms at the airport *détaxe* (refund) desk. The most convenient way of getting the refund is to charge the purchase to a credit card and get a credit for the tax refund applied to your credit card account.

TELEPHONES

All telephone numbers in France have 10 digits. The code for Paris and its region is 01, which is part of the 10-digit phone number and must be dialed to make the call go through. Direct-dial to the US can be made by dialing 001, then the area code and number. Phone rates are much cheaper after 10PM than in the daytime. Telephone calls made from hotels are expensive; if you are making a long-distance call, it is worth having a phone card.

Phone booths adorn half the street corners in Paris. Most operate only with *télécartes*, special phone cards that are sold at post offices, métro stations, and *tabacs*. To use phones in cafés, you may have to purchase a *jeton* (phone token) at the bar.

Two agencies that rent *portables*, as the French call cell phones, are **George V Telecom**, 46 Rue Pierre Charon, opposite the Four Seasons George V Hotel (01.47.20.30.40; fax 01.47.20.42.48; www.george-v-telecom.com), and **Rent A Cell Express**, 116 *bis* Ave des Champs-Elysées (suite 440), next to the Lido (01.53.93.78.00; fax 01.53.93.78.09; www.rent-a-cell.com). Both agencies will deliver the phone to your hotel or residence 7 days a week.

TICKETS

"Everything that exists elsewhere exists in Paris," said Victor Hugo in *Les Misérables*. So it goes for the array of entertainment options available to both the spectator and the participant in this city. For a daily recording (in English) of exhibitions and concerts, call 01.49.52.53.56. There is a kiosk at the **Place de la Madeleine** that sells half-price tickets to about 120 different events in Paris—including plays, concerts, ballets, and operas—on the day of the performance.

TIME ZONE

France is 1 hour ahead of Greenwich Mean Time (GMT); throughout most of the year, when it's 9PM in Paris it's 8PM in London, 3PM in New York, and noon in Los Angeles. However, Europe starts and ends *l'heure d'été* (daylight saving time) several weeks before North America, so between about the end of March and the end of April, France is 7 hours ahead of New York, and between the end of September and the end of October, it is 5 hours ahead.

Phone Book

EMERGENCIES

AIDS Hot Line 01.44.93.16.69

Ambulance 15

Burn Center 01.42.34.17.58

Crisis Line (English-language, 3-11PM) ....
....01.47.23.80.80

Dental Emergency (SOS Dentaire) 01.43.37.51.00

Doctor (SOS Médecins) 01.43.07.77.77

Fire 18

Lost or Stolen Credit Card: 08.36.69.08.80

Pharmacy (British and American) 01.47.42.49.40

Pharmacy (24-hour) 01.45.62.02.41

Poison Center.......................................01.40.05.48.48

Police (emergency) 17

Police (nonemergency) 01.53.73.53.73

Roadside Emergency (Automobile Club
de l'Ile-de-France) 01.40.55.43.01

HOSPITALS

American Hospital 01.46.41.25.25

American Hospital Hotline 01.47.47.70.15

British Hospital 01.46.39.22.22

VISITORS' INFORMATION

Métro 08.36.68.77.14

Road Conditions Paris 01.48.99.33.33

Time 36.99

Tourist Information...............................08.92.68.31.12

Weather ....08.36.68.02.75 or 32.50

TIPPING

Because a 15% service charge is added to restaurant bills in Paris and throughout France, a supplementary tip is not necessary. However, you may leave an additional 5% for *service extraordinaire*. Tip cabdrivers 10% to 15% of the fare. It is not obligatory, but is certainly much appreciated, to tip hotel porters and maids (10 francs or 2 Euros per bag for the former; 10 francs or 2 Euros a day for the latter).

VISITORS' INFORMATION CENTERS

The **Office de Tourisme de Paris** (127 Ave des Champs-Elysées, between Rues Galilée and de Presbourg; 08.92.68.31.12; fax 01.49.52.53.00; www.paris-touristoffice.com), the city's official tourist bureau, offers help with hotel reservations in French and English, information about exhibitions, free maps and brochures, and sight-seeing information and tour bookings; it's open daily except 1 May. Between May and September, another tourist office operates daily at the **Eiffel Tower** (01.45.51.22.15). A smaller *Bureau d'Accueil*, open Monday through Saturday between 8AM and 8PM, is located in the **Gare de Lyon** (01.43.43.33.24).

L'Espace Tourisme du Carrousel du Louvre (Carrousel du Louvre, 99 Rue de Rivoli; 08.03.81.80.00; www.paris-ile-de-france.com) offers tourist information about the **Ile de France**, the region surrounding Paris, which includes **Versailles**, **Fontainebleau**, and **Chartres**. It is open Monday and Wednesday through Sunday.

Detail from Musée Carnavalet

FÊTES ET FOIRES (FESTIVALS AND FAIRS)

Paris has a full calendar of special events, celebrations, and trade expositions throughout the year that attract Parisians and visitors alike. For additional details on the events listed and others, consult the **Office de Tourisme** (127 Ave des Champs-Elysées, between Rues Galilée and de Presbourg, 08.92.68.31.12; www.paris-touristoffice.com). It publishes a free annual calendar of events and offers extensive listings on its web site. Also check the weekly listings in *Pariscope* and *L'Officiel des Spectacles* (available at newsstands).

January

Fashion Shows   The haute couture summer season kicks off this month with much fanfare. Many of the shows are held in the **Carrousel du Louvre**. For more information, call 01.43.16.47.47.

Fête des Rois (Feast of the Kings)   Called the **Feast of the Epiphany** in English-speaking countries, this religious holiday (6 January), which commemorates the visit to the infant Jesus by three kings, is also an excuse for a tasty treat: a round, buttery almond-paste cake called a *galette des rois*. Inside the cake is hidden a tiny charm, and whoever finds it gets to be king or queen for the day, donning the crown that comes with the cake. The cakes are sold all month long.

February

Tournoi des Cinq Nations (Five Nations Trophy)   This international rugby tournament is held in mid-February at the **Stade de France** (01.42.31.31.31).

Salon International de l'Agriculture   This is a vast farming fair featuring the animals and products of French and foreign *agriculteurs* and a sampling of regional food and wine. It's held for one week in late February at **Paris Expo**, the huge exposition center at the Porte de Versailles. For more information, call 01.49.09.60.00.

March

Salon du Livre   This big annual book, magazine, and multimedia fair is held for one week in mid-March at the **Paris Expo** at the Porte de Versailles. For more information, call 08.92.68.00.51.

Foire du Trône   The largest fair and carnival in France takes place from the last week of March until the end of May in the **Bois de Vincennes**. For more information, call 01.43.43.92.92.

Salon de Mars   Paris's most important antiques fair is held in the **Parc du Champ-de-Mars** during the last week of March.

April

Paris Marathon   The race, held during the first week of April, starts from the **Place de la Concorde** and ends on

Avenue Foch. The best place to catch a glimpse of the runners is along the **Avenue des Champs-Elysées**. For more information, call 01.53.17.03.10.

Salon de la Jeune Peinture   The work of young contemporary artists is exhibited at the **Grand Palais** for 2 weeks in mid-April. For more information, call 01.44.13.17.17.

Shakespeare Garden Festival   In a small open-air theater in the **Bois de Boulogne**, set in a garden blooming with flora described by Shakespeare, classic plays (usually by French writers such as Beaumarchais and Molière) are performed between the end of April and the beginning of October. Occasionally there are English-language performances. For more information, call 01.42.71.44.06.

May

May Day   On the French **Labor Day** (1 May), most shops and museums are closed and trade unions and left-wing parties organize marches. Bouquets of *muguet* (lily of the valley) are sold all over Paris.

French Open   This prestigious tennis tournament, held in the **Stade Roland Garros** during the last week of May or the first week of June, is the Wimbledon of France. Advance tickets can be purchased starting in January (write to Stade Roland Garros, 2 Ave Gordon-Bennett, 75016 Paris, 01.47.43.48.00); they're also available at the stadium 1 week before tournament.

June

Fête du Cinéma   For 3 days in late June, cinema-lovers get to watch as many films as they want in any movie theater in Paris for a mere € 1.50 per ticket, after paying full price for the first movie and receiving a cinema "passport."

Fête de la Musique   On the longest day of the year (21 June), live bands play throughout the city until the wee hours. It's a great party.

International Rose Competition at Bagatelle   Prizes for the best roses are given on 21 June, but the public can view the competitors in the **Bois de Boulogne**'s **Jardins de Bagatelle** from 22 June though the end of September. For more information, call 01.40.67.97.00.

Gay Pride Parade   The largest gay and lesbian parade

in France takes place on the last Saturday in June. It follows different routes every year. For more information, call 08.92.68.11.31.

Garçons de Café Hundreds of café waiters and waitresses run around the city, each carrying a tray with a bottle and glass; any spillage or breakage disqualifies the entrant. The race takes place at the end of the month. For information on the schedule and route, call 08.92.68.31.12.

July

Fashion Shows Winter haute couture collections are launched in the **Carrousel du Louvre**. For more information, call 01.43.95.10.10.

Bastille Day The French national holiday (14 July) celebrates the 1789 storming of the **Bastille** prison by the revolutionary masses with an impressive military parade down the Champs-Elysées and a fireworks show at the **Palais de Chaillot**.

La Villette Jazz Festival This 10-day festival at the **Parc de La Villette** in late June and early July draws top jazz artists from Europe, Africa, and North and South America. Concerts are held in **La Grande Halle** and **La Cité de la Musique** and on the open lawns of the park. For more information, call 08.03.30.63.06.

Tour de France After pedaling for three weeks and 2,301 miles (3,835 kilometers), cyclists in the world's most famous bicycle race complete the last leg on the streets of Paris and arrive at the finish line on the Champs-Elysées. For more information, call 01.49.35.69.00.

August

Fête de L'Assomption (Feast of the Assumption) The 15 August procession in front of **Notre-Dame** and the accompanying Mass are memorable experiences.

September

Les Journées du Patrimoine (Heritage Days) On the third Saturday and Sunday of September, 300 historic buildings and sites that are usually closed to the public are open free of charge, giving history and architecture buffs the chance to explore private houses, *hôtels particuliers*, and other historic structures, including the **Palais d'Elysée**, the French presidential palace. The **Office de Tourisme** has the full list.

October

Fêtes des Vendanges à Montmartre (Wine Harvest Festival) The only vineyard left in Paris is no bigger than a baseball diamond and produces 500 bottles of Clos Montmartre every year. On the first Saturday in October, the basement of the *mairie* (town hall) of the 18th arrondissement (métro: Jules Joffrin) becomes a winery, and festivals and parades liven the tiny crooked streets of **Montmartre**. For more information, call 01.42.52.42.00.

Prix de l'Arc de Triomphe This event marks the opening of the horse-racing season and is attended by the fashionable Chanel-suit, Hermès-scarf, and Gucci-bag crowd. The races take place during the first week of October at the **Hippodrome de Longchamp** (01.44.30.75.00) in the **Bois de Boulogne**.

FIAC (Foire Internationale d'Art Contemporain) For one week in mid-October, French and foreign gallery owners gather in the large exhibition space of **Paris Expo** (08.92.68.00.51) at the **Porte de Versailles** to show artists' work. This is a very important event for the international contemporary art world.

November

Armistice Day In a somber ceremony in remembrance of those who died in the two world wars, the French president lays wreaths at the **Tomb of the Unknown Soldier** under the **Arc de Triomphe** on 11 November.

Beaujolais Nouveau Day Posters proclaiming that the *"Beaujolais Nouveau est arrivé"* announce the day (the third Thursday in November) that the first wine of the Beaujolais vintage, pressed and drunk without the aging process, arrives in Paris. Cafés, wine bars, bistros, and wine shops all join together in a countrywide wine-tasting party. Beaujolais Nouveau is never a sophisticated wine, but it can be pleasantly light and fruity.

December

Illuminations de Noël Between 15 November and 5 January, all the trees along **Avenue Montaigne** and **Avenue des Champs-Elysées** are festooned with dainty white Christmas lights between 5PM and midnight. This is Paris at its most enchanting.

Crèche de Notre-Dame A life-size Nativity scene stands under a large tent in the square in front of **Notre-Dame** between early December and early January. Proceeds go to the **Notre-Dame Foundation**. For more information, call 01.56.56.44.22.

Christmas Eve Mass Both **Notre-Dame** and **St-Eustache Cathedrals** have memorable Masses that include impressive organ music on Christmas Eve (24 December). The holiday services draw ample crowds.

The Islands: Ile de la Cité and Ile St-Louis

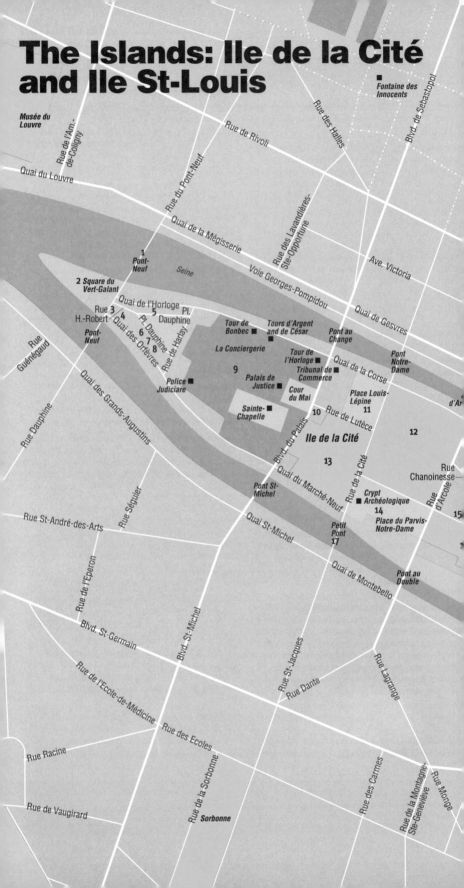

Musée du Louvre

Rue de l'Am.-de-Coligny

Rue de Rivoli

Rue des Halles

Fontaine des Innocents

Blvd. de Sebastopol

Quai du Louvre

Rue du Pont-Neuf

Quai de la Mégisserie

Rue des Lavandières-Ste-Opportune

Voie Georges-Pompidou

Ave. Victoria

1 Pont-Neuf

Seine

2 Square du Vert-Galant

Quai de l'Horloge

Pl. Dauphine

Tour de Bonbec

Tours d'Argent and de César

Pont au Change

Quai de Gesvres

Rue 3 H.-Robert 4

Pl. Dauphine

La Conciergerie

Tour de l'Horloge

Quai de la Corse

Pont Notre-Dame

5

Rue de Harlay

Tribunal de Commerce

Pont-Neuf

Quai des Orfèvres

6 7 8

Rue Guénégaud

Police Judiciare

9

Palais de Justice

Cour du Mai

Place Louis-Lépine

d'Ar

Quai des Grands-Augustins

Sainte-Chapelle

Blvd. du Palais

10 Rue de Lutèce

11

Rue Dauphine

Ile de la Cité

12

13

Rue de la Cité

Rue Chanoinesse

Rue Séguier

Pont St-Michel

Quai du Marché-Neuf

Rue d'Arcole

Rue St-André-des-Arts

Quai St-Michel

Crypt Archéologique

14

15

Rue de l'Eperon

Petit Pont

17

Place du Parvis-Notre-Dame

Quai de Montebello

Pont au Double

Blvd. St-Michel

Blvd. St-Germain

Rue de l'Ecole-de-Médicine

Rue St-Jacques

Rue Dante

Rue Lagrange

Rue des Ecoles

Rue Racine

Rue de la Sorbonne

Rue des Carmes

Rue de la Montagne-Ste-Geneviève

Rue Monge

Rue de Vaugirard

Sorbonne

THE ISLANDS: ILE DE LA CITÉ AND ILE ST-LOUIS

At the heart of Paris are two islands: the sloop-shaped Ile de la Cité, which cradles the **Cathédrale de Notre-Dame de Paris** in its stern, and Ile St-Louis, which follows in the wake. Although the islands have no grand hotels, major restaurants, cinemas, or designer shops, they do possess two gems of Gothic architecture (Notre-Dame and **Sainte-Chapelle**), a world-famous prison, an elegant 17th-century subdivision, some of the city's most beautiful private mansions, the nation's law courts and police headquarters, an Art Nouveau métro station, a flower and bird market, 15 bridges, and one too many souvenir shops selling miniature Napoléon busts and "I Love Paris" bumper stickers.

The following sites serve as an introduction to the islands. If you happen to tour this area on a Sunday, additional attractions include Notre-Dame's morning Mass (10:30AM) and late-afternoon organ concerts and the bird market at **Place Louis-Lépine**. If visiting the Ile St-Louis galleries and boutiques and the **Palais de Justice** is more your style, a weekday would be a better time to drop by. You might begin with a stop at a pastry shop to purchase croissants and brioches in time for a boat trip up the **Seine** (tour boats leave from the **Pont-Neuf**). Then, after stopping at the flower market and Notre-Dame, have lunch at a tea salon on Ile St-Louis before strolling down to look at the exterior of the 17th-century **Hôtel de Lauzun**. Top off your day with a candlelit concert in Sainte-Chapelle, followed by dinner at the exceedingly fancy **L'Orangerie** or the ever lively and more plebeian **Brasserie de l'Isle Saint-Louis**.

ILE DE LA CITÉ

The birthplace of Paris, the Cité (as the island is called) was founded by the Parisii in the third century BC and overtaken by the Romans in 52 BC. It survived attacks by Germans and barbarians, floods, and famine but succumbed to a Frenchman, Baron Georges-Eugène Haussmann, Napoléon III's prefect (1853-1870). Baron Haussmann ordered the Cité's "hygienizing," in the process destroying 90 streets and most of its medieval and Louis XIII homes. In their place, he constructed four architecturally dull buildings (**Hôtel-Dieu Hospital**, the **Préfecture de Police**, the **Tribunal de Commerce**, and the **Palais de Justice**) and increased by six times the size of the square in front of **Notre-Dame**.

1 PONT-NEUF

Despite its name (New Bridge), Paris's most famous bridge is also its oldest. Completed in 1607, it was the city's original pedestrian bridge as well as the first in Paris to be constructed without houses on top of it. Crossing the Seine at the river's widest point, it's also the city's grandest bridge; designed by **Androuet du Cerceau**, it features 12 broad arches and a series of turrets for street vendors, jugglers, and acrobats. It was completed under the popular Henri IV (Henri of Navarre), who inaugurated the bridge by galloping his charger across it. The bronze equestrian statue of Henricus Magnus (Henri the Magnificent, as the king was also called) at the bridge's center is an 1818 replacement; the original, erected two centuries earlier by the king's wife, Marie de Médicis, was melted down to make cannons during the revolution. The cornices overlooking the river have a carved frieze of grimacing caricatures, perhaps of King Henri's ministers and courtiers.

The bridge became such a well-traveled thoroughfare that, legend held, it was impossible to cross without encountering a monk, a prostitute, and a white horse. One of the most notorious Pont-Neuf charlatans was the Great Jean Thomas, who in 1715 set up a stall on the bridge to peddle bottles of an odorous elixir called Solar Balm. As part of an inventive advertising campaign, he hawked his wares dressed in a scarlet suit, a hat of peacock feathers, and a string of human teeth hung around his neck. The bridge has been sketched by J. M. W. Turner among others, rhapsodized by poets such as Victor Hugo and Jean Loiret, and (in 1985) wrapped by Bulgarian artist Christo in acres of beige canvas and more than 7 miles of rope. ♦ Métro: Pont-Neuf

2 SQUARE DU VERT-GALANT

Borrowing Henri IV's nickname (which translates roughly as "Gay Old Dog" or "Old Flirt"), this cobblestoned spit of land may be reached by steps behind the king's statue in the middle of Pont-Neuf. A haunt of anglers by day and of lovers on warm summer nights, the square, lush with chestnut trees, affords the best fish-eye view of Paris. Departing from here are 1-hour boat tours of the Seine offered by **Bateaux Vedettes Pont Neuf** (01.46.33.98.38). Between March and October the tours leave daily every 30 minutes between 10:30AM and noon, 1:30 and 8PM, and 9 and 10:30 PM. Between November and February, weekday trips depart between 10:30AM and noon, 2 and 6:30PM, and 8 and 10PM; weekend trips depart between 10:30 AM and noon, 2 and 6:30PM, and 8 and 10PM. There is commentary in English. ♦ Just west of Pl du Pont-Neuf. Métro: Pont-Neuf

3 TAVERNE HENRY IV

★★$ Named after the king in bronze across the street, this reasonably priced bistro serves delicious *charcuterie*, regional cheeses, and goose *rillettes* and is well stocked with Bordeaux and Burgundy wines. ♦ M-F, lunch and dinner; closed 15 August to 15 September. No credit cards accepted. 13 Pl du Pont-Neuf (at Rue Henri-Robert). 01.43.54.27.90. Métro: Pont-Neuf

4 QUAI DES ORFÈVRES (GOLDSMITHS QUAY)

This is the Scotland Yard of Paris, home of the city's detective force, the *police judiciare*, or the PJ. Perhaps the most famous member of the PJ is Inspector Maigret, the protagonist of the detective stories by the late Georges Simenon. ♦ Between Rue de Harlay and Pont-Neuf. Métros: Cité, St-Michel

On Quai des Orfèvres:

AU RENDEZ-VOUS DES CAMIONNEURS

★$$ Owner-chef Alain Haye creates simple but tasty fare at this cozy restaurant. Start with his mussels and shrimps with minced leeks and cream or smoked haddock, followed by poached eggs with onion chutney or *blanquette de veau* (veal in a white sauce); for dessert, the *truffé au chocolat* and *charlotte aux fraises* (trifle with strawberries) should satisfy any sweet tooth. ♦ Daily, lunch and dinner. No. 72 (between Rue de Harlay and Pl du Pont-Neuf). 01.43.54.88.74

5 PLACE DAUPHINE

Once the royal garden, this tranquil triangle of stone and redbrick town houses dates from 1607 and takes its name from Henri IV's son, the princely dauphin who became Louis XIII. The square was one of Henri IV's first city-planning projects in the 17th century and regrettably lost its third side with the expan-

Ile de la Cité

sion of the **Palais de Justice**. Surrealist poet André Breton (1896-1966) called it "one of the most secluded places I know." ♦ Métro: Pont-Neuf

5 LA ROSE DE FRANCE

★★$$ This tiny restaurant with an outdoor terrace specializes in tasty *côtelettes d'agneau* (lamb chops with *herbes de Provence*), *coquille St. Jacques avec poireau et beurre blanc* (scallops and leeks in butter sauce), and *filet de boeuf en croûte* (tenderloin of beef in a pastry crust). ♦ M-F, lunch and dinner; closed the last 3 weeks of August and Christmas through New Year's Day. No. 24 Pl Dauphine (between Rues de Harlay and Henri-Robert). 01.43.54.10.12. Métro: Pont-Neuf

6 HÔTEL HENRI IV

$ The wallpaper is peeling, the rooms are tiny, and the showers and bathrooms are in the hall, but that's a minor price to pay for a room with a view of one of the prettiest squares in Paris and a daily rate that's less than the cost of a decent bottle of wine. There are only 22 rooms at this very popular hostelry, so reserve well in advance. There's no restaurant. No. 25 Pl Dauphine (between Rues de Harlay and Henri-Robert). 01.43.54.44.53. Métro: Pont-Neuf

7 LE CAVEAU DU PALAIS

★★$$ Charming and comfortable, this restaurant is wedged between the Quai des Orfèvres and Place Dauphine. Sample the *salade de gambas* (fresh shrimp salad), *filet de boeuf à la moutarde de Meaux* (tenderloin of beef with mustard sauce), grilled grouper with basil, and *fondant au chocolat*. Dine inside under the exposed wood beams in winter, and on the terrace facing Place Dauphine in summer. ♦ M-Sa, lunch and dinner. Open every day in the summer. No. 19 Dauphine (between Rues

More than half of French families own their own homes. One in eight owns a holiday home, often one that belongs to the extended family. Two-thirds of these are in the country and the other third by the sea or in the mountains.

The croissant, that most French of pastries, actually originated in Budapest. According to the story, when the Turks besieged Budapest in 1686, they dug underground passages to reach the city center. Bakers, working during the night, heard the noise made by the invaders and sounded an alarm. The Turks were defeated, and the bakers who had saved the city were granted the privilege of creating a special pastry, which took the form of a *croissant* (crescent), the emblem on the Ottoman flag.

de Harlay and Henri-Robert). 01.43.26.04.28. Métro: Pont-Neuf

7 LE BAR DU CAVEAU

★$ Managed by Le Caveau du Palais next door, this wine bar serves light meals: *charcuterie*, country cheese, and a variety of Bordeaux and Beaujolais. ♦ Daily, breakfast, lunch, and snacks until 8PM. No. 19 Pl Dauphine (between Rues de Harlay and Henri-Robert). 01.43.54.45.95. Métro: Pont-Neuf

RESTAURANT PAUL

8 RESTAURANT PAUL

★★$$ Long marble tables set with cloth napkins as big as dish towels dominate this spot. Try the skate with capers or roast free-range chicken, and for dessert try *baba au rhum flambé* (a yeast cake flambéed with rum) with red currant jam or *mousse au chocolat*. ♦ Tu-Su, lunch and dinner. Closed second week of August. 15 Pl Dauphine (between Rue de Harlay and Pl du Pont-Neuf) and 52 Quai des Orfèvres (between Rue de Harlay and Pl du Pont-Neuf). 01.43.54.21.48. Métro: Pont Neuf

9 PALAIS DE LA CITÉ

This massive interlocking series of structures has been occupied by the French government since 52 BC, first as the palace of Roman prefects, later as the Gothic palace of the first 12 kings of France. In the 13th century it was the residence of St. Louis (Louis IX), who lived in the upper chambers (now the **First Civil Court**). The king meted out justice beneath a tree in the courtyard. All that remains of the original palace is the breathtaking **Sainte-Chapelle** and the gloomy **Conciergerie**, one of history's most hideous and brutal prisons. (See below for details on both places.) Most of the original site was covered by the **Palais de Justice**, which was built after the great fire of 1776 and greatly expanded by Baron Haussmann under Napoléon III. ♦ Bounded by Blvd du Palais and Rue de Harlay and Quais des Orfèvres and de l'Horloge. Métros: Cité, St-Michel

Within the Palais de la Cité:

TOURS DE BONBEC, D'ARGENT, AND DE CÉSAR (BABBLE, MONEY, AND CÉSAR TOWERS)

Along the Quai de l'Horloge side of the old palace is a set of round, imposing towers. The first is **Tour de Bonbec**, nicknamed "the babbler" because it was used as a torture chamber during the Reign of Terror, a period of brutal purges following the revolution. Next are the **Tour d'Argent**, where the royal treasure was once kept, and the **Tour de César**, two steepled gate towers beside the entrance to the **Conciergerie**. The tower interiors are not open to the public. ♦ Quai de l'Horloge (between Blvd du Palais and Rue de Harlay)

LA CONCIERGERIE

After the bloody mob revolt led by Etienne Marcel in 1358, young King Charles V moved the royal residence to the Marais but left behind the royal dungeon and Supreme Court in the charge of the king's caretaker, known as the *Comte des Cierges* (Count of Candles), or *Concierge*. Among the dungeon's long list of former residents are such notorious criminals as Ravaillac, the fanatic who murdered the popular Henri IV and was imprisoned and tortured here before his execution. During the revolution, the Tribunal commandeered the palace and administered its own ruthless form of justice. The **Conciergerie** became the antechamber to the guillotine during the Reign of Terror between January 1793 and July 1794. About 2,600 Parisians were condemned to death, among them Charlotte Corday, who had stabbed Marat in his bath, and, perhaps the best-remembered inmate, Marie Antoinette, the Austrian queen who had reputedly scoffed at the starving French masses with the phrase "Let them eat cake." Shortly after the Tribunal executed her husband, King Louis XVI, she was held here in a tiny cell between August and October 1793, when she was delivered to the guillotine. Royalty were not the only victims during this tumultuous time; no one in a position of authority was safe. Revolutionary Danton, who had ordered the execution of 22 people, was in turn condemned to death by citizen Robespierre, who later was sent to the guillotine by a panel of judges, the Thermidor Convention. At the end of the terror, the Tribunal's own public prosecutor, Fouquier-Tinville, was dragged off to the gallows shouting, "I am the ax! You don't execute the ax!"

Put yourself in the shoes of Marie Antoinette as she walked down the prison's Rue de Paris (which during the Reign of Terror led to the quarters of an executioner known as Monsieur de Paris). She was jailed in dank **cell No. VI**; in the cell next door, both Danton and Robespierre were held on death row, and, in the adjoining chapel, the 22 condemned Girondins heard Mass before their execution. All these rooms, as well as the *salle de la dernière toilette*, from which prisoners were led to the block, have been restored to their original state.

On your way out, duck into the magnificent medieval vaults of the four-aisled **Salle des Gens d'Armes** (Hall of the Men-at-Arms), frequently used these days for classical concerts, theater performances, and wine tastings. The spiral staircase at the far end of the hall is worth a peek. Also be sure to stroll through the 14th-century kitchen that served some 3,000 guests and had large walk-in ovens. The souvenir shop near the exit sells replicas of revolutionary playing cards that replace kings, queens, and jacks with humbly clothed men and women personifying common virtues such as industry and justice. The original deck (1793) by Jaume and Dugorc is kept in the **Bibliothèque Nationale**. ♦ Admission. Daily. Audio guide available in English; schedule of tours in English variable, posted at the entrance. 1 Quai de l'Horloge (between Blvd du Palais and Rue de Harlay). 01.53.73.78.50

TOUR DE L'HORLOGE (CLOCK TOWER)

This tower was the site of the city's first public clock (1334). Today's more Baroque version is set in a constellation of golden fleurs-de-lis and flanked by angels, rams, and royal shields. Until the French Revolution, the clock signaled royal births and deaths by pealing nonstop for 3 days. ♦ Quai de l'Horloge and Blvd du Palais

PALAIS DE JUSTICE (LAW COURTS)

Behind the lusciously gilded Louis XVI railing and portal gates on the Boulevard du Palais is the main entrance to the **Palais de Justice** and the **Cour du Mai** (May Courtyard). The courtyard was the last stop for the condemned before they left by wooden carts, or tumbrils, for the gallows in the Place de la Concorde. Look above the door at the top of the marble steps for the words *Liberté, Egalité, Fraternité*. On the right in the lobby (Salle des Pas-Perdus, literally "Room of the Wasted Steps") is an amusing statue of Berryer, a 19th-century barrister. To his right sits a sculpted muse with her foot on a turtle, a jab at the speed of the legal process. Behind the door to the left is the gorgeous blue-and-gold Première Chambre, also known as the *Chambre Dorée* (Gilded Chamber), where the Revolutionary Tribunal sat on 6 April 1793 and sentenced Queen Marie Antoinette to death. In the "cathedral of chicanery," as Balzac called the Law Courts, a thicket of police, public *écrivains* (letter writers), and prisoners used to gather while hawkers sold newspapers and rented black

---

judicial robes. Today, the lobby is still a chaos of black-robed barristers, plaintiffs, and judges dashing about. If you'd like to see a French Perry Mason putting *liberté*, *égalité*, and *fraternité* into action, visit on a weekday, when courtroom proceedings (except the juvenile court) are in session. ♦ M-Sa. 2 Blvd du Palais (between Quais des Orfèvres and de l'Horloge). 01.44.32.50.00. Métro: Cité

Within the Palais de Justice:

SAINTE-CHAPELLE

After **Notre-Dame**, this is the city's most significant medieval monument. St. Louis (Louis IX, 1214-1270), France's only canonized king, erected this Gothic jewel of a chapel in 1248 to enshrine the relics he bought from Venetian merchants during his first crusade. His purchases included Christ's Crown of Thorns, two pieces of the True Cross, a nail from the cross, the Roman soldier's lance that pierced Christ's side, and several drops of Christ's blood. For the relics, he paid 35,000 *livres* in gold, a sum far in excess of what it cost to construct this building. **Sainte-Chapelle** (the name means "holy chapel") was built in fewer than 5 years and is thought to have been designed by **Pierre de Montreuil**. It soars 67 feet without the aid of flying buttresses, a daring architectural feat in those days. In medieval times the chapel was connected to the palace of Louis IX, but today it's hidden away in a side courtyard of the 19th-century Palais de Justice. The interior has two tiers—the royal family worshiped upstairs in the light and airy **Chapelle Haute**, out of view of the court members who prayed on the somber ground floor.

The chapel suffered considerable damage during the revolution, when the gold reliquary was melted down and the structure was put to use as a flour warehouse. In the 19th century the chapel was thoroughly made over by **Eugène-Emmanuel Viollet-le-Duc** (1814-

1879), one of the Baron Haussmann–hired architects who also restored Notre-Dame and cathedrals at Amiens and St-Denis. **Louis Charles Auguste Steinheil**, a compatriot of Balzac and Baudelaire, restored the windows. Of the 12 apostle statues, only one (the bearded apostle fifth down on the left side) is original. Portions of the damaged originals are on exhibit in the **Musée de Cluny**. The chapel's spectacular windows are older than Notre-Dame's and comprise the largest expanse of stained glass in the world—1,500 square yards, enough to cover three basket-ball courts. Created in an age of mass illiteracy, this pictorial Bible consists of 1,134 scenes. Start at the lower left panel of each window and read from left to right, row by row from bottom to top. The narrative begins with Genesis and continues through the Crucifixion (illustrated in the choir apse), with scenes and figures from both the Old and New Testaments interspersed throughout. The concluding windows (on the left side of the church as you face the rose window) depict Louis IX's acquisition of the holy relics, the construction of the chapel, and, finally, the Apocalypse. Notice that a liberated Louis IX devoted entire windows to two women of the Old Testament, Judith and Esther.

Because the windows are backlit by the sun, different ones are more brightly illuminated at different times of day; you have to get up early to catch the Battle of Jericho and must come after lunch for David and Goliath. If the flies on Pharaoh's face interest you, bring your opera glasses, because details of many of the panels, particularly the highest ones, are nearly impossible to decipher with the naked eye. Anyone who identifies even a few Bible characters in a short visit is doing well. A while back, a Belgian Benedictine monk arrived here with his Bible and a pair of binoculars; it took him 2 full weeks, gazing every day from dawn to dusk, to complete the cycle.

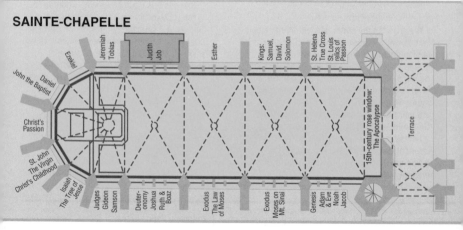

SAINTE-CHAPELLE

Sainte-Chapelle

For an initial visit, the best approach is to set aside your guidebook and gaze upward. Note how the thick, predominantly red- and blue-dyed glass of the 15 main windows contrasts sharply with the green and yellow hues of the flamboyant rose window (restored by Charles VIII in 1485) illustrating the Apocalypse. Imagine yourself among the royal family in the 13th century watching as Louis IX mounted the stairs to the gold reliquary to display the sacred Crown of Thorns. (The crown now resides in Notre-Dame and is exhibited only on Good Friday.) In addition to its visual splendors, Sainte-Chapelle is renowned for its acoustics; Couperin played the organ here in the 17th century. Nowadays, rather expensive evening concerts of classical music are held here every evening between 15 March and October. ◆ Admission. 2 Blvd du Palais (between Quais des Orfèvres and de l'Horloge). 01.42.77.65.65; concerts 01.42.50.96.18

10 BRASSERIE DES DEUX PALAIS

★$ This corner café with 1920s-style mirrored columns serves omelettes, good coffee, and hot lunch specials. ◆ Daily breakfast, lunch, and dinner. 3 Blvd du Palais (at Rue de Lutèce). 01.43.54.20.86. Métro: Cité

11 PLACE LOUIS-LÉPINE

Named after a Belle Epoque police chief remembered for having armed Parisian policemen with whistles and truncheons, this square is a charming urban Eden surrounded by the grim walls of Hôtel-Dieu Hospital, the Préfecture de Police, and the Tribunal de Commerce. One of the largest flower markets in Paris blooms here year-round with everything from chrysanthemums to lemon trees. On Sunday, the square is transformed into a bird market selling cages, seed, and a palette of colorful canaries, finches, and parrots. ◆ Rue de la Cité (between Rue de Lutèce and Quai de la Corse) Métro: Cité

On Place Louis-Lépine:

CITÉ MÉTRO STATION

This is one of the original 141 Art Nouveau "dragonfly" métro station entrances designed by **Hector Guimard** in 1900.

12 HÔTEL-DIEU HOSPITAL

Behind the double row of chestnut trees along the north end of the parvis is "God's Hostel," founded by St. Landry, Bishop of Paris. The original hospital building was erected here in AD 651. In 1400, this became the site of the oldest known cabaret in Paris, **La Pomme de Pin**; it was frequented by Rabelais, Villon, Molière, and Racine. The present hospital building was built here in the mid-19th century by Baron Haussmann as part of his urbanization project; in the latter part of that century it was an important training facility for US doctors. ◆ Pl du Parvis Notre-Dame (between Rues d'Arcole and de la Cité). Métros: Cité, St-Michel

Everything I saw—the chestnut trees scattering their leaves along the walks, the wide bridges clustered with bookstalls at either end of the medieval town of Ile de la Cité over which Notre-Dame raised its ponderous, Gothic stones—evoked that strange pang which even first-time visitors to Paris recognize, with some astonishment, as *nostalgia*. A buried memory seems to stab at your consciousness in Paris, and you follow in the steps of an elusive phantom *déjà vu*, but never quite catch up. So deeply embedded in the world's dream of freedom, youth, art, and pleasure has this city become, that the feeling that the stranger in Paris has is feeling of *return*. Perhaps one misses friends so keenly there because all of one's senses are pitched to such a keen note of receptivity, and one vibrates with an awareness that one longs to share.

—John Clellon Holmes, *Displaced Person*, 1987

13 PRÉFECTURE DE POLICE

A bunker of a building, this structure is the headquarters of the fictional Inspector Clouseau of *Pink Panther* fame and the very real Paris police. On 19 August 1944, during the liberation of Paris, about a thousand Paris police officers revolted against the German occupation, barricaded themselves inside, hoisted the tricolor to a rousing chorus of the *Marseillaise*, and held off Nazi tanks and artillery for 4 days until the Allies arrived. In the ensuing battle, 280 died, and buildings around **Notre-Dame**'s parvis are still pockmarked with bullet holes. ♦ 1 Rue de la Cité (between Quai du Marché-Neuf and Rue de Lutèce). Métros: Cité, St-Michel

14 PLACE DU PARVIS-NOTRE-DAME

In the Middle Ages, when miracle plays were performed, the square in front of Notre-Dame represented *paradis*, or paradise, a name contracted over the centuries to *parvis*. Critics of Baron Haussmann, who enlarged the parvis sixfold in the 19th century, called it the "paved prairie." Métros: Cité, St-Michel

Beneath the Place du Parvis-Notre-Dame:

CRYPTE ARCHÉOLOGIQUE (ARCHEOLOGICAL CRYPT)

In 1965, while excavating for an underground parking lot, city workers unearthed Gallo-Roman and medieval ruins, now preserved in this slightly eerie but intelligently designed archeological site/museum beneath the Place du Parvis-Notre-Dame. The crypt, designed by **André Hermant**, is worth a quick visit, if only to see the museum's interesting scale models of Paris, which show its evolution from a Celtic settlement during the Second Iron Age to a Roman city in 50 BC. Notice that the Romans, in anticipation of another barbarian invasion, reinforced the original ramparts with a second wall. This is one of the city's most accessible museums, with information in English and French. If you're lucky, you may even see a few archaeologists still carefully digging away. ♦ Admission. Tu-Su. Enter at the west end of Place du Parvis-Notre-Dame. 01.43.29.83.51

On the Place du Parvis-Notre-Dame:

RUE DE VENISE

Paris in the Middle Ages was a snarl of narrow horse paths. Marked in the pavement of the parvis in front of the cathedral is the former position of this 1-yard-wide medieval alley, no doubt once the narrowest street in Paris.

STATUE DE CHARLEMAGNE

On the south side of the parvis rests a bronze statue, created in 1882, of Charlemagne, the Frank who was crowned the first Holy Roman Emperor in AD 800. The center of Charlemagne's empire was at Aix-la-Chapelle; under Charlemagne and his successors, Paris was merely a provincial town. (If you happen to be looking for public toilets, follow the tail of Charlemagne's prancing horse; it points west to nearby stairs leading underground.)

POINT ZÉRO

All distances in France are measured from this brass compass star (Point Zéro des Routes de France) fixed in the pavement in front of Notre-Dame. Throughout France, highway signs tell you how far away you are (in kilometers) from Paris.

15 LE VIEUX BISTRO

★★$$ Far removed from the traffic and crush of tourists is this quiet, charming restaurant featuring the cuisine of Lyons. The *civet de canard* (duck stew) and the Burgundy sausage are both delicious choices. ♦ Daily, lunch and dinner. Reservations recommended. 14 Rue du Cloître-Notre-Dame (between Rues Massillon and d'Arcole). 01.43.54.18.95. Métro: Cité

16 9-11 QUAI AUX FLEURS

The sculpted heads on the façade of this 19th-century building commemorate two of history's most famous lovers, Héloïse and Abélard, who today cast plaintive glances at couples strolling arm in arm along the Quai aux Fleurs (where, by the way, no flowers are sold). In 1118 Pierre Abélard (1079-1142), an iconoclastic theologian who helped found the **University of Paris**, fell in love with one of his students. She was Héloïse (1101-1164), the brilliant niece of Fulbert, the foul-tempered canon of **Notre-Dame**. "Under the guise of study, we gave ourselves to love," wrote Abélard. ". . . We exchanged more kisses than sentences." The passionate affair was brought to an abrupt, brutal, and tragic end by Fulbert, whose thugs emasculated Abélard. Héloïse and Abélard lived on, cloistered separately for many years, but were buried side by side in **Père-Lachaise Cemetery**. ♦ 9-11 Quai aux Fleurs (at Rue des Chantres). Métros: Cité, Hôtel de Ville

17 PETIT PONT

The "Little Bridge" was first built in 1185 by Bishop Maurice de Sully, who also oversaw the construction of Notre-Dame. In the Middle Ages, minstrels were allowed to cross the bridge without paying the toll. A 19th-century version now stands. ♦ Between Quais St-Michel and du Marché-Neuf. Métros: Cité, St-Michel

18 CATHÉDRALE DE NOTRE-DAME DE PARIS (CATHEDRAL OF OUR LADY OF PARIS)

"The cathedral of Notre-Dame," wrote e.e. cummings, "does not budge an inch for all the idiocies of this world." For 6 centuries, this world-famous masterpiece of the Middle Ages has endured as a sonnet in stone, harmonizing mass and elegance, asymmetry and perfection. Among its architectural triumphs are the Gothic ribbed vaulting and the flying buttresses, which opened up the church by permitting the erection of higher, more slender walls pierced by glorious stained glass.

In 1163 no less a personage than Pope Alexander III laid the cathedral's foundation stone, but the final masterful touches were not completed until 1345—almost two centuries later. (Sainte-Chapelle, by comparison, was erected in 5 years.) The design followed the sketches executed in 1159 by Bishop Maurice de Sully and was implemented by architects **Pierre de Montreuil**, who was responsible for Notre-Dame's south transept, and **Jean de Chelles**, as well as generations of anonymous workers.

To tour the cathedral is to stroll through French history. On this site, the Romans built a temple in antiquity to Jupiter and the emperor Tiberius. In the cathedral during the Middle Ages, the homeless slept and were fed, trade unions met, passion plays were performed, and merchants from the Orient sold everything from ostrich eggs to elephant tusks. During the 12th century the cathedral's adjoining school became an intellectual center known throughout Europe; it eventually gave birth to the **Sorbonne**. During the revolution the cathedral was rechristened the "Temple of Reason"; shortly thereafter, it was auctioned off to a demolition contractor for scrap building material. Though never demolished, Notre-Dame was in shambles in 1804 when Napoléon Bonaparte called Pope Pius VII from Rome to officiate at his coronation, which was held before the cathedral's high altar. After the anointing, Napoléon defiantly snatched the crown from the pontiff and crowned himself emperor, a dramatic scene captured by Jacques-Louis David in his famous painting, which hangs in the **Louvre**.

West Façade At the base of the west façade, which is topped by two 69-meter (226-foot) towers, are three famous portals. The ones on the left and right honor the Virgin Mary and her mother, St. Anne, respectively; the one in the center depicts the Last Judgment. Royalty also managed to get into the picture; in the tympanum of the portal to St. Anne, a kneeling King Louis VII (far right) dedicates the cathedral with Bishop Sully (on the left with a crook in his hand), as the bishop's faithful secretary takes notes straddling a Gothic stool. The presence of Barbedor, the scribe, represents one of the first times an intellectual was honored in a cathedral façade.

Notre-Dame

Above the three portals is the **Gallery of Kings**, Eugène-Emmanuel Viollet-le-Duc's 19th-century replicas of medieval masterpieces, which were once painted in vibrant yellow, cobalt, and scarlet. The 28 kings represent the kings of Judea and Israel, thought by the Catholic Church to be the ancestors of Christ. In 1793 revolutionaries mistook them for the kings of France and toppled and decapitated them. Fortunately, an educator spirited away the heads and buried them in his yard at 20 Chaussée d'Antin, near the present site of the **Opéra Garnier**. They languished there until 1977, when they were unearthed during excavations for a bank vault and put on exhibit at the **Musée de Cluny**.

The entire façade of the cathedral was cleaned and restored for the 2000 millennium and is now in splendid condition.

North and South Towers   Enter the **North Tower** from a separate entrance at its foot. At the end of a spiraling 255-step climb you will find not Victor Hugo's tormented hunchback, Quasimodo, but an equally unsettling sight: Viollet-le-Duc's stone bestiary of gargoyles, gremlins, and demons. It was believed that

the gargoyles kept evil spirits from the cathedral; a number of them also serve as downspouts, squirting rain from their mouths—an entertaining sight during spring showers. The 90-meter (297-foot) spire was added during the heavy-handed Gothic Revival restoration of 1860. Viollet-le-Duc placed a statue of himself alongside the copper apostles and evangelists. The apostles stand on the cathedral roof looking outward, blessing the city, but the architect looks upward, admiring his work. For a bird's-eye view of the Viollet-le-Duc statue, the celebrated flying buttresses, and the splendid chain of bridges over the Atlantic-bound Seine, climb the last 125 steps to the top of the **South Tower**. The tower also houses the cathedral's famous 13-ton **Emmanuel Bell**, tolled on solemn occasions.

Interior   A recent cleanup of the cathedral's interior has made it much brighter and easier

to see its splendors. One of them is the massive **organ**. It is France's largest, a masterwork installed in the mid-19th century by Aristide Cavaillé-Coll and recently brought up to the highest standards of present-day audio technology. Following in the tradition of François Couperin, César-Auguste Franck, and Olivier Messiaen, all of whom performed here, some of Europe's greatest organists offer free recitals every Sunday afternoon between 5:15 and 6PM. These concerts, as well as the candlelight Easter vigil and Christmas Eve Mass, draw ample crowds, as does the deeply moving cathedral service held each 11 November, when the Royal British Legion honors British and Commonwealth soldiers who died on French soil during World War I. The cathedral's capacity is 3,000, with 1,400 seated.

Mays Paintings   During the Middle Ages, the Orfèvrerie (the gold workers' union) presented paintings to the cathedral each May. The paintings, called Mays, were originally hung between the church pillars; today, they are displayed in the side chapels. Among them are works by Charles Le Brun (1619-1690) and Eustache Le Sueur (1616-1655).

Windows   New windows were installed in the cathedral's clerestory after World War II, but not because of damage caused by the Germans. In the 18th century Louis XV declared stained glass déclassé and destroyed the Gothic glass in the upper-level nave windows, replacing it with clear glass. (The rest of the stained-glass windows were left intact.) The change gave the interior a bright, Protestant appearance. It was not until after the war that contemporary glass replicas of the original upper-nave Gothic windows were installed. Of Notre-Dame's three famous rose windows (north, south, and west), only the north has the original 13th-century glass. The south and west rose windows glow most brilliantly at twilight, whereas the north window is best viewed in morning light. The stained-glass windows of the 13th and 14th century are thick, with small images and a predominance of deep reds, blues, and purples. (The colors are actually dyed into the glass.) Over the centuries, it became possible to make thinner glass. Images became larger and were hand-painted on the glass surface, and ways of making brighter greens and yellows were discovered. These developments are evident in the differences between the original windows and the modern replicas.

Wood Sculpture   One of the cathedral's most charming decorations is the 14th-centuries Gothic relief on the north side of the chancel that depicts the life of Christ from the Nativity to the Last Supper.

The new altar (in front of the old altar) reflects the liturgical changes in the 1960s that allowed the priest to say Mass facing the congregation instead of turning his back. In addition, Mass is now said in French instead of Latin (although the cathedral's echoing acoustics sometimes make it hard to figure out what language is being spoken). ♦ 6 Pl Parvis du Notre-Dame (at Rue du Cloître-Notre-Dame). 01.42.34.56.10, 01.44.32.16.70 for tour information. Métros: Cité, St-Michel

19 SQUARE JEAN-XXIII

Cherry trees blossom here in the spring, lime trees provide shade in the summer, and the chestnut leaves are heaped ankle-deep in autumn. **Notre-Dame**'s west face is towering but flat compared to the south and east sides, shored by dramatic flying buttresses that loom above this park. Here is a place to pause and feed the birds or to perch on a wooden bench during one of the occasional outdoor concerts given by a local police officers' orchestra. ♦ Quai de l'Archevêché and Rue du Cloître-Notre-Dame. Métros: Cité, Maubert-Mutualité

20 MÉMORIAL DE LA DÉPORTATION (DEPORTATION MEMORIAL)

Designed by **G. H. Pingusson** in 1962, this structure commemorates the 200,000 people, most of them Jewish, who were deported from France and died during the Holocaust. Some 30,000 people from Paris alone were sent to Nazi death camps during World War II. Reflecting the Jewish tradition of paying homage to the dead by placing a stone on the grave, the memorial is constructed around a tunnel of 200,000 quartz pebbles. It also contains small tombs with earth from each of the concentration camps. Visitors descend a narrow stair to an open space where they can look out at water through iron-barred windows. From there they pass through a door to a low, enclosed room where they can look through other barred windows into the tunnel of pebbles. The visitor here feels trapped visually and psychologically by the low ceiling and iron bars. Stark and simple, the memorial is one of the city's most moving monuments. ♦ Free. Daily. Sq de l'Ile-de-France. Métros: Cité, Maubert–Mutualité

21 PONT ST-LOUIS

Step lightly; this pedestrian bridge is the ninth on a site that has had a shaky history. The first bridge linking Ile de la Cité and Ile St-Louis was erected in 1634 by developer Jean-Christophe Marie; it crumbled on opening day, drowning 20 people. But that wasn't the worst of Marie's bridge disasters; his Pont-Marie, built the following year, later collapsed during a flood, killing 121 people. ♦ Between Quais d'Orléans and de l'Archevêché. Métros: Cité, Pont-Marie

ILE ST-LOUIS

A world apart from the rest of Paris, this once-bucolic cow pasture and site of sword duels is jammed today with grand 17th-century town houses (which with few exceptions are closed to the public) and fashionable shops. Somehow it remains a peaceful oasis in the heart of a bustling city. Ile St-Louis is named after Louis IX, the saintly French king who recited his breviary here among the cows. Voltaire considered this island the "second best" location in the world (his first choice was the straits of the Bosporus separating Europe from Asia).

People have lived here for only 300 years, yet the island is the oldest fully preserved section of the French capital, bisected by a single commercial street. When Henri IV decided to "urbanize" the pastoral Ile St-Louis for his courtiers as an extension of Place des Vosges, he hired developer Jean-Christophe Marie. Between 1614 and 1630, Marie laid out one of the city's first real-estate developments with straight streets on a grid, an avant-garde idea in an age when streets followed meandering medieval cow paths.

Only six blocks long and two blocks wide, Ile St-Louis is an isolated village with no subway stop, four small hotels, and a baker whose ovens are fueled with wood. *Louisiens* (as island residents are called) are a proud, independent breed who don't always take kindly to interlopers. (Ile St-Louis was the first quarter in Paris to chase out the Nazis during the Liberation.) The list of former island residents includes Apollinaire, Balzac, Voltaire, Zola, Baudelaire, Cézanne, Courbet, Daumier, Delacroix, Colette, George Sand, and Georges Pompidou. When *Louisiens* leave the island, they say they are going to Paris or to the continent or to the mainland, a voyage that's less than the length of a football field. Many of the elder residents have not been off the island in years, and up until the 1970s there was so little traffic here on Sunday that the islanders played *boules* (boccie) in the streets.

Soon after **Berthillon** opened its doors here in 1954, ice cream became the rage of Paris and the island was rediscovered. Along with the notoriety came the inevitable chic tea salons and hordes of tourists. Nonetheless, Ile St-Louis retains its own distinctive identity and charm and remains one of the most exclusive addresses in the city.

22 LA BRASSERIE DE L'ISLE SAINT-LOUIS

★★$$ This Alsatian brasserie-tavern comes complete with the regional mascot—a stork perched on the old wooden bar. The bird, of course, is stuffed, and soon so are the neighborhood habitués who sit elbow to elbow dining on sausage, sauerkraut, ham knuckles,

---

Restaurants/Clubs: Red | Hotels: Purple | Shops: Orange | Outdoors/Parks: Green | Sights/Culture: Blue

PARIS IN PRINT

Some of history's most compelling stories have been set in the French capital. The following is a survey of three centuries of Paris-inspired literature.

The Age of Reason by Jean-Paul Sartre (Vintage Books, 1992): The author's 1945 novel is set in 1938 Paris. This is the story of Mathieu, a professor of philosophy, who is motivated by an idealistic obsession to remain free, particularly when his mistress becomes pregnant.

The Ambassadors by Henry James (Oxford University Press, 1986): In this Henry James 1903 classic, Lambert Strether is sent to Paris by Mrs. Newsome, a wealthy widow whom he plans to marry, to persuade her son Chad to come home. Strether gradually realizes that life may hold more meaning for Chad in Paris than in Massachusetts.

The American by Henry James (Buccaneer Books, 1990): This 1877 novel describes how a rich, self-made American goes to Paris to enjoy his wealth and becomes engaged to a beautiful young French widow from a noble family. But problems develop as cultural differences between the French family and the American emerge.

Banners of Silk by Rosalind Laker (Doubleday, 1981): A historical romance portraying the rags-to-riches story of two couturiers, Charles Worth and Louise Vernet, in the world of 19th-century Paris fashion.

The Blessing by Nancy Mitford (Carroll & Graf, 1989): Grace, a beautiful but dull English woman, marries a dashing French marquis and is swept into the complexities of Parisian society.

Camille by Alexandre Dumas *fils* (New American Library, 1984): First published in 1848, this novel depicts Camille, a beautiful courtesan in the fashionable world of 19th-century Paris, who rejects a wealthy count for her penniless lover Armand Duval. They escape to the country, but at the request of his family she pretends she no longer loves him and goes back to her life in Paris. The story ends with a tragic reunion between the lovers.

Du Côté de Chez Swann (*Swann's Way*) by Marcel Proust (1913, available in various English translations): The first volume of Proust's magnificent series of interlocking novels about high society in Belle Epoque Paris, *A la Recherche du Temps Perdu* (*In Search of Lost Time*), centers on the obsessive love of Charles Swann, a wealthy and well-connected art expert, for the devious *demimondaine* Odette de Crécy and the effects of this amour on Swann and his circle. The first section, **Combray**, contains the famous *madeleine* scene, in which the taste of the little cake dipped in tea triggers the narrator Marcel's flood of childhood memories.

Cousin Pons by Honoré de Balzac (Viking Press, 1978): Part of the 1848 series *Scenes of Parisian Life*, this book focuses on the friendship of two old musicians, Schmucke and Cousin Pons, and is set in the sordid mid-19th-century Parisian society of minor theaters, innkeepers, and impoverished artists and other bohemians.

Down and Out in Paris and London by George Orwell (Harvest, 1961): First published in 1933, this colorful account of the penniless writer's sojourn among the low-lifes of Paris in the late 1920s contains a hilarious exposé of the sanitary conditions in posh French restaurants, where he worked as a *plongeur* (dishwasher).

Explosive Acts: Toulouse-Lautrec, Oscar Wilde, Félix Fénéon and the Art & Anarchy of the Fin de Siècle by David Sweetman (Simon & Schuster, 2000). Through the author's revealing portraits of these three personalities a vivid picture of *la vie parisienne* at the close of the nineteenth century and onset of the twentieth—in all its glamour and grit—emerges as crisp as an autumn night in Montmartre.

The Flâneur by Edmund White (Bloomsbury, 2001): A *flâneur* is one who ambles through a city without any fixed purpose but is secretly attuned to the history of the place and in search of adventure, aesthetic or erotic. This "stroll through the paradoxes of Paris" takes us into fascinating little-known places and spheres of interest that this finely attuned writer discovered in his 16 years in the city and opens our eyes and minds to the unexpected.

Gigi by Colette (French & European Publications, 1979): The 1952 story of a young girl brought up to be a high-class mistress, who maneuvers a marriage proposal from a sophisticated man-about-town.

Giovanni's Room by James Baldwin (Laureleaf, 1985): In this groundbreaking gay novel, first published in 1956, most of the story takes place in Paris, where a young American man is involved with both his fiancée and another man.

Good Morning, Midnight by Jean Rhys (W. W. Norton & Company, 1986): A middle-aged woman, lonely and adrift in Paris, seeks consolation in a relationship with a gigolo.

Héloïse and Abélard by George Moore (W. W. Norton & Company, 1974): This fictionalized version of the tragic 12th-century love affair between Héloïse, a beautiful and learned woman, and Pierre Abélard, the brilliant philosopher who served as her tutor, was first published in 1921.

The Hunchback of Notre Dame by Victor Hugo (Longmeadow Press, 1991): First published in 1830, this classic is set in Paris during 1482. With the harshness of medieval life and the grandeur of **Notre-Dame** as backdrops, the strange and fantastic romance between the hunchback Quasimodo and his Esmeralda unfolds.

Imagining Paris: Exile, Writing, and American Identity by J. Gerald Kennedy (Yale University Press, 1993): An exploration of the imaginative process of five expatriate American writers (Gertrude Stein, Ernest Hemingway, Henry Miller, F. Scott Fitzgerald, and Djuna Barnes) demonstrates how the experience of living in Paris shaped their careers and literary works.

Is Paris Burning? by Larry Collins (Simon & Schuster, 1965): A suspenseful and exciting retelling of the story of the liberation of Paris in 1944 and one German general's decision to save the city from being burned to the ground.

Le Rouge et le Noir (*The Red and the Black*) by Stendhal (French & European Publications, 1958): Published in 1830, this tale follows the fall of Napoléon, as protagonist Julien's scandalous adventures take him to Paris.

Les Claudine by Colette (French & European Publications, 1969): Four semiautobiographical novels written from 1900 to 1903 follow Claudine through precocious girlhood, young womanhood in Paris, marriage, and an unusual love affair.

Les Enfants Terribles by Jean Cocteau (EMC Corp., 1977): In this historically and psychologically significant novel, two wild, poetic children withdraw to a small room in the midst of Paris after their mother's death.

Les Liaisons Dangereuses (*Dangerous Liaisons*) by Pierre Choderlos de Laclos (Knopf, 1991): Condemned in 1782 for being scandalous, this ruthless portrayal of sexual intrigue is a powerful moral analysis of the decadent society of mid-18th-century France.

Les Misérables by Victor Hugo (Penguin USA, 1982): A tale of the poor and the outcast in the early 19th century. First published in 1862, it recounts how an unjust system labels the noble Jean Valjean a criminal; other suffering victims of society are Fantine, her daughter Cosette, and Cosette's lover Marius.

Love in the Days of Rage by Lawrence Ferlinghetti (E.P. Dutton, 1988): Set against the turbulence and energy of the 1968 student riots in Paris, the love between a French banker and an expatriate American woman grows as revolutionary ideas are debated in cafés.

The Mandarins by Simone de Beauvoir (W.W. Norton & Company, 1991): This 1954 book paints a portrait of the existentialist clique and its adversaries, and re-creates the ambiance of Paris after the German occupation.

Mrs. 'arris Goes to Paris by Paul Gallico (International Polygonics Ltd., 1989): A middle-aged London cleaning woman, determined to own a designer gown, invades Paris's Christian Dior salon in this 1958 classic tale.

A Moveable Feast by Ernest Hemingway (Scribner, 1996): Published posthumously in 1964, Papa's sketches of his years as a young writer in Paris (1921–1926) are noted for their lovely descriptions of his Left Bank haunts, hatchet jobs on writers who befriended and helped him—Gertrude Stein and Scott Fitzgerald in particular—and self-pity about how the world somehow caused him to break up his idyllic first marriage.

The Notebooks of Malte Laurids Brigge by Rainer Maria Rilke (W.W. Norton & Company, 1992): A young Danish poet of noble birth moves to Paris and lives in poverty. This 1910 novel is written as if it were a series of diary entries, with observations of the poet's suffering and squalor and speculations on art and life.

Overhead in a Balloon: Twelve Stories of Paris by Mavis Gallant (W.W. Norton & Company, 1988): Twelve stories interconnected by characters who jump from one tale to another. Parisian life is well captured in pieces about a bourgeois debate over real-estate law,

roommates discussing domestic arrangements, and dissatisfied lovers.

Paris: Capital of the World by Patrice Higonnet (Harvard University Press, 2002): A professor of French history at Harvard takes an unusual and incisive look at the life and times of Paris from the mid-eighteenth century to World War II. By deconstructing the myths that have grown up around the French capital, the author sheds light on how Paris came to be considered the capital of such wide-ranging domains as art, science, revolution, pleasure, and the American imagination. Not a history book per se but encyclopedic in scope, Higonnet's ruminations are not only intellectually challenging but full of little-known bits of Paris trivia divulged like a true insider.

Paris Noir by Tyler Stovall (Houghton Mifflin, 1996): A richly detailed account of the long, mutually stimulating cultural relationship between France and the many African-American writers, artists, and musicians who have lived and worked in the City of Light.

The Scarlet Pimpernel by Baroness Emmuska Orczy (Buccaneer Books, 1984): Sir Percy Blakeney, a foppish young Englishman, is found to be the daring Scarlet Pimpernel who rescues aristocrats from the guillotine during the French Revolution.

The Sun Also Rises by Ernest Hemingway (Scribner, 1954): This classic tale of Jake Barnes, Lady Brett Ashley, and the Lost Generation of disillusioned World War I veterans in Paris was published in 1926 at the height of the postwar expatriate migration to **Montparnasse**. A literary sensation, it immediately established Hemingway as the dominant prose stylist in the English language.

Sylvia Beach and the Lost Generation by Noel Riley Fitch (Norton, 1985): This lively biography of the creator of the Shakespeare and Company bookshop, friend of Hemingway, Fitzgerald, Pound, Joyce, and numerous other expatriate writers and the courageous publisher of Joyce's *Ulysses*, is the best single volume on the English-language literary explosion in Paris in the 1920s and 1930s.

A Tale of Two Cities by Charles Dickens (Buccaneer Books, 1987): This 1859 Dickens classic, set against the bloody French Revolution, has memorable scenes in the **Bastille** prison and the working-class **Faubourg St-Antoine** quarter.

Tender Is the Night by F. Scott Fitzgerald (Scribner, 1934, and numerous paperback editions): The tragic story of Dr. Dick Diver and his beautiful but mentally fragile wife Nicole unfolds against the sumptuous backdrops of the Côte d'Azur and Paris, where key scenes in this haunting reflection on the failed dreams of the 1920s take place at the **Ritz Hotel**.

Tropic of Cancer by Henry Miller (Grove Press, 1989): Published in 1934, this explosive autobiographical novel recounts Miller's adventures as a hungry, but by no means sex-starved, American in the Paris of the early 1930s.

blueberry tarts, and *chopes* (steins) of Mutzia beer. The 1913 silver-plated espresso machine is a museum piece. The servers are paragons of patience and good cheer when talking to foreigners. ♦ F-Tu, lunch and dinner; Th, dinner; closed in August. 55 Quai de Bourbon (at Rue St-Louis-en-l'Ile). 01.43.54.02.59. Métro: Pont-Marie

23 LA MAISON LAFITTE

Magret de canard (duck fillet), *confit d'oie* (goose confit), foie gras, and other gourmet by-products of force-fed fowl are preserved, packaged, and ready to be taken home in your suitcase. ♦ Tu-Sa. 8 Rue Jean-du-Bellay (between Rue St-Louis-en-l'Ile and Quai de Bourbon). 01.43.26.08.63. Métro: Pont-Marie

24 LE FLORE EN L'ILE

★$ A three-star view of the Panthéon on the Left Bank and the flying buttresses of Notre-Dame is the main draw of this Viennese-style tearoom. Other highlights include music by Mozart, good breakfasts, a hearty onion soup, traditional *plats du jour*, and delicious fruit tarts. Regrettably, however, the waiters do their utmost to live up to the bad old stereotype of Parisian service. ♦ Daily, breakfast, lunch, and dinner until 2AM. 42 Quai d'Orléans (at Rue Jean-du-Bellay). 01.43.29.88.27. Métro: Pont-Marie

24 LA CHAUMIÈRE EN L'ILE

$$ In a rustic setting of stone walls and oak beams, this little restaurant serves such traditional French dishes as onion soup, foie gras, roast salmon, beef Bourgignon, cassoulet, and crème brûlée. The attraction here is more in the charm of the surroundings than in the quality of the cuisine. ♦ Daily, lunch and dinner. 4 Rue Jean-du-Bellay (at Rue St-Louis-en-l'Ile). 01.43.54.27.34. Métro: Pont-Marie

The term *hôtel* in Paris often refers not to an overnight lodging place but rather to an *hôtel particulier*, meaning a town house or mansion.

The guillotine was proposed by Dr. Joseph Guillotin in 1791 as an instantaneous and more humane method of execution. The beheading device was adopted for all capital crimes in France in 1792. Contrary to common lore, Dr. Guillotin was not killed by the machine that bears his name; he died in his bed in 1814 at age 76.

25 ALAIN CARION

You'll find minerals, geodes, meteorites, and minuscule fossilized black nautiluses fashioned into earrings at this rock collector's paradise of international renown. ♦ Tu-Sa. 92 Rue St-Louis-en-l'Ile (between Rues Le Regrattier and Jean-du-Bellay). 01.43.26.01.16. Métro: Pont-Marie

25 AU LYS D'ARGENT

★$ For light fare that's also light on your pocketbook, pop into Lucy Rouffet's cheerful, mirrored *glacier-crêperie–salon de thé*. In addition to 24 crêpes, 25 kinds of tea, and the mouthwatering array of ice cream and pastries, copious salads and omelettes and a daily big brunch are offered. ♦ Daily, lunch and dinner. 90 Rue St-Louis-en-l'Ile (between Rues Le Regrattier and Jean-du-Bellay). 01.46.33.56.13. Métro: Pont-Marie

26 HÔTEL ST-LOUIS

$$ The cousin of **Hôtel de Lutèce** and **Hôtel des Deux-Iles** (see below for both), this 21-room hostelry has exposed wooden beams, Louis XIII furniture, thick carpeting, and modern bathrooms, but *petits* bedrooms. Fifth-floor rooms have a view of the rooftops. There's no restaurant. Reserve far in advance. ♦ 75 Rue St-Louis-en-l'Ile (at Rue Boutarel). 01.46.34.04.80; fax 01.46.34.02.13. Métro: Pont-Marie. www.hotelsaintlouis.com

26 LE MONDE DES CHIMÈRES

★★$$ This stone-and-beam bistro is a strong favorite of Ile St-Louis natives. Among the specialties of chef Cécille Ibane are 40-garlic chicken, *brandade de morue* (codfish puréed with olive oil, garlic, and milk), duck with apples, and an assortment of crêpes. ♦ Tu-Sa, lunch and dinner. 69 Rue St-Louis-en-l'Ile (between Rues Le Regrattier and Boutarel). 01.43.54.45.27. Métro: Pont-Marie

27 HÔTEL DE LUTÈCE

$$$ Named after the first Roman settlement in Paris, this restored 17th-century town house is now a hotel offering 23 comfortable rooms. The small breakfast room opens onto a flowered atrium. Ask for one of the brighter rooms on the top floor; they offer exquisite views of the island's rooftops and the dome of the Panthéon across the river. Reserve far in advance. ♦ 65 Rue St-Louis-en-l'Ile (between Rues Le Regrattier and Boutarel). 01.43.26.23.52; fax 01.43.29.60.25. Métro: Pont-Marie. lutece@hotel-ile-saintlouis.com; www.hotel-ile-saintlouis.com

28 AUX ANYSETIERS DU ROY

★$$ Originally called Au Petit Bacchus (the scorched remains of a 300-year-old effigy of the god of drink and revelry slouch above the entrance), this tavern used to serve the gamblers and jocks who frequented the ancient *jeu de paume* (tennis) court across the street at No. 54. The chef recommends the foie gras, *magret de canard au miel et aux raisins* (duck breast with honey and grapes), and the apple tart with vanilla ice cream. Don't leave without washing your hands in the 17th-century pewter bathroom sink upstairs. ♦ Daily, lunch and dinner. Reservations recommended. 61 Rue St-Louis-en-l'Ile (at Rue Le Regrattier). 01.56.24.84.58. Métro: Pont-Marie.

28 HÔTEL DES DEUX-ILES

$$$ An abundance of fresh flowers adorns this 17th-century mansion-turned-hotel. The hotel bar, which has a fireplace, and the Renaissance-style ceramic tiles in the bathrooms are adequate compensation for the 17 smallish Provence-inspired rooms. There's no restaurant. Reserve far in advance. ♦ 59 Rue St-Louis-en-l'Ile (between Rues Budé and Le Regrattier). 01.43.26.13.35; fax 01.43.29.60.25. Métro: Pont-Marie. hotel.2iles@free.fr

28 PYLÔNES

The fanciful rubber jewelry and accessories displayed here sell as briskly as hot chestnuts on a winter afternoon. In lieu of that Boucheron diamond bracelet, wouldn't you rather be wearing a fanciful cactus, fish skeleton, monkey, or maybe the pyramids of Giza on your wrist? Other novelties include children's bibs, fanciful bike bells, brightly colored computer mouses, *Star Wars* chess sets, and New Wave egg cups. ♦ Daily. 57 Rue St-Louis-en-l'Ile (between Rues Budé and Le Regrattier). 01.46.34.05.02. Métro: Pont-Marie

29 HÔTEL CHENIZOT

This former residence of the city's archbishops was also the home of Theresa Cabarrus, a noblewoman of insatiable sexual appetite. She offered herself to drawing-room revolutionaries and as a result of this gesture was dubbed **Notre Dame de Thermidor**. Although the plaster cornucopia and ferns in the first courtyard date from an 18th-century restoration, the mythological sea god over the front door and the sundial in the damp rear courtyard are original 17th-century decorations. This is now an apartment building with a restaurant and shop on the ground floor (see below). ♦ 51 Rue St-Louis-en-l'Ile (between Rues Budé and Le Regrattier). Métro: Pont-Marie

Within Hôtel Chenizot:

LA CASTAFIORE

LA CASTAFIORE

★★$$ In 1988 a North American and an Englishman left the advertising business to open Ile St-Louis's only Italian restaurant. The result was this dining spot with terra-cotta walls, white tablecloths, and a warm ambiance in which to enjoy *tagliatelles aux St. Jacques* (pasta with scallops) or saltimbocca. Don't pass up the homemade tiramisù or the *poire au Barolo* (fresh pear in wine sauce) for dessert. ♦ Daily, lunch and dinner. Reservations recommended. 01.43.54.78.62

L'EPICERIE

French gourmands will feel right at home in this tiny shop packed to the rafters with delicacies to do penance for. Champagne mustard, *terrine de canard lapin* (duck casserole), fois gras, homemade wild strawberry jam, and beautifully wrapped bonbons are but a few of the treats. ♦ Daily, 10:30AM-9PM. 01.43.25.20.14

30 LA PETITE SCIERIE

Nothing but duck by-products are sold at this retail outlet of the well-known duck farm of the same name (which means "the little sawmill") in Pouilly-sur-Loire. Jars of *confit de canard* (preserved duck breast), *confit de canard* with broad beans, *choucroute de canard* (duck with sauerkraut), preserved duck gizzards, and other emanations of our fine feathered friend fill the shelves from floor to ceiling, and foie gras is available either in bulk or—for those like their fat liver on the go—in the foie gras sandwiches that the shop sells. Daily, 10AM-8PM. 60 Rue St-Louis-en-l'Ile (between Rues des Deux-Ponts and Le Regrattier). 01.55.42.14.88. Métro: Pont-Marie

---

Restaurants/Clubs: **Red** | Hotels: **Purple** | Shops: Orange | Outdoors/Parks: **Green** | Sights/Culture: Blue

Hôtel du
jeu de paume

31 HÔTEL DU JEU DE PAUME

$$$ Deftly fashioned around a royal tennis court dating from 1624 (*jeu de paume* is the medieval precursor of the game now played at Wimbledon, Flushing Meadow, and Roland-Garros), this refined 28-room hotel was opened in the 1980s. There's no restaurant. Reserve far in advance. ♦ 54 Rue St-Louis-en-l'Ile (between Rues des Deux-Ponts and Le Regrattier). 01.43.26.14.18; fax 01.40.46.02.76. Métro: Pont-Marie. info@jeudepaumehotel.com; www.jeudepaumehotel.com

32 NOS ANCÊTRES LES GAULOIS

★$$ Tackily decorated with sheepskins, battered shields, and mounted heads of wild boars (in sunglasses) to loosely evoke the Middle Ages, this cavernous, all-you-can-eat establishment seats 240 people. Earthy do-it-yourself salads, greasy sausage platters, grilled meat, chocolate mousse, and barely drinkable red wine are perennial hits with starving students and rowdy German tour groups. It's always crowded; arrive early and avoid Saturday nights, when the ambiance is raucous, bordering on Neanderthal. ♦ M-Sa, dinner until 1AM; Su, lunch and dinner until 1AM. Reservations required. 39 Rue St-Louis-en-l'Ile (between Rues des Deux-Ponts and Budé). 01.46.33.66.12. Métro: Pont-Marie

Le Relais de l'Isle
J a z z   R e s t a u r a n t

32 LE RELAIS DE L'ISLE

★★$$ Jazz buff Christophe Lepelletier's intimate restaurant features top Paris-based pianists such as Bobby Few nightly, either solo or accompanied by bass, guitar, or drums, with guests like famed jazz singer Joe Lee Wilson, who lives on the island, occasionally sitting in. Solid French family fare is served: foie gras or warmed goat cheese on toast with salad for a starter; main courses of shrimps and scallops cooked in olive oil, breast of crispy duck, lamb shanks, or the vegetarian plate of the day; and for dessert, *moilleux au chocolat amer* (bitter chocolate that's crusty on top, melted inside) or pears marinated in red wine and cinnamon. That such a tiny place as this (it seats only 24) can offer its customers so much for the modest prices it charges is somewhat of a miracle.

Only a *fou de jazz* could pull it off. There are good, filling, inexpensive luncheon specials with the best in recorded jazz. ♦ M, Th-Su, lunch and dinner; W, dinner; music nightly, 7:30PM-1AM. Reservations recommended. 37 Rue St-Louis-en-l'Ile (between Rues des Deux-Ponts and Budé). 01.46.34.72.34. Métro: Pont-Marie

33 BERTHILLON

This Ile St-Louis landmark is so popular that around Christmastime police officers direct the flow of Parisians queuing up for what is undeniably the best ice cream and sorbet in Paris. Its position as the city's preeminent ice-cream shop is so secure that it has the nerve to close 2 days a week, on school holidays, and for 6 weeks in summer, the prime ice-cream–eating season. Women in pink aprons scoop up more than 70 flavors, all made without a single artificial ingredient. Sample the exotic fruit flavors in season: rhubarb, black currant, fig, kumquat, and fresh melon. ♦ W-Su; closed school holidays and mid-July through August. ♦ 31 Rue St-Louis-en-l'Ile (between Rues Poulletier and des Deux-Ponts). 01.43.54.31.61. Métro: Pont-Marie

34 AU GOURMET DE L'ISLE

★$$ Famous for its *andouillette* (sausage with tripe)—a nice dish if you can stomach it—this bargain bistro is a bustling place. Other less challenging specialties: artichoke hearts and pork in red wine sauce, fruit tarts, and Auvergne wines. ♦ W-Su, lunch and dinner; Tu, dinner. Reservations recommended for dinner. 42 Rue St-Louis-en-l'Ile (between Rues Poulletier and des Deux-Ponts). 01.43.26.79.27. Métro: Pont-Marie

34 BOULANGERIE MARTIN

Once you've taken a bite of Philippe Martin's *baguette à l'ancienne*, it's so hard to stop eating it that some people think he must doctor the recipe with some controlled substance (a conjecture that M. Martin denies). However he does it, his crisp-crusted, chewy-hearted old-style baguette is one of the best in the city. ♦ Tu-Sa. 40 Rue St-Louis-en-l'Ile (between Rues Poulletier and des Deux-Ponts). 01.43.54.57.59. Métro: Pont-Marie

35 L'AUBERGE DE LA REINE BLANCHE

★★$$ Named for the mother of the island's patron, St. Louis, this pretty pale apricot dining room offers dependable French classics: *canard* (duck) *à l'orange*, coq au vin, and *boeuf bourguignon*. Catch the cute dollhouse furniture displayed on the walls. ♦ M-Tu, F-Su, lunch and dinner; Th, dinner. Reservations recommended. 30 Rue St-Louis-en-l'Ile (between Rues Poulletier and des

Deux-Ponts). 01.46.33.07.87. Métro: Pont-Marie

35 L'ORANGERIE

★★★$$$ A mini Maxim's, with 18th-century décor and background harpsichord music, this restaurant specializes in elegant late suppers. Chateaubriand, leg of lamb (cooked over a wood fire), rich Bordeaux reds, and sophisticated ambiance cause Rolls-Royce traffic jams out front. Actor Jean-Claude Brialy is the owner. Jackets and ties required for men. ♦ Daily, dinner; closed the last 3 weeks of August. Reservations required. 28 Rue St-Louis-en-l'Ile (between Rues Poulletier and des Deux-Ponts). 01.46.33.93.98. Métro: Pont-Marie

35 LIBRAIRIE ULYSSE

In 1971 the free-spirited Catherine Domain opened this vest-pocket shop specializing in travel books. She has crammed in, higgledy-piggledy, 20,000 French and English titles on everything from trekking in the Himalayas to canoeing in South America, a large collection of road and topographical maps, and of course, many books on Paris and France. Fellow residents of small islands (ones with fewer than 3,000 residents and whose circumference can be walked in less than 24 hours) are entitled to a free passport from the Ulysse Little Island Club that offers many free services and contacts in Paris. ♦ Tu-Sa, 2-8PM. 26 St-Louis-en-l'Ile (between Rues Poulletier and des Deux-Ponts). 01.43.25.17.35; fax 01.43.29.52.10. Métro: Ponte-Marie. ulysse@ulysse.fr; www.ulysse.fr

35 LA CHARLOTTE DE l'ISLE

★★$ For a diabolically delicious treat, order *gâteau du diable* (devil's cake), half-moon cookies, or witch's brooms (chocolate-dipped orange rinds) at this little-known tea salon. Sylvie Langlet, the hospitable, kimono-clad owner who presides over this fairyland, serves freshly brewed Chinese tea at one of four tiny tables nestled in the back room or three in the front among the clutter of puppets, dried-flower bouquets, and an old stereo playing Poulenc. Puppet shows and piano concerts are regular events here. ♦ Tea: Th-Su, noon-8PM. Puppet shows: W, 3PM, by reservation. Piano concerts: F, 6-8PM. Closed July through August. 24 Rue St-Louis-en-l'Ile (between Rues Poulletier and des Deux-Ponts). 01.43.54.25.83. Métro: Pont-Marie

36 ST-LOUIS-EN-L'ILE

Popular for weddings and candlelit concerts, this Jesuit Baroque–style church was built in 1726; it follows plans created by island resident **Louis Le Vau**, the great French architect who designed portions of the **Louvre** and **Versailles**. Inside is a statue of St. Louis in chain mail and crusader's sword, and next to the tomb of a Polish freedom fighter with a daunting name (Damaiowicestrzembosz) is a 1926 plaque that bears the inscription: "In grateful memory of St. Louis in whose honor the City of St. Louis, Missouri, USA, is named." The church was vandalized during the revolution. For example, the empty-handed carved cherubs over the massive wooden west portal once held the king's fleur-de-lis. The only reason the statues of St. Geneviève and the Virgin Mary survived the revolution is that they were disguised as the goddesses of Reason and Freedom. Evening concerts are held here frequently. ♦ 3 Rue Poulletier (at Rue St-Louis-en-l'Ile). 01.46.34.11.60. Métro: Pont-Marie

37 PONT-MARIE

King Louis XIII laid the first stone of this bridge, which was completed in 1635. Twenty-three years later, a spring thaw caused a flood that partially destroyed the bridge; 22 of the four-story houses above the structure fell into the Seine, drowning 121 residents and shopkeepers. The bridge is not named after Marie de Médicis, Henri IV's widow, who commissioned the work, but after Jean-Christophe Marie, the contractor hired to develop Ile St-Louis and the quais. ♦ Between Quais d'Anjou and de Hôtel-de-Ville. Métro: Pont-Marie

39 3 QUAI DE BOURBON

The plainness of the façade of this real-estate agency is a story in itself. The sumptuous Empire-style windows and storefront that once adorned the building were purchased by J. Pierpont Morgan and in 1926 were moved to the Metropolitan Museum of Art in New York. They now serve as the entrance to the museum's Wrightsman Galleries, which house a superb collection of Louis XVI furniture and porcelain. ♦ Between Rues des Deux-Ponts and Le Regrattier. Métro: Pont-Marie

39 BOULANGERIE RIOUX

Old-fashioned bread is baked in a *four chauffé au bois* (wood-burning oven) at this traditional bakery. ♦ M-W, Sa-Su. 35 Rue des Deux-Ponts (between Rue St-Louis-en-l'Ile and Quai de Bourbon). 01.43.54.57.59. Métro: Pont-Marie

39 LES FOUS DE L'ILE

★$ Brass candlesticks on old wooden bistro tables, wacky monthly art exhibitions, and music from Paganini to Pearl Jam make this roomy converted *épicerie* (food market) the

---

Restaurants/Clubs: Red | Hotels: Purple | Shops: Orange | Outdoors/Parks: Green | Sights/Culture: Blue

island's most relaxing and hip restaurant-café. At lunch, famished students arrive for the warm goat cheese salad, *tagliatelles au saumon fumé* (pasta and smoked salmon) with caviar, *magret de canard* (duck breast) in cherry sauce, and cheesecake. Unlike most eating places on the island, here the diner has plenty of room. ♦ Tu-F, lunch, dinner, and tea; Sa, tea and dinner; Su, brunch and tea. Live music Tu and W. 33 Rue des Deux-Ponts (between Rue St-Louis-en-l'Ile and Quai de Bourbon). 01.43.25.76.67. Métro: Pont-Marie

40 37 QUAI D'ANJOU

When he returned to France in 1921 after the acceptance of his first major novel, *Three Soldiers*, ex–World War I ambulance driver John Dos Passos rented a room in this apartment building. ♦ Between Rues Poulletier and des Deux-Ponts. Métro: Pont-Marie

41 29 QUAI D'ANJOU

In 1922, with a hand-printing press, North American William Bird established his Three Mountains Press in this building. Under the editorial aegis of Ezra Pound, it published Ernest Hemingway and Ford Madox Ford. ♦ Between Rues Poulletier and des Deux-Ponts. Métro: Pont-Marie

42 HÔTEL DE LAUZUN

Louis Le Vau built this mansion in 1656 for a corrupt French army caterer, Charles Gruyn des Bordes, who was arrested soon afterward. That is why the building is named for its second tenant, the dandy Duke of Lauzun. The roll call of residents and visitors to the **Hôtel de Lauzun** includes Rilke, Wagner, Daumier, Delacroix, and **Louis Charles Auguste Steinheil** (who restored the **Sainte-Chapelle** windows). In 1834 Baudelaire gathered his bohemian "hashish club" in an upstairs room and conducted the hallucinatory research for his book *Les Paradis Artificiels*. Some of the gaudiest suites in all of Paris are the **Chambres de Parade** (parade rooms), which are cluttered with golden nymphs, cut-velvet walls, trompe l'oeil murals, and allegorical figures. In 1928 the city bought and restored it as a residence for visiting heads of state. ♦ Tours one Tuesday per month, by appointment only; reserve at least a year in advance. 17 Quai d'Anjou (between Rues St-Louis-en-l'Ile and Poulletier). 01.42.76.57.99. Métros: Pont-Marie, Sully–Morland

43 9 QUAI D'ANJOU

Nineteenth-century illustrator and satirist Honoré Daumier lived in this apartment building off and on for 17 years in the company of such distinguished islanders as poet Charles Baudelaire and fellow artist Ferdinand Delacroix. It was on the Ile St-Louis that Daumier sketched his mordant portrayals

of life and politics and painted masterpieces such as *La Blanchisseuse* (*The Washer Woman*), which hangs in the **Louvre**. ♦ Between Rues St-Louis-en-l'Ile and Poulletier. Métros: Pont-Marie, Sully–Morland

44 HÔTEL LAMBERT

Probably the most opulent of 17th-century private residences in Paris, this frescoed and pilastered *hôtel particulier* was designed by **Louis Le Vau** in 1640 for Lambert the Rich. Its lavish gilded ceilings by Charles Le Brun predate and rival his **Great Hall of Mirrors** at **Versailles**. After the 1830-1831 insurrection, Polish prince Adam Czartoryski fled to France, married King Louis-Philippe's granddaughter, and bought the **Hôtel Lambert** for his personal residence. Over the years, Czartoryski's home served as a salon for expatriate Polish royalty and intelligentsia, as well as a rehearsal hall for Frédéric Chopin. Later it functioned as a girls' finishing school and a safe house for Allied fighter pilots whose planes had been shot down in France. Voltaire briefly nested here with his lover, the Marquise de Châtelet, while writing the *Henriade*. Since 1972 the house has belonged to the Rothschilds. Behind the locked gate is a horseshoe-shaped courtyard and the famous **Galerie d'Hercule**, containing the Eustache Le Sueur frescoes and Jacques Rousseau trompe l'oeil landscape paintings. The building is open to the public only on rare occasions. ♦ 2 Rue St-Louis-en-l'Ile (between Quai d'Anjou and Rue Poulletier). Métros: Pont-Marie, Sully–Morland

45 5 RUE ST-LOUIS-EN-L'ILE

The expatriate literary agent William Aspenwall Bradley, who represented such authors as Thornton Wilder, Edith Wharton, Katherine Anne Porter, and John Dos Passos, lived in this apartment building. Bradley was the one who closed the deal for publication of the *Autobiography of Alice B. Toklas* by Gertrude Stein. ♦ Between Quai d'Anjou and Rue de Bretonvilliers. Métros: Pont-Marie, Sully–Morland

46 RUE DE LA FEMME SANS TESTE (STREET OF THE HEADLESS WOMAN)

Shortly after the revolution, the Rue Le Regrattier (named in the 17th century for an entrepreneur in the island development consortium) was dubbed the "Street of the Headless Woman" (in old French, *tête* was spelled with an s) after a decapitated statue at the corner of Rue Le Regrattier and Quai de Bourbon. "Headless woman" is a misnomer, however; the robed stone figure, severed at the torso, is believed to be St. Nicholas, the patron saint of boatmen. His statue stands at the top of the stairs that once led down to the ferry. ◆ Rue Le Regrattier. Métro: Pont-Marie

46 6 RUE LE REGRATTIER

Jeanne Duval, the voluptuous West Indian mistress of Charles-Pierre Baudelaire who was known as the Black Venus, lived here. It's still a private residence. ◆ Between Quai d'Orléans and Rue St-Louis-en-l'Ile. Métro: Pont-Marie

47 18-20 QUAI D'ORLÉANS

Columnist Walter Lippmann lived here in 1938. It remains a private residence. ◆ Between Rues Budé and Le Regrattier. Métro: Pont-Marie

48 10 QUAI D'ORLÉANS

James Jones, the author of *From Here to Eternity*, resided here with his family between 1958 and 1975 and entertained such famous writers and artists as Henry Miller, Alexander Calder, William Styron, Sylvia Beach, and James Baldwin. This is still a residential building.◆ At Rue Budé. Métro: Pont-Marie

49 MUSÉE ADAM MICKIEWICZ

The life and times of exiled Mickiewicz, the "Byron of Poland," as well as the poet's relationships with great Romantic French authors and musicians, are brought to life on the second floor of this exquisite library and museum. The private library, established in 1852, contains some 200,000 volumes as well as copies of nearly every Polish newspaper published in the 19th century. In the Chopin Room on the first floor are composer Frédéric Chopin's frayed armchair, his hand-penned mazurka scores, a death mask, and the world's only daguerreotype of the young pianist. ◆ Admission. Tu-F, 2-6PM; Sa, 10AM-1PM. Guided tours: Th, 2-5PM, on the hour. 6 Quai d'Orléans (between Rues des Deux-Ponts and Budé). No phone. Métro: Pont-Marie

" ISAMI "

49 ISAMI

★★★$$ Small, simple, and casual, the only Japanese restaurant on the island specializes in sushi and sashimi but also serves such dishes as oyster salad with vinegar and steamed *daurade* (sea bream). You will be reassured by seeing that many of your fellow diners are from Japan. ◆ Tu-Sa, lunch and dinner; Su, dinner. 4 Quai d'Orléans (between Rues des Deux-Ponts and Budé). 01.40.46.06.97. Métro: Pont-Marie

50 24 QUAI DE BÉTHUNE

In 1935 Helena Rubinstein demolished one of the island's finest town houses (constructed in 1642) and built an Art Deco structure in its place. She reigned from the new building's rooftop apartment. This remains a residential building. ◆ At Rue Poulletier. Métro: Pont-Marie

51 FLOOD MARKER

Written on the wall along Quai de Béthune are the words *Crue Janvier 1910* and a line marking the astounding level, or *crue*, the Seine reached during the *inondation* (flood) of January 1910, when many streets became canals and rowboats were the preferred form of transportation. ◆ Quai de Béthune (between Blvd Henri-IV and Rue des Deux-Ponts). Métro: Pont-Marie

52 SQUARE BARYE

At the eastern tip of Ile St-Louis, this pocket park is all that remains of the terraced gardens of Duc de Bretonvillier. You might glimpse sunbathers or witness a schoolboys' fishing competition here on the cobblestone quay. ◆ Métros: Pont-Marie, Sully–Morland

---

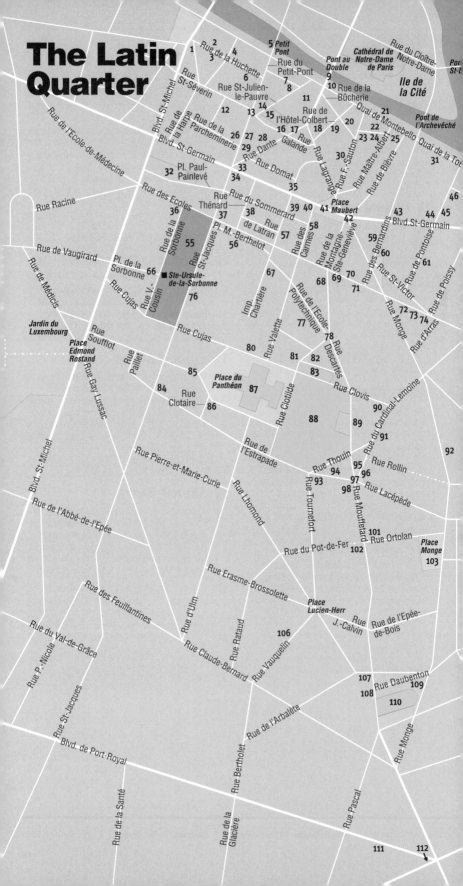

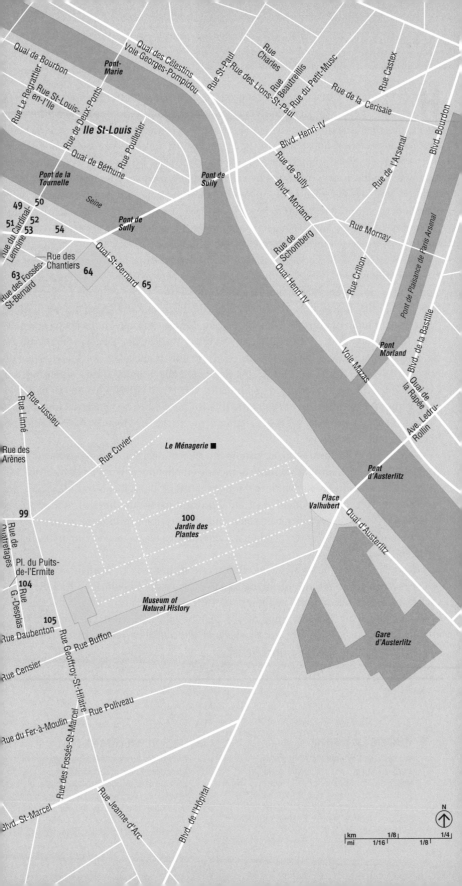

THE LATIN QUARTER

Home to Roman Paris, the **Sorbonne**, and the bohemian quarter, the Latin Quarter is a cultural mecca. The Henri Murger novel *Scènes de la Vie de Bohème*, which became the Puccini opera *La Bohème*, was set in this district. Verlaine and Descartes lived here, and today old bookshops, student cafés, publishing houses, jazz clubs, and, more recently, expensive boutiques grace the streets of the Latin Quarter. For 7 centuries, this was a city within a city, inhabited by Latin-speaking scholars who were exempt from civil law and recognized no authority other than the pope. Latin, which hasn't been spoken here since the revolution, has been replaced on the streets of the Left Bank by the Moroccan, Greek, and Vietnamese of immigrant families selling couscous, souvlaki, and imperial rolls to supplement the basic bohemian diet of coffee and cheap cigarettes.

This overview of the Latin Quarter begins at the **Pont de la Tournelle**, in front of the famed penthouse restaurant **La Tour d'Argent**. From here you can browse the bookstalls along the **Seine** and enjoy a splendid view of **Notre-Dame**'s flying buttresses. Next come two funny, offbeat museums, the **Musée des Hôpitaux de Paris–Assistance Publique** (Museum of Public Health and Welfare) and the **Musée des Collections Historiques de la Préfecture de Police** (Police Museum); and then the **Rue des Ecoles**, which leads to the **Sorbonne** and the **Collège de France**, for centuries the most celebrated seats of learning in Europe. At the end of the street are the **Roman Baths** adjoining the extraordinary medieval **Musée de Cluny**. As you climb **Montagne Ste-Geneviève**, named after the patron saint of Paris, you'll pass King Philippe Auguste's 13th-century city wall and the **Panthéon**, a classical monument and the final resting place of Voltaire, Rousseau, and Victor Hugo.

At the **Place de la Contrescarpe**, visitors can embark on a detour that passes a Roman arena and a Moorish mosque en route to the zoo and botanical gardens—a nice spot for a picnic lunch purchased in the **Place-Monge** market or along **Rue Mouffetard**. On this medieval market street frequented in the 20th century by the likes of young Ernest Hemingway, you can meander past stalls selling everything from tropical mangoes to African monkey bread and then end up at **Gobelins**, the old royal weaving mills, for an afternoon tour.

For a quick bite while sight-seeing, stop at one of the many inexpensive Vietnamese or Greek shish kebab restaurants along Mouffetard around **Gobelins**. To find the Latin Quarter's fancier restaurants, including **La Tour d'Argent**, head toward the Rue des Ecoles and the Seine. The area's nightspots, including **Paradis Latin, Les Trois Maillets**, and the **Caveau de la Huchette**, are also located here and are an appropriate way to end a day spent in the bohemian Latin Quarter.

1 RUE DE LA HARPE

Named after Reginald the Harper, this medieval street, along with **Rue de la Huchette**, is one of the city's oldest. A youthful air emanates from the cheap restaurants jammed with students along this bustling byway. ◆ Métros: St-Michel, Cluny–La Sorbonne

2 RUE DE LA HUCHETTE

In medieval times this ancient thoroughfare was called Street of Roasters because it had a plethora of barbecue pits. Couscous and shish kebab joints continue the carnivorous tradition by roasting whole lambs and pigs in their front windows. You can always find cheap, sometimes risky, street food here. The narrow walking street runs between Rue du Petit-Pont and Blvd St-Michel. Métro: St-Michel

On Rue de la Huchette:

10 RUE DE LA HUCHETTE

For several months here in 1795, a young brigadier general languished in a sparsely decorated back room. Unemployed, unloved, and (he thought) dying of hunger, he saw no hope for the future. Soon thereafter, he dispersed a mob by firing grapeshot into its midst, and from then on Napoléon Bonaparte was never ignored. ♦ Métro: St-Michel

28 RUE DE LA HUCHETTE

Outside the **Hôtel Mt-Blanc** is one of the many wall plaques in Paris commemorating World War II Resistance fighters. It reads "Here fell Jean-Albert Bouillard, dead in the course of duty, killed by the Gestapo 17 May 1944 at 20 hours." ♦ Between Rue Xavier-Privas and Pl St-Michel. Métro: St-Michel

3 THÉÂTRE DE LA HUCHETTE

Ever since Eugène Ionesco finished them in the mid-1950s, two of his plays, *The Bald Soprano* and *The Lesson*, have been running nonstop at this 85-seat theater. ♦ Box office: M-Sa. 23 Rue de la Huchette (between Rues Xavier-Privas and de la Harpe). 01.43.26.38.99. Métro: St-Michel

4 RUE DU CHAT-QUI-PÊCHE

The Street of the Fishing Cat, most likely named for a medieval fishmonger, is one of the shortest, narrowest, and, arguably, grungiest alleys in Paris. ♦ Between Rue de la Huchette and Quai de Montebello. Métro: St-Michel

5 PETIT PONT

Bishop Maurice de Sully was responsible for the construction of this little bridge, built in 1185 and rebuilt in the 19th century. Formerly located at the end of the bridge was the **Petit Châtelet** fortress and prison, a more diminutive version of the **Grand Châtelet** on the Right Bank. ♦ Métros: St-Michel, Cité

6 CAVEAU DE LA HUCHETTE

This is another crowded, dingy jazz cellar on a street that once rang with bebop but now has retrogressed to Dixieland and swing; there's a dance floor. Prices for admission and drinks are remarkably modest. ♦ Cover; student discount available. Daily, 9:30PM-2:30AM, ending later on weekends. 5 Rue de la Huchette (between Rues du Petit-Pont and Xavier-

Privas). 01.43.26.65.05. Métro: St-Michel

7 RUE DE LA BÛCHERIE

A *bûcherie* is a woodshed, and this part of the quay is where firewood-laden barges dropped their cargo. ♦ Between Rues St-Julien-le-Pauvre and du Petit-Pont. Métros: Maubert–Mutualité, St-Michel, Cité

On Rue de la Bûcherie:

SHAKESPEARE AND COMPANY

With its cavalcade of book-jammed shelves and bins encroaching on a floor space that wasn't vast to begin with, this old-time bookstore bespeaks either secret-attic allure or airless fire-hazard nonpareil, and doubtless receives a good deal of its foot traffic from those seeking out the ghost of Ernest Hemingway. It isn't here, though: the original **Shakespeare and Company** that belonged to Sylvia Beach (and was immortalized by the young Hem in *A Moveable Feast*) on Rue de l'Odéon is long gone, though part of its collection went into this shop run by cantankerous nonagenarian George Whitman. The inventory is eclectic, unabashedly leftward leaning politically, and organized only in the most arcane fashion if at all, but none of that prevents tourists from hunting down this old dinosaur, impervious to the clean efficiencies of amazon.com after all these years. Each book purchased in the shop is stamped with an inscription that reads "Shakespeare and Company Kilometer Zero Paris." Daily, noon-midnight. No. 37 Rue de la Bûcherie. 01.43.26.96.50

LA BÛCHERIE

★★$$$ With the grand **Notre-Dame** view from its dining terrace, this is a delightful spot for lunch or dinner in clement weather, and when it gets chilly, reserve a table near the crackling fireplace in the sleek yet cozy dining room (but avoid sitting behind the chimney, where famished customers can go unnoticed for days). Among the specialties are ravioli stuffed with snails from Burgundy with tomatoes and basil; shellfish casserole with vegetables and a dash of cayenne; and *confit de canard* (preserved duck) with delicate mushrooms in red-wine sauce. ♦ Daily, lunch and dinner. Reservations

Parlez-Vous Anglais?

If English is your first—or only—language, and you need a book fix in Paris, here are the English-language bookstores of choice:

Abbey Bookshop 29 Rue de la Parcheminerie (between Rues de la Harpe and Boutebrie). 01.46.33.16.24

Albion 13 Rue Charles-V (between Rues Beautreillis and St-Paul). 01.42.72.50.71

Brentano's 37 Ave de l'Opéra (between Rues Danielle-Casanova and d'Antin). 01.42.61.52.50

Galignani 224 Rue de Rivoli (between Rues d'Alger and de Castiglione). 01.42.60.76.07

San Francisco Book Company 17 Rue Monsieur le Prince (between Rues Dubois and Dupuytren). 01.43.29.15.70

Shakespeare and Company 37 Rue de la Bûcherie (between Rues St-Julien-le-Pauvre and du Petit-Pont).

01.43.26.96.50

Tea and Tattered Pages 24 Rue Mayet (between Rues du Sevres and Cherche-Midi). 01.40.65.94.35

The Village Voice 6 Rue Princesse (between Rues Guisarde and du Four). 01.46.33.36.47

W.H. Smith and Son 248 Rue de Rivoli (at Rue Cambon). 01.44.77.88.99

And if you need a library:

American Library in Paris 10 Rue du Général-Camou (between Aves Rapp and de La Bourdonnais). 01.53.59.12.60

British Cultural Center 9 Rue de Constantine (at Rue St-Dominique). 01.49.55.73.23

recommended. 41 Rue de la Bûcherie. 01.43.54.24.52

8 Esmeralda

$$ This atmospheric 19-room hotel is a favorite with traveling writers and professors. The garrulous owner, artist Michèle Bruel, seems to have stepped right out of the 19th century. Some of the guest rooms have views of **Notre-Dame**. There is no restaurant. ♦ No credit cards accepted. 4 Rue St-Julien-le-Pauvre (between Rues Galande and de la Bûcherie). 01.43.54.19.20; fax 01.40.51.00.68. Métros: Maubert-Mutualité, St-Michel, Cité

9 Pont au Double

The name derives from the fact that this was the only bridge in Paris whose toll was 2 *sous* instead of 1. ♦ Métros: Maubert-Mutualité, St-Michel

10 Quai de Montebello Booksellers

The *bouquinistes* who work in the shadow of **Notre-Dame** practice one of the city's oldest trades, selling old Daumier prints, volumes on everything from Balzac to bebop to girlie magazines, and the occasional naughty postcard out of their green boxes on the quay. These famous, free-spirited cowboys of the book business open and close their sidewalk stalls when they please and sell only what interests them. ♦ Daily, depending on the weather. Quai de Montebello (between Pont de l'Archevêché and Pont au Double). Métros: Maubert-Mutualité, St-Michel

11 Square René-Viviani

In this lovely little park stands what is reputed to be the oldest tree in Paris. This false acacia (*Robinia pseudoacacia*) leans on concrete crutches, infirm but erect, and blooms every spring. Not bad for a sprout that crossed the ocean from Guyana to be planted in 1680 by Jean Robin. Sit for a moment on one of the park benches and notice the pieces of worn and broken statuary surrounding you; they were once part of **Notre-Dame**. ♦ Métros: Maubert-Mutualité, St-Michel

12 Rue St-Julien-le-Pauvre

The magnificent gate at **No. 14** marks the 17th-century home of the governor of the old **Petit-Châtelet** prison. Also don't miss the house of the dwindling windows at **No. 10**; they start with the largest ones on the ground floor and shrink all the way up to the maids' rooms in the attic. Métros: Maubert-Mutualité, St-Michel, Cité

the tea caddy

12 The Tea Caddy

★$ Looking like a prim and proper English great-aunt's library, with dark wood paneling and thick-paned windows, this is the place for afternoon tea and assorted pastries. Light meals of quiche, salads, and omelettes are also served. ♦ Daily. 14 Rue St-Julien-le-Pauvre (between Rues Galande and de la

Bûcherie). 01.43.54.15.56. Métros: Maubert–Mutualité, St-Michel, Cité

12 St-Séverin

This lesser-known edifice, which was constructed around 1220 on the burial site of a sixth-century hermit named Séverin, is the official church of the **University of Paris**. Recognized as the city's richest example of flamboyant Gothic architecture, it was expanded between 1414 and 1520 with a bullet-shaped nave, a gaggle of gargoyles, and a five-aisled symphony of ribbed vaulting and stained glass. In 1673, the distinguished **Jules Hardouin-Mansart** tried his hand at enhancing the church, adding a small communion hall. Don't miss the double ambulatory's slender medieval columns that shoot into vaulted arches, creating an effect that Joris-Karl Huysmans compared to being in a palm grove. The modern windows are by Jean Bazaine, the French abstract painter who created the mosaics for the **UNESCO** building and the **Cluny–La Sorbonne** métro station. Saint-Saëns and Fauré performed on the 18th-century rococo organ in front of the west window; today the organ is frequently used for recitals. ♦ Rue des Prêtres-St-Séverin and St-Séverin. Métros: St-Michel, Cluny–La Sorbonne

13 Les Trois Maillets

The "Three Mallets" began in the 13th century as a tavern that served the stonemasons constructing **Notre-Dame**. Some 700 years later it was transformed into a postwar jazz club first frequented by North American GIs. Entertainment still includes jazz but also belly dancing, rap, rock, Latino music, and French pop, and it has one of the best piano bars in Paris. ♦ Cover. Daily, 6PM-6AM; live music begins at 11PM. No. 56 Rue Galande (at Rue du Petit Pont). 01.43.54.00.79

15 St-Julien-le-Pauvre

Named in honor of St. Julian the Poor, a martyred third-century bishop who gave all his money to the penniless, this church, an odd, graceless amalgam of Romanesque and Gothic architecture, has no bell tower, transepts, or organ and squats on a small square lined with acacia trees. With its iron-caged well in front, it looks more like a humble country church than a Parisian monument. Founded in 1165 (and restored in 1250 and 1651), this is one of several structures that claims the title of oldest church in Paris. Although the construction of **Notre-Dame** began 2 years earlier, St-Julien-le-Pauvre was completed first, and though **St-Germain-des-Prés** is older, it originally stood

outside the city walls and therefore was not, strictly speaking, a Parisian church. In the 12th century, when renegade theologian Pierre Abélard quit Notre-Dame, he took more than 3,000 students along with him and established a new university here. The church thus became the seat and meeting place of the new **University of Paris**. In 1524, students critical of a new rector ransacked and nearly destroyed the church. After the revolution, St-Julien-le-Pauvre was used variously as a salt storehouse, wool market, and flour granary. Since 1889 it has belonged to the Greek Orthodox Church, and there are numerous Byzantine-style icons. The enormous stone slab beside the well came from the fourth-century Roman highway that became **Rue St-Jacques**. ♦ 1 Rue St-Julien-le-Pauvre (at Sq René-Viviani). 01.43.54.52.16. Métros: Maubert–Mutualité, St-Michel, Cité

16 Rue Galande

The beginning of the old Roman road to Lyon, this meandering street was named in 1202 after a family who lived nearby. It was one of the fancier neighborhoods in 17th-century Paris. ♦ Métro: Maubert–Mutualité

16 Studio Galande

Catch one of the cinema's weekend showings of *The Rocky Horror Picture Show*. Watching funkily costumed French college students enjoying their umpteenth viewing of this crazy cult film—singing, dancing, and shouting at the on-screen characters—is guaranteed to have you in stitches. Outside the theater, glance up at the 14th-century stone relief of St. Julien crossing the Seine, which originally stood over the portal of nearby **St-Julien-le-Pauvre** church. ♦ 42 Rue Galande (between Rues du Fouarre and St-Julien-le-Pauvre). 01.43.26.94.08. Métro: Maubert–Mutualité.

17 Rue du Fouarre

Seated on *fouarres* (bundles of straw), undergraduates in the Middle Ages attended open-air lectures presented in this alley by rowdy intellectuals, notorious throughout

St. Geneviève (ca. 423-500), the patron saint of Paris, was said to have holy powers from birth. The story goes that Geneviève's mother lost her eyesight when she hit the young girl. The little saint restored her mother's sight by bathing her eyes with water from a well in the Paris suburb of Nanterre. The well is revered for its healing powers to this day.

Restaurants/Clubs: Red | Hotels: Purple | Shops: Orange | Outdoors/Parks: Green | Sights/Culture: Blue

Europe. In an attempt to ease tensions in 1358, Charles V chained the street at both ends and closed it at night. During his visit to Paris in 1304, even Dante harkened to the scholars here and later made reference in his writing to this *vico degli strami* (the road of straws). ◆ Métro: Maubert-Mutualité

On Rue du Fouarre:

17 LA FOURMI AILÉE

★★$ On a chilly day come to this charming tearoom and women's bookstore and order a hot goat cheese salad, sit back in a caned bentwood chair by the fireplace, and peruse a book by Simone de Beauvoir. ◆ Daily, noon-1AM. No. 29. 01.43.29.40.99

18 LES BOUCHONS DE FRANÇOIS CLERC

★★$$ François Clerc sells the well-selected wines and champagnes in his cellar in his restaurant at cost. The wine prices are only one reason to rush to this dining spot: The wood-beamed dining room is sophisticated and cozy, the homemade bread is warm and crusty, the waiters are young and bubbly, and the menu features such original dishes as *salade folle de Bouchons* (mixed green salad with beef carpaccio and foie gras slices), *filet de boeuf rôti au sautoir, ragoût de févettes à la bordelaise* (fillet of beef slices with tender beans and bordelaise sauce), and *coulant chaud au chocolat, glace vanille bourbon* (melted chocolate sauce over superb vanilla ice cream). This place is popular, so book well in advance. ◆ M-F, lunch and dinner; Sa, dinner. Reservations required. 12 Rue de l'Hôtel-Colbert (between Rues Lagrange and de la Bûcherie). 01.43.54.15.34. Métro: Maubert-Mutualité

MELIÁ COLBERT
Boutique HOTEL

19 MELIA COLBERT

$$$ From 9 of the 36 comfortable rooms in this former 17th-century residence, you can contemplate **Notre-Dame** while having breakfast in bed. All the guest rooms have been newly renovated and are decorated in traditional French style and now have modern bathrooms, air-conditioning, satellite TV, and Internet access. The place has an interesting history: Parts of the building date back to 1500, and an animal hospital sponsored by the Duke of Windsor once stood on the site of the present courtyard garden. There's no restaurant. ◆ 7 Rue de l'Hôtel-Colbert (at Rue de la Bûcherie). 01.56.81.19.00; fax 01.56.81.19.02. Métro: Maubert-Mutualité. melia.colbert@ solmelia.com; www.solmelia.com

20 GALERIE URUBAMBA

Traditional indigenous art and culture from the Americas—weavings, masks, headdresses, and more—is the specialty of this gallery-folk art shop. A bookshop affords visitors a selection of over 2,000 titles and catalogs. The gallery also organizes language and fabric-weaving classes. ◆ Tu-Sa, 2-7:30PM. 4 Rue de la Bûcherie (between Rue du Haut Pavé and l'Hotel-Colbert). 01.43.54.08.24. Métro: Maubert-Mutualité

22 DEGRÉS DE NOTRE DAME

$$ In this picturesque little hotel directly across the river from **Notre Dame**, all 10 rooms have exposed beams and are delightfully decorated to accent the old-time charm, but they also offer up-to-date bathrooms, phones, TV, and plenty of closet space. The front rooms overlook a quiet street; the back rooms, the cathedral; and Room 510, which takes up the entire top floor, is a spacious atelier with skylights and a breathtaking Notre Dame view. There's a cozy, wood-beamed restaurant and bar on the ground floor. The only drawback: There's no elevator. ◆ 10 Rue des Grands Degrés (between Rue Frédéric-Sauton and Quai de Montebello). 01.55.42.88.88; fax 01.40.46.95.34. Métro: Maubert-Mutualité

23 LE KIOSQUE FLOTTANT

★$ Moored across the river from the south side of the Notre Dame from spring to fall, this cute old double-decker café boat gives you double value for your money—decent light fare and refreshments and one of the most dramatic views there is of the cathedral and its flying buttresses. ◆ Daily, 10-2AM Apr-Sept. Port de Montebello, Quai de Montebello (by the foot of the Pont de l'Archevêché). 01.43.54.19.51. Métro: Maubert-Mutualité

23 PATCHWORKS DU ROUVRAY

Like the **Galerie Urubamba** across the square, this quilt emporium is run by a North American woman. Diane de Obaldia's shop is named after a 14th-century farmhouse near Chartres, where she started her business. Today she sells traditional patchwork quilts of the 1930s. She also offers many quilting classes (in French and English) and 1,500 varieties of cotton fabric for inspired quilters. ◆ M-Sa. 3 Rue de la Bûcherie (corner of Rues de la Bûcherie and Frédéric-Sauton). 01.43.25.00.45. Métro: Maubert-Mutualité

24 LE REMINET

*$$ This bistro has seen its popularity grow steadily thanks to its charming sidestreet location and inventive menu that changes frequently. How inventive? For starters, try prawn fritters with tandoori avocado purée or parsley and garlic-flavored pig's ears with preserved gizzards and warm foie gras. Desserts could include the likes of Earl Grey tea mousse with crispy eggplant leaves, sesame biscuits and bergamot oil, peaches flambé with nutmeg, and cognac brioche with apricot sorbet. Young chef Hugues Gourney executes such oddities with skill but portions are almost uniformly on the *petite* side. M, Th-Su, lunch and dinner. 3 Rue des Grands-Degrés (between Rues du Haut-Pavé and Maître Albert). 01.44.07.04.24. Métro: Maubert-Mutalité or St-Michel

25 JEAN-PIERRE STELLA

Legions of lead soldiers stand at attention in this little shop on the quay. Military medals, Napoleonic helmets, and vintage weaponry are also sold. ♦ M-Sa, 2-7PM, and by appointment in the mornings; closed mid-July through August. 67 Quai de la Tournelle (between Rues de Bièvre and Maître Albert). 01.46.33.40.50. Métro: Maubert-Mutalité. Also at 32 Blvd St-Germain (between Rues de Pointoise and Poissy). 01.46.33.61.60

25 ATELIER MAÎTRE ALBERT

★★★$$ For a romantic dining experience, try this fine, elegant, surprisingly affordable restaurant named for the celebrated 13th-century University of Paris *doctor universalis* Albert le Grand. The rustic stone walls, rose-toned tapestries, exposed wood-beam ceiling, gold-framed mirrors, candlelit tables, and magnificent 16th-century fireplace give the spacious main dining the look and feel of a Renaissance manor house, whereas in the smaller, more intimate dining rooms, modern art decorates the walls. The fixed-price luncheon and dinner menus offer a grand array of starters, main courses, cheeses, and desserts,

with a half-bottle of wine or other beverage included. Some items featured are roasted quail on a bed of green salad with a poached egg; marinated and poached salmon terrine with leeks, truffles, and French dressing; roasted sea bass with lemon and black olive sauce; roasted guinea fowl; rack of lamb with garlic cream; hot chocolate cake with vanilla ice cream; and homemade apple tart with caramel sauce. Come here on a cold winter day when the fireplace is crackling away. ♦ M-Sa, lunch and dinner. Reservations recommended. 1 Rue Maître-Albert (at Quai de la Tournelle). 01.46.33.13.78. Métro: Maubert-Mutalité

26 RUE DE LA PARCHEMINERIE

In the Middle Ages this narrow street was crammed with scribes, copyists, and parchment peddlers. It runs between Rue St-Jacques and Rue de la Harpe. Métro: Cluny-La Sorbonne

On Rue de la Parcheminerie:

ABBEY BOOKSHOP

A long, narrow shop stacked to the rafters with more books than you'd think it could possibly hold, this Canadian-owned store sells new and used books by Canadian, US, British, and other anglophone authors, travel books, maps, and translated works by French and world writers. The shop also buys used books. ♦ M-Sa. 29 Rue de la Parcheminerie (between Rues de la Harpe and Bouterbrie), 01.46.33.16.24

27 RUE ST-JACQUES

The city's oldest street originated as a Roman road. A thousand years later, it was named after St. Jacques (St. James), whose body is believed to have miraculously appeared in Spain in the ninth century. Paris was the principal starting point of a thousand-mile pilgrimage to Santiago de Compostela in Spain, where the saint's body was buried. In medieval times, pilgrims wearing scallop shells (the symbol of St. James) would set off down this street. The delicious contents of such shells are now served throughout Paris as *coquilles St-Jacques*. ♦ Métros: St-Michel, Cluny-La Sorbonne, Maubert-Mutalité

美 麗 華 酒 家
MIRAMA

27 MIRAMA

★$ With glazed, roasted ducks hanging in the window and a cauldron whose contents

Restaurants/Clubs: **Red** | Hotels: **Purple** | Shops: **Orange** | Outdoors/Parks: **Green** | Sights/Culture: **Blue**

47

bubble mysteriously just inside the door, this informal Chinese restaurant at first seems suspect. Yet it's crowded all day long, and deservedly so: The ingredients are fresh and the price is right. Try the noodle soup with shrimp dumplings, sweet-and-sour chicken, crispy mixed vegetables, pork ribs in black bean sauce, and, of course, the *canard laqué* you saw on the way in. ♦ Daily, lunch and dinner. 17 Rue St-Jacques (between Blvd St-Germain and Rue Galande). 01.43.54.71.77. Métros: Maubert–Mutualité, St-Michel

28 LIBRAIRIE GOURMANDE

The celebrated *bouquiniste* Mme. Baudon moved to this shop from her stall on the quay, where she sells books on food and wine from the 17th century to the present. ♦ Daily. 4 Rue Dante (between Blvd St-Germain and Rue Galande). 01.43.54.37.27. Métros: Maubert–Mutualité, St-Michel

29 27 RUE ST-JACQUES

More than a hundred sundials can be found in Paris, but few were created by artists of worldwide repute. Surrealist Salvador Dalí designed this *cadran solaire* for friends whose furniture store was located here. The timepiece's completion in 1968 was televised, with Dalí mounting a cherry picker to carve his signature into the still-wet cement. Set on the south face of the building, the sundial depicts a female face in the form of a *coquille St-Jacques* (scallop shell). ♦ Between Blvd St-Germain and Rue Galande. Métros: Maubert–Mutualité, St-Michel

Restaurant de Haute Mer

29 LE BAR À HUITRES

★★$$ Fresh oysters and scallops arrive daily from the Normandy and Brittany coasts to

become components in sumptuous platters of mollusks and crustaceans. Fish specialties include monkfish curry in winter and roast turbot with wine and butter sauce in summer. Served with velvety *beurre blanc* for dipping, the grilled lobster is heavenly. The bar outside sells oysters and such for takeout, making this place truly a paradise for shellfish lovers at among the best prices in town. ♦ Daily, lunch and dinner until 2AM. 33 Rue St-Jacques (between Blvd St-Germain and Rue Galande). 01.44.07.27.37. Métros: Maubert–Mutualité, Cluny–La Sorbonne, St-Michel. Also at 112 Blvd du Montparnasse (at Blvd Raspail). 01.43.20.71.01. Métro: Vavin; 33 Blvd Beau-marchais (at Rue du Pas-de-la-Mule). 01.48.87.98.92. Métros: Bastille, Chemin Vert

Chieng-Mai
Spécialités Thaïlandaises

30 CHIENG-MAI

★★$$ An excellent Thai restaurant, this eatery serves beef satay, squid and mint salad, spicy pork brochette, and, for dessert, grilled flan with coconut milk. The pineapple salad is divine. Red is the predominant color in the two warm and inviting dining rooms. ♦ Daily, lunch and dinner. Reservations required. 12 Rue Frédéric-Sauton (between Rues Lagrange and de la Bûcherie). 01.43.25.45.45. Métro: Maubert–Mutualité

31 MUSÉE DES HÔPITAUX DE PARIS—ASSISTANCE PUBLIQUE (MUSEUM OF PUBLIC HEALTH AND WELFARE)

Tucked away in this 17th-century mansion, which was converted into the central pharmacy for the city's hospitals after the revolution, is one of Paris's most offbeat yet entertaining museums. Unknown to most Parisians (and visitors), this repository of French medical history contains an extraordinary collection of old ceramic apothecary jars, Roman medicine vials, hospital rosters, pewter syringes, copper basins, blocks of marble that were pulverized to powder baby bottoms, and a model of a quasi–night deposit box that 19th-century nuns invented for abandoned babies. ♦ Admission. Tu-Su; closed in August and on holidays. 47 Quai de la Tournelle (between Rues de Pontoise and des Bernardins). 01.40.27.50.05; fax: 01.40.27.46.48. Métro: Maubert–Mutualité

31 45 QUAI DE LA TOURNELLE

Shortly after being discharged from the American Ambulance Corps in the spring of 1919, John Dos Passos sublet a playwright's

---

I needed Paris. It was a feast, a grand carnival of imagery, and immediately everything good there seemed to offer sublimation to those inner desires that had for so long been hampered by racism back in America. For the first time in my life I was relaxing from tension and pressure. My thoughts, continually rampaging against racial conditions, were suddenly becoming as peaceful as snowflakes. Slowly a curtain was dropping between me and those soiled years.

—Gordon Parks,
Voices in the Mirror, 1990

apartment here and began what would become his first successful novel, *Three Soldiers*. It remains a residential building. ♦ Between Rues de Pontoise and des Bernardins. Métro: Maubert-Mutualité

32 HÔTEL DE CLUNY, MUSÉE DE CLUNY (MUSÉE NATIONAL DU MOYEN-AGE), AND PALAIS DES THERMES

Constructed by the abbots of Cluny in 1330 and rebuilt in 1510, this magnificent mansion is one of the oldest private residences in Paris. It straddles the ruins of second-century **Roman baths** and contains one of the world's finest collections of French medieval art, including the exquisite *Lady and the Unicorn* tapestries.

The baths date from Marcus Aurelius (AD 161-80); Julian the Apostate, proclaimed Roman emperor in 360, lived in the adjoining palace. The baths and palace were sacked during numerous barbarian invasions, and in 1340 Pierre de Châlus, abbot of Cluny, the wealthy Benedictine abbey in Burgundy, bought the ruins and erected the **Hôtel de Cluny** as a pied-à-terre for the abbots when they visited Paris. Shortly after the revolution, the hotel was occupied by a cooper, a laundress, French navy astronomers, and a surgeon who used the chapel for his dissections. Among the mansion's tenants in 1833 was Alexandre du Sommerard, an art collector who had specialized in Gothic and Renaissance art. When he died in 1842, the state bought the building as well as du Sommerard's collection and appointed his son Edmond as the first curator of the **Musée de Cluny**, also known as the **Musée National du Moyen-Age** (National Museum of the Middle Ages).

As you enter the museum courtyard by the Rue du Sommerard, notice the polygonal stair tower sprinkled with carved shells (*coquilles St-Jacques*), the symbol of the patron saint of Jacques d'Amboise, the abbot of Jumièges, who between 1485 and 1510 rebuilt the hotel in its present Flamboyant Gothic style. The first rooms of the museum are replete with delicate ivory carvings, embroidered Egyptian silks, and Flemish tapestries of gentlemen setting off for the hunt. ♦ Admission. M, W-Su 9:15AM–5:45PM. One-hour guided tours in English Sa-Su, 11:15PM. 6 Pl Paul-Painlevé (at Rue du Sommerard). 01.53.73.78.00; information, 01.53.73.78.16. Métro: Cluny–La Sorbonne. www.musee-moyenage.fr

Within the Hôtel de Cluny, Musée de Cluny, and Palais des Thermes:

NOTRE-DAME GALLERY

In this stark white room are the sculpted stone heads of 21 noseless but nevertheless majestic monarchs (1210-30). They represent the kings of Judea and Israel, who, according to St. Matthew's genealogy, were ancestors of Christ. Like most men too closely associated with religion and royalty at the time of the revolution, they lost their heads. But theirs was a case of mistaken identity. The full-length statues of the kings were originally enshrined in the **Gallery of Kings** on **Notre-Dame**'s west façade, but they were beheaded in 1793 by an angry mob who assumed they depicted the kings of France. The statues have stood decapitated since that time, and for nearly 2 centuries the heads were considered lost. But in 1977, during excavations for a new bank in the **Hôtel Moreau** near the **Opéra**, they were unearthed; the discovery is considered one of the 20th century's major archeological finds.

ROMAN BATHS

The towering roof of the *frigidarium* (cold bath) is the largest Roman vault in all of France. The ceiling has survived 18 centuries of wear and tear, even withstanding being topped with 8 feet of topsoil and an abbot's apple orchard and kitchen garden. The ship prows decorating the base of the groined vaulting are the building signatures of the powerful Boatmen's Guild of Paris. Nearby is the *Boatmen's Pillar*, one of the oldest pieces of sculpture in Paris. It was dedicated to the god Jupiter by the Boatmen's Guild during the reign of Roman emperor Tiberius (AD 14-37) and was later discovered beneath **Notre-Dame**.

TREASURY

Upstairs, above the baths, is a dazzling display of Gallic, Barbarian, and Merovingian jewelry, including six gold Visigoth crowns, two 13th-century gold double crosses, and the sublimely delicate 14th-century *Golden Rose* that was presented to the Bishop of Basel by Pope Clement V.

STAINED GLASS

Among the medieval stained-glass windows in the upstairs corridor are religious scenes from **Sainte-Chapelle** and the **Basilique de St-Denis**. Take a close look; in the actual churches—even with a strong pair of opera glasses and a craned neck—you won't get this good a view. Three large windows and the surrounding stonework come from the church of **St-Jean-de-Latran**, demolished in 1859 to make way for the Rue des Ecoles built between the **Cluny** and the **Sorbonne**.

ABBOTS' CHAPEL

One of the few surviving interior details of the original mansion, this chapel was the abbots' oratory and is an architectural masterpiece. The elaborate vaulting sprouts palmlike from a single slender pillar. In a room near the chapel is a 1383 eagle lectern and a 12th-century gilt copper altar table.

TAPESTRIES

Saving the best for last, enter the rotunda on the top floor, dimly lit to protect the world-famous *Lady and the Unicorn* tapestry series. In 1844, quite by accident, writer George Sand discovered the tapestries hanging at the Château de Boussac; supposedly they were a wedding present in the 15th century from magistrate Jean Le Viste to his bride (the Le Viste coat of arms appears in each panel). The artist, who remains unknown, is thought to have designed the similar set of six tapestries that is now hanging in the Cloisters museum in New York City. The delicate tapestries allegorically depict the five senses. In the one representing sight, for instance, the noble unicorn gazes into the mirror of a bejeweled blond woman. In the mysterious sixth tapestry, the woman's tent is emblazoned with the words *A Mon Seul Désir* (To My Only Desire), thought to represent mastery of all five senses. Notice that the woman on the red *millefleur* (literally, "one thousand flowers") background changes from one sumptuous gown to another in a veritable fashion show as you progress around the room.

Outside the Hôtel de Cluny:

JARDIN DE CLUNY

To further enliven our the appreciation of the life and arts of the Middle Ages, the museum has created a charming contemporary garden of medieval inspiration on its grounds. Laid out in neat geometrical plots are a variety of types of garden of the period—a kitchen garden, a medicinal garden, a perfumed *jardin d'amour*, a celestial garden bursting

with flowers symbolizing the Virgin. Boardwalks make for easy viewing, and clearly written descriptive panels in French, English, and Spanish explain the practical uses and symbolic meanings of the many plants and flowers in medieval times. ♦ Free. Daily during daylight hours. Bounded by Blvds St-Michel and St-Germain, Rue de Cluny, and the rear of the Hôtel de Cluny. Entrances on Blvd St-Michel, Blvd St-Germain, Rue de Cluny. Métro: Cluny–La Sorbonne

33 A L'IMAGERIE

The largest old print and poster shop in Paris specializes in original Art Deco, Art Nouveau, and late 19th-century Japanese prints and stamps. ♦ M, 10AM-3PM; Tu-Sa, 10AM-6PM. 9 Rue Dante (at Rue Domat). 01.43.25.18.66. Métros: Cluny–La Sorbonne, Maubert–Mutualité

34 ALBUM

From Action comics to Zot, Donald Duck to Dick Tracy, this *bande dessinée* (comic strip) shop specializes in new and vintage North American comic books. For the seriocomic art collector, there are oil paintings of Batman and portraits and statues of Mr. Spock. Two sister shops are just around the corner at Nos. 6 and 7 Rue Dante. ♦ M-Sa. 67 Blvd St-Germain (at Rue St-Jacques). 01.53.10.00.60. Métros: Cluny–La Sorbonne, Maubert–Mutualité

35 RUE DES ANGLAIS

In medieval times this street was a favorite haunt of English students attending the Sorbonne. ♦ Between Blvd St-Germain and Rue Lagrange. Métro: Maubert–Mutualité

36 BRASSERIE BALZAR

★★$$ Camus and Sartre had their last argument at this eatery, and James Thurber, Elliot Paul, William Shirer, and the old *Chicago Tribune* crowd gathered here for the beer and *choucroute* (sauerkraut) *garni*. The faithful clientele, old wood paneling and mirrors, and waiters in long white aprons create an ambiance that makes this one of the best brasseries in Paris. Getting a table for lunch is not difficult; dinner, however, is a different story. At night, especially after the theater, the vinyl banquettes are jammed with university professors, actors, editors, journalists, and aspiring poets dining on hearty fare such as *cervelas rémoulade* (sausage with mustard and herb dressing), *cassoulet*, and calf's liver, all washed down with a bottle of Bordeaux. But don't count on stellar service. ♦ Daily, breakfast, lunch, and dinner. Reservations recommended. 49 Rue des Ecoles (at Rue de la Sorbonne). 01.43.54.13.67. Métro: Cluny–La Sorbonne

Eighty-six years in the making, one of the world's largest sundials has finally been installed at Place de la Concorde, as part of the Year 2000 festivities of the City of Paris. It takes an approach more cerebral than celebratory. The sundial's pointer, or gnomon, is the 109-foot Obelisk of Luxor. Its base is the northern half of Place de la Concorde.

—Rose Marie Burke,
   Sundial Aids Millennium Countdown,
   the *Wall Street Journal*, 26 Oct 1999

FLEA MARKETS

In the late 19th century, textile merchants started laying out cheap clothes and fabrics at stands on the outer fringes of Paris, and on weekends shop girls and factory workers would flock there, rummage through the material, and get bitten by *puces* (fleas)—which is how the *marché aux puces*, or "flea market," got its name. Over the years, bric-a-brac, antiques, artwork, furniture, and all sorts of other goods joined the textiles, particularly at the **Porte de Clignancourt**, where the world's largest flea market developed. Cheap clothes and junk can still be found there, but the typical shopper these days—the typical foreign shopper in particular—comes here in search of high-quality, original, one-of-a-kind products, rather than cheap goods. Most dealers now have permanent shops at the market and so have less incentive to get rid of their merchandise at the end of the day, so don't expect many bargains. Shoppers in search of cheap goods would be better off at the *puces* at **Montreuil** or **Vanves** (see below).

Marché aux Puces de St-Ouen   Popularly known as the Porte de Clingancourt flea market, this vast maze of more than 2,000 stalls and shops, many of them in large covered pavilions, spreads out over 75 acres in the suburb of **St-Ouen** on the northern edge of the city. It lies directly north of the Porte de Clignancourt métro station (the last stop on the No. 4 line northbound), just beyond the overpass of the peripheral highway. Ten separate *marchés* make up the whole. To get to them, follow Avenue Michelet to Rue des Rosiers, which branches off to the left. The first one you come to is **Marché Vernaison** on the north side of Rue des Rosiers (at No. 99), the oldest building at the *puces*, dating from 1918. Its 300 dealers sell a mind-boggling variety of items, from old postcards and books to pottery and 18th-century furniture, at generally lower prices (and presumably lower quality) than the others. Next (at No. 85) is the **Marché Biron**, called "the Faubourg St-Honoré of the *puces*," with 220 dealers offering fine antiques of all categories from jewelry, crystal chandeliers, and rugs to massive, beautifully finished armoires. The smaller **Cambo** at No. 75 has furniture and old paintings. On the south side of Rue des Rosiers, two new pavilions offer a pleasant shopping atmosphere, with escalators and benches and cafés: the side-by-side **Marché Malassis** at No. 142, opened in 1990, and the **Marché Dauphine** at No. 140, opened in 1992. Between them, they boast more than 500 shops on two levels covering all fields of antiques. The next building, **Marché des Rosiers**, specializes in the late 19th century. The last one on Rue des Rosiers is the **Marché Serpette** at No. 110, which, combined with the adjoining outdoor **Marché Paul Bert**, is the most "professional" of the antiques markets. Dealers from all over the world come to buy and sell every kind of antique, from 18th century to Art Deco. The general level of quality is quite high.

For bric-a-brac of all sorts, head for **Marché Jules Vallès** at 7 Rue Jules Vallès. For clothes, shoes, and fashion accessories, **Marché Malik** at 53 Rue Jules Vallès specializes in *fripes* (secondhand clothing), and the shops lining Rue Paul Bert offer all manner of contemporary gear. This little street becomes a youth fashion *boom* on weekends.

The market is held on Saturday, Sunday, and Monday between 5AM and 6PM.

For a wildly entertaining lunch, you can't beat **Chez Louisette** at 130 Avenue Michelet in the Marché Vernaison, where Edith Piaf imitators wring hearts with *La Vie en Rose* and *Je Regrette Rien* amid a décor of year-round Christmas ornaments and flea market rejects for furniture. Steamed mussels and *frites* (French fries) are the things to eat here. Open Saturday, Sunday, and Monday, noon to 6PM. Always crowded, no reservations. Métro: Porte de Clignancourt.

Marché de Puces de Montreuil   This market at the **Porte de Montreuil** on the eastern edge of Paris is far more rough-and-tumble than the mega-*puces* at **St-Ouen**, and its merchandise is strictly garage-sale. But, as at a garage sale, there is always the chance of tumbling on a real bargain, if you know what you're looking for. The ambiance is very lively. The market draws lots of youngsters who rummage through mountains of *fripes* and military surplus gear, and one of the most popular stands here sells old theater costumes. Costume jewelry is also big. Open Saturday, Sunday, and Monday, 7:30AM to 7PM. Métro: Porte de Montreuil.

Marché aux Puces de Vanves   At this smallest and most laid-back of the markets, you have to come early to shop for antiques, because most of the antique dealers pack up and leave at 2PM. The story is that dealers from the Clignancourt market come here on Saturdays at dawn to stock up on goods that they sell at much higher prices in their shops. Small furniture, cutlery, china, glassware, pewter, jewelry, and paintings are the big items here. Artists and craftspeople also display their products alongside the antique dealers, and there are stamp and postcard sellers galore. Open Saturday, Sunday, and Monday, 7:30AM to 7PM. Métro: Porte de Vanves.

There is also an antiquarian and secondhand-book market at **Parc Georges Brassens** at **Porte de Vanves** on Saturday and Sunday.

Restaurants/Clubs: Red | Hotels: Purple | Shops: Orange | Outdoors/Parks: Green | Sights/Culture: Blue

37 RUE DES ECOLES

This street name celebrates the presence of all the academic institutions and universities hereabouts. ◆ Métros: Maubert–Mutualité, Cardinal-Lemoine

37 AU VIEUX CAMPEUR

France's best mountain-climbing outfitters this side of Chamonix carry pitons, ice axes, alpine sleeping bags, and giant spools of brightly colored climbing rope for your next ascent of Everest or the Eiffel Tower. Even if a bivouac at a wine bar atop the Montagne Ste-Geneviève's slopes is more your style, pause on the sidewalk and watch France's next generation of rock climbers testing new equipment, rappelling down an indoor version of what looks like the Eiger's North Face. This is one of twenty **Vieux Campeur** stores within a few blocks in the Latin Quarter. ◆ M-Sa. 48 Rue des Ecoles (between Rues Thénard and St-Jacques). 01.53.10.48.48. Métros: Cluny–La Sorbonne, Maubert–Mutualité. Also at numerous locations throughout the city

38 HÔTEL COLLÈGE DE FRANCE

$$ This is a simple-but-comfortable 29-room bed-and-breakfast inn on a quiet street in the middle of the Latin Quarter. There's no restaurant. ◆ 7 Rue Thénard (between Rues de Latran and du Sommerard). 01.43.26.78.36; fax 01.46.34.58.29. Métros: Maubert–Mutualité, St-Michel. hotel.du.college.de.france@wanadoo.fr

39 CLUB JEAN DE BEAUVAIS

Work off those gourmet French meals at this classy health club, where visitors to Paris are welcome to sign up for daily or weekly

---

The ubiquitous green trash bins of Paris are called *poubelles* in honor of Eugène Poubelle, the prefect of the Seine between 1883 and 1896. In 1884, he issued the order that all trash must be deposited in receptacles.

More than 500 people died daily in Paris during the Black Plague of 1348-1349.

Eight million traffic tickets are issued in Paris every year, 7.5 million of them for illegal parking.

---

memberships. The good-looking staff members offer advice and support while members huff and puff through their cardiovascular circuits and weight-training programs. Classes in aerobics, stretching, toning, and yoga are given daily. Somehow, the modern exercise equipment is right at home amid the beautifully renovated stone walls and wood-beamed ceilings of the 17th-century salons. This is where Jodie Foster exercises when she is in Paris. ◆ Daily. 5 Rue Jean-de-Beauvais (between Rue du Sommerard and Blvd St-Germain). 01.46.33.16.80. Métro: Maubert–Mutualité

40 THANH BINH

This little Vietnamese grocery store supplies the many Southeast Asian restaurants and families clustered around Place Maubert. The exotic spices and bewildering assortment of food (rice steamed in banana leaves, tapioca in grape leaves, shrimp muffins) will transport you to the Mekong Delta. ◆ M-Sa. No. 29 (at Blvd St-Germain). 01.40.46.06.15. Métro: Maubert–Mutualité

41 PLACE MAUBERT

The name *Maubert* is probably a contraction of *Maître* (Master) *Albert*, who was a Dominican teacher at the **University of Paris** in the Middle Ages. For centuries, this wide spot in the road was a crime-ridden skid row, a resort for tramps drinking *gros rouge* (cheap red wine), and the site of public executions. Here, in 1546, during the reign of François I, printer and humanist philosopher Etienne Dolet was burned at the stake as a heretic; his own books were used to kindle the fire. In addition to serving as an execution ground, from the Middle Ages hence this crossroads has been a bustling open-air market. ◆ Market: Tu, Th, Sa, 7AM-1PM. At Blvd St-Germain and Rues Monge and Lagrange. Métro: Maubert–Mutualité

42 BOULANGERIE KAYSER

Eric Kayser bakes some of the finest breads in Paris, all made from organically grown wheat and natural leaven, including his famed crusty and chewy *baguette de farine de froment*. ♦ M-Sa. 8 Rue Monge (between Place Maubert and Rue des Bernardins). 01.44.07.01.42. Métro: Maubert–Mutualité

Au Pactole
Restaurant

43 AU PACTOLE

★★$$ With vivacious manager Nedra Gara firing up the signature dish of steak tartare flambé with cognac or vodka in the bright, cheerful dining room and chef Hans-Stéphane Durant concocting imaginative dishes in the kitchen, this duo, which took over the restaurant in 2000, has made it an adventurous place for a meal. Truffle-flavored salmon, quail preserved in virgin oil roasted in vinegar, lobster stew with fine herbs, soufflé of lemon sole with hazelnuts and potato croquettes, and mango ice-cream soufflé with candied orange peel are just a few of the inventive treats you might find on the constantly evolving menu. ♦ M-F, lunch and dinner; Sa, dinner; closed 2 weeks in mid-August. Reservations recommended. 44 Blvd St-Germain (between Rues de Pontoise and des Bernardins). 01.46.33.31.31. Métro: Maubert–Mutualité

44 DIPTYQUE

Run by English and French artists who met while studying at the **Ecole des Beaux-Arts** after World War II, this tiny corner shop specializes in elegant antique bead necklaces, perfumed soaps, eau de toilette, and candles scented like the forest floor on a damp May morning. ♦ M-Sa. 34 Blvd St-Germain (at Rue de Pontoise). 01.43.26.45.27. Métro: Maubert–Mutualité

45 LA MARÉE VERTE

★★★$$ A nautical décor of marine blue with yellow accents and prints of grand old ocean liners on the walls make for a charming setting in which to enjoy the ever-popular and impeccably fresh fish platter of salmon, cod, scallops, and scorpion fish; skate wings with *tapenade* (Provençal olive paste) and capers; roast duckling with blueberries; or lamb chops in parsley and garlic sauce with vegetables. The restaurant is also known for its exhilarating foie gras, fine vegetarian platters, *café glacé* that is the soul of coffee in ice, and a good and very affordable wine list. Besides superb food and wine and

reasonable prices, the warm, serene ambiance created by owners Hélène and Julvic Thomas has kept this restaurant a favorite of neighborhood regulars, figures from the worlds of politics (the late President Mitterrand dined here often), show business personalities, and foreigners in Paris for more than 20 years. The Thomases admit to a particular *faible* (soft spot) for North Americans—there's even a perfect translation of the menu items from French to English, a rarity in a French restaurant. ♦ M, dinner; Tu-Sa, lunch and dinner. Reservations recommended. 9 Rue de Pontoise (between Blvd St-Germain and Rue Cochin). 01.43.25.89.41. Métro: Maubert–Mutualité

46 CHEZ TOUTOUNE

★★$$ Colette DeJean, nicknamed "Toutoune," offers a fine home-style Provençal cuisine at old-fashioned prices. Specialties include *abondance de cagouilles à la créme d'ail doux* (little snails served in creamy garlic sauce), *filets de rouget-barbet, étuvée de legumes aux tomates fraîches* (sweet red mullet cooked with tomatoes), *rable de lapin mitonné à la sauge* (saddle of rabbit with sage), and an assortment of unusual desserts. ♦ Tu-Su, lunch and dinner. Reservations recommended for dinner. 5 Rue de Pontoise (at Rue Cochin). 01.43.26.56.81. Métro: Maubert–Mutualité

47 VIVARIO

★$$ This small, lively neighborhood restaurant is serious about the quality of the Corsican meals it serves. Its menu changes daily to make the most of what's fresh, but it always includes delicious pasta dishes. Terrace dining in the summer. ♦ Tu-F, lunch and dinner; M, Sa, dinner; closed at Christmas. 6 Rue Cochin (between Rues de Poissy and de Pontoise). 01.43.25.08.19. Métro: Maubert–Mutualité

48 BOULANGERIE BEAUVALLET JULIEN

Modesty may prevent M. Ousbih and his family from putting their bakery's name in the window, but they won't divulge the recipe that results in the best baguettes in the Latin Quarter. Thin and crusty with the tang of sour-

---

Restaurants/Clubs: **Red** | Hotels: **Purple** | Shops: **Orange** | Outdoors/Parks: **Green** | Sights/Culture: **Blue**

dough, one of these baguettes is the perfect base for building a picnic to take down to the quay. Fresh loaves come out of the oven at 7AM, 11AM, and 1PM. ♦ M-Tu, Th-Su; closed in August. 6 Rue de Poissy (at Rue Cochin). 01.43.26.94.24. Métro: Maubert–Mutualité

49 LES COMPTOIRS DE LA TOUR D'ARGENT

If you want to take one of the **Tour d'Argent** restaurant's trademark blue-and-white Limoges plates home as a souvenir, walk across the street to the gourmet boutique of **Claude Terrail**, the enterprising restaurateur who has become the Pierre Cardin of French cuisine. Here, instead of dinner for $180, you can buy a menu for $20, fresh *foie gras de canard* (duck liver pâté) to go, or an entire **Tour d'Argent** place setting, including fluted champagne glass, coffee spoon, and ashtray. Also on sale are such items as Dijon mustard and wine. ♦ Tu-Su, until midnight. 2 Rue du Cardinal-Lemoine (at Quai de la Tournelle). 01.46.33.45.58. Métros: Cardinal-Lemoine, Maubert–Mutualité

50 *STATUE DE STE-GENEVIÈVE*

On the Pont de la Tournelle, one of the Seine's relatively new bridges (1928) and the fifth in a long line that dates back to 1369, is a missilelike statue of the city's patron saint. Apparently ready for a heavenly liftoff, the angular obelisk of St. Geneviève by Landowski turns her back on **Notre-Dame** and faces upriver, guarding the city as her spirit has done since 450. In that year, the prayers of the then 27-year-old nun were credited with halting Attila the Hun's advance on Paris, after his army of barbarians had just sacked Cologne and brutalized 10,000 of its maidens. In 473, while the city was under siege by the Franks, Geneviève courageously smuggled 11 boatloads of food through enemy lines to feed starving Parisians. She lived on **Montagne Ste-Geneviève** until the age of 89. Like France's other virgin saint, Joan of Arc, Geneviève was eventually consigned to flames, but not until 1,281 years after her death, when fanatical anticlerics of the revolution burned her remains and cast the ashes into the river. ♦ Pont de la Tournelle and Quai de la Tournelle. Métros: Cardinal-Lemoine, Pont-Marie

51 CHEZ RENÉ

★$$ An authentic old-fashioned bistro with amusing waiters, this eatery offers tasty daily Lyonnaise specials that range from Wednesday's *pot-au-feu* to Friday's *blanquette de veau* (veal in a white sauce). Also on the menu are cucumbers and cream, country sausages, mutton with white beans, *entrecôte*, and, in autumn, *pleurottes*

provençales (fresh wild mushrooms baked with garlic). ♦ Tu-Sa, lunch and dinner; closed in August. Reservations recommended. 14 Blvd St-Germain (at Rue du Cardinal-Lemoine). 01.43.54.30.23. Métros: Cardinal-Lemoine, Maubert-Mutualité

52 LA TOUR D'ARGENT

★★★★$$$$ This may no longer be the top restaurant in Paris, but its penthouse panorama of **Notre-Dame**'s flying buttresses and the barges passing on the **Seine** have helped make it the city's most famous and spectacular eating establishment, and one of its most expensive. The renowned dining spot stands on the site of the **Café Anglais**, which opened in 1582. The café was mentioned by Mme. de Sévigné in her famous letters and provided the setting for a Dumas novel; it is also said to be where the fork was first used in Paris. On the ground floor of the restaurant is a table set with the silver, crystal, and china used at a dinner here on 7 June 1867 that was attended by Czar Alexander II, the Czarevitch, Wilhelm I, and Bismarck. Touches of class are found throughout the establishment, from the Grand Siècle–style elevator to the traditional blue cornflower in the jacket lapel of restaurant owner and dandy Claude Terrail. The kitchen's pièce de résistance is pressed duck flambé, first served in 1890 to Edward VII, then Prince of Wales. The kitchen keeps a running tally of the number of ducklings pressed, and each order arrives at the table with a numbered card. (Almost 1 million ducklings later, the dish is still a hit.) Other recommended dishes include *filet de sole Cardinal* (with crayfish), flambéed peaches, and *fondant au chocolat* (soft, rich chocolate cake). The wine list draws from the 300,000 bottles in the vaulted cellars underground. Tables in the rooftop dining room must be reserved far in advance; ask for one by the picture window. Bear in mind, however, that lunch is half the price of dinner, and midday is when Parisians eat out. The restaurant is popular with North American and Japanese tourists, and at dinnertime the waiters may be the only French speakers in the place. ♦ Tu-Su, lunch and dinner. Reservations required. 15-17 Quai de la Tournelle (between Blvd St-Germain and Rue du Cardinal-Lemoine). 01.43.54.23.31. Métros: Cardinal-Lemoine, Maubert-Mutualité

52 LA RÔTISSERIE DU BEAUJOLAIS

★★$$ Owned by Claude Terrail of the pricey **Tour d'Argent** next door (see above), this boisterous bistro serves Lyonnaise specialties and rotisserie-roasted meat. Try the coq au vin and the *canette rôtie* (roast duck, which comes from the same farm that supplies **La Tour d'Argent** with its birds). Drink in the warm, jolly atmosphere along with a bottle of Moulin-à-Vent, the richest of the Beaujolais, while you consider Terrail's philosophy: "Simple things are what people want, even those in fur coats." ♦ Tu-Su, lunch and dinner. 19 Quai de la Tournelle (at Rue du Cardinal-Lemoine). 01.43.54.17.47. Métros: Cardinal-Lemoine, Maubert–Mutualité

53 L'ATLAS

★★$$ Chef El Jaziri Binjamin likens himself to a culinary ambassador promoting unique dishes from his native Morocco. The tasty *tajines* (stews) include lamb with forest mushrooms and lustily spiced fish with saffron. The elegant *couscous de L'Atlas*, with veal, meatballs, and lamb, is another fine main course. Have sweet mint tea with orange blossom nectar to end the meal on a soothing note. ♦ Daily, lunch and dinner. 12 Blvd St-Germain (at Rue du Cardinal-Lemoine). 01.46.33.86.98, 01.44.07.23.66. Métros: Cardinal-Lemoine, Maubert–Mutualité

54 LE RALLYE

★$ Locals right out of central casting lunch on sandwiches and the *plat du jour* here, but when an earthy crowd takes over at night, the café comes to resemble an Amsterdam bar. Just down the street but a world away in spirit from **La Tour d'Argent**, it has a collection of Tintin cartoon memorabilia on display. ♦ Café: daily, breakfast and lunch. Bar: daily, 7AM-2AM. 11 Quai de la Tournelle (between Blvd St-Germain and Rue du Cardinal-Lemoine). 01.43.54.29.65. Métros: Cardinal-Lemoine, Maubert–Mutualité

55 SORBONNE

France's most famous university began in 1253 as humble lodgings for 16 theology students. In medieval times, the university was not a mass of edifices, pedants, and bureaucrats; it was a loose assembly of soapbox academics giving street-corner lectures to students who boarded at inns throughout Paris. However, by the end of the 13th century, when the Sorbonne became the administrative headquarters for the **University of Paris**, there were 15,000 undergraduates studying in the city. St. Thomas Aquinas and Roger Bacon were among the Sorbonne's great teachers; St. Ignatius Loyola, Dante, Erasmus, and John Calvin were students here. As the Sorbonne grew in size and power, it frequently contradicted the authority of the French throne. During the Hundred Years' War (1337-1453), the university had the audacity to side with England against France. It recognized Henry V as king of France and cravenly sent one of its best prosecutors to Rouen to try Joan of Arc.

In 1642 Cardinal Richelieu was elected grand master of the Sorbonne; he commissioned architect **Jacques Lemercier** to restore the dilapidated college buildings and erect a Jesuit-style church. During the revolution the university closed down and remained empty until 1806, when Napoléon headquartered his **Académie de Paris** here. Following the May 1968 student-worker demonstration, the state unceremoniously rechristened the Sorbonne "Paris University IV," tossing it into the archipelago of institutions of higher learning scattered about the city.

Don't be shy about wandering down the university's long stone corridors or visiting the lecture halls, including the **Amphithéâtre Descartes** and the **Salle Doctorat**. (Unfortunately, the ornate **Grand Amphithéâtre** with its famous Puvis de Chavannes fresco is strictly reserved for ceremonies of state.) If you decide to enroll in a 4-month crash course in French (as hundreds of North Americans do every year), you will come to know the dusty domed ceiling and stiff wooden benches of the **Amphithéâtre Richelieu** intimately. For an admission application, contact Cours de Civilisation Française de la Sorbonne, Galerie Richelieu, 45-47 Rue des Ecoles, 75005 Paris. 01.40.46.26.70. www.fle.fr/sorbonne. ♦ 45-47 Rue des Ecoles (between Rues St-Jacques and de la Sorbonne). University main number: 01.40.46.22.11. Métro: Cluny–La Sorbonne. www.paris4.sorbonne.fr

Within the Sorbonne:

STE-URSULE-DE-LA-SORBONNE

Nothing of Cardinal Richelieu's **Sorbonne** remains save **Jacques Lemercier**'s chapel (1642), which was the first completely Roman-style building in 17th-century Paris. Richelieu is buried here. Above François Girardon's beautiful white marble tomb (1694), which depicts a half-recumbent Richelieu, his red cardinal's hat still hangs by a few slender threads from the ceiling. According to tradition, the hat will remain there until Richelieu's soul is freed from Purgatory, at which time the threads will rot and the hat will drop. ♦ The chapel is closed to the public except during special exhibitions of stained glass, tapestry, and old manuscripts. Church services are held in the chapel on 21 October (the feast day of St. Ursula) and 4 December (the anniversary of Richelieu's death). Pl de la Sorbonne and Rue de la Sorbonne. 01.40.46.20.52

Restaurants/Clubs: Red | Hotels: Purple | Shops: Orange | Outdoors/Parks: Green | Sights/Culture: Blue

56 COLLÈGE DE FRANCE

First called the **Collège des Trois-Langues** (Three-Languages College) because Hebrew and Greek were taught here as well as Latin, this institution, founded by François I in 1529, counts among its famous faculty Frédéric Joliot-Curie (son-in-law of Marie and Pierre Curie), who split the uranium atom; the physicist André-Marie Ampère, after whom a unit of measuring electric current is named; poet Paul Valéry; and the more contemporary scholars Roland Barthes, Michel Foucault, and Claude Lévi-Strauss. ♦ 11 Pl Marcelin-Berthelot (between Rues Jean-de-Beauvais and St-Jacques). 01.44.27.12.11. Métro: Maubert-Mutualité. www.college-de-france.fr

57 EGLISE ROUMAINE (ROMANIAN CHURCH)/BEAUVAIS COLLEGE CHAPEL

One of the Sorbonne's first college chapels, this structure was built in 1380. The restored sanctuary has been used since 1882 by the Romanian Orthodox Church. ♦ 9 bis Rue Jean-de-Beauvais (between Rues des Ecoles and du Sommerard). 01.43.54.67.47. Métro: Maubert-Mutualité

58 MUSÉE DES COLLECTIONS HISTORIQUES DE LA PRÉFECTURE DE POLICE (POLICE MUSEUM)

This fascinating, often grisly little collection surveys the city's most notorious crimes, from the 16th century to the present. Exhibits include a graphic representation of the 1563 punishment accorded the Duc de Guise's murderer (quartering by four horses), orders for the arrest of Dr. Guillotin in 1795, an account of Charlotte Corday's murder of Marat in his bath, Verlaine's statement of his attempted murder of fellow poet Rimbaud, and a book stained with blood from the 1932 assassination of French President Paul Doumer. Among the more ingenious weapons on display are a strangling cord made of twisted paper and a

knife concealed in a lady's fan. There's also a guillotine blade used during the revolution. ♦ Free. M-Sa. 1 bis Rue des Carmes (between Rue des Ecoles and Pl Maubert). 01.44.41.52.50. Métro: Maubert-Mutualité

59 LES DEUX TISSERINS

Marie-Claude Leblois's little toy shop, crammed with some of the most unusual playthings in Paris, is a veritable wonderland of rocking horses, marionette theaters, finger puppets, mobiles, sailboats, wooden trains, spinning tops, stuffed animals, dolls, and music boxes. Lebois's famous line of children's clothing includes gaily patterned flannel pajamas, hooded jackets, and cotton dresses; her monogrammed sacs à dos (backpacks) have been favorites of Parisian children for years. ♦ Tu-Sa. 36 Rue des Bernardins (between Rue Monge and Blvd St-Germain). 01.46.33.88.68. Métro: Maubert-Mutualité

60 ST-NICOLAS-DU-CHARDONNET

Built in 1709, this church was originally a 13th-century chapel standing in a field of chardons (thistles). Later redesigned by Charles Le Brun, it now houses the Le Brun family chapel, along with Charles Le Brun's painting The Martyrdom of St. John. The beautiful wood carving over the side door on the Rue des Bernardins is also his work. This also happens to be one of the most conservative churches in Paris: Mass is still said entirely in Latin. ♦ Sq de la Mutualité and Rue des Bernardins. Métros: Cardinal-Lemoine, Maubert-Mutualité

61 CLUB QUARTIER LATIN

The pretty indoor pool at this athletic club is one of the few in Paris where lap swimming is the norm and lane markers are respected. Downstairs are four squash courts, saunas, dance classes, a lounge, and a snack bar where salads and fruit juices are served. Day passes are available. ♦ M-F, 9AM-11:30PM; Sa-Su. 19 Rue de Pontoise (between Rue St-Victor and Blvd St-Germain). 01.55.42.77.88. Métros: Cardinal-Lemoine, Maubert-Mutualité

62 MAISON DE LA VANILLE

This charming tea salon–cum-crêperie is a welcome addition to a city frothing over with chocoholics and the establishments that cater to them. Purchase pure Bourbon vanilla extracts (named for the purity, not because of any alcoholic content), have a cake made with vanilla, or indulge in one of three varieties of hot chocolate, each one à la vanille. W-Sa, lunch and tea; Su, brunch and tea. 18 Rue du Cardinal Lemoine (between Rues des Ecoles and Blvd St-Germain). 01.43.25.50.95. Métro: Cardinal Lemoine

---

The life expectancy of French women is the highest in Europe: 82.1 years.

The correct number of kisses hello or good-bye varies from region to region in France. In Paris, it's usually two, but they are not real kisses. They are hugs and light brushes of the lips on each cheek, or even the suggestion of a kiss without the lips actually touching the cheeks.

CHILD'S PLAY

In addition to such obvious child-pleasers as the **Eiffel Tower**, Paris is filled with other attractions that will amuse and amaze young visitors. Here are 10 favorites:

1. **Jardin du Luxembourg** is the most marvelous garden in Paris, where children love to play and adults will recapture their childhood. There are special play areas for wee ones, with sandboxes and a lawn where, contrary to the usual Paris law, playing on the grass is allowed. Older children can enjoy the large playground crammed with numerous slides, swings, and monkey bars. Other delights include pony, donkey, and go-cart rides; a pond where you can rent toy boats to sail; and **Théâtre des Marionnettes** puppet shows.

2. The **Cité des Enfants** at the **Parc de La Villette** has a grand array of stimulating interactive games and science displays for children between ages 3 and 12.

3. **Musée de la Poupée** (Doll Museum) has a collection of more than 200 French porcelain dolls dating from 1860 to 1960. Stuffed animals and limited editions of porcelain dolls can be purchased in the museum's gift shop.

4. **Musée Carnavalet**, housed in a splendid 16th-century mansion, is the **Historical Museum of the City of Paris**, with exhibits on four centuries (1500-1900) of Parisian life. On the ground floor is an entire room full of old shop signs created to be understood by a population that was mostly illiterate—a bakery sign features a stalk of wheat, a butcher sign depicts a pig, and a locksmith sign is in the shape of a giant key. Also of interest to young museum-goers is the exhibit on the French Revolution, which includes a rope ladder used by a prisoner to escape from the **Bastille**, a model of the guillotine, and a pair of revolutionary drums. Tours for children are offered on Wednesdays, Saturdays, and school holidays.

5. **The Seine** offers tired little feet (and big ones too) boat tours along the river in a *bateau mouche*. These excursions are especially dramatic on summer nights, when the buildings visible from the river are spectacularly, fantastically lit. Highlights include **Notre-Dame**, the **Conciergerie**, the **Louvre**, and the **Eiffel Tower**.

6. The **Sewers** of Paris afford children a place to explore underground Paris. The hour-long visit includes a film and a walk through the tunnels.

7. **Disneyland Paris** is a definite quick fix of American culture, where kids of all ages can spend a day with Mickey and Minnie. The theme park is similar to those in Florida and California, with the requisite **Frontierland**, **Fantasyland**, **Adventureland**, **Discoveryland**, and **Main Street**.

8. The **Zoological Park** in the **Bois de Vincennes**, one of Europe's most beautiful zoos, is home to over 110 species of mammals and 115 types of birds. Visitors can help feed the animals their daily meals: pandas at 9:30AM and 5PM, pelicans at 2:15PM, penguins at 2:30PM, and seals and otters at 4:30PM. On weekends, a small train takes passengers on a tour of the zoo.

9. The **Louvre** is a daunting prospect to anyone, so when visiting the world's largest art museum with children, limit your itinerary to one museum department per day. A good place to start is the **Egyptian Antiquities Collection**, always a favorite of fledgling art connoisseurs. Highlights include Akhout-Hetep's *mastaba* (funeral chapel); Middle Kingdom tomb objects, including model boats to help the deceased on their journey in the afterlife and blue-glazed terracotta hippopotami; and furniture, games, jewelry, and other objects illustrating daily life in the New Kingdom period.

10. The **Museum of Natural History** in the **Jardin des Plantes** possesses one of the world's richest mineral collections and some of the oldest fossilized insects on earth. The **Grande Galerie de l'Evolution** houses a superb display on the evolution of life. Highlights are a giant whale skeleton; an impressive grouping of stuffed African savannah animals, including giraffes, lions, and elephants; and an extinct and endangered species exhibit.

63 MOISSONNIER

★★$$ Earthenware bowls spilling over with Lyonnaise salads, a friendly wait staff, generous *charcuterie*, and a homey setting have earned this Left Bank establishment a loyal clientele. Specialties include kidneys with mustard, tripe baked with onions and white wine, creamy au gratin potatoes, and delicious Beaujolais. ♦ Tu-Sa, lunch and dinner; closed in August. 28 Rue des Fossés-St-Bernard (between Rues Chantiers and des Ecoles). 01.43.29.87.65. Métros: Jussieu, Cardinal-Lemoine

64 INSTITUT DU MONDE ARABE (ARAB INSTITUTE)

Opened in 1987, this sociocultural institution was established to promote relations between France and the Arab world. It contains a library, exhibition space, and a top-floor restaurant

Restaurants/Clubs: Red | Hotels: Purple | Shops: Orange | Outdoors/Parks: Green | Sights/Culture: Blue

that serves Moroccan specialties (see below). The architect, **Jean Nouvel**, who received the Aga Khan prize for his design, has given Islamic architectural elements a stunning space-age interpretation. Notice Nouvel's treatment of the south façade: The wall is made up of thousands of camera-like shutters that open and close automatically according to the sun's brightness, thus regulating the amount of light let inside the building. ♦ Tu-Su. 1 Rue des Fossés-St-Bernard (at Quai St-Bernard). 01.40.51.38.38. Métros: Jussieu, Cardinal-Lemoine. www.imarabe.org

Within the Institut du Monde Arabe:

Le Ziryab

★★$$ The river view from this rooftop Moroccan restaurant is better than that of **La Tour d'Argent**—at a fraction of the price. Start a meal with one of the hot and cold hors d'oeuvres, such as marinated salmon or mini chicken brochettes. Move on to *zaalouk d'aubergines* (eggplant pâté), *kefta* (a mixture of minced beef and lamb with seven spices), a *tagine* (spicy North African stew), or couscous (steamed semolina wheat, stewed vegetables in broth, and a choice of meats), then end the repast with an assortment of Oriental pastries and mint tea. Linger at a table on the terrace on a balmy summer evening. ♦ Tu-Su, lunch and dinner. Reservations recommended. Ninth floor. 01.40.51.38.38

65 Musée de Sculpture en Plein Air

This outdoor sculpture museum, built in 1980, was once the site of Henri IV's bathing beach. Here the king would pour water from a royal hat over the young Dauphin as the preamble to a swimming lesson. Today this long grassy lawn on the banks of the **Seine** is dotted with large modern sculptures in stone, wood, and steel, and there are benches for quiet contemplation of the river and a playground for children. But don't come here after dark; a less desirable brand of exhibitionist prowls then. ♦ Quai St-Bernard (between Pl Valhubert and Pont de Sully). No phone. Métros: Gare d'Austerlitz, Jussieu

According to the *International Herald Tribune*, France remains the world's top tourist destination, with 75 million foreign visitors in 2000.

In Paris I find everything that appeals to me: lights, noises in the night, places where one has fun according to one's liking, a sympathetic and tolerant world, in sum, a true civilization.

—Harlem Renaissance poet Countee Cullen

66 Place de la Sorbonne

This square, lined with cafés and lime trees, was a focal point of the student-worker protest of 1968. That year, on 10 and 11 May, police and students clashed violently, resulting in the injury of 400 participants and the arrest of hundreds of others. In the square stands a graffiti-marred statue of Auguste Comte (1798-1857), who was fired from his job as examiner in mathematics at the prestigious **Ecole Polytechnique** for his revolutionary ideas. Comte is best remembered as the founder of Positivism, a philosophy that strongly influenced John Stuart Mill. Between Rue de la Sorbonne and Blvd St-Michel. Métro: Cluny–La Sorbonne

On Place de la Sorbonne:

SELECT
HOTEL

Select Hôtel

$$ A bright, cheerful hotel tastefully modernized and conveniently located on the Place de la Sorbonne, this 68-room hotel is an ideal base for exploring the Latin Quarter. In 1937, 25-year-old Eric Sevareid checked into a 50-cents-a-night room here and headed off to work for the *Paris Herald*, soon accomplishing such feats as an interview with Gertrude Stein. There's no restaurant, but there's a vaulted stone breakfast room and a comfy little bar. ♦ No. 1 (at Rue Victor-Cousin). 01.46.34.14.80; fax 01.46.34.51.79. Select.Hotel@wanadoo.fr; www.selecthotel.fr

67 Le Coupe-Chou

★$$ This seductive inn with an impressive fireplace occupies the site of a 16th-century barbershop whose proprietor slit the throats of his customers and then gave their bodies to a *charcutier* across the street to be made into pâté. If you can cast that grisly chapter from your mind, you will probably enjoy this attractive dining spot, which serves *escalopes de saumon à la crème d'estragon* (salmon with tarragon cream sauce), lamb with mint, *magret de canard* (duck fillet) with peaches, and *millefeuilles maison* (homemade puff pastries), a specialty—though you may want to skip the pâté. ♦ M-Sa, lunch and dinner; Su, dinner. Reservations recommended. 11 Rue de Lanneau (at Impasse Chartière). 01.46.33.68.69. Métro: Maubert-Mutualité

68 Montagne Ste-Geneviève

The central point of the old **University of Paris**, this French Parnassus is named after one of Paris's two patron saints (St. Denis is her male counterpart). It is admittedly steep, but to call any of the city's seven hills a mountain is certainly an example of Roman grandiloquence. The summit of Ste-Geneviève is gracefully crowned with the Panthéon (see page 62), whose columned dome dominates the Left Bank. This is a vicinity rich in intellectual history: Here was the convent where St. Thomas Aquinas wrote his *Summa Theologica*, on which the orthodox philosophy of Catholicism is based; here both St. Ignatius Loyola and Calvin studied; here Marat drew up his pamphlets; and here Pascal died a stone's throw from the place where Verlaine was to pass away many generations later. The hill counts among its educational institutions the world-famous **Sorbonne**, the **Collège de France**, prestigious medical and law schools, and three large secondary schools and was at one time the site of the **Ecole Polytechnique**, the French equivalent of MIT. In 1804 the Rue de la Montagne-Ste-Geneviève was the scene of a plot to murder Napoléon Bonaparte. ◆ Métro: Maubert-Mutualité

69 LIBRAIRIE PRÉSENCE AFRICAINE

Need a few Wolof lessons before visiting Gambia? Looking for a Senegalese cookbook? Want to hear a black gospel concert on the Left Bank? This African bookstore includes a Third World periodical section and a bulletin board. ◆ M-Sa. 25 *bis* Rue des Ecoles (between Rues des Bernardins and de la Montagne-Ste-Geneviève). 01.43.54.15.88. Métros: Maubert-Mutualité, Cardinal-Lemoine

70 DA CAPO

Charles Recht runs this postage stamp–size shop dealing in 78-rpm records, old sheet music, and opera programs. ◆ Tu-Sa, noon-6:30PM; closed in August. 14 Rue des Ecoles (between Rues des Bernardins and de la Montagne-Ste-Geneviève). 01.43.54.75.47. Métros: Maubert-Mutualité, Cardinal-Lemoine

71 HÔTEL RÉSIDENCE HENRI IV

$$$ Talk about *petite*—this small Belle Epoque–style hotel at the end of a quiet impasse and across from a rare wedge of green space has just nine rooms and five two-room apartments, replete with small kitchenettes, marble bathrooms, and such features as cable television, minibar, and direct phone line. If you want to hide away close to the heart of it all, this might be the place for you. 50 Rue des Bernardins (at Rue des Ecoles). 01.44.41.31.81; fax 01.46.33.93.22. Métro: Maubert-Mutualité. *henri4@hotellerie.net*

72 BREAKFAST IN AMERICA

**$ Visitors who come to Paris for any length of time soon realize that the proud French breakfast tradition is neither proud nor a tradition; in fact, by North American standards it isn't even breakfast. Elegant it may be, but the café/croissant combo seems more like a concession to the imperative of digesting a little something before lunch than an actual meal. Not so at this Formica-countered, red-boothed diner, brainchild of friendly expat Craig Carlson. This friendly Californian brings to Paris pancakes as fluffy as any you'll find stateside, not to mention burgers, homemade chili con carne, and a solid triple-decker club. (If you want your bread extra crispy, just pop it into one of the toasters that accompany every table.) Add to all this a bottomless cup of coffee and it's no wonder the place is so popular with...the French. Daily, breakfast, lunch, and dinner. 17 Rue des Ecoles (between Rues d'Arras and Monge). 01.43.54.50.28. Métros: Maubert-Mutualité, Cardinal-Lemoine, Jussieu.

73 FAMILIA HÔTEL

$$ In this well-named hotel, amiable owner-managers Eric and Sylvie Gaucheron and Eric's parents, Bernard and Colette, make their guests feel right at home. The 30 rooms in this century-old, Haussmann-style building combine modern conveniences (up-to-date bathrooms, cable TV, and soundproofing) and old-fashioned charm. Nineteen guest rooms are decorated with frescos of Paris, many have exposed wood-beam ceilings, and many are furnished with antiques. Eight rooms have balconies, and the five on the upper two floors have views of the **Notre-Dame**. There's no restaurant. ◆ 11 Rue des Ecoles (between Rues d'Arras and Monge). 01.43.54.55.27; fax 01.43.29.61.77. Métros: Maubert-Mutualité, Cardinal-Lemoine, Jussieu. www.hotel-paris-familia.com

73 MINERVE HÔTEL

$$ Standing shoulder to shoulder with the **Familia**, this 52-room hotel was acquired by the Gaucheron family and renovated from top to bottom in 2000. It matches the attractiveness and high comfort level of the **Familia** in every way, and the front rooms on the top floors have the same **Notre-Dame** view. There's no restaurant. ◆ 13 Rue des Ecoles (between Rues d'Arras and Monge). 01.43.26.26.04; fax 01.44.07.01.96. Métros: Maubert-Mutualité, Cardinal-Lemoine, Jussieu. minerve@hotellerie.net; www.hotel-paris-minerve.com

74 LIBERTEL QUARTIER LATIN

$$$ A contemporary hotel in the Latin Quarter? It does exist, and though this 29-room hotel is part of a large chain, it is exceedingly clean and comfortable all around. The lobby is done up as a library, a reflection of the neighborhood's rich literary history, and guests can borrow whatever they fancy from the bilingual selection. Guest rooms feature dark woods and simple but sophisticated pale blue or yellow color schemes, and sparkling bathrooms feature stylish fixtures and oversize mirrors. 9 Rue des Ecoles (between Rues d'Arras and Monge). 01.44.27.06.45; fax 01.43.25.36.70. Métros: Maubert-Mutualité, Cardinal-Lemoine, Jussieu. H2782@accor-hotels.com

75 LE PARADIS LATIN SIDNEY

Israël's glittering nightclub stages one of the city's top floor shows. The food is not the main focus here, but the dinner, the *spectacle*, and **Gustave Eiffel**'s magnificent 1889 theater—a national landmark—make for a memorable evening out. It's also possible to see the show without dining. ♦ Cover. M, Tu, Th-Su, dinner, 8PM. Show: M, Tu, Th-Su, 9:30PM (arrive 30 minutes in advance). Reservations required. 28 Rue du Cardinal-Lemoine (between Rue des Ecoles and Blvd St-Germain). 01.43.25.28.28. Métro: Cardinal-Lemoine. www.paradis-latin.com

---

At any season, and all year long, in the evening the view of the city from the bridges was always exquisitely pictorial. One's eyes became the eyes of a painter, because the sight itself approximated art, with the narrow, pallid façades of the buildings lining the river; with the tall trees growing down by the water's edge; with, behind them, the vast chiaroscuro of the palatial Louvre, lightened by the luminous lemon color of the Paris sunset off toward the west; with the great square, pale stone silhouette of Notre-Dame to the east. The stance from which to see Paris was any one of its bridges at the close of day.

—Janet Flanner, *Paris Was Yesterday*, 1972

I therefore will not pretend to have been looking at Paris with new eyes, or to have gathered on the banks of the Seine a harvest of extraordinary impressions. I will only pretend that a good many old impressions have recovered their freshness, and that there is a sort of renovated entertainment in looking at the most brilliant city in the world with eyes attuned to a different pitch.

—Henry James, *Portraits of Places*, 1883

76 LYCÉE LOUIS LE GRAND

Founded in 1550, this 1,500-student state-run high school numbers among its former pupils Molière; Voltaire; Robespierre; Hugo; Baudelaire; French presidents Pompidou, Giscard d'Estaing, and Chirac; and Léopold Senghor, the ex-president of Senegal. It's closed to the public. ♦ 123 Rue St-Jacques (between Rue Cujas and Pl Marcelin-Berthelot). Métro: Cluny–La Sorbonne

77 ECOLE POLYTECHNIQUE

These massive buildings once housed the French MIT. The school was founded as an army-run engineering school by Gaspard Monge, the mathematician who accompanied Napoléon to Egypt, and its best-known graduates are car designer André Citroën and former French president Valéry Giscard d'Estaing. Its annual grand ball at the **Opéra** is also famous. In 1976 the prestigious university moved to the suburbs; the buildings here are now used for scientific research. ♦ Rue de l'Ecole-Polytechnique (between Rues de la Montagne-Ste-Geneviève and Valette). Métros: Cardinal-Lemoine, Maubert–Mutualité

78 LA NEF PARISIENNE

Affixed on this small square, as on city schools and other public structures throughout Paris, is the image of a sailing vessel known as *La Nef Parisienne*. The image has been Paris's coat of arms since 1260, when St. Louis appointed the boatmen's guild to administer the affairs of the city. *Fluctuat nec mergitur* ("float never sink") is the city motto. In addition to adorning buildings, the coat of arms is embossed on everything from the mayor's stationery to police officers' badges. ♦ Rues Descartes, de la Montagne-Ste-Geneviève, and de L'Ecole-Polytechnique. Métros: Cardinal-Lemoine, Maubert-Mutualité

79 LE BUISSON ARDENT

**$$ The name of this restaurant, which translates as "the burning bush," is a reference to a biblical scene once etched above a nearby doorway that is said to have been one of the old gates to the city. With its high ceilings, rustic 1920s painted murals of the four seasons, and décor that's somewhere between dowdy and dapper, this is a quietly Parisian setting for bistro fare with a comfortably contemporary outlook. Main courses include the likes of *magret de canard*, cooked to taste and delicately sliced over a tangy risotto, and codfish with tapenade and fennel compote. The wine list is moderately priced and easy to follow and desserts are both creative and uniformly generous: try the melting chocolate cake with vanilla pecan ice cream or vanilla- and orange-crème-stuffed crepes with a dollop of citrus sorbet. M-F, lunch and dinner. 25 Rue Jussieu (between Rue des Fossés St-Bernard and Pl Jussieu). 01.43.54.93.02. Métro: Jussieu

80 BIBLIOTHÈQUE STE-GENEVIÈVE

This beautiful library, constructed in 1850 on the Place du Panthéon, occupies the site of the old **Collège Montaigu**, where Erasmus, Calvin, and St. Ignatius Loyola studied. Architect **Henri Labrouste**'s revolutionary use of steel-frame-and-masonry construction (further elaborated in his other library, the **Bibliothèque Nationale**, which was finished in 1868) makes this building one of the most important 19th-century forerunners of modern architecture. Though you may peek inside, the library itself is restricted to visitors with valid readers' cards except during limited touring hours. ♦ Tours: M-F, 9-9:45 AM, by appointment only. Pl du Panthéon (between Rues Valette and Cujas). 01.44.41.97.97. Métro: Cardinal-Lemoine

81 CROCOJAZZ

This cubbyhole of a record shop resounds with the music of Art Blakey, Miles Davis, Louis Armstrong, and Coleman Hawkins. Jack Daniel's whiskey bottles on the wall, the occasional country twang of Hank Thompson and Ricky Skaggs, and the worn Levi's jeans and ersatz cowboy boots of the French clientele round out the ambiance here. ♦ Tu-Sa. 64 Rue de la Montagne-Ste-Genevieve (at Pl Ste-Genevieve). 01.46.34.78.38. Métro: Maubert–Mutualité

82 51 RUE DE LA MONTAGNE-STE-GENEVIÈVE

The Irish author James Joyce shared a flat here with French writer Valéry Larbaud. It's still a residential building. ♦ Between Rues St-Etienne-du-Mont and Descartes. Métro: Cardinal-Lemoine

83 ST-ETIENNE-DU-MONT

The combination of a Gothic rose window, triple classical pediments, a medieval-style belfry, and a Renaissance dome in this church defies the laws of architectural purity. Its low-hanging chandeliers are a menace to anyone over 6 feet tall. And it must be the only church in Paris that closes for lunch. But *mon Dieu*, it's beautiful! Completed in 1626, the church is home to two graceful 16th-century spiral staircases, an extraordinary wooden pulpit (1650) shouldered by a grimacing Samson, and the only rood screen left in Paris, as well as the tombs of Pascal, Racine, and Marat. The church surrounds a shrine to

St. Geneviève, which Paris fathers have visited the first Sunday of each year for centuries. During the annual pilgrimage on 3 January 1857, while bowing to bless a child, Monseigneur Sibour, Archbishop of Paris, was stabbed to death by a defrocked priest named Verger, who apparently objected to the ban on marriage that compels priestly celibacy. A marker at the rear of the center aisle indicates the spot where the murder was committed. ♦ Pl Ste-Geneviève (between Rues Clovis and St-Etienne-du-Mont). 01.43.54.11.79. Métro: Cardinal-Lemoine

84 PERRAUDIN

★★$ Popular among Sorbonne students and their profs (come early to be assured a table), this bargain canteen has the archetypal bistro décor (lace curtains, red-and-white-checkered tablecloths, and Art Deco tile floors). On the menu is a panoply of *cuisine bourgeoise*: lamb and kidney beans, beef stew, au gratin potatoes, and modestly priced wines. For dessert try the pear sorbet laced with *poire William* liqueur. ♦ M-F, lunch and dinner; Sa, dinner; closed the last 2 weeks of August. 157 Rue St-Jacques (between Rues des Fossés-St-Jacques and Soufflot). 01.46.33.15.75. RER: Luxembourg

85 RUE SOUFFLOT

Looking down this street (named for the architect of the **Panthéon**), you will see two matching buildings: the City Hall of the fifth arrondissement and the **University of Paris Faculty of Law** building, with the **Luxembourg Gardens** and **Eiffel Tower** in the distance. Eighteen feet below Rue Soufflot lie the remains of a Roman forum, discovered by 19th-century archeologists; the ruins are not open to the public. ♦ Métros: Cardinal-Lemoine, Maubert–Mutualité

On Rue Soufflot:

LES FONTAINES

★$$ This bustling bistro may look as if it lost its soul somewhere in all the cigarette smoke, but it serves surprisingly good, hearty fare at honest prices. Main courses include *lapin entier* (whole roast rabbit) with mustard sauce, *gigot d'agneau* (leg of lamb), *coquelet* (small chicken) with sautéed potatoes, and *fricassé de lotte* (monkfish stew) in wine sauce with basil, and there's a very good *tarte Tatin* (apple tart). ♦ M-Sa, lunch and dinner. No. 9 (at Rue Paillet). 01.43.26.42.80

86 HÔTEL DES GRANDS HOMMES

$$$ Comfortable and right in the heart of the Latin Quarter, this serene 31-room hotel

---

Restaurants/Clubs: Red | Hotels: Purple | Shops: Orange | Outdoors/Parks: Green | Sights/Culture: Blue

boasts views of the Panthéon and the spire of Notre-Dame from some of its top-floor rooms. Surrealism may have had its start at this hotel, as André Breton and Philippe Soupault invented automatic writing here in 1919. There's no restaurant. ♦ 17 Pl du Panthéon (between Rues d'Ulm and Clotaire). 01.46.34.19.60; fax 01.43.26.67.32. Métro: Cardinal-Lemoine. reservations@ hoteldesgrandeshommes.com; www. hoteldesgrandeshommes.com

87 PANTHÉON

When Louis XV recovered from gout at Metz in 1744, he vowed, in gratitude, to build a great temple honoring St. Geneviève. The architect, **Jacques-Germain Soufflot**, chose to construct a classical edifice based on the form of a Greek cross (339 feet long and 253 feet wide). Soufflot, who had been inspired by his trips to Italy, intended his building to resemble the Pantheon in Rome; however, the Paris version's lofty 52-pillar dome and handsome Corinthian colonnade wound up being much more reminiscent of St. Paul's Cathedral in London. Finished in 1850 by **Guillaume Rondelet**, one of Soufflot's students, the building was secularized into the **Temple of Fame**, a necropolis for the distinguished atheists of France. In its rather depressing crypt lie Voltaire, Rousseau, Victor Hugo (whose coffin passed a ceremonial night under the **Arc de Triomphe** and was carried here in the hearse of the poor), Gambetta, Emile Zola, Louis Braille (the 19th-century Frenchman who, blinded at age 3, went on to invent the system of embossed dots that enables the sightless to read), Jean Jaurès (the celebrated leftist politician and orator who was assassinated in 1914), and Jean Moulin (the Resistance leader in World War II who was tortured to death during the Occupation). After the revolution, the building's 42 tall windows were walled up, and today the monument looms over the square like a prison, grandiose and austere. ♦ Admission. Daily. Pl du Panthéon. 01.44.32.18.00. Métros: Cardinal-Lemoine, Maubert-Mutualité

88 LYCÉE HENRI IV

Dating from Napoleonic times, this is one of the city's most prestigious high schools; Jean-Paul Sartre, the French novelist and playwright

The word *boulevard* was originally a military term for an embankment behind a rampart where cannons were placed. When the wall that stood along the current route of the Grands Boulevards was torn down in the late 18th century, the wide civilian roadway took its old martial name.

who refused the Nobel prize for literature in 1964, taught here. The school's most notable architectural feature is the Tour de Clovis, a Gothic belfry. The tower is all that remains of the Abbaye Ste-Geneviève, built by King Clovis after he was converted to Christianity by his wife, Clotilde of Burgundy, and St. Geneviève herself. St. Thomas Aquinas (1225-1274) taught at the abbey. The school is closed to the public. ♦ 23 Rue Clovis (at Rue Clotilde). Métro: Cardinal-Lemoine

89 RUE DESCARTES

This street carries the name of French mathematician and philosopher René "I-think-therefore-I-am" Descartes (1596-1650). He lived on Montagne-Ste-Geneviève between 1613 and 1619 and again in 1625 but it is doubtful he ever lived on this street, which was then known as Rue des Bordels (street of brothels). Descartes emigrated to Sweden, where he died in the arms of Queen Christina. Métro: Cardinal-Lemoine

On Rue Descartes:

NO. 39 RUE DESCARTES

A plaque below the awning marks the house where poet Paul Verlaine (1844-1896) died. Later there was a hotel at this same address; in 1922 Ernest Hemingway rented a room in the hostelry, which he later described in *A Moveable Feast*. It's now an apartment building with restaurants on the ground floor. ♦ Between Rues Thouin and Clovis

NO. 47 RUE DESCARTES

At the end of the passageway through this historic 17th-century, half-timbered Norman-style house is a section of King Philippe Auguste's medieval city wall. Visitors may enter the passageway to see the wall. ♦ Between Rues Thouin and Clovis

90 RUE CLOVIS

This short street is named after Clovis (AD 466-511), king of the Franks, who defeated the Romans at Soissons, ending the Roman Empire's dominion of Gaul and founding France. The narrow sidewalk on the south side of the street (near **No. 5**) is practically blocked by the ivy-draped ruins of King Philippe Auguste's fortified wall. It was originally 33 feet high, with a pathway on top, and was patrolled by city sentries. (During the 19th century, a bronze regiment of these sentries was enshrined on the roof of the **City Hall** in the Place de l'Hôtel-de-Ville). Construction of the wall started in 1190, and it marked the city limits of Paris until the 17th century. The wall was pulled down when Louis XIV left Paris for **Versailles**. At the bottom of the hill at **No. 67** Rue du Cardinal-Lemoine is the house where Pascal died in 1662. ♦ Métro: Cardinal-Lemoine

91 HÔTEL DES GRANDES ECOLES

$$ Entering the courtyard here is like stepping into an Impressionist painting. This homey, family-run establishment comprises three ivy-covered houses set in a lush garden. Each of the 51 delightful rooms is decorated differently; ask for one with a garden view. On cool mornings, enjoy your croissants and café au lait in the charming lace-curtained break-fast room; in summer, you can eat amid the trees and flowers. (There's no restaurant.) Guests return year after year, so make reservations well in advance. ♦ 75 Rue du Cardinal-Lemoine (between Rues Rollin and Monge). 01.43.26.79.23; fax 01.43.25.28.15. Métros: Cardinal-Lemoine, Place Monge. Hotel.Grandes.Ecoles@wanadoo.fr; www.hotel-grandes-ecoles.com

92 ARÈNES DE LUTÈCE (ROMAN ARENA)

After the **Roman Baths** at the **Musée de Cluny**, this 1st-century amphitheater is the city's most important Roman ruin. Accidentally discovered (and partially destroyed) in 1869, the 325- by 425-foot oval once seated 15,000 spectators. With its surrounding gardens and benches, the arena provides an island of tranquillity for young parents pushing strollers and old men playing *boules* (boccie); in summer, campy medieval jousts take place here. It's a nice spot for a picnic lunch of sourdough rye bread and *charcuterie* from the Place Monge market. ♦ Pl Emile-Mâle and Rue de Navarre. Métro: Place Monge

92 HÔTEL RÉSIDENCE MONGE

$ For those who reserve early, this cheerful hotel located only 10 meters from the Arènes de Lutèce offers four rooms with views over-looking the ancient amphitheater: numbers 31, 41, 51, and 61. All 36 rooms are plain but neat, well equipped, and comfortable. The rooms without views are very modestly priced; the deluxe rooms are a bit more expensive. There is no restaurant. ♦ 55 Rue Monge (between Rues Lacépède and Cardinal-Lemoine). 01.43.26.87.90; fax 01.43.54.47.25. Métro: Place Monge. hotel-monge@gofornet.com; www.hotelmonge.com

93 9 RUE BLAINVILLE

The first public library in Paris was once housed in this building. ♦ At Rue Tournefort. Métro: Place Monge

94 LA TRUFFIÈRE

★★$$ Rich specialties from Périgord—the very antithesis of nouvelle cuisine—are served at this rustic eatery: black truffles, foie gras, and generous portions of goose and duck prepared in every conceivable fashion. Have an aperitif near the fireplace in the sitting room before proceeding to dinner and dine in the romantic vaulted cellar. ♦ Tu-Su, lunch and dinner. Reservations required. 4 Rue Blainville (between Rues Mouffetard and Tournefort). 01.46.33.29.82. Métros: Cardinal-Lemoine, Place Monge

95 CAFÉ DELMAS

★$$ Anyone hunting for **La Chope**, the old café where young Hemingway rubbed shoul-ders with the sturdy butchers, bakers, and tradesmen of the *quartier*, has been deprived of that particular plunge into nostalgia by the conversion of the Place Contrescarpe landmark into a trendy eatery in 2001. Instead of the atmospheric, if down-at-the-heels, neighborhood café, we now have mood lighting, scrubbed stone walls, sleek modern café chairs, and a wise-mouthed wait staff with minimal attention spans. The menu offers an uninspiring mix of salads, a *plat du jour*, and, luckily, Bertillion ice cream for dessert. The impressive range of modish drinks seems to be the main attraction for the young profes-sionals who now gravitate here. ♦ Daily breakfast, lunch, and dinner until 2AM. 2 Pl de la Contrescarpe (at Rue Cardinal-Lemoine). 01.43.26.51.26. Métro: Place Monge

95 74 RUE DU CARDINAL LEMOINE

Ernest and Hadley Hemingway lived on the fourth floor of this working-class building from the beginning of 1922 to the summer of 1923. It was their first apartment in Paris, lovingly recalled in *A Moveable Feast*. ♦ Between Rue Thouin and Pl de la Contrescarpe. Métro: Cardinal-Lemoine

96 1 PLACE DE LA CONTRESCARPE

The name **Maison de la Pomme de Pin** (Pine Cone Cabaret) is carved into the wall above the *boucherie* (butcher's shop) at this address. It marks the site of an old café frequented by satirist François Rabelais (1494-1553), author of *Pantagruel* and *Gargantua*. ♦ At Rue du Cardinal-Lemoine. Métro: Place Monge

---

Restaurants/Clubs: Red | Hotels: Purple | Shops: Orange | Outdoors/Parks: Green | Sights/Culture: Blue

97 PLACE DE LA CONTRESCARPE

In the Middle Ages, this dark, dangerous neighborhood lay outside King Philippe Auguste's city wall, beyond the moat, on the counterescarpment. Since the days of Hemingway's *A Moveable Feast*, the public urinals and bus stop have disappeared, but a certain seediness remains. In winter, the local *clochards* (street people) still huddle over the heating duct and live off spoils from the markets and spare change from tourists. On summer weekends, harmless bikers in black leather congregate here. ♦ Métro: Place Monge

98 RUE MOUFFETARD

Leading out of the Place de la Contrescarpe is the 13th-century **Rue Mouffetard**. As you descend the narrow street, let your imagination take you back to the time when it was the main Roman road to the southeast, Lyon, and Italy. During the 12th century the area near the Bièvre River was filled with the country homes of rich Parisians. Within four centuries the Bièvre became a foul-smelling stream polluted by the animal wastes and dyes dumped by tanners, skinners, and the Flemish tapestry weavers from the **Gobelins** factory. In 1910 the river was covered over and incorporated into the sewer system.

Some guess that the name "Mouffetard" comes from *mouffette*, French for "skunk"; more likely it is a corruption of the Roman name of the hill it traverses, Mont Cétar. Prior to the revolution the poor of Paris lived here in utter wretchedness. The unadorned mansard-roofed 17th-century houses that still line the Rue Mouffetard were built for ordinary folk. In the 1600s one French writer said more money could be found in one single house of the **Faubourg-St-Honoré** than in all of those combined on the Rue Mouffetard.

Sadly, this thoroughfare, long beloved by gourmets and gourmands, has become more and more tacky with each passing year, as quaint old shops have given way to fast-food joints. The upper half of the street is filled with restaurants, many Greek, but a bustling pedestrian street market at the bottom of the hill that has convened ever since 1350 has managed to retain a good deal of its authenticity and charm. The outdoor market section (see page 66) runs from Rue de l'Epée-de-Bois to Rue Censier, with the liveliest area near Rue Censier. ♦ Between Rues Censier and Thouin. Métros: Place Monge, Censier–Daubenton.

98 12 RUE MOUFFETARD

Above this *charcuterie* is an astounding painting that looks more suited to early Atlanta than Paris. *Le Nègre Joyeux* (*The Happy Negro*) portrays a stereotyped grinning black servant in striped pants serving tea to his mistress. ♦ At Rue Blainville. Métro: Place Monge

99 HÔTEL JARDIN DES PLANTES

$$ Guests of this tranquil 33-room hotel in a quiet neighborhood can enjoy breakfast and lunch surrounded by flowers on the rooftop terrace. Many of the rooms have views of the magnificent botanical garden nearby. It's a member of the Timotel chain. ♦ 5 Rue Linné (between Rues Lacépède and des Arènes). 01.47.07.06.20; fax 01.47.07.62.74. Métros: Jussieu, Place Monge. jardin-des-plantes@timhotel.fr; www.timhotel.com

100 JARDIN DES PLANTES

It was begun in 1626 by Louis XIII as a royal medicinal herb garden planted on an old rubbish heap. Today the 74-acre botanical garden hosts a floral orgy of peonies, irises, roses, geraniums, and dahlias between April and October. The garden, bounded by streets named after great French naturalists and botanists (Jussieu, Geoffroy St-Hilaire, and Buffon), contains a pedestal inscribed to the French scientist Lamarck, the author of the doctrine of evolution (tough luck, Charles Darwin), and another honoring Chevreul, the director of the **Gobelins** dye factory who lived to 103 and whose color-spectrum research informed the work of the Impressionist painters

Within the park is France's oldest public zoo, **Le Ménagerie**, which has a rather pathetic history. Established shortly after the revolution to display survivors from the **Royal Menagerie at Versailles** (one hartebeest, one zebra, one rhinoceros, and a sheepdog), it was originally called the **People's Democratic Zoo**. In 1795 the first elephants arrived, in 1805 the bear pit opened, and in 1827 an Egyptian prince contributed a giraffe. The zoo grew in size and popularity until the Siege of Paris in 1870 and 1871, when the poor beasts were eaten. For several weeks, it is said, the privileged of Paris dined on elephant steaks the size of manhole covers. The zoo has never recovered from the slaughter, and conditions remain on the shabby side. (Animals are still jailed in Second-Empire pavilions, and rumors of stray cats being fed to snakes and reptiles proliferate.) Children still seem to love it, though. A 248-kilo (545-pound) male tortoise named Kiki lives here. He arrived from the Seychelles in 1923, is 125 years old, shares a cage with two female tortoises named Joséphine and Mégane, and does not act his age.

Legend holds that the park's famous Cedar of Lebanon, now 40 feet in circumference, traveled in 1735 as a seedling in the hat of naturalist Bernard de Jussieu, who had carefully preserved it during confinement as a prisoner of war. But in truth, it was given to him after his release.

The park's **Museum of Natural History** has five departments (paleontology, paleobotany, mineralogy, entomology, and zoology), and it possesses one of the world's richest mineral collections and some of the oldest fossilized insects on earth. The **Grande Galerie de l'Evolution** houses a superb display on the evolution of life. Highlights include giant whale skeletons, a majestic parade of stuffed African Savannah animals, and a moving exhibit on extinct and endangered species. ◆ Admission to zoo and museum. Garden and zoo: daily. Museums and greenhouses: M, W-Su. Bounded by Pl Valhubert, Quai St-Bernard, and Rues Geoffroy-St-Hilaire, Buffon, and Cuvier. 01.40.79.30.00. Métros: Gare d'Austerlitz, Jussieu, Place Monge

101 51 TO 55 RUE MOUFFETARD
In 1938 workers discovered 3,351 coins of 22-karat gold weighing 16.3 grams each and bearing the image of Louis XV hidden inside the wall here. The buried treasure, according to an accompanying note, belonged to Louis Nivelle, the royal counselor who mysteriously disappeared in 1757. ◆ At Rue Ortolan. Métro: Place Monge

102 FONTAINE DU POT-DE-FER
What appears to be an Italianate roadside dungeon is actually a restored historic monument. Behind this wall is one of the 14 fountains constructed in 1624 at the behest of Marie de Médicis. The fountain was designed to handle the overflow from the Gallo-Roman aqueduct that she had refurbished to supply water for her new palace in the **Luxembourg Gardens**. ◆ 60 Rue Mouffetard (at Rue du Pot-de-Fer). Métro: Place Monge

103 PLACE MONGE
This square is named for the mathematician Gaspard Monge (1746-1818), who in 1794 founded the prestigious **Ecole Polytechnique**. Near the bustling small farmers' market is the old barracks of the Garde Républicaine, whose famous horse guards parade down the Champs-Elysées on Bastille Day, 14 July. ◆ Market: W, F, Su, 7AM-1PM. Métro: Place Monge

104 LA MOSQUÉE DE PARIS
This Moorish ensemble of soaring minarets, pink marble fountains, and crescent moons is the oldest mosque in France. In gratitude for North African support during World War I, France gave the French Arab community the funds to build the mosque. It was constructed in 1926 by Arab artisans and three French architects. Arabs from the poor Belleville and Barbès quarters gather at this enclave of Islam to read the Koran at the **Institut Musulman**. During Ramadan, hundreds of people kneel facing Mecca and pray to Allah on a sea of Persian carpets spread beneath the mosque's delicately carved dome. Nearby, behind a dark curtain, the women intone their prayers. Though unfortunately brief, the guided tour of the building, central courtyard, and Moorish garden offers a worthwhile introduction to Islam. You may leave feeling as though you've passed the time in Riyadh or Istanbul. ◆ Admission. M-Th, Sa-Su. Pl du Puits-de-l'Ermite and Rue Georges-Desplas. 01.45.35.97.33/34/35. Métro: Place Monge

105 SALON DE THÉ DE LA MOSQUÉE
★$ Flaky Moroccan pastries, sweet mint tea, and Turkish coffee are served during the summer on a charming white patio shaded by leafy fig trees. In winter, warm up with tea in a quiet lounge adjoining the *hammam* (Turkish steam bath). No alcohol is served. ◆ Daily, breakfast, lunch, and dinner until 10PM; closed in August. 2 Rue Daubenton (at Rue Geoffroy-St-Hilaire). 01.43.31.38.20. Métros: Censier-Daubenton, Place Monge

106 10 RUE VAUQUELIN

Working in a ramshackle ground-floor laboratory here at the **Sorbonne School of Physics and Chemistry** (which is now housed in a shiny new redbrick-and-glass building), Marie Curie and her husband, Pierre, discovered radium on 26 December 1898. The discovery of radioactivity not only earned them a Nobel prize in 1903 (the first of two for Marie) but triggered a fundamental rethinking of theoretical physics. A few months after their achievements, the quantum theory was published. ♦ Between Rue Claude-Bernard and Pl Lucien-Herr. Métro: Censier–Daubenton

107 RUE MOUFFETARD MARKET

Among the gastronomic items purveyed at this outdoor market are mangoes, blood oranges, horse meat, wild boar, sea urchins, Colombian coffee, and hundreds of marvelously smelly cheeses. Take a self-guided tour: Just follow your nose. Be sure to go down the **Rue Daubenton** and **Passage Passé Simple** to visit the flower shops and the stalls specializing in Auvergnat sausage. As you wander, remember the two cardinal rules of marketing in Paris: First, don't touch the produce; and second, the vendor, not the customer, is always right. ♦ Tu-Sa; Su, 9AM-1PM, 4-7:30PM. Between Rues Censier and de l'Epée-de-Bois. Métro: Censier–Daubenton

107 LE MOUFFETARD

★★$ The croissants, brioches, and fruit tarts are made fresh daily by the friendly Chartrain family, owners of the best café on the street. It's noisy, always crowded with vendors and students, and in winter the windows steam up, thanks to the animated conversation. Hearty traditional food. ♦ Tu-Su, breakfast, lunch, and dinner; closed in mid-July for 3 weeks. 116 Rue Mouffetard (at Rue de l'Arbalète). 01.43.31.42.50. Métro: Censier–Daubenton

108 A LA BONNE SOURCE

This bas-relief of two boys drawing water, whose title means "At the Good Spring," dates from the time of Henri IV (1589-1610). It's the oldest house sign on the street. ♦ 122 Rue Mouffetard (between Rues Edouard-Quénu and de l'Arbalète). Métro: Censier–Daubenton

109 LA TUILE À LOUP

Run by the affable Marie-France and Michel Joblin, this crowded shop specializes in French regional arts and crafts. The shelves are stocked with earthenware dishes, hand-carved wooden bowls, toys by well-known French artist Roland Roure, and a vast selection of books on French folklore, rural architecture, and ecology. ♦ M, afternoon; Tu-Sa; closed in summer. 35 Rue Daubenton (between Rues Monge and Mouffetard). 01.47.07.28.90. Métro: Censier–Daubenton

110 ST-MÉDARD

Built in 1773, this rustic village church is an architectural conglomeration of Flamboyant Gothic and Renaissance styles and has a story for every predilection. French literature majors may remember this as the church in which Jean Valjean accidentally encounters Javert in Victor Hugo's Les Misérables. Trade unionists point out that the church was turned into the **Temple of Labor** during the revolution. Art historians will recall the notorious painting of St. Geneviève, which for centuries was erroneously ascribed to Watteau. And the occultists in the crowd will appreciate a most famous corpse buried here, that of a church deacon named François Paris, a saintly young Jansenist who died in 1727. Rumors of miraculous cures drew huge crowds of convulsionary hysterics to his grave within 2 years of his death. (The frenzied gatherings were finally outlawed by Louis XV in 1732, but Paris's tomb remains beneath the unmarked stones of what is now the Chapel of the Virgin.) The majority of the church's construction was financed by fines imposed on Protestants; the money ran out while the vaulted ceiling was being installed, so it was completed in wood. At least that's how the story goes. ♦ 141 Rue Mouffetard (at Sq St-Medard). 01.44.08.87.00. Métro: Censier–Daubenton

111 AU PETIT MARGUERY

★★$$ The jovial Cousin brothers' 1900s-style neighborhood bistro presents such hearty dishes as cassoulette de gros escargots de Bourgogne (Burgundy snails in casserole), roasted skate wing with mustard seeds, rump steak with shallots, and roast pheasant, partridge, or venison in season, washed down by one of their fine, reasonably priced Burgundy wines. A very lively and popular spot despite its somewhat remote location. ♦ Tu-Sa, lunch and dinner; closed in August. Reservations recommended. 9 Blvd de Port-Royal (between Blvd Arago and Rue Pascal). 01.43.31.58.59. Métro: Les Gobelins

112 MANUFACTURE DES GOBELINS (GOBELINS TAPESTRY FACTORY)

The factory, the avenue, and the neighborhood all take their name from the brothers Jean and Philibert Gobelin, who in the 15th century established their famous dye works along the stinking Bièvre River. Although the name "Gobelins" has become synonymous with tapestry, the two brothers never wove a thread. Their claim to fame in the tapestry world was making a special scarlet dye. In 1662 Jean-Baptiste Colbert,

Louis XIV's famous minister, persuaded the king to take over the Gobelins property. There, under the management of court painter Charles Le Brun, Colbert assembled a crafts colony of about 250 Flemish weavers. His goal was twofold: to compete with Flanders's tapestry industry and to cover the vast expanse of walls in the Sun King's sumptuous palace at **Versailles**. In time, the tapestry factory became so celebrated that Marie Antoinette and Louis XVI (in 1790) and the pope (in 1895) paid personal visits to the humble workshops.

Today scores of weavers at the factory manufacture tapestries using ancient techniques, working on century-old wooden looms. Using wools from a palette of 14,920 colors, weavers may spend 2 to 4 years completing woven panels, the designs of which are based on modern paintings by artists such as Matisse, Picasso, and Miró. Three days a week, the state-owned mills offer 75-minute guided tours of the tapestry factory and the allied **Savonnerie** (carpet) and **Beauvais** (horizontal loom weaving) workshops, a treat for anyone interested in weaving and crafts. You can visit the studios where weavers, trained from the age of 16, work quietly, occasionally glancing up at mirrors before them to view the reverse side of the tapestry. If you can't get to the factory, you can see Gobelins tapestries hanging at **Versailles** as well as other places reserved for the privileged: the **Paris Opéra**, the **National Library**, the **Elysée Palace**, and the **Luxembourg Palace**. The Mobilier National (National Storehouse) is also housed within these compounds. ♦ Admission. Tours: Tu-Th, 2:45PM. To arrange group tours, call Caisse Nationale des Monuments Historiques at 01.44.54.19.30/31. 42 Ave des Gobelins (between Rues Croulebarbe and des Gobelins). 01.44.08.52.00. Métro: Les Gobelins

St-Germain

Quai Anatole-France

2

1

Rue de la Légion d'Honneur

Rue de Lille

3

Pont Royal

Rue de Soufflot

4

5

Rue de l'Université

Rue de Poitiers

6

Rue de Verneuil

7

8

Quai Voltaire

Rue de l'Université

Rue du Bac

11

12

9

10

Rue de Beaune

16

Blvd. St-Germain

Rue S-Bottin

17

Rue de Montalembert

27

24

25

26

28

Rue du Bac

Rue du Pré-aux-Clercs

Rue de St-Simon

37

Blvd. St-Germain

Rue de Bellechasse

38

39

40

41

Rue de Grenelle

Blvd. Raspail

52

53

Rue des Sts-Pères

Rue de Varenne

75

61

73

76

77

Rue St-Guillaume

Rue Vaneau

74

78

94

95

96

104

103

Rue de la Planche

111

Rue du Dragon

1

Rue de Babylone

Rue Chomel

119

112

Rue du Fou

Rue du Bac

Rue Velpeau

120

121

Rue du Vieux-Colombier

128

129

Rue de Sèvres

127

Rue du Cherche-Midi

136

Place Alphonse-Deville

137

Mada

Rue de Sèvres

Rue de Mézière

145

Rue St-Placide

Rue d'Assas

Rue Cassette

144

151

Rue de Rennes

Rue du Regard

N

For nos. 157-176, see pg. 105

km
mi   1/16   1/8   1/8   1/4

ST-GERMAIN

The tree-lined **Boulevard St-Germain** originates near the tip of Ile St-Louis, then traverses the heart of literary Paris and finally arrives back at the Seine at the **Pont de la Concorde** in the noble faubourg fashionable during the reign of Louis XV. This is the home of the **Académie Française**, the world's oldest café (**Le Procope**), prestigious publishing houses, bookbinders, and a conclave of intellectuals' watering holes where Fitzgerald, Hemingway, and other North American scriveners wrote or drank in the Jazz Age of the 1920s, and where Sartre, Camus, and company made existentialism a household name in the 1940s and 1950s.

The St-Germain quarter is also the home of the inviting **Jardin du Luxembourg** (Luxembourg Gardens), the **Ecole des Beaux-Arts** (School of Fine Arts), and a plethora of art galleries. In this neighborhood, the painter Corot walked the quays; Manet lived on **Rue Bonaparte**; and Delacroix resided in the **Place de Furstemberg**. Ingres, Baudelaire, and Wagner stayed on **Quai Voltaire**, and Picasso painted *Guernica* on **Rue des Grands-Augustins**.

This St-Germain itinerary covers the boulevard's most interesting portion, in the vicinity of the church of **St-Germain-des-Prés**, site of the remains of the city's oldest abbey. The route leads down alleys where bookshops, poster stores, antiques dealers, and picture restorers do business side by side with chic dress shops and cafés frequented by students. In the 1990s, the high-fashion industry invaded the old stomping ground of Sartre, de Beauvoir, and Camus. Some might bemoan the *quartier*'s drift from Sartre to the sartorial, but the new trend has reenergized an area that had been drifting into lethargy. And there are still plenty of places left that keep the myth of St-Germain alive.

Start at the **Musée d'Orsay**, a former Belle Epoque train station that is now devoted to art and culture between 1848 and World War I. En route to the Boulevard St-Germain, take **Rue du Bac** and stop at **Deyrolle**, an amusing taxidermy shop. On the boulevard is **Madeleine Gély**'s handmade-umbrella shop, an essential stop during those frequent April or November downpours. Consider having an early lunch and watching the world go by at one of the area's literary shrines such as **Café de Flore** or **Les Deux Magots**. When you can't drink one more cup of café au lait, visit the shaded Place de Furstemberg to look for the old studio of Delacroix, browse for antiques along **Rue Jacob**, pause for tea and macaroons at **Ladurée**, or tour the African art galleries along **Rue de Seine**.

Also on this tour is the narrow **Cour du Commerce St-André**, where the guillotine was invented and where firebrand Marat had his printing press. You'll pass Le Procope, where Voltaire and Robespierre were among the regulars, and the **Rue de Buci**, the street market where Picasso bought his sausages. From the **Odéon**, where Sylvia Beach had her famous bookshop, nature lovers will want to detour through the **Jardin du Luxembourg**, one of Queen Marie de Médicis's legacies to the city. Those nostalgic for the Paris of the North American expatriates in the 1920s can proceed to neighboring **Montparnasse** and visit favorite haunts of writers and artists of that period that are still going strong, such as the **La Closerie des Lilas**, **Le Sélect**, and **La Coupole**.

At day's end, consider dining at a classic Old World bistro such as **Allard**. Or catch an early Cary Grant film at the **Action Christine**, then dine in the splendor of **Jacques Cagna** around the corner on Rue des Grands-Augustins. Then wander toward the river, stopping at **La Palette** for a beer, or stroll along the **Pont des Arts**, with its superb view of the Ile de la Cité, and ponder the magnificence that is Paris at night.

1 HÔTEL D'ORSAY

$$ Forty-one bright, airy rooms with Oriental rugs, pastel walls, and floral wallpaper are available here at the former **Hôtel Solférino**, which was enlarged, renovated, and renamed in 1998. There's also a veranda where you can enjoy breakfast (but no restaurant). ♦ 93 Rue de Lille (between Rue de Solférino and Blvd St-Germain). 01.47.05.85.54; fax 01.45.55.51.16. Métros: Solférino, Assemblée Nationale. hotel.orsay@wanadoo.fr

2 PALAIS DE LA LÉGION D'HONNEUR

Built by Pierre Rousseau for German prince Frédéric III de Salm-Kyrbourg in 1786, this palace is architecturally the most significant Louis XVI building in Paris. It inspired Thomas Jefferson, the American ambassador to France at the time, in his architectural vision for the future capital of the United States. In 1804 Napoléon acquired it for the Légion d'Honneur. The *légion* was a society started by Napoléon to honor men, and later women, for outstanding service to France. Members may wear a woven bud of red wool stitched to their left lapel. The palace houses the **Musée de la Légion d'Honneur et des Ordres de Chevalerie**, which exhibits medals, insignia, and decorations related to the history of the *légion*. Included in the collection is Napoléon's Légion d'Honneur medal and his sword and breastplate. The California Palace of the Legion of Honor in San Francisco, which has an extensive collection of French art, is based on the palace here. ♦ The Museum is closed for renovations until 2005: 2 Rue de la Légion d'Honneur, formerly named Rue de Bellechasse (at Quai Anatole-France). RER: Musée d'Orsay.

3 MUSÉE D'ORSAY

What was once an imposing turn-of-the-19th-century train station, the **Gare d'Orsay**, is now a magnificent showcase for 19th-century art and culture. Opened in 1986, this museum houses the art that chronologically links the **Louvre** collections with those of the **Pompidou Center**, bridging the end of Romanticism and the origins of modern art. The museum transports visitors back to a time of grace and wit conveyed in the works of such geniuses as writers Henry James and Marcel Proust, actress Sarah Bernhardt, and artists Edouard Manet and James McNeill Whistler.

The collection (see diagram at right) includes all the Impressionist paintings formerly in the **Jeu de Paume**; the post-Impressionist and Nabi works from the **Palais de Tokyo** (among them are 400 paintings by Odilon Redon); and selected works that were formerly in the Louvre, including paintings and sculptures by artists who were born after 1820, such as Courbet and Millet, and various late paintings by Delacroix, Corot, Ingres, and the Barbizon landscape painters.

The Quai d'Orsay site was once occupied by the **Palais d'Orsay**, a government building that was devastated (as were the **Hôtel de Ville** and the **Tuileries Palace**) by the May 1871 fires set by the Commune at the end of France's tragic civil war period. The Orléans Rail Company bought the property and hired **Victor Laloux** (1850-1937), the architect who had rebuilt the **Hôtel de Ville**, to design a railway station and hotel. Construction lasted from September 1898 to July 1900 and was accomplished by a crew of 380 men working in round-the-clock shifts.

At one time, 200 trains a day used the **Gare d'Orsay**, but the growing electrification and lengthening of trains made its short platforms obsolete in the late 1930s. Over the years, the station took on other functions. Prisoners of war were garrisoned here after the liberation; General de Gaulle announced his return to power at the **Gare d'Orsay** hotel on 19 May 1958; Orson Welles made a film version of

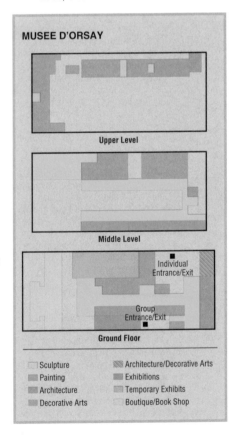

MUSEE D'ORSAY

Upper Level

Middle Level

Individual Entrance/Exit

Group Entrance/Exit

Ground Floor

Sculpture
Painting
Architecture
Decorative Arts
Architecture/Decorative Arts
Exhibitions
Temporary Exhibits
Boutique/Book Shop

---

the Franz Kafka book *The Trial* here in 1962; and in 1970, Bernardo Bertolucci used it as a setting for part of his film *The Conformist*.

As early as 1961, plans to raze the station and build a modern 870-room hotel complex were nearly realized; **Le Corbusier** even competed for the design job. But in 1971 the station was declared a historic landmark, and 8 years later **ACT Architecture** (a group of three associated architects: **Pierre Colboc**, **Renaud Bardon**, and **Jean-Paul Philippon**) was selected to renovate the building for use as a museum. Famed Italian designer **Gae Aulenti** planned the interior.

The famous French Impressionist collection is displayed on the ground and upper levels of the museum. The term *Impressionism* was coined by a derisive critic after seeing Monet's painting *Impression: Sunrise*. The name stuck, and the movement effected as dramatic a change in the course of art history as the Renaissance had. Instead of choosing heroes, mythic deities, or saints for their subject matter, the Impressionists painted ordinary people in cafés as well as trains chugging into **Gare St-Lazare** with vivid color and undisguised brush strokes.

The museum collection also features paintings by more than 36 North American artists, including John Singer Sargent, William Merritt Chase, Robert Henri, Winslow Homer, and Henry Ossawa Tanner, many of whom worked and studied in Paris. And this is where you can visit that emblem of North American art, *Arrangement in Grey and Black: The Artist's Mother*, by Whistler. A restaurant, rooftop café, bookstore, gift shop, and 380-seat auditorium round out the museum complex. ♦ Admission. Tu, W, F, Sa, 10AM-6PM; Th, 10AM-9:45PM; Su, 9AM-6PM (from June 20 the museum opens at 9AM); closed Mondays, closed Christmas, 1 January, and 1 May. 1 Rue de la Légion d'Honneur, formerly named Rue de Bellechasse (at Quai Anatole-France). 01.40.49.48.48 for information for individuals; 01.40.49.49.94 for information for groups. Métro: Solférino; RER: Musée d'Orsay. www.musee-orsay.fr

Within the Musée d'Orsay:

Ground Level. This floor features painting, sculpture, photography, and decorative arts dating from 1848 to 1870. The front of the gallery contains flamboyant sculptures by Rude, Préault, and Pradier and a great animal bronze by Barye. Don't miss the Daumier room to the left of the front of the gallery for his scathing satirical prints and amazing clay busts of corrupt and immoral contemporaries. At the rear of the gallery stands *The Dance* by Carpeaux. Rooms at the end of the courtyard are dedicated to the **Paris Opéra** and its architect, **Charles Garnier.**

To the right of the central court are paintings by Romantics such as Delacroix and Ingres, as well as works by the eclectics and symbolists, including Puvis de Chavannes and Gustave Moreau, along with the pre-1870 work of Edgar Degas. To the left of the courtyard are works by Realists, including Daumier, Corot, Millet, and the Barbizon painters. They are neighbors to the masterpieces of Edouard Manet, such as *Olympia* and *Déjeuner sur L'Herbe*, and to the pre-1870 work of Monet, Bazille, and Renoir.

Upper Level. To follow the chronological order of the artwork, ascend from the ground floor to the museum's upper level, where the light streaming through the glass roof shows off the post-1870 flowering of Impressionism. Here Manet, Degas, Monet, and Renoir are joined by Sisley, Pissarro, van Gogh, and Cézanne. Nearby, works by such post-Impressionists as Seurat, Signac, Cross, and Gauguin are shown with art from the Pont Aven and Nabi schools, including Denis, Bonnard, Vallotton, and Vuillard. Henri Rousseau's famous *Charmeuse de Serpents*, a room of Toulouse-Lautrec's works, and Matisse's landmark 1904 painting *Luxe, Calme et Volupté* are found here. There's also a special room devoted to graphic arts and photography between 1880 and 1914, including the works of early photographers Atget, Emerson, Steichen, and Stieglitz. On a landing between the upper and middle levels are works by Nadar, Legray, Baldus, Carroll, and Cameron.

Middle Level. The terraces above the central court display the sculpture of Rodin, Maillol, and Bourdelle. The rooms along the **Seine** have figures created during the Third Republic, including works by symbolists Burne-Jones and Delville. Eight rooms are devoted to the era of Art Nouveau, with pieces by Belgians Horta and van de Velde, by Gallé and Majorelle of the Nancy School, by Guimard, and by Thonet, the dean of bentwood furniture. On the Rue de Lille side are the 20th-century paintings of Klimt and Matisse, heralding the advent of modern art. Also on this level is an exhibition showing the evolution of the film industry.

RESTAURANT DU MUSÉE D'ORSAY

★★$ Housed in the dining room of the old hotel on the museum's middle level, the restaurant is an ornately gilded period piece that has a ceiling covered with painted deities by Gabriel Ferrier, winner of the 1872 Prix de Rome. The décor may be the main attraction here, but the traditional French *menu du jour* is honest and inexpensive at 14 euros, and the 15-dish Nordic buffet is a bargain at 15 euros. ♦ Tu-W, F-Su, lunch and afternoon tea; Th, dinner; closed Christmas, 1 January, and 1 May. 01.45.49.47.03

CAFÉ DES HAUTEURS

★$ Dominated by one of the gigantic see-through clocks of the old railway station, this airy café serves salads, snacks, light meals, and liquid refreshments. Service is cafeteria-style except during lunch and dinner hours. There's a grand view of the **Seine**, the **Tuileries**, and the **Louvre** from the balcony outside the café. ♦ Tu-W, F-Su; Th, until 9:30PM; closed Christmas, 1 January, and 1 May. No phone

4 BONPOINT

This pricey store offers exquisite couture for the little darlings in your life. Nearby on the same street are two sister stores—**No. 65** for womenswear and **No. 86** for clothes for infants up to 3 months of age, whereas **No. 7 Rue Solférino** on the corner of Rue de l'Université carries a large assortment of household items. ♦ M-Sa. 67 Rue de l'Univer-sité (at Rue de Solférino). 01.45.55.63.70. Métro: Solférino. Also at 15 Rue Royale (between Rue St-Honoré and Place de la Madeleine). 01.47.42.52.63. Métros: Concorde, Madeleine; 12 Avenue Montaigne (between Place de l'Alma and Rue Boccador). 01.47.20.42.10. Métro: Alma-Marceau; and 50 Rue Etienne Marcel (between Rue du Louvre and Place des Victoires). 01.40.26.20.90. Métro: Sentier

5 LE TÉLÉGRAPHE

★★$$ The splendid Art Nouveau dining hall of the **Maison des Dames des Postes, Télégraphe et Téléphones**, a dormitory built for female operators and postal clerks in 1905, has been converted into a glamorous restaurant and bar, with a quiet garden open for lunch only in fair weather. The neoclassical French fare includes such starters as lobster raviolis with fresh herb dressing and preserved tomato tart with fillets of sardine; main courses of fillet of line-caught bass with Nice olives and rack of lamb with sage; and *fondant au chocolat* (soft chocolate cake with a warm, runny center) for dessert. After a long day at the **Musée d'Orsay**, get off your feet in the magnificent barroom, the perfect spot to prolong the Belle Epoque mood. ♦ M-F, lunch and dinner; Sa-Su, dinner. Reservations recommended, especially for lunch in the garden. 41 Rue de Lille (between Rues de la Légion and de Poitiers). 01.42.92.03.04. Métro: Rue du Bac; RER: Musée d'Orsay

TAN-DINH

6 TAN-DINH

★★★$$ The most elegant—and expensive—Vietnamese restaurant in Paris is conveniently located around the corner from the **Musée d'Orsay**. Delicate smoked-goose ravioli, light noodles with piquant shrimp, and lobster beignets with ginkgo are prepared by the affable Vifian brothers, who alternate nights in the kitchen. The exotic sorbets and remarkable Bordeaux are also memorable. ♦M-Sa, lunch and dinner; closed in August. Reservations recommended for dinner. 60 Rue de Verneuil (between Rues du Bac and de Poitiers). 01.45.44.04.84. Métro: Solférino

7 RAVI

★★$$$ Spicy and pricey, this aptly named Indian restaurant (*ravi* means "sun" in Hindi) outshines its competitors with Madras curries, kabobs, and outstanding tandoori prawns. The small dining room is charming and welcoming. ♦ M-F, lunch and dinner; Sa, dinner. Reservations recommended. 50 Rue de Verneuil (between Rues du Bac and de Poitiers). 01.42.61.17.28. Métro: Solférino

8 MAXOFF

★$$ Such specialties as *tarama* (salmon roe spread), Baltic salad, beef stroganoff, Iranian caviar, *caviar d'aubergines* (eggplant caviar), Ukrainian borscht, blintzes, and strudel are served in a warm and convivial atmosphere in this cute little restaurant with only six tables. ♦ M-F, lunch and dinner; Sa, dinner; closed in August. Reservations recommended. 44 Rue de Verneuil (between Rues du Bac and de Poitiers). 01.42.60.60.43. Métro: Solférino

9 50 Rue de l'Université

This is the former site of the **Hôtel de l'Intendance**, where Edna St. Vincent Millay wrote her Pulitzer prize–winning book of poems *The Harp Weaver* in 1921. The hotel has since been replaced by an unattractive modern structure. ◆ Between Rues du Bac and de Poitiers. Métro: Rue du Bac

10 Rue du Bac

The barracks that housed the swashbuckling heroes of *The Three Musketeers* by Alexandre Dumas were located on this street, which was built in 1564 and named after the *bac* (ferry) that used to transport Vaugirard quarry stone across the **Seine** to the construction site of the **Tuileries Palace**. ◆ Between Rues de l'Université and de Verneuil. Métros: Rue du Bac, Sèvres Babylone

10 Lefèbvres & Fils

Among those who shopped for earthenware china and fanciful trompe l'oeil dishes at this firm established in 1881 were Victor Hugo, Marcel Proust, and Georges Feydeau. ◆ M–Sa; closed in August. 24 Rue du Bac (between Rues de l'Université and de Verneuil). 01.42.61.18.40. Métro: Rue du Bac

11 Le Bistrot de Paris

★★$$ This fashionable bistro has an innovative one-two punch: ravishing 1880s décor with Belle Epoque mosaics and a Provençal menu, with the specialties changing with the seasons. Lots of *gibier* (wild game) is featured during the hunting season. ◆ M–Su, lunch and dinner. Reservations recommended. 33 Rue de Lille (between Rues de Beaune and du Bac). 01.42.61.16.83, 01.42.61.15.84. Métro: Rue du Bac

12 9 Rue de Beaune

While living here at the **Hôtel Elysée** in July 1920, Ezra Pound convinced James Joyce to move from Trieste and bring his family to Paris, where Pound settled them in a small hotel nearby at 9 Rue de l'Université. Today this is a residential building. ◆ At Rue de Lille. Métro: Rue du Bac

12 7 Rue de Beaune

In 1872 young Henry James, whose future novels *The American* and *The Ambassadors* would feature North American expatriates in Paris, came to this residential building to visit fellow Bostonian James Russell Lowell and as a bonus found Ralph Waldo Emerson and his daughter Ellen in the sitting room. It was, as he wrote home, "a little Cambridge on the Seine." ◆ Between Rue de Lille and Quai Voltaire. Métro: Rue du Bac

13 Quai Voltaire

This quay honors Voltaire, whose return to Paris in 1778 after a 30-year absence was greeted by a torchlight parade that wound from the **Comédie Française** (where his tragedy *Irène* had just opened) across the river to **No. 27 Quai Voltaire**, where he died on 30 May 1778. The quay's history involves many artists: Jean-Dominique Ingres died on 14 January 1867 at **No. 11**; Delacroix and Corot, at different times, rented the top-floor studio at **No. 13**; in the hotel at **No. 19**, Baudelaire penned *Les Fleurs du Mal* in 1857, and Wagner composed *Die Meistersinger* here between 1861 and 1862. Today, it is a bazaar of first-rate antiques shops and galleries. Side by side are well-known dealers such as **Galerie Berès Bailly** (No. 25, 01.42.61.27.91) and **Anthony Embden** (No. 15, 01.42.61.04.06). ◆ Between Ponts du Carrousel and Royal Métro: Rue du Bac

13 Hôtel du Quai Voltaire

$$ Charles-Pierre Baudelaire, Oscar Wilde, Richard Wagner, and Jean Sibelius each came to this hotel looking for a room with a view. Do the same: Ask for a front room (if you don't mind traffic noise) and wake up to a vista of the Seine and the **Tuileries**. There are 32 fairly comfortable guest rooms. There's no restaurant, but there is a bar that serves only drinks. The staff members at reception aren't very helpful. ◆ 19 Quai Voltaire (between Rues des Sts-Pères and de Beaune). 01.42.61.50.91; fax 01.42.61.62.26. Métro: Rue du Bac. www.hotelduquaivoltaire.com

14 Sennelier

The Left Bank's finest painters patronize this celebrated art-supply store. Even if you can't draw an apple to save your life, step inside and rub shoulders with the Beaux-Arts students shopping for linseed oil, blocks of brilliantly colored pastel chalks, and wooden palettes. ◆ M, afternoons; Tu–Sa, all day. 3 Quai Voltaire (between Rues des Sts-Pères and de Beaune). 01.42.60.72.15. Métros: Rue du Bac, St Germain-des-Prés. Also at 4 *bis* Rue de la Grande Chaumière (between Rue Notre Dame-des-Champs and Blvd du Montparnasse). 01.46.33.72.39. Métro: Vavin

15 Pont des Arts

Providing a pedestrian crossing between the **Institut de France** and the **Louvre**, this wooden-planked structure with latticed arches was the first iron bridge in Paris. Designed by an engineer named Dillon in 1804, the footbridge was originally landscaped with potted orange trees, rosebushes, and hothouses full of exotic tropical plants. Hordes of easel-toting artists from the nearby **Ecole des Beaux-Arts** come here to sketch and paint that familiar compact view spanning the Ile de la Cité, the rose-gray façade of Place Dauphine, and the dignified form of the Pont-Neuf, as well as the spires of **Notre-Dame** and **Ste-Chapelle** in the distance. ♦ Between Quais de Conti and du Louvie. Métro: Pont-Neuf

16 LE CABINET DE CURIOSITÉ

Lined with panels from an Empire-period pharmacy, this amusing shop displays stuffed monkeys, brass hourglasses, women's shoes from the Louis XVI epoch, strange old primitive paintings, apothecary jars, an exquisite collection of Gothic keys and locks, and iron cork-crushers shaped like crocodiles. Owner Claudine Guerin is an expert in fine wrought iron. ♦ M–Sa; closed in August. 23 Rue de Beaune (between Rues de Verneuil and de Lille). 01.42.61.09.57. Métro: Rue du Bac

Hôtel
de
l'université ***

PARIS

17 HÔTEL DE L'UNIVERSITÉ

$$$ This sedate hotel in a 17th-century town house has exposed stone walls and wooden beams, tapestries, antiques, and a small private courtyard. It offers 27 quaint, comfortably modernized rooms, but no restaurant. ♦ 22 Rue de l'Université (between Rues des Sts-Pères and de Beaune). 01.42.61.09.39; fax 01.42.60.40.84. Métro: Rue du Bac. hoteluniversite@gofornet.com

18 ECOLE DES BEAUX-ARTS (SCHOOL OF FINE ARTS)

The city's fine arts school was established by Louis XIV and trained many of the architects and artists who have designed and decorated Paris over the centuries. It's worth a quick detour to view the lovely Renaissance archway, fountain, and sculpture and the changing exhibitions of student work. Two well-known architects, **Richard Morris Hunt** and **Bernard Ralph Maybeck**, were among the first North Americans to be educated here, and each employed his own version of the Beaux Arts style in the US during the late 19th century. Ellsworth Kelly studied here after World War II. ♦ Daily. 14 Rue Bonaparte (between Rue Jacob and Quai Malaquais). 01.47.03.50.00. Métros: Rue du Bac, St-Germain-des-Prés

19 8 RUE BONAPARTE

The young Corsican conqueror once lived here, but this street wasn't named for him until 1852, when his nephew, Napoléon III, became emperor. ♦ Between Rue Jacob and Quai Malaquais. Métro: St-Germain-des-Prés

20 ROGER-VIOLLET

The more than eight million black-and-white and color photographs for sale at this press agency document the history of humankind from antiquity to the present. Stored here are glossies of the Temple of Ramses at Abu Simbel, the interior of a 14th-century baker's shop, Louis Armstrong, and the demolition of the Berlin Wall. Curious tourists are not admitted, but journalists, students, and other researchers are welcome. ♦ M–F. 6 Rue de Seine (between Rue des Beaux-Arts and Quai Malaquais). 01.55.42.89.00. Métros: Odéon, St-Germain-des-Prés

21 INSTITUT DE FRANCE

Situated across the Pont des Arts from the **Louvre**, this 17th-century masterpiece, designed by **Louis Le Vau** at the same time as he was working on the **Louvre**, houses five academies, including the prestigious **Académie Française**. The academy began in 1635 as a salon of intellectuals who gathered informally to discuss French rhetoric and usage. Shortly thereafter, Cardinal Richelieu charged them with the protection and dissemination of the French language, hoping that Parisian French would eventually obliterate the less-refined regional dialects.

Academy membership is limited to 40 "immortals." At their induction ceremonies, the members wear silver-embroidered green robes and cocked admirals' bonnets and carry jeweled swords. The immortals don their robes for closed-door meetings, which are held every Thursday afternoon. Among their responsibilities are safeguarding the mother tongue and preparing new editions of the academy's dictionary, which first appeared in 1694.

Election to the academy is reserved for great writers, and even the list of also-rans comprises a pantheon of French literature: Descartes, Diderot, de Maupassant, Balzac, Flaubert, Verlaine, Stendhal, and Proust among them. Molière, the playwright-director-actor, was invited to join the academy on the condition that he give up acting. He refused the honor. No actor has ever been admitted to date. Emile Zola campaigned unsuccessfully for election 13 times; Nobel prize–winners André Gide and Albert Camus never even tried. Late North American–born novelist Julian

Green, who wrote his works in French, was elected in 1971. In 1981, history was made when Marguerite Yourcenar was inducted into the sacred ranks of the academy and became the first female immortal. (The cloak she wore at the presentation was personally designed by Yves Saint Laurent.)

The left wing of the institute (toward the mint building) is the site of the notorious **Tour Nesle**, from where, according to Dumas, Queen Margot (the first wife of Henri IV) would catapult that night's lover into the **Seine**. Among the exemplary statuary in the institute rotunda is a nude bust of Voltaire by Houdon. ♦ Open to cultural groups by appointment. 23 Quai de Conti (at Pl de l'Institut). 01.44.41.44.41. Métro: Pont-Neuf

22 12 Rue Mazarine

Here young Molière made his acting debut and later, with an inherited nest egg, opened a theater in an abandoned tennis court; this was the genesis of the **Comédie Française**. In 1673, after he died onstage, the theater company was orphaned and evicted. But the troupe started performing once again in another old tennis court at 14 Rue de l'Ancienne-Comédie after more than a decade of inactivity. ♦ Between Rues Jacques-Callot and de Seine. Métros: Odéon, Mabillon

23 Galerie Larock-Granoff

One of the city's most reputable modern art galleries sells works of the masters. ♦ M, 2-6:30PM; Tu-Sa. 13 Quai de Conti (at Impasse Conti). 01.43.54.41.92. Métro: Pont-Neuf

23 Impasse de Conti

On this street in 1792, a young Corsican named Napoléon Bonaparte rented an attic room in the **Hôtel de Guénégaud** (now part of the **Hôtel des Monnaies**) built by **François Mansart** in 1659. Twelve years later, he conquered Europe and crowned himself emperor of France. ♦ Métro: Pont-Neuf

24 Librairie Elbé

At this gallery, easily among the most atmospheric in Paris, you can buy the original versions of the old advertisements of French tobacco, biscuits, and spirits that are so crassly copied at the city's postcard racks. But there's more to what meets the eye in the

"Vive la difference" is still the order of the day in France. Although French women got the vote in 1946, they have yet to fare well at the polls. Only 10.9% of the members of parliament are women, compared to 30.9% in Germany and 42.7% in Sweden.

attractive window displays: first-run prints of antique maps, engravings of wildlife and hunting scenes, and (in the basement) vintage travel posters. Items are on the pricey side, but friendly staff make browsing a pleasure. Tu-Sa, 10AM-PM and 2PM-6:30PM. 213 *bis*, Blvd St-Germain (at Rue de St-Simon). 01.45.48.77.97. Métro: Rue du Bac

25 Galerie Maeght/Librairie Maeght

The owner of this art gallery and art shop comes from a famous family of modern art dealers and sells paintings, drawings, and original graphics, along with a huge selection of prints by modern artists from Matisse to Cucchi, deluxe art books, art exhibition posters, Miró T-shirts, and postcards. ♦ M-Sa. 42 Rue du Bac (between Blvd St-Germain and Rue de l'Université). 01.45.48.45.15. Métro: Rue du Bac

25 Deyrolle

This 150-year-old taxidermy shop has everything from mounted polar bears, ostriches, lions, and bewildered baby elephants to cobras, wild boars, and other citizens of Noah's Ark, all staring out of glass eyes. Deyrolle also acquires rare butterflies, tastefully stuffed cocker spaniels, and just about every crystal, geode, and mineral on earth. Kids could be left here for hours. ♦ M-Sa. 46 Rue du Bac (between Blvd St-Germain and Rue de l'Université). 01.42.22.30.07. Métro: Rue du Bac. Also at 29 rue Greuze (corner of Rue de Sablons and Rue Greuze). Métro: Trocadero

26 Hôtel Pont Royal

$$$$ Gone is the legendary bar in the basement that was favored by Sartre, de Beauvoir, Camus, Styron, Garcia Márquez, and many another famous writer during Paris's post–World War II era of literary glory. Neglected in recent years, it fell victim to a thorough renovation of the hotel for the year 2000, successful despite that nostalgic loss. Earth tones, abundant mahogany, and boldly striped fabrics warm the ambiance of this elegant hotel. Rooms are comfortably appointed, if not always particularly spacious. There are modern conference rooms and a small fitness center in the basement. At press time the much-anticipated restaurant **L'Atelier de Joël Robuchon** was slated to open in the hotel. 7 Rue de Montalembert (between Rues Sébastien-Bottin and du Bac). 01.42.84.70.00; fax 01.42.84.71.00. Métro: Rue du Bac. hpr@hotel-pont-royal.com; www.hotel-pont-royal.com/hpr

26 Hôtel Montalembert

$$$$ This chic Left Bank luxury hotel is popular with people from the worlds of publishing, fashion, and the fine arts.

Designer Christian Liaigre's tasteful furnishings for the lobby and 56 rooms boast a wondrous attention to detail, from handcrafted leather furniture to cast-bronze door handles. The modern guest rooms with customized furniture will suit guests who prefer contemporary style, while the Louis Philippe rooms with finely restored period furniture will please traditionalists. Everyone staying here should plan a few long, bubbly soaks in the opulent bathrooms, done in gray marble and chrome. ♦ 3 Rue de Montalembert (between Rues Sébastien-Bottin and du Bac). 01.45.49.68.68; fax 01.45.49.69.49. Métro: Rue du Bac. welcome@hotel-montalembert.fr; www.montalembert.com

Within the Hôtel Montalembert:

RESTAURANT MONTALEMBERT

★★$$ The congenial atmosphere and the creations of chef Fréderic Deswarte have made this intimate café a popular meeting place for Parisians. You can't go wrong with the poached chicken salad with lemon and poppy-seed sauce, mixed salad with *tapenade* and roasted goat cheese, roast lamb with polenta, or the apple and rhubarb crumble. ♦ M-Su, breakfast, lunch, and dinner. Reservations recommended. 01.45.49.68.68

27 LENOX

$$$ The then–22-year-old T.S. Eliot spent a romantic summer here in 1910 on the old man's money, just before he took a job in a London bank and wrote "The Love Song of J. Alfred Prufrock." Restored with chic simplicity and a slightly New Wave bar, the 34-room hotel is a favorite of visiting fashion models. Ask for one of the top-floor rooms—they have balconies and exposed beams. There's no restaurant, but the bar is open daily between 4PM and 2AM, with live music Tuesday through Thursday between 6:30 and 9:30PM. ♦ 9 Rue de l'Université (at Rue du Pré-aux-Clercs). 01.42.96.10.95; fax 01.42.61.52.83. Métros: Rue du Bac, St-Germain-des-Pres. hotel@lenoxsaintgermain.com; www.lenoxsaintgermain.com

28 2-4 RUE DE L'UNIVERSITÉ

In 1776 Benjamin Franklin lived here at the former Hôtel d'Entragues while he was drumming up support for the American Revolution. It's still a residential building. ♦ At Rue des Sts-Pères. Métros: Rue du Bac, St-Germain-des-Pres

29 RUE JACOB

Named after the Old Testament patriarch, this street is chock-full of book and antiques shops selling everything from autographs and old manuscripts to theater props and scientific instruments. ♦ Between Rues des Sts-Pères and de Seine. Métros: St-Germain-des-Prés, Mabillon

29 56 RUE JACOB

The Treaty of Paris, by which England recognized the independence of the 13 American colonies, was signed in this building, formerly the Hôtel d'York, on 3 September 1783. Benjamin Franklin, John Jay, and John Adams endorsed the document on behalf of the US; David Hartley and Richard Oswald represented England. ♦ Between Rues Bonaparte and des Sts-Pères. Métro: St-Germain-des-Prés

ALAIN BRIEUX

SCIENCES · TECHNIQUES · MÉDECINE

30 ALAIN BRIEUX

This eclectic curio shop specializes in prints, Arabic astrolabes, and rare medical books that date back to the 16th century. Everything in the store is for sale except the crocodile hanging from the ceiling. This item was a traditional feature in old apothecaries and alchemists' labs. ♦ M-F; Sa, 2-6PM; closed in August. 48 Rue Jacob (between Rues Bonaparte and des Sts-Pères). 01.42.60.21.98. Métro: St-Germain-des-Prés

31 ANGLETERRE

$$$ Among the notables who have stayed in this 18th-century hostelry are Washington Irving, Sherwood Anderson, and young Ernest Hemingway. It's now a picturesque 27-room hotel with a garden patio. The bar is open 24 hours for hotel guests only; there's no restaurant. ♦ 44 Rue Jacob (between Rues Bonaparte and des Sts-Pères). 01.42.60.34.72; fax 01.42.60.16.93. Métro: St-Germain-des-Prés. anglotel@wanadoo.fr

32 24 RUE BONAPARTE

In the spring of 1928, Henry Miller stayed here with his wife, June. The building now has both residential and commercial space. ♦ Between Rue Jacob and Quai Malaquais. Métro: St-Germain-des-Prés

33 24 RUE VISCONTI

This was once the home of Racine. According to a historian's account, the brilliant 17th-century dramatist died here on 21 April 1699 of a combination of dysentery, erysipelas, rheumatism, a liver ailment, and, possibly, "the chagrin of no longer being in favor with the king." The building is still a private residence. ♦ Between Rues de Seine and Bonaparte. Métro: St-Germain-des-Prés

34 L'HÔTEL

$$$$No two rooms in this sumptuous hideaway hotel are alike, but delightful as the Jacques Garcia (designer of the **Hôtel Costes**) décor may be, it will never be this address's chief claim to fame. That's because in 1900, when it was called the **Hôtel d'Alsace**, Oscar Wilde died here, abhorring the then tacky wallpaper and writing to a friend "I am dying beyond my means." It is possible to stay in Wilde's room, refurbished to look like his London town house, but other guest rooms and suites are not without allure. There is, for example, the Cardinal Suite, with views of the St-Germain-des-Prés rooftops, an Art Deco bedroom inspired by dance-hall belle Mistinguett's stay, and the Marco Polo Room with Far Eastern stylings. The hotel features a unique six-story light well and a small underground swimming pool. 13 Rue des Beaux-Arts (between Rues de Seine and Bonaparte). 01.44.41.99.00; fax 01.43.25.64.81. Métro: St-Germain-des-Prés. reservation@l-hotel.com; www.l-hotel.com

Within L'Hôtel:

LE BELIER BAR

A favorite among the art and antiques dealers in the neighborhood, this opulent bar and restaurant feels like the salon of a wealthy Parisian's home. Bar open daily, 2-11PM; restaurant, Tu-Sa, lunch and dinner. 01.44.41.99.00

France grants new mothers 16 weeks of paid maternity leave.

Over 91.2% of French people approve of premarital sex, the highest percentage of any country in Europe.

Though Paris is by far the most populous municipality in France, with 2.15 million people, it ranks only 113th in land surface, with 10,540 hectares (26,044 acres).

34 GALERIE CLAUDE BERNARD

One of the city's best, this internationally known gallery shows such modern heavyweights as Balthus, Giacometti, David Hockney, Louise Nevelson, and Jim Dine. ♦ Tu-Sa. No credit cards accepted. 7-9 Rue des Beaux-Arts (between Rues de Seine and Bonaparte). 01.43.26.97.07. Métro: St-Germain-des-Prés

35 5 RUE DES BEAUX-ARTS

Edouard Manet was born here in 1835. ♦ Between Rues de Seine and Bonaparte. Métro: St-Germain-des-Prés

36 HÔTEL DES MONNAIES/MUSÉE DES MONNAIES (MINT/MONEY MUSEUM)

The austere classical-style French mint is where the nation's centime and franc coins were designed and struck. In 1775, shortly after the original mint by **Jules Hardouin-Mansart** was demolished, the present edifice was built by **Jacques-Denis Antoine**. The museum traces the history of French coins back to Charlemagne's day and houses a collection of medals, currency, and commemorative coins. Hundreds of gold and silver medals are also for sale in the museum shop (2 Rue Guénégaud, 01.40.46.58.58). ♦ Admission. Museum: Tu-F, 11AM-5:30PM; Sa-Su, noon-5:30PM; Th, 11AM-9PM. Tours of mint production area: W, F, 2:15PM. Museum shop: M-Sa. 11 Quai de Conti (between Rue Guénégaud and Impasse de Conti). 01.40.46.55.33. Métro: Pont-Neuf

37 HÔTEL DUC DE ST-SIMON

$$$ Two Swedish friends own this cozy antiques-furnished 34-room hotel on a hidden street just off the Boulevard St-Germain. It's popular among transatlantic diplomats, intellectuals, actors (including Lauren Bacall), writers (Nobel prize–winner Toni Morrison, John Irving, P.D. James, and Nadine Gordimer stay here), film director Arthur Penn, and his photographer brother Irving. But despite the eminence of the company, the ambiance remains very relaxed. Reservations for newcomers may be difficult to come by, but keep trying. Garden lovers should ask for room **No. 25**, which has a flower-bedecked terrace, if they don't mind a room that's a bit small. ♦ 14 Rue de St-Simon (between Rue de Grenelle and Blvd St-Germain). 01.44.39.20.20; fax 01.45.48.68.25. Métro: Rue du Bac

38 PLEATS PLEASE/ISSEY MIYAKE

A fashion purist, Tokyo-based designer Miyake creates all his own fabrics and dresses his followers for maximum comfort and ease of motion. Miyake's haute couture shop is in the Marais along with two others. ◆ M-Sa. 201 Blvd St-Germain (between Rue St-Guillaume and Blvd Raspail). 01.45.48.10.44. Métro: Rue du Bac. Also at 3 Pl des Vosges (between Rues de Birague and des Francs-Bourgeois). 01.48.87.01.86; 3 *bis* Rue des Rosiers (between Vieille du Temple and Rue de Pavée). 01.40.29.99.66; 47-49 Rue des Francs Bourgeois (at the corner of Rue Veille du Temple). 01.44.54.07.05. Métros: St-Paul, Bastille

39 MADELEINE GÉLY

Since 1834 the finest umbrella shop in Paris has been selling and repairing handmade *parapluies*. The narrow little boutique is crammed with umbrellas—large, small, new, and antique. And you needn't have a bad leg to buy one of Madeleine Gély's 400 new or antique canes. They include duck- and bulldog-headed canes, watch canes, whiskey-flask canes, and even a cane to measure the withers of a horse. There are also sturdy utilitarian models. ◆ Tu-Sa; closed in August. 218 Blvd St-Germain (between Rues St-Guillaume and du Bac). 01.42.22.63.35. Métro: Rue du Bac

40 COFFEE SAINT-GERMAIN

★$$ In the former space of the Coffee Parisien, *américainophile* owner Bruno Rivière continues to serve such North American–style culinary treats as pancakes with maple syrup, eggs Benedict, bagels and cream cheese, and bacon cheeseburgers and hash browns. Brunch is offered all day. ◆ Daily, lunch, brunch, and dinner until midnight. 5 Rue Perronet (between Rues des Sts-Pères and St-Guillaume). 01.40.49.08.08. Métros: Rue du Bac, St-Germain-des-Prés

41 DEBAUVE AND GALLAIS

This wood-paneled chocolate shop with a semicircular counter began as a pharmacy nearly 200 years ago, when medicated chocolate was a nostrum for flatulence, anemia, and other ills. Today, in addition to delicious nonmedicinal chocolate, the shop

sells such delights as *croquamandes* (almonds roasted with caramelized sugar), hot chocolate mix, and real chocolate gift boxes. The old metal tea canisters date from 1804. ◆ M-Sa. 30 Rue des Sts-Pères (between Rues Perronet and de l'Université). 01.45.48.54.67. Métros: Rue du Bac, St-Germain-des-Prés

42 DÉMONS ET MERVEILLES

You'll find folk costumes from Romania, Hungary, Poland, Afghanistan, Tibet, and India; big silver bracelets from Morocco, Algeria, and the Middle East; and heavy iron crucifixes from Ethiopia here. Faty, the Tunisian owner, left his law practice to start this shop. ◆ M-Sa. 45 Rue Jacob (between Rues St-Benoît and des Sts-Pères). 01.42.96.26.11. Métro: St-Germain-des-Prés

43 LE PETIT ST-BENOÎT

★★$ Offering indigent Left Bank intellectuals *blanquette de veau* (veal in a white sauce), shepherd's pie, and salted pork with lentils since 1901, this popular coach-house bistro has prices that are difficult to beat. The rest room features a celebrated blue-and-white-checkered washbowl. ◆ M-Sa, lunch and dinner. 4 Rue St-Benoît (between Blvd St-Germain and Rue Jacob). 01.42.60.27.92. Métro: St-Germain-des-Prés

44 LADURÉE

★★★$ With this sumptuous *salon de thé* and upscale treat emporium the celebrated Right Bank *pâtissier* makes the jump to St.-Germain. Much more than a branch of the other Ladurées, this place merits a special trip for its décor. An Empire-period "Botanical" room leads to a spacious, light-flooded veranda with golden palms, Oriental-style sofas, rust-red cast-iron tables, and a gorgeous fresco. There's additional seating in the Prussian Blue Room upstairs. Take time out for the company's first chocolate boutique, adjoining the takeaway pastry counter on the ground floor. As if having to decide which flavors of macaroons to buy weren't hard enough, now you can add an array of

---

THE BEST

Paule Caillat

Promenades Gourmandes

I love my little neighborhood in the third arrondissement, which has become very hip in the last few years.

The **Square du Temple**, typically Haussmannien with a lake, a music kiosk, and a big lawn where sunbathing is allowed. Early in the morning, residents of the nearby Chinese community practice tai chi.

Restaurants

Chez Omar, on rue de Bretagne, with the most likable couscous in Paris.

SI for the best decor, nicest service, and great Italian-style vegetables.

R'ALIMENTS for semi-organic food and great wok dishes in an avant-garde setting.

Shops

L'Habilleur on rue de Poitou for discounted designer clothes for men and women, always a great selection.

Patyka, on rue Rambuteau, carries a line of natural plant-based products for the face and body, made in Hungary. Their "huile absolue" is truly the best.

RTA (René Talmon l'Armée) at 3, rue Cunin Gridaine 75003 (between rue de Turbigo and Rue Saint-Martin) for contemporary jewelry from a young designer from Berlin whose workshop is on the premises.

Last but not least, for the greatest haircut in Paris : **Rita Del'orco** (tel. 06.10.82.41.14). This Italian artist works only for magazines, but if you call her, she will come to you with her suitcase and style your hair memorably.

---

ganaches, pralines, nougat, marzipan, truffles, *mendiants* (dark chocolate rounds with dried fruit and nuts) and *fruits déguisés* (chocolate-dipped fruits) to your wish list. Daily, breakfast, lunch, and afternoon tea, 8:30AM-7:30PM. 21 Rue Bonaparte (at Rue Jacob). 01.44.07.64.87. Métro: St-Germain-des-Prés.

45 17 RUE VISCONTI

Young Balzac set up his print shop at this address. A few years later, in 1836, Delacroix moved in. It was here that he painted his portraits of George Sand and Frédéric Chopin. It is now a private residential–commercial building. ♦ Between Rues de Seine and Bonaparte. Métro: St-Germain-des-Prés

45 CLAUDE BOULLÉ

For a quarter of a century, Claude Boullé has been selling his landscapes represented in natural stones, cut and polished. Some of them are the mineral counterparts of Turner's seascapes on canvas. ♦ M-Sa. 28 Rue Jacob (between Rues de Seine and Bonaparte). 01.46.33.01.38. Métro: St-Germain-des-Prés

45 LA MAISON RUSTIQUE

Those with green thumbs will enjoy browsing in this agricultural and horticultural bookstore. ♦ M-Sa. 26 Rue Jacob (between Rues de Seine and Bonaparte). 01.42.34.96.60. Métro: St-Germain-des-Prés

Four fifths of Paris's parkland is located on the edges of the city in the Bois de Boulogne and the Bois de Vincennes.

46 LIBRAIRIE FISCHBACHER

Along with a stunning collection of fine arts editions, this shop has history books on fine and primitive arts, critical studies, and biographies in French, English, German, and Italian. ♦ M-Sa. 33 Rue de Seine (between Rues Jacques-Callot and Mazarine). 01.43.26.84.87. Métros: Mabillon, St-Germain-des-Prés

47 LA PALETTE

★★$ This bohemian café is right out of a Jean Rhys novel. In fact, James Ivory filmed part of the down-and-out tale *Quartet* (with Alan Bates, Maggie Smith, and Isabelle Adjani) here in 1981. The artists' palettes that hang on the wall are more interesting than the paintings themselves, but don't miss the humorous 1920s tiled murals in the back room. House specialties include Gruyère omelette, chef's salad, country ham served on Poilâne country bread, and a delicious *tarte Tatin*. Bearded waiter Jean-François is grouchy but kindhearted and plays the part of a little Bonaparte; you must order quickly and without indecision or he'll ignore you until you've learned your lesson. One Aussie regular calls the crouch-style toilet an "authentic porcelain kangaroo trap." ♦ M-Sa, breakfast and lunch until 2PM; closed in August. No credit cards accepted. 43 Rue de Seine (at Rue Jacques-Callot). 01.43.26.68.15. Métros: Mabillon, St-Germain-des-Prés

48 GALERIE J.C. RIEDEL

One of the most successful galleries in Paris, this springboard for European talent boasts the works of such promising and well-received artists as S.W. Hayter, François Audrum, Sanyu, and Garcia Tella. ♦ Sa, 2-7PM. 12 Rue Guénégaud (between Rue Mazarine and Quai de Conti). 01.46.33.25.73. Métro: Odéon

48 MICHEL CACHOUX

Dig through the fossils, lapis, amethysts, and star-shaped calcites—there's something for everyone's hard-rock fantasy here. ♦ Tu-Sa; closed in August. 16 Rue Guénégaud (between Rue Mazarine and Quai de Conti). 01.43.54.52.15. Métro: Odéon

49 RUE DE NEVERS

Dating from the 13th century, this alley ends near a remnant of the King Philippe Auguste city wall (ca. 1200). It passes beneath an arch chiseled with an excerpt of the 17th-century poem *Le Paris Ridicule* by Claude Le Petit, which forecast the collapse of Henri IV's noble Pont-Neuf. The paper edition of this caustic verse was publicly burned in the Place de Grève (today's place de l'Hotel-de-Ville) along with its author. ♦ Between Rue Dauphine and Quai des Grands-Augustins. Métro: Pont Neuf

50 7 RUE DES GRANDS-AUGUSTINS

From 1936 to 1955, Pablo Picasso lived in this imposing house, where he painted *Guernica* in 1937. His friends Gerald and Sara Murphy, the quintessential North American expatriates in the 1920s, had an apartment in the pink building around the block on the Quai des Grands-Augustins. It was Picasso who got them work painting sets for Diaghilev and the Ballets Russes. They were also the models Fitzgerald used for Dick and Nicole Diver in *Tender Is the Night*. ♦ Between Rue de Savoie and Quai des Grands-Augustins. Métro: St-Michel

51 LES BOOKINISTES

★★$$ The enterprising Guy Savoy opened this attractive bistro on a quay by the Seine where book peddlers ply their trade. The contemporary décor by Daniel Humair and Léopold Gest features large mirrors with colorful hand-painted frames, cheerful red-and-yellow lampshades, and black modern chairs. In the

kitchen, Savoy's protégé, William Ledeuil, has made a name for the restaurant with his imaginative combinations of raw and cooked products and sweet-and-sour flavors. Roasted sea bass with black beans, sweet red peppers, and lemon grass and roasted young rabbit in peanut and mustard crust with Swiss chard and grilled mushrooms are a couple of examples. There's also a vegetarian menu. The staff members are alert and friendly, and the prices are quite reasonable for the high quality and culinary inventiveness of the cuisine. ♦ M-F, lunch and dinner; Sa, dinner. Reservations required. 53 Quai des Grands-Augustins (at Rue des Grands-Augustins). 01.43.25.45.94. Métro: St-Michel

51 QUAI DES GRANDS-AUGUSTINS

In 1313, one of the first *quais* (embankments) in Paris was constructed next to the monastery of St. Augustine. Hundreds of years later, Thomas Jefferson idled away many an afternoon here, browsing along this stretch of riverside, which is still known for its book- and print-sellers. Between Blvd St-Michel and Rue Dauphine. Métro: St-Michel

51 LAPÉROUSE

★★$$$ This glamorous Old World quayside restaurant is housed in the former town mansion of the Comte de Bruillevert, Master of Waters and Forests under Louis XIV. In 1766 it was transformed by Lefèvre, the king's official wine merchant, into a public meeting place that was renowned for the quality of wines it served. In 1840 the establishment was named in honor of the French navigator Lapérouse and thrived as a watering hole for such literary figures as Guy de Maupassant, Emile Zola, Alexandre Dumas, Victor Hugo, and Colette. Specialties include roasted Dublin prawns with tangerine dressing, baked scallops with truffles, crusty fillet of sea bass with caviar, roasted Bresse farm hen, and intriguing desserts, including a soufflé flavored with Southern Comfort and macaroons. ♦ M-F, lunch and dinner; Sa, dinner. Reservations required. 51 Quai des Grands-Augustins (between Rues Seguier and Grands-Augustins). 01.43.26.68.04. Métro: St-Michel

52 FRANCO MARIA RICCI EDITORE

This is the Paris shop of the celebrated Milan publisher whose eclectic and elegant series of fine arts books and literature ranges in subject from decorative ceramics and iconography to deluxe Italian reissues of Saki, Kafka, Borges, and Poe. ♦ M-Sa. 189 Blvd St-Germain (between Rues St-Guillaume and du Bac). 01.45.49.10.94. Métro: St-Germain-des-Prés

THE CITY OF LIGHT ON THE BIG SCREEN

With its dramatic buildings, beautiful boulevards, and enduring air of romance, mystery, and sophistication, Paris has an undeniable star quality. It's little wonder, then, that the city has been the setting for scores of films from the early days of the motion-picture industry to the present. The following, arranged alphabetically, are some of the movies in which Paris plays a featured role.

A Bout de Soufflé (*Breathless*; 1959): One of the first and most influential of the French New Wave films, directed by Jean-Luc Godard, tells the story of a young car thief who kills a policeman and goes on the run with his American girlfriend. This classic stars Jean-Paul Belmondo and Jean Seberg.

An American in Paris (1951): Directed by Vincente Minnelli and featuring music by George Gershwin, this enthusiastic MGM musical stars Gene Kelly and Leslie Caron. The sets of the fabulous ballet sequence are inspired by famous French paintings.

Belle de Jour (1967): In this surreal Luis Buñuel classic, Catherine Deneuve plays a bored *haute bourgeoise* Paris housewife with disturbing sexual fantasies who goes to work in a high-class brothel.

The Bourne Identity (2002): This slick spy thriller starring Matt Damon features a breathtaking car chase that gives one pause about driving in Paris. A mad dash through the city streets culminates with Damon thrusting his tiny car against the flow of traffic on one of the boulevards that straddles the Seine.

Camille (1937): Based on the play by Alexandre Dumas *fils*, this classic MGM flick starring Greta Garbo shows Belle Epoque Paris through the misty eyes of Hollywood. A fatally ill courtesan falls for an innocent young man (Robert Taylor) who loves her.

Casque d'Or (1952): Simone Signoret, Serge Reggiani, and Claude Dauphin are featured in this beautiful and tragic romance, set in the Paris slums of 1898.

Charade (1963): The city becomes the perfect setting for Audrey Hepburn and Cary Grant to fall in love in this comedy-thriller directed by Stanley Donen.

Diva (1981): In Jean-Jacques Beineix's stylish, offbeat thriller, a young opera fan's obsession with a diva (Wilhelmina Wiggins Fernandez) gets him mixed up with a bizarre bunch of underworld characters. An aria was filmed at the Bouffes du Nord theater, and there are motor scooter chases that give viewers a good look at the streets of Paris.

Everyone Says I Love You (1996): The Paris segment of one of Woody Allen's most delightful comedies includes scenes of a **Montmartre** apartment with a jaw-dropping view of **Sacré-Coeur** and a particularly memorable dance number in which Goldie Hawn struts and flutters into the air above the quays along the Seine by Notre-Dame.

Forget Paris (1995): Debra Winger plays an Air France employee in Paris who helps Billy Crystal find his lost luggage (his father's body) and fulfill his father's dream

of being buried in Normandy. This offbeat comedy provides some memorable Paris streetscapes.

Frantic (1988): A Roman Polanski thriller features Harrison Ford as an American doctor in Paris who becomes embroiled with Arab terrorists while hunting fo his kidnapped wife.

French Can-Can (1955): This Jean Renoir film explores how the can-can was launched in Paris nightclubs and features great scenes of ramshackle Paris.

Funny Face (1957): Fred Astaire, Audrey Hepburn, and Kay Thompson star in the story of a fashion editor and photographer who discover a fashion model working in a bookshop. Great music, dancing, and art direction.

Gigi (1958): Based on the novel by Colette, this voluptuous MGM musical directed by Vincente Minnelli is set in fin de siècle Paris. A young girl (Leslie Caron) is trained by her aunt (Hermione Gingold) to be a kept woman, and a dashing, rich gentleman (Louis Jourdan) falls in love with her. Delightful scenes feature 1890s Parisian haunts, and sly old *boulevardier* Maurice Chevalier steals the show with such Lerner and Loewe tunes as "Thank Heaven for Little Girls."

Hôtel du Nord (1938): People with problems congregate at a small hotel on the **Canal Saint-Martin** in Paris; with Annabella, Louis Jouvet, Jean-Pierre Aumont, and Arletty. Lots of *atmosphère*.

The Hunchback of Notre-Dame (1939): Charles Laughton and Maureen O'Hara star in the Hollywood version of the Victor Hugo novel about the deformed bell ringer of **Notre-Dame** who rescues a young Gypsy woman from her evil guardian.

Irma La Douce (1963): Shirley MacLaine and Jack Lemmon star in this saucy Billy Wilder film about a Paris policeman who falls for a prostitute and becomes her pimp. The street and café scenes offer classic images o Paris.

Last Tango in Paris (1972): Marlon Brando stars in thi Bernardo Bertolucci film as a middle-aged man who has a doomed love affair with a young Frenchwoman. The most memorable scenes take place in a Paris bathtub.

Le Dernier Métro (*The Last Metro*; 1980): François Truffaut's drama of a theatrical company in Paris during the dark days of the Nazi occupation, starring Catherine Deneuve and Gérard Depardieu.

Le Fabuleux Destin d'Amélie Poulain (*Amélie*; 2001): In this poetic film by Jean-Pierre Jeunet, an enchanting young woman (Audrey Tautou) works behind the scenes to transform the destinies of unfortunates around her in Montmartre, and she ends up with a surprising and upbeat *destin* of her own.

Les 400 Coups (*The 400 Blows*; 1959): In François Truffaut's autobiographical film, an alienated 12-year-old boy (Jean-Pierre Léaud), unloved by his selfish parents, grows up wild in the city, gets thrown into a reformatory, and escapes at the end. The film gives a vivid impression of working-class Paris street life.

Les Amants (*The Lovers*; 1958): This Louis Malle film, starring Jeanne Moreau and Alain Cuny, tells the story of the secret life in Paris of a rich wife who abandons everything for a passionate romance with a young man.

Les Amants du Pont-Neuf (*The Lovers of the Pont-Neuf*; 1991): An artist who fears she is going blind ends up on the Pont-Neuf with other down-and-out characters. This movie, directed by Léos Carax and starring Juliette Binoche, Denis Lavant, and Klaus-Michael Gruber, was one of the most expensive French films ever made, mainly because the City of Paris refused to let the film be shot on the **Pont-Neuf**, and the producers had to build an elaborate set re-creating the bridge and its surroundings elsewhere.

Les Enfants du Paradis (*Children of Paradise*; 1945): A street mime falls in love with an elusive young woman whose problems with other men keep them apart. Jean-Louis Barrault, Arletty, and Pierre Brasseur star in this epic melodrama set in the world of mid–19th-century popular theater in Paris, considered by some to be the greatest French film of all time.

Les Misérables (1935): Based on the Victor Hugo novel, this film tells the story of Jean Valjean (Frederic March), unjustly convicted and sentenced to years in prison, who emerges to rebuild his life but is hounded by cruel police officer Javert (Charles Laughton).

Love Me Tonight (1932): A Parisian tailor (Maurice Chevalier) pitches French-accented woo at a vain princess (Jeanette MacDonald) to the tune of a grand Rodgers and Hart score ("Isn't It Romantic?", "Lover," "Mimi") in this scintillating musical comedy by Rouben Mamoulian, featuring one of the greatest openings of any movie, as working-class Paris awakens one morning.

Midnight (1939): Delightful screwball comedy by writers Billy Wilder and Charles Brackett and director Mitchell Leisen about a resourceful young American (Claudette Colbert) who arrives in Paris from Monte Carlo with nothing but the gown on her back, impersonates a Hungarian countess amid high society (John Barrymore, Mary Astor, and friends), and is pursued by a love-struck taxi driver (Don Ameche) named Czerny.

Paris Blues (1961): Two American jazz musicians in Paris (Paul Newman and Sidney Poitier) fall in love with two tourists (Joanne Woodward and Diahann Carroll) in

this Martin Ritt film with a great Duke Ellington score, fine black-and-white location shooting, and convincing performances all around.

Paris Underground (1945): Two women (Constance Bennett and Gracie Fields) who are caught in Paris when the Nazis invade continue their Resistance activities.

Paris Vu Par . . . (*Six in Paris*; 1965): Six short stories, set in different parts of Paris, are told by six French New Wave directors.

Paris When It Sizzles (1963): A filmwriter and his secretary try out several script ideas together. William Holden and Audrey Hepburn star in the Hollywood remake of the 1952 French film *La Fête à Henriette*.

Phantom of the Opera (1925): This silent-film classic is the story of a disfigured man (Lon Chaney) who abducts the prima donna of the **Paris Opéra** (Mary Philbin) and brings her to his lair in the sewers below.

Playtime (1968): Barbara Dennek, Jacqueline Lecomte, and Henri Piccoli appear in this Jacques Tati romp in which Hulot and a group of American tourists are bewildered by life in an airport, a business block, and a restaurant.

Prêt-à-Porter (*Ready to Wear*; 1995): Robert Altman's satirical look at the world of haute couture includes performances by Julia Roberts, Chiara Mastroianni, Sophia Loren, and Lauren Bacall. Paris, the fashion capital of the world, serves as the backdrop for this parody.

Round Midnight (1986): Real-life sax great Dexter Gordon turns in a brilliant performance in Bernard Tavernier's film about an alcoholic American jazz musician in Paris who is befriended by a French fan (François Cluzet), with a fine studio re-creation of jazz-crazy **St-Germain-des-Prés** in the 1950s and an Oscar-winning score by Herbie Hancock, who appears in the film.

Sabrina (1954): Audrey Hepburn plays a chauffeur's daughter who is wooed by Humphrey Bogart and William Holden. A scene in which Hepburn takes a cooking class at the **Cordon Bleu** inspired an actual course at the famous culinary institution.

Subway (1985): Luc Besson directs Isabelle Adjani and Christopher Lambert in this stylish comedy-melodrama about an eccentric man on the run from thugs who takes refuge overnight in the platforms and tunnels of the Paris métro.

The Trial (1962): Kafka's nightmarish story of a man who is tried and convicted for an unspecified crime is directed by Orson Welles and features Welles, Jeanne Moreau, and Anthony Perkins. The old **Gare d'Orsay** (now the **Musée d'Orsay**) is the set for a huge office space with endless rows of desks.

53 THAN

★$ This tiny Asian canteen is a popular bargain in the pricey St-Germain quarter. The affable Mr. Than has been packing them in with his delicious and affordable Cantonese and Vietnamese specialties since 1968. He is especially proud of the lacquered duck and caramelized spare ribs. Regular diners include neighborhood editors, publishers, shop clerks, and medical students. ♦ Tu-Sa, lunch and dinner; M, dinner. 42 Rue des Sts-Pères (between Blvd St-Germain and Rue Perronet). 01.45.48.36.97. Métros: Rue du Bac, St-Germain-des-Prés

54 LE PETIT ZINC

★★$$ Not so *petit* anymore since doubling its size in its big Year 2000 renovation, this turn-of-the-19th-century bistro blends sumptuous Art Nouveau and Art Deco décor in its multilevel dining space. Fresh shellfish, fillets of bass cooked in their skins, fillet of beef with Béarnaise sauce, and thick-sliced veal liver *meunière* are a few of its specialties. It attracts a pleasant mix of Parisians and visitors and is a lively spot for a late-night meal. ♦ Daily, noon-2AM. 11 Rue St-Benoît (corner of Rue Guillaume-Apollinaire). 01.42.86.61.00. Métro: St-Germain-des-Prés

55 ST-GERMAIN-DES-PRÉS

$$ In the heart of bustling St-Germain, this 30-room hotel is convenient though hardly tranquil. Breakfast is served in the garden room, but there's no restaurant. *New Yorker* magazine columnist Janet Flanner, who wrote under the nom de plume of Genêt, lived here between 1925 and 1938. ♦ 36 Rue Bonaparte (between Rues de l'Abbaye and Jacob). 01.43.26.00.19; fax 01.40.46.83.63. Métro: St-Germain-des-Prés. Hotel-Saint-Germain-des-Pres@wanadoo.fr

56 27 RUE JACOB

The prestigious French publishing house Editions du Seuil has its offices in the building where Ingres, the master of French classical painting, lived more than 150 years ago. ♦ Between Rues de Furstemberg and Bonaparte. Métro: St-Germain-des-Prés

57 HÔTEL DES MARRONNIERS

$$ All you can glimpse of this 41-room hotel from the street is a couple of potted palms and a sliver of courtyard inviting you to take a closer inspection. Do you so and you'll find an address that Frenchmen from the provinces have long favored for their sojourns in Paris. The hotel is clean and traditional, even if that means some of the bathrooms are a bit outmoded, with a small garden atrium where guests can have breakfast. This hotel's affordable rates in an increasingly chic neighborhood make it very popular, so book ahead. 21 Rue Jacob (between Rues de Furstemberg and Bonaparte). 01.43.25.30.60; fax 01.40.46.83.56. Métro: St-Germain-des-Prés

Librairie maritime outremer

58 LIBRAIRIE MARITIME OUTREMER

This bookstore specializes in maritime books. ♦ M-Sa. 17 Rue Jacob (between Rues de Furstemberg and Bonaparte). 01.46.33.47.48. Métro: St-Germain-des-Prés. Also: Librairie Le Yacht, 55 Ave de la Grande Armee (at Place du Général Patton). 01.45.00.17.99. Métro: Argentine

59 14 RUE JACOB

German opera composer Richard Wagner lived here in 1841-1842. The building now has both residential and commercial space. ♦ Between Rues de Furstemberg and Bonaparte. Métro: St-Germain-des-Prés

La Cafetière

60 LA CAFETIÈRE

★★$$ This cozy restaurant features inventive Italian cuisine, varied with a few meat and fish daily specials prepared *à la française*. Among the Italian dishes are *bresaola girolles* (cured beef with hot mushrooms), lasagna with foie gras, and seafood risotto. For dessert, try the *cioccolata morbibo*, a "death by chocolate" mousse. *Cafetière* means "coffeepot"—hence the collection that's scattered all about. ♦ Tu-Sa, lunch and dinner; closed month of August. Reservations recommended. 21 Rue Mazarine (between Rues Dauphine and Guénégaud). 01.46.33.76.90. Métro: Odéon

61 ST-VLADIMIR LE GRAND

Come on a Sunday morning and watch the rosy grandmothers wearing babushkas enter this Ukrainian church. ♦ 49-51 Rue des Sts-Pères (at Blvd St-Germain). Métros: Rue du Bac, St-Germain-des-Prés

62 LE BILBOQUET

★$$ On the former site of **Club St-Germain**, an old existentialist haunt, this upbeat dinner-jazz club serves grilled rack of lamb and sides of beef in a 1950s ambiance. ♦ Daily, dinner. Music: daily, 10:30PM-1:30AM. 13 Rue St-Benoît (corner of Rue Guillaume-Apollinaire). 01.45.48.81.84. Métro: St-Germain-des-Prés

Réunion
des Musées
Nationaux

Librairie des Musées

63 RÉUNION DES MUSÉES NATIONAUX

It's Tuesday. You forgot to buy a poster or catalog at the **Louvre** to take home, and now the museum is closed. Don't fret. This book-store stocks all the catalogs and posters published by the national museums in France since 1966 along with jewelry, assorted gifts, and reproductions of artifacts. ♦ M-Sa. 10 Rue de l'Abbaye (between Rues de Furstem-berg and Bonaparte). 01.43.29.21.45. Métros: St-Germain-des-Prés, Mabillon

64 YVELINE

Tucked away in Place de Furstemberg is this charming antiques shop that is a fascinating place to browse. ♦ M-Sa; closed in August. 4 Rue de Furstemberg (between Rues de l'Abbaye and Jacob). 01.43.26.56.91. Métros: St-Germain-des-Prés, Mabillon

64 MUSÉE EUGÈNE DELACROIX

The old atelier of Eugène Delacroix, where he lived, worked, and, in 1863, died, is now a mu-seum displaying his paintings, sketches, and letters. A quick tour will give you some idea of why Baudelaire described Delacroix as a "vol-canic crater artistically concealed beneath bou-quets of flowers." ♦ Admission. M, W-Su. 6 Rue de Furstemberg (between Rues de l'Ab-baye and Jacob). 01.44.41.86.50. Métros: St-Germain-des-Prés, Mabillon

64 PLACE DE FURSTEMBERG

Named after Egon de Furstemberg, a 17th-century abbot of St-Germain-des-Prés, this hidden treasure attracts French filmmakers, flamenco guitarists, and harpists who like to play in the courtyard because of its extraordi-nary acoustics. At the center of the square is a white-globed lamppost and four paulownia trees that Henry Miller described as having "the poetry of T.S. Eliot." Unfortunately, only one of the four elegant trees he described remains standing. The others fell victim to disease and were replaced by young trees in 1999. ♦ Rue de Furstemberg (between Rues de l'Abbaye and Jacob). Métros: St-Germain-des-Prés, Mabillon

65 7 RUE JACOB

In 1656, at the age of 17, Racine lived here with his uncle. It's still a residential–commercial building. ♦ Between Rues de Furstemberg and Bonaparte. Métro: St-Germain-des-Prés

66 MANUEL CANOVAS

This showroom exhibits wallpaper and fabrics by the famed designer whose sumptuous works are often featured in *Vogue* and *Archi-tectural Digest*. ♦ M-Sa. 5 Rue de Furstemberg (between Rues de l'Abbaye and Cardinale). 01.43.25.75.98. Métros: St-Germain-des-Prés, Mabillon

66 2 RUE CARDINALE

The Black Sun Press operated at this address under the aegis of Harry and Caresse Crosby, a wild and wealthy couple of Americans in Paris in the 1920s. They were the first to publish D.H. Lawrence's *Sun* and Hart Crane's *The Bridge*. Harry, who was a nephew of J.P. Morgan, died in a double suicide with one of his many mistresses at the Hôtel des Artistes in New York. ♦ Between Rues de l'Abbaye and de Furstemberg. Métros: St-Germain-des-Prés, Mabillon

67 HÔTEL DE SEINE

$$$ Once a family-run pension, this 30-room hotel has lost its bohemian charm of yore, but it's nonetheless a well-located and comfort-able place that strives to please. Beat poet

---

Lawrence Ferlinghetti, owner of City Lights Bookstore in San Francisco, used to stay here. There's no restaurant. ♦ 52 Rue de Seine (between Rues de Buci and Jacob). 01.46.34.22.80; fax 01.46.34.04.74. Métro: Mabillon

67 COSI

★★$ This gourmet Italian sandwich and salad counter serves everything from salmon carpaccio to roasted red peppers—all on bread baked in wood-fired pizza ovens. Tuscan wines, opera by Verdi, and daily editions of *La Repubblica* add to this place's Latin charm. Take your order to go, or if you prefer, eat here in the upstairs seating area. ♦ Daily, lunch and dinner until 11PM. 54 Rue de Seine (between Rues de Buci and Jacob). 01.46.33.35.36. Métro: Mabillon

67 FISH

★★$ Occupying the lofty, wood-beam-ceilinged site of a turn-of-the-19th-century *poissonnerie* (fishmonger's shop) with a colorful mosaic façade of fish and seashells, this easygoing seafood restaurant calls itself "La Boissonnerie" (the drinkmonger's shop) to point up the equal importance of its wines with its eats. American Juan Sanchez, owner of **La Dernière Goutte** wine shop (see page 91), masterminds the predominantly southern

French wine list, while his partner Drew Harré, a New Zealander who owns **Cosi** across the street (see above), supervises the food. The largely international clientele feasts on risotto with squid ink, grilled tuna with garlic purée, *rouget* (red mullet) *provençal*, lamb ribs and purée of fennel with thyme, and other Mediterranean fare. Or they just come in for a glass of one of Juan's wines at the long, convivial wooden bar. ♦ Tu-Sa, lunch and dinner. 69 Rue de Seine (between Rues de Buci and Callot). 01.43.54.34.69. Métro: Mabillon

68 GALERIE DOCUMENTS

Opened in 1954 by Michel Romand and now run by his daughter Mireille, this is the city's most distinguished antique poster shop, specializing in *affiches* from 1875 to 1930, particularly the works of Toulouse-Lautrec, Grasset, Mucha, and Steinlen. ♦ M, 2:30-7PM; Tu-Sa. 53 Rue de Seine (between Rues de Buci and Jacques-Callot). 01.43.54.50.68. Métro: Mabillon

69 ALCAZAR

★★$$ British design and restaurant mogul Sir Terence Conran opened his new-fashioned version of the old-fashioned brasserie in 1998. A former nightclub, the two-story, glass-domed space is now an ultramodern 250-place dining room, decorated in white, red, and gray, with a glassed-in kitchen where diners can watch their meals being prepared. Some traditional brasserie items are available—notably raw shellfish, which is impeccably fresh—but the menu is largely Mediterranean-inspired, with lots of fish, fresh vegetables, and goat cheese. With chef Guillaume Lutard, formerly of Taillevent, assuring the quality of the cuisine, a bright, enthusiastic young team of servers, and a spectacular décor, everything is in place for an enjoyable dining experience. The only drawback is the rather high noise level. The large open bar **L'AZ** on the mezzanine serves salads and other reasonably priced light fare and wine by the glass. Sunday brunch features a pianist, and a DJ entertains every night until 2PM. This has become a prime spot for *les before*, where hip young clubgoers congregate beween 9PM and midnight, before heading off into the Parisian night, though some opt for *les after* at Conran's on-premises nighclub Le Wagg. ♦ Daily, lunch and dinner until 1AM. 62 Rue Mazarine (between Carrefour de Buci and Rue Jacques-Callot). 01.53.10.19.99. Métro: Odéon

70 RUE DAUPHINE

The construction of the Pont-Neuf (see page 22) channeled traffic over to the Left Bank and led to this street's construction. When Henry IV's original request to put a highway through a monastery's vegetable gardens was denied, he snapped, "I will open the new road with cannonballs!" The gardens were sacrificed, and the new road, named after the king's son, was built. Today the narrow road is lined with shops, little restaurants, and café-tabacs (cafés that sell tobacco). ♦ Métro: Pont-Neuf

70 LE MONDE EN MARCHE

Step into a magical world of wooden toys, puppets, and puzzles that are gaily colored and made by hand. ♦ M-Sa, 10:30AM-7:30PM; closed in August. 34 Rue Dauphine (between Carrefour de Buci and Rue de Nesle). 01.43.29.09.49. Métro: Odéon

71 LA RÔTISSERIE D'EN FACE

★★$$ Across the street from Jacques Cagna's famous namesake restaurant is his unpreten-tious bistro, where good, simple meals can be enjoyed in an agreeable setting. The menu features meats cooked on the rotisserie—chicken served with mashed potatoes, prime ribs of beef, and lamb with thyme. The *pastilla de pintade* (crispy pastry filled with guinea fowl, onion, eggplant, and mild spices) is a popular dish, and Cagna's mother has contributed family recipes, including *joues de cochon aux carottes et pommes de terre fondantes*, which translates inelegantly as pig cheeks with carrots and mashed potatoes. For dessert, the bistro's chocolate mousse rivals the best. ♦ M-F, lunch and dinner; Sa, dinner.

Reservations recommended. 2 Rue Christine (at Rue des Grands-Augustins). 01.43.26.40.98. Métros: Odéon, St-Michel

71 ACTION CHRISTINE

Two adjacent revival movie houses keep aficionados of Hitchcock and Lubitsch, as well as fans of Bogie and Bacall classics, happy. ♦ Daily. 4 Rue Christine and 10 Rue des Grands-Augustins. 01.43.29.11.30. Métros: Odéon, St-Michel

72 JACQUES CAGNA

★★★$$$$ In his elegant old inn, Cagna features traditional French cuisine with a nouvelle flourish. The prices are weighty, but the sauces are light, and the vegetables are treated with the gentleness they deserve. Specialties include escargots, Breton lobster salad, and foie gras; roasted turbot with crisply fried and puréed Granny Smith apples; roast Aveyron lamb; suckling pig casserole; Houdan farm hen; wild game in season; and a wild strawberry mille-feuille with light vanilla cream. The wine cellar stocks 60,000 bottles in 550 varieties. Most of the patrons are affluent older people. ♦ M, Sa, lunch only; Tu-F, lunch and dinner; closed in August, 1 week at Christmas, and holidays. Reservations required. 14 Rue des Grands-Augustins (at Rue Christine). 01.43.26.49.39. Métros: Odéon, St-Michel

72 RELAIS CHRISTINE

$$$$ A 16th-century monastery was converted into this plush, well-run, fashionable hotel in 1980. It offers 51 rooms with either modern or antique furnishings as well as single or split-level apartments, some of which have luxurious marble bathrooms and access to a secluded courtyard. The basement breakfast room alone is worth the visit to this hotel (there's no restaurant). ♦ 3 Rue Christine (between Rues des Grands-Augustins and Dauphine). 01.40.51.60.80; fax 01.40.51.60.81. Métros: Odéon, St-Michel. relais_ch@club-internet.fr; www.relais-christine.com

72 5 RUE CHRISTINE

After being evicted from their famous atelier at 27 Rue de Fleurus, Gertrude Stein and

Alice B. Toklas moved here in 1938. During the war, they fled to the countryside; in their absence, 5 Rue Christine was visited by the Gestapo, who attached a note to one of Stein's Picasso paintings reading "Jewish trash, good for burning." Stein died on 27 July 1946, and Toklas lived on here for another 18 years. The two women are buried side by side in Père-Lachaise Cemetery. ♦ Between Rues des Grands-Augustins and Dauphine. Métros: Odéon, St-Michel

73 LA COUR DE VARENNE

The back door of Etienne Lévy's antiques store opens onto a lovely courtyard where Madame de Staël's servants' quarters still stand. There are two floors of clocks, 17th- and 18th-century furniture, Oriental lacquer, mother-of-pearl–framed mirrors, and much more. ♦ Tu-Sa; closed in August. 42 Rue de Varenne (between Rues du Bac and de Bellechasse). 01.45.44.65.50. Métro: Rue du Bac

74 OLIVIER DE SERCEY

Ambassadors and government ministers from nearby offices frequent this tiny printing and engraving shop that makes dignified business cards. Wedding and party invitations are also a specialty. ♦ M-F; closed in August. 96 Rue du Bac (between Rues de Varenne and de Grenelle). 01.45.48.21.47. Métro: Rue du Bac

La Boîte à Musique

antiquités
bibelots

74 LA BOÎTE À MUSIQUE

This antiques shop specializes in 19th-century music boxes from France, England, and Switzerland. ♦ M, 2-7PM; Tu-Sa; closed in August. 96 Rue du Bac (between Rues de Varenne and de Grenelle). 01.42.22.01.30. Métro: Rue du Bac

75 SUPERLATIF

Popular with locals is this stationery shop that sells a wide variety of colored paper, designer pens, and assorted doodads. ♦ M-Sa. 86 Rue du Bac (between Rues de Varenne and de Grenelle). 01.45.48.84.25. Métro: Rue du Bac

76 MUSÉE MAILLOL—FONDATION DINA VIERNY

Located in an 18th-century mansion next to Bouchardon's splendid **Fontaine des Quatre Saisons** (see below), this museum is the result of the partnership of sculptor-painter Aristide Maillot and his model, Dina Vierny, whom he met when she was 15. Their collaboration lasted for 10 years until his death at 83 in 1944. Vierny's sublime form is seen in works such as *La Montagne*, *L'Air*, *La Rivière*, and Maillot's ultimate work, *Harmonie*. She went on to become a successful Paris art dealer and worked for 30 years to create this foundation dedicated primarily to Maillot's work. The museum also includes pieces by such other 20th-century artists as Dufy, Matisse, Bonnard, Poliakoff, Kandinsky, Kabakov, and Duchamp. It mounts first-rate temporary exhibits as well, including big ones in recent years on Frida Kahlo, Bonnard, and nudes by Klimt, Schiele, and other Austrian Expressionists. A pretty café in the vaulted basement serves light meals. ♦ Admission; free for children under age 18. M, W-Su, 11AM-6PM. 59-61 Rue de Grenelle (between Blvd Raspail and Rue du Bac). 01.42.22.59.58. Métro: Rue du Bac. www.museemaillol.com

76 FONTAINE DES QUATRE SAISONS (FOUR SEASONS FOUNTAIN)

In the early 18th century, this, the wealthiest quarter in Paris, was almost totally without water. To remedy that problem, in 1739 sculptor Edme Bouchardon was commissioned to design this fountain to supply water to neighborhood residents. The Ionic-pillared fountain is adorned with a seated figure of Paris looking down on reclining personifications of the **Seine** and **Marne Rivers**. The sides are decorated with figures of the seasons and reliefs of cherubs. Voltaire protested the placement of this fountain in a narrow and confined street, arguing that "fountains must be elevated in public places and, like all beautiful monuments, be viewed on all sides." ♦ 57-59 Rue de Grenelle (between Blvd Raspail and Rue du Bac). Métro: Rue du Bac

77 ROLAND BARTHÉLEMY FROMAGER

The **Elysée Palace** buys its cheese at this shop, which offers more than 50 kinds of fresh goat cheese, the finest *vacherin* (from October through February), and its special *boulamour*, a ball of enriched cow's cheese covered with kirsch-soaked raisins. ♦ Tu-Sa. 51 Rue de Grenelle (between Blvd Raspail and Rue du Bac). 01.45.48.56.75. Métro: Rue du Bac

78 KENZO STAR

Japanese designer Kenzo splashes gorgeous colors over amusing, informal clothes and accessories. This is one of his eight shops in

Paris. His flagship store is on Place des Victoires. ♦ M-Sa. 17 Blvd Raspail is men's-wear only (at Rue de Grenelle). 01.45.49.33.75. Womenswear is across the street at 16 Blvd Raspail. 01.42.22.09.38. Métro: Rue du Bac. Also at 3 Pl des Victoires (between Rues Etienne-Marcel and Croix-des-Petits-Champs). 01.40.39.72.03. Métro: Bourse

shu uemura
tokyo paris new york

79 SHU UEMURA

This classy Japanese cosmetics shop features compacts, lipstick, nail polish, creams, and brushes in every hue and shape imaginable. It's one of an international 6,000-shop chain started in 1986 by makeup artist Shu Uemura, who perfected the faces of Japan's most famous movie stars. ♦ M-Sa. 176 Blvd St-Germain (between Rues St-Benoît and des Sts-Pères). 01.45.48.02.55. Métro: St-Germain-des-Prés

79 CAFÉ DE FLORE

★★$$ Jean-Paul Sartre wrote of hanging out in this great café during World War II: "Simone de Beauvoir and I more or less set up house in the Flore. We worked from 9AM till noon, when we went out to lunch. At 2PM we came back and talked with our friends till 4PM, when we got down to work again till 8PM. And after dinner, people came to see us by appointment. It may seem strange, all this, but the Flore was like home to us: even when the air-raid alarm went, we would merely feign leaving and then climb up to the first floor and go on working." The drink to order here in winter is hot grog (rum, tea, and lemon slices); be sure to ask for extra lemon because they never bring enough. For early birds this is an excellent place to scrutinize le monde and have a breakfast of oeufs sur le plat (fried eggs), bacon, and croissants. Salads, sandwiches, and other typical café fare are served at lunch and dinner. The endearingly worn Art Deco interior—all red, mahogany, and mirrors—has changed little since the war. Many writers and journalists who live in the neighborhood still call this café their second home. Philosophy discussions are held monthly in English. ♦ Daily, breakfast, lunch, and dinner until 1:30AM. 172 Blvd St-Germain (at Rue St-Benoît). 01.45.48.55.26. Métro: St-Germain-des-Prés

80 KOREAN BARBECUE

★$$ The fare here includes marinated beef and vegetables that you grill over a gas stove at your table. The décor is clean, simple, and no-nonsense. ♦ Daily lunch and dinner.1 Rue du Dragon (at Blvd St-Germain). 01.42.22.26.63. Métro: St-Germain-des-Prés

81 BRASSERIE LIPP

This ersatz Alsatian eatery may still be something of a national landmark, but that doesn't necessarily mean it's worth your adulation, to say nothing of your time or money: indeed, those looking for polite service, serviceable food, and celebrity sightings in St-Germain-des-Prés would do well to look elsewhere—across the street at Café de Flore, for example. Daily, 8:30AM-2AM. 151 Blvd St-Germain (between Rues de Rennes and du Dragon). 01.45.48.53.91. Métro: St-Germain-des-Prés

82 LA HUNE

Wedged between **Café de Flore** and **Les Deux Magots** is one of the liveliest bookstores in Paris. It provides literary sustenance to the Parisian men and women of letters (and those trying to resemble them) who frequent the nearby shrines. ♦ M-Sa, 10AM-midnight. 170 Blvd St-Germain (at Rue St-Benoît). 01.45.48.35.85. Métro: St-Germain-des-Prés

82 LES DEUX MAGOTS

★★$$ The best-situated terrace in St-Germain-des-Prés is right here at this glamorous old café. From the tables fronting on the boulevard, patrons can indulge in the French national sport of people watching at its finest, whereas those on the more sedate Place St-Germain-des-Prés side can watch the sidewalk performers in the square in front of the church, who are always amusing and occasionally brilliant. The café's name comes from the two statues of paunchy Chinese commercial agents—magots—that sit high on the center pillars inside. The menu calls this place "The Rendezvous of the Intellectual Elite"—no empty boast. Like the **Café de Flore**, this place long attracted poets, writers, and artists, including Paul Verlaine, Arthur Rimbaud, Stéphane Mallarmé, André Breton, Antonin Artaud, Jean Giraudoux, Oscar Wilde, and Picasso, who met Dora Marr here. Among the many North American regulars were Ernest Hemingway, New Yorker columnist Janet Flanner, Djuna Barnes, and Richard Wright. Today, though, you'll find mostly tourists. ♦ Daily, breakfast, lunch, and dinner until 1:30AM. 6 Pl St-Germain-des-Prés (at Blvd St-Germain). 01.45.48.55.25. Métro: St-Germain-des-Prés

82 ARTHUS-BERTRAND

This establishment dating from 1803 casts reproductions of some of the **Louvre**'s treasures in sterling or in 18-karat gold. It also supplies 80% of the military medals and decorations used by African nations. For $6,000 to $20,000, it custom-designs the ceremonial swords worn by the "immortals" accepted into the **Académie Française**. The firm has a seriousness and a price list that will curb any idle browser. ♦ M-Sa. 6 Pl St-Germain-des-Prés (between Blvd St-Germain and Rue Guillaume-Apollinaire). 01.49.54.72.10. Métro: St-Germain-des-Prés

EMPORIO ARMANI
CAFFE

83 EMPORIO ARMANI

Shoulder to shoulder with **Brasserie Lipp**, a bastion of Paris's 20th-century literary aristocracy, Georgio Armani's ultraminimalist fashion boutique is a stronghold of today's St-Germain-des-Prés ascendancy—*la mode*. Here fashion victims will find four floors of sleek men's and women's ready-to-wear clothing, including the famed Armani jeans, shoes, jewelry, watches, sunglasses, fashion magazines, and daily newspapers in several languages. ♦ M-Sa. 149 Blvd St-Germain (at Rue de Rennes). 01.53.63.33.50. Métro: St-Germain-des-Prés

Within Emporio Armani:

CAFFÉ ARMANI

★★$$ The shopping set's favorite place for a Left Bank rendezvous is this café on the second floor overlooking Place St-Germain-des-Prés. Here the décor matches or even exceeds the austerity of the rest of the boutique, with gray, gray, and more gray as the color scheme. Well-prepared Northern Italian classics are featured—antipasti, carpaccio, pasta in several forms, risotto, scampi, vegetables grilled in olive oil, and fish of the day—and there's a fine list of Italian

wines. ♦ M-Sa, 11AM-11:30PM. Second floor. 01.45.48.62.15.

84 EMBÂCLE

This sculpture (whose name means "blockage") is not a ruptured water main but a practical joke of a fountain by Charles Daudelin. It was created in 1985. ♦ Pl du Quebec. Métro: St-Germain-des-Prés

85 ST-GERMAIN-DES-PRÉS

For more than 15 centuries a church has stood on this corner, which in Roman times was a *pré* (open pasture). The first church, built in AD 452 by Merovingian king Childebert, was repeatedly destroyed by invading Normans and finally rebuilt to last in 1163. The Romanesque western gate tower is faintly reminiscent of the great abbeys on the outskirts of Paris. During the Middle Ages, this church, named after St. Germanus (AD 496–576), Bishop of Paris, became a focal point for Easter fairs, with hundreds of stalls, performing theater troupes, live "statues," and dancing bears.

Inside the church is an altar dedicated to the victims of the September 1793 massacre, a shameful chapter of French history, when Paris was ruled by a bloodthirsty mob called the *sans-culottes* (because they wore linen trousers instead of aristocratic knee breeches). In 1793, after a mock trial on the weekend of 2-3 September, almost 200 prisoners sequestered in the church were led into the courtyard (at the corner of what is now Rue Bonaparte and Blvd St-Germain), where they were stabbed and hacked to death by hired killers. Ministers of Louis XVI, his father confessor, and the Swiss Guards were slaughtered. The carnage was followed by an auction of the victims' personal effects. The skull of René Descartes, the 17th-century mathematician and philosopher, along with the body of John Casimir, a 17th-century king of Poland who was abbot of St-Germain, are buried inside the church.

Today, however, the edifice is best known for its evening concerts of classical music. It also provides a cool place to meditate on muggy summer days. ♦ Guided tours: Tu, Th, 1-5PM. Pl St-Germain-des-Prés (between Blvd St-Germain and Rue de l'Abbaye). 01.43.25.41.71; concerts, 01.42.77.65.65. Métro: St-Germain-des-Prés

Next to St-Germain-des-Prés:

HOMMAGE À APOLLINAIRE

In the small park to the left of the main portal of St-Germain-des-Prés is a memorial to the poet Guillaume Apollinaire (1880-1918), who lived and died at 202-204 Blvd St-Germain. Of Polish origin (his last name was Kostrowitzki), Apollinaire wrote the famous

> The Parisian travels little, he knows no language but his own, reads no literature but his own, and consequently he is pretty narrow. However, let us not be too sweeping; there are Frenchmen who know languages not their own: these are the waiters.
>
> —Mark Twain, *Paris Notes*, 1882

Alcools in 1913 and was an early leader of the Paris avant-garde. Eventually renowned for his poetry, Apollinaire was best known in his time as the man who stole the *Mona Lisa*. The scandal began when Apollinaire's former personal secretary lifted two inconsequential Phoenician statues from the **Louvre** and sold them to Picasso. Coincidentally, the *Mona Lisa* disappeared shortly afterward. Apollinaire, trying to protect his secretary and Picasso from suspicion and incarceration, turned in the statues and was jailed for 4 days. The *Mona Lisa* eventually resumed her place in the Louvre, and Apollinaire was exonerated. He never, however, recovered his self-esteem. The *Hommage à Apollinaire* memorial originally had a bronze bust of a woman by Pablo Picasso on it, given to the city in 1958 in honor of his old friend. In a sad echo of the *Mona Lisa* affair, the Picasso bust was stolen in 1999 and has yet to be recovered. A short street nearby also honors Apollinaire.

86 RUE DE BUCI

The once certifiably quaint street market here has gone upscale, to the delight of shoppers who love crowds and spend with plastic and the detriment of what could be called local color. Few vestiges of the food market that once thrived here—with operatic hawkers hustling everything from endive to homemade fettuccine, freshly ground Colombian coffee, wild strawberries, cherries, hot baguettes and pink tulips—remain, though you can still pick up fruit and a roast chicken or two. Today, though, cafés and boutiques predominate.

From here, Rue de Seine shoots off toward the river, becoming a thoroughfare of art galleries. Bear that in mind when passing by in the early evening: A crowded gallery is most likely a *vernissage* (literally, a "varnishing," the French name for an exhibition opening). Put on your best French accent, join the party, and talk art while sipping a glass of champagne. Between Rues St-André-des-Arts and du Four. Métros: Mabillon, Odéon

At Rue de Buci:

LE CHAI DE L'ABBAYE

★$ Typical French fare is served here at one of the few good wine bars in Paris not crawling with yuppies. M-Sa, breakfast, lunch, and dinner until 2AM; Su, to 11PM. No. 26 (at Rue du Bourbon-le-Château). 01.43.26.68.26

TASCHEN

If you fancy a beautiful coffee-table book, either for yourself or as a gift, this is the place to come. Taschen publishes sumptuous books on subjects as diverse as popular film (a gorgeous tome dedicated to *Some Like It Hot* is one example), fashion photographers, and midcentury modern architecture. Unlike at some smaller bookstores, browsing is encouraged here. Daily, 11AM-8PM. No. 2 (at Rue Mazarine). 01.40.51.79.22

2 RUE DU BOURBON-LE-CHÂTEAU

Buzz yourself in and have a look at the circular-well courtyard in this 1824 apartment building. (**L'Hôtel** on Rue des Beaux-Arts is another example of this architectural device.) Try to imagine how items such as grand pianos are hoisted up to the fifth floor. ♦ At Rue de Buci. Métro: Mabillon

"vins de propriétaires"

LA DERNIÈRE GOUTTE

Genial Miami-born American Juan Sanchez has made himself one of Paris's top *cavistes*, specializing entirely in French wines that he finds and purchases directly from the châteaux and sells in his shop by the **Rue de Buci** market. Distinguished *vignerons* from all wine regions of France come here to present their wares at wine tastings every Saturday between 10:30AM and 8PM. Juan's selections from the South of France can also be sampled at **Fish**, a Mediterranean eatery around the corner on **Rue de Seine** (see page 86). ♦ M, 4PM-9PM; Tu-F, 9:30AM-1:30PM and 4PM-9PM; Sa, 9:30AM-9PM; Su, 10:30AM-3PM and 4PM-7PM. 6 Rue du Bourbon-le-Château (between Rue de Buci and Rue de l'Echaudé). 01.43.29.11.62. Métro: Mabillon

87 HÔTEL LE RÉGENT

$$$ Tastefully converted from a 1730 mansion, this comfortable 25-room hotel is nicely situated between the **Seine** and **Rue de Buci**, which boasts one of the prettiest outdoor markets in Paris. There's no restaurant. ♦ 61 Rue Dauphine (between Rues

St-André-des-Arts and André-Mazet).
01.46.34.59.80; fax 01.40.51.05.07. Métro:
Odéon. hotel.leregent@wanadoo.fr

88 ST-ANDRÉ-DES-ARTS

$$ A friendly staff runs this modest but
comfortable 35-room hotel that was the 17th-
century residence of the king's musketeers.
The rooms are small, but they all have their
original wood beams, and the bathrooms are
perfectly modern. There's no restaurant. ♦ 66
Rue St-André-des-Arts (at Rue André-Mazet).
01.43.26.96.16; fax 01.43.29.73.34. Métro:
Odéon. hsaintand@minitel.net

89 46 RUE ST-ANDRÉ-DES-ARTS

e.e. cummings rented a single room in this
building housing two bookshops. Today the
structure has both residential and commercial
space. ♦ Between Rues Séguier and des
Grands-Augustins. Métros: Odéon, St-Michel

90 28 RUE ST-ANDRÉ-DES-ARTS

In *Satori in Paris*, Jack Kerouac described
pleasant evenings spent here at what was
then a bar called **La Gentilhommière** (ca.
1962) and is now a pizzeria. ♦ At Rue Gît-le-
Coeur. Métro: St-Michel

91 RUE GÎT-LE-COEUR

The name means "where the heart lies," a
French phrase that's a good deal more
romantic than the street's preceding moniker:
Gilles-le-Cook. **Nos. 1-9** were originally one
mansion, built in the 16th century by François
I for his love at the time, the Duchesse
d'Etampes. ♦ Métro: St-Michel

On Rue Gît-le-Coeur:

RELAIS HÔTEL DE VIEUX PARIS

$$$ In the 1950s this was a seedy crash pad
known as "the Beat hotel," where Allen
Ginsberg, Gregory Corso, Jack Kerouac, and
William S. Burroughs holed up for long
periods, and where Ginsberg helped
Burroughs edit *Naked Lunch*. They'd be
shocked if they could see it now: In 1991, the
hotel underwent a total renovation, and its
bohemian atmosphere gave way to distinctly
more upscale charm, with 20 comfortable,
tastefully decorated, traditionally French
rooms. The old days have not been forgotten,
however: photos of the Beats taken here in
the 1950s hang in the lobby. There is no
restaurant. ♦ No. 9 (at Rue de l'Hirondelle).
01.44.32.15.90; fax 01.43.26.00.15.
VieuxParis@sollers.fr; www.sollers.fr.rhvp

92 L'ECLUSE

★★$ A spectrum of 60 reds (18 of which can
be ordered by the glass) are offered at this
wine bar overlooking the **Seine**. Bordeaux is
the specialty, a wine that goes wonderfully

with the plates of smoked goose, carpaccio,
and Chavignol cheese served here. ♦ Daily,
lunch and dinner until 1AM. Reservations
recommended. 15 Quai des Grands-Augustin
(between Pl St-Michel and Rue Gît-le-Coeur).
01.46.33.58.74. Métro: St-Michel. Also at 6
Rue François-1er (between Rues Lincoln and
Quentin-Bauchart). 01.47.20.77.09. Métro:
George-V; 15 Pl de la Madeleine (between
Blvd Malesherbes and Rue Chauveau
Lagarde). 01.42.65.34.69. Métro: Madeleine
13 rue de Roquette (between Place de la
Bastille and Rue Daval). 01.48.05.19.12.
Métro: Bastille

93 CAVEAU DE LA BOLÉE

A wooden door leads into a 13th-century
dungeonlike cavern filled with late-night chess
and checkers players, once a haunt of Baudelaire and his mistress Jeanne Duval, Verlaine,
and Oscar Wilde. Dinner is served upstairs
starting at 9PM and downstairs before the
show; a cabaret act is performed Monday
through Saturday starting at 10:30PM. ♦ Daily
dinner and late-night snacks. 25 Rue de
l'Hirondelle (between Pl St-Michel and Rue Gît
le-Coeur). 01.43.54.62.20. Métro: St-Michel

94 DINERS EN VILLE

Tablecloths, candlesticks, china, earthenware
flatware—everything for the well-dressed table
is available here. There's a wide selection of
tinted wine and aperitif glasses from all over
the world. ♦ M, 2-7PM; Tu-Sa, 27 Rue de
Varenne (at Rue du Bac). 01.42.22.78.33.
Métro: Rue du Bac

95 LA MAISON DE VERRE (GLASS HOUSE)

Seeing the extraordinary glass house of **Pierr**
Charreau and **Bernard Bijovet** is a must for
any student of 20th-century design. You can
get a glimpse of the exterior from the
courtyard, but for a look at the inside of the
early 1930s building—a tour de force in glass
block-and-steel construction—you must make
a reservation. Send inquiries to A. P. Vellay-
Dalsace, 31 Rue St-Guillaume, 75006 Paris.
♦ Donation requested; send with reservations
request. 31 Rue St-Guillaume (between Rue
de Grenelle and Blvd St-Germain). Métros:
Sèvres-Babylone, Rue du Bac

96 SABBIA ROSA

Sexy teddies and other alluring lingerie can b
purchased for or by the femme fatale. ♦ M-
Sa; closed second week of August. 71-73
Rue des Sts-Pères (between Rue de Grenelle
and Blvd St-Germain). 01.45.48.88.37.
Métros: St-Sulpice, St-Germain-des-Prés

96 Y's YOHJI YAMAMOTO

Shop here for an outfit that's actually both
fashionable and comfortable. This Japanese

designer creates basic, high-style clothes for men and women. ♦ M-Sa. 69 Rue des Sts-Pères (between Rue de Grenelle and Blvd St-Germain). 01.45.48.22.56. Métros: St-Sulpice, St-Germain-des-Prés. Also at 25 Rue du Louvre (between Rue du Louvre and Etienne Marcel). 01.42.21.42.93. Métro: Etienne Marcel

96 HÔTEL DES STS-PÈRES

$$$ This tastefully renovated 39-room hotel was designed in 1658 by **Alphonse Daniel Gittard**, who founded the Academy of Architecture under Louis XIV. If dozing off while staring up at a 17th-century ceiling painting of the crowning of Jupiter is your idea of luxury, ask for room 100. There's no restaurant, but the hotel has a pretty garden for breakfast in fair weather. ♦ 65 Rue des Sts-Pères (between Rue de Grenelle and Blvd St-Germain). 01.45.44.50.00; fax 01.45.44.90.83. Métros: St-Sulpice, St-Germain-des-Prés. hotelst.peres@wanadoo.fr

97 RUE DES CISEAUX

Named after a scissors craftsman who once resided here, this short street is home to three Japanese restaurants and a pizzeria. Métro: St-Germain-des-Prés

la rhumerie

98 LA RHUMERIE

Upper-crust imbibers, along with the rabble out for a good time, keep this place packed. The stiff punches made with 130 kinds of the tropical liquor make it worth fighting for a table. In addition to the usual daiquiris and planter's punch, try the Père Serge, which is named after a priest at St-Germain-des-Prés and is made with rum, lemon, and sugarcane syrup. The liquid refreshments are the real draw here, but meat and fish dishes are served at lunch and snacks such as *boudin* (sausage), *akra de morue* (fish fritters), and crab *farci* (stuffed and spiced crab) are available throughout the day and night. ♦ Daily, 9AM-2AM. 166 Blvd St-Germain (between Rues de Buci and de l'Echaudé). 01.43.54.28.94. Métro: Mabillon

99 RUE ST-ANDRÉ-DES-ARTS

This narrow street lined with food stalls, a cinéma, book and poster merchants, and an eclectic mix of other shops seems more like a pedestrian mall. ♦ Métros: Odéon, St-Michel

99 THE MAZET

Once a hangout for seedy street musicians and pinball players, this former café-bar-restaurant has cleaned up its act and become a drinking establishment only. The customers for its two floors of bars are students from the many language and design schools in the area and the **University of Paris** and locals who appreciate the relaxed ambiance and wide range of beverages. ♦ Su-Th, 4PM to 2AM, F-Sa until 5AM. 61 Rue St-André-des-Arts (between Rues de l'Eperon and de l'Ancienne-Comédie). 01.43.54.68.81. Métro: Odéon

99 COUR DU COMMERCE ST-ANDRÉ

Built in 1776, the city's first covered shopping mall was a hive of activity during the revolution and inspired 17 other passages that sprang up on the Right Bank in the 19th century. Through the windows at **No. 4**, you can glimpse the remains of one of the towers in the city wall. At **No. 8** in 1789, Marat printed revolutionary exhortations in his inflammatory journal *L'Ami du Peuple*. Nearby, a German carpenter named Schmidt patiently perfected the guillotine (named after Dr. Guillotin, who recommended this apparatus for decapitation as a humane means of execution). Schmidt practiced on sheep, and the street ran red with the blood of the unfortunate beasts. It was also here that the artist Balthus had a studio and painted his famous picture *Le Passage du Commerce St-André* in 1954. (Don't look for the shop with the golden key in the painting; it was abandoned long ago.) **La Maison de la Catalogne** (01.40.46.85.28), Catalonia's attractive tourist office, art gallery, gift shop, café, and restaurant, occupies **Nos. 4, 6**, and **8**. ♦ 59-61 Rue St-André-des-Arts (between Rues de l'Eperon and de l'Ancienne-Comédie). Métro: Odéon

Within the Cour du Commerce-St-André:

A LA COUR DE ROHAN

★★$ This English-style tearoom with apricot walls and paisley tablecloths offers fish or onion soup; melted goat cheese on toast; savory tarts; toothsome cakes, scones, and crumbles; exotic teas; and a 17th-century heirloom recipe for spicy marmalade. No smoking is allowed. ♦ M-W, Su, lunch, afternoon tea, and dinner until 7:30PM; in the summer, until 11PM; closed in August. 01.43.25.79.67

100 ALLARD

★★$$ One of the old-time, honest bistros, this place has two zinc bars and a rotating selec-

---

tion of *plats du jour* as perennial as the clientele. The Allard family, who played host here to the Aga Khan, Brigitte Bardot, and Georges Pompidou, has sold the restaurant, but the place still retains much of the old feeling. ♦ M-Sa, lunch and dinner; closed the first 3 weeks of August. Reservations required. 41 Rue St-André-des-Arts (at Rue de l'Eperon). 01.43.26.48.23. Métros: Odéon, St-Michel

101 PLACE ST-MICHEL

A relatively nonviolent crowd of students, bikers, and drug dealers gathers here on hot Saturday nights. The passable restaurants around the square cater to pizza and souvlaki eaters. ♦ Métro: St-Michel

On Place St-Michel:

FONTAINE ST-MICHEL (ST. MICHAEL FOUNTAIN)

In 1860 Gabriel Davioud designed this 75-foot-high and 15-foot-wide spouting monster. The bronze of St. Michael fighting the dragon is by Duret.

102 AU ST-SÉVERIN

★$ The best people-watching perch in Place St-Michel has the famous Berthillon ice cream. The hot chocolate isn't bad either. ♦ Daily, 7AM-2AM. No. 3 Rue St-Séverin (at Rue de la Huchette). 01.43.54.19.36 Métro: St-Michel

103 110 RUE DU BAC

After the sale of *Arrangement in Grey and Black: The Artist's Mother* to the French government in 1893, James McNeill Whistler moved into a ground-floor apartment here and consorted with such artist-intelligentsia friends as Henry James, Edgar Degas, Edouard Manet, and Henri de Toulouse-Lautrec. It remains a residential building. ♦ Between Rues de Babylone and de Varenne. Métros: Rue du Bac, Sèvres–Babylone

> I cannot conceive any place so perfectly and wonderfully expressive of its own character; its secret character no less than that which is on the surface; as Paris is. I walked about streets—in and out, up and down, backwards and forwards—during the two days we were there; and almost every house, every person I passed, seemed to be another leaf in the enormous book that stands wide open there. I was perpetually turning over, and never coming any nearer the end. There never was such a place for a description.
>
> —Charles Dickens,
> Letter to Count d'Orsay, 7 August 1844

104 EDITIONS DE PARFUMS FRÉDÉRIC MALLE

If row upon row of packaged perfume à la Sephora leaves your nostrils numb, here's one possible antidote: a small, sophisticated boutique that sells small batches of scents "published" by some of France's leading perfumers. Customers familiarize themselves with such perfumes as *Musc Ravageur*, *Iris Poudre*, and *Angéliques Sous la Pluie* by inhaling their emanations from transparent "fragrance columns," which supposedly give a clearer idea of the perfumes' aura. M-Sa. 37 Rue de Grenelle (between Rues des Sts-Pères and St-Guillaume). 01.42.22.77.22. Métro: Rue du Bac

BAXTER

*Gravures Anciennes
& Encadrements*

105 BAXTER

Old prints, etchings, and lithographs abound in this charming shop that specializes in European architectural and botanical illustrations from the 17th to 19th centuries. The friendly staff has both a knowledge of and affection for the wares. Framing services are available. ♦ M, 1-7PM; Tu-Sa. 15 Rue du Dragon (at Rue Bernard-Palissy). 01.45.49.01.34. Métro: St-Germain-des-Prés

106 LA LOUISIANE

$$ If you want to stay right in the heart of Paris, this 80-room property is a good choice. The hotel has hosted some famous French literati, including Jacques Prévert, Jean-Paul Sartre, and Simone de Beauvoir, who lived in one of the hotel's coveted oval rooms for years, and it was the favorite of North American jazz musicians during the heyday of the St-Germain jazz caves in the 1950s. The noise level can be high, so light sleepers should go elsewhere. There's no restaurant. ♦ 60 Rue de Seine (between Blvd St-Germain and Rue de Buci). 01.44.32.17.17; fax 01.46.34.23.87. Métro: Mabillon. hotel@lalouisiane.net

107 VAGENENDE

★★$$ With the full effulgence of an 1885 Belle-Epoque-and-Tiffany-glass décor, this poor man's Maxim's has starred in films such as *Travels with My Aunt* and *Murder on the*

Orient Express. Homemade foie gras, fresh shellfish, and grilled fish are good dishes to try. ♦ Daily, lunch and dinner until 1AM. 142 Blvd St-Germain (between Rues Grégoire-de-Tours and de Seine). 01.43.26.68.18. Métros: Mabillon, Odéon

108 HÔTEL LEFT BANK ST-GERMAIN

$$$ Best Western comes to France, offering 31 rooms with flowered wallpaper, heavy furniture, white marble bathrooms, and such modern amenities as air conditioning and cable television. The central location means the hotel is near the lively Carrefour de l'Odéon, but the rooms are well insulated against the noise. The top-floor penthouse suite has a splendid rooftop view of **Notre-Dame**. There's no restaurant. ♦ 9 Rue de l'Ancienne-Comédie (between Blvd St-Germain and Rue St-André-des-Arts). 01.43.54.01.70; fax 01.43.26.17.14. Métro: Odéon. lbank@paris-hotels-charm.com

109 LE PROCOPE

★★$$ This colorful eatery bills itself as the world's oldest café. It was founded in 1686 by Sicilian Francesco Procopio dei Coltelli, the man credited with introducing coffee to France. The opening of the **Comédie Française** in a tennis court–turned-theater across the street in 1689 ensured its success. Over the centuries, customers have included 17th-century writers La Fontaine, Rousseau, and Voltaire; 18th-century revolutionaries Benjamin Franklin, Thomas Jefferson, Robespierre, Danton, Bonaparte, and Marat; such ageless literati as Victor Hugo, Honoré de Balzac, Paul Verlaine, George Sand, and Mallarmé; and in the 1950s, when the tavern-café became a restaurant, Simone de Beauvoir and Jean-Paul Sartre. The 18th-century décor is sumptuous, all red and gold, mirrors and crystal chandeliers, and there's furniture that belonged to Voltaire and Rousseau. The cuisine was long dismissed as bland and uninteresting, but the menu has improved over the past few years. The fresh shellfish platters, grilled lobster, *coquilles St.-Jacques*, and duck breast with orange are quite good, and the prix-fixe menus are surprisingly reasonable. ♦ Daily, lunch and dinner until 1AM. Piano bar: M-Sa, 10PM-1AM. 13 Rue de l'Ancienne-Comédie (between Blvd St-Germain and Rue St-André-des-Arts). 01.40.46.79.00. Métro: Odéon

109 PUB ST-GERMAIN-DES-PRÉS

$$ Along with 26 brands of draft beer and 450 international varieties of bottled brew, this 600-seat pub offers such basic grub as mussels and chicken cooked with—guess

what?—beer. By the end of the evening, you may feel that you have been similarly stewed yourself. The menu also offers hamburgers and lots of beef. Open around the clock, it's a favorite of North American students abroad. ♦ Daily, 24 hours. 17 Rue de l'Ancienne-Comédie (between Blvd St-Germain and Rue St-André-des-Arts). 01.43.29.38.70. Métro: Odéon

110 BOULEVARD ST-MICHEL

This was one of the long, broad, tree-lined boulevards that Baron Haussmann scythed through the heart of Paris in the mid-19th century. Running uphill from the **Seine** to Boulevard Montparnasse, it divided the Left Bank in two, with the Latin Quarter to the east and the St-Germain-des-Prés area to the west. The street was named in 1867 in memory of the ancient **chapel of St-Michel** that stood here once upon a time. ♦ Between Ave de l'Observatoire and Pl St-Michel. Métros: St-Michel, Cluny–La Sorbonne

110 ST-MICHEL MÉTRO

This is one of the Art Nouveau métro entrances designed by **Hector Guimard** in 1900. ♦ Pl St-André-des-Arts and Rue Danton

110 LA MAISON DE LA LOZÈRE

★★$$ This crowded canteen with bare wooden tables is a trip straight to the Lozère region in France's heartland. Try one of the robust regional specialties such as *aligot d'Aubrac* (a heavenly concoction of mashed potatoes, garlic, and *tomme*, a cheese, served only on Thursday), *maoucho* (grilled sausage stuffed with cabbage and other vegetables and ground pork), *assiette de cochonnailles* (a platter of cold sausage, ham, and pâté from the region), grilled Lozère lamb chops, bleu d'Auvergne cheese, and good *vin de pays* in carafes. ♦ Tu-Sa, lunch and dinner; closed mid-July through mid-August and the last week of December. Reservations recommended. 4 Rue Hautefeuille (between Rue Serpente and Pl St-André-des-Arts). 01.43.54.26.64. Métro: St-Michel

MAUD FRIZON
PARIS

111 MAUD FRIZON

More than 1,500 styles of handcrafted haute couture footwear are carried here. ♦ M-Sa. 83 Rue des Sts-Pères (at Rue de Grenelle). 01.42.22.06.93. Métro: Sèvres–Babylone. Also at 90 Rue du Faubourg St-Honoré (at Pl Beauvau). 01.42.65.27.96. Métro: Miromesnil

Restaurants/Clubs: Red | Hotels: Purple | Shops: Orange | Outdoors/Parks: Green | Sights/Culture: Blue

111 CASSEGRAIN

There's nothing quite like a proper thank-you note or an engraved-in-gold place card. This stationer has been setting the standard since 1919. ♦ M-Sa. 81 Rue des Sts-Pères (between Rue de Grenelle and Blvd St-Germain). 01.42.22.04.76. Métros: St-Sulpice, Sèvres–Babylone

112 31 RUE DU DRAGON

The **Académie Julian**, which was once here, admitted hundreds of aspiring North American painters who were hoping to study on the GI bill after World War II but were unable to meet the stricter entrance requirements of the **Ecole des Beaux-Arts**. The building now has both residential and commercial space. ♦ Between Carrefour de la Croix-Rouge and Rue Bernard-Palissy. Métro: St-Sulpice

112 CHEZ CLAUDE SAINLOUIS

★★$ Since opening in 1959, the unfailingly popular restaurant of ex-stuntman Claude Piau (Sanlouis was his *nom de cinéma*) has played it safe, serving an unchanging menu of traditional dishes. Steak, lamb chops, fish, scrumptious *pommes frites*, and chocolate mousse are served against a backdrop of bright red banquettes and photos of numerous French presidents, who apparently appreciated the no-frills cooking of the place. This is a good alternative to the overrated **Brasserie Lipp** nearby. Tu-Sa, lunch and dinner; closed in August and one week at Christmas. Reservations recommended. 27 Rue du Dragon (between Carrefour de la Croix-Rouge and Rue Bernard Palissy). 01.45.48.29.68. Métro: St-Sulpice

113 VIA PALISSY

★★$$ Climb to the tiny, crooked dining room of this Italian restaurant to sample risotto Milanese, gnocchi with Gorgonzola, and homemade tiramisù. ♦ Tu-Sa, lunch and dinner; closed 3 weeks in August. Reservations recommended. 11 Rue Bernard-Palissy (at Rue du Sabot). 01.45.44.02.52. Métro: St-Germain-des-Prés

114 YAKIJAPO MITSUKO

★★$$ One of the best sushi bars in Paris also serves sashimi and yakitori at reasonable prices in a simple, elegant dining room. ♦ Daily, lunch and dinner. 8 Rue du Sabot (between Rues du Four and Bernard-Palissy). 01.42.22.17.74. Métro: St-Sulpice

115 VILLAGE VOICE

In the intelligent tradition of those famous Left Bank bookstore-salons run by such women as Sylvia Beach and Adrienne Monnier, the English bookshop of Odile Hellier is a busy crossroads for anglophone writers, artists, and literati in Paris. Hellier has something for everyone: a fine selection of classical, contemporary, and small-press fiction, exceptional author readings, and the latest issues of the *New York Review of Books*, the *New Yorker*, and (naturally) the *Village Voice*. ♦ M, 2-8PM; Tu-Sa; Su, 2-7PM. 6 Rue Princesse (between Rues Guisarde and du Four). 01.46.33.36.47. Métro: Mabillon

115 COFFEE PARISIEN

★★$ Framed dollar bills on the wall, a 1950s Lucky Strike ad, the *New York Times* front page from the day President John F. Kennedy was assassinated in Dallas, and other Americana set the tone for Franco–New Yorker Jonathan Goldstein's Big Apple–style luncheonette in the City of Light. Nachos, guacamole and tortilla chips, chicken wings, spinach salad, pastrami sandwiches, cheeseburgers, hash browns, eggs Benedict, grilled tuna, vegetarian plate, cheesecake, Bud, Corona, Ben & Jerry's—it's all there, just like *chez vous*. ♦ Daily, noon to midnight. 4 Rue Princesse (between Rues Guisarde and du Four). 01.43.54.18.18. Métro: Mabillon. Also at 7 Rue Gustave Courbet (between Rues de Longchamp and de la Pompe). 01.45.53.17.17. Métro: Rue de la Pompe

116 CHEZ GEORGES

On an alley called Duckling Street, surrounded by a wealth of Italian restaurants, is this classic old French bar wallpapered with mug shots of the singers who once performed in the old cabaret downstairs. It's a nice place for a glass of Côtes-du-Rhône or Beaujolais before dining on cannelloni and pizza down the street. ♦ Tu-Sa, noon-2AM. No credit cards accepted. 11 Rue des Canettes (between Rues Guisarde and du Four). 01.43.26.79.15. Métro: Mabillon

17 LE GOLFE DE NAPLES

★$ The best pizza in Paris is found at this little *ristorante* across the street from the Marché St-Germain. The pies come in 17 varieties, from the simple *Napoletana* to the appetite-sating *Amoureuse*, heaped with fresh shrimp, squid, mussels, and mushrooms. Italian appetizers, salads, pasta, meat, and fish dishes are also served at prices that are easy on the pocket. With its red tablecloths, big wood-burning oven, and happily chattering diners, the tone is decidedly upbeat. The late Marcello Mastroianni used to eat here every week during his frequent stays in Paris. There's a sidewalk terrace for alfresco dining in summer. A word of caution: The Neapolitan nonchalance of the wait staff can be a problem for those in a hurry. ◆ Daily, lunch and dinner. 5 Rue de Montfaucon (at Rue Clément). 01.43.26.98.11. Métro: Mabillon

Hôtel de Fleurie
★ ★ ★
Saint-Germain-des-Prés

18 HÔTEL DE FLEURIE

$$$ This renovated 18th-century town house in the heart of St-Germain-des-Prés offers 29 quiet, air-conditioned rooms, including some in the attic with high ceilings and wood beams. Downstairs is a handsome stone-vaulted breakfast room, where the Marolleau family serves an excellent continental breakfast—slices of *quatre-quarts* (French pound cake), crisp baguettes, cheese, and freshly squeezed orange juice. There's no restaurant. ◆ 32-34 Rue Grégoire-de-Tours (between Rue des Quatre-Vents and Blvd St-Germain). 01.53.73.70.00; fax 01.53.73.70.20. Métro: Odéon. bonjour@hotel-de-fleurie.tm.fr; www.hotel-de-fleurie.tm.fr

18 CASA BINI

★★$$ Anna Bini and her family have prepared meals for Catherine Deneuve and Marcello Mastroianni at this casual, friendly Tuscan restaurant. Florentine appetizers include *crostini* with mozzarella and ham, and swordfish carpaccio with herbs. There are new pasta, meat, and fish specials every day. Ask about Madame Bini's cultural and culinary tours to Italy. ◆ M-Sa, lunch and dinner; Su, dinner; closed 1 week in mid-August. Reser-vations recommended. 36 Rue Grégoire-de-Tours (between Rue des Quatre-Vents and Blvd St-Germain). 01.46.34.05.60. Métro: Odéon

119 LA CIGALE

★★$$ The portions may be small and the prices as inflated as this backstreet bistro's celebrated soufflés (count on 15 euros or so per puff), but when everything tastes this good, it's hard indeed to complain. For starters try a simple green salad or vegetable raviolis in a succulent butter sauce, or go straight in for the kill with some of the lightest, dreamiest soufflés you'll find anywhere. The Henry IV is a cheese rendition that comes with a savory mustardy sauce, complete with small chicken chunks, on the side. Broccoli and goat cheese is another good bet. For dessert, try a classic chocolate soufflé or a vanilla soufflé with a pot of warm caramel sauce on the side. This very traditional dining spot is a perennial favorite with locals and shoppers taking a break from the nearby **Le Bon Marché** department store, so whether for lunch or dinner, reservations are imperative. M-F, lunch and dinner; Sa, dinner. 11 *bis* Rue Chomel (between Rue de Babylone and Blvd Raspail). 01.45.48.87.87. Métro: Sèvres-Babylone

LE RÉCAMIER

RESTAURANT

120 LE RÉCAMIER

★★★$$$ Situated in a serene cul-de-sac in the well-trodden St-Germain shopping district, this elegant restaurant caters to the Paris publishing crowd and has one of the city's most peaceful outdoor terraces. Owner and certified wine expert Martin Cantegrit features dishes from his native Burgundy—fricassee of snails and wild mushrooms, *boeuf bourguignon sans pareil*, chateaubriand Récamier—as well as salmon tartare (raw chopped salmon, served with a sauce of herbs and spices), an excellent summer starter. Cantegrit's wine list, which he calls "my little Bible," merits the appellation. ◆ M-Sa, lunch and dinner. 4 Rue Récamier (at Rue de Sèvres). 01.45.48.86.58. Métro: Sèvres–Babylone

121 RUE DES STS-PÈRES

Known in the 13th century as the Chemins aux Vaches (Cow Path), this street became Rue de St-Pierre in the 16th century because of a nearby chapel dedicated to St. Peter. By

---

Restaurants/Clubs: **Red** | Hotels: **Purple** | Shops: **Orange** | Outdoors/Parks: **Green** | Sights/Culture: **Blue**

97

1652, people had worn the name down to ♦ Rue des Sts-Pères. Métros: Sèvres–Babylone, St-Germain-des-Prés

121 AU SAUVIGNON

★$ This old wine bar is predictably papered with maps of French wine regions. Still, in summer it's not such a bad thing to enjoy a plate of country-cured ham, some *cantal* cheese, and a Sancerre rosé while sitting at one of the sidewalk tables watching the world stroll by. ♦ M-Sa, breakfast, lunch, and dinner until 10PM; closed in August. 80 Rue des Sts-Pères (at Rue de Sèvres). 01.45.48.49.02. Métro: Sèvres–Babylone

122 PIERRE HERMÉ

Macaroons flavored with the likes of milk chocolate and passion fruit and dessert creations like the Ispahan, a rose macaroon filled with rose-petal cream, whole raspberries and litchis, have helped generate so much buzz around this slender pastry shop that it is frequently impossible to get inside the door. If impatience gets the best of you, by no means despair: These sweet treats may be unassailably imaginative, but Pierre Hermé—who cut his sweet tooth at Ladurée—by no means has a monopoly on scrumptiousness. This is, after all, Paris. ♦ M-Sa. 72 Rue Bonaparte (between Rues du Four and du Vieux Colombier). 01.43.54.47.77

123 BIRDLAND

The jazzy bar serves chili con carne and plays classic John Coltrane and Charlie Parker. ♦ M-Sa, 7PM-dawn; Su, 11PM-dawn. 20 Rue Princesse (at Rue Guisarde). 01.43.26.97.59. Métro: Mabillon

123 CHEZ HENRI

★★$ This first-rate neighborhood bistro with a convivial ambiance is known for its delicious *magret de canard* (duck fillet), green bean vinaigrette, *foie de veau* (veal liver), lamb shanks cooked with prunes and cinnamon, baked goat-cheese salad, au gratin potatoes, and homemade tarts. ♦ M-Sa, lunch and dinner. Reservations recommended. No credit cards accepted. 16 Rue Princesse (between Rues Guisarde and du Four). 01.46.33.51.12. Métro: Mabillon

124 AUX CHARPENTIERS

★★$$ Formerly the lunch hall of an 18th-century carpenters' guild, this reasonably priced bistro serves chef Pierre Bardeche's simple but well-prepared bacon and lentils, beef stew, sautéed veal, and other daily specials. ♦ Daily, lunch and dinner. Reservations recommended. 10 Rue Mabillon (between Rues Guisarde and du Four). 01.43.26.30.05. Métro: Mabillon

124 CASTEL'S

This private club caters to dandies, backbiting gossips, BCBGs (for *bon chic bon genre*, the French term for preppy), and former cabinet ministers with socialites on their arms. Technically, no one crosses the fabled threshold unaccompanied by a card-carrying member (some 2,500 privileged people), but if you're acceptably dressed (jacket and tie for men) and have made a dinner reservation, chances are good you'll be permitted to join the elite. ♦ Tu-Sa, dinner. Disco: Th-Sa from 11PM-dawn. 15 Rue Princesse (between Rues Guisarde and du Four). 01.40.51.52.80. Métro: Mabillon

125 MARCHÉ ST-GERMAIN

An old covered market has been converted into a bright, modern mall with **The Gap** and several other youth-oriented clothing boutiques and **Coolin**, a convivial Irish pub (01.44.07.00.92). But the fishmongers, cheese and wine merchants, florists, and dairymaids are still to be found in the south side of the building, fronting on Rue Lobineau. Under the market building are a basketball court and a 25-meter (82.5-foot) public swimming pool, the **Piscine St-Germain** (01.43.29.08.15). ♦ Market: Tu-Sa; Su morning. Pool: Tu-Su; hours vary. Rues Mabillon and Lobineau. Métro: Mabillon

Christian Tortu

126 CHRISTIAN TORTU

Since opening in 1984, this has been one of the hottest florists in town, creating opulent and original designs with flowers and vegetables. Garden furniture is also sold. Tortu's home decoration boutique is just down the street (see page 96). ♦ M-Sa. 6 Carrefour de l'Odéon (between Rue des Quatre-Vents and Blvd St-Germain). 01.43.26.02.56. Métro: Odéon

126 CARREFOUR DE L'ODÉON

A crossroads of sorts is ruled over by a great pigeon-christened bronze of Georges-Jacques Danton. This revolutionary leader's statements such as "We need audacity, more audacity, audacity forever . . ." cost him his head. Robespierre sent him to the guillotine in 1794. ♦ At the corner of Rues des Quatre-Vents and de l'Odéon. Métro: Odéon

127 HÔTEL LUTETIA

$$$$ The Left Bank's grandest of grand hotels, this seven-story, 250-room gem opened in 1910, and its interior is a

veritable museum of Art Deco style. In more recent times the hotel was refurbished by decorator Sybille de Margerie, who kept the '30s feel intact. The guest rooms are large and luxurious, some with views of the gilded dome of the **Invalides** and the **Eiffel Tower**. Among the suites, the most remarkable is the penthouse Arman suite, designed by (and sometimes the Parisian residence of) the sculptor, featuring a bed with a violin-shaped headboard and a red velvet sofa with stacked suitcases for armrests. The two principal dining spots are the highly rated gourmet restaurant **Paris** (01.49.54.46.90), designed by Sonia Rykiel, and the spacious modern **Brasserie Lutetia** (01.49.54.46.76). The intimate **Bar Lutèce** (01.49.54.46.09) attracts the likes of neighborhood resident Catherine Deneuve and offers intimate jazz four nights a week (W-Sa, 10PM-1AM). Vivacious vocalist Cynthia MacPherson, a longtime American in Paris, sings regularly. Check the hotel's web site for the schedule of artists. ♦ 45 Blvd de Raspail (at Rue de Sèvres). 01.49.54.46.46 or 800.888.4747; fax 01.49.54.46.00. Métro: Sèvres-Babylone. www.lutetia-paris.com

128 POILÂNE

Oftentimes a line forms to get inside the door of this bakery, renowned for the round sourdough country loafs churned out from antique wood-fired ovens in the cellars. In opening his shop, Lionel Poilâne, who died tragically with his wife in a helicopter crash in Brittany on 31 October 2002, continued a family tradition started by his Norman father, Pierre, in 1933. He was a driving force behind the renaissance in authentic French baking, and the signature Poilâne loaves are found today on tables in some 400 Parisian restaurants as well as in gourmet shops in New York, London, and Tokyo. Various kinds of breads are available as well as a small selection of excellent *pâtisseries* and bars of gourmet chocolate. ♦ M-Sa. 8 Rue du Cherche-Midi (between Pl Alphonse-Deville and Carrefour de la Croix-Rouge). 01.45.48.42.59. Métro: St-Sulpice

129 MARITHÉ & FRANÇOIS GIRBAUD

You can get your cool jeans fix with a complimentary serving of nature at this trendy shop (one of several in Paris), of which an entire wall serves as a vibrant vertical greenhouse. Mostly you'll find chic, casual women's wear here, though there is a small men's section on the basement level. ♦ M-Sa. 7 Rue du Cherche-Midi (between Rues de Sèvres and d'Assas). 01.53.63.53.63

130 ANNICK GOUTAL

Original perfumes, precious oils, lotions, and soaps are purveyed at this ivory- and gold-toned boutique. Goutal's beautifully packaged products celebrate nature with such women's and men's fragrances as Eau d'Hadrien, Eau du Ciel, Gardénia Passion, and Rose Absolute. The knowledgeable salespeople will cheerfully assist you in choosing the right scent. This is one of nine stores in Paris. ♦ M-Sa. 12 Pl St-Sulpice (between Rues des Canettes and Bonaparte). 01.46.33.03.15. Métro: St-Sulpice

131 LE PETIT VATEL

★$ At one of St-Germain's smallest and least expensive restaurants, with only 16 places around its handful of tables, owner Catherine Grandjacques and her garrulous chef Sixte, who is fluent in French, English, and Spanish, offer an amazing array of choices, given the minuscule size of the place. They serve a different soup every day, including lime soup in the summer; homemade pâté; *pot au feu*; vegetarian plate; *pamboli* (mountain cheese and Spanish ham baked in an oven over toast with olive oil, a Catalan specialty); grilled, boiled, and baked sausages; lamb stew; moussaka; roast pork; chocolate cake; and *gratin de pommes* (baked apple casserole). ♦ Tu-Sa, lunch and dinner. No credit cards accepted. 5 Rue Lobineau (between Rues de Seine and Mabillon). 01.43.54.28.49. Métros: Mabillon, Odéon

SOULEIADO®

132 SOULEIADO

Souleiado means "sunny" in the Provençal language, and here at its Paris boutique the famed southern French manufacturer offers a dazzling array of its colorfully patterned Provençal cloth items, from tablecloths, place mats, and napkins to scarves, shawls, cosmetic bags, stuffed toys, photo albums, datebooks, and eyeglass cases. Hundreds of choices of yard goods are also available for wall coverings and drapes, lampshades, sheets, pillowcases, quilted bedspreads, and even towels. There are skirts, blouses, and jackets in the women's wear section, and for men there are snappy sports shirts and ties. Be sure not to miss the dinnerware from Solafrance and the

---

Restaurants/Clubs: Red | Hotels: Purple | Shops: Orange | Outdoors/Parks: Green | Sights/Culture: Blue

handblown bubble glass pitchers and drinking glasses from the Verrerie de Biot on the Côte d'Azur. ◆ M-Sa. 78 Rue de Seine (at Rue Lobineau). 01.43.54.62.25. Métros: Odéon, Mabillon

133 CHRISTIAN TORTU BOUTIQUE

Impeccably elegant flowerpots in amazing shapes and materials, ceramic trays, smooth stone soap dishes and ashtrays, everything in soothing shades of gray-green, gray, dark cherry, and silver, and floral-patterned tableware are sold in this little annex of the famed flower shop. ◆ M, 2PM-7PM; Tu-Sa. 17 Rue des Quatre-Vents (between Carrefour de l'Odéon and Rue de Tournon). 01.43.26.02.56. Métro: Odéon

134 SAN FRANCISCO BOOK COMPANY

A few steps from Sylvia Beach's original Shakespeare and Company bookshop, Jim Carroll and Phil Wood carry on the worthy tradition of offering English-language books in a small but remarkably well-stocked store. They sell used books only, hardcover and paperback, covering literature, music, art, film, philosophy, and the social sciences, and try to keep prices low to promote turnover. They also buy and swap books. ◆ M-Su. 17 Rue Monsieur-le-Prince (between Rue Antoine-Dubois and Carrefour de l'Odéon). 01.43.29.15.70. Métro: Odéon

135 RUE DE L'ECOLE-DE-MÉDECINE

During the revolution, Jean-Paul Marat founded the biting journal *L'Ami du Peuple* and was forced to hide in the Paris sewers. The radical democrat was elected to the National Convention 3 years later with the support of Danton and Robespierre but soon learned that you can't please all of *le peuple* all of the time. On 13 July 1793 Marat was stabbed while taking a bath in his house on this street. His killer was Girondist Charlotte Corday, who had hidden a knife in her bodice. For a surprisingly ungory depiction of the assassination, see David's painting in the **Louvre**'s **Salle des Etats**. ◆ Métros: Odéon, Cluny-La Sorbonne

136 LE BON MARCHÉ

The granddaddy of all Paris department stores, which was founded in 1852, underwent *un lifting* (a major overhaul) during the 1990s and is as up-to-date now as its big Right Bank competitors. Ready-to-wear collections include those of Corrine Saurrut, Ralph Lauren, Vivienne Westwood, and Comme des Garçons, and the store has its own line of menswear called Balthazar. Its gorgeous gourmet food market, **La Grande Epicerie**, is especially famous, and with more than 9,000 square feet of floor space, it is one of the largest of its kind in the city. Everything from fresh oysters to foie gras and superb wines is sold here. This is the only department store on the Left Bank. ◆ Store: M-Sa. Epicerie: M-Sa, 10AM-9PM. 22 Rue de Sèvres (at Rue du Bac). Store: 01.44.39.80.00. Epicerie: 01.44.39.81.00. Métro: Sèvres–Babylone

137 RUE DU CHERCHE-MIDI

This street's name, which literally means "seek noon," has nothing to do with telling time, despite the astronomically themed frieze set above the doorway at No. 19. It's supposedly a 16th-century reference to a kind of parasite (real or imagined) that made its presence felt at midday—just in time to get fed. But the street has long since taken a more salubrious turn and today is packed with chic boutiques, especially the stretch from the Rue de Sèvres to the Rue d'Assas. ◆ At Carrefour de la Croix-Rouge. Métro: St-Sulpice

138 PLACE ST-SULPICE

One of the most serene squares in Paris has a café, pink-flowering chestnut trees, and the marvelous stone **Fontaine des Quatre Points Cardinaux** (Fountain of the Four Cardinal Points) by Visconti. The fountain features four famous French clergymen oriented north, south, east, and west, with four regal lions snarling at their feet. Once flanked by shops peddling ivory crucifixes, rosary beads, and clerical garments, the square today is graced by two Yves Saint Laurent boutiques. It hosts antiques and book fairs in summer and what many consider the finest of the Bastille Day balls. ◆ Métro: St-Sulpice

139 ST-SULPICE

Interrupted by insurrection, insolvency, and even bolts of lightning, the construction of this church required the services of architects, including the notable **Louis Le Vau**, over a span of 134 years. Its dramatic classical style was the inspiration of **Giovanni Servandoni**, a Florentine known for his theater and stage-set designs. The disparity of the two towers, an odd couple indeed, was the result of shifting architectural sands and patronly indecision. Named after St. Sulpicius, the sixth-century archbishop of Bourges, and dubbed the **Temple of Victory** during the revolution, the church hosted a lavish banquet for 1,200 after Napoléon returned from his victories in Egypt. Inside the front door are two holy-water stoups made from enormous shells given to François I by the Venetian Republic. The first chapel on the right was frescoed by an aging Eugène Delacroix. In a chapel at the rear of the church is the extraordinary *Virgin and Child* by Jean-Baptiste Pigalle. The organ, designed in 1776 by **Jean-François Chalgrin**, with 6,588 pipes, numbers among the largest in the world. In the floor, running along the north–south transept, is a bronze meridian line, a testament to France's 19th-century passion for science. Three times a year, on the equinoxes and the winter solstice, sunlight strikes the line so precisely that light runs along the metal strip, glances off an obelisk and globe at its top, and finally illuminates across. The inscription on the obelisk translates, more or less, as "Two Scientists with God's Help." ♦ Pl St-Sulpice (between Rues Palatine and St-Sulpice). 01.46.33.21.78. Métro: St-Sulpice

Marie,
Mercié
23 rue St Sulpice
Paris 75006

40 Marie Mercié

The custom-made hats in Mercié's summer and winter collections here range from classic chapeaux to the amusing befeathered, beribboned fantasies that have earned her an international reputation. ♦ M-Sa. 23 Rue St-Sulpice (between Rues de Tournon and Garancière). 01.43.26.45.83. Métros: Mabillon, Odéon

41 12 Rue de l'Odéon

From 1921 to 1940 this was the famous bookstore **Shakespeare and Company**, run by Sylvia Beach, daughter of a Presbyterian minister from Princeton, New Jersey. Her shop was a Parisian hearth and home for North American and British writers, including Ezra Pound,

Archibald MacLeish, Thornton Wilder, and F. Scott Fitzgerald, to whom Beach served as guardian angel. She was constantly lending books and money to Ernest Hemingway, who came to Paris in 1921 and, after the publication of *The Sun Also Rises* in 1926, became the city's most famous writer from across the Atlantic. Beach was devoted to literature in general and to one writer in particular: James Joyce. If it hadn't been for this amazing woman, the most important literary event of the day—publication, in full, of *Ulysses*— might never have happened. Beach became Joyce's secretary, editor, agent, and banker, and nearly bankrupted her bookstore in the process of publishing the book. A plaque on the building commemorates her achievement. The building now has residential and commercial space. ♦ Between Pl de l'Odéon and Carrefour de l'Odéon. Métro: Odéon

142 Chez Maître Paul

★★$$ This quaint little restaurant that opened in 1945 looks like a country cottage hidden deep in the Franche-Comté region in the Jura Mountains in eastern France. The kitchen is famous for its variety of wine sauces and a winning way with chicken and veal. Specialties include free-range chicken in a sauce made with *vin jaune* (a wine similar to sherry), and calf's liver cooked with *vin de paille* (a Sauternes-like wine). ♦ Daily, lunch and dinner. Closed Su, M in July and August. Reservations recommended. 12 Rue Monsieur-le-Prince (at Rue Casimir-Delavigne). 01.43.54.74.59. Métro: Odéon

143 Grand Hôtel des Balcons

$$ This comfortable 50-room hotel, very reasonably priced for this area, is just down the street from the **Théâtre de l'Odéon**. There's no restaurant, but a buffet breakfast is served. ♦ 3 Rue Casimir-Delavigne (between Pl de l'Odéon and Rue Monsieur-le-Prince). 01.46.34.78.50; fax 01.46.34.06.27. Métro: Odéon. resa@balcons.com; www.balcons.com

144 Atelier Guillaume Martel

Have a special 17th-century portrait or modern print you need framed? Martel, a graduate of the prestigious **Ecole du Louvre**, specializes in *dorure froide* (a cold-gilding technique) frames for both antique and contemporary prints. ♦ Tu-Sa, 10AM-6PM; closed in August. 2 Rue du Regard (at Rue du Cherche-Midi). 01.45.49.02.07. Métro: Sèvres–Babylone

145 Hôtel de l'Abbaye

$$$ Stone arches, antique furniture, and fresh-cut flowers enhance this exquisite 18th-

---

century convent-turned-hotel. There are 40 peaceful rooms; ground-floor rooms **Nos. 2**, **3**, and **4** open onto the trellised garden. There's no restaurant, but breakfast is served in the garden in fair weather, in the charming breakfast room when it's not. ◆ 10 Rue Cassette (at Rue de Mézières). 01.45.44.38.11; fax 01.45.48.07.86. Métro: St-Sulpice. hotel.abbaye@wanadoo.fr; www.hotel-abbaye.4in.com

146 RUE FÉROU

This street has housed a number of artists over the years. Painter-photographer Man Ray occupied an atelier with a high ceiling at **No. 2** in 1951. Ernest Hemingway lived in the sphinx-protected *hôtel particulier* at **No. 6** in 1926, having left his wife, Hadley, for French *Vogue* staffer Pauline Pfeiffer. Painter Henri Fantin-Latour had an apartment at **No. 13** in 1858, where he was sketched by his friend James McNeill Whistler (whose drawing was later purchased by the **Louvre**). ◆ Métro: St-Sulpice

147 AU BON ST-POURÇAIN

★$$ At this authentic old neighborhood bistro, Chef Franck Pasquet fuels his St-Germain regulars with escargots, *compote de lapereau* (young rabbit stew), cassoulet, beef with olives, and sole meunière, which they wash down with good, modestly priced St-Pourçain wine. ◆ M-Sa, lunch and dinner. 10 *bis* Rue Servandoni (between Rues de Vaugirard and du Canivet). 01.43.54.93.63. Métros: St-Sulpice, Mabillon

148 19 RUE DE TOURNON

In May 1790 American revolutionary naval officer John Paul Jones, having served a year in the Russian navy, moved to Paris, where he was welcomed as a national hero for his epic 1779 capture of the *Serapis*, a British warship. When he told Ambassador Benjamin Franklin that he wanted to learn French, the wise old gentleman advised him to get "a walking dictionary." Jones died destitute in a second-floor flat in this building on 18 July 1792; he received a full-scale state funeral paid for by the French government. This is still a residential building. ◆ Between Rues de Vaugirard and St-Sulpice. Métro: Odéon

149 LA MÉDITERRANÉE

★★$$ Stunning interiors and good, fresh seafood continue to attract a stylish clientele at this glamorous old haunt of Marlene Dietrich, Orson Welles, Man Ray, Marc

Chagall, and Jean Cocteau. Offerings range from fresh shellfish, marinated mussels, and sea bream with creamy polenta to more sophisticated dishes, including *chipirons* (little Basque squid) sautéed in herbs, tartare of fresh tuna, bouillabaisse, and fillet of bass roasted with dried tomatoes. ◆ Daily, lunch and dinner. 2 Pl de l'Odéon (at Rue de l'Odéon). 01.43.26.02.30. Métro: Odéon

150 BOUILLON RACINE

★★$$ Built in 1906, this ornate Art Nouveau bouillon, a type of soup restaurant popular in Paris in the early 20th century, had great success in those days, but it eventually went downhill and was abandoned. The building was classified a historical monument, which meant that its interior could not be altered. A young Belgian chef, Olivier Simon, found it and fell in love with it in the early 1990s, and he and his partners spared no expense restoring it. When they opened in 1996, the mosaic floors, floral tile walls, serpentine chandeliers, and myriad other design elements were revealed once again in their full Belle Epoque efflorescence.

The cuisine is mainly Belgian, with beer used in many of the sauces. *Waterzooi* (Belgian *pot au feu*) is always on the menu, as is *carbonade de thon à la flamande* (Flemish-style tuna) and *pastilla* (duck and onions candied in beer with figs and fresh mint). But the menu changes frequently and offers such non-Belgian choices as ostrich steak or salmon sautéed with tandoori spices as well. And of course there's a vast array of Belgian beers, both bottled and on tap. The young staff is cheerful and efficient, the atmosphere lively. Reserve a table in the main dining room upstairs. Hot chocolate at the bar is not to be missed. An annex next door serves more contemporary fare. ◆ Daily, lunch and dinner. Reservations recommended. 3 Rue Racine (between Blvd St-Michel and Rue Monsieur-le-Prince). 01.44.32.15.60. Métro: Cluny–La Sorbonne

151 CAFÉ PARISIEN

★★$ This modest café has garnered a large reputation. Its weekend brunches, hearty *plats du jour*, and *moelleux au chocolat* (soft chocolate cake) draw a lively, often literary, throng. If you can't get in, a branch, **Le Petit Café Parisien**, is just up the street at 35 Rue de Vaugirard (between Rues Jean Bart and d'Assas; 01.45.49.47.15). ◆ M-F, lunch and dinner; Sa-Su, brunch and dinner. No credit cards accepted. Reservations recommended. 15 Rue d'Assas (between Rues de Vaugirard and de Rennes). 01.45.44.41.44. Métro: Rennes

152 42-44 RUE DE VAUGIRARD

In a top-floor flat of this apartment building, William Faulkner set to work on his first novel

Mosquitoes, in the summer of 1925. ♦ At Rue Servandoni. Métros: St-Sulpice, Mabillon

153 THÉÂTRE DE L'ODÉON

City architects **Marie-Josephe Peyre** and **Charles de Wailly** designed this rather clumsy building in 1782, intending it to look like an ancient temple. With 1,913 seats, it was the largest theater in Paris at the time. Beaumarchais's *Marriage of Figaro* premiered here on 27 April 1784 in an atmosphere of success and scandal; the author was jailed. After World War II, Jean-Louis Barrault and Madeleine Renaud revived interest in the theater with their productions of works by Beckett, Ionesco, Albee, and Claudel that became the talk of the town and, for a short period, made the theater the most popular in Paris. ♦ Box office: Daily, 11AM-6:30PM. 1 Pl Paul-Claudel (at Rue Corneille). 01.44.41.36.36. Métro: Odéon; RER: Luxembourg. www.theatre-Odéon.fr

154 LE MONITEUR

The best shop in Paris for books on architecture and landscape design also has a large selection of international design magazines and an array of unusual guidebooks and postcards. ♦ M-Sa. 7 Pl de l'Odéon (at Rue Racine). 01.44.41.15.75. Métro: Odéon

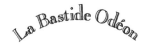

155 LA BASTIDE ODÉON

★★$$ Fine Provençal cooking and a superb selection of Bandol, Palette, Cassis, Bellet, Châteauneuf du Pape, and other southern French wines await you in chef Gilles Ajuelos's sunny yellow-ocher restaurant by the side of the **Théâtre de l'Odéon**. *Anchoïde de saumon cru* (purée of anchovies, olive oil, and vinegar with raw salmon), *rascasse à l'aïoli* (Mediterranean scorpion fish with a garlicky blend of eggs and olive oil), and lamb with spices and preserved lemon are a few of his savory specialties. ♦ Tu-Sa, lunch and dinner; closed 3 weeks in August. Reservations recommended. 7 Rue Corneille (between Rues de Vaugirard and Racine). 01.43.26.95.34. Métro: Odéon

156 RUE MONSIEUR-LE-PRINCE

Monsieur-le-Prince is what every French king's brother was traditionally called. Since the early 19th century, this street has been a veritable North American alley, as evidenced by the events that took place at the following addresses. **No. 14**: A plaque on the building commemorates African-American novelist Richard Wright, who lived in a third-floor apartment between 1948 and 1959, when Martin Luther King, Jr. II visited him there. **No. 22**: In 1892 James McNeill Whistler had a studio on the courtyard, where he completed a portrait of Count Robert de Montesquiou-Fezensac, the model for Baron de Charlus in Proust's *In Search of Lost Time*. (Years later, the count sold the painting for an exorbitant sum, thereby greatly offending Whistler. The portrait is now part of the Frick Collection in New York City.) **No. 49**: Poet Henry Wadsworth Longfellow lived here in June 1826. For $36 a week, he received a room in the *pension de famille* of Madame Potet, French lessons with her daughters, and free laundry service. **No. 55**: Oliver Wendell Holmes lived here (now the site of the **Lycée St-Louis**) between 1833 and 1835 while he studied to be a doctor. To be on the safe side, the following year he obtained a second medical degree from Harvard. ♦ Métro: Odéon; RER: Luxembourg

156 POLIDOR

★★$ For well over a century and a half, the home cooking served here has lured such struggling writers as Verlaine, Joyce, Valéry, and Hemingway out of their garrets for the earthy consolations of lentil or bean soup, chicken in cream sauce, curried pork, and guinea fowl with bacon. Since its founding in 1845, little has changed; it's still a classic bistro with the traditional bistro décor, complete with lace curtains and tiny wooden drawers where the regulars store their linen napkins. Diners sit shoulder to shoulder at long tables, and the ambiance is very convivial. The food is good, there are plenty of choices, and the prices have stayed within a garret-dweller's means. ♦ Daily, lunch and dinner. No credit cards accepted. 41 Rue Monsieur-le-Prince (between Rues de Vaugirard and Racine). 01.43.26.95.34. Métro: Odéon

157 27 RUE DE FLEURUS

The most famous of all North American expatriate addresses, this is where Gertrude Stein lived between 1903 and 1938, first with her brother Leo, then with her devoted

---

companion, lover, and muse, Alice B. Toklas. The walls of this large atelier were crammed with great Impressionist, Fauvist, and Cubist paintings. Gertrude and her family were among the first to buy works by Matisse and Picasso, who became regulars at her legendary Saturday night salons. An avant-garde writer and literary guru, she influenced many writers who visited her here, most notably the youthful Ernest Hemingway, in a friendship that eventually went sour. Stein gave her amusing account of their relationship in *The Autobiography of Alice B. Toklas*, but Hem got the vindictive last word in *A Moveable Feast*. Stein's atelier is on the ground floor of the pavilion at the rear of the garden. It can be seen from the street through the glass doors of the main building, but the view from the inner court is better, if you can get someone to buzz you in. A wall plaque commemorates her residence here. ♦ Between Rue D'Assas and Blvd Raspail. Métros: St-Placide, Rennes

Christian Constant

158 CHRISTIAN CONSTANT

★★$ This tearoom-cum-chocolate-and-pastry shop serves 32 kinds of tea accompanied by 5 varieties of sugar, acacia honey, and fresh brioches, as well as luscious lemon meringue tarts. The pièce de résistance, however, is the pure bittersweet chocolate bar. ♦ Daily, breakfast, lunch, and tea. 37 Rue d'Assas (at Rue de Fleurus). 01.53.63.15.15. Métros: St-Placide, Rennes

159 58 RUE MADAME

The oldest brother of Gertrude Stein, Michael Stein, and his artist wife, Sarah, moved into a loft in this Protestant church building in 1903 and soon began buying canvases of then-unknown Henri Matisse, who became a close friend. In a little more than a decade, Michael and Sarah, together with Gertrude and their brother Leo, had assembled one of the finest collections of Matisses, Renoirs, Cézannes, and Picassos in the world. ♦ Between Rues de Fleurus and de Vaugirard. Métros: St-Placide, Rennes

160 PERREYVE

$$ A quiet, modestly priced 30-room hotel, this place is just a minute's stroll from the **Luxembourg Gardens**. There's no restaurant. ♦ 63 Rue Madame (at Rue de Fleurus). 01.45.48.35.01; fax 01.42.84.03.30. Métros: St-Placide, Rennes. www.paris-hotel.com/PERREYVE

161 HÔTEL DE L'AVENIR

$$ Conveniently located one block from the **Luxembourg Gardens**, this unassuming hotel has 35 neat, quiet, comfortable rooms at rates that are, as the French say, *très correct*. There's no restaurant. ♦ 65 Rue Madame (at Rue de Fleurus). 01.45.48.84.54; fax 01.45.49.26.80. Métros: St-Placide, Rennes

162 JARDIN DU LUXEMBOURG (LUXEMBOURG GARDENS)

In the heart of the Left Bank, this 60-acre playground is graced with fountains, sculptures, ponds, flower beds, tennis courts, pony rides, a marionette theater, and outdoor band concerts. The *buvette*, a small open-air café (where, at the neat, modern public toilet in the basement, the cheerful attendant charges €0.40 per visit), is dappled with light filtered through the leaves of the surrounding trees, recalling the most pleasant moods of Impressionism. As a part of his draconian remodeling of Paris, Baron Haussmann had a plan to change this precious green expanse by turning part of it into roadways but was thwarted when 12,000 Parisians signed a petition to save the park. A team of officious *gardiens* keeps the park under heavy surveillance, enforcing the following regulations: "The park is out of bounds to the drunk, beggars, and the indecently dressed; the playing of cards is restricted to the northwest corner of the gardens; the kicking of balls and sitting on the grass is prohibited entirely; and the park must be vacated precisely 30 minutes before sunset." These uniformed guards trill their whistles to chase lingerers from the gardens.

As for those ever-amusing North Americans in Paris: In 1900 Isadora Duncan was wont to dance here at 5AM, when the gardens opened, and Ernest Hemingway's destitute painter protagonist in *Islands in the Stream* captured and strangled pigeons for lunch. Don't miss the garden's many hidden delights: the small bronze replica of the Statue of Liberty; a series of statues of French queens and famous 19th-century women standing among the crocuses, daffodils, and azaleas; a beekeeping school run by André Lumaire, curator of the apiary, who gives practical classes between February and mid-September through the **Centrale d'Apiculture** (41 Rue Pernety, between Rues Raymond-Losserand and de l'Ouest, 01.45.42.29.08); and the *pétanque* bowlers and chess players sequestered in their respective corners of the gardens. On the weekend, smartly dressed Latin Quarter grade-schoolers romp here and compete in the park's tricycle races and toy sailboat regattas held in the octagonal basin at the center of the park. ♦ Entrances at Pl Paul-Claudel and Rue de Médicis. Métro: Odéon, Pl Edmond-Rostand and Blvd St-

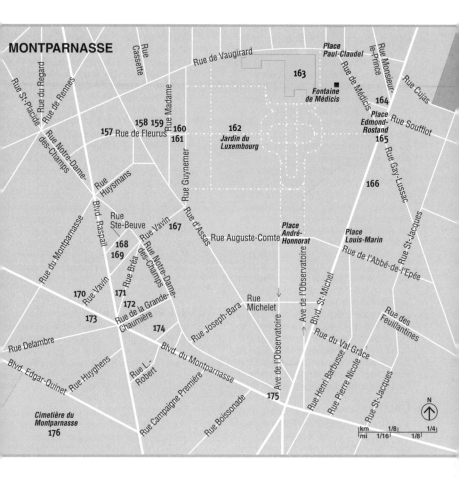

MONTPARNASSE

Rue Cassette

Rue de Vaigirard

Place Paul-Claudel

Rue Monsieur-le-Prince

Rue Cujas

Rue du Regard

Rue St-Placide

Rue de Rennes

163

Fontaine de Médicis

Rue de Médicis

164

Rue Souflot

Rue Madame

158 159 160

157 Rue de Fleurus 161

162

Jardin du Luxembourg

Place Edmond-Rostand

165

Rue Notre-Dame-des-Champs

Rue Huysmans

Rue Guynemer

166

Rue Gay-Lussac

Blvd.- Raspail

Rue Ste-Beuve 167

Rue Vavin

Rue d'Assas

Rue Auguste-Comte

Place André-Honnorat

Place Louis-Marin

Rue St-Jacques

168

169

Rue Bréa

Rue Notre-Dame-des-Champs

Rue de l'Abbé-de-l'Epée

Rue du Montparnasse

170 Rue Vavin 171

172

173 Rue de la Grande-Chaumière

174

Rue Joseph-Bara

Rue Michelet

Ave de l'Observatoire

Blvd. St-Michel

Rue du Val Grâce

Rue des Feuillantines

Rue Delambre

Blvd. Edgar-Quinet Rue Huyghens

Rue L.-Robert

Blvd. du Montparnasse

Ave de l'Observatoire

Rue Henri Barbusse

Rue Pierre Nicole

Rue St-Jacques

Rue Campagne Première

175

Rue Boissonade

Cimetière du Montparnasse

176

N

| km | | 1/8 | 1/4 |
| mi | 1/16 | | 1/8 |

Michel. RER: Luxembourg, Pl André-Honnorat and Rue Auguste-Comte; Luxembourg, Rue Guynemer (between Rues d'Assas and de Vaugirard). Métros: Notre-Dame des Champs, Rennes; Rue de Vaugirard (between Pl Paul-Claudel and Rue Guynemer). Metros: St-Sulpice, Rennes, Mabillon

Within the Jardin du Luxembourg:

FONTAINE DE MÉDICIS (MEDICI FOUNTAIN)

At the end of a long, somewhat slimy pool filled with goldfish is one of the few Italianate stonework remnants of Marie de Médicis's day. White marble nude lovers, *Acis* and *Galatea*, are eyed from above by the bronze Cyclops *Polyphemus*, who waits to do the mythic Greek version of kicking sand in the face of the 98-pound weakling before making off with the girl. Notice that the water appears to flow uphill into the grotto. On the back side

of the fountain is a delightful bas-relief of *Leda and the Swan* by Valois.

163 PALAIS DU LUXEMBOURG (LUXEMBOURG PALACE)

The assassin Ravaillac could hardly have imagined that his murder of Henri IV in 1610 would result in the creation of this splendid palace and gardens. (Indeed, he didn't live long enough after committing his dastardly deed to imagine much of anything.) The widow of Henri IV, Queen Mother Marie de Médicis, grew tired of the **Louvre** and decided to build a palace that would recall her native Italy. She bought this vast property at the southern edge of the city from Duke François de Luxembourg and dispatched an architect to Florence to study her family residence, the Pitti Palace, before making plans for the new palace. Obediently, **Salomon de Brosse** designed this palace for her. Work began in 1615, but by the time

---

Restaurants/Clubs: Red | Hotels: Purple | Shops: Orange | Outdoors/Parks: Green | Sights/Culture: Blue

the residence reached completion in 1631, Marie had been banished by her own son, Louis XIII, for turning against Cardinal Richelieu. She died penniless in Cologne 11 years later. During the revolution, the palace served a short stint as a prison; it was here that British-born North American "Citizen Tom Paine" languished as an enemy Englishman for more than 10 months during the 1793 Reign of Terror and narrowly escaped execution. Subsequently, the palace was remodeled to house the newly created French **Senate**, which met for the first time in 1804 and still resides here. Few of the trappings of Marie de Médicis's time remain; the 19th-century architect **Jean-François Chalgrin** (who also designed the **Arc de Triomphe**) made sure of that in his democratic remodeling. The 24 large canvases of the queen's life story created by Rubens were moved to the Louvre and the Uffizi Gallery in Florence. Chalgrin festooned the library with the paintings of Delacroix in homage to Virgil, Homer, and Dante. On the one day each month that the palace is open, visitors line up around the block. ♦ Admission. First Sunday of the month (call 01.42.34.20.60 before the 15th of the previous month to make a reservation for the guided tour). Rue de Vaugirard (between Pls Paul-Claudel and Guynemer). Métro: Odéon

164 DALLOYAU

★★$$ To sip a civilized cup of Chinese tea and indulge in a scoop of homemade ice cream or a delicate pastry while gazing over the **Luxembourg Gardens** from the terrace of this pastry shop and tea salon is to taste the luxury and leisure of an earlier, more gracious, era. ♦ Daily, breakfast, lunch, and afternoon tea. 2 Pl Edmond-Rostand (at Blvd St-Michel). 01.43.29.31.10. Métro: Luxembourg (RER). Also at 101 Rue du Faubourg St-Honoré (between Rues du Colisée and La Boétie). 01.42.99.90.00; 5 Blvd Beaumarchais (between Rues de la Bastille and du Pas de la Mule). 01.48.87.89.88; 63 Rue Grenelle (between Rue du Bac and Blvd Raspail). 01.45.49.95.30; 25 Blvd Capucines (between Rues de la Michodière and Choiseul). 01.47.03.47.00; and Lafayette Gourmet in the Galeries Lafayette, 48–52 Blvd Haussmann (between Rues Charras and Mogador). 01.53.20.05.00

165 LE PETIT JOURNAL

This old-time jazz boîte features French Dixieland and swing groups and the occasional piano trio. Frequent performers include clarinetist Claude Luter, Sidney Bechet's longtime partner, and renowned pianist Claude Bolling. Clients can either pay a charge for the music and a drink, or enjoy the show over a prix-fixe dinner; prices for both options are quite reasonable. ♦ M-Sa,

until 1:30AM; closed in August. 71 Blvd St-Michel (between Pl Louis-Marin and Rue Gay-Lussac). 01.43.26.28.59. RER: Luxembourg. Also at 13 Rue du Commandant-René-Mouchotte (between Pl de Catalogne and Ave du Maine). 01.43.21.56.70. Métros: Gaîté, Montparnasse-Bienvenue

166 93 BOULEVARD ST-MICHEL

Sylvia Beach, founder of the famous Paris **Shakespeare and Company** bookstore (see page 43), holed up here in a top-floor kitchen after spending 6 months in a Nazi detention camp in Vittel. The first "liberator" she encountered was her old friend Ernest Hemingway, then a war correspondent, on 26 August 1944. They met in the street in front of her abandoned bookshop. As she later recalled, "We met with a crash; he picked me up and swung me around and kissed me while people on the street and in the windows cheered." ♦ Between Pl Louis-Marin and Rue Gay-Lussac. RER: Luxembourg

167 JEAN-PAUL HÉVIN

Mispronounce this master chocolatier's last name and you have an idea of just how delicious his chocolate confections are: from florentines to flavored ganaches and truffles to fine pastries, this sleek shop is pure choco-heaven. The chocolate leaves, flavored with hazelnuts, pistachios, orange zest, or almonds, are sold by weight and presented in attractive carry-away sachets. The shop on the Right Bank has a second-floor tea salon. Daily, 10AM-7:30PM. 3 Rue Vavin (between Rues d'Assas and Notre-Dame-des-Champs). 01.43.54.09.85. Métro: Vavin. Also at 231 Rue St-Honore (at Rue de Castiglione). M-Sa, 10AM-7:30PM. 01.55.35.35.97. Métro: Palais-Royale-Musée du Louvre.

168 LA TABLE DE FÈS

★★$$ Excellent North African couscous, chicken and lemon *tajine* (stew), and peppery *merguez* (lamb sausage) keep this friendly Moroccan restaurant crowded and hopping. The spicy change of pace from all those buttery French cream sauces is welcome. This spot is best late at night, when things are at their liveliest. ♦ M-Sa, dinner; closed the last 2 weeks of August. Reservations required on Saturday. 5 Rue Ste-Beuve (between Blvd Raspail and Rue Notre-Dame-des-Champs). 01.45.48.07.22. Métros: Vavin; Notre-Dame-des-Champs

168 LE SAINTE-BEUVE

$$$ Ideally situated equidistant from **La Coupole** and the **Luxembourg Gardens**, this handsome hotel was decorated by master designer **David Hicks**. It offers 22 refined and relaxing rooms in various shades of pastel. All are furnished in antiques, with air conditioning, great bathrooms, and cable TV.

There's no restaurant, but drinks are served by the fireplace in the little lobby bar, which, like the rooms, combines comfort with elegance. ◆ 9 Rue Ste-Beuve (between Blvd Raspail and Rue Notre-Dame-des-Champs). 01.45.48.20.07; fax 01.45.48.67.52. Métros: Vavin, Notre-Dame-des-Champs. www.paris-hotel-charme.com

169 26 RUE VAVIN

This luxury terraced apartment building was designed in 1925 by French architect **Henri Sauvage**. The splendid blue-and-white-tile complex, complete with ground-floor shops and indoor parking, was an early attempt at a self-contained building—what Le Corbusier would call a *unité d'habitation*. ◆ Between Blvd Raspail and Rue Notre-Dame-des-Champs. Métros: Vavin, Notre-Dame-des-Champs

Within 26 Rue Vavin:

MARIE · PAPIER

CREATION / MARIE-PAULE ORLUC / 26 RUE VAVIN
75006 PARIS. TÉL : 01.43.26.46.44. FAX : 01.46.34.64.45
e-mail:mariepap@aol.com

MARIE-PAPIER

Attracting customers from Los Angeles to Tokyo, this famous French stationery store sells an elegant line of colored paper in single sheets or large albums. ◆ M-Sa. 01.43.26.46.44

ROUGE ET NOIR

Games galore! This handsome shop sells finely crafted miniature billiard tables, roulette wheels, hand-carved dominoes, Chinese checkers, Monopoly, and, yes, even Trivial Pursuit. Ask to see the reproductions of 15th-through 18th-century playing cards, as well as those with World War I, wine, and old costumes as themes—*les cartes à jouer* are kept in albums and are not on display. ◆ Tu-Sa. 01.43.26.05.77

170 LE SÉLECT

★★$ With its tan walls, kitsch ceiling molding, brown banquettes, and old-fashioned globe lighting fixtures, this café, which opened in 1923, is the least altered of the hangouts favored by Kiki, Foujita, Ernest Hemingway, F. Scott Fitzgerald, Hart Crane, Henry Miller, and other writers and artists in the heyday of Montparnasse. It remains a colorful spot where neighborhood regulars meet for coffee or a drink or to partake of the fine selection of salads, omelettes, and sandwiches. The delicious *croque "Sélect" pain Poilâne complet* (grilled ham, tomato, and egg sandwich on Poilâne sourdough bread) is a meal in itself. Grilled meat and bistro dishes are also served. ◆ M-Sa, 7AM-2:30AM; Su, 8:30AM-2:30AM. 99 Blvd Montparnasse (at Rue Vavin). 01.45.48.38.24. Métro: Vavin

171 DOMINIQUE

★★$$ This restaurant-deli is as Russian as balalaikas. Grab a stool at the counter and snack on smoked salmon, pressed caviar, hot borscht, and blintzes with sour cream. Takeout

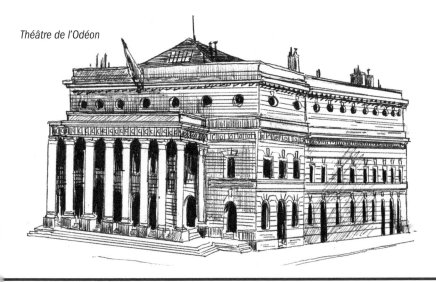

Théâtre de l'Odéon

is available. In the rear is an intimate restaurant for candlelight dining under a portrait of the Czar Nicholas II. ◆ Daily dinner; lunch at bar only. Closed between mid-July and mid-August. Reservations recommended. 19 Rue Bréa (between Blvd Raspail and Rue Notre-Dame-des-Champs). 01.43.27.08.80. Métro: Vavin

172 Académie de la Grande-Chaumière

Any closet Cézannes, budding Bonnards, or rising Renoirs in your traveling party? At this modest art academy you can draw or paint your own masterpiece from live models and carry it home for less than the cost of those imitation Toulouse-Lautrec posters sold on Rue de Rivoli. ◆ Painting and drawing: M-Sa, 9AM-noon. Sketching: M-Sa, 2-5PM. Closed in August. 14 Rue de la Grande-Chaumière (between Rue Notre-Dame-des-Champs and Blvd Montparnasse). 01.43.26.13.72. Métro: Vavin

173 La Coupole

★★$$ Along with Brasserie Lipp and Brasserie Balzar, this is a brasserie with a history. The landmark was the brainchild of **René Lafond** and his brother-in-law **Ernest Fraux**. While working at Le Dôme, Montparnasse's most popular café, in 1926, they took a 20-year lease on a wood-and-coal depot just down the street and transformed it into a huge dining room with red-velvet booths, jazz-age chandeliers, and its most original feature: 33 pillars and pilasters painted by Montparnasse artists. Painter **Alexandre Auffray**, whose studio was nearby, came up with the idea and recruited 31 artists from the *quartier* to do the painting. Lafond paid for the supplies and gave each artist a few good meals as an honorarium. Many had studied under Matisse, Léger, and Friesz, all of whose stylistic influences can be detected. In fact, the Cubist bathing beauty on the second pilaster to the left of the bar was long attributed to Léger but turns out to have been done by his protégé Otto Gustav Carlsund. The most striking images were painted by Marie Vassillief: the elegant black man with a monocle and top hat, and the black rat dancing on the head of a flutist; they can be seen on the two center pilasters on the rear wall. Although these artists never achieved great renown, their paintings burst with the vibrant spirit of Montparnasse when the brasserie opened on the night of 20 December 1927 at the height of *Les Années Folles*.

Purchased for more than $10 million in 1988 and restored by brasserie czar Jean-Paul Bucher, the cavernous dining room has been classified as a historic monument (thus ensuring that its columns will be preserved). The restaurant seats 450 diners, and the tables are full every night. It's a watering hole for politicos, neighborhood merchants, aspiring actors, wandering poets, Scandinavian models, editors, and suburban hordes that invade the Montparnasse movie theaters on weekends, and there's no lack of tourists, of course. It is most chic to make an appearance Sunday night, but on any night the atmosphere will be festive. This is no *restaurant gastronomique*, but the traditional French and brasserie fare is reasonably good and the big seafood bar by the right-hand entrance serves excellent *plateaux de fruit de mer* (seafood platters). A word of caution: The decibel level is high. This is no place for a quiet tête-à-tête.

In the basement is an enormous ballroom where dancers literally kick off their shoes. There is salsa on Tuesday night, 1970s and 1980s music with a live band Friday and Saturday evenings, and tea dancing Saturday and Sunday afternoon. ◆ Restaurant: daily, breakfast, lunch, and dinner, Su-Th, until 1AM, and F-Sa, until 1:30AM. Ballroom: W, 8PM-4AM; F-Sa, 9PM-4AM; tea dancing, Sa-Su, 3-7PM. No reservations taken after 9PM. 102 Blvd Montparnasse (between Rues Delambre and Montparnasse). 01.43.20.14.20. Métro: Vavin

174 Le Caméléon

★★$$ A bohemian bastion for famished painters in the 1960s, this eatery has become a thriving neighborhood bistro serving classic smoked Auvergne sausage, Mediterranean-style cod with *aïoli* (reddish garlic mayonnaise), swordfish on a bed of zucchini, fillet of beef with pink pepper, filet mignon of pork, and a wide selection of salads. Those with a sweet tooth might go for the iced soufflé of fresh mint tea. Splurge on a delicious old Bourgueil wine with your meal. ◆ M-F, lunch and dinner; Sa, dinner; closed the first 3 weeks in August. Reservations recommended for dinner. 6 Rue de Chevreuse (between Blvd Montparnasse and Rue Notre-Dame-des-Champs). 01.43.20.63.43. Métro: Vavin

175 La Closerie des Lilas

★★$$$ Since it opened in 1808, this legendary restaurant where lilacs once bloomed has attracted writers and artists, and the big names can be found engraved on the tables inside. Baudelaire, Verlaine, and Jarry drank here in the 19th century, Paul Fort held weekly poetry recitals in the years before World War I, and the Dadaists and Surrealists met here after the war. But the café is best known as one of Ernest Hemingway's favorite hangouts, where he wrote "true sentences" in notebooks and talked life and literature with John Dos Passos, Archibald MacLeish, and F. Scott Fitzgerald. In *The Sun Also Rises*, part of which Hem wrote here, Lady Brett, Jake, and Bill

Gorton stop in for a drink. Today the place is frequented by young French film stars; people in publicity, communications, and fashion; and writers and artists with money. It's expensive and a bit pretentious but fine for an after-dinner drink or a weekend lunch in the mottled light of its outdoor terrace in August, when the rest of Paris shuts down. Try the steak tartare, *pigeon de Bresse rôti* (roasted pigeon from Bresse), *rumsteck flambé au cognac* (beefsteak flambéed with cognac), or the best-selling *turbotin grillé* (grilled turbot). The piano kindles a certain warmth as well. ♦ Daily, lunch and dinner until 1:30AM. Reservations required. 171 Blvd Montparnasse (between Ave de L'Observatoire and Rue de Chevreuse). 01.40.51.34.50. RER: Port Royal

176 CIMETIÈRE DU MONTPARNASSE (MONTPARNASSE CEMETERY)

The Left Bank's largest cemetery is the final address of many world-renowned writers and artists. Appropriately, Jean-Paul Sartre and Simone de Beauvoir, who dominated the intellectual life of the *quartier* from the end of World War II until their respective deaths in 1980 and 1986, lie side by side to the right as you enter the main gate, along the wall. Other famous writers in graves and tombs along the neat lime tree–shaded alleys are Charles Baudelaire, Guy de Maupassant, Tristan Tzara, Robert Desnos, Josef Kessel (the author of *Belle de Jour*), Samuel Beckett, Marguerite Duras, and songwriter Serge Gainsbourg. Photographer Man Ray, painter Chaim Soutine, sculptor Henri Laurens, composer Camille Saint-Saëns, actress Maria Montez, Captain Alfred Dreyfus of the famous affair, and World War II collaborationist Prime Minister Pierre Laval, executed for treason in 1945, are also here, as is sculptor Frédéric Auguste Bartholdi, the creator of the Statue of Liberty, whose magnificent *Lion of Belfort* can be seen nearby in the center of Place Denfert-Rochereau. The most amusing grave is that of the inventor of a portable petrol-fueled lamp, one M. Pigeon, portrayed full-figure in bronze reclining in bed reading by the light of his lamp, with Mme. Pigeon asleep at his side. A detailed map is free for the asking at the cemetery's entrance. ♦ Daily. 3 Blvd Edgar-Quinet (between Blvd Raspail and Rue de la Gaîté). Métros: Blvds Edgar-Quinet, Raspail

Restaurants/Clubs: **Red** | Hotels: **Purple** | Shops: **Orange** | Outdoors/Parks: **Green** | Sights/Culture: **Blue**

109

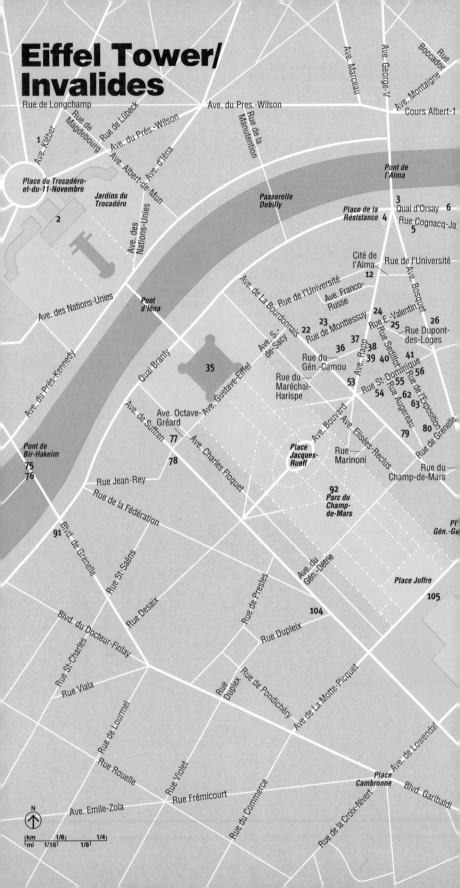

Eiffel Tower/
Invalides

Rue de Longchamp

Ave. du Pres.-Wilson

Ave. Marceau

Ave. George-V

Ave. Montaigne

Rue Boccador

Rue de Magdebourg

Rue de Lübeck

Rue de l'Université

Ave. du Prés.-Wilson

Ave. Albert-de-Mun

Ave. d'Iéna

Rue de la Manutention

Cours Albert-1

1

Ave. Kléber

Place du Trocadéro-
et-du-11-Novembre

Pont de
l'Alma

Jardins du
Trocadéro

Passerelle
Debilly

Place de la
Résistance   4

3

Quai d'Orsay   6

2

Ave. des Nations-Unies

Ave. des Nations-Unies

Pont
d'Iéna

Rue Cognacq-Ja
5

Cité de
l'Alma

Rue de l'Université
12

Ave. Bosquet

Ave. de La Bourdonnais

Rue de l'Université

Ave. Franco-
Russe

Rue E.-Valentin

24

26

Rue de Monttessuy

23

25

Rue Dupont-
des-Loges

Ave. S.
de-Sacy

22

Rue Sedillot

37

Rue du
Gén.-Camou

36

38

Quai Branly

35

Ave. Gustave-Eiffel

39   40

41

55

Ave. Rapp

53

Rue St-Dominique

56

Rue du
Maréchal-
Harispe

54

63

Ave. Octave-
Gréard

Ave. de Suffren

77

Rue de l'Exposition

Ave. Elisées-Reclus

79

80

Rue de Grenelle

Pont de
Bir-Hakeim

75
76

78

Ave. Charles Floquet

Ave. Bouvard

Place
Jacques-
Rueff

Rue
Marinoni

Rue du
Champ-de-Mars

Rue Jean-Rey

Rue de la Fédération

92
Parc du
Champ-
de-Mars

Pl
Gén.-G

91

Blvd. de Grenelle

Rue St-Saëns

Rue Desaix

Ave. du
Gén.-Détrie

Place Joffre

105

Rue de Presles

104

Rue Dupleix

Blvd. du Docteur-Finlay

Rue St-Charles

Rue Viala

Rue
Dupleix

Rue de Pondichéry

Ave. de La Motte-Picquet

Rue de Lourmet

Rue Rouelle

Rue Violet

Ave. de Lowendal

Rue Frémicourt

Rue du Commerce

Place
Cambronne

Blvd. Garibaldi

Ave. Emile-Zola

Rue de la Croix-Nivert

N

km   1/8   1/4
mi   1/16   1/8

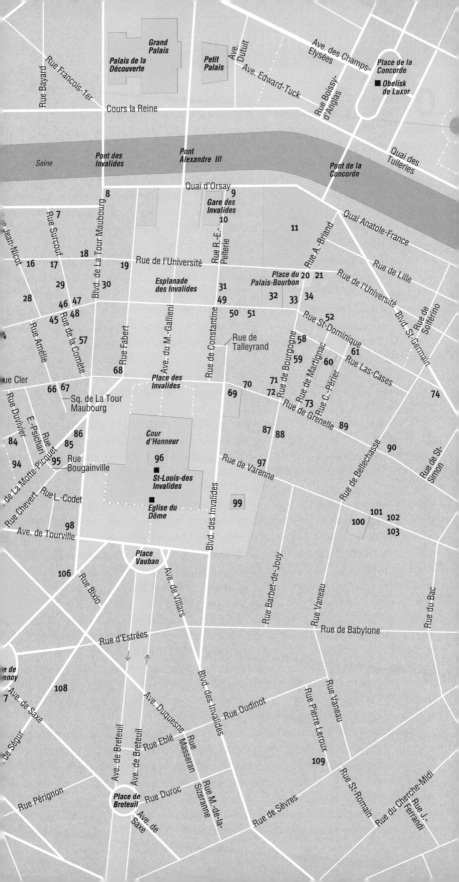

Overshadowed by the lacy mast of the **Tour Eiffel** (Eiffel Tower) and the sparkling gold dome of the **Hôtel des Invalides** (under which rest the remains of Napoléon Bonaparte), this district is one of pomp and grandeur. But nestled among the high-profile monuments are intimate streets lined with fancy food shops that cater to the residents of this upscale *quartier* (neighborhood), and some of the best restaurants in the city.

The following route encompasses two sectors bisected by the **Esplanade des Invalides**. The area to the east of **Les Invalides** is home to the **Assemblée Nationale**, situated in the elegant **Place du Palais-Bourbon**, and is scattered with stately 17th- and 18th-century mansions, including the **Hôtel de Biron**, where the famous sculptor Rodin lived and worked. The mansion is now the **Musée Rodin**.

The affluent neighborhood to the west of the esplanade is dominated by the symbol of Paris, the Eiffel Tower, which forms part of the grand axis from the **Ecole Militaire** along the **Parc du Champ-de-Mars**, and across the river to the **Palais de Chaillot**. To learn some of the secrets of this neighborhood, meander in and out of the side streets off **Rue St-Dominique**, which are lined with exceptional restaurants, small antiques shops, Art Nouveau apartment houses, candy shops, and patisseries; this is also the site of the city's ritziest street market.

Keep in mind that much of this area shuts down in August, when the French take their annual vacation, and many of the restaurants here are closed for Saturday lunch and all day Sunday year-round.

To begin your explorations, set your watch by the clock over the courtyard façade of the Assemblée Nationale in the Place du Palais-Bourbon and grab a breakfast of coffee and croissants alongside publishers, *députés* (parliament members), and diplomats at the **Brasserie Bourbon**. If it's Saturday, you can start with a morning tour of the Assemblée Nationale, France's parliament building. Otherwise, head down the **Rue de Bourgogne**, taking detours onto **Rue de Varenne**, **Rue de Grenelle**, and **Rue St-Dominique** to view the neighborhood's 17th- and 18th-century mansions, including the **Hôtel Matignon** and the **Hôtel de Galliffet**. You may be able to catch only a glimpse of these fancy former residences, however; many of them are now ministries and embassies sequestered behind stone portals and off-limits to the public. Upon reaching the **Hôtel de Biron**, spend the remainder of the morning in the **Musée Rodin**; be sure to take some time to stroll in the garden among some of the sculptor's best-known works.

This district's superb restaurants offer lunch possibilities to fit any pocketbook. Indulge in a meal at one of the neighborhood's elegant and pricey establishments, such as **Arpège**, or cross the Esplanade des Invalides to **Le Divellec** or **Petrossian**. Less expensive but also delicious alternatives are lunch at the classic family-run bistro **Thoumieux** and **La Poule au Pot**; **Bar au Sel** is a good place for fish; or, on the trendy side, try **L'Esplanade**. Those who want to save their three-star appetites (and budgets) for dinner could pick up a light bite at **Café Lunch**.

Spend the early afternoon touring the **Hôtel des Invalides**, a monumental 17th-century complex commissioned by Louis XIV to house the nation's veterans. This ensemble of buildings includes the magnificent Baroque **Eglise du Dôme** (Dome Church), which crowns the burial place of Napoléon Bonaparte, and the **Musée de l'Armée**, with its large collection of military paraphernalia.

Wander west along the Rue St-Dominique and notice its distinctly different character as compared to its sister leg to the east. With the distant Eiffel Tower beckoning as you inal destination, investigate the side streets such as **Rue Surcouf, Rue Malar,** and **Rue Augereau.** Peruse the city's classiest street market along the **Rue Cler** and take in the beautiful displays of produce, baked goods, cheese, *charcuterie,* and flowers. If hunger sets in, stop for a coffee and *pain au chocolat* at **Jean Millet** or stroll a little farther for tea and scones at the lovely *salon de thé* **Les Deux Abeilles.**

As you reach the vicinity of the **Parc du Champ-de-Mars,** stroll among some of the small side streets, which play peek a boo with the Eiffel Tower, noticing the elegant apartment houses along the way. Cross the **Pont d'Iéna** to reach the **Palais de Chaillot,** which houses three museums—the **Musée de la Marine,** the **Musée de l'Homme,** and the **Musée des Monuments Français.** From the building's terrace is a striking view of the Eiffel Tower, sweeping across the **Champ-de-Mars** to the **Ecole Militaire,** the military school that numbers Napoléon Bonaparte as its most famous cadet.

Dining spots abound in this neighborhood; you could end your day with dinner at **Vin sur Vin** or really celebrate Paris with a table at **Le Jules Verne** within the weightless filigree of the Eiffel Tower. Linger after dinner over a good cognac and ponder the glorious nighttime perspective of the City of Light.

1 LA BUTTE CHAILLOT

★★$$ Enter this breezily modern bistro, a stone's throw from the Palais de Chaillot, via an unusual white plastic walkway. But what really sets this restaurant a notch above others in the area is that it's owned by Guy Savoy, whose culinary prowess shines through on a menu that includes, notably, creative fish dishes such as a starter of seared tuna steak with poppy seed, apple-and-celery remoulade, and an entrée of caramelized seabream fillet with a Parmesan-and-vegetable risotto. The place is a good choice for a mid-week lunch. M-F, Su, lunch and dinner; Sa, dinner. 110 bis Ave Kléber (between Pl du Trocadéro and Rue de Longchamp). 01.47.27.88.88. Métro: Trocadéro

2 PALAIS DE CHAILLOT

Perched on its hill across the Seine from the **Eiffel Tower,** this palace serves as the Right Bank termination of the monumental axis that sweeps up across the **Champ-de-Mars** from the **Ecole Militaire.** The white sandstone twin pavilions of the palace were built for the **1937 Exposition Universelle,** replacing the earlier **Palais du Trocadéro,** a massive barrel-shaped building erected for the 1878 exhibition. Although its stark forms and groups of heroic statuary uncomfortably recall the type of fascist architecture that emerged during the period in Germany and Italy, the palace succeeds both as a monument and a cultural complex. Within its two curving wings (which cradle a series of descending gardens and pools) are three museums and a theater, library, and restaurant.

At press time the left wing of the palace was closed for a major renovation; it is expected to reopen sometime in 2003 as the home of the **Cité de l'Architecture et du Patrimoine** (see page 114). The **Musée du Cinéma Henri Langlois** and the screening room of the **Cinémathèque Français,** formerly located in the left wing, are expected to move to the fanciful building designed by **Frank Gehry** for the now-defunct **American Center** in the **Parc de Bercy** in eastern Paris; it has been purchased by the French Ministry of Culture and will reopen as a cinema museum at some yet-to-be-determined date. In the right wing of the palace, the **Musée de la Marine,** the **Musée de l'Homme,** and the **Théâtre National de Chaillot** remain open (see page 114).

The palace's terrace offers a spectacular view of the Eiffel Tower directly across the river. ♦ Pl du Trocadéro-et-du-11-Novembre (between Aves Paul Doumier and du Président-Wilson). Métro: Trocadéro

Within the Palais de Chaillot:

MUSÉE DE LA MARINE

Founded in 1827 by order of Charles X and moved here in 1943, the museum displays magnificent scale models of ships; artifacts and mementos of naval heroes; and exhibits on the scientific and technical aspects of the history of navigation. ♦ Admission. M, W-Su. 01.53.65.69.69; www.musee-marine.fr

THE BEST

Amy Serafin
Editor, WHERE Paris

The neo-Gothic façade of the **Conciergerie** lit up at night, best viewed from the Quai de la Mégisserie.

The **Louvre** museum, an obvious choice but still the best. You could go a thousand times and have a different experience each visit.

Strolling under the arcades at the **Palais Royal** gardens.

Gourmet grocery shopping at **La Grande Epicerie**, behind **Le Bon Marché**. There's always something you didn't realize you absolutely need.

Guy Savoy's artichoke-and-black-truffle soup, so delicious you could eat it as starter, main dish, and dessert.

The falafels at **L'As du Falafel**, on the rue des Rosiers, as good as any you'll find in the Middle East.

The rose-raspberry-litchi "Ispahan" by the world's most incredible pastry chef, Pierre Hermé.

Early morning coffee at the Café de la Nouvelle Mairie, a delightful neighborhood spot in a quiet square in the fifth arrondissement.

Meeting friends at Le Baratin, a lively wine bar in the 20th with simple homecooked meals and an authentic Belleville ambiance.

MUSÉE DE L'HOMME (MUSEUM OF HUMANKIND)

The museum traces human history through a series of anthropological, archeological, and ethnological displays. ♦ Admission. M, W-Su. 01.44.05.72.72; www.mnhn.fr

Within the Musée de l'Homme:

LE TOTEM

★$$ This cavernous restaurant, named for its array of giant totem poles from the owner's native Canada, offers a sensational view of the **Eiffel Tower** across the river. The outdoor dining terrace is one of the most romantic spots in Paris in the late afternoon and evening, when the weather allows. Sophisticated bistro fare is served, or you can stop in for snacks and drinks. ♦ Daily, noon to 1AM. Reservations recommended. Access (at no charge) through the main entrance of the Musée de l'Homme, 17 Place du Trocadéro. 01.47.27.28.29. Métro: Trocadéro

THÉÂTRE NATIONAL DE CHAILLOT

Located beneath the **Palais Terrace**, this theater seats 1,200 people in the main Salle Jean Villar and features productions of mainstream European classics and musical reviews. The 400-seat Salle Gémier stages more experimental works. ♦ Box office: daily. 01.53.65.30.00

Two unwritten rules of etiquette when dining at someone's home in France: Arrive 10 to 20 minutes late for a dinner party, but on time for lunch.

CITÉ DE L'ARCHITECTURE ET DU PATRIMOINE

Scheduled to open sometime in 2003, this museum combines the collections of the **Musée des Monuments Historiques** (which occupied half of this wing before it closed) and the **Institut Français d'Architecture**. This collaboration will present the full history of France's architectural heritage from the Middle Ages to the present. Created in 1880, the older collection was the brainchild of **Eugène Emmanuel Viollet-le-Duc**, who restored **Notre-Dame**, **Mont St-Michel**, and **Carcassone** in the 19th century. Through drawings, models, and reproductions, visitors can trace the development of monumental sculpture, statuary, and mural painting on buildings from the early Romanesque period to the decoration of the great Gothic cathedrals, and, thanks to the newly added collection, follow the story into the 20th century. ♦ Admission. M, W-Su. 01.44.05.39.10

3 EGOUTS (SEWERS)

The *égouts* of Paris are always a popular underground attraction. This 1,305-mile network of tunnels was constructed during the reign of Napoléon III and is considered one of Baron Haussmann's finest achievements. If laid end to end, the tunnels would reach from Paris to Istanbul. The sewers house freshwater pipes, telephone wires, traffic-light cables, and the city's pneumatic postal network, which was shut down in 1984. The hour-long sewer tour includes a film, a photograph exhibition, and a walk through the 18-foot-high by 14-foot-wide tunnels. Ever since a notorious bank heist in which the robbers made their getaway via the sewers, underground boat cruises have not been permitted. ♦ Admission. Sa-W. Quai d'Orsay (at Pont de l'Alma). 01.53.68.27.81. RER: Pont de l'Alma

4 PLACE DE LA RÉSISTANCE

This intersection was named for the French forces who fought to free Paris from Nazi control from 1940 to 1944. RER: Pont de l'Alma

5 RUE COGNACQ-JAY

Opened in 1928, this street bisected the land owned by M. Cognacq and his wife, whose maiden name was Jay. The two were philanthropists and founders of **La Samaritaine** department store. The area between Rue Malar and Avenue Bosquet was occupied in 1910 by an amusement park called **Magic City**, which disappeared in 1925. ♦ RER: Pont de l'Alma

6 53-65, 67-69, AND 71-91 QUAI D'ORSAY

Between 1829 and 1909 this area was the site of a tobacco manufacturing center. A factory specializing in the fabrication of cigars with tobacco from Havana once stood at **Nos. 53-65**; in 1862 it employed more than 700 workers.♦ Between Rue Malar and Pl de la Résistance. Métro: Invalides; RER: Pont de l'Alma

At 65 Quai d'Orsay:

AMERICAN CHURCH

Built in 1931 by **Carrol Greenough** in the Gothic style, this interdenominational church serves the spiritual and social needs of the English-speaking community in Paris. Up to 3,000 people per day come to participate in activities that include AA and Al-Anon meetings, dance and theater classes, gymnastics, judo, and karate. There's an information center for newcomers to Paris open Mondays and Tuesdays between 10 AM and 1PM, plus a bulletin board renowned by apartment hunters for its listings of housing available in the city. There are free classical concerts on Sundays at 6PM, and every Monday at 6PM a free English–French conversation group gathers in the basement. Within the church complex are also the bilingual Montessori and Lenen Schools. ♦ 01.40.62.05.00

7 BAR AU SEL

★★$$ There has always been a café or restaurant on the site that this intimate, friendly eatery has occupied since the beginning of the century. But carnivores beware: Chef Jean-Jacques Philletas serves only seafood. Dublin Bay prawns in "raviolis" with

parsley, fresh salmon carpaccio with basil, and Mont St-Michel mussels are some of the starters; main dishes include sea bass or sea bream *en croûte de sel* (salt-crusted), scallops *à la provençale*, or fresh roasted cod with flavored olive oil. ♦ Daily, lunch and dinner. Reservations required. 49 Quai d'Orsay (at Rue Surcouf). 01.45.51.58.58. Métro: Invalides

8 THIOU

★★★$$ Named for its petite Thailand-born female chef, this restaurant has been a hit since it opened in 2000, as the beautiful ones of *le tout Paris* trailed this former cook at the celebrity-rich **Bains-Douches** nightclub across Paris to her intimate, contemporary-style eatery in the sedate 7th arrondissement. Though she came to Paris to become a pianist, she has made her mark in the art this town appreciates above all others, with some of the freshest, most delicately flavorful Thai cuisine you could hope to find. Among her offerings are assorted hors d'oeuvres, grilled chicken and prawns on bamboo skewers, marinated grilled beef, sautéed shrimp with crispy basil, chicken with green curry, and a score of other treats that this self-trained natural chef learned from her mom in Bangkok.♦ M-F, lunch and dinner; Sa, dinner; closed in August. Reservations required. 49 Quai d'Orsay (at Blvd. de La Tour Manbourg). 01.45.51.58.58 Métro: Invalides

9 MINISTÈRE DES AFFAIRES ETRANGÈRES (MINISTRY OF FOREIGN AFFAIRS)

The façade, roof, grand stairs, and garden statuary of this structure, built by **Lacornée Lacornée** in 1845, are classified with the *Monuments Historiques*. ♦ 37 Quai d'Orsay (between Rues Aristide-Briand and Robert-Esnault-Pelterie). Métro: Invalides

10 RUE ROBERT-ESNAULT-PELTERIE

Since 1965 this street has borne the name of the French astronomical engineer and pioneer of aviation (1881-1957) who lived at 23 Rue de Constantine. ♦ Métro: Invalides

On Rue Robert-Esnault-Pelterie:

GARE DES INVALIDES

At the Air France *aérogare* (air terminal), you can catch a bus to **Orly Airport**, which leaves every 12 minutes; change your Air France ticket; or rent a car at the **Hertz**, **Avis**, or **Europcar** counters. Be forewarned: If you want to drop off a rental here, get very clear instructions about where to park it in the underground garage beneath the Esplanade des Invalides and where to deposit the key in one of the hard-to-find boxes; even the French are confused by the drop-off procedures. ♦ 5 Rue Constantine

11 PALAIS BOURBON/ASSEMBLÉE NATIONALE

The home of the French parliament was constructed in 1728 for the Duchess of Bourbon, one of Louis XIV's daughters. In 1807 **Bernard Poyet** designed the mansion's north façade for Napoléon in the Greek Revival style, to mirror the **Madeleine** across the river; it now houses the **Assemblée Nationale** (the lower house of the French parliament). Nearly 600 deputies convene in a chamber decorated in crimson and gold and adorned with a large Napoleonic eagle. Even the president of France is denied entrance into this exclusive club's assemblies. Ordinary people, however, can watch sessions from a public gallery, provided they have a pass signed by a deputy. If you tour the building, don't miss Delacroix's allegorical *History of Civilization* on the library ceiling. ♦ Free. Guided tours: Sa, 10AM, 2PM, and 3PM; identification necessary; groups must call in advance. To arrange a group tour or to attend an assembly debate (October through June), call the administrative office of the Assemblée Nationale (01.40.63.64.08). Entrance at 33 Quai d'Orsay (between Rues Aristide-Briand and Robert-Esnault-Pelterie). 01.40.63.60.00. Métro: Assemblée Nationale

12 LES DEUX ABEILLES

★★$ Here is a cozy tea salon that feels like a grandmother's cottage, with pink-flowered fabric on the walls, terra-cotta tiles, lace curtains, wooden sideboards, and homemade tarts cooling in the window. The food is substantial and good: omelettes with *cèpes*,

---

The new automated sidewalk in the central transfer tunnel of the Montparnasse-Bienvenue métro station moves at 5.6 miles per hour—three times as fast as the older ones on either side of it. It accelerates as passengers step on and decelerates at the other end, 200 yards later.

But Paris was a very old city and we were young and nothing was simple there, not even poverty, nor sudden money, nor the moonlight, nor right nor wrong nor the breathing of someone who lay beside you in the moonlight.

—Ernest Hemingway, A Moveable Feast, 1964

---

tomato and thyme tarts, and *salade de feuilleté au roquefort* (salad with Roquefort cheese). Desserts include Berthillon ice cream; a light, smooth *tarte Tatin* served with homemade whipped cream; pear-and-rhubarb crumble; and raspberry tart soufflé. Teatime treats include scones with butter and confiture, warm cinnamon brioches, and *chocolat à l'ancienne* (old-fashioned hot chocolate) with cream. Everything is made daily by mother and daughter Anne and Valeria Arella, who opened the tearoom in 1985. They or the soft-spoken waitresses serve steamy hot tea in pink-flowered cups. ♦ M-Sa, breakfast, lunch, and tea until 7PM. 189 Rue de l'Université (between Aves Rapp and Franco-Russe). 01.45.55.64.04. RER: Pont de l'Alma

13 MICHEL CHAUDUN

Once chief *chocolatier* at **Maison du Chocolat**, Chaudun now turns out his own confections. Chocolate Eiffel Towers and Statues of Liberty, *colombes* (white and dark chocolate discs), a white-chocolate Tutankhamen, and several African totem sculptures in dark chocolate are on display. ♦ Tu-Sa; closed in August. 149 Rue de l'Université (at Rue Malar). 01.47.53.74.40. Métro: La Tour Maubourg; RER: Pont de l'Alma

14 BEATO

★★$$ This classy Italian restaurant with colors reminiscent of Siena is popular with good reason: Its savory specialties include *triglie al pesto di basilico risotto al nero* (fillets of red mullet with risotto in octopus ink), spaghetti Stromboli (with olives, capers, and anchovies), *scaloppine al limone* (veal scallopini with lemon), *scampi e zucchine fritti*, and coffee tiramisú. The prix-fixe lunch is a remarkable value. ♦ M-Sa, lunch and dinner; closed 3 weeks in August. 8 Rue Malar (between Rues St-Dominique and de l'Université). 01.47.05.94.27. Métro: La Tour Maubourg; RER: Pont de l'Alma

15 L'AFFRIOLÉ

★★$$ In a relaxed bistro setting, diners can feast on the imaginative cuisine of young chef Thierry Verola, an alumnus of Alain Senderens's, Alain Dutournier's, and Jacques Cagna's distinguished kitchens. Seasonal offerings might include *lisettes* (little mackerel) marinated in lemon, cannellonis of salmon marinated in anise, raviolis of spinach and mushrooms with ginger, breast of guinea fowl with spice bread, and preserved lamb shoulder in pastry with eggplant. ♦ M-F, lunch and dinner; Sa, dinner; closed first 3 weeks of August. 17 Rue Malar (between Rues St-Dominique and de l'Université). 01.44.18.31.33. Métro: La Tour Maubourg; RER: Pont de l'Alma

16 RUE JEAN-NICOT

This street is named after the 17th-century gentleman who introduced tobacco to France. ♦ RER: Pont de l'Alma

16 CONSERVATOIRE MUNICIPAL

With its bold design of intersecting white forms and geometric cutouts, this structure is one of architect **Christian de Portzamparc**'s first well-known projects. After designing it in the 1980s, he went on to the **Café Beaubourg** and, more recently, the **Cité de Musique** at **Parc La Villette**. The building houses the seventh arrondissement's conservatory, where students are trained in music, dance, and dramatic arts. ♦ 135 Rue de l'Université (at Rue Jean-Nicot). Métro: La Tour Maubourg

17 LA POULE AU POT

★★$ "If God grants me a longer life, I will see to it that no peasant in my kingdom will lack the means to have a chicken in the pot (*une poule dans son pot*) every Sunday," promised King Henri IV. At this popular restaurant with prices a peasant could almost afford, you can enjoy comforting chicken stew every day but Sunday (when the restaurant is closed). *Poule* alone does not account for the always-full tables, however. Other tasty options include salad of warm foie gras with cèpes, *filet au poivre* (fillet of beef flambéed with Armagnac and served with Béarnaise sauce), and *andouillette au chablis* (tripe sausage grilled in white wine). Dessert might be *croustillant poires au chocolat* (pear-filled pastry covered with chocolate). Come in anytime for a coffee or a *pression* (draft beer) and a warm welcome at the zinc bar. This restaurant belongs to the Dumond family, who own the equally friendly restaurant **Le Trumilou** on the Quai de l'Hôtel de Ville. ♦ M-F, breakfast, lunch, and dinner; Sa, dinner. 121 Rue de l'Université (at Rue Surcouf). 01.47.05.16.36. Métros: La Tour Maubourg, Invalides

18 PETROSSIAN

Parisians have flocked here since the 1920s for caviar, smoked salmon, foie gras, truffles, and natural and flavored vodkas. Sit down at one of the shop's three tables to sample some of its wares and a glass of champagne in an elegant atmosphere. The shop also sells exquisite silver and crystal caviar bowls and crystal vodka glasses and carafes. ♦ M-Sa. 18 Blvd de La Tour Maubourg (at Rue de l'Université). 01.44.11.32.22. Métros: Invalides, La Tour Maubourg

Within Petrossian:

PETROSSIAN RESTAURANT

PETROSSIAN RESTAURANT

★★★$$$ With its pale gray walls, large mirrors, and ample light from the French windows, this spacious upstairs restaurant shimmers with cool, silvery elegance. As to be expected, there's smoked salmon, foie gras, and caviar galore on the menu, or the risotto sautéed with foie gras or smoked swordfish salad with tomatoes and mozzarella might tempt you. Blini are also a specialty, available with sea scallops and red onions (*St-Jacques poêlées et blin-d'oignons rouge*), shoulder of lamb with dried fruits and raisins (*épaule d'agneau de Lozere confite et blin-palet de fruits secs et raisins*), or other savory melanges. But save room for the "Teaser," a secret dessert made daily and served in special glasses designed by M. Petrossian. ♦ Tu-Sa, lunch and dinner; closed 2 weeks in the middle of August. Reservations required. 01.44.11.32.32

19 LE DIVELLEC

★★★$$$ The tasteful nautical decor of chef Jacques Le Divellec's restaurant leaves no doubt that the focus here is the sea. Le Divellec's book of seafood recipes, *Les Bons Plats de la Mer*, is none too discreetly displayed at the restaurant's entrance foyer. Some of his exceptional dishes include red-tuna and blue-lobster tartare, Dublin Bay prawns steamed in seaweed, pan-roasted mullet with eggplant "caviar," and braised turbot with truffles. For dessert, top the meal off with an iced cognac and a hot-pear and bitter-chocolate soufflé. ♦ M-F, lunch and dinner. Reservations required. 107 Rue de l'Université (at Rue Fabert). 01.45.51.91.96. Métro: Invalides

20 PLACE DU PALAIS-BOURBON

This square boasts an elegant ensemble of Louis XVI buildings constructed in 1776. The

---

Restaurants/Clubs: Red | Hotels: Purple | Shops: Orange | Outdoors/Parks: Green | Sights/Culture: Blue

place is dominated by the main-entrance façade of the Palais Bourbon and a view of its inner courtyard. The façade and courtyard are the only surviving elements of the original mansion. ♦ Rues de Bourgogne and de l'Université. Métro: Assemblée Nationale

21 BRASSERIE BOURBON

★★$$ The seasonally changing Alsatian and fish specialties served here are appreciated by the politicians from the Assemblée Nationale who lunch in the comfortable dining room and on the terrace. A winter meal could start with *moules marinières* (mussels steamed in white wine), foie gras, or *saumon fumé*, followed by sirloin steak with *frites* (french fries) or *saucisson sec de montagne* (dry mountain sausage) and sauerkraut. In spring and summer diners might start with *coquilles St-Jacques à la provençale* (scallops in a sauce of olive oil, garlic, onions, tomatoes, and herbs) or a grilled fish plate. A good bottle of Gewürztraminer or Riesling will bring out the best in any of these dishes. ♦ M-Su, breakfast, lunch, tea, and dinner. Reservations recommended. No. 1 Place du Bourbon (at Rue de l'Université). 01.45.51.58.27

22 PÂTISSERIE DE LA TOUR EIFFEL

★$ Before attempting a trip to the summit of the **Eiffel Tower**, enjoy a novel view of the edifice's east leg from the terrace of this *patisserie*, which doubles as a tea salon. Fortify yourself for the ascent with a hot chocolate and a *tarte de framboise*. Lots of tasty salads, too. ♦ Tu-Su, 6AM-8PM. 21 Ave de La Bourdonnais (at Rue de Monttessuy). 01.47.05.59.81. RER: Pont de l'Alma

22 VIN SUR VIN

★★★$$$ Sunny yellow walls, flowers, and crisp white linen tablecloths on the nine comfortably spaced tables greet diners as they enter this small but oh-so-elegant restaurant. The atmosphere is warm yet discreet, like a private club. As its name indicates, the wine here is even more important than the food. Genial owner Patrice Vidal's list is magnificent, with more than 500 fine French vintages drawing from all the regions of the country; it includes some that are modestly priced. The menu features a seasonally changing array of original dishes. Some past favorites include fresh scallop salad; lamb with slices of bacon, artichoke, and celery purée; *turbot rôti à huile d'olive* (roasted turbot in olive oil); *baba au rhum* with oranges; crème brûlée; and a bitter-chocolate tart. ♦ Tu-F, lunch and dinner; M, Sa, dinner. Reservations required. 20 Rue de Monttessuy (between Aves Rapp and de La Bourdonnais). 01.47.05.14.20. RER: Pont de l'Alma

23 RUE DE MONTTESSUY

This otherwise unremarkable street is impressive for its angular view of one of the **Eiffel Tower**'s legs. The famous monument, usually depicted in its totality, becomes a revelation when seen at such close proximity and from such a refreshing perspective. ♦ RER: Pont de l'Alma

23 AU BON ACCUEIL

★★$$ For gourmet meals at reasonable prices, its location convenient to the **Eiffel Tower**, and the warm welcome its name promises, this place is hard to beat. Chef Jacques Lacipière prepares a new menu daily, depending on what inspires him when he makes his rounds at the **Rungis** wholesale food market at 2AM. Since opening their doors in 1986, he and his gracious wife, Catherine, who oversees the two dining rooms (an airy coral-and-white one in front and the more intimate one in the rear), have built a loyal following of residents of this affluent and famously gourmand arrondissement and staff members of the nearby **American University** and **American Library**. The prix-fixe menu is a real bargain: A typical meal might consist of a starter of crème of lentils with truffles, a main course of sole in lemon butter sauce or roasted young veal with truffles, and, for dessert, roasted apricots in thyme with vanilla ice cream. The wine list matches the sophistication of the cuisine. ♦ M-F, lunch and dinner. Reservations recommended. 14 Rue de Monttessuy (between Aves Rapp and de La Bourdonnais). 01.47.05.46.11. RER: Pont de l'Alma

24 PHARMACIE RAPP

Worth a peek even if you don't need *un adhésif* (adhesive bandage) or *l'aspirine*, this corner pharmacy has an 1899 interior that's a pretty assemblage of delicately carved wood cupboards and reliefs of medicinal plants. Notice the original *pots à pharmacie* (blue glass jars) in the windows. ♦ M-Sa. 23 Ave Rapp (at Rue Edmond-Valentin). 01.47.05.41.25. RER: Pont de l'Alma

25 7 RUE EDMOND-VALENTIN

Irish writer James Joyce lived here between 1935 and 1939. It's still a residential building. ♦ Between Ave Bosquet and Rue Dupont-des-Loges. RER: Pont de l'Alma

26 THE AMERICAN UNIVERSITY OF PARIS

Established in 1962 as an independent arts and sciences institution, this university currently has 112 faculty members and over 800 students from 85 countries. Thirty-five percent of the students are from the United States, many on junior-year exchange programs from other schools. The largest department is international business administration, but the university is also strong in art history, comparative literature, European cultural studies, and international economics. This building houses some of the school's administrative offices, a student café, and some classrooms. The library, which is open only to university students, is located at 9 *bis* Rue de Monttessuy. Other school facilities are at 147 Rue de Grenelle. If you want to sit in on a class or enroll in a summer course, contact the director of admissions (admissions@aup.fr). ♦ 31 Ave Bosquet (between Rues St-Dominique and de l'Université). 01.40.62.07.20; fax 01.47.05.34.32. RER: Pont de l'Alma. www.aup.edu

27 CHEZ L'AMI JEAN

★$$ Here is a Basque restaurant full of sports memorabilia that is frequented by players of rugby and *pelota* (a Basque game similar to jai alai). Owner Jean, himself a former *pelotari* from Basque country, offers paunchy former ballplayers and other patrons such dishes as *confit de canard des Landes* (preserved duck breast), *pot au feu* (boiled beef with vegetables in broth), paella Valenciana, fresh anchovies, foie gras, and Basque-style chicken, along with a selection of regional red wines. ♦ M-Sa, lunch and dinner; closed in August. 27 Rue Malar (between Rues St-Dominique and de l'Université). 01.47.05.86.89. Métro: La Tour Maubourg

28 POUJAURAN

One of the pioneers of the organic bread movement in France, Jean-Luc Poujauran made his name as a young *boulanger* (baker) in the early 1980s with his chewy *baguette biologique* made with organically grown, stone-ground wheat. He also makes a superb sourdough *pain de campagne*, flavored breads (e.g., apricot, fig), and a popular raisin-nut loaf. He is equally famous for his pastries. Poujauran's *galette des rois* is as light and flavorful as that traditional almond cake can get. ♦ Tu-Sa, 8AM-8:30PM. 20 Rue Jean-Nicot (between Rues St-Dominique and de l'Université). 01.47.05.80.88. Métro: La Tour Maubourg

29 LE BELLECOUR

★★★$$ This small, cozy dining room recalls the bistros of days gone and offers classic and refined seasonal Lyonnaise specialties that have earned the owner and co-chef, Gerald Goutagny, a Michelin star. Specialties include pike dumplings, *tablier de sapeur* (breaded, pan-roasted tripe), chicken in vinegar, tartare of oysters and sea scallops, roasted fillet of duck with spices, and iced

vacherin (baked meringue) with grilled coffee cream. TV journalists frequent the place and keep things lively. ♦ M-F, lunch and dinner; Sa, dinner; closed in August. Reservations required. 22 Rue Surcouf (between Rues St-Dominique and de l'Université). 01.45.51.46.93. Métros: La Tour-Maubourg, Invalides

RESTAURANT

Une cuisine de femme

29 AU PETIT TONNEAU

★★$$ Ginette Boyer has been preparing *"une cuisine de femme"* for businesspeople, artists, and locals since 1979. In her cheerful dining room, with its compelling run-down charm, she serves *salade Bressane* (with chicken livers in raspberry vinaigrette), *rognons de veau* (veal kidneys) with Madeira sauce, *châteaubriand au poivre* (with pepper), and chocolate profiteroles. The *plat du jour* of fish changes depending on the day's catch; occasional specials are *coquilles St-Jacques* and *turbot au beurre blanc* (turbot in a butter sauce with vinegar and shallots) with fresh sorrel. There's a nice selection of wines, predominantly from Ginette's native Loire Valley. ♦ Daily, lunch and dinner. 20 Rue Surcouf (between Rues St-Dominique and de l'Université). 01.47.05.09.01. Métros: La Tour Maubourg, Invalides

30 LE MANDARIN DE LA TOUR MAUBOURG

★$ One of many Chinese restaurants that dot the *quartier*, this informal place is always full. Its loyal local clientele appreciates the wide range of Mandarin dishes, including spring rolls, roasted spareribs, spicy Peking soup, Chinese raviolis soup, and roast duck. ♦ M-Sa, lunch; M-Tu, Th-Su, dinner. 23 Blvd de La Tour Maubourg (between Rues St-Dominique and de l'Université). 01.45.51.25.71. Métro: La Tour Maubourg

31 CANADIAN CULTURAL SERVICES

This branch of the Canadian embassy helps Canadian artists find contacts. It often hosts visual-arts shows and theater productions, and changing sculpture exhibits are displayed in the courtyard. There's also a large English–French documentation center that anyone can use. ♦ M, W, F, 10AM-6PM; Th,

---

Restaurants/Clubs: **Red** | Hotels: **Purple** | Shops: **Orange** | Outdoors/Parks: **Green** | Sights/Culture: **Blue**

A Loaf of Bread . . .

From time immemorial, a chunk of bread, supplemented with a bit of cheese or a scrap of meat if they were lucky, was the daily staple that kept poor people alive in France generation after generation. Bread remained the staff of life until widespread prosperity came along in the latter half of the 20th century, and the French moved off in new, vastly expanded dietary directions—and cut back drastically on bread. *Boulangeries* went out of business right and left, and quality declined in the face of public disinterest. But in the 1980s and 1990s, a new wave of artisan *boulangers* came along and reawakened the French taste for bread. They did it through quality bread-making, stimulating the public's taste buds by reviving long-forgotten styles of bread and introducing new ones, such as Lionel Poilâne's now world-famous sourdough bread and Jean-Luc Poujauran's chewy *baguette biologique*. As a result, Paris has become a better bread town than at any time in its history, offering such a stupendous range of original, intriguing, lovingly baked loaves that even French people have a hard time making up their mind what to buy. And they are buying it now for taste rather than survival. To be sure of getting the real thing, shop at a *boulangerie artisinale*—one that chooses its own flour, makes its own dough, and bakes the bread in its own ovens. Since 1997, when the French government passed a law to protect artisanal bakers from big mass-production outfits, no bakery shop has the right to call itself a *boulangerie* unless it meets those demanding conditions.

There are hundreds of kinds of bread available—almost as many as cheeses. To help you cope with the inevitable bread shock, here are some of the main varieties:

baguette: literally "wand," the familiar long, thin French loaf, the bread most commonly served in restaurants, always the same weight (250 grams) no matter what its size

baguette à l'ancienne: old-style baguette

ficelle: "thread," a thin, crusty baguette

flûte: a short, slim baguette

bâtard: "bastard," halfway between a *baguette* and a *pain* (a full-size loaf)

brioche: soft, sweet, puffy bread made with eggs, generally eaten at breakfast

pain biologique: organic bread

pain de campagne: crusty, loaf-shaped rustic white bread, often served with *charcuterie*

pain aux céréales: multigrain bread (with 6, 8, or 12 different kinds of grain)

pain complet: a whole-grain bread; can be any size loaf

pain au froment: made with stone-ground wheat flour

pain aux noix: walnut bread

pain de siegle: dense rye bread, always served with fresh oysters

pain au son: bran bread

pain Poilâne: the big circular sourdough loaf created by Lionel Poilâne, sold whole, in halves, or in quarters all over Paris and all over the world but never better-tasting than the loaves baked at his home *boulangerie* (see below).

Some outstanding *boulangeries*:

Kayser 8 Rue Monge (between Blvd St-Germain and Rue des Bernardins; Métro: Maubert–Mutualité). 01.44.07.01.42

Carton 6 Rue de Buci (between Carrefour de Buci and Rue de Seine; Métro: Odéon). 01.43.26.04.13

Poilâne 8 Rue du Cherche-Midi (between Rue d'Assas and Carrefour de la Croix-Rouge; Métro: Sèvres–Babylone). 01.45.48.42.59

Poujauran 20 Rue Jean Nicot (between Rues de l'Université and St-Dominique; Métro: La Tour Maubourg; RER: Pont de l'Alma). 01.47.05.80.88

René-Gérard Saint-Ouen 111 Blvd Haussmann (at Rue d'Argenson; Métro: Miromesnil). 01.42.65.06.25

Alain Rioux 35 Rue des Deux-Ponts (between Rue St-Louis-en-l'Ile and Quai de Bourbon; Métro: Pont-Marie). 01.43.54.57.59

Hubert 23 Rue Daval (between Rue St-Sabin and Blvd Richard Lenoir; Métro: Bastille). 01.48.05.63.28

10AM-9PM; Sa, 2-6PM. 5 Rue de Constantine (between Rues St-Dominique and de l'Université). 01.44.43.21.90. Métro: Invalides

32 28 Rue St-Dominique

Pierre Lassurance, one of the builders of mansions in the Faubourg St-Germain area, constructed this *hôtel* in 1703. In 1764 it was owned by Maurice de Riquet, Comte de Caraman, who had a celebrated garden that Marie Antoinette visited in 1771 to get some ideas about how to transform her **Jardin de Trianon** at **Versailles**. In 1929 it became the headquarters for the Union Internationale de Chimie (International Union of Chemists). ◆ Between Rues de Bourgogne and de Constantine. Métros: Assemblée Nationale, Invalides

33 Galerie Naïla de Monbrison

If you're looking for a gift or souvenir that's out of the ordinary, you'll find it in this small, narrow jewelry shop and art gallery designed by **Patric Naggar** and **Dominique Lachevsky**. Such unassuming materials as glass, particleboard, oxidized bronze, and lead are fashioned into well-crafted display cases that contrast with and complement the precious materials of the jewelry they contain. Mme. de Monbrison offers a superb collection of ethnographic jewelry, and drawers hold bounties of colorful handcrafted trinkets from Asia, Africa, Siberia, Turkey, and North America. Contemporary art jewelry is also featured in the gallery's expositions. ♦ Tu-Sa; closed in August. 6 Rue de Bourgogne (between Rue St-Dominique and Pl du Palais-Bourbon). 01.47.05.11.15. Métro: Assemblée Nationale

34 MARIE-PIERRE BOITARD

A silver baby rattle, silver key chains with elegant tassels, and fine Hungarian china are displayed on tables draped with fancy brocades and embroidered fabrics and sold by equally resplendent but somewhat serious saleswomen. Check out the hand-painted goblets made especially for the shop by Mrs. Boitard. ♦ M-Sa. Nos. 9-11 Pl du Palais-Bourbon (at Rue de Bourgogne). 01.47.05.13.30. Métro: Assemblée Nationale

35 RUE DE BOURGOGNE

Opened in 1719, this street, named for Louis, Duc de Bourgogne (1682-1712), the son of Louis XIV, originally extended to the quay but was modified in 1778 when the Place du Palais-Bourbon was created. ♦ Métros: Assemblée Nationale, Varenne

34 HÔTEL BOURGOGNE ET MONTANA

$$$ This elegant hotel's name has nothing to do with the state of Montana; its previous owner hailed from Montana, Switzerland. The refined decoration of the 32 rooms is in keeping with the upscale neighborhood. The buffet breakfast offers eggs, omelettes, ham, sausage, and cheese. ♦ 3 Rue de Bourgogne (between Rue St-Dominique and Pl du Palais-Bourbon). 01.45.51.20.22; fax 01.45.56.11.98. Métro: Assemblée Nationale. info@bourgogne-montana.com

34 TANTE MARGUERITE

★★★$$$ The second of renowned Burgundy chef Bernard Loiseau's three Paris "aunts,"

this restaurant exudes a sense of serenity with its rosy wood-paneled walls, comfortable upholstered chairs and banquettes, crisp white tablecloths, and discreetly elegant table settings, and its *cuisine bourgeoise* is prepared and presented with consummate skill. The menu changes daily, but some starters you may encounter are the *soupe de poireaux* (leek soup) with sour cream and croutons or *ragoût d'escargots* (snail stew), main dishes of baked turbot with tarragon sauce or *épaule d'agneau de lait des Pyrénées et cassoulet de hariots tarbais* (casserole of spring lamb and white-bean stew), and for dessert, pears in red wine and *cassis* (black-currant liquor) or the restaurant's famous and incredibly delicious *moelleux au chocolat* (runny chocolate cake). The friendly staff helps make the dining experience a real pleasure. ♦ M-F, lunch and dinner; closed in August. Reservations recommended. 5 Rue de Bourgogne (between Rue St-Dominique and Pl du Palais-Bourbon). 01.45.51.79.42. Métro: Assemblée Nationale. Also: Tante Louise, 41 Rue Boissy d'Anglas (between Rue St-Honoré and Blvd Malesherbes). 01.42.65.06.85. Métro: Madeleine; and Tante Jeanne, 116 Blvd Péreire (between Pl du Maréchal Juin and Rue Eugène Flachat). 01.43.80.88.68. Métro: Péreire

35 TOUR EIFFEL (EIFFEL TOWER)

In 1889, the world was drunk on science. The decade had produced one technological marvel after another: the automobile, the telephone, the electric light, and the **Eiffel Tower**. First dubbed a monstrosity, then considered the definitive symbol of Paris, the tower was built to commemorate the centennial of the storming of the **Bastille** and to stand as the centerpiece of the **1889 International Exhibition of Paris**. The now-classic structure by **Gustave Eiffel** beat 700 other entries in the design competition. (Among the losers, for obvious reasons, were a giant guillotine and a mammoth lighthouse.) The tower was the tallest structure in the world until 1930, when the title was usurped by New York's Chrysler Building. Eiffel, who also engineered the iron bones of that city's Statue of Liberty (undergirding the Frédéric Bartholdi copper structure), was himself a diminutive man, only 5 feet tall.

Spanning 2.5 acres at its base, the tower is made of 18,000 metal parts held together with 2.5 million rivets and covered with 50 tons of brown paint. (The structure is repainted every 7 years and at last count received its 17th coat.) A thousand feet high, it weighs at least 10,000 tons and sways no

---

more than 4.5 inches in strong winds. The weight is distributed so elegantly that it exerts no more pressure on the ground per centimeter than does a stone wall 9 meters high. Three platforms are built into the tower—at 57 meters (187 feet), 115 meters (377 feet), and 276 meters (899 feet)—and elevators and staircases serve each level. There are 1,665 steps to the top level. The overall height is 324 meters (1,062 feet).

When the tower was first completed, much of Paris was unimpressed. Its stark, geometric structure offended the prevailing Beaux Arts sensibility. Prominent critics, including such luminaries as Paul Verlaine, Guy de Maupassant, the younger Dumas, and Emile Zola, denounced it as the "Tower of Babel" and a dishonor to Paris. Maupassant used to say he liked to have lunch at the tower because it was the only place in Paris he didn't have to look at.

In later years it was discovered that the tower could function as the world's largest antenna, and during World War I it became one of France's most vital weapons. Since then, it has served as a radio and meteorological post, and in 1985 was fitted with broadcasting equipment for France's fifth television channel.

A long line of innovative novels that were considered too sexually explicit for US censorship laws were first published in Paris. (Some of these later became the basis of landmark court challenges that struck down those laws.) James Joyce's *Ulysses* was published by Sylvia Beach in 1922 and promptly banned as pornography by the US government. In a famous decision in 1933, US District Court Judge John M. Woolsey lifted the prohibition on the book, stating: "My considered opinion, after long reflection, is that whilst in many places the effect of 'Ulysses' is somewhat emetic, nowhere does it tend to be an aphrodisiac." Henry Miller's *Tropic of Cancer*, a far more blatantly erotic novel, was published by Jack Kahane's Obelisk Press in 1934. It didn't appear in the US, however, until 1964, when the Supreme Court ruled in favor of its being published there. This decision is considered a major step in the liberalization of the US's censorship laws. Other innovative and erotically uninhibited English-language novels originally published in Paris because of restrictive British and US laws are D.H. Lawrence's *Lady Chatterley's Lover*, Lawrence Durrell's *The Black Book*, Henry Miller's *Tropic of Capricorn* and *Rosy Crucifixion* trilogy, Anaïs Nin's *The House of Incest*, Vladimir Nabokov's *Lolita*, J.P. Donleavy's *The Ginger Man*, and William Burroughs's *Naked Lunch*.

Despite these eminently utilitarian applications, the Eiffel Tower's primary effect is to excite the imagination. One man tried to fly from it and was killed when his wings failed him. In 1923 a bicycle-riding journalist careened down the steps to the ground from the top floor. A team of mountaineers scaled it in 1964, an event transmitted live on Eurovision, and in 1984 two Englishmen parachuted from it.

In 1989, a 9-year renovation program was completed in time for the tower's 100th birthday on the bicentennial of the French Revolution. About 1,500 tons of extraneous concrete (mostly in the form of concession areas) were removed from the first platform; four new electronic glass elevators and new visitors' facilities were installed; and the pavilion housing the tower's main restaurant, **Le Jules Verne** (see below), was remodeled. The most dramatic change of all, however, was a modern interior lighting system with 352 sodium lamps inaugurated on New Year's Eve 1986, replacing the old floodlights in the **Champ-de-Mars**. The new lights illuminate the entire structure from within the framework, creating a golden tracery against the sky at night. ♦ Admission varies for each of the three levels. Daily, 9:30AM–11PM, Jan-June, Sept-Dec; daily, 9AM–midnight, mid-June to end of Aug. Ave Gustave-Eiffel (between Aves Silvestre-de-Sacy and Octave-Gréard). 01.44.11.23.23. RER: Champ-de-Mars–Tour Eiffel. www.eiffel-tower.com

Within the Tour Eiffel:

LE JULES VERNE

★★★★$$$$ One of the most beautiful views of Paris, day or night, is from this aerie in the second level of the **Eiffel Tower,** reached by the restaurant's direct private elevator. With the commotion of the city 123 meters below, giant elevator gears turning in silence outside the double-paned windows, and famous monuments in all directions vying for your gaze, the atmosphere here is completely unique. Sleek and seductive, the all-black décor is an elegant backdrop for the restaurant's chic clientele and the creative and refined cuisine of chef Alain Reix. Breast of Bresse chicken in a truffle consommé; baked line-caught sea bass with port *jus* and peas and chickpeas puréed separately with olive oil; skewer of roasted Dublin Bay prawns and grated potatoes with wild mushrooms and vanilla oil; and caramel *fleur de sel* soufflé served with banana *fromage blanc* are just some of the reasons that reservations here, particularly for dinner, are booked months in advance. A fixed-price, three-course lunch menu available during the week is a relative bargain at around $50 per person, but there's no way of getting around a relentlessly pricey wine list. One strategy for securing a table that works: fax the restaurant as far ahead of time as possible and specify your hotel or other phone number while in Paris. Daily, lunch and dinner. Reservations required. Second level (elevator at south pier). 01.45.55.61.44; fax 01.47.05.29.41

ALTITUDE 95

★★$$ This silvery metallic restaurant wedged in among the 19th-century brown steel girders of the first level of the **Eiffel Tower** takes its design inspiration from a 19th-century vision of the future, the interior of a fantasy dirigible: There are shiny bolts on the tables, silver-riveted bucket seats on wheels, and altimeters reminding you of your elevation of 95 meters (312 feet) above sea level. Besides the great view, the restaurant offers honest cuisine at reasonable prices if you stick with the prix-fixe menus that feature dishes from several regions in France. You might start with oysters from Brittany, then have a Franche-Comté–inspired fillet of trout, followed by Provençale goat cheeses, and a dessert of crepes flambéed with Grand Marnier from the Ile-de-France. The wine is overpriced, unfortunately, but parents will be pleased with the inexpensive children's menu. ♦ Daily, lunch, tea, and dinner. Reservations recommended. First level (elevator at north pier). 01.45.55.20.04

36 AMERICAN LIBRARY IN PARIS

Founded in 1920, this is the largest English-language library in continental Europe, with more than 100,000 volumes. Anyone can become a member and partake of a collection that includes fiction, nonfiction, reference books, audio- and videocassettes, a CD-ROM and Internet reference center, more than 450 current periodicals, and 8,000-plus children's books. There's a yearly fee for membership, but visitors can join for as little as a day. A free story hour is held every Wednesday afternoon in the children's room. Roughly once a month, the library hosts Evenings with an Author, a series of talks and readings by well-known English-language writers that is free and open to the public. Short-story writer Mavis Gallant, novelists William Wharton and Diane Johnson, biographer John Baxter, and *New Yorker* writer Adam Gopnik are some of the authors who have appeared in recent years. ♦ Tu-Sa; limited hours in August. 10 Rue du Général-Camou (between Aves Rapp and de La Bourdonnais). 01.53.59.12.60; fax 01.45.50.25.83. RER: Pont de l'Alma. alparis@noos.fr; www.americanlibraryinparis.org

37 LE SANCERRE

★$ Jean-Louis Guillaume's atmospheric wine bar takes its name from the rich, dry, full-bodied Loire Valley wine that he features on his menu. Wine is the primary focus here; the menu offers very simple fare. Snuggle up in the warm, woody dining room and order a bottle with some *jambon fumé* (smoked ham), an omelette, or hot goat cheese on toast. Those who have a problem with the dense cloud of cigarette smoke in the main room can find relief in the *non-fumeur* alcove in the rear. ♦ M-F, breakfast, lunch, and dinner; Sa, lunch; closed 2 weeks in August. 22 Ave Rapp (between Rues du Général-Camou and de Monttessuy). 01.45.51.75.91. RER: Pont de l'Alma

38 PUYRICARD

M. and Mme. Roelandts's shop features delectable chocolates from Aix-en-Provence. Heavenly coconut-praline, raspberry-marzipan, apricot-truffle, and mandarin-orange chocolates are some of the irresistible, award-winning fantasies available here. ♦ M, 2-6:30PM; Tu-Sa, 10AM-6:30PM. 27 Ave Rapp (between Sq Rapp and Rue Edmond-Valentin). 01.47.05.59.47. RER: Pont de l'Alma

38 29 AVENUE RAPP

Paris's prime example of Art Nouveau architecture won designer **Jules Lavirotte** first prize at the Concours des Façades de la Ville de Paris in 1901. A sense of humor can be seen in this apartment building's glazed terra-cotta decoration of animal and flower motifs intermingled with female figures, which was deliberately erotic and subversive for its day. ♦ Between Sq Rapp and Rue Edmond-Valentin. RER: Pont de l'Alma

39 SQUARE RAPP

This small private way was called Villa de Monttessuy before receiving its current name from the neighboring Avenue Rapp. Notice the trompe l'oeil perspective created by the dark green lattice on the building at the end of the street. ♦ RER: Pont de l'Alma

On Square Rapp:

No. 3

Another **Jules Lavirotte** construction, this 1899 apartment building features a wild conglomeration of balconies, railings, glazed-brick and terra-cotta decoration, and a watchtower whose finial seems to be a hybrid of Tintin's rocket and the dome of **Sacré-Coeur**.

SOCIÉTÉ THÉOSOPHIQUE DE FRANCE

This curious and ponderous brick building is the headquarters of the French Theosophical Society. The interior lobby, a cubic space surmounted by a dome, is somewhat reminiscent of the architecture of India but unfortunately comes across as heavy and clunky rather than uplifting and inspirational. The society sponsors some lectures (often on Sunday) and classes in religion and theosophy. ♦ Tu-Sa. 4 Sq Rapp. 01.47.05.26.30

At the Société Théosophique de France:

LIBRAIRIE ADYAR

The society's bookstore stocks volumes about spirituality, psychology, parapsychology, and astrology, with some titles in English. You'll also find candleholders, crystal pyramids, tarot cards, incense, meditation tapes, and anything else you might need to start your journey toward enlightenment. ♦ Tu-Sa. 01.45.51.31.79

40 18 RUE SEDILLOT

The vaguely Baroque overtones of this turn-of-the 19th-century building by **Jules Lavirotte** are typical of the sinuous style employed by the Art Nouveau architect on several Paris apartment buildings. ♦ Between Rues St-Dominique and Edmond-Valentin. RER: Pont de l'Alma

41 DUCHESNE BOULANGER PÂTISSIER

This pastry shop is most notable for its Louis XV–style interior of ornate wood paneling, mirrors, and mosaics, although the selection of pastries also makes it worth a stop. Enjoy a treat and a cup of coffee or tea at one of the four tables. Great sandwiches also. ♦ M-Sa; closed 1 month in summer. 112 Rue St-Dominique (between Rues Dupont-des-Loges and Sedillot). 01.45.51.31.01. Métro: Ecole Militaire

42 ST-PIERRE DU GROS CAILLOU

In 1652 the inhabitants of this neighborhood, then called **Gros-Caillou**, decided that their parish church of **St-Sulpice** was just too far away. It took 86 years to realize, but in 1738 the small chapel of **Notre-Dame-de-Bonne-Délivrance** was erected on this site. The present church, with its austere Doric façade and interior coffered vault, replaced the chapel in 1922. ♦ 92 Rue St-Dominique (at

Rue Pierre-Villey). 01.45.55.22.38. Métro: L Tour Maubourg

43 HÔTEL DE LA TULIPE

$$ This hotel's lively owner, former actor Jea Louis Fortuit, claims that the rooms in his charming hotel were once the cells of monks and that the small rounded structure jutting out into the lush plant-filled courtyard was th chapel. Whatever the story, the atmosphere this cottagelike hostelry is relaxed and friendly, and many of the guests are Fortuit's actor friends. Each of the 22 rooms is slightl different, and many have rustic wood beams and exposed stone walls. There's no restaurant. The name was inspired by a Belgian tul seller who rented the entire hotel for four months during a Salon d'Agriculture in the 1950s. ♦ 33 Rue Malar (between Rues St-Dominique and de l'Université). 01.45.51.67.21; fax 01.47.53.96.37. Métr La Tour Maubourg. www.hoteldelatulipe.com

44 JEAN MILLET

Pastry chef Denis Ruffel makes dreamy hone *madeleines* and croissants, and his *pain au chocolat* has two sticks of chocolate instead of the typical one. Indulge in an afternoon snack of a St-Marc pastry (made with chocolate, Chantilly cream, and a caramelized cookie) and an espresso at one of the invitin tables. There are also sandwiches, salads, and a daily lunch special. ♦ M-Sa; Su, 8AM-1PM. 103 Rue St-Dominique (between Rues Amélie and Cler). 01.45.51.49.80. Métro: L Tour Maubourg

45 81 RUE ST-DOMINIQUE

In the mid-18th century this building housed a cabaret called the **Canon-Royal**. It's now the site of several shops. ♦ Between Rues d la Comète and Amélie. Métro: La Tour Maubourg

45 93 RUE ST-DOMINIQUE

All that's left of the clockmaker's workshop that was on this site in the early 19th centur is its sign, which is composed of three bells, lantern, shells, garlands of fruits and flowers and, of course, a clock. It's classified with th *Monuments Historiques*. The building today a mix of commercial and residential space. ♦ Between Rues de la Comète and Amélie. Métro: La Tour Maubourg

46 BOULANGERIE GISQUET

The interior of this bakery is registered as a historic monument; notice the decorative faïence tiles and the painting on the trompe l'oeil ceiling that depicts a view of the sky from underneath an oval balustrade. Much more re are Mme. Gisquet's enticing country breads, fruit tarts, and macaroons. Don't leave without mille-feuille of pears with a caramelized topping, or a Balkan made with Chantilly cream, *fromage blanc* (sour cream), and raspberries. ◆ M-Sa, 7AM-9PM. 64 Rue St-Dominique (between Rues Surcouf and Jean-Nicot). 01.45.51.70.46. Métro: La Tour Maubourg

46 HÔTEL LE PAVILLON

$$ In 1889, when the **Eiffel Tower** was nearing completion and Paris buzzed in anticipation of the World's Fair, many former monastery and convent buildings became hotels to accommodate the flood of visitors to the city. This one, part of a convent built in 1585 by the Ursuline nuns, once sat in a large open field that extended all the way to the **Seine**. Today it is a humble 18-room hostelry that's inexpensive, well located, and quiet. An arched iron gate and a well-planted courtyard separate the building from the street. Regular guests return year after year. There's no restaurant. ◆ 54 Rue St-Dominique (between Rues Surcouf and Jean-Nicot). 01.45.51.42.87; fax 01.45.51.32.79. Métro: La Tour Maubourg. patrickpavilloon@aol.com

46 HÔTEL SAINT DOMINIQUE

$$ Another former-convent-turned-hotel, this one has 34 well-equipped *chambres*, a breakfast room in the vaulted basement (but no restaurant), and exposed beams in the lobby. The small courtyard has cheerful yellow-painted walls. ◆ 62 Rue St-Dominique (between Rues Surcouf and Jean-Nicot). 01.47.05.51.44; fax 01.47.05.81.28. Métro: La Tour Maubourg. hotel.saint.dominique@ wanadoo.fr

47 RUE SURCOUF

In 1728 this street was called **Rue de la Boucherie-des-Invalides** because a slaughterhouse was located at its terminus on Rue St-Dominique. By 1867 the *boucherie* had disappeared; the street's name was changed to honor corsair Robert Surcouf (1773-1827). ◆ Métros: La Tour Maubourg, Invalides

48 THOUMIEUX

★★$$ For those seeking honest regional fare, here is an authentic bistro that has been in Jean Bassalert's family for more than 75 years. The comfortable dining room, with its sophisticated 1930s charm, glows with the warmth of a place well loved, and attentive but discreet waiters deliver impeccable service. The menu includes many specialties from the La Corrèze region in southwest France and changes daily according to what's fresh at the market. Experiment with a Correzien appetizer such as the earthy *soupe de châtaignes* (chestnut soup) or the *pâté de pomme de terre* (a pastry made with potatoes, pork, and garlic), then have a main course of steak frites, *confit de canard* (preserved duck breast), grilled beef with bordelaise sauce, or *gigot d'agneau rôti* (roast leg of lamb) with ratatouille. Your wine choice might be a lush Bordeaux, such as the Château David 1996, or a Nuits-St-Georges 1997 from Burgundy. For dessert the crème brûlée is warm and velvety, and the *gâteau Thoumieux crème anglaise* (chocolate cake with custard sauce) is as rich and delicious as it sounds. The banquet room is the site of a monthly wine class (normally for groups, but there is often an extra space or two) during which six types of wine are served with six accompanying dishes. There's also a small hotel upstairs (see below). ◆ Daily, lunch and dinner. Reservations recommended. 79 Rue St-Dominique (between Blvd de La Tour Maubourg and Rue de la Comète). 01.47.05.49.75. Métro: La Tour Maubourg

At Thoumieux:

HÔTEL THOUMIEUX

$$ If you can land one of the 10 modern rooms here, you will be surrounded by the amiable young staff members of the restaurant downstairs. You could even indulge in dinner at **Thoumieux** every night! ◆ 01.47.05.49.75; fax 01.47.05.36.96

49 BRITISH CULTURAL CENTER

The aim of the center, which is under the aegis of the British Council, is to promote cultural and scientific links between Great Britain and France by organizing exchange programs for French and British scientists, offering English-language classes, and operating a lending library of English-language books as well as a young learners' center. The council promotes young artists and musicians and brings such British orchestras and theater companies as the Royal Shakespeare Company to France. ◆ Free. M-F, 9:30AM-5:30PM. 9 Rue de Constantine (at Rue St-Dominique). Center: 01.49.55.73.00. Library: 01.49.55.73.23. Métro: Invalides. www.britishcouncil.fr

50 57 RUE ST-DOMINIQUE

This grand mansion, visible through iron gates, is separated from the street by an unpaved courtyard and symmetrical fountains on either side of the entrance. Known as the

Hôtel de Monaco de Sagan, it was built in 1784 by **Alexandre Théodore Brongniart**, for the Princess of Monaco. Until 1825 it was the British Embassy. It was acquired in 1838 by Dutch banker William Hope, who distorted it by raising the first floor, moving the stairs, and adding three dining rooms. Hope also enlarged the grounds, incorporating a little chapel dating from 1706 belonging to the Filles de Ste-Valère. Today the building houses the Polish Embassy. ♦ Between Rues de Bourgogne and de Constantine. Métros: Assemblée Nationale, Invalides

51 53 RUE ST-DOMINIQUE

Today home to the Ministry of Cultural Affairs, this mansion was built in 1770. Past renovations united its garden with that of **Nos. 43** and **55** Rue St-Dominique. ♦ Between Rues de Bourgogne and de Constantine. Métros: Assemblée Nationale, Invalides

52 14-16 RUE ST-DOMINIQUE

The **Hôtel de Brienne**, built in the early 18th century, was the home of Letizia Bonaparte, Napoléon's mother, between 1806 and 1817. Today it is occupied by the Ministry of Defense. ♦ Between Rues de Solférino and de Bourgogne. Métros: Solférino, Assemblée Nationale

53 AVENUE DE LA BOURDONNAIS

Opened in 1770, this avenue once had five entrance gates leading to the **Parc du Champ-de-Mars** along its route. The last survivor, the **Porte Rapp**, existed until 1920. Take time to explore this upscale residential neighborhood by strolling along the short, perpendicular streets (such as Avenue Silvestre de Sacy, Rue du Maréchal-Harispe, and Rue Marinoni) that lead from the **Avenue de la Bourdonnais** into the park. Here beautiful apartment buildings and gardens are set back from the street behind iron gates, and well-heeled women in fur coats walk their well-coiffed dogs. Métro: Ecole Militaire; RER: Pont de l'Alma

53 KNIAZ IGOR

★$$ The atmosphere is all red velvet and balalaika music, and Beluga caviar, borscht with sour cream, chicken Kiev, *roulade de filet de boeuf* (rolled beef fillet), and vodka sorbet are featured menu items at this Russian restaurant. Faded photos of past dinner guest Roman Polanski are proudly displayed in the window. ♦ M-Sa, dinner; closed last 2 weeks of July. Reservations recommended. 43 Ave de La Bourdonnais (between Pl du Général-Gouraud and Rue du Général-Camou). 01.45.51.91.71. RER: Pont de l'Alma

54 ARYLLIS

The master florist in the back room of this flower shop makes artful arrangements out of the long-stemmed roses, tulips, lilies, and ferns sumptuously displayed in urns and baskets. ♦ M-Sa. 141 Rue St-Dominique (at Rue Augereau). 01.47.05.86.26. Métro: Ecole Militaire (RER)

54 LE CHARIOT DU ROY

At first glance one wonders whether the vibrant colors of the fruits and vegetables here are due to trickery with lighting: The strawberries, green beans, pencil-thin asparagus, mangoes, kiwis, kumquats, miniature bananas, and other deluxe fruits and vegetables look too perfect to be real. There's also a cheese counter, a selection of nuts and dried fruits, and assorted delicacies such as quail eggs. ♦ Tu-Sa; Su, 8AM-1PM; closed in August. 145 Rue St-Dominique (between Rue Augereau and Pl du Général-Gouraud). 01.47.05.07.08. Métro: Ecole Militaire

54 DUBERNET

Behind the wood-columned façade is a megaselection of tins and jars of foie gras, *confit d'oie* (goose confit), *boudin blanc truffé* (blood sausage with truffles), pâtés, *pot au feu*, and *gésiers de canard* (duck gizzards). On the last Friday and Saturday of each month, the boutique sells its delicacies at a 25% to 30% discount. ♦ Tu-Sa; closed in August. 2 Rue Augereau (at Rue St-Dominique). 01.45.55.50.71. Métro: Ecole Militaire

55 HÔTEL DE LONDRES EIFFEL

$$ This calm, quiet, 30-room hotel just off Rue St-Dominique has some fifth- and sixth-floor rooms that look out on the top of the **Eiffel Tower**; these are also the smallest rooms on the premises (the double beds are a tight squeeze), but for many that's a small price to pay for a view of Paris's most famous edifice. Continental breakfast (not included in the room rate) is served in the breakfast room; there's no restaurant. ♦ 1 Rue Augereau (at Rue St-Dominique). 01.45.51.63.02; fax 01.47.05.28.96. Métro: Ecole Militaire. info@londres-eiffel.com; www.londres-eiffel.com

55 CHEZ AGNÈS

★★$$ In a homey salon with rows of tables in the front room and a discreet dog named Gipsy in the back, Agnès offers such fare from Les Landes as *salade au foie gras*, *pavé de saumon sauce poivre vert* (salmon steak with green pepper sauce), and *daube Landais* (beef stew with wine and Armagnac sauce). ♦ M-Sa, lunch and dinner; Su, dinner; closed 2 weeks in August. 1 *bis* Rue Augereau (at Rue St-Dominique). 01.45.51.06.04. Métro: Ecole Militaire

56 LA FONTAINE DE MARS

★★$$ Ever popular, Mme. Boudon's gem of bistro is comfortable and cozy, with small dining rooms and a lively atmosphere. Locals keep coming back for the southwest-style cooking. Those looking for light fare might try the warm *pâté de cèpes*, poached fillet of turbot, *sole meunière*, and *pruneaux à l'Armagnac* (prunes in Armagnac), whereas diners with heartier appetites could opt for the *boudin aux pommes* (blood sausage with apples), duck cassoulet, or *carré d'agneau roti au romarin* (roast lamb with rosemary), with a *truffé au chocolat* for dessert. A bottle of Madiran Château Bouscassé or Cahors Château Eugénie will aid in digestion. The outdoor dining terrace on the little square is delightful in warm weather. ♦ M-Su, lunch and dinner. Reservations recommended. 129 Rue St-Dominique (between Ave Bosquet and Rue de l'Exposition). 01.47.05.46.44. Métro: Ecole Militaire

LA FONTAINE DE MARS

56 FONTAINE DE MARS

This freestanding fountain by **Henri Beauvarlet** was once situated in the center of a semicircle of poplars, replaced in 1859 with the present arcaded square. The fountain's bas-relief represents Hygeia, the goddess of health, giving a drink to Mars, the god of war. Between the pilasters are vases encircled by serpents, the symbol of Aesculapius, the god of medicine. ♦ Rues St-Dominique and de l'Exposition. Métro: Ecole Militaire

56 LA CROQUE AU SEL

★$ Two different prix-fixe menus are offered at this turn-of-the-19th-century-style bistro. *Pot au feu* (boiled beef with vegetables in broth) is the specialty, along with *sauté de boeuf* (pan-fried beef), grilled pork chops, and other grilled meats and fish. The high ceilings, whirling fans, and palms give the restaurant a breezy, summery air, and the covered terrace makes a nice dining spot in the warm-weather months. ♦ M-F, lunch and dinner; Sa, dinner. 131 Rue St-Dominique (at Rue de l'Exposition). 01.47.05.23.53. Métro: Ecole Militaire

57 LE BISTROT DU 7ÈME

★★$ The warmth that emanates from this neighborhood bistro may have less to do with the simple, traditional French food it serves than with Argentine Mme. Beauvallet, who, with her husband, owns this cozy spot. Changing daily specials might include *bavette aux échalottes* (steak with shallots), *soupe de poissons* (fish soup), trout meunière, grilled

pork sausage, crème brûlée, iced chocolate charlotte, and a fruit or chocolate tart. The restaurant's only nod to Mme. Beauvallet's Argentine roots is the inclusion of plump little bottles of San Felipe Tinto, an Argentine red wine, nestled among all the Bordeaux, Bourgognes, and Beaujolais. ♦ M-F, lunch and dinner; Sa-Su, dinner. Reservations recommended. 56 Blvd de La Tour Maubourg (between Rues de Grenelle and St-Dominique). 01.45.51.93.08. Métro: La Tour Maubourg

ombeline
Paris

58 OMBELINE

Maud Frizon sold the name of her famous line of haute couture shoes; switched to her married name, Maud de Marco; and opened this shop. However, her stunning and creative footwear still has the same high quality and wild heel shapes that made her original line of shoes famous. ♦ M-Sa. 17 Rue de Bourgogne (between Rues de Grenelle and Las-Cases). 01.47.05.56.78. Métros: Assemblée Nationale, Varenne

59 CAROLE DE VILLARCY

At this tiny boutique you can find top-quality women's haute couture (including clothing by Chanel, Guy Laroche, Yves Saint Laurent, and other designers) from seasons past at a fraction of the original prices. ♦ M, 2-7PM; Tu-Sa; closed in August. 27 Rue de Bourgogne (between Rues de Grenelle and Las-Cases). 01.45.51.28.38. Métros: Assemblée Nationale, Varenne

60 BASILIQUE STE-CLOTHILDE

This neo-Gothic church, designed in 1846 by Christian Gau, was the first of its kind to be built in Paris. It is the product of mid–19th-century enthusiasm for the Middle Ages, inspired by such writers as Victor Hugo. The church is notable for its prominent twin towers, a landmark visible from across the river. Composer César Franck was organist here from 1858 until his death in 1890, and a monument commemorating him stands in the pretty neighborhood park opposite the church. ♦ 23 bis Rue Las-Cases (between Rues Casimir-Périer and de Martignac). 01.44.18.62.60. Métro: Solférino

61 LE SQUARE

★★$$ On this forbidding stretch of Rue St-Dominique dominated by Ministry of Defense buildings, the one refuge for conviviality is this bar and restaurant owned and operated by an enterprising group of young friends. At the long modern brass bar, you can pop in for coffee or a drink anytime, or you can settle down for a bite in one of the airy, contemporary dining rooms with hand-rubbed tan-ocher walls and handsome conical wrought-iron lighting fixtures. Like the décor, the cuisine's accent is southern: risotto with mussels, gnocchis with salmon, spinach salad with raw mushrooms and Parmesan cheese, chicken stew with lemon, *filets de rougts* (little red mullet), and duck's breast roasted with figs. ♦ M-Sa, lunch and dinner. Reservations recommended. 31 Rue St-Dominique (at Rue Casimir-Périer). 01.45.51.09.03. Métro: Varenne

62 CAFÉ DE MARS

★★$$ This relaxed café has a sunny décor and a welcome to match, thanks to the warmth of Solange and Laurence. They offer grilled vegetables with olive oil, chicken wings with barbecue sauce, a choice of carpaccios with mashed potatoes, Peruvian beer, and a rich chocolate cake for dessert. On weekends, students from the nearby **American University of Paris** come here to unwind. ♦ M-F, lunch and dinner; Sa, dinner; closed 2 weeks of August. 11 Rue Augereau (between Rues de Grenelle and St-Dominique). 01.47.05.05.91. Métro: Ecole Militaire

63 AUBERGE DU CHAMP DE MARS

★$ Michel Duclos wears the chef's hat while his wife, Madeleine, plays host in this softly lit, red-velvet-upholstered restaurant. The prix-fixe, three-course menu includes such appetizers as avocado and smoked salmon salad or *escargots à la bourguignonne* (snails with butter, garlic, and parsley), a main course of *poulet Normandie* (chicken in a mushroom cream sauce) or turbot in hollandaise sauce, and a dessert of profiteroles with warm chocolate sauce or warm apple tart. ♦ M-F, lunch and dinner; Sa, dinner; closed 2 two weeks in August. 18 Rue de l'Exposition (between Rues de Grenelle and St-Dominique). 01.45.51.78.08. Métro: Ecole Militaire

64 THE REAL McCOY

Longing for Pop-Tarts, Reese's Peanut Butter Cups, marshmallows, a peanut butter–and–jelly sandwich, or a sesame-seed bagel? You've come to the right place. This tiny grocery also has five small tables for homesick North Americans and local aficionados of exotic treats from across the Atlantic. ♦ Daily. 194 Rue de Grenelle (between Rue Cler and Ave Bosquet). 01.45.56.98.82. Métro: Ecole Militaire

65 RUE CLER

At Paris's most exclusive street market you'll see the best-dressed shoppers in town choosing from the colorful, bountiful displays of butchers, bakers, *fromagers* (cheese sellers), greengrocers, wine merchants, and florists that spill out onto the cobblestone street. This market, like most, is especially lively on Saturday morning. ♦ Tu-Sa, morning. Between Ave de La Motte-Picquet and Rue de Grenelle. Métros: Ecole Militaire, La Tour Maubourg

65 LE REPAIRE DE BACCHUS

This small wine shop has a big selection of *grands vins français*, as well as many labels from small regional producers. The salespeople are expert wine counselors, able to offer advice on just the right wine to have with a particular dish or to help you select something for your wine cellar back home. You could try an inexpensive bottle of Vieille Ferme Côte du Ventoux 1999, with its distinct perfume of wood and raspberries, or splurge with a Château Lethil 1998 that envelops the mouth with its refined flavors. The shop also carries over 60 types of whiskey, including some rare bottles. ♦ Tu-Sa; Su, morning. 29 Rue Cler (between Rues du Champ-de-Mars and de Grenelle). 01.45.56.99.99. Métro: Ecole Militaire. Also at 147 Rue St-Dominique (between Rue Augereau and Pl du Général-Gouraud). 01.45.51.77.21. Métros: Ecole Militaire, La Tour Maubourg

65 FROMAGERIE CLER

Bleu de Bresse, creamy chèvre, and Morbier are just a few of the cheeses sold at this well-stocked shop that you could design a picnic around. ♦ Tu-Sa; Su, 8AM-1PM. 31 Rue Cler (between Rues du Champ-de-Mars and de Grenelle). 01.47.05.48.95. Métros: Ecole Militaire, La Tour Maubourg

66 ST-JEAN

This small Lutheran evangelical church was built in the neo-Gothic style in 1911; the interior is intimate and full of light, with a timber ceiling of boat hull construction. In 1990 the **American University** took out a 50-year lease on the land directly behind the church and constructed a new building to house its classrooms, computer lab, and faculty offices. The university's main building is located at 31 Avenue Bosquet. ♦ 147 Rue de Grenelle (between Sq de La Tour Maubourg and Cité du Général-Négrier). Métro: La Tour Maubourg

67 SQUARE DE LA TOUR MAUBOURG

Dating from 1897, this peaceful private drive is decorated with an ornamental pool that matches one in the Place François-1er across the river. ♦ Métro: La Tour Maubourg

café *de l'*esplanade

68 L'ESPLANADE

★★$$ Decorated by star designer **Jacques Garcia** (no minimalist, he), the long vaulted dining room is lined with upright replicas of 17th-century cannons with fanciful iron chandeliers with clusters of cannonballs overhead, all painted black, with broad swaths of gold trim here and there and reddish velvet *Directoire* chairs for dashes of color. The large glass doors, which are opened in fine weather, offer grand views of the **Hôtel des Invalides**, as do the tables on the *terrasse*. The food is World: spinach salad, shrimp soup with coconut milk, melted goat cheese and light Provençal vegetable soup, risotto with spicy shrimps, swordfish with coriander, duck breast with Szechwan pepper. Or you can simply have an omelette or a club sandwich. Unlike the resolutely international *carte*, the small, astute selection of wines is entirely French. Opened in the fall of 2000, this is one of the latest additions to the Costes brothers' classy and rapidly expanding hotel and restaurant empire. The clientele is chic, but not oppressively so, and the attractive young waiters and waitresses are efficient and cordial. ♦ Daily, 8AM-1AM. Reservations recommended. 52 Rue Fabert (between Rues de Grenelle and St-Dominique). 01.47.05.38.30. Métro: La Tour Maubourg

69 HÔTEL DU CHÂTELET

This mansion is a fine example of the Louis XV style, built in 1770 for the Duc du Châtelet, who was later beheaded in *la Terreur*. It was confiscated in 1796 to house a civil engineering school. In 1835 it became the Turkish embassy, in 1843 the Austrian embassy, and from 1849 to 1906 it was the Archbishop's Palace. Since then it has housed the Ministry of Employment. The courtyard façade is ornamented with four composite columns supporting an entablature and balustrade that extend along the whole façade. Several of the salons have their original Louis XV and XVI decoration, and the arched porte cochere is in the Tuscan style. ♦ 127 Rue de Grenelle (at Blvd des Invalides). Métro: Varenne

70 HÔTEL DU CHANAC DE POMPADOUR

Designed by architect **Pierre-Alexis** in 1704, this mansion has housed the Swiss Embassy since 1938. Inside is a subterranean swimming pool, surrounded by 20 Tuscan columns, with five niches for statues. Unfortunately, it is open to the public only 2 days a year, on the *journées du patrimoine*, the third Saturday and Sunday of September. ♦ 142 Rue de Grenelle (between Rues de Bourgogne and de Talleyrand). Métro: Varenne

71 CLUB DES POÈTES

★★$ "*La poésie est vivante. Vive la poésie!*" (Poetry is alive. Long live poetry!) proclaims Jean-Pierre Rosnay, well-known French poet and owner of this dimly lit, cozy restaurant where actors read works by poets from all over the world in the evenings. There are French poems from poets Villon to Boris Vian and North American verses from Walt Whitman to Lawrence Ferlinghetti and Jack Kerouac. Diners savor leek and vegetable pie, pâté, *salade Drômoise* (with tomatoes, St-Marcellin cheese, and walnuts), *grillade St-Tropez* (beef with tomatoes and herbs), and *gâteau de Sarah* (chocolate cake from an old family recipe). Rosnay's wife and son are both poets, and together the family puts out a poetry journal three times a year, runs a radio station devoted to poetry, and started the Festival of Poetry in Paris. Visitors from the US will enjoy a warm welcome here; Rosnay, a Resistance fighter during World War II, loves North Americans. ♦ M-Sa, lunch and dinner; closed in August. Reservations recommended. 30 Rue de Bourgogne (between Rues de Grenelle and St-Dominique). 01.47.05.06.03. Métros: Assemblée Nationale, Varenne

Trenta Quattro
Ristorante Italiano

72 TRENTA QUATTRO

★★$$ Charming Francesca Ciardi serves delectable Italian fare in her cozy dining room. Ricotta-and-spinach ravioli, risotto with blueberries and cèpes, and veal in white wine or lemon Marsala sauce are all worthy dishes. If you have any room left at the end of the meal, share the rich zabaglione and blueberries with your dinner companion. ♦ M-F, lunch and dinner; Sa-Su, dinner. Reservations recommended. 34 Rue de Bourgogne (at Rue de Grenelle). 01.45.55.80.75. Métro: Varenne

73 CAFÉ LUNCH

★$ This busy little lunch counter might be more at home at San Francisco's North Beach than among the mansions of this stately neighborhood. There's a selection of panini—try the Sicilian (with tomatoes, mozzarella, basil, and olive oil); various salads; quiche of the day; and such desserts as *tarte au citron* (lemon tart), apple crumble, and brownies. The cappuccino is made with aromatic and rich Segafredo brand coffee beans. Order from the take-out window or eat inside at the counter. ♦ M-Sa, breakfast and lunch until 5:30PM. 130 Rue de Grenelle (at Rue de Martignac). 01.45.55.15.45. Métro: Varenne

74 RUE ST-DOMINIQUE

Between 1355 and 1643 this street had nine different names; its present appellation comes from a monastery for Dominican novices that was once located here. The street originally stretched to Rue des Sts-Pères, but a large portion of it was amputated to make room for the opening of Boulevard St-Germain in 1866. Rue St-Dominique is more like two streets: The segment to the east of Esplanade des Invalides—often called St-Dominique–St-Germain—is characterized by fine *hôtels particuliers* that now hold government offices and can rarely if ever be visited; the sector to the west of the esplanade—known as St-Dominique-Gros-Caillou—is largely a local shopping street that offers glimpses of the **Eiffel Tower** along its course. ♦ Métros: Solférino, Invalides, La Tour Maubourg

74 5 RUE ST-DOMINIQUE

The 18th-century **Hôtel de Tavannes**, once the property of the **Dames de Bellechasse** religious order, housed the important literary salon of Sophie Soymonof, wife of General Svetchine and known as the Russian Mme. de Sévigné, between 1818 and 1857 that was frequented by many distinguished personalities. Illustrator **Gustave Doré**, who had his atelier nearby at 27 *bis* Rue de Bellechase,

George Gershwin loved Paris and visited it as often as possible. He attended the Paris premieres of *Rhapsody in Blue, Concerto in F,* and *An American in Paris.* He wrote part of the last here and also bought French taxi horns to simulate the sound of the traffic.

lived here from 1832 until his death in 1883. The private mansion is one of the few in the city that's open to the public (albeit for a limited time and just the courtyard and staircase). It has an elegant arched doorway surmounted by a scallop and crowned by a triangular pediment. Inside there's a fine stair well with a wrought-iron balustrade. ♦ Daily, 9:30AM–noon, 2:30-6PM, 20 Aug-30 Sept. Between Blvd St-Germain and Rue de Bellechasse. Métro: Solférino

75 PONT DE BIR-HAKEIM

Along the top of this double-decker bridge runs one of the only aboveground métro lines in Paris, which provides a spectacular view of the **Eiffel Tower** as it is approached from the **Seine**. Board at the **Passy** station, just across the river, and travel toward **Nation**. The lower bridge is for pedestrians. It was constructed in 1903 to replace an inadequate pedestrian bridge, the Pont de Passy. In 1949 it was named for the 1942 Battle of Bir-Hakeim in the Libyan desert, when the Free French forces held off Rommel's armored divisions. ♦ Métros: Passy, Bir-Hakeim

76 ALLÉE DES CYGNES

A small narrow islet that divides the **Seine** provides a pleasant promenade from the Pont de Bir-Hakeim to the Pont de Grenelle with a view of **Radio France** (a modern building that housed the **French Broadcasting Service** until 1975) on the Right Bank and the **Front de Seine** (a modern urban-renewal project integrating high-rise apartment and office towers, public buildings, and a shopping center) on the Left Bank. On the upriver side of Pont Bir-Hakeim is a 1930s equestrian statue named **La France Renaissante** by Danish sculptor **Wederkinch**, and downriver of the Pont de Grenelle is a small replica of the **Statue of Liberty** donated by the North American community in Paris in 1885. ♦ Métros: Passy, Bir-Hakeim

Ribe

77 CHEZ RIBE

★★$$ The exquisite wood paneling dates from 1900, but the specialties on Jean-Antoine Père's prix-fixe menu are as fresh as can be. Start with tartare of smoked salmon, then try the swordfish or tuna (*espadon* or *thon*) with olive oil, or the *carbonnade flamande* (beef cooked in beer). For dessert, order the *délice viennois* (coffee mousse). ♦ M-Su, breakfast, lunch, and dinner; closed in August. Reservations recommended. 15 Ave de Suffren (at Ave Octave-Gréard).

01.45.66.53.79. RER: Champ de Mars–Tour Eiffel

78 AVENUE DE SUFFREN

Like Avenue de la Bourdonnais, this avenue opened in 1770 as a perimeter road around the **Parc du Champ-de-Mars**. It was named after Vice Admiral Bailli Pierre André de Suffren (1726-1788), the justice administrator of St-Tropez and commander of the Ordre de Malte, who fought for the Americans during the Revolutionary War. ♦ Métros: La Motte-Picquet-Grenelle, Segur, Sevres-Lecourbre; RER: Champ-de-Mars-Tour Eiffel

78 PARIS HILTON

$$$$ Built in 1966, this sleek, International-style hotel has 11 stories of concrete and glass and a vast, airy marble-floored lobby. It looks more like a corporate headquarters than a Parisian luxury hotel, but then, the hostelry makes no pretensions to Old World grandeur. Set in a quiet park overlooking the **Eiffel Tower** and the **Palais de Chaillot**, it offers 462 first-rate modern rooms and suites, along with several conference rooms and ballrooms. The 10th and 11th floors are the executive floors, with a private lounge and other extras. ♦ 18 Ave de Suffren (at Rue Jean-Rey). 01.44.38.56.00; fax 01.44.38.56.10. RER: Champ-de-Mars-Tour Eiffel. www.hilton.com

Within the Paris Hilton:

PACIFIC EIFFEL

★★$$ Reckoning that Paris has all the French restaurants it needs, this eatery has placed its emphasis on a different culinary appeal: California cuisine, enlivened by touches of the Mediterranean and the Far East, with grilled fish and meat from the rotisserie featured. There is an attractive all-you-can-eat buffet at both lunch and dinner. The wines come from California, Australia, and South Africa, with a good selection from the main wine regions of France. The restaurant is a big, rambling double-decker with a cheerful red, blue, and yellow color scheme, and its sweeping white metal staircase with pipe banisters gives it the feel of a modern cruise ship. Although the restaurant is on the ground floor of the hotel, it has a separate entrance and identity. ♦ Daily, breakfast, lunch, and dinner. 01.44.38.57.77, 01.44.38.56.00

LE BAR SUFFREN

The staff at this comfy English-style bar with Robert Doisneau photos on the walls have invented some novel cocktails, including the Aristobar (vodka, champagne, and wild strawberry liqueur) and the nonalcoholic Soleil Rouge (fresh grapefruit and orange juice, lemonade, and grenadine). Croissants and coffee are served in the morning, and snack service is offered all day. There is a terrace for alfresco sipping in good weather. ♦ Daily, 10AM-2AM. 01.44.38.56.00

LE TOIT DE PARIS

★★$$ "The rooftop of Paris," this grill on the hotel's top floor offers a superb view of the nearby **Eiffel Tower**. It is open to the public only on Sunday, for a champagne brunch buffet featuring main courses of lobster, prime rib, and salmon, and a large selection of salads and pastries. ♦ Su, 11AM-3PM. 01.44.38.56.00

79 DÉCEMBRE EN MARS

A large variety of stuffed animals, Bauhaus blocks, Annette Himstadt dolls, hobbyhorses, spinning tops, wooden trains, and wonderful French hand puppets are just a few of the colorful delights sold in this little toy store. ♦ Tu-Sa; closed in August. 65 Ave de La Bourdonnais (between Rue de Grenelle and Pl du Général-Gouraud). 01.45.51.15.45. Métro: Ecole Militaire

80 RUE DE L'EXPOSITION

Formerly known as the Passage de l'Alma, this quiet, narrow street received its current name at the time of the **1867 Exposition Universelle**. ♦ Métro: Ecole Militaire

80 HÔTEL DE L'ALMA

$$ A comfortable 31-room hotel on a calm street offers all the modern conveniences and makes no attempt at false charm. The lobby is pleasantly decorated with rattan furniture. Many North Americans stay here. ♦ 32 Rue de l'Exposition (between Rues de Grenelle and St-Dominique). 01.47.05.45.70; fax 01.45.51.84.47. Métro: Ecole Militaire. almahotel@minitel.net

81 DAVOLI

Also known as La Maison du Jambon (The House of Ham), this shop has Parma hams hanging from the ceiling and is literally stuffed with sausages and such take-out dishes as lasagna, salads, and an assortment of tarts. It also sells marvelous *choucroute*, the Alsatian sauerkraut specialty. ♦ Tu, Th-Sa; W, Su, 8AM-1PM; closed 15 July-15 August. 34 Rue Cler (between Rues du Champ-de-Mars and de Grenelle). 01.45.51.23.41. Métro: Ecole Militaire

82 CAFÉ DU MARCHÉ

★★$ Escape the bustling Rue Cler street market by ducking into this cordial and very

---

popular café for a quick coffee at the attractive copper bar, or stay for a lunch of *confit de canard*, farm chicken, or supersize fresh salads. You can also order a crepe at the little stand outside and eat it at a table inside. ◆ M-Sa, 7AM-midnight; Su, 11:30AM-3PM. 38 Rue Cler (at Rue du Champ-de-Mars). 01.47.05.51.27. Métro: Ecole Militaire

83 HÔTEL CHAMP-DE-MARS

$ You'll wake up to the Rue Cler market when you stay at this charming 25-room *hôtel familial*. Adding to the appeal are the accommodating young owners; the friendly resident spaniel, Chipie; and the unbeatable prices. There's a downstairs breakfast room with high-backed tapestry-covered chairs; breakfast can be served in rooms. **No. 2** and **No. 4** have small terraces. There's cable TV but no restaurant. ◆ 7 Rue du Champ-de-Mars (between Rue Cler and Ave Bosquet). 01.45.51.52.30; fax 01.45.51.64.36. Métro: Ecole Militaire. stg@club-internet.fr; www.hotel-du-champ-de-mars.com

83 RAGUT CHARCUTERIE

The mouthwatering take-out dishes displayed here make it difficult to leave empty-handed. Choices include trout with almonds, langoustine thermidor, paella, bouillabaisse, avocado stuffed with shrimp or crab, quiche lorraine, Hungarian goulash, beef brochettes, spinach in cream, coq au vin, duck with peaches—the list goes on and on. ◆ M-Sa. 40 Rue Cler (at Rue du Champ-de-Mars). 01.45.51.29.35. Métro: Ecole Militaire

84 3 RUE DU CHAMP-DE-MARS

Buzz yourself into the entrance foyer of this Art Nouveau apartment house to see how the leaf-and-lily design that appears on the façade's masonry and on the iron gates is repeated in the lovely tile mosaic on the floor. ◆ Between Rues Duvivier and Cler. Métro: Ecole Militaire

85 LE CHAMBRELAIN

The hand-painted Limoges porcelain dishes here are exquisitely decorated with fruits, flowers, and fish and come in handsome black gift boxes that accentuate the precious quality of this expensive tableware. Those on tighter budgets might consider buying dishes decorated by the traditional method known as

décalcomanie; you can take home a set adorned with artichokes, rutabagas, pea pods, roses, and irises for about half the price of the hand-painted porcelains. Chambrelain has been in the business since 1946 and had a big workshop that supplied **Bergdorf Goodman** and **Neiman Marcus** before he decided to scale down to this smaller boutique. The smell of turpentine permeating the shop emanates from the backroom atelier where Mme. Marteau gives courses in hand-painting porcelain. ◆ M-F; closed in August. 11 Ave de La Motte-Picquet (between Rue Bougainville and Blvd de La Tour-Maubourg). 01.45.55.03.45. Métro: La Tour Maubourg

86 CAFÉ MAX

★$ One of the only beacons in this nighttime desert is this cozy French bistro that's particularly animated on Saturday nights. The place is agreeably dingy, with banquettes, mismatched chairs and tables, and such flea-market memorabilia as a stuffed swordfish and street signs on its red walls and wooden shoe lasts hanging from the ceiling. Jovial owner Max, who speaks very good English, presides over the dining room while his wife, Lili, rules in the kitchen. The food is simple and includes *cassoulet landais* (a casserole of duck confit, garlic, sausage, beans, and ham), Lyons sausages, ham and potato salad, and *tarte Tatin* (apple tart). For an aperitif, order a kir Max, the house cocktail made with sparkling white wine and crème de cassis. ◆ M, dinner; Tu-Sa, lunch and dinner; closed in August. Reservations recommended 7 Ave de La Motte-Picquet (between Rue Bougainville and Blvd de La Tour Maubourg). 01.47.05.57.66. Métro: La Tour Maubourg

87 HÔTEL DE VARENNE

$$ The entrance to this tranquil hotel is through a flower-filled courtyard with white iron garden furniture. Guests staying in the 24 fresh, pretty rooms can have breakfast alfresco in the spring and summer. There's no restaurant. ◆ 44 Rue de Bourgogne (between Rues de Varenne and de Grenelle). 01.45.51.45.55; fax 01.45.51.86.63. Métro: Varenne. hotel.varenne@wanadoo.fr; www.hotelvarenne.com

Le Garde Manger

88 LE GARDE MANGER

★★$$ In the back of this little wine and gourmet-food boutique you can take a table alongside *députés* from the **Assemblée Nationale** and staff members of the **Musée Rodin** to savor a lunch of foie gras or smoked salmon from the shop's shelves. Changing *plats du jour* might include salmon with curry, Perigord cassoulet (bean and meat stew), and sautéed veal, and such desserts as crème brûlée and *tarte aux pommes* (apple tart). Try one of the fine wines—perhaps the Bordeaux Pessac Léognan—with your repast. ♦ Restaurant: M-F, lunch; Sa, lunch and dinner. Shop: M-F, 10AM-6PM. Closed in August. Reservations required. 51 Rue de Bourgogne (between Rues de Varenne and de Grenelle). 01.45.50.23.93. Métro: Varenne

89 PETIT HÔTEL DE VILLARS

This *hôtel* with elegant twin garlanded oval windows was constructed in 1712 by **Germain Boffrand**, as an addition to the 1709 mansion he built next door, at **No. 116**, for the Duc de Villars. It is now the Lycée Paul Claudel, a private high school. ♦ 118 Rue de Grenelle (between Rues de Bellechasse and Casimir-Périer). Métros: Solférino, Varenne

90 TEMPLE DE PENTÉMONT

This handsome Baroque chapel was built by **Constant d'Ivry** in 1750 for the Abbaye de Pentémont, a convent where Joséphine de Beauharnais, future wife of Napoléon, lived for several years. The convent's main buildings (some are still visible at 37-39 Rue de Bellechase) housed an aristocratic school, famous for educating young ladies from the noble families of Paris. Thomas Jefferson's daughter was a student here when he was America's ambassador to France between 1785 and 1789. The church can only be visited during the weekly services at 10:30AM Sundays and on the French national *Journées du Patrimoine*, the third Saturday and Sunday of September. ♦ 104-106 Rue de Grenelle (between Rues de St-Simon and de Bellechasse). Métro: Rue du Bac

91 8 BOULEVARD DE GRENELLE

A plaque records the roundup of thousands of Parisians, most of them Jews, in the *vélodrome* (cycling track) here on 16 July 1942 before their deportation to Nazi concentration camps. Of the approximately 150,000 adults and 20,000 children arrested by the Germans and the cooperating Paris police, only 3,000 adults and 6 children survived. The *vélodrome* was demolished in 1959. ♦ Métro: Bir-Hakeim

92 PARC DU CHAMP-DE-MARS

🔟 Named for the god of war, this large rectangular park stretching from the **Ecole**

Militaire to the **Eiffel Tower** has long been a site of battles, both actual and preparatory. Here, in 52 BC, Roman legions defeated the Parisii; in 886 the Parisians beat back the invading Vikings; and, in the early 18th century, when this was the parade ground for the Ecole Militaire, Napoléon drilled with his fellow cadets. Now the park, adorned with flowering trees, shrubs, and miniature cascades, is the site of pony rides, marionette theaters, organ-grinders, occasional parades for children, and Christmastime fairs and pageantry. You can do almost anything in the **Champ-de-Mars** except have a picnic on the lawns. French grass is sacred grass, and a bluecoat (guard) will appear and order you off before you've even had time to unwrap your salami and uncork the Bordeaux. ♦ Bounded by Allées Adrienne-Lecouvreur and Thomy-Thierry, and Pl Joffre and Ave Gustave-Eiffel. Métro: Ecole Militaire; RER: Pont de l'Alma, Champ-de-Mars-Tour Eiffel

93 HÔTEL RELAIS BOSQUET

$$ The automatic sliding doors are the first tip-off that this 40-room establishment is strong on modern conveniences and limited in the charm department. However, you can count on a comfortable stay enhanced by CNN, hair dryers, and an iron and ironing board in your room. Some of the fifth- and sixth-floor rooms have a view of the tip of the **Eiffel Tower**. All rooms have electric blackout window shades for late-night revelers. There's no restaurant, but the breakroom really is divided into smoking and nonsmoking sections. ♦ 19 Rue du Champ-de-Mars (between Rue Cler and Ave Bosquet). 01.47.05.25.45; fax 01.45.55.08.24. Métro: Ecole Militaire. hotel@relaisbosquet.com; www.relaisbosquet.com

94 LE LUTIN GOURMAND

This candy shop with the whimsical name (it means "gourmet imp") has something for everyone: glass cases full of colorful hard candies and mints, lollipops shaped like animals and hearts; tempting hazelnut treats called *feuilletés aux noisettes*. ♦ Tu-Sa. 47 Rue Cler (between Ave de La Motte-Picquet and Rue du Champ-de-Mars). 01.45.55.29.74. Métro: Ecole Militaire

95 AU LIÉGEUR

Cork is the name of the game here: cork trivets, sheets of cork, corkscrews, and just plain old corks that come from the company's (what else?) cork factory. The shop carries a nice assortment of decanters, decorative corks, and the coveted *bouchon universel*, a cork specially designed to fit bottles of all sizes. Other than cork, there are maps of wine routes and exquisite Riedel wine glasses for sale. ♦ Tu-Sa; closed in August. 17 Ave de La Motte-Picquet (between Rue Bougainville and Blvd de La Tour Maubourg). 01.47.05.53.10. Métros: Ecole Militaire, La Tour Maubourg

95 RESTAURANT LE CHAMP DE MARS

★★$$ At this comfortable restaurant you might start with Normandy oysters, then have a main course of stuffed duck with green-pepper sauce, roast lamb with herbs, or a variety of fish dishes, followed by a dessert of nougat ice cream with *coulis de framboises* (raspberry sauce) and *profiteroles au chocolat*. ♦ Tu-Su, lunch and dinner; closed mid-July to mid-August. Reservations recommended. 17 Ave de La Motte-Picquet (at Rue Bougainville). 01.47.05.57.99. Métros: Ecole Militaire, La Tour Maubourg

96 HÔTEL DES INVALIDES

Louis XIV ordered **Libéral Bruant** to erect this monumental group of buildings to house the king's old soldiers, many of them invalids who had been reduced to begging or seeking shelter in monasteries. When the *hôtel* was completed in 1676, 6,000 aging pensioners moved in. It is still used as a home for old soldiers, though only 100 or so still live here. The year after its completion, the Sun King (Louis XIV's nickname, derived from his brilliance and his fondness for gold) commissioned a second church for the complex, which was built by **Jules Hardouin-Mansart**. Attached Siamese-twin–style to **Bruant**'s original church, **St-Louis-des-Invalides**, the **Eglise du Dôme** (Dome Church) is one of the most magnificent Baroque churches of the **Grand Siècle**. Its dome is decorated with garlands and crowned with a 351-foot-tall spire.

France's bravest soldiers and greatest warriors are entombed in the Eglise du Dôme: Turenne, Vauban, Duroc, Foch, and, of course, Napoléon. "I do not think that there is a more impressive sepulchre on earth than that tomb; it is grandly simple," wrote Theodore Roosevelt of Napoléon's resting place. "I am not easily awestruck, but it certainly gave me a solemn feeling to look at the plain, red stone bier which contained what had once been the mightiest conqueror the world ever saw."

Concealed by the outward simplicity of the red porphyry tomb, Napoléon's remains are contained in seven coffins, one inside the other, made of iron, mahogany, lead, ebony, oak, and marble. Napoléon was originally interred on the island of St-Helena, where he died in 1821. The British finally agreed to repatriate his remains in 1840, thus fulfilling the emperor's wish to be buried "on the banks of the Seine among the people of France whom I have loved so much." The tomb of Napoléon's son, the king of Rome, who died in Vienna at age 21, sounds a morbid footnote to history. In 1940 his remains were given to Paris in a grandiose gesture by a heady Hitler.

Bruant's church, St-Louis-des-Invalides, where the occupants of the *hôtel* worshiped, is separated by a glass barrier from the domed edifice. One of the church's most impressive features is the collection of captured banners hanging from the upper galleries. Among these tattered mementos of French military victories there is even the flag with the rising sun of Japan, a relic of World War II. In 1837 Berlioz's Requiem was performed here for the first time.

Visitors enter St-Louis-des-Invalides from the **Cour d'Honneur**, an impressive courtyard also designed by Bruant. This is where French army officer Alfred Dreyfus was publicly disgraced and where de Gaulle kissed Churchill. The statue of Napoléon by Seurre, which used to be on the top of a column in Place Vendôme, now stands in this courtyard. Among the other Napoleonic memorabilia exhibited here are the emperor's death mask, his dinner jacket, and the dog, now stuffed for posterity, that was his companion during his years on the island of Elba. ♦ Admission. Daily. Pl Vauban 01.44.42.37.72. Métros: Invalides, La Tour Maubourg, Varenne, St-Francois-Xavier. www.invalides.org

Within the Hôtel des Invalides:

MUSÉE DE L'ARMÉE (ARMY MUSEUM)

At the north end of the **Invalides** complex, this museum houses one of the largest collections of military paraphernalia in the world. Swords, guns, suits of armor, flags, and other articles are on display, along with innumerable models, maps, and images that trace the evolution of warfare from prehistoric times through World War II. Understandably, Napoleonic souvenirs are most conspicuous, but there are also intriguing exhibitions of medieval, Renaissance, and Asian militaria, and the new wing devoted to World War II, opened in 2000, offers a fascinating and well-balanced view of the progress of the war in Europe, the Soviet Union, and the Pacific. The story of France's national anguish is recounted in detail through excellent maps, models, photos, audiovisual displays, uniforms, weapons, and other well-chosen memorabilia from the Fall of France in 1940 and General de Gaulle's famous broadcast from London, through the rise of *La Résistance*, the landings in Normandy and Provence, and the eventual *Libération* and defeat of the Nazis. ♦ Admission. Daily. Pl des Invalides (between Blvds des Invalides and de La Tour Maubourg). 01.44.42.37.72. Métros: Invalides, La Tour Maubourg, Varenne, St-Francois-Xavier. www.invalides.org

97 RUE DE VARENNE

The name of this street, like that of Rue de Grenelle, evolved over time from the word *garenne* (rabbit warren); **Rue de Varenne** was laid out in 1605 along a *garenne* belonging to the abbey of **St-Germain-des-Prés**. Today, the street is lined with ministries and foreign embassies housed in attractive old mansions. Métros: Varenne, Rue du Bac, Sèvres–Babylone

97 ARPÈGE

★★★★$$$$ Daring but respectful of tradition, chef Alain Passard executes a brilliant menu that includes *crème de truffe du Périgord noir aux oeufs* (egg mousse with thin slices of Parmesan cheese and truffles); lobster, removed from its shell, with sweet-and-sour rosemary sauce and candied turnips; or braised sole in white wine with candied sweet onions and lemon grass. Desserts include *Guanaja et Manjari moelleux au basilic* (a very black chocolate cake with a liquid interior served with basil ice cream) and his most famous invention, *tomate confite farcie aux douze saveurs* (candied red tomato stuffed with fresh and dried fruits, roots, and spices, served with anise ice cream). The wine list is one of the best in Paris. The skillful servers may add the final touches to dishes at your table. The mood of the small dining room is modern and subdued, with low lighting, wood paneling, sumptuous carpets, and classical-style nude figurines in crystal. Many gourmets consider this the greatest restaurant in Paris. ♦ M-F, lunch and dinner. Reservations required. 84 Rue de Varenne (between Rue de Bourgogne and Blvd des Invalides). 01.45.51.47.33. Métro: Varenne

98 LE MAUPERTU

★★$$ This intimate spot will convince you that dining in Paris can indeed be both grand and affordable. The décor is a blend of terra-cotta and marble and the menu is pleasing to the palate. The expertly prepared French specialties include *mille-feuille de torteau aux crevettes* (crab and shrimps in a flaky pastry) and *ravioli de champignons au coulis de cèpes* (ravioli stuffed with wild mushroom with a sauce of cèpes). Such desserts as wafer-thin slices of chocolate and white-chocolate mousse served with light egg custard are superb. There's also an excellent wine list. Reserve a table under the glass roof, with its lovely view of the gilded dome of the **Hôtel des Invalides**; it's especially splendid at night. ♦ M-F, lunch and dinner; Sa, dinner. Reservations recommended. 94 Blvd de La Tour Maubourg (between Ave de Tourville and Rue Louis-Codet). 01.45.51.37.96. Métro: Ecole Militaire

99 MUSÉE RODIN

The **Hôtel de Biron**, which houses this museum, is a Regency masterpiece of columns and pediments originally built in 1730 by **Jean Aubert** and **Jacques-Ange Gabriel** for a wealthy wigmaker named Abraham Peyrenc. In 1753 it was bought by the Maréchal-Duc de Biron, who indulged quite a passion for gardening in the years before he went to the guillotine during the Reign of Terror; he spent 200,000 *livres* each year on tulips alone. During an unfortunate stint as a convent school, the *hôtel's* gold-and-white wood paneling was ripped out by the mother superior, who deemed it too Baroque and materialistic.

The Hôtel de Biron was subsequently subdivided into a cluster of artists' studios. In 1908, Auguste Rodin (1840-1917) moved in and stayed until his death. His neighbors in the *hôtel* included Rainer Maria Rilke, Jean Cocteau, Isadora Duncan, and Henri Matisse.

After viewing the ground-floor exhibits of Rodin works, which include *The Kiss*, bear left and gradually spiral upstairs. The works are displayed chronologically, beginning with Rodin's academic paintings and his sketches in both classic and modern modes. Notice that Rodin usually depicts only right hands; the one exception to this rule is *The Hand of the Devil*, which shows Satan's left hand crushing humanity.

The room containing Rodin's *Sculptor with His Muse* also displays several works by Camille Claudel, the talented sculptor who became Rodin's muse, model, and lover at the age of 17. Her portrait of Rodin, executed in 1888 at the peak of their affair, when he was nearly 50, reveals a rather cold man with small eyes.

Upstairs is a series of studies of Balzac created in the early 1890s. In one of them, a

---

Restaurants/Clubs: Red | **Hotels: Purple** | Shops: Orange | **Outdoors/Parks: Green** | Sights/Culture: Blue

bronze, the writer stands stark naked and is 90% paunch. In the final version, which stands at the corner of Rue Vavin and Boulevard Montparnasse, Rodin draped Balzac in a concealing cloak.

The museum also has a number of fine paintings that belonged to the artist, including a portrait of Rodin by Sargent, three superb van Goghs (*Le Père Tanguy*, *Vue du Viaduc d'Arles*, and *Les Moissoneurs*), Monet's *Belle-Ile*, and Renoir's *Femme Nue*.

The lovely garden, the third largest of any of the *hôtels* in Paris (after those of the **Elysée Palace** and the **Hôtel de Matignon**), provides the setting for some of Rodin's best-known works, *The Thinker*, *The Burghers of Calais*, *The Gates of Hell*, and, on an island in the center of the pool, the *Ugolin* group. On 30 January 1937, Helen Keller visited here and was permitted to touch the sculptures with her hands. Of *The Thinker*, she said: "In every limb I felt the throes of emerging mind." Keller said the sculpture of the *Burghers of Calais*, who surrendered their lives to the English to save their city, was "sadder to touch than a grave."

The museum's tree-shaded **cafeteria** in the garden is a serene spot for lunch or refreshments in clement weather. ◆ Admission. Tu-Su. 77 Rue de Varenne (between Rue Barbet-de-Jouy and Blvd des Invalides). 01.44.18.61.10. Métro: Varenne. www.musee-rodin.fr

101 HÔTEL DE GOUFFIER DE THOIX

Built in 1719 for the Marquise de Gouffier de Thoix, this *hôtel particulier* was confiscated during the revolution and later won in a lottery by a jeweler. The family of the original owners returned to Paris in the 19th century to reclaim it. Notice the magnificent doorway surmounted by a shell carving. It is now a government administration building. ◆ 56 Rue de Varenne (between Rues du Bac and de Bellechasse). Métros: Rue du Bac, Varenne

102 HÔTEL DE GALLIFFET

This handsome 1739 mansion, with an Ionic peristyle facing the interior courtyard, is the only important *hôtel particulier* from the Faubourg St-Germain's 18th-century heyday that you can easily visit. Now housing the Istituto Italiano di Cultura (Italian Cultural Institute), its library, *médiathèque*, Italian language courses, art exhibitions, concerts, and lectures are open to the public. Visitors who just want to look at the mansion and its lovely garden are welcome. Many of the rooms have their original decoration, and the stairwell is ornamented with false windows framed by Ionic columns and lit by a cupola. Be sure not to miss the magnificent eight-column peristyle in the interior courtyard. ◆ M-F, 9:30AM-1PM and 3-6PM. 50 Rue de Varenne (between Rues du Bac and de Bellechasse). 01.44.39.49.39. Métros: Rue du Bac, Varenne. www.iicparis.org

100 HÔTEL MATIGNON

Behind the immense *porte cochere* flanked by two pairs of Ionic columns is one of the most beautiful mansions in the city, built by **Jean Courtonne** in 1721. Inside are beautiful salons sumptuously decorated in period styles, the largest private garden in Paris, and a music pavilion. Former owners include Talleyrand, the diplomat who lived here between 1808 and 1811 and held infamous parties and receptions, and, later in the century, Mme. Adelaïde, the sister of Louis-Philippe. Since 1958 it has been the residence of the French prime minister. It's off-limits to the public except for *les Journées du Patrimoine* (Patrimony Days), the third Saturday and Sunday of September. ◆ 57 Rue de Varenne (between Rues du Bac and Vaneau). Métros: Rue du Bac, Varenne

103 HÔTEL DE BOISGELIN

This mansion was constructed in 1732 by **Jean Sylvain Cartaud** and has been the Italian Embassy since 1938. The general public may visit it only on the third Saturday and Sunday of September, *les Journées du Patrimoine*. ◆ 47 Rue de Varenne (between Rues du Bac and Vaneau). Métros: Rue du Bac, Varenne

106 AUBERGE D'CHEZ EUX

★★$$$ In the shadow of the **Hôtel des Invalides**, Jean-Pierre Court and his father have specialized in a *cuisine familiale* from France's southwest since 1963. The restaurant's enclosed terrace is draped with red-and-white-striped fabric and is a perfect spot for feasting on the homemade *foie gras d'oie* (goose-liver pâté), which comes with a glass of Château Loubens Bordeaux Blanc; *cuisses de grenouilles provençales* (frogs' legs sautéed in olive oil, garlic, and tomatoes); *magret de canard* (sliced fresh roasted duck breast) with honey vinegar; roast lamb chops; or *pavé de saumon d'Ecosse poêlé sauce Béarnaise* (sautéed Scottish salmon steak with Béarnaise sauce). Wines are reasonably priced; the Cahors Château Lagineste would be a good choice with any of the meat dishes. ◆ M-Sa, lunch and dinner; closed 3 weeks in August. Reservations recommended. 2 Ave de Lowendal (at Blvd de La Tour Maubourg). 01.47.05.52.55. Métro: Ecole Militaire

104 74 AVENUE DE SUFFREN

During the **1900 Exposition Universelle**, this was the site of the **Grande Roue de Paris**, a 350-foot Ferris wheel (one-third the height of the **Eiffel Tower**). The wheel had 40 wooden cars divided into five series of 8 cars; it took five stops, boarding 8 cars at a time, to load the whole wheel. In what is perhaps a metaphor for the French mentality, each 8-car unit was composed of 6 second-class cars, 1 first-class car, and a restaurant. The Ferris wheel's axis was supported by two pylons set in concrete foundations; between them was a garden that was the site of a theater, restaurant, hotel, several souvenir stands, and a number of duels. Today the area is built up with a variety of structures, none as fanciful as the late lamented Ferris wheel. ♦ At Rue Dupleix. Métro: La Motte-Picquet-Grenelle

05 ECOLE MILITAIRE

In an attempt to rival the **Hôtel des Invalides** of Louis XIV, Louis XV and his mistress, Mme. de Pompadour, hired **Jacques-Ange Gabriel**, the architect who created the Place de la Concorde in the 1770s, to design a military school. Raising money for the project was a problem until Beaumarchais, who wrote *The Marriage of Figaro* and gave harp lessons to Louis XV's daughters, came up with the idea of paying for the building through a lottery and a tax on playing cards. Standing at the foot of the **Champ-de-Mars**, the school, with its Corinthian columns, statues, dome, double colonnade, and elegant wrought-iron fence, is one of Gabriel's masterpieces. The most famous graduate of the school, which is still in operation, was Napoléon Bonaparte. He spent a year here and left as a lieutenant when he was 16 with the comment on his report card: "Will go far if circumstances permit." ♦ By appointment only. For information write to Direction Générale, Ecole Militaire, 1 Pl Joffre, 75007 Paris. 1 Pl Joffre (at Ave de La Motte-Picquet). No phone. Métro: Ecole Militaire

07 UNESCO SECRETARIAT

This building was designed by architects from three member countries: **Bernard Zehrfuss** of France, **Luigi Nervi** of Italy, and **Marcel Breuer** of the US. When it was built in the late 1950s, the headquarters of the 158-member **United Nations Educational, Scientific, and Cultural Organization** was a hopeful symbol of a new era of international cooperation. The main building with its three crescent glass-and-concrete wings in the shape of a Y is a veritable time capsule of cutting-edge architecture of that period. Likewise, its art collection is a treasure trove of works by mid-20th-century masters: Henry Moore's *Reclining Figure*; a black metal Calder mobile; two ceramic walls executed by Artigas after designs by Miró; a sculpture by Giacometti; a fresco by

Tamayo; a relief by Jean Arp; and a mural by Picasso, *The Victory of the Forces of Light and Peace over the Powers of Evil and Death*. An enchanting Japanese garden has a fountain designed by Noguchi. The gift shop in the lobby has a fine selection of handicrafts from around the world. Visitors must present their passports to pass through security. ♦ M-F. Group tours by appointment. 7 Pl de Fontenoy (between Aves de Saxe and de Lowendal, directly across the square from the Ecole Militaire). 01.45.68.10.00. Métros: Ségur, Cambronne, Ecole Militaire. www.unesco.org

108 LES OLIVADES

★★$$ Avignon-born chef Flora Mikula trained under grand master Alain Passard at **Arpège** before opening her sunny Provençal bistro in this otherwise somber part of town. It is favored by the **UNESCO** crowd, Americans in Paris, and others with a taste for light, healthy olive oil–based cuisine. Some of her specialties are rockfish soup with croutons and aioli (a garlicky blend of eggs and olive oil), quail preserved in olive oil, grilled sea bass with truffle-laced mashed potatoes, and roast lamb with roasted garlic cloves. The fresh goat cheeses from the Alps of Provence are superb. For dessert try the soft chocolate cake with lavender ice cream. There's a fine selection of wines from the South of France. ♦ Tu-F, lunch and dinner; M, Sa, dinner. Reservations recommended. 41 Avenue de Ségur (between Rues de Saxe and Duquesne). 01.47.83.70.09. Métro: Ségur

109 CHEZ GERMAINE

★★$ Slightly off the beaten track but well worth the effort to get there, this friendly seven-table eatery offers perhaps the best food for the money of any restaurant in Paris. And for this swanky *quartier*, the prices are truly amazing. The menus change every day, but some savory family-style offerings that may be on it when you go there are leeks *vinaigrette*, a steaming plate of lentils, roast pork with sage, *brandade de morue* (garlicky purée of salt cod and potatoes), and *lapin chasseur* (rabbit roasted with wine and mushrooms), and for dessert, delicious *clafoutis*, soft tarts made with apples or other fruits. If cherries are in season, be sure to choose the *clafoutis aux cerises*. The house wine is inexpensive and good. If you're alone, expect to be seated at a table with fellow diners. They don't make 'em like **Chez Germaine** anymore. ♦ M-F, lunch; and dinner; Sa, lunch; closed in August. No smoking; no credit cards. 30 Rue Pierre Leroux (between Rues de Sèvres and Oudinot). 01.42.73.28.34. Métros: Vaneau, Duroc

Restaurants/Clubs: Red | Hotels: Purple | Shops: Orange | Outdoors/Parks: Green | Sights/Culture: Blue

The Louvre and
the Champs-Elysées

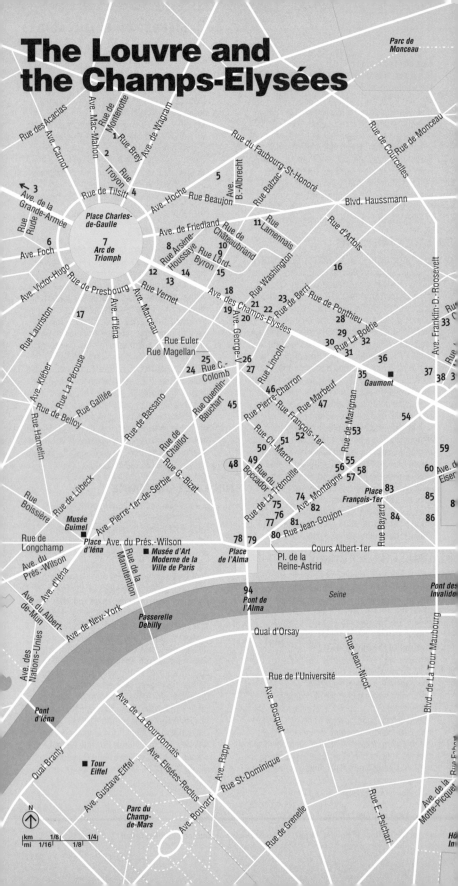

Parc de Monceau

Rue des Acacias
Ave. Mac-Mahon
Rue de Montenotte
Ave. de Wagram
Rue Brey
1 Rue Brey
Ave. Carnot
2
Rue de Monceau
Rue de Courcelles
Rue du Faubourg-St-Honoré
Rue Troyon
Rue de Tilsitt 4
3
Ave. de la Grande-Armée
Rue Rude
5
Ave. B.-Albrecht
Rue Balzac
Ave. Hoche
Rue Beaujon
Blvd. Haussmann
Place Charles-de-Gaulle
7
Arc de Triomph
6
Ave. Foch
Ave. de Friedland
Rue de Chateaubriand
Rue Lamennais
11
Rue d'Artois
8
Ave. Arsène-Houssaye
10
Rue Lord-Byron
15
Rue Washington
16
12
13
14
Ave. Victor-Hugo
Rue de Presbourg
Rue Vernet
Ave. Marceau
18
Ave. des Champs-Elysées
Rue Washington
23
Rue de Berri
Rue de Ponthieu
17
21
22
19
20
28
Ave. Franklin-D.-Roosevelt
33
Rue Lauriston
Ave. d'Iéna
Rue Euler
Rue Magellan
25
26
Ave. George-V
Rue Lincoln
29
30
Rue La Boétie
31
32
36
37
38
Ave. Kléber
Rue La Pérouse
Rue Galilée
24
Rue C.-Colomb
27
35
Gaumont
Rue de Belloy
Rue de Bassano
Rue Quentin-Bauchart
45
46
Rue Pierre-Charron
Rue Marbeuf
47
Rue de Marignan
53
54
Rue Hamelin
Rue de Chaillot
Rue Cl.-Marot
51
Rue François-1er
52
Rue Boissière
Rue de Lübeck
Rue G.-Bizet
48
50
49
Rue du Boccador
55
56
57
58
59
60
Ave. d' Eisen
Musée Guimel
Ave. Pierre-1er-de-Serbie
Rue de La Trémoille
74
Ave. Montaigne
Place François-1er
83
85
8
Rue de Longchamp
Place d'Iéna
Ave. du Prés.-Wilson
Rue de la Manutention
Musée d'Art Moderne de la Ville de Paris
75
76
77
81
82
84
Rue Bayard
86
Ave. du Prés.-Wilson
78
79
80
Rue Jean-Goujon
Cours Albert-1er
Ave. d'Iéna
Place de l'Alma
Pl. de la Reine-Astrid
Ave. du Albert-de-Mun
Ave. de New-York
94
Pont de l'Alma
Seine
Pont des Invalides
Ave. des Nations-Unies
Passerelle Debilly
Quai d'Orsay
Pont d'Iéna
Rue de l'Université
Rue Jean-Nicot
Blvd. de la Tour Maubourg
Quai Branly
Ave. de La Bourdonnais
Ave. Rapp
Ave. Bosquet
Tour Eiffel
Ave. Gustave-Eiffel
Ave. Elisées-Reclus
Rue St-Dominique
N
Parc du Champ-de-Mars
Ave. Bouvard
Rue de Grenelle
Rue E.-Psichari
Ave. de la Motte-Picquet
Hô In
km 1/8 1/4
mi 1/16 1/8

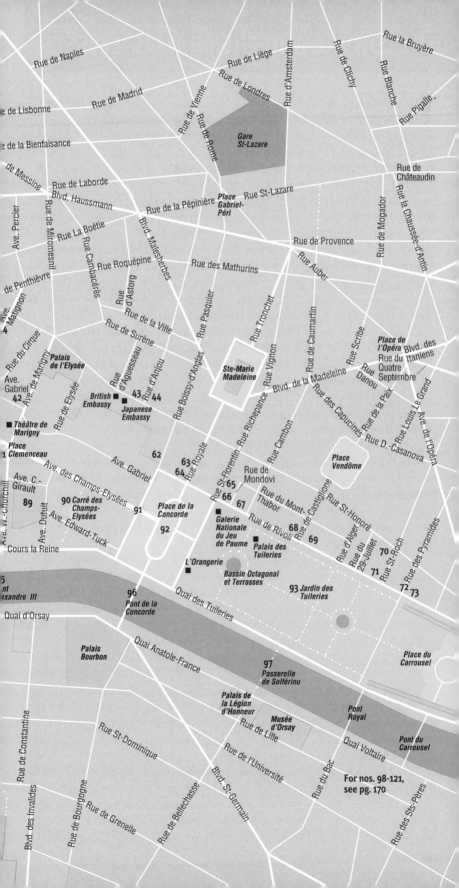

This superlative stroll includes the largest museum in the Western world (the **Louvre**), the world's most famous boulevard (the **Champs-Elysées**), the most ancient monument in Paris (the 3,300-year-old Egyptian **Obelisk of Luxor**), the best 360-degree view of Paris (from **La Samaritaine**'s rooftop café), some of the city's grandest hotels (the **Meurice, Crillon, Plaza Athénée,** and **George V**), its oldest métro station (**Franklin-D.-Roosevelt**), its most elegant tea salon (**Angélina**), its best-stocked English paperback bookshops (**Galignani** and **W.H. Smith**), the world's most magnificent square (**Place de la Concorde**), the largest concert hall in Paris (**Théâtre du Châtelet**), the "hautest" of haute couture (the boutiques along **Avenue Montaigne**), the sexiest cabaret in Paris (the **Crazy Horse**), some of the city's best gourmet restaurants (**Les Ambassadeurs, Ledoyen, Laurent, Taillevent, Alain Ducasse au Plaza Athénée, Le Cinq, Pierre Gagnaire, Guy Savoy**), and the world's biggest triumphal arch (**L'Arc de Triomphe**). That's a lot to absorb in one day, so get an early start, put on your most comfortable shoes, and *bon courage*—that's French for "keep a stiff upper lip."

Monday may be the best day for our hypothetical hike through this area, for it's the only day the **Hôtel de Ville** (City Hall) is open, and the lines at the Louvre Museum slack off (on the first Sunday of the month, when admission to the Louvre is free, it's a mob scene). Monday is also discount night at the cinemas on the Champs-Elysées. Begin your tour with the Hôtel de Ville, then walk along the **Seine** past the pet and plant shops on **Quai de la Mégisserie** and stop for morning coffee and a spectacular panorama atop **La Samaritaine** department store. Next comes the Louvre Museum with all its wonders—take a 2- to 3-hour whirlwind tour of the history of art here that includes those three remarkable Mediterranean ladies: *Venus de Milo,* the *Winged Victory of Samothrace,* and the *Mona Lisa.* After the Louvre, take a break at the nearby **Jardin des Tuileries** (Tuileries Gardens), then either splurge for lunch at Ledoyen or join the fashion models with fierce sweet cravings who order the Mont Blanc dessert at Angélina. En route to the Place de la Concorde, you might stop at W. H. Smith for the latest *New Yorker* or an English-language novel to read on the plane home.

From the base of the Obelisk of Luxor, it is a mile to the **Arc de Triomphe**. If you need motivation to keep walking, consider the delights that lie ahead: the major art exhibition that can always be found under the huge glazed dome of the **Grand Palais**, the high-fashion boutiques of the **Triangle d'Or**, and chef Alain Ducasse's pheasant cooked with foie gras and black truffles at the Restaurant Alain Ducasse au Plaza Athénée. The eastern half of the Champs-Elysées is bordered by gardens (designed by André Le Nôtre, a gardener for Louis XIV, who also landscaped **Versailles**) that have not changed since novelist Marcel Proust played there as a child. On the right, you pass behind three fine structures: the **British Embassy,** the **Japanese Embassy,** and the **Palais de l'Elysée.** At the **Rond-Point des Champs-Elysées,** a roundabout in the middle of the Champs-Elysées, shoppers should veer left to Avenue Montaigne, the high-fashion row, whereas art buffs and philatelists will want to go directly to the galleries on **Avenue Matignon** and to the stamp stalls on **Avenue Gabriel.**

The last stretch of the Champs-Elysées, which leads up to Napoléon's triumphal arch, is meant to be strolled in the evening, when Paris more than lives up to its nickname, the City of Light. High rollers will want a cocktail on the terrace at **Fouquet's,** and dinner at **Taillevent, Chiberta,** or, perhaps, upstairs at **Lasserre,** where the ceiling rolls back for stargazing between courses. Those who are on a tighter budget might

atch a first-run movie at the **Gaumont** or a Beckett play at the **Théâtre du Rond-**
·oint and then enjoy a late-night supper at the vivacious Art Deco brasserie **Le Boeuf**
ur le Toit or the spectacular **Man Ray**, then dance the night away at **Queen**.

When the day's strolling is over, you may feel as if you've completed the **Tour de**
rance, the world's greatest bicycle race, which ends each July on the Champs-Elysées—
lso the finishing line for your 1-day *"Tour de Paris."*

---

1 L'ETOILE VERTE

★★$$ Coq au vin, sautéed veal, and
chateaubriand Béarnaise are just some of the
basic, well-prepared fare served at this little
neighborhood eatery. With its pleasant décor
of light wood-paneled walls, white tablecloths,
and red banquettes, its jolly wait staff, and
good food at remarkably reasonable prices for
this high-rent part of town, it's little wonder
this restaurant is packed at lunchtime every
day. ◆ Daily, lunch and dinner. 13 Rue Brey
(between Ave de Wagram and Rue de
Montenotte). 01.43.80.69.34. Métro:
Charles-de-Gaulle–Etoile

2 GUY SAVOY

★★★★$$$$ This spacious contemporary
dining room, redone in 2000 by architect
Jean-Michel Wilmotte and decorated with
modern-art paintings and African sculptures,
perfectly complements the cuisine of noted
Chef Savoy. Try the artichoke soup with
Parmesan and truffles, pan-fried mussels and
wild mushrooms, *bar en écaille grillé aux*
epices douces (sea bass grilled in sweet
spices), and wild fruits in aspic flavored with
Damson plums. Rely on head sommelier Eric
Mancio, one of the best in France, to help
select your wine from his amazing *cave*. Every-
thing looks as good as it tastes—and vice
versa. The clientele is suitably glamorous. ◆
M-F, lunch and dinner; Sa, dinner; closed the
last week of July and the first 3 weeks of
August. Reservations recommended. 18 Rue
Troyon (between Aves de Wagram and Mac-
Mahon). 01.43.80.40.61. Métro:
Charles-de-Gaulle–Etoile

5 ROYAL MONCEAU

$$$$ This luxurious hotel has a decidedly
theatrical air, with a vast marble-floor,
mirrored lobby bedecked with huge arrange-
ments of flowers, and 220 rooms and suites
that are correspondingly grand. Not surpris-
ingly, it has hosted such celebrities as Arnold
Schwarzenegger, Sylvester Stallone, Tina
Turner, Sting, and Madonna, who shot a video
here. The saunas, steam rooms, herbal
massages, and "spa cuisine" dining at the
sumptuous **Thermes Health Spa** are open to
hotel guests. There are also two exceptionally
fine restaurants. ◆ 37 Ave Hoche (between
Ave Berthie-Albrecht and Rue Beaujon).
01.42.99.88.00; fax 01.42.99.89.90. Métro:
Ternes. royal_monceau@jetmultimedia.fr;
www.royalmonceau.com

Within the Royal Monceau:

LE JARDIN

★★★$$$ Set in the hotel's garden, this pretty
glass dining pavilion is the best address in
Paris for Mediterranean-Provençal cuisine.
(Michelin awarded it one star.) Trained by
Jacques Maximin and Alain Ducasse in their
Côte d'Azur palaces, supervising chef Bruno
Cirino has proved himself an imaginative
creator in his own right in this savory and
certifiably healthy olive oil–based style of
cooking. For a starter, try a generous portion
of cèpes sautéed with tiny breaded wild nuts,
or succulent roasted *écrevisses* (little fresh-
water crayfish) on a bed of truffle-laced
spaghetti. Main courses of note include a
casserole of langoustine tails and fresh
peppers served with grilled langoustine heads
stuffed with a peppery green roe; line-caught
Mediterranean bass with seasonal garniture;
and rack of lamb with pine nuts and summer
savory. For dessert try the astounding dark
chocolate ravioli with licorice ice cream. To
accompany this feast, ask sommelier
Stéphane Lochon to choose from his remarkable selection of southern French wines. The
waiters are warm and relaxed but very attentive, and the restaurant's flowery garden
setting makes it a bright, cheerful place for
lunch, and quiet and romantic for a candlelight dinner. ◆ M-F, lunch and dinner.
01.42.99.98.70

LE CARPACCIO

★★$$ This airy Italian restaurant with sunny
yellow Venetian décor and Murano glass

---

chandeliers features the cuisine of distinguished chef Angelo Paracucchi, who owns a restaurant in Rome and writes a weekly food column for *Il Messaggero*, an Italian daily newspaper. His specialties include carpaccio with white truffles; risotto with scampi; grilled fish of the day; sautéed bass with artichokes and asparagus; grilled lamb cutlets; and a grand array of antipasti, pastas, and Italian desserts. Bruno Malara, the sommelier here since 1983, was chosen sommelier of the year for 1999 by Le Pudlo de Paris Gourmand for his astute selection of Italian wines. Jeanne Moreau, Catherine Deneuve, Ornella Mutti, Jean-Paul Belmondo, and other celebrities in love with Italian cooking can often be found dining here. ♦ Daily, lunch and dinner; closed in August. Reservations recommended. 01.42.99.98.90

3 LE MÉRIDIEN ETOILE

$$$$ Conveniently located across from the **Palais des Congrès**, this 1,025-room hotel, completely renovated and refurbished in 2001, is perfect for the business traveler. The hotel's **Le Club Président** is a 112-room hotel-within-the-hotel on two adjoining floors, designed to resemble a private British club; it offers quick check-in/-out service, meeting rooms, traditional business services, voice mail, and individual fax and phone lines on request.♦ 81 Blvd Gouvion-St-Cyr (between Pl de la Porte-Maillot and Rue Belidor). 01.40.68.34.34; fax 01.40.68.31.31. Métro: Porte-Maillot. www.lemeridien-etoile.com

Within Le Méridien Etoile:

L'ORÉNOC

★★$$ Named for Venezuela's vast tropical Orinoco River and featuring exotic modern décor by **Pierre-Yves Rochon**—lots of red ocher and dark, moody spotlighting—the restaurant offers appropriately tropical cuisine but also traditional French dishes and the Asian-tinted melange known as World food: lightly grilled Breton crab spring roll with Thai spices; bass steamed with ginger, sesame oil,

and soy sauce; duck marinated in satay with wok-fried vegetables. The menu was conceived by famed chef Michel Rostang and is executed by Guy Guénégo. ♦ Daily, lunch and dinner. Reservations recommended. 01.40.68.30.40

LIONEL HAMPTON JAZZ CLUB

Known throughout Paris for its high-quality music, this hospitable club attracts well-known international jazz and blues players and bands. Performers here have included B.B. King, Oscar Peterson, the Count Basie Orchestra, and Fats Domino. ♦ Cover. M-Sa, 10:30PM-2AM. Reservations recommended. 01.40.68.30.42

4 14 RUE DE TILSITT

In April 1925 novelist F. Scott Fitzgerald, his wife Zelda and their young daughter Scotty moved into an apartment at this address. *The Great Gatsby* had just come out to excellent reviews, but sales were disappointing. Fitzgerald's drinking, always a problem, went from bad to worse. He would stumble into the Paris bureau of the *Chicago Tribune* and make a scene, and his pals William L. Shirer and James Thurber had to drag him back to **Rue de Tilsitt** in a taxi. This is still an apartment building. ♦ At Ave de Wagram. Métro: Charles-de-Gaulle–Etoile

6 LE DUPLEX

★★$$ The beautiful people who frequent this restaurant and nightclub come to see and be seen. If you don't want to stand outside under bright lights hoping you're cool enough to be allowed into the nightclub, make dinner reservations. You'll enjoy typical bistro food along with a stupendous view of the **Arc de Triomphe**, and afterward you can go directly downstairs to the club, which boasts the best sound system in Paris. ♦ Restaurant: Tu-Sa, dinner. Nightclub: daily, 11PM-4AM. Reservations recommended. 8 Ave Foch (between Rues de Presbourg and Rude). 01.45.00.45.00. Métro: Charles-de-Gaulle–Etoile

11 TAILLEVENT

★★★★$$$$ This is as close as a restaurant comes to perfection. Chef **Alain Solivères**, a Montpellier native, brings his reputation for reinventing southern French cooking to bear on the menu of one of the top dining spots in Paris. It is in the former town house of the Duc de Morny, with high ceilings, oak-paneled walls, and Louis XV furniture; the décor by **Pierre-Yves Rochon** gives the place the feel of a grand bourgeois private club. Its namesake is Guillaume Tirel (aka Taillevent), the 14th-century royal cook who wrote the first treatise on French cooking, and it offers such innovative dishes as scallops with diced Lucques olives, chorizo, and Parmesan, tuna strip steak garnished with Esplette peppers, lemon, capers, and Serrano ham, and sea bass in shellfish *jus* with baby clams and artichokes. The wine list draws on a cellar of 130,000 bottles ranging from such collector's items as a Lafite-Rothschild 1806 to a less risky and far less expensive Château Haut Brion. This is the perfect choice for a top-of-the-line business lunch or that once-in-a-lifetime dining experience. ♦ M-F, lunch and dinner; closed in August. Reservations required well in advance. 15 Rue Lamennais (between Rue Washington and Ave de Friedland). 01.44.95.15.01. Metro: George-V

7 PLACE CHARLES-DE-GAULLE

Once called **Place d'Etoile** (Square of the Star), this square was created by Baron Haussmann in 1854 when he added seven avenues to the existing five to form a 12-pointed star. Although the area is a snarl of traffic, it was always the street where the rich and famous, such as Aristotle Onassis, Maria Callas, Claude Debussy, the Shah of Iran, and Prince Rainier of Monaco, lived. One of the avenues that begin here, Avenue Foch, is the widest (390 feet) in Paris; it leads to the **Bois de Boulogne**. ♦ At Aves des Champs-Elysées and de la Grande-Armée and Aves Kléber and de Wagram. Métro: Charles-de-Gaulle–Etoile

On Place Charles-de-Gaulle:

L'ARC DE TRIOMPHE

If Emperor Napoléon hadn't changed his mind in the nick of time, Parisians would be staring not at this magnificent arch but at a 160-foot-high elephant squirting water from its trunk. The decision was so close that a model of the elephant was made and stood for a while at the Place de la Bastille. In the end, Napoléon chose the more tasteful triumphal arch to honor his army's victory at the Battle of Austerlitz. (The sun sets exactly along this axis on 2 December, the anniversary of that victory.) His triumphal arch is 164 feet high and 148 feet wide.

Construction of the arch began in 1806, and the walls had scarcely risen above the ground by the time Napoléon divorced the childless Empress Josephine and wed Princess Marie Louise of Austria in 1810. The bridal procession passed through a fake arch of canvas, hastily constructed for the occasion by the architect **Jean-François Chalgrin**. The arch was not completed until 1836, well after Napoléon's downfall; only 4 years later, a chariot bearing his body would pass beneath the arch on its way to the **Invalides**. On 14 July 1919, victorious French soldiers marched through the structure. The following month,

pilot Sergeant Godefroy flew a plane with a wingspan of 29 feet through the 48-foot-wide arch. On 11 November 1920 the body of the Unknown Soldier was laid in state here to commemorate the dead soldiers of World War I. The eternal flame at the tomb (first kindled in 1923) is lit each evening at 6:30. On 26 August 1944, after the Germans had been routed from the capital, General Charles de Gaulle led a jubilant crowd to the arch, then walked down the Champs-Elysées to **Notre-Dame**, where the *Te Deum* Mass was celebrated in thanksgiving. On state occasions, an enormous French flag hangs inside the arch.

It would be suicide to cross the Place Charles-de-Gaulle on foot (cars have a hard enough time); pedestrians can take an underground passage. An elevator or 284 steps will take you (during daylight hours only) to the platform at the top, which affords a magnificent panorama of Paris.

On the Arc de Triomphe:

DEPARTURE OF THE VOLUNTEERS

Known as *La Marseillaise*, this sculpture by **François Rude** is the arch's most inspired and noteworthy stonework. (It is on your right when your back is to the Champs-Elysées.) In 1916, on the day the Battle of Verdun started, the sword brandished by the figure representing the Republic broke and fell off. The disarmed sculpture was immediately hidden to conceal the accident from the superstitious, who might have seen it as a bad omen.

8 CHIBERTA

★★★$$$ The most chic nouvelle cuisine restaurant in Paris is made even more hip by its Art Deco décor. Chef Eric Coisel offers such seasonal specialties as wild mushroom fricassee in winter, truffle-and-parsley ravioli in autumn, and salmon with fresh artichokes and asparagus come spring. For dessert try the poached pear on crumbled biscuits in spiced syrup. The house Bordeaux is more than passable and the service good-natured and impeccable. This dining spot caters to a business clientele at noontime and an upscale international crowd in the evening. ♦ M-F, lunch and dinner; Sa, dinner; closed in August. Reservations recommended. 3 Rue

Arsène-Houssaye (between Aves des Champs-Elysées and de Friedland). 01.53.53.42.00. Métro: Charles-de-Gaulle-Etoile

9 RUE BALZAC

**\$\$\$ You'd never guess it from the bright, contemporary design (think whimsical wall stenciling and gold chandeliers with an upside down fleur-de-lis motif), but this decidedly upscale eatery is owned by Johnny Hallyday, who is loosely the French equivalent of Elvis. The only hint comes from the menu, from which you can order pasta with green olives "Johnny's way." Though the dish is very good, the rest of the Michel Rostang–formulated menu offers more gutsy fare, such as fillet of sea bass à la plancha with red-beets-and-garlic confit; braised lamb with forest mushrooms; and roast wild duck with figs and bittersweet pumpkin. Desserts shine, from the selection of homemade ice creams and sorbets served in a row of shot glasses to a divine almond-milk soufflé glacé studded with amarena cherries. Service is attentive even if you're not a celebrity, and tables are amply spaced apart—a luxury in oftentimes cramped Parisian restaurants. Here quality overrides trendiness, making it a hip spot to have a quality meal just steps from the Champs-Elysées fray. M-F, lunch and dinner; Sa-Su, dinner. 8 Rue Lord-Byron (at Rue Balzac). 01.53.89.90.91. Métro: George-V

10 HÔTEL DE VIGNY

\$\$\$\$ Sumptuous wood paneling, a lobby resembling a private London club, and 37 bright and airy rooms that are royally furnished with antiques, puffy down comforters, and private Jacuzzis are just some of the features of this hostelry. There's an attractive bar where sandwiches and salads are served, but no restaurant. ♦ 9–11 Rue Balzac (at Rue Lord-Byron). 01.42.99.80.80; fax 01.42.99.80.40. Métros: George-V, Charles-de-Gaulle-Etoile. De.Vigny@wanadoo.fr

12 133 AVENUE DES CHAMPS-ELYSÉES

After World War II, General Dwight D. Eisenhower, supreme commander of the Allied Forces in Europe, had his headquarters here in what was the old **Hôtel Astoria**. He asked for a room with a view of the **Arc de Triomphe**, his favorite structure in Paris. The

hotel was destroyed in a fire in 1972; the present building houses offices and a drugstore. ♦ At Rue de Presbourg. Métro: Charles-de-Gaulle-Etoile

Within 133 Avenue des Champs-Elysées:

DRUGSTORE DES CHAMPS-ELYSÉES

In addition to aspirin and bandages, this drugstore sells gourmet groceries, quick brasserie meals, wristwatches, banana splits, and Cuban cigars. ♦ Daily, 9AM-2AM. 01.44.43.79.00, 01.47.20.39.24

13 OFFICE DE TOURISME DE PARIS

Home of the city's official tourist bureau, this office provides visitors with free maps and brochures, sight-seeing information, and same-day hotel reservations for those stuck without a room for the night. ♦ Daily, 9AM-8PM. 127 Ave des Champs-Elysées (between Rues Galilée and de Presbourg). 08.36.68.31.12; fax 01.49.53.53.00. Métros: Charles-de-Gaulle-Etoile, George-V. www.paris-touristoffice.com

14 LA BUTIK

The makings of a real Danish smorgasbord—pickled herring, eel, marinated salmon, shrimp salad, roast beef with onions, Aarlborg aquavit, Ceres beer—abound at this cheerful take-out shop fronting on the Champs-Elysées. The Danish pastries are superb. ♦ Daily, 9AM-10PM; Su, 11AM-8PM. 142 Ave des Champs-Elysées (between Rues Balzac and Arsène-Houssaye). 01.43.59.20.41. Métro: Charles-de-Gaulle-Etoile

14 LE RESTAURANT FLORA DANICA

★★\$\$ Refined Nordic cuisine is served at this Danish restaurant in a secluded setting on the ground floor to the rear of La Butik. Here salmon is featured in many incarnations (poached with dill, smoked, marinated, or grilled) and served with draft Danish beer or French wine. This place is famous for its flaky pastries. In summer, meals are served in a lovely umbrella-shaded courtyard and in a tranquil garden shaded by big leafy trees, a welcome respite from the bustle of the Champs-Elysées. The rest of the year, you dine in the pleasant Danish Modern dining room or on stools at the restaurant's cheerful bar. ♦ Daily, lunch and dinner. 142 Ave des Champs-Elysées (between Rues Balzac and Arsène-Houssaye). 01.44.13.86.26. Métro: Charles-de-Gaulle-Etoile

14 CPH

★★★\$\$\$ Upstairs from **Le Restaurant Flora Danica** and **La Butik**, this restaurant, whose initials stand for "Copenhagen," serves more sophisticated and more expensive, gourmet Danish cuisine in an elegant modern dining room with big windows overlooking the Champs-Elysées or on a dining terrace in the rear overlooking the Restaurant Flora Danica's dining terrace and garden. Reindeer terrine, marinated herring, roasted cod with Greenland shrimps, presalted duck *à la danoise*, and rhubarb compote with strawberries and vanilla cream are among chef Georges Landriot's specialties. The restaurant has long sported a prestigious Michelin star. ♦ M-F, lunch and dinner; Sa, dinner; closed in August and the first week of January. 142 Ave des Champs-Elysées (between Rues Balzac and Arsène-Houssaye). 01.44.13.86.26. Métro: Charles-de-Gaulle–Etoile

15 PIERRE GAGNAIRE

★★★★$$$$ This dining spot has garnered rave reviews from the moment it opened. One of the most skilled practitioners of blending exotic ingredients, Chef Gagnaire prepares such dishes as poached salmon with chutney, duck foie gras wrapped in bacon, roasted duck topped with lime and served with bitter melons, veal with tomato marmalade and tiny squid, and herbed sea bass with fresh vegetables. His use of sweet and sour is legendary. Desserts are just as captivating—the dried grapefruit *dacquoise* (filled meringue) is a hit. Here the décor is minimalist, almost self-effacing, as if to highlight the creativity of the cuisine, which has elevated this restaurant to the apotheosis of Michelin three-stardom. ♦ M-F, dinner; closed the last 2 weeks of July. Reservations recommended. 6 Rue Balzac (between Ave des Champs-Elysées and Rue Lord-Byron). 01.44.35.18.25. Métro: Charles-de-Gaulle–Etoile

16 GYMNASE CLUB

The largest health club in Paris offers five floors of aerobics studios, bodybuilding equipment, saunas, Jacuzzis, a solarium, and juice bar. ♦ M-Sa. 26 Rue de Berri (between Rue de Ponthieu and Rue d'Artois). 01.43.59.04.58. Métro: George-V

17 RAPHAEL

$$$$ This luxurious 87-room lodging place with Louis XVI and Louis XV décor attracts Italian and North American movie stars. There's a sumptuously decorated restaurant. ♦ 17 Ave Kléber (at Ave des Portugais). 01.44.28.00.28; fax 01.45.01.21.50. Métro: Kléber. management@raphael-hotel.com; www.raphael-hotel.com

18 LIDO

The largest cabaret in Paris, this lavish extravaganza outglitters Las Vegas with its $15 million revue starring the famous **Bluebell Girls**, whose dance numbers are choreographed by computer and who wear $4 million worth of high-tech costumes incorporating fiber optics, fake fur, leather, and the obligatory feathers and sequins. Dazzling special effects include aerial and aquatic ballets, a motorized flying dragon, water sprays, and a skating rink that rises out of the floor. Throw in a few jugglers, acrobats, and bare-breasted dancers decorously lowered from the ceiling and you have your basic night at the **Lido**. It's always packed with Japanese tourists, car salesmen, and sailors on leave. Famed chef Paul Bocuse is the food consultant for the international menu. ♦ Cover. Shows: daily, 10PM and midnight; doors open at 8PM for dinner and dancing before the show. Reservations recommended. 116 *bis* Ave des Champs-Elysées (between Rues Washington and Balzac). 01.40.76.56.10. Métro: George-V. www.lido.fr

JL
LANCASTER

23 LANCASTER

$$$$ With just 60 guest rooms and suites, this small luxury hotel is a haven of tranquillity a stone's throw from the commotion of the Champs-Elysées. The building was constructed in 1889 as a town house for a Spanish nobleman, converted into a hotel in 1930, and beautifully restored by hotelier extraordinaire Grace Leo Andrieu in 1996. Illustrious guests have included Greta Garbo and Marlene Dietrich, whose favorite color, lilac, predominates in the eponymous suite where she lived with her daughter for three years. A wealth of antiques and Louis XV and Louis XVI furniture generates a stately feel, and the air of discretion still makes the hotel a popular choice for discriminating stars, such as Matt Damon. One of the unusual features is the Zen garden, a quiet riot of jasmine and other flowers, ferns overhanging screens of woven wicker, and a fountain: a great place for a breakfast or lunch alfresco. Noted chef Michel Troisgros created the menu for the hotel's restaurant. ♦ 7 Rue Berri (between Rue d'Artois and Ave des Champs-Elysées). 01.40.76.40.76 or 800/223.6800 from the U.S.; fax 01.40.76.40.10. Métro: Frankin D. Roosevelt. reservation@hotel-lancaster.fr, www.hotel-lancaster.fr

---

Restaurants/Clubs: Red | Hotels: Purple | Shops: Orange | Outdoors/Parks: Green | Sights/Culture: Blue

17 THE CHICAGO PIZZA PIE FACTORY

★$ Midwesterners pining for a taste of home should descend to the cavernous brick basement, bright with red-and-white-checkered tablecloths and reverberating with Chuck Berry, where they can order a deep-dish pizza with such traditional toppings as pepperoni and mushrooms. ♦ Daily, 11:30AM-1AM. Happy hour: M-F, 4-7PM. 5 Rue de Berri (between Rue d'Artois and Ave des Champs-Elysées). 01.45.62.50.23. Métro: George-V

19 BARFLY

★★$$ Food is secondary here—getting a chance to gawk at the international assemblage of the rich and almost famous is more to the point. However, there is a perfectly acceptable eclectic menu of Japanese sushi or traditional French fare, including puff-pastry desserts. As reservations can be hard to come by, dropping in for a drink at the bar is the quicker way to check out the scene. ♦ Daily, lunch and dinner until 1AM. Reservations recommended. 99 Ave des Champs-Elysées (at Ave George-V). 01.47.23.70.60. Métro: George-V

19 LOUIS VUITTON

The flagship store of the ultrachic retailer sells Marc Jacobs's ready-to-wear suits, coats, sweaters, and shoes and its famous monogrammed leather briefcases, handbags, and luggage that attract armies of Japanese shoppers day in and day out. ♦ M-Sa, 101 Ave des Champs-Elysées (at Ave George-V). 01.53.57.24.60. Métro: George-V

20 FOUQUET'S

★★$$$ This famous café has been a watering hole for **show-biz** celebrities, the glamour set, and big names in literature and the arts since it opened in 1899. James Joyce dined here almost every night once he got in the chips (there's a dining room upstairs named after him), and every March the French film industry selects the nominees for the Césars, its version of Hollywood's Oscars, in the sumptuous banquet room. The restaurant serves traditional French fare, including some specialties that have been on the menu for the past 50 years: *maquereaux* (mackerel) in white wine, *merlan au colbert* (fried whiting), and *hachis parmentier* (mashed potatoes mixed with beef and spices). The big outdoor terrace with its trademark red awning straddles the southwestern corner of Avenue George-V and the Champs-Elysées and is a popular spot for lunch or a drink. Some of the best people-watching in Paris is found here. Sit on the George-V side to rub shoulders with celebrities. ♦ Daily, breakfast, lunch, and dinner until 1AM. Reservations recommended. 99 Ave des Champs-Elysées (at Ave George-V). 01.47.23.70.60. Métro: George-V

21 LE QUEEN

As the name may suggest, this ultra-*in* (pronounced "ultra-*een*") disco started out being almost exclusively for gay men, but it is now somewhat more mixed, except for Saturday and Sunday when gay guys take over big time. Straight men and women are especially welcome Wednesday nights if they're young enough and chic enough to get by the doorman. Top DJs from Paris and London provide the music. It's jammed every night, and the dance floor is pure delirium, with drag queens galore. ♦ Cover. Daily, midnight-dawn. 102 Ave des Champs-Elysées (between Rues de Berri and Washington). 01.53.89.08.90. Métro: George-V

22 1 RUE DE BERRI

On 17 October 1785, 42-year-old Thomas Jefferson succeeded Benjamin Franklin as minister to France and moved into this mansion, the **Hôtel de Langeac**, designed by architect **Jean-François Chalgrin**. Jefferson resided here for the next 4 years. It's now divided into shops and offices. ♦ At Ave des Champs-Elysées. Métro: George-V

24 16 RUE CHRISTOPHE-COLOMB

In 1898 Henry Adams, grandson of John Quincy Adams and professor of history at Harvard University, stayed in several rooms in this apartment building while reading medieval manuscripts for his book on art and culture, *Mont-Saint-Michel and Chartres*. ♦ Between Rue Magellan and Ave Marceau. Métro: George-V

25 HÔTEL FRANÇOIS I

$$$$ Decorated by **Pierre-Yves Rochon**, this luxurious 40-room hostelry on a quiet street

two short blocks off the Champs-Elysées is a favorite of business travelers. The spacious lobby and bar feature a subtle melange of Renaissance and modern décor elements. All rooms afford luxurious bath amenities, minibar, room service, and Internet connection. ◆ 7 Rue Magellan (between Rues Christophe-Colomb and de Bassano). 01.47.23.44.04; fax 01.47.23.93.43. Métro: George-V. hotel@hotel-francois1er.fr

26 JEAN-PAUL GAULTIER

The bad boy of French fashion himself hand-picks the creations on display in this beautifully lit boutique designed by **Philippe Starck**. There is more menswear to choose from here than at the larger store in the Galerie Vivienne and a different selection of accessories—all supposedly handpicked by Gaultier himself. Lionel Ritchie is one of the many celebrity customers who shop here. ◆ M-Sa. 44 Ave George-V (at Rue François-I). 01.44.43.00.44. Métro: George-V. Also at: 6 Rue Vivienne (Galerie Vivienne). 01.42.86.05.05. Métro: Bourse

27 L'ECLUSE

★★$$ The second in a chain of six classy wine bars, this place offers vintage Bordeaux and light meals of smoked salmon, carpaccio, and goat cheese. ◆ Daily, lunch and dinner until 1AM. 64 Rue François-1 (between Rues Lincoln and Quentin-Bauchart). 01.47.20.77.09. Métro: George-V. Also at numerous locations throughout the city

28 RÉGINE'S

Régine, the celebrated (and now septuagenarian) doyenne of Paris nightlife no longer has a stake in the club that still bears her name, but the beat goes on under the management of young Laurent de Gourcuff, who has kept the original allure intact: dim lighting, floor-to-ceiling mirrors, and lots of red and gold. The '70s decadence may be gone, but card-carrying members of the **Ritz/Tour d'Argent/Maxim's** crowd still come here to party three nights a week. If you want help in getting in, have your hotel concierge make the call. Cover. ◆ Th-Sa. 49 Rue de Ponthieu (between Rues La Boétie and de Berri). 01.43.59.21.60. Métro: Franklin-D.-Roosevelt

29 CHESTERFIELD CAFÉ

This large brick-walled Tex-Mex café puts on free concerts by an all–North American lineup of rising rock and R&B artists and big names on the comeback trail. Alanis Morissette, the Spin Doctors, Widespread Panic, Jeff Healey, Southside Johnny, Eagle Eye Cherry, and many others have performed here. There is live gospel on Sundays between 2 and 5PM. ◆ Daily, 11AM-5AM; Su, brunch noon-5PM. Live music: Tu-Sa, midnight-2AM. Happy hour: M-F, 4-8PM. 124 Rue La Boétie (between Rue de Ponthieu and Ave des Champs-Elysées). 01.42.25.18.06. Métro: Franklin-D.-Roosevelt

30 GUERLAIN INSTITUT DE BEAUTÉ

Make an appointment at least a week in advance if you wish to visit this Regency-paneled beauty salon and undergo the royal treatment from the perfumed ladies in pink. ◆ M-Sa. 68 Ave des Champs-Elysées (between Rues La Boétie and de Berri). 01.45.62.11.21. Métro: George-V

31 VIRGIN MEGASTORE

This majestic music and multimedia shop looks like a Cecil B. DeMille movie set, complete with a monumental marble staircase. Its various levels are replete with a mind-bending selection of records, CDs, tapes, and videos (in English and French), as well as books on music and stereo equipment. ◆ M-Sa, 10AM-midnight; Su, noon-midnight. 52-60 Ave des Champs-Elysées (at Rue La Boétie). 01.49.53.50.00 (recorded message); 01.49.53.52.45. Métro: Franklin-D.-Roosevelt

Within the Virgin Megastore:

VIRGIN CAFÉ

★$ After buying your CD, head for this relaxed, modern, moderately priced café on the second floor for tempura with vegetables, carpaccio, or roast guinea fowl with thyme, or just a coffee or one of the wines on its very creditable list. ♦ Daily, 10AM-midnight

32 INSTITUT GÉOGRAPHIQUE NATIONAL

The French counterpart of the National Geographic Society in Washington, DC, is a cartographer's heaven, selling maps of the entire universe (at least that which is recognized by the French) and more. You may purchase wall-size maps of the Paris métro, navigation charts of the Seine, infrared satellite photos of France, 1618 city maps of Paris, and 4-by-4-foot color aerial photographs of different sectors of downtown Paris so detailed you can make out pedestrians on the Champs-Elysées. ♦ M-Sa. 107 Rue La Boétie (between Rue de Ponthieu and Ave des Champs-Elysées). 01.43.98.80.00. Métro: Franklin-D.-Roosevelt

33 LE BOEUF SUR LE TOIT

★★$$ With its high mirrored walls, period chandeliers, and velvet banquettes, this 1930s Art Deco gem is the most glamorous of Jean-Paul Bucher's vintage brasseries in Paris (the others are **Flo**, **Julien**, **Terminus Nord**, **Vaudeville**, **La Coupole**, and **Le Balzar**). Named after a 1919 musical by Jean Cocteau and Darius Milhaud, Le Boeuf had the hottest jazz, the prettiest women, and the best gossip in Paris at its earlier location during *Les Années Folles* of the 1920s. Cocteau, Picasso, the Dadaists, the Surrealists— everyone who was anyone in the arts came to see and be seen. The memorabilia collection by the front door recalls those days. There's no jazz band now, just the tinkling of a cocktail piano, but the aura of glamour remains strong. Fashion models, actors, and others who seek the good life still pack the place, especially after the theaters let out. This is one of the most stimulating spots in Paris for a late-night snack or supper. Fresh

---

There are 240 *bouquinistes* plying their bookselling trade from outdoor stalls, mainly along the banks of the Seine.

The oldest house in Paris is at 51 Rue de Montmorency (between Rues Beaubourg and St-Martin) in the third arrondissement. It was built by alchemist Nicholas Flamel in 1407.

When Benjamin Franklin died in 1790, the French Assembly went into mourning for 3 days, and the restaurant Le Procope was draped in black in honor of one of its patrons, who was France's favorite North American.

---

shellfish, grilled fish, *tajine de lotte aux olives et gingembre* (a spicy Moroccan stew of monkfish with olives and ginger), and well-prepared brasserie fare are served. ♦ Daily, lunch and dinner until 2AM. Reservations recommended. 34 Rue du Colisée (between Rue du Faubourg St-Honoré and Ave Franklin-D.-Roosevelt). 01.53.93.65.55. Métros: St-Phillipe-du-Roule, Franklin-D.-Roosevelt

33 ESCROUZAILLES

★★$$ This friendly and refreshingly simple restaurant with a sunny décor serves mouth-watering specialties from France's gastronomic heartland, the Massif Central. Appetizers include pumpkin soup, duck foie gras, and sautéed goose gizzards with lima beans. For the main course, try the roast salmon, honeyed roast lamb, or the remarkable *croustillant quercynois en croûte de pomme de terre* (two crispy potato wafers filled with preserved duck breast, foie gras, and potato gratin). Wild game is served in season. A bottle of Château Montus Madiran red goes beautifully with everything. Be sure to save room for either one of the homemade fruit sherbets or the *tout chocolat noir* (a square of dark mousselike chocolate). The good, honestly priced food and wine keep the place filled with business people at lunch and Parisian regulars and foreign visitors at dinner ♦ Daily, lunch and dinner. Reservations recommended. 36 Rue du Colisée (between Rue du Faubourg St-Honoré and Ave Franklin-D.-Roosevelt). 01.45.62.94.00. Métros: St-Philippe-du-Roule, Franklin-D.-Roosevelt. Also at 83 Avenue de Ségur (between Avenue de Suffren and Blvd Garibaldi). 01.40.65.99.10. Metro: Ségur

34 AVENUE MATIGNON

This is "gallery alley" for Right Bank art and antiques. Take note of the stamp collectors' market along this street and the connecting **Avenue Gabriel** that is held Thursdays, Saturdays, Sundays, and holidays. ♦ Between Rond-Point des Champs-Elysées and Rue de Penthièvre. Métro: Franklin-D.-Roosevelt

On Avenue Matignon:

LE BERKELEY

★$$ A classic oysters-and-champagne, steak-and-fries restaurant, **Le Berkeley** features designer **Jacques Garcia**'s red walls with oil paintings and twin crescent wooden staircases to the mezzanine library. Once a stomping ground of Cocteau, Garbo, Dietrich, and the Windsors, the place still draws its fair share of celebrities at night. ◆ Daily, breakfast, lunch, and dinner until 2AM. Reservations recommended. 7 Ave Matignon (at Rue de Ponthieu). 01.42.25.72.25. Métro: Franklin-D.-Roosevelt

MARKET

$$*** Jean-Georges Vongerichten, the celebrity chef behind such renowned restaurants as Jean-Georges, Vong, and Mercer Kitchen (all in New York) opened this unstuffily chic and all-round superior eatery in the Christie's building to much fanfare in 2001. The Christian Liaigre interior, with its gray wood-and-stone walls, a sprinkling of African and Pacific masks, and transparent tables, is well suited to occasions festive or formal. Service is both flawless and friendly and the menu is driven by the freshest and best things the seasonal markets have to offer, meaning what you order could just as easily be of French inspiration as it could be Asian or Italian. Start with the "black plate" special for two, an assortment of dishes such as shrimp satay, lobster daikon, and quail with Thai spices, or opt for appetizers à la carte such as crab salad with mango, cumin crisps and grainy mustard, or a delectable goat cheese, tomato, and arugula pizza. Main courses could include steamed black sea bass with carrot confit in an orange-and-cumin sauce with couscous, lobster terrine with fenugreek, lemongrass, and snow peas, or roast farm chicken with an olive *tapenade* and goat-cheese-and-beet tart. Sommelier Patrice Aignan-Lassagne does an expert, graceful job of finding the perfect wine to accompany each course, and the wine list is full of unusual vintages. Standouts among desserts, like other courses generously portioned, include profiteroles with pecan ice cream instead of the usual vanilla, and passion-fruit cheesecake. Under the capable stewardship of young American chef de cuisine Eric Johnson, who worked with Vongerichten for more than 4 years in New York, Market has shaped up as one of the most enjoyable tables in Paris. ◆ Daily, lunch and dinner; Sa-Su, brunch, lunch, and dinner. Reservations recommended. 15 Avenue Matignon (between Rues de Ponthieu and Rabelais). 01.56.43.40.90. Métro: Franklin-D.-Roosevelt

35 FRANKLIN-D.-ROOSEVELT MÉTRO STATION

This is the oldest métro station in Paris. The *métro* (short for *métropolitain*) was born on 4 October 1898, when men with picks and shovels began digging a labyrinth beneath the city as directed by engineer Fulgence Bienvenue. ◆ Rue de Marignan and Ave des Champs-Elysées

36 HÔTEL COLISÉE

$$ Quilted bedspreads and bamboo furniture embellish the 44 rooms of this comfortable, well-located member of the Best Western hotel group. There's no restaurant. ◆ 6 Rue du Colisée (between Rue de Ponthieu and Ave des Champs-Elysées). 01.56.88.26.26; fax 01.56.88.26.00. Métro: Franklin-D.-Roosevelt. info@bw-colisee.com; www.bw-colisee.com

37 JADIS ET GOURMANDE

A chocolate lover's sweetest dream, this candy store sells chocolate letters of the alphabet to compose messages, Arcs de Triomphe, chocolate Bordeaux bottles filled with coffee beans, and dozens of other original ideas for gifts. ◆ M-Sa. 49 *bis* Ave Franklin-D.-Roosevelt (between Rond-Point des Champs-Elysées and Rue de Ponthieu). 01.42.25.06.04. Métro: Franklin-D.-Roosevelt

38 YVAN

★★★$$ In his handsome *restaurant gastronomique*, personable blond chef Yvan Zaplatilek, a darling of *le tout Paris*, attracts a glamorous clientele. The cuisine is largely influenced by his Belgian roots: duck-liver pâté with four spices and onion jam, poultry ravioli with truffle oil, lamb chops with barigoule tarragon, broiled fillet of *daurade* (sea bream) with green cabbage stew, and *gâteau au chocolat* (chocolate cake). The pastel-and-ivory dining room is filled with fresh flowers and softly lit with chandeliers and candlelight. ◆ M-F, lunch and dinner; Sa, dinner. Reservations required. 1 *bis* Rue Jean-Mermoz (at Rond-Point des Champs-Elysées). 01.43.59.18.40. Métro: Franklin-D.-Roosevelt

Le Petit Yvan

38 LE PETIT YVAN

★★$$ Chef Yvan Zaplatilek's little bistro is cheery, with brightly colored mismatched plates, red paper napkins, a hodgepodge collection of art on the walls, and a polite young staff. It's a tight squeeze, but the beautiful people here don't seem to mind rubbing elbows with one another. The inexpensive prix-

AMERICANS IN PARIS

For much of the 20th century, the City of Light was an essential place of pilgrimage for American writers, artists, musicians, and anyone else with a taste for culture and a certain worldly conception of freedom. As longtime expatriate Irwin Shaw put it in *Paris, Paris!*, "It all may have started with the reading of Dumas or Théophile Gauthier or Balzac or a book by Fitzgerald or seeing a movie about fighter pilots in World War One, or just by sensing something in the general climate of the time that made one feel that no artist could consider himself fully prepared for his life work without eating a croissant for breakfast in the capital of France."

Ernest Hemingway, F. Scott Fitzgerald, Ezra Pound, Josephine Baker, Sidney Bechet, Gertrude Stein, Man Ray, Alexander Calder, Aaron Copland, Langston Hughes, Henry Miller, Richard Wright, James Baldwin, Allen Ginsberg, and William Burroughs all came to Paris, found inspiration here, and made crucial contributions to the vibrant new American culture that was emerging. Now travelers come to Paris from all over the world to walk in the footsteps of these colorful individuals.

Young Hemingway's Paris

The quintessential literary guide to the Left Bank of the 1920s is, of course, Hemingway, who wrote beautifully about it in *The Sun Also Rises*, and *A Moveable Feast*. The starting point is **Place de la Contrescarpe** (between Rues Lacépède and Mouffetard; Métros: Cardinal-Lemoine, Place Monge). In January 1922, young Hem and his bride Hadley settled into their first apartment, a plain four-floor walk-up with no toilet or hot water at 74 Rue du Cardinal-Lemoine, just down the hill from the Contrescarpe. The small oval *place* retains much of the working-class grit Hemingway described. The cafés are more savory than they were in Hem's day, but the daily Rue Mouffetard market exudes an atmosphere of Old Paris.

The **Closerie des Lilas**, 71 Boulevard du Montparnasse (at Avenue de l'Observatoire; Métro: Port Royal RER), 01.40.51.34.50, was a rustic café on the eastern fringe of Montparnasse long favored by *hommes de lettres* where the struggling young writer found the best ambiance for writing his stories. Here he had long discussions with John Dos Passos, Scott Fitzgerald, Ezra Pound, and Archibald MacLeish. Today the Closerie is an attractive upscale café and restaurant that prides itself in its illustrious literary past.

In *A Moveable Feast*, Hem wrote about walking in the lovely **Luxembourg Gardens** to avoid food smells when he was too poor to buy anything to eat. He crossed the gardens to get to Gertrude Stein's home on the west side of the park. The gardens are bordered on the east and west by Boulevard St-Michel and Rue Guynemer, on the north and south by Rues de Vaugirard and Auguste-Comte; Métros: Luxembourg (RER), Notre-Dame-des-Champs, St-Sulpice.

27 Rue de Fleurus

Avant-garde writer, art collector, and literary guru Gertrude Stein lived in a garden pavilion at the rear of this building between 1903 and 1938, first with her brother Leo, then with her lover Alice B. Toklas from 1910 on. The walls of the spacious atelier were covered with Cézannes, Matisses, Picassos, and other Impressionist, Fauvist, and Cubist paintings that Stein and her family were among the first to collect. Matisse and Picasso became friends and fixtures at her Saturday-night *salons*, and Picasso painted a famous portrait of his chunky hostess. Miss Stein could be overbearing, especially about her own writing ("20th century literature is Gertrude Stein"), but many budding authors visited her and valued her advice. Young Hemingway, 23 years old when he met Stein, became her prize protégé. Their friendship eventually went bad, though, and they wrote their conflicting accounts of it in *The Autobiography of Alice B. Toklas* and *A Moveable Feast*. A wall plaque on the building commemorates Stein's residence here. 27 Rue de Fleurus is between Rue d'Assas and Boulevard Raspail (Métros: St-Placide, Notre-Dame-des-Champs).

Boulevard Montparnasse

Boulevard Montparnasse at the intersection of Boulevard Raspail was the special turf of American expatriates in the 1920s. Eight decades later, "the Quarter," as they called it, would be perfectly recognizable to them, with the big café-restaurants like the **Dôme** and **La Coupole** facing the **Rotonde** and **Le Sélect**, but they would find that only two have retained their true Jazz Age flavor: Le Sélect and La Coupole.

Le Sélect, 99 Boulevard du Montparnasse (between Rues Vavin and Peguy; Métro: Vavin), 01.45.48.38.24, opened in 1923 and quickly became a favorite of such lively local characters as Kiki de Montparnasse and Foujita. Hemingway preferred it to the other cafés in "the Quarter," and he set important scenes in *The Sun Also Rises* here. Hart Crane got drunk (not unusual for him), slugged a cop, and ended up in jail. Henry Miller cadged many a meal in the 1930s. The atmosphere is little changed from those days, particularly on the inside, where the tan walls, kitsch ceiling molding, old brown banquettes, and beaten-up wooden chairs and tables make it a comfortable spot for neighborhood regulars and nostalgics alike to have a drink or a bite.

La Coupole, 102 Boulevard du Montparnasse (between Rues Delambre and Montparnasse; Métro: Vavin), 01.43.20.14.20, is a vast brasserie decorated by local artists that became an instant hit with writers and artists when it opened in December 1927. Josephine Baker promenaded among the tables with her pet cheetah. Henry Miller, Alfred Perlès, Lawrence Durrell, and Anaïs Nin were regulars in the 1930s, either sipping on the open-air terrace (now glassed in) or eating in the grand dining hall, where Nin usually footed the bill. La Coupole is refreshingly Hemingway-free, since he had moved to Key West by the time it opened. The original artwork was fully restored in 1988, and the restaurant remains a very exciting place to see and be seen.

Odéon

12 Rue de l'Odéon (between Place de l'Odéon and Carrefour de l'Odéon; Métro: Odéon) is where Sylvia Beach's **Shakespeare and Company** bookshop was in the 1920s and 1930s. Beach is best known for publishing James Joyce's *Ulysses*, a novel literary historians rate as one of the 20th century's greatest, and she nurtured many American writers, including Thornton Wilder, Archibald MacLeish, F. Scott Fitzgerald, and (of course) young Ernest Hemingway. A wall plaque recounts her great publishing feat.

14 Rue Monsieur-le-Prince (between Carrefour de l'Odéon and Rue Casimir Delavigne; Métro: Odéon) was the home of Richard Wright, the author of *Native Son* and *Black Boy*, between 1948 and 1959. Like many African-American writers, artists, and musicians (James Baldwin, Chester Himes, and Sidney Bechet among them), Wright found the racially tolerant atmosphere of Paris much more to his liking than that of pre–civil rights America. He became a close friend of Sylvia Beach, still living around the corner on Rue de l'Odéon. She admired him greatly. "Fellas like Hemingway appear uncouth beside Dick Wright," she confided to her sister. There is a wall plaque in Wright's honor.

St-Germain-des-Prés

Jean-Paul Sartre and other French intellectuals gravitated to **St-Germain-des-Prés** during the World War II occupation because there were too many Germans in the big Montparnasse cafés. After the Liberation, they stayed and were joined by the next wave of American expatriates in the existentialist years of the late 1940s and the 1950s.

Café de Flore, 172 Boulevard St-Germain (at Rue St-Benoît; Métro: St-Germain-des-Prés), 01.45.48.55.26, has long been a great favorite of the literary crowd. The Flore came to its greatest fame when Sartre and Simone de Beauvoir set up shop here in the late 1940s and 1950s. Richard Wright became a companion of theirs.

James Baldwin also became a regular, but upstairs—the sanctuary for gay men in that period.

Among the many, many Americans who have favored glamorous **Les Deux-Magots**, Place St-Germain-des-Prés (at Boulevard St-Germain; Métro: St-Germain-des-Prés), 01.45.85.55.25, were novelist Djuna Barnes and *New Yorker* columnist Janet Flanner, who lived in hotels down the street; Hemingway, who really got around for a young man who claimed to be poor; and Harry Crosby, who first met Hart Crane here and agreed to publish his poem *The Bridge*.

Brasserie Lipp, 151 Boulevard St-Germain (between Rues de Rennes and du Dragon; Métro: St-Germain-des-Prés), 01.45.48.53.91, is a bastion of the French literary establishment, but it has also had a fair number of notable American clients. In *A Moveable Feast*, Hemingway describes a memorable meal he had there when he was young and poor. In 1949, an angry exchange took place here between Richard Wright and his former protégé James Baldwin over Baldwin's attack on him in a literary magazine, the start of a feud that never healed.

The Right Bank

Hôtel Ritz, 15 Place Vendôme (Métros: Madeleine, Opéra, Tuileries), 01.43.16.30.30: Scott Fitzgerald had more drinks than were good for him at the Ritz Bar in the 1920s but put it to great use as a setting in "Babylon Revisited" and *Tender is the Night*. War correspondent Hemingway and his band of irregulars "liberated" the Ritz in August 1944 after the Germans had pulled out of Paris, and he got a bar in the hotel named after him.

In the magnificent 1913 Art Nouveau **Théâtre des Champs-Elysées**, 15 Rue Montaigne (between Rue Boccador and Pl de l'Alma; Métro: Alma–Marceau), 01.49.52.50.00, a number of American events electrified Paris in the 1920s. In 1925, Josephine Baker's sensational dancing in the black American show *La Revue Nègre* made her the toast of Paris. The following year, young American expatriate composer George Antheil set off a riot with his *Ballet Méchanique*, and in 1928 George Gershwin, a great lover of this city, attended the premiere of the Ballet Russes' *Rhapsodie en Bleu*.

To literally walk in the footsteps of these interesting Americans, contact **Paris Walking Tours** (01.48.09.21.40; fax 01.42.43.75.51; Paris@paris-walks.com; www.pariswalkingtours.com), which offers walks through virtually every district in Paris with lively and informative commentary in English.

fixe menu offers such dishes as salmon carpaccio with dill and ginger; tomatoes stuffed with goat cheese, basil, and coriander; breast of duck in sweet-and-sour sauce; lamb curry; and apple tart with apple brandy sorbet. ♦ M-F, lunch and dinner; Sa, dinner. Reservations recommended. 1 *bis* Rue Jean-Mermoz (at Rond-Point des Champs-Elysées). 01.42.89.49.65. Métro: Franklin-D.-Roosevelt

39 MATHIS BAR

This plush and very red bar, tucked into the small Elysées Matignon hotel, is one of the swishest spots to have a drink (or several, if you can afford it) in Paris. The look is mid-'70s disco glam, with music to match, and the crowd is relentlessly posh. Come after midnight, look the part (think Prada, not Gap), and bring a friend or two, the better to edge your way past an almost impossibly icy hostess. ♦ Daily from 10PM. 01.53.76.01.62. 3 Rue de Ponthieu (between Ave Matignon and Rue Jean Mermoz). Métro: Franklin-D.-Roosevelt

40 RESTAURANT LAURENT

★★★$$$$ Just down the street from the official residence of the French president, the parking lot of this restaurant is always crowded with chauffeured limousines bearing diplomatic license plates. The drawing cards here are the lovely garden terrace, impeccable service, and *nouvelle cuisine bourgeoise*, which includes salmon carpaccio with caviar, rack of lamb, *langoustines* in pastry crust, roast lobster, and warm raspberry soufflé. The chef is Philippe Braun, a disciple of Joël Robuchon, and the aptly named Philippe Bourguignon oversees the wine list. In addition to the terrace, there are tables in a covered garden pavilion and in dining rooms on two floors in the 19th-century building. The interior décor is plush, with high ceilings, Impressionist paintings, and a nostalgic Belle Epoque theme. ♦ M-F, lunch and dinner; Sa, dinner. Reservations required. 41 Ave Gabriel (between Aves de Marigny and Matignon). 01.42.25.00.39. Métro: Champs-Elysées–Clemenceau

41 RÉSIDENCE MAXIM'S

$$$$ Near the intersection of the Champs-Elysées and the Place de la Concorde, Pierre Cardin has created a 43-room confection, most of it Art Nouveau, that accommodates visiting executives, sheiks, and the rich and famous for anywhere from $400 to $3,000 per night. There are 38 suites and 4 rooms. Be sure to look at the two Toulouse-Lautrec

paintings in the classic Belle Epoque bar and restaurant. ♦ 42 Ave Gabriel (between Rue du Cirque and Ave Matignon). 01.45.61.96.33; fax 01.42.89.06.07. Métro: Champs-Elysées–Clemenceau

43 COMME DES GARÇONS

Red is the new black—so says **Rei Kawakubo**, the Japanese designer behind this glitzy brand, and her expansive, expensive Paris boutique, designed by British team **Abe Rogers** and **Shona Kitchen**, shows she wasn't joking. A pimiento-red ultralong acrylic counter runs against shimmering walls of scarlet fiberglass, creating an energizing backdrop for the men's and women's collections. Kawakubo's line features characteristically bold cuts, patterns, and colors. So what if the least pricey item is a 75-Euro T-shirt? This is fashion as wearable art, and as such merits at least a look. So, too, does the "chill-out" zone across the courtyard, a room full of mechanized chili-pepper-red cube seats that glide across the floor by remote control. ♦ M-Sa, 11AM-7PM. 54 Rue du Faubourg St-Honoré (between Rues d'Anjou and d'Aguesseau). 01.53.30.27.27. Métro: Concorde

42 1 AVENUE DE MARIGNY

In 1954, when novelist John Steinbeck and his family moved into this house, he described it in a letter to Richard Rodgers and Oscar Hammerstein: "It is next to the Rothschilds and across the street from the president of France. How's that for an address for a Salinas kid?" It's still a private residence. ♦ At Ave Gabriel. Métro: Champs-Elysées–Clemenceau

FOUR SEASONS HOTEL
George V

45 FOUR SEASONS HOTEL GEORGE V PARIS

$$$$ Opened in 1928, this hotel named for the British king during World War I was among the most glamorous and expensive in Paris and attracted a long parade of celebrities and extremely wealthy people over the years. In 1996, one of the latter, Prince al-Waleed of Saudi Arabia, bought the hotel and commissioned designer **Pierre-Yves Rochon** to refurbish the property. When it finally reopened in December 1999, it was everything that a hotel at the pinnacle of *le luxe* should be—thoroughly modern in its comforts and conveniences while fully main-

taining its Old World charm. There are 245 luminous and supremely elegant guest rooms (including 61 suites)—all with grand marble bathrooms, huge closets, and Internet connection via cable television, and 30 have private balconies large enough to breakfast on. The hotel has an outstanding gourmet restaurant, **Le Cinq** (see below); an English-style bar, **Le Bar George V Cinq** (see below); and an exquisite lounge, **La Galerie** (see below), and there is a fitness center with pool and spa reserved for the use of the hotel's guests. The flower arrangements in the marble lobby and other public rooms are absolutely dazzling. The Four Seasons hotel group manages the property. ♦ 31 Ave George-V (between Ave Pierre-1ᵉʳ-de-Serbie and Rue Quentin-Bauchart). 01.49.52.70.00; fax 01.49.52.70.10. Métro: George-V. par. reservations@fourseasons.com; www.fourseasons.com

Within the Four Seasons Hotel George V Paris:

Le Cinq

★★★★$$$$ Elegant, yet intimate, like the dining room of a lovely château, all gray and gold with Wedgwood cameo-style friezes in the walls, this restaurant provides the perfect setting for the stunning cuisine of Philippe Legendre, one of the great chefs of Paris, who flew from his Michelin-three-star nest at **Taillevent** to take charge of the kitchen here when the George V reopened. He changes his repertoire and recomposes the menu each season, but some of his specialties that have drawn raves are his lobster *boudin*, a light, sausage-shaped lobster mousse as a starter; pan-fried sole with seaweed in *marinière* sauce; casserole of young Bresse chicken and lobster; and for dessert, peach poached in cassis sauce or open chocolate biscuit filled with runny chocolate and served with coffee sauce. Add to the cuisine champion sommelier Eric Beaumard's magnificent wine list, the friendly service, and the gorgeous flower arrangements, and you have a dining experience of the loftiest order. Between May and October, meals are also served in the **Cour de Marbre**, the marble courtyard in the heart of the hotel. ♦ Daily, breakfast, lunch, and dinner. Reservations required long in advance. 01.49.52.71.54

Le Bar George V Cinq

A spacious mahogany-paneled room decorated with old prints of equestrian scenes and landscapes, all very Englishy, for lunch, drinks, and refreshments. ♦ Daily, 10:30AM-1AM weekdays; 2AM weekends.

La Galerie

This exquisite gallery with Savonnerie carpets, 17th-century tapestries from Flanders, and French windows looking out on the hotel's marble courtyard is a delightful spot for breakfast, light lunch, afternoon tea with piano accompaniment, or a drink, and there's jazz piano and bass Friday, Saturday, and Sunday evenings to 1AM. ♦ Daily, 8AM-1AM; afternoon tea, 3-6PM.

44 1728

***$$$ Here's a café for the ambassadorial set. A series of sumptuously restored salons in the town house where the Marquis de Lafayette once lived is the rarified setting for afternoon tea featuring pastries by Pierre Hermé and teas by Yang Lining. You don't have to dream about taking home some the elegant surroundings: the collection of 17th-20th—century paintings is also for sale. There is also restaurant service. M-F, lunch, tea, and dinner; Sa, tea and dinner. 8 Rue d'Anjou (at Rue du Faubourg St-Honoré). 01.40.17.04.77. Métro: Concorde

45 37 Avenue George-V

On their honeymoon in 1905, Franklin and Eleanor Roosevelt visited Franklin's aunt Deborah Delano, who had an apartment at this address. She used to take the newlyweds driving; in fact it was in the **Bois de Boulogne** that FDR learned to drive. ♦ Between Ave Pierre-1ᵉʳ-de-Serbie and Rue Quentin-Bauchart. Métro: George-V

46 La Maison du Chocolat

There are many chocolate shops in Paris, but this one, part of a small chain founded by Robert Linxe, is among the best. It's the perfect place for the kind of chocolate lover for whom a Hershey bar would be something close to mass-market poison: even the décor, like all the packaging a study in brown, bespeaks the seriousness and subtleness of Linxe's gourmet endeavor. Best-known here are the decadent truffles and dark chocolate ganaches with various fruit and herbal infusions. On a cold day sidle up to a small bar for a gourmet cup of hot chocolate—so thick (but smooth) it's served with a glass of water on the side. M-Sa. 52 Rue François-1ᵉʳ (at Rue Pierre-Charron). 01.47.23.38.25. Métro: Franklin-D.-Roosevelt

47 Man Ray

★★$$ Converted from an old Champs-Elysées movie theater by **Miguel Canico**

Martins of **Buddha Bar** fame, this vast restaurant and music venue is similarly Asian-flamboyant in style, with two giant statues of Tibetan lady percussionists overlooking the gym-size dining room, and there is a mezzanine bar with photos by **Man Ray** lining the walls. The cuisine is World—Thai and Japanese, ravioli, gazpacho, chicken **tagine** with olives and lemons, a French dish or two—but food here is of little importance. The look and the feeling are all, particularly at night, when the models, publicists, and wanabees flock in for the vibes and the hope of spotting Johnny Depp, Sean Penn, and John Malkovitch, who are part owners, and some of their glamorous friends. Live bossa nova, Latin, cool, and classic jazz are performed Monday to Thursday between 7 and 9PM. Dancing to recorded music starts nightly around 12:30AM except Friday nights, when celebrated DJs play house, techno, garage, or whatever else happens to be in vogue at the club's Ceyla Parties, which go on to the wee hours. It's worth stopping in for a drink at the bar just to see the place. ◆ M-F, lunch and dinner; Sa-Su, dinner. Reservations required for dinner. 34 Rue Marbeuf (between Ave des Champs-Elysées and Rue François-1er). 01.56.88.36.36. Métro: Franklin-D.-Roosevelt

48 AMERICAN CATHEDRAL

This spired Gothic Revival church was designed by **George Edmund Street**, the architect of London's New Law Courts, and consecrated in 1886. It has 42 Pre-Raphaelite stained-glass windows and a fine 15th-century triptych by the Roussillon Master, probably Gaubert Gaucelm. In addition to its Anglican-Episcopalian services in English held on Monday through Friday and Sunday, the church presents numerous choral concerts and organ recitals. ◆ 23 Ave George-V (between Pl de l'Alma and Ave Pierre-1er-de-Serbie). 01.53.23.84.00. Métro: Alma–Marceau

49 LA FERMETTE MARBEUF 1900

★★$$ In 1978, when Jean Laurent purchased what had been a self-service restaurant since 1950, he had no idea of the treasure that lay behind the plastic and Formica. Renovations began, and as workers were tearing down the partition walls, they discovered the tile, stained glass, and cast-iron pillars of a spectacular Art Nouveau room that had been hidden for 30 years. The room, it turns out, had been created in 1898 by two young, unknown designers named **Hutre** and **Wielharski**. Although the real star here is the décor, the cuisine runs a close second. Among the delectations are crabmeat with avocado, green beans, and mayonnaise; grilled young turbot with Béarnaise sauce; saddle of rabbit stuffed with fennel; prime ribs of beef; peach soup with apricots and Beaumes de Venise liqueur; and mint-flavored dark- and white-chocolate cake. A fine selection of *eaux-de-vie*, cognacs, and liqueurs await the end of your meal. ◆ Daily, lunch and dinner. Reservation required. 5 Rue Marbeuf (at Rue du Boccador). 01.53.23.08.00. Métro: Alma–Marceau

49 24 RUE DU BOCCADOR

In the late 1940s this apartment building was rife with such movie stars as Brigitte Bardot, Ivy League CIA agents posing as novelists, and legitimate North American writers, including Theodore H. White, Art Buchwald, and Irwin Shaw. This is where White, after working for 6 years as *Time* magazine's Beijing bureau chief, wrote his Pulitzer prize–winning World War II novel, *The Mountain Road*. In a fifth-floor studio, Buchwald wrote his "Paris After Dark" column for the *Herald Tribune*, and Shaw, in much grander digs, completed his best-selling novel *The Young Lions*, which was published in 1948. ◆ Between Rue Marbeuf and Ave George-V. Métro: Alma–Marceau

50 RISTORANTE ROMANO

★★$$ Highlights of this simple, casual, and warm Italian eatery include its smiling owner Romano and a seasonally changing menu that might include *insalata caprese* (mozzarella, tomato, and basil), spaghetti *alle vongole* (with clams), ravioli in a morel sauce, scampi, and saltimbocca with mozzarella. ◆ Daily, lunch and dinner. Reservations recommended. 11 Rue Marbeuf (between Rues du Boccador and Clément-Marot). 01.47.20.85.98. Métro: Alma–Marceau

51 CHEZ ANDRÉ

★★$$ Unchanged since 1938, this bistro bustles at lunchtime with the dressed-for-success crowd from the Champs-Elysées and matronly waitresses loping through with hot plates. Recommended dishes include poached haddock, short ribs, roast leg of lamb with mashed potatoes, sponge cake with rum sauce, and the affordable house Muscadet and red Graves. ◆ Daily, lunch and dinner until 1AM. Reservations recommended. 12 Rue Marbeuf (at Rue Clément-Marot). 01.47.20.59.57. Métro: Franklin-D.-Roosevelt

52 CLARIDGE-BELLMAN

$$$ Decorated with antiques, paintings, 17th-century tapestries, Chinese vases, and other costly objets d'art, this posh 42-room hotel is home to Italian couturiers during the seasonal fashion shows. The quietly elegant dining room is open to the public. Reserve well in advance. ♦ 37 Rue François-1ᵉʳ (at Rue Marbeuf). 01.47.23.54.42; fax 01.47.28.08.84. Métro: Franklin-D.-Roosevelt. claridge-bellman@wanadoo.fr

53 SPOON FOOD & WINE

★★$$ Back from a global trot, world-famous chef Alain Ducasse offers his take on World food—which comes mainly from Asia, the Americas, and Italy—in this bright, modern, and resolutely un-French bistro. Even the menu is un-French—the dishes are described first in English, then translated (in smaller print) into *français*. Diners can mix and match their dishes from all over the globe: pork or shrimp ravioli, seviche, Thai squid in curry sauce, a BLT or pastrami sandwich, pan-seared tuna with satay sauce, or barbecued spareribs. And for dessert, what else but Ben & Jerry's ice cream? The wine list is equally eclectic. Half the 120 selections come from the US; the rest come mainly from Chile, South Africa, and Australia, with only 10% hailing from France. It was a bold culinary experiment to begin with, and it has definitely caught on, proving that Paris is indeed hot to globe-trot. ♦ M-F, lunch and dinner; closed the last week of July and the first 3 weeks of August. Reservations recommended. 14 Rue de Marignan (between Rue François-1ᵉʳ and Ave des Champs-Elysées). 01.40.76.34.44. Métro: Franklin-D.-Roosevelt

54 AVENUE MONTAIGNE

This street is to haute couture what the **Louvre** is to art. The swank avenue is lined with high-fashion temples (**Christian Dior**, **Nina Ricci**, **Jean-Louis Scherrer**, **Valentino**, **Louis Vuitton**, **Ungaro**, **Prada**, and **Laroche**). You will also find the **Canadian Embassy**, the luxurious **Plaza Athénée** hotel, and two smart theaters (the **Comédie des Champs-Elysées** and the **Théâtre des Champs-Elysées**). ♦ Between Rond-Point des Champs-Elysées and Pl de l'Alma. Metros: Alma–Marceau, Franklin-D.-Roosevelt

54 ARTCURIAL

An essential stop for art lovers, this prestigious gallery and bookstore sells modern and contemporary prints, sculptures, original art objects and jewelry, and art books in the glamorous new space it settled into in 1998. ♦ Tu-Sa; closed 3 weeks in August. 61 Ave Montaigne (between the Rond-Point des Champs-Elysées and Rue François-1ᵉʳ). 01.42.99.16.16. Métro: Franklin-D.-Roosevelt

$$\left\{ \begin{array}{c} \text{AVENUE} \\ \text{41, AV. MONTAIGNE} \end{array} \right\}$$

55 L'AVENUE

★★$$ In this chic brasserie restaurant located on one of the most sumptuous avenues in the world, the Costes brothers and designer **Jacques Garcia** have done it again, resuscitating a moribund place and making it *un must* for the beautiful ones. The most restrained of Garcia's many restaurant makeovers features violet walls, candy-striped banquettes, comfortable burgundy velvet chairs, and antlerlike white wood chandeliers. The waitresses are attractive and pleasant, a hallmark of the Costeses' establishments, and the food is quite good and remarkably low-priced, given the ultrahaute location just across the street from **Chanel** and **Dior** and **Nina Ricci**. Tomatoes with mozarella, rocket with Parmesan, carpaccio, risotto with gambas, sole meunière, duck breast—this is the sort of fresh, plain, well-prepared fare you'll find here. No wonder everyone looks so good. ♦ Daily, breakfast, lunch, afternoon tea, and dinner to 1AM. Reservations recommended. 41 Ave Montaigne (at Rue François-1ᵉʳ). 01.40.70.14.91. Métros: Franklin-D.-Roosevelt, Alma–Marceau

56 NINA RICCI

Perhaps the most beautiful lingerie in the world is sold here, along with a stylish array of dresses, scarves, scents, and jewelry. **The Ricci Club**, an elegant menswear shop, is next door at 19 Rue François-1ᵉʳ, and around the corner at 17 Rue François-1ᵉʳ this haute couture designer's fashions from the year before are sold at a discount. ♦ M-Sa. 39 Ave Montaigne (at Rue François-1ᵉʳ). All three stores 01.49.52.56.00. Métros: Alma–Marceau, Franklin-D.-Roosevelt

57 CHRISTIAN DIOR

In 1949 Dior signed the first designer licensing contract (for stockings). Today, women can dress in his wares from head to toe. Roam through this ultrachic gray-and-white complex, which sells dresses, furs, jewelry, makeup, accessories, and gifts, to select your ensemble. ◆ M-Sa. 30 Ave Montaigne (between Rue François-1er and Pl de la Reine-Astrid). 01.40.73.54.00. Métros: Franklin-D.-Roosevelt, Alma–Marceau

57 26 AVENUE MONTAIGNE

In 1857, when he was 14, Henry James moved into this apartment building with his family. ◆ Between Rue François-1er and Pl de la Reine-Astrid. Métro: Alma–Marceau

CHANEL

58 CHANEL

The dashing Chanel collections are displayed here to their best advantage in a setting of crisp white walls, gleaming mirrors, and spacious dressing rooms. ◆ M-Sa. 42 Ave Montaigne (between Rues Bayard and François-1er). 01.47.23.74.12. Métros: Alma–Marceau, Franklin-D.-Roosevelt

59 THÉÂTRE DU ROND-POINT

Modern French theater, including the works of Camus and Claudel, is featured at this prestigious theater just off the Champs-Elysées. ◆ Call for box office hours. 2 bis Ave Franklin-D.-Roosevelt (between Ave du Général-Eisenhower and Rond-Point des Champs-Elysées). 01.44.95.98.00. Métros: Champs-Elysées–Clemenceau, Franklin-D.-Roosevelt

Within the Théâtre du Rond-Point:

THÉÂTRE DU ROND-POINT RESTAURANT

★$$ On the theater's lower level, this restaurant serves reasonably priced traditional French and international dishes. Try such items as smoked salmon with shallot cream, grilled peppers with a poached egg,

The systematic numbering of houses began under Napoleon in 1805, based on the relation of the street to the river. For streets running parallel to the Seine, the numbers follow the flow of the river, roughly east to west. No. 1 is at the upriver (eastern) end, and numbers ascend in the downriver direction. For streets that run perpendicular to the river, the numbers start at the river and mount as they move outward.

blanquette de veau, steak and fries, smoked veal cutlets, and baba au rhum for dessert. I the summer, dine on the delightful terrace overlooking the gardens along the Champs-Elysées. ◆ Daily, lunch, afternoon tea, and dinner. Reservations recommended. 01.44.95.98.44

60 25 AVENUE FRANKLIN-D.-ROOSEVELT

Between 1862 and the end of the US Civil War, John Slidell, the Confederate commissioner to France, vainly attempted to gain diplomatic recognition and financial support for the Southern cause. After the Confederacy's defeat, Slidell chose to remain in this house in Paris. It's still a private home ◆ Between Rue Jean-Goujon and Impasse d'Antin. Métro: Franklin-D.-Roosevelt

61 STATUE DE CLEMENCEAU

Georges Clemenceau (1841-1929) was the outspoken French politician who formed a coalition government in 1917 and galvanized French morale in the final phases of World War I. Sculptor **François Cogne** has capture Clemenceau's trademarks in bronze: the walrus mustache, high leather boots, walking stick, and wool scarf flapping in the wind. ◆ Clemenceau (at Ave des Champs-Elysées). Métro: Champs-Elysées–Clemenceau

62 AMERICAN EMBASSY

Designed in 1933 by the New York firm **Delan and Aldrich** and flanked by two bald eagles in stone, the embassy and nearby consulate are staffed with about 500 people working for an alphabet soup of agencies, including the IRS, CIA, and FBI, and the Departments of Defense State, Agriculture, and Commerce. ◆ Rue Boissy-d'Anglas (between Ave Gabriel and Rue du Faubourg St-Honoré). 01.43.12.22.22. Métro: Concorde

63 MAXIM'S

★★$$$$ Paris without **Maxim's**? Pas possible. Where would all those rich business executives lunch? And where would the bona fide blue-bloods, glitzy jet-setters, and fashionably late diners find such a Belle Epoque setting? This venerable dining spot has given the royal treatment to Edward VIII of England and Leopold II of Belgium, as well as to such prominent North Americans as John Paul Getty, Jackie Onassis, and Elizabeth Taylor. Not everyone is admitted to this Pierre Cardin–owned landmark, which has been cloned in Beijing, Brussels, Mexico City, Moscow, Nagoya, New York, Rio de Janeiro, Shanghai, Singapore, and Tokyo. If you are lucky enough to be allowed to pass through the doors, however, expect unsurpassed champagne and service, better food than you may be expecting (new chef Bruno Strill is working hard to restore the cuisine to its Belle Epoque best), and a splendid and expensive Parisian evening. ♦ M-Sa, lunch and dinner. Reservations required. 3 Rue Royale (between Pl de la Concorde and Rue du Faubourg St-Honoré). 01.42.65.27.94. Métro: Concorde

64 NORTH FAÇADE OF PLACE DE LA CONCORDE

When royal architect **Jacques-Ange Gabriel** designed the Place de la Concorde, he made sure that buildings would face only its north side, and in 1757, work began on the two matching neoclassical north façades separated down the middle by Rue Royale. The façade's design was borrowed from the **Louvre** colonnades, which Gabriel himself had restored. The **Hôtel de la Marine**, part of the façade east of Rue Royale, was intended to be a lodging for foreign ambassadors but became first a royal-furniture storehouse and then, in 1792, the Admiralty (now known as the Ministry of the Navy). L'Automobile Club de France and the very elegant **Hôtel Crillon** (see below) now occupy the building on the opposite corner. On 6 February 1778, Louis XVI and American diplomats (including Benjamin Franklin) met at the Crillon to sign the Treaty of Friendship and Trade, which recognized the independence of the 13 American states. ♦ Between Rues St-Florentin and Boissy-d'Anglas. Métro: Concorde

64 HÔTEL CRILLON

$$$$ The hotel with the best address in Paris, anchoring the northern edge of the Place de la Concorde, has a lot more going for it than location. History, for example: The façade was designed in 1758 by **Jacques-Ange Gabriel** for the Count of Crillon. The family managed to hold onto the mansion right through the revolution, in spite of the fact that the guillotine was set up practically on its doorstep. Today the 90-room, 57-suite institution is the last of the palace-style Parisian hotels that is totally under French ownership, and general manager Philippe Krenzer oversees a sizable staff who continue a tradition of grand hospitality *à la française*. Guest rooms are elegantly decorated in Louis XV and Louis XVI style, with regal carpets, bedspreads, and modern, sparkling marble bathrooms. From the three Presidential Suites and somewhat smaller (but no less luxurious) Duke of Crillon and Leonard Bernstein Suites there are jaw-dropping views over the Place de la Concorde and beyond. If the luxury of the hotel isn't tonic enough, you can repair to the small but complete fitness center or adjacent Guerlain Institute day spa. Among the notables who

have made the Crillon their Parisian *pied-à-terre* are Mary Pickford and Douglas Fairbanks, who stopped in during their 1920 honeymoon, newspaper magnate William Randolph Hearst and his girlfriend, Marion Davies, and Greta Garbo. Today, this is where the Pet Shop Boys stay when they perform in Paris. The hotel's proximity to the American and British embassies ensures a steady roster of diplomats, royalty real and wishful, and wealthy movers and shakers of international provenance. 10 Pl de la Concorde (between Rues Royale and Boissy d'Anglas). 800.888.4747, 800.223.6800, or 01.44.71.15.00; fax 01.44.71.15.02. Métro: Concorde. reservations@crillon.com, www.crillon.com

Within the Hôtel Crillon:

LES AMBASSADEURS RESTAURANT

★★★$$$$ In this magnificent dining room, with marble walls, elaborate mirrors, 20-foot-high ceilings, and massive crystal chandeliers, innovative chef Dominique Bouchet concocts a cuisine that measures up to the setting. Medallion of lobster with chives, small ravioli with duck foie gras, braised St-Pierre (John Dory), Brittany lobster, filet mignon of suckling pig, Vendée pigeon glazed with honey, and warm *grand cru* chocolate tart are among the specialties. The exemplary fare is complemented by outstanding views of the Place de la Concorde. ♦ Daily, lunch and dinner. Reservations required. 01.44.71.16.16

L'OBÉLISQUE

★★$$ Serving delicious pasta and regional cheeses, this discreet eatery with wood-paneled walls offers meals suitable for lighter appetites and slimmer purses while remaining in step with the hotel's elegant atmosphere. ♦ Daily, lunch and dinner; closed in August. Reservations recommended. 01.44.71.15.15

BAR PIANO CRILLON

International journalists and visiting diplomats often stop here for a glass of champagne before dinner. Its hot *feuilletés* (croissantlike pastries) are great snacks. ♦ Daily, 11AM-2AM. 01.44.71.15.39

65 LESCURE

★★$ Come to this busy and unspoiled bistro to enjoy such dishes as *poule au pot* (boiled chicken with herb stuffing), *confit de canard* (preserved duck breast), rabbit and sorrel, dandelion-green salad, and wild game during hunting season (autumn). ♦ M-F, lunch and dinner; closed in August. Reservations recom-

---

Restaurants/Clubs: Red | Hotels: Purple | Shops: Orange | Outdoors/Parks: Green | Sights/Culture: Blue

mended. 7 Rue de Mondovi (between Rues de Rivoli and du Mont-Thabor). 01.42.60.18.91. Métro: Concorde

66 HÔTEL TALLEYRAND/AMERICAN CONSULATE

Designed by **Jacques-Ange Gabriel**, the architect for Louis XV, and **Jean-François Chalgrin**, who designed the **Arc de Triomphe**, this *hôtel* was originally the residence of diplomat par excellence Charles-Maurice de Talleyrand-Périgord and subsequently housed Czar Alexander I, several French Rothschilds, and, during World War II, the German navy, which kept prisoners of war in the cellars. Today this historic building houses the **American Consulate**, best known among travelers as the office where they replace lost or stolen passports. ♦ 2 Rue St-Florentin (at Rue de Rivoli). 01.43.12.22.22. Métro: Concorde

67 W.H. SMITH

This British bookstore on two levels has 70,000 titles available and is strong in current, recent, and classic fiction; history; travel books; and maps. It's also the best place in Paris to find English-language periodicals. The magazine section carries over 500 titles, and all major British, Irish, and North American international newspapers are delivered daily. ♦ M-Sa. 248 Rue de Rivoli (at Rue Cambon). 01.44.77.88.99. Métro: Concorde

68 HÔTEL INTER-CONTINENTAL PARIS

$$$$ Designed in 1878 by **Charles Garnier**, who built the **Opéra Garnier**, this 450-room establishment has three salons that are classified as historical landmarks. The fanciest receptions in town—including those celebrating the new haute couture collections of Yves Saint Laurent, Guy Laroche, and Jean Patou—take place in these ornate rooms. This hotel has always drawn a varied clientele: Victor Hugo and the Empress Eugénie were

fans, as is Jerry Lewis. The rooms offer both turn-of-the-century elegance and modern conveniences. ♦ 3 Rue de Castiglione (between Rues de Rivoli and du Mont-Thabor). 01.44.77.11.11; fax 01.44.77.14.60. Métros: Concorde, Tuileries paris@interconti.com; www.interconti.com

Within the Hôtel Inter-Continental Paris:

RESTAURANT 234 RIVOLI

★★$$ This airy restaurant overlooking the **Tuileries** features such dishes as terrine of wil duck and dried figs, fresh goat cheese with preserved tomatoes and coriander, lobster ste with fresh pasta, or medallion of venison in honey vinegar during hunting season. If the prices for these à la carte delicacies are beyond your budget, there's a more affordable prix-fixe menu. There's also a lavish buffet breakfast. The restaurant can be entered eithe from the hotel lobby or the street entrance at 234 Rue de Rivoli. ♦ Daily, breakfast, lunch, and dinner to 11PM. 01.44.77.10.40

TERRASSE FLEURIE

★★$$ This flowery terrace restaurant in the hotel's secluded central Cour d'Honneur courtyard serves summery fare from May through September. It is a lovely spot for a buffet lunch, late-afternoon snack, or romantic candlelight dinner. ♦ Daily, lunch and dinner; May-Sept. 01.44.77.10.44

TUILERIES BAR

The perfect spot for a tryst, this cozy and peaceful bar with soft lighting and dark red velvet walls serves sandwiches, snacks, and *plats du jour*. A piano player entertains Tuesday through Saturday between 10PM an closing. ♦ Daily, breakfast, lunch, and dinner until 1AM. 01.44.77.10.47

69 GALIGNANI

Established in 1802, the grande dame of Paris bookstores still sells plenty of books in French, but most of its works are now in English. The store is strong in literature, current affairs, politics, and history, and its international art book section is the most extensive in France. ♦ M-Sa. 224 Rue de Rivoli (between Rues d'Alger and de Castiglione). 01.42.60.76.07. Métros: Concorde, Tuileries

The first Paris métro line opened in 1900, running between Porte Maillot and Porte de Vincennes. The No. 1 is still in operation but has been extended by three stops to Grande Arche de La Défense on the Porte Maillot end and by three stops to Château de Vincennes in the eastern part of the city.

69 ANGÉLINA

★★★$$ The Rolls-Royce of Parisian tea salons, this place originally went by the name **Rumpelmayer's**. It was founded in 1903 on the former site of the king's stables. Amid marble pedestal tables, landscapes by Lorrant-Heilbronn, and gilt décor, the hardworking wait staff deliver justly celebrated pastries, sumptuous hot chocolate, and *Mont Blanc*, a weighty concoction of chestnut cream purée (a favorite of the Aga Khan). The whipped cream is fresh and the ice water is served on silver trays. In spring and autumn, get a table near Rue de Rivoli, where you can watch top models and fashion designers returning from the ready-to-wear collection fashion shows. ♦ Daily, breakfast, lunch, and afternoon tea. 226 Rue de Rivoli (between Rues d'Alger and de Castiglione). 01.42.60.82.00. Métros: Concorde, Tuileries

69 HÔTEL MEURICE

$$$$ For the better part of 2 centuries heads of state (vacationing and exiled), artists, writers, and other celebrities have favored this refined 160-room property. Alphonse XIII of Spain stayed here for years, and Salvador Dalí made it his Paris home for 3 decades. During World War II, the hotel served as German army headquarters; it was here that Commandant General von Cholitz, after disobeying Hitler's orders to burn Paris, surrendered to the Allies in August 1944. Since the hotel opened in 1817, it has attracted many famous North American visitors, including Herman Melville, Henry James, Henry Wadsworth Longfellow, and Wilbur and Orville Wright, who stayed here in 1907 while trying to sell their airplane to the French. (The Wrights used the familiar argument that their invention was the weapon to end all wars. The French military didn't buy that, but the public was captivated by the biplane that the Wrights had shipped all the way to Paris from Dayton, Ohio.)

The hostelry was extensively renovated in 2000—the number of rooms was reduced from 180 to 160 to make room for more suites (including a huge penthouse with a 360-degree view of Paris); a new sub-basement was dug to house the heating and air-conditioning units; the electrical and plumbing systems were modernized; a winter garden was created; and a fully up-to-date health spa featuring Candalie-wine grape-seed-extract treatments was installed. The styles of Louis XV and XVI still prevail throughout the hotel. Tea under the Art Nouveau glass dome of the **Jardin d'Hiver** is a discreet pleasure, especially in the late afternoon after the pianist settles at the keys, and the wood-paneled **Bar Fontainebleau** with its comfortable red leather club chairs offers a choice of 90 cocktails.

Note: There's no charge for children 13 and under when sharing a room with a parent or guardian, and pets are free of charge. ♦ 228 Rue de Rivoli (between Rues d'Alger and de Castiglione). 01.44.58.10.10; fax 01.44.58.10.19. Métros: Concorde, Tuileries. reservations@meuricehotel.com; www.meuricehotel.com

Within Hôtel Meurice:

LE MEURICE

★★★$$$$ In this opulent dining room directly inspired by the royal apartments of the Château de Versailles, you may feast like a king on chef Marc Marchand's *mille-feuille de tomate et chèvre frais au basilic* (puff pastry of tomato and goat cheese with basil), nuggets of lamb with dried fruits, tuna steak pan-fried in olive oil, and his remarkable coconut biscuit with coconut sorbet. Sommelier Antoine Zochetto's awe-inspiring wine list includes 850 entries. ♦ Daily, breakfast, lunch, and dinner. 01.44.58.10.55

70 COMFORT HOTEL LOUVRE MONTANA

$$ Clean, modern, and conveniently located near the Tuileries and St-Roch (which has marvelous evening concerts), this 25-room hotel is an isle of economy in an archipelago of extravagance. There's no restaurant. ♦ 12 Rue St-Roch (between Rues de Rivoli and St-Honoré). 01.42.60.35.10; fax 01.42.61.12.28. Métro: Tuileries. lm@hotels-emeraude.com; www.hotels-emeraude.com

71 ST-JAMES ET ALBANY

$$$ Portions of this elegant hotel date back to the reign of Louis XIV, which is appropriate because for years its clientele was strictly old European aristocracy. It now offers 202 rooms, suites, duplexes, and home-away-from-home studios equipped with kitchenettes. The nicest accommodations are nestled in the attic beneath low-beamed ceilings. The hotel incorporates parts of the old **Noailles Mansion**, where General Lafayette married one of the Noailles daughters in 1774, and where Queen Marie Antoinette paid a visit in 1779. It is built around a garden and interior courtyard, away from the traffic noise of Rue de Rivoli. ♦ 202 Rue de Rivoli (between Rues St-Roch and du 29-Juillet). 01.44.58.43.21; fax 01.44.58.43.11. Métro: Tuileries. hotel@clarionsaintjames.com; www.clarionsaintjames.com

---

Restaurants/Clubs: Red | Hotels: Purple | Shops: Orange | Outdoors/Parks: Green | Sights/Culture: Blue

Within St-James et Albany:

LE NOAILLES

★$$ Love will blossom when you stroll through the **Tuileries** with that special someone and then dine tête-à-tête in the courtyard of this elegant dining spot. Recommended dishes include *pavé de cabillaud mi-fumé* (lightly smoked cod) and pork tenderloin with apples and Calvados. ♦ Daily, lunch and dinner. 01.44.58.43.40, 01.44.58.43.21

BAR ST-JAMES

★★$$ This library-turned-bar is one of coziest spots in town for a quiet drink or a light lunch. The luncheon special, which changes daily, is dependable and inexpensive. ♦ Bar: 5PM-1AM. Restaurant: daily, lunch. 01.44.58.43.44

72 STATUE DE JEANNE D'ARC

This gilded equestrian statue by 19th-century sculptor Frémiet honors Joan of Arc (1412-1431), the French national hero and Roman Catholic saint. Born during the Hundred Years' War (1337-1453), this charismatic peasant girl claimed she heard the voices of saints urging her to save France from the English. She was able to convince the dauphin Charles VII to provide her with troops that, under her generalship, took back Orléans and routed the English forces in the Loire. In 1429, during an unsuccessful attempt to liberate Paris from the occupying English army, Joan stationed a cannon on Butte St-Roch (leveled some 3 centuries ago as landfill for the Champ-de-Mars) to attack the St-Honoré Gate (which is now 163 Rue St-Honoré). A year later Joan of Arc was captured by Burgundians and turned over to the English, and the following year she was convicted of witchcraft and heresy by a tribunal of French clerics who supported the English, then burned at the stake in Rouen. She was canonized in 1920, and today France honors her with a national holiday. ♦ Pl des Pyramides (between Rues de Rivoli and des Pyramides). Métro: Tuileries

73 HÔTEL REGINA

$$$$ Offering a splendid view of the **Tuileries Gardens**, this quiet 120-room hotel is furnished with antiques, crystal chandeliers, and a Louis XV-style elevator cage that has been retired from service and put on display in the lobby. The Belle Epoque-style restaurant serves standard French fare. ♦ 2 Pl des

> I got the impulse for doing things my way in Paris.
> —Alexander Calder

Pyramides (at Rue de Rivoli). 01.42.60.31.10; fax 01.40.15.95.16. Métro Tuileries. helene@regina-hotel.com; www.regina-hotel.com

74 PLAZA ATHÉNÉE

$$$$ Elegant and charming, this 187-room and suite property has long enjoyed a reputation as the most fashionable palace hotel in Paris, largely because its **Relais Plaza** restaurant (see page 161) remains the favored lunchtime hangout of Paris couturiers. In fact when the great designer Pierre Balmain died, the management retired his table. Also on the premises are three Michelin-star restaurants; **Le Bar** (see page 161); the **Cour Jardin** (see page 161) for summertime dining; and a classic Parisian gathering place for tea or a drink, the **Galerie des Gobelins** (see page 161). The Louis XV- and XVI-style décor features a profusion of flowers—the hotel staff boasts that the monthly florist's bill is higher than the electric bill. In 1918 West Point graduate Captain George Patton stayed here while learning to fence at the French Military Academy in Saumur. While in residence, Patton discussed combat with then 28-year-old Charles de Gaulle. Marlene Dietrich, Grace Kelly, Gary Cooper, and Jacqueline Kennedy also stayed here. Today the hotel's select out-of-town clientele includes Rockefellers, rich Brazilians, and the like. The rooms and suites on the first six floors are decorated in Louis XV, Louis XVI, and Regency style, and on the seventh and eighth floors in Art Deco, with original sketches by great fashion designers decorating the corridors and suites, all in the most exquisite of taste. The hotel was entirely refurbished and now offers all up-to-date audio, video, and personal communication technologies in every room, including Internet access via television cable. ♦ 25 Ave Montaigne (between Rues Clément-Marot and du Boccador). 01.53.67.66.65; fax 01.53.67.66.66. (From the US, toll-free: 800.223.6800.) Métro: Alma-Marceau. www.plaza-athenee-paris.com

Within the Plaza Athénée:

RESTAURANT PLAZA ATHÉNÉE

★★★★$$$ The décor of this elegant Regency-style dining room *"relooké"* by

Patrick Jouin—the big crystal chandelier encircled in a gauzy gray web, the Louis XVI chairs upholstered in gun-metal–gray fabric—tips the diners off right away to what they can expect: a blithe spirit that also extends to the cuisine proposed here at the flagship of the world's most famous chef, Alain Ducasse, whose network of restaurants extends to two others in Paris, one each in Tokyo, New York, and London, and several in Monte Carlo and Provence. Under the day-to-day direction of his right-hand chef Jean-François Piège, Ducasse offers such starters as jellied tomato in Parmesan granita, squab and foie gras wrapped in a cabbage leaf, sea scallops with white truffles and lettuce cream, and crayfish tails with wild mushrooms in shellfish juice. For main courses there are milk-fed lamb with preserved lemon and bits of dried fruit, lobster curry (to shake up the traditionalists), and Bresse chicken with *albuféra* sauce. For dessert, choose between Ducasse's legendary sheep's-cheese curd with caramel mousse and honey ice cream and his equally legendary *baba au rhum*. This is one of the world's most expensive restaurants, but if you can afford it (or the company's paying), eating here is an experience you'll never forget. In summer the restaurant serves at a few tables on a terrace overlooking the hotel's central courtyard. ♦ Th, F, lunch and dinner; M, Tu, W, dinner; closed mid-July to mid-August. Reservations required months in advance. 01.53.67.65.00

LE BAR

★★$$ Between the décor and the drinks, this is one hot hotel bar. The former is the creation of **Patrick Jouin** and features a long illuminated bar fashioned of sculpted and sandblasted glass as well as reproductions of 17th-century landscape paintings with frames so deep that you can sit inside them. Libations run the gamut from simply elegant—the Rose Royale is made with champagne and fresh raspberry purée—to simply outrageous: the Bubblegum has strawberry liqueur and vodka jelly studded with strawberry pieces, a layer of bubblegum ice cream mixed with vodka, and, *mais oui*, a piece of pink Malabar chewing gum at the bottom. Daily, 6PM-2AM.

RELAIS PLAZA

★★$$ As with all food served at the hotel, this chic brasserie with superb 1930s Art Deco décor inspired by the dining room of the ocean liner *Normandie* is under the culinary direction of Alain Ducasse, and the master's touch is happily in evidence. Try the fresh shellfish-and-lobster-salad; one of the grilled fish, poultry, or meat dishes accompanied by a good house wine; and for dessert, a fresh fruit salad or one of the house's own fruit sorbets. The restaurant has long been a lunchtime favorite of *le tout Paris* of the arts, the neighborhood's many fashion designers in particular, and of the after-theater and -concert crowd in the late evening. ♦ Daily, lunch and dinner. Reservations recommended. 01.53.67.64.00

COUR JARDIN

★★$$ With its big red umbrellas, climbing vines, and Mediterranean-accented summer cuisine, this alfresco restaurant set up in the hotel's peaceful interior courtyard is a charming spot for lunch or dinner when the weather gets warm and the Paris traffic gets noisy. ♦ Daily, lunch and dinner, May-Sept. 01.53.67.66.02

GALERIE DES GOBELINS

Named for its Gobelins carpets, this long, elegant gallery along the courtyard dotted with cozy alcoves is a lovely spot for breakfast, a light lunch, or afternoon tea, when the sumptuous pastry cart comes along, and you may order drinks anytime. Come here after a performance at the **Théâtre des Champs-Elysées** and mix with the concert crowd and the South American night owls staying at the hotel. ♦ Daily, 8AM-midnight

75 HÔTEL DE LA TRÉMOILLE

$$$$ This impressive-yet-relaxed 107-room hotel is a bit of *vieux France* in the heart of the high-fashion district. The rooms are furnished with antiques and feature sumptuous bathrooms. After an afternoon of shopping at **Christian Dior** and **Nina Ricci**, dine here or at one of the restaurants in the nearby **Plaza Athénée** and charge your meal to your room. ♦ 14 Rue de La Trémoille (at Rue du Boccador). 01.56.52.14.00; fax 01.40.70.01.08. Métro: Alma-Marceau. 100750.1177@compuserve.com

Within the Hôtel de la Trémoille:

LE LOUIS D'OR

★★$$$ A fire burns in the *cheminée* (fireplace) of this elegant but cozy dining room. With an emphasis on traditional cuisine, a fine meal here might consist of a starter of potato cakes with truffles and port or scallop salad with lime, a main course of sole meunière or roast lamb with fresh thyme, and a dessert of crème brûlée or *tarte Tatin*

(apple tart). ♦ M-F, breakfast, lunch, and dinner; Sa-Su, breakfast and lunch. Reservations required. 01.47.23.34.20

ⓥ VALENTINO

76 VALENTINO

The Milan designer's Paris boutique, all beige marble and glass, shows his sophisticated men's and women's fashions as well as the casual, less expensive clothes sold under his younger label, Miss Valentino. ♦ M-Sa. 17-19 Ave Montaigne (at Rue du Boccador). 01.47.23.64.61. Métro: Alma–Marceau

77 THÉÂTRE DES CHAMPS-ELYSÉES

Here, on 29 May 1913, the **Ballets Russes** of Sergei Diaghilev first performed to the music of the Stravinsky piece Le Sacré du Printemps. Riots followed the performance, which was shocking in its originality and modernity. Diaghilev, Stravinsky, Nijinsky, and Cocteau fled the mobs for the **Bois de Boulogne** and drove around while Diaghilev wept.

Inaugurated in 1913, the theater was one of the first buildings of reinforced concrete in Paris; it was designed by **Auguste Perret**, who was later hired to reconstruct the entire port city of Le Havre after World War II. Today it is the city's most celebrated classical music venue; it also hosts opera and dance performances.

North American footnotes: On 2 October 1925 La Revue Nègre opened here; John Dos

---

What is most striking about [the "Lost Generation"] is the superficial nature of their relation to the capital. The Paris that they treasured was a Paris that never existed, a Paris found only in tourist brochures. . . . Would anyone reading the work of these writers come away with the slightest notion of what France had suffered in the First World War, of how bitter the aftermath of that war was, of how deep were the country's economic difficulties, or of how fascism first began to make its presence known?

—Patrice Higonnet, Paris: Capital of the World, 2002

The gnarled robinia pseudoacacia (false acacia) tree that can be seen alongside the St-Julien-le-Pauvre church was planted in 1602 or 1680—either date would make it the likeliest candidate for oldest living tree in Paris.

Passos painted the show's stage set, Sidney Bechet played clarinet, and Josephine Baker danced to "Yes, Sir, That's My Baby." In May 1927 a Charles Lindbergh autograph sold for $1,500 at an auction held at the theater. (Th name of his plane, The Spirit of St. Louis, pleased the French, who associated it not with Missouri but with the saintliest of their line of kings.) And on 16 April 1928, the Gershwins attended the opening of a performance of La Rhapsodie en Bleu by the Ballet Russes. ♦ Box office: M-Sa. No performances 1 July through the first week of September and holidays. 15 Ave Montaigne (between Rue du Boccador and Pl de l'Alma). 01.49.52.50.00. Métro: Alma–Marceau

Atop the Théâtre des Champs-Elysées:

◼ maisonblanche
restaurantbar

MAISON BLANCHE

★★★$$$ The arrival of Pourcel twins Laurent and Jacques of the Michelin-three-star Jardin des Sens restaurant in Montpellier was one o the haute cuisine events of 2001 in Paris, bringing a new élan to this already glamorous restaurant high atop the **Théâtre des Champs-Elysées**. The cuisine here is Mediterranean, featuring tiny sea urchins stuffed with crabmeat and caviar, salad of raw and cooked vegetable of the moment with a red-beet caramel sauce, rouget (red mullet), sea bass baked with preserved lemons, and roasted leg of milk-fed lamb from the Pyrénées with a thick layer of herbs. There is a dazzling selection of southern French wines. The airy, all-white décor and spectacular view of the **Eiffel Tower** through the two-story-high plate-glass front wall give you the feeling of being on a deluxe rooftop bateau mouche. The restaurant remains a great favorite of people from the nearby haute couture houses and from the world of entertainment, who come here to see and especially to be seen, so dress accordingly—you will be seen. ♦ M-F lunch and dinner; Sa, dinner. 15 Ave Montaigne (between Rue du Boccador and Pl de l'Alma). 01.47.23.55.99. Métro: Alma–Marceau

chez francis

78 CHEZ FRANCIS

★★$$ Formerly a relais de poste (stable for the post office's horses), this bistro boasts a three-star view of the **Eiffel Tower** and the largest outdoor terrace in Paris. A show-biz crowd assembles here for fresh seafood platters, grilled sole, roasted Scottish salmon with bacon and lentils, poached skate, roasted chicken with tandoori sauce, and lamb kebab. ◆ Daily, lunch and dinner. Reservations recommended. 7 Pl de l'Alma (at Ave George-V). 01.47.20.86.83. Métro: Alma-Marceau

79 AVENUE GEORGE-V

Along this grand avenue named after the English king, you will find the **American Cathedral**; the salons of **Givenchy** and **Balenciaga**; the Chinese and Mexican Embassies; the elegant **Four Seasons Hotel George V**; and the **Crazy Horse**, with its sophisticated girlie shows. ◆ Between Pl de l'Alma and Ave des Champs-Elysées. Métros: Alma-Marceau, George-V

79 MARIUS ET JANETTE

★★★$$$ For a taste of some of the finest *provençale* cuisine available in Paris, reserve a table at this gracious seafood restaurant, which is set on a large yacht. Chef Laurent Odiot serves classic bouillabaisse, lobster salad, sea bass flambé, and a selection of other seafood dishes. A favorite of celebrities (Sylvester Stallone, Michelle Pfeiffer, and Robert De Niro have all dined here), this place has an appropriately nautical feel, with lots of wood and photos of fishers on the walls. Note: Bouillabaisse lovers must call 2 days in advance to order the dish. ◆ Daily, lunch and dinner. Reservations recommended. 4 Ave George-V (between Pl de l'Alma and Rue de La Trémoille). 01.47.23.41.88. Métro: Alma-Marceau

79 LE BISTROT DE MARIUS

★★$$ Pagnol's Marius may have run away to sea, but the chef here seems to have just returned. The bill of fare at this warm, *provençale*-style spot revolves around the freshest of raw shellfish, rockfish soup, sea scallops, and, for carnivores, roast lamb fillets with sautéed potatoes. ◆ Daily, lunch and dinner. 6 Ave George-V (between Pl de l'Alma and Rue de la Trémoille). 01.40.70.11.76. Métro: Alma-Marceau

79 CRAZY HORSE SALOON

The originality of *l'art du nu* (the art of the nude) in Paris's sexiest floor show lies in the play of light patterns projected onto the nearly nude bodies of the 18 women dancers—"living pictures," as the spectacle's creator, **Alain Bernardin**, called them. Updated every

year, the show has attracted millions of spectators since the club opened in 1951. The women come from all over Europe, but they must be of uniform height—between 5 feet 4 inches and 5 feet 5 inches tall—so that their salient features line up neatly on stage. The performers adopt fanciful stage names—Choo Choo Nightrain, Fuzzy Logic, Lola Fragola, Tita de Cucufa, and Pussy Duty-Free were just some of the more appealing appellations at press time. The show also features brilliant puppet and magic acts. The club has arrangements with neighboring **Chez Francis** (see above) and **Fouquet's** (see page 146), where spectators can dine either before or after the show. ◆ Cover. Shows: M-F, Su, 8:30PM, 11PM; Sa, 7:30PM, 9:45PM, 11:50PM. Reservations recommended. 12 Ave George-V (between Pl de l'Alma and Rue de la Trémoille). 01.47.23.93.90. Métro: Alma-Marceau. www.crazy-horse.fr

80 2 AVENUE MONTAIGNE

Back when this was the **Hôtel Elysée-Bellevue**, Sinclair Lewis passed the winter of 1924 here writing *Arrowsmith*. It is now a private residential building. ◆ At Pl de la Reine-Astrid. Métro: Alma-Marceau

81 BAR DES THÉÂTRES

★★$$ This lively bar-restaurant is patronized during the day by a democratic mix of shoppers, local business- and tradespeople, and workers from nearby construction sites who pop in for a beer; in the evening by theatergoers and critics before, during, and after performances; and by actors and actresses unwinding after the curtain comes down. The fare is simple: *charcuteries*, smoked salmon, steak with pepper sauce, *choucroute*, osso buco, and the like. Service with a smile by the veteran team of waiters. ◆ Daily, lunch and dinner until 2AM. 6 Ave Montaigne (between Rue François-1ᵉʳ and Pl de la Reine-Astrid). 01.47.23.34.63. Métro: Alma-Marceau

82 PRADA

When good fashion victims die, as Oscar Wilde might have said, they go to Prada. ◆ M-Sa. 10 Ave Montaigne (between Rue François-1ᵉʳ and Pl de la Reine-Astrid). 01.53.23.99.40. Métro: Alma-Marceau

83 SAN RÉGIS

$$$$ This sophisticated and discreet 44-room hotel has hosted Raquel Welch and Lauren Bacall. It's decorated with fine antiques and paintings and sits close (but not

too close) to the Champs-Elysées. There's a restaurant and a bar. ♦ 12 Rue Jean-Goujon (between Ave Franklin-D.-Roosevelt and Pl François-1er). 01.44.95.16.16; fax 01.45.61.05.48. Métro: Franklin-D.-Roosevelt. message@hotel-sanregis.fr; www.hotel-sanregis.fr

84 7 RUE FRANÇOIS-1ER

During World War II, this building, formerly the **Hôtel du Palais**, was the headquarters of the American Red Cross. It was here that North American poet e.e. cummings, a volunteer ambulance driver, spent a glorious May in 1917, accidentally detached from his unit. This was the start of a series of tragicomic events that led to his spending 6 months in a French prison, an experience that provided cummings with ample material for his autobiographical prose work, *The Enormous Room*, published in 1922. The building is now privately owned. ♦ Between Cours Albert-1er and Pl François-1er. Métro: Franklin-D.-Roosevelt

85 LASSERRE

★★★$$$$ In the same luxurious league (and price range) as the **Tour d'Argent** and **Grand Véfour**, this restaurant is famous for its caviar, 1930s ocean-liner décor, and service bordering on perfection. (Owner René Lasserre got his start in the restaurant business washing dishes at the age of 13, and all that experience shows.) Located in a small town house, the main dining room is reached by a velvet-lined elevator. In warm weather, the ceiling, painted by **Touchagues**, rolls away, providing patrons with a view of the stars and a little cool air. Masterpieces from the repertoire include lobster salad with warm potatoes and artichokes with a Chardonnay vinaigrette; slices of turbot roasted with butter, salt, and vinegar juice and served with purée of mushrooms and radishes; morsels of lamb with a scent of winter simmered with figs and exotic vegetables; and *crêpes flambées au* Grand Marnier. The restaurant's illustrious wine cellar

has 140,000 bottles. ♦ M, dinner; Tu-Sa, lunch and dinner; closed in August. Reservations required; jackets required. 17 Ave Franklin-D.-Roosevelt (between Rues François-1er and Jean-Goujon). 01.43.59.53.43. Métro: Franklin-D.-Roosevelt

86 FRANCE AMÉRIQUE

If you want to give a party and insist on nothing less than a Second Empire town house for your setting, consider this place, which rents its three Louis XVI rooms (200 square meters/660 square feet) for festivities lasting just until midnight. Have **Angélina** (see page 159) take care of the catering for the perfect lavish bash. ♦ 9 Ave Franklin-D.-Roosevelt (between Rues François-1er and Jean-Goujon). 01.43.59.51.00. Métro: Franklin-D.-Roosevelt

87 PALAIS DE LA DÉCOUVERTE

The western part of the **Grand Palais** houses a sprawling science museum offering holography exhibitions, Jacques Cousteau festivals, daily demonstrations on everything from ants to astronomy, and 9,000 stars twinkling on the ceiling of its celebrated planetarium. Kids love the Madagascar agate and, of course, the metal replicas of dinosaurs. ♦ Admission. Tu-Su. Ave Franklin-D.-Roosevelt (between Cours la Reine and Ave du Général-Eisenhower). 01.56.43.20.21. Métro: Franklin-D.-Roosevelt. www.palais.decouverte.fr

88 GRAND PALAIS

Along with the **Pont Alexandre III** and the **Petit Palais**, this exuberant stone, steel, and glass structure is an example of Art Nouveau architecture at its most excessive. Like the Petit Palais, the **Grand Palais** was built for the **1900 Exposition Universelle**. Famous for its vast domed and vaulted glass roof and superb staircase, the Grand Palais was the work of three architects: **Henri Deglane** designed the principal façade; **Albert Thomas**, the rear façade; and **Louis-Albert Louvet**, the rest. With 54,000 square feet of floor space (equivalent to nearly 14 basketball courts), this structure is used for blockbuster art exhibitions. ♦ Admission. Open only for special exhibitions and events; call for schedule or check *Pariscope* or *L'Officiel des Spectacles*. Ave Winston-Churchill (between Cours la Reine and Pl Clemenceau). 01.44.13.17.17. Métro: Champs-Elysées–Clemenceau

89 PETIT PALAIS

This turn-of-the-century palace, which is *petit* only by comparison to the leviathan **Grand Palais** across the street, houses the fine arts museum of the City of Paris. Its collection of 10,000 paintings, sculptures, and objets d'art

---

The Brigade Fluviale (River Brigade) of the City of Paris employs 50 divers full-time. Every year they fish about 100 people out of the Seine, half of them alive (accidents or failed suicide attempts) and half of them *perdus aux eaux*—lost to the waters.

The French will only be united under the threat of danger. No one can simply bring together a country that has over 265 kinds of cheese.

—Charles de Gaulle

is strongest in 19th-century French painters such as Delacroix, Courbet, Monet, Cézanne, and Bonnard. Architect **Charles Girault**, who designed the building for the **1900 Exposition Universelle**, the first world's fair in Paris, crowned it with a graceful cupola and decorated its two wings with Ionic columns and rococo embellishments. The museum is currently closed for a complete renovation and is scheduled to reopen at the beginning of 2005. ♦ Admission. Tu-Su. Ave Winston-Churchill (between Cours la Reine and Ave Charles-Girault). 01.42.65.12.73. Métro: Champs-Elysées–Clemenceau

90 LEDOYEN

★★★$$$$ During the reign of Louis XVI (1774-1792), this dining spot on the south side of the Champs-Elysées was a country inn and dairy bar serving fresh milk to travelers. Dinner here can still seem pleasantly bucolic; the view of the Champs-Elysées from the elegant upstairs dining room is superb. Young chef Christian Le Squer has made himself right at home here with his imaginative, exquisitely prepared and served offerings. For starters, choose from whole-roasted foie gras–stuffed Landes duckling sliced at your table, giant langoustines served both deep-fried on a bed of angel-hair noodles and roasted in their own shells, or simple and elegant grilled *coquilles St-Jacques* (scallops). Main courses include sole sautéed in sage butter with a rémoulade of cucumber and fresh ginger, and braised turbot and mashed potatoes with truffle butter. The desserts are stupendous, and the restaurant has one of the finest wine lists in Paris. ♦ M-F, lunch and dinner; closed the month of August. Jacket and tie required. Reservations required. Carré des Champs-Elysées (off Ave Edward-Tuck). 01.53.05.10.01. Métro: Champs Elysées–Clemenceau

91 CHEVAUX DE MARLY (MARLY HORSES)

The two sculptures of rearing horses at the entrance to the Champs-Elysées are actually replicas. The originals by Nicolas and Guillaume Coustou, called *Africans Mastering the Numidian Horses*, were taken from the **Château de Marly** (the Louis XIV château that was destroyed in the revolution) and placed here in 1795. Sixteen horses dragged the statues to Paris in 5 hours, a transportation feat considered so marvelous that the vehicle in which they were carried is exhibited in the **Conservatoire des Arts et Métiers**. In 1994, the original Coustou sculptures were moved to **La Cour Marly**, a glass-covered courtyard in

the **Louvre**. ♦ Ave des Champs-Elysées (at Pl de la Concorde). Métro: Concorde

91 AVENUE DES CHAMPS-ELYSÉES

The neighborhood that is now the site of the world's most famous boulevard was forsaken marshland, unsafe after dark, until 1616, when Marie de Médicis, the wife of Henri IV, had a fashionable carriage-drive, the Cours-la-Reine (Queen's Way), built west of the **Tuileries** along the **Seine**. A half-century later, master landscaper **André Le Nôtre** planted double rows of chestnut trees to create another avenue to the northwest. Originally called the Grand Cours, this second avenue was later renamed the Avenue des Champs-Elysées (Elysian Fields). In 1724 the boulevard was extended to the top of the Butte de Chaillot. Fifty years later, architect **Jacques-Germain Soufflot** leveled it by 16 feet to ease the climb for carriage-towing horses.

Since its creation, the Champs-Elysées has always been the place to promenade. Processions marking the liberation of Paris (26 August 1944), the student-worker demonstrations (30 May 1968), the death of Charles de Gaulle (12 November 1970), and the French soccer team's victories in the 1998 World Cup and the 2000 European Football Championship all made their way down this street. If you fancy pomp and pageantry, show up here on Bastille Day (14 July), when the jets of the French air force streak overhead; Armistice Day (11 November), when the president lays a wreath on the **Tomb of the Unknown Soldier**; in late July when the grueling 3-week Tour de France bicycle race ends here; and at Christmastime, when the avenue's trees twinkle with tiny white lights. The eastern half of the boulevard, from Place de la Concorde to Rond-Point des Champs-Elysées, is bordered by lush gardens of azaleas and mature chestnut trees. Within the gardens are theaters (the **Théâtre de Marigny** and **Théâtre du Rond-Point**) and exclusive restaurants with pretty garden terraces, such as **Ledoyen** and **Laurent**. The western half of the avenue leads from the Rond-Point des Champs-Elysées to the Place Charles-de-Gaulle, also known as Place d'Etoile, where the **Arc de Triomphe** hulks large at the top of the wide, tree-lined avenue. A major face-lift of this commercial section of the Champs-Elysées in the 1990s gave it new wide granite sidewalks, ended on-street parking, and toned down the garish décor of certain fast-food outlets that had tarnished the avenue's aristocratic image. Banks, airline offices, shops and shopping arcades, numerous cafés, restaurants, fast-food businesses, ice-

Avenue des Champs-Elysées

cream parlors, and several big cinemas line this lively stretch where strolling has become a delight once again, night or day. ♦ Between Pls de la Concorde and Charles-de-Gaulle. Métros: Concorde, Champs-Elysées–Clemenceau, Franklin-D.-Roosevelt, George-V, Charles-de-Gaulle–Etoile

92 PLACE DE LA CONCORDE

The largest square in Paris, covering 21 acres, was a swamp until royal architect **Jacques-Ange Gabriel** was asked by Louis XV to find a setting appropriate for an equestrian statue of the king himself. The statue stood on the square, originally named for Louis XV, for less than 20 years; it was removed during the revolution. On Sunday, 21 January 1793, the guillotine was set up on the square's west side (near the spot where the statue of Brest sculpted by Cortot stands today). Louis XVI was beheaded, and the 13-month Reign of Terror began. Among its thousands of victims were Marie Antoinette, Madame du Barry, Charlotte Corday, and Danton. On the evening of 28 July 1794, more than 1,300 townspeople gathered here to watch the execution of Robespierre. During the revolution, no fewer than 1,343 victims were executed on the **Place de la Révolution** (as it was known then), and the square so reeked of gore that herds of oxen balked at crossing it. The *place* subsequently was given the name *concorde* (peace) as a way of laying to rest its violent past. ♦ Between Jardin des Tuileries and Ave des Champs-Elysées. Métro: Concorde

On Place de la Concorde:

OBELISK OF LUXOR

This 3,300-year-old, 220-ton Egyptian obelisk is unquestionably the oldest monument in Paris. Originally erected around the 13th century BC in the Temple of Luxor, the 76-foot-tall monument was a gift to Louis Philippe from Mohammed Ali Pasha, who was viceroy of Egypt, in 1831. (He also gave Queen Victoria Cleopatra's Needle, a slightly shorter obelisk taken from Heliopolis.) The pink-granite Paris obelisk, which replaced the equestrian statue of Louis XV that was removed during the revolution, traveled 600 miles by barge down the Nile to Alexandria, was towed across the Mediterranean and up the Atlantic, was carted through Normandy, and finally was erected at Place de la Concorde in 1836, ending a political squabble over whose monument should adorn a square dedicated to neither a French king nor Napoléon's army. The designs on the pedestal are meant to illustrate the technological wizardry involved in the obelisk's journey from Egypt to Paris.

Visitors be forewarned: Pedestrians crossing the **Place de la Concorde** on foot are taking their lives in their hands. But go ahead; you only live once, and the obelisk is worth a close look. What's more, the island surrounding it provides an unobstructed view of the Champs-Elysées. Cross at the light!

SCULPTURE AND FOUNTAINS

Adorning Gabriel's original octagonal square are several groups of statuary, allegorical figures representing Bordeaux, Brest, Lille, Marseilles, Nantes, Rouen, and Strasbourg. Believe it or not, the tiny two-room pavilions underneath the statues were once rented out as dwellings. North and south of the obelisk stand two fountains, one representing maritime navigation, and the other, river navigation. The latter, ironically, is the farthest from the **Seine**. The fountains' sea nymphs and water gods are replicas of those found in fountains in St. Peter's Square in Rome.

93 JARDIN DES TUILERIES (TUILERIES GARDENS)

The elegant gardens *à la française* were designed in 1664 for Louis XIV by **André Le Nôtre**, the king's gardener, who was born in a cottage on the royal grounds. Le Nôtre also designed the gardens at **Versailles**, **Chantilly**, and the **Château Vaux-le-Vicomte**. It's hard to believe that this lovely and serene spot was the site of such violence during the revolution (the **Palais des Tuileries**, then the home of the royal family, was attacked by an angry mob in 1792). Stroll through the manicured hedges and lawns near the 18 bronze nudes by Aristide Maillol. In 1998, 12 works by Rodin and such modern artists as Giacometti, Laurens, Max Ernst, Dubuffet, and Germaine Richier were permanently installed here for the pleasure of the six million people who visit the gardens every year. You'll see old women feeding the pigeons, vendors lofting mechanical birds into the air in hope of attracting a sale, and kids racing sailboats on the fountain under the watchful eyes of their governesses. Four refreshment stands, a small merry-go-round, a swing set, and subdued pony rides for children are available.

From the upper terrace of the gardens is a splendid view of the **Seine**, the **Musée d'Orsay**, and the **Palais de la Légion d'Honneur**, which was begun by Napoléon to laud French accomplishment. Farther in the distance, you can glimpse the stern neoclassic **Palais Bourbon**, where the Chambre des Députés, France's congress, holds its sessions. This terrace has become known as a gathering spot for gay men. ♦ 7AM-8:30PM between 31 March and the last weekend in September; 7:30AM-7:30PM the rest of the year. Bounded by Ave du Général-Lemonnier and Place de la Concorde and Quai des Tuileries and Rue de Rivoli. Métros: Tuileries, Concorde

Within the Jardin des Tuileries:

GALERIE NATIONALE DU JEU DE PAUME

The name of this museum, built in 1853 by Napoléon III, refers to the building's original function as an indoor court where royalty played the racket sport that was the precursor of tennis. The sport was created by medieval monks who started swatting wads of rags around the monastery courtyard with the palm of their hands; *jeu de paume* meaning literally "the game of the palm." Rackets came later. In 1907, a group of painters called Impressionists commandeered the building and used it as a gallery. From 1947 until 1986, the **Louvre**'s collection of French Impressionist masterpieces was housed here, making this the most visited museum in the world relative to its size. The Impressionist collection was moved across the river to St-Germain's **Musée d'Orsay**, and since 1991 the renovated galleries here have hosted changing exhibitions by contemporary artists. On the terrace to the south of the museum is a monument to Charles Perrault, the 17th-century fabulist who convinced Colbert to make the Tuileries public. ♦ Call ahead for opening times; Tu, noon-9:30PM; W-F, noon-7PM; Sa-Su, 10AM-7PM. Northwest corner (at Pl de la Concorde). 01.47.03.12.52 www.jeudepaume.org

PALAIS DES TUILERIES (TUILERIES PALACE)

Designed in 1564 by **Philibert Delorme**, this palace stood until 1884. It connected the two corner pavilions of the **Louvre** (paralleling what is today Avenue du Général-Lemonnier) and took its name from the *tuile* (tile) factories that had previously stood on the site. Catherine de Médicis, for whom the palace was built, moved out after her astrologer, Ruggieri, told her she would die close to St-Germain. Because the Tuileries was in the parish of **St-Germain-l'Auxerrois**, Catherine built another palace near what is today the **Bourse du Commerce** (Commercial Stock Exchange), and there she died. As for Ruggieri's prediction: The priest who administered the last rites to Catherine de Médicis was named Julien de St-Germain.

Napoléon's second wife gave birth in the palace to a short-lived imperial heir, l'Aiglon, who was named the king of Rome. Subsequent royal residents included Charles X and Louis-Philippe, who ruled between 1831 and 1848 and was popularly known as the "Grocers' King" for his custom of carving the

---

Sunday roast himself. In 1871, during the Siege of Paris, the Communards set the palace afire. It burned for 3 days while the **Louvre Museum** staff members worked frantically to save the collections. The palace was razed between 1882 and 1884; a single bay was preserved and stands unmarked in a remote corner of the **Tuileries Gardens** behind the **Jeu de Paume**.

BASSIN OCTAGONAL ET TERRASSES (OCTAGONAL FOUNTAIN AND TERRACES)

Between the **Jeu de Paume** and **L'Orangerie** (see below) are a series of 18th-century statues representing the Nile, the Tiber, the Loire and Loiret, the Marne, and the Seine Rivers, part of an overall garden design that also includes the adjoining **Octagonal Fountain**, terraces, slopes, and stairways. North of the fountain is a modest bust of André Le Nôtre, the landscape architect. The **Tuileries** is framed from the west by Coysevox's two winged horses, erected in 1719 at the western edge of the garden, along Place de la Concorde.

The first human ascent in a hydrogen balloon, on 1 December 1783, was launched beside the Octagonal Fountain. Thousands packed the park to watch the historic flight of physician J.A.C. Charles and his mechanic Noel Robert. Among the spectators were Benjamin Franklin and French philosopher Denis Diderot, who conjectured that one day human beings might go to the moon. The hot-air balloon rose more than 2,000 feet and carried its passengers safely 25 miles to the north of Paris. Now, every New Year's Day, the celebrity-studded Paris–Dakar overland motor race across Europe and North Africa begins here. ◆ Between L'Orangerie and the Jeu de Paume

CAFÉ VÉRY

★$ Located on the central alleyway a few steps east of the **Bassin Octagonal**, this café is the best place in the park to pause for liquid or solid refreshment—particularly in fair weather, if you're lucky enough to secure a table outdoors. The Dame Tartine group runs this café, and it features the same range of imaginative salads, sandwiches, and light dishes (smoked salmon on a bed of endives with fresh ginger sauce, and duck stew with orange and mint leaves) as at the other locations. If the gates to the park are closed in the evening, tell the guard on duty you are going to the restaurant, and you will be let in; the closest gate is the Grille d'Honneur on the Place de la Concorde side.◆ Daily, noon–11PM. 01.47.03.94.84. Also at 2 Rue Brisemiche (Pl Igor-Stravinsky). 01.42.77.32.22. Métros: Hôtel de Ville, Rambuteau; 59 Rue de Lyon (between Rue Lacuée and Pl de la Bastille). 01.44.68.96.95. Métro: Bastille

L'ORANGERIE

This former citrus nursery is the permanent home of the Walter-Guillaume Collection of paintings, including 144 masterworks by such artists as Renoir, Monet, Cézanne, Henri Rousseau, Soutine, Picasso, Modigliani, Derain, and Matisse. The artists best represented are Pierre-Auguste Renoir (24 works) and André Derain (28 paintings). The Cézannes are exceptional, particularly *Apples and Biscuits*, whose audacious composition is held together by a drawer latch placed dead center in the picture. On the lower floor, mounted on curved panels, are Claude Monet's eight giant water-lily murals, *Les Nymphéas*. ◆ Admission. Closed for restoration until early 2004. Southwest corner (at Pl de la Concorde). 01.42.97.48.16

94 PONT DE L'ALMA

Built in 1855 to honor the first French victory in the Crimean War (1854), this bridge is decorated with a statue of a Zouave soldier that acts as a watermark; during the flood of 1910, the **Seine** reached his chin. The *bateaux mouches* and dinner cruises embark on their tours of the Seine from the quay below Place de l'Alma. In 1987 the *International Herald Tribune* erected a full-scale replica of the torch of the Statue of Liberty on Place de l'Alma by the Right Bank end of the bridge to commemorate the newspaper's 100th anniversary. When Princess Diana and Dodi al-Fayed died in an automobile crash in 1997 in the underpass beneath this spot, the torch instantly became an ad hoc memorial to them. For a year after the tragedy, mourners heaped the monument with flowers and plastered it with poems and placards in their honor. To this day people still bring notes and flowers to this spot and cover the torch and the walls near it with affectionate and sometimes weird graffiti. ◆ Between Quai d'Orsay and Ave de New-York. Métro: Alma–Marceau

95 PONT ALEXANDRE III

Between the **Grand Palais** and the **Invalides** is an elegant Belle Epoque bridge embodying the architectural giddiness that celebrated the French spirit of ingenuity and optimism at the turn of the 19th century. The bridge is encrusted with every Greco-Roman frippery in the book: human-size cupids; lavish garlands; huge golden statues of Pegasus and Renown; prides of lions; and a plethora of trumpets, tridents, shells, and shields. Built to commemorate the 1892 French–Russian alliance, the bridge bears the Russian and French coats of arms side by side and teams a sculptural allegory of the Seine with one of the Neva. ◆ Between Quai d'Orsay and Cours la Reine. Métro: Champs-Elysées–Clemenceau

96 PONT DE LA CONCORDE

This five-arched bridge designed in 1791 by civil engineer **Jean Rodolphe Perronet** is constructed in part with stone souvenirs from the 1789 storming and demolition of the **Bastille**, allegedly so that people could forever trample the ruins of the old fortress. ◆ Between Quai d'Orsay and Cours la Reine. Métro: Concorde

97 PASSERELLE DE SOLFÉRINO

Opened in 2000, the city's newest bridge provides pedestrian passage between the **Jardins des Tuileries** and the **Musée d'Orsay**. Constructed of a special type of steel used in naval architecture, the wood-planked *passerelle* (footbridge), designed by engineer **Marc Mimram**, is the first to span the **Seine** with only one arch. ◆ Between Quais Anatole-France and des Tuileries. Métros: Tuileries, Musée d'Orsay

98 LE FUMOIR

LE FUMOIR

★★$$ Polished wood floors, antique tables, comfortable leather armchairs, a bar with a soul from a Jazz Age Philadelphia speakeasy, and a cozy 3,000-book library–dining room in the rear give this bar and restaurant its special charm. Ask for a table in the library, where you can leaf though a book while having a drink (or swap some of your books for theirs if you wish), or you can dine on the modern concoctions of the French-Swedish team of Michel Portos and Henrick Anderson. Herrings marinated with sherry on toast with creamed cucumbers; sautéed fillet of *rascasse* (scorpion fish) with tomatoes, anchovies, and parsley; breast of guinea fowl with sage and Parma ham; and steak with Béarnaise sauce are a few of the choices they offer. There's a superb selection of wines, and the bar makes an excellent martini, much appreciated by the young professionals who frequent the place. ◆ M-Su, lunch and dinner; drinks, 11AM-2AM; happy hour, 6-8PM. Reservations recommended. 6 Rue de l'Amiral-Coligny (between Quai du Louvre and Rue de Rivoli). 01.42.92.00.24. Métro: Louvre

98 LOUVRE–RIVOLI MÉTRO STATION

The platform is a museum in itself, with softly illuminated copies of the sculptures found above it in the **Louvre**. This and the **Varenne** métro station (with replicas of Rodin sculptures) are two of the prettiest in Paris. ◆ Rues de l'Amiral-de-Coligny et de Rivoli

99 RUE DE RIVOLI

On this arcaded street, an incongruous mix of luxury hotels and tacky souvenir shops lies demurely behind a graceful but rather monotonous First Empire colonnade designed by **Charles Percier** and **Pierre Fontaine** in 1811 at the behest of Napoléon. The street was named after the Italian town where the emperor thrashed the Austrians in 1797. Strict rules pertaining to the arcades forbade leasing shops to any entrepreneur using ovens or metal tools, thus excluding such riffraff as bakers and butchers. ◆ Between Rues St-Florentin and de Sévigné. Métro: Louvre–Rivoli

99 RUE DE L'ARBRE-SEC

This short street is long and rich in history. D'Artagnan of the Three Musketeers lived at **No. 4** (formerly the **Hôtel des Mousquetaires**, now **La Samaritaine** department store); at **No. 52** is the **Hôtel de Trudon**, the former home of Louis XV's wine steward; nearby is the **Hôtel de François Barnon**, named after Louis XIV's barber. The name *arbre-sec* (which literally means "dry tree") refers to a tree in ancient Palestine that supposedly lost its leaves the day of Christ's crucifixion. ◆ Between Pl de l'Ecole and Rue St-Honoré. Métro: Pont-Neuf

99 CHEZ LA VIEILLE

★★$$ True to its name, this bistro features fare that would make a French country grandmother proud. A typical meal that young chef Frédérique Pasturel prepares is *foie gras de canard* (duck-liver pâté); followed by lamb shoulder with herbs from Provence, veal liver with shallots, or fish from the market; and for dessert, a grand selection from the *chariot* (cart). There's a well-chosen list of wines, mostly Bordeaux. The welcoming owner Marie-José Cervoni presides over the tiny five-table dining room. ◆ M-W, F, lunch; Th, lunch and dinner; closed in August. Reservations recommended for lunch; required for dinner. 1 Rue Bailleul (at Rue de l'Arbre-Sec). 01.42.60.15.78. Métros: Louvre-Rivoli, Pont-Neuf

100 LA GALCANTE

Despite the fact that it's on the ground level, walking into this big, no-nonsense shop is like stumbling into the attic of the French grandmother you never had. First, it's in the back of a courtyard almost totally hidden from the street. Second, it's literally overflowing with the original pages from old newspapers, magazines, and catalogs, mostly (but not

---

Restaurants/Clubs: Red | Hotels: Purple | Shops: Orange | Outdoors/Parks: Green | Sights/Culture: Blue

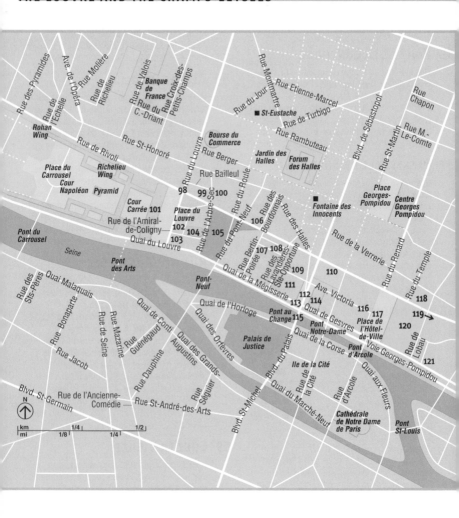

exclusively) French. Whether you're looking for an issue of *Paris-Match* with Greta Garbo on the cover or food or fashion advertisements from the 1920s to French up your home, you will doubtless find the goods here—and possibly for a good deal less than the book-sellers by the Seine. There's more organization here than first meets the eye, and staff are only too happy to help locate that special something. ♦ Tu-Sa, noon-7PM. 52 Rue de l'Arbre-Sec (between Rue de Rivoli and Rue St-Honoré). 01.44.77.87.47. Métro: Louvre-Rivoli. lagalcante@lagalcante.com

101 MUSÉE DU LOUVRE

This is the single largest building in Paris, the largest palace in Europe, the largest museum in the Western world, and probably the most dominating symbol of art and culture the world has ever known. "I never knew what a palace was until I had a glimpse of the Louvre," said 19th-century North American author Nathaniel Hawthorne. It has 224 halls,

and its enormous **Grande Galerie** is longer than three football fields. It took 7 centuries to build, spanning the lives of 17 monarchs and countless architects.

The word *louvre*, though its origin is obscure, is believed to be either a derivation of the Old French word *louverie*, which meant "wolf lodge," or a variation of an Old Flemish word meaning "fortress." In 1190 King Philippe Auguste began surrounding Paris with a 30-foot-high city wall that included the fortified structure known as the **Louvre**. More than 3 centuries later, François I agreed to live in this fortress at the request of Parisian citizens who had ransomed him from captivity in Italy. In 1527 he tore down most of the old building, and by 1546 he had constructed the **Cour Carrée** (Square Courtyard).

In 1578 Catherine de Médicis built a new palace, the **Tuileries**, at the far end of the present Louvre. The two palaces were joined by Henri IV, who created a number of apartments in the long gallery for the use of court painters and their families in 1608. This same Henri was stabbed by an assassin here in 1610. (He was the only king to die within the Louvre's walls.) In the late 1660s, Colbert, a minister of finance to Louis XIV, hired the acclaimed Roman architect **Giovanni Bernini** to redesign the Louvre. But when Bernini suggested knocking the whole place down and starting from scratch, Colbert sent him packing. Louis XIV proceeded to reconstruct the Cour Carrée to his own tastes, consulting architect **Louis Le Vau**, painter Charles Le Brun, and Claude Perrault, a Parisian physician whose brother Charles was the author of "Puss in Boots." After renovating the palace, Louis XIV established an artists' colony here; residents included painters such as Coustou, Boucher, and Coypel. Louis XIV left Paris for **Versailles** in 1678, and without royal occupants, the Louvre fell into disrepair. Overrun by freeloaders and squatters, it soon became a slum, and a shantytown of bars and brothels sprang up outside its walls.

After being dissuaded from tearing the structure down, Louis XVI magnanimously put some of the royal art collection on display in the Louvre shortly before he and Marie Antoinette were beheaded in 1793. Following his rise to power, Napoléon moved into the **Tuileries Palace** and built Rue de Rivoli for quick access to the Louvre. Napoléon also built the **Arc du Carrousel**, an arch celebrating some of his military victories (see page 173). During the Second Empire, Napoléon's nephew Napoléon III and Baron Georges-Eugene Haussmann, the radical urban planner, completed the Louvre (or so they thought) by building the **North Wing**, the **Flore** and **Marsan Pavilions**, and all the façades of the **Cour Napoléon**.

The Louvre's art collection began with 12 paintings—including works by Titian, Raphael, and Leonardo da Vinci—that François I looted in Italy. (He took not only the *Mona Lisa* but also the man who had painted it, inviting Leonardo to his château at Amboise, where the artist remained until his death.) By the time of Louis XIV (who reigned from 1643 to 1715), the royal collection numbered more than 2,500 items. Until the revolution, works in the Louvre were strictly for the pleasure of the kings and their courtiers. In 1793, after nearly burning the palace to the ground, the revolutionaries opened the collection to the masses. Today the museum possesses more than 350,000 works of art, only 30,000 of which are on display at any given time. In a morning's hoofing, however, you can see many of the Louvre's greatest hits: the *Venus de Milo*, the *Winged Victory of Samothrace*, the *Mona Lisa*, the *Crown Jewels*, the *David* works, the *Eagle of Sugerius*, the *Law Code of Hammurabi*, the **Rubens Gallery**, Michelan-

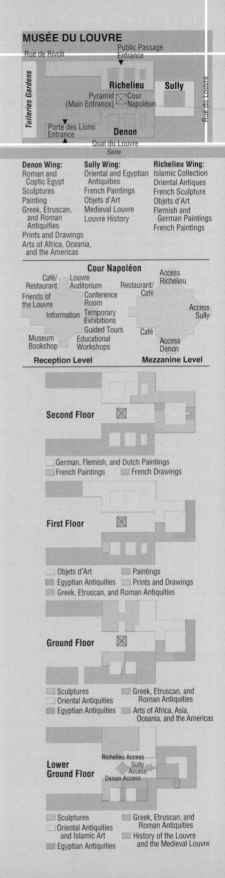

gelo's *Slaves*, the *Seated Scribe*, and other highlights of art history.

The collection is divided into seven main categories (see floor plan on page 171): Oriental antiquities (and Arts of Islam); Egyptian antiquities; Greek, Etruscan, and Roman antiquities; paintings; sculptures; objets d'art; and prints and drawings. In 2000 the Louvre added a small but dazzling collection of primitive works from Africa, Oceania, and the Americas; it will be on display until at least 2004, when it will be transferred to the new museum of primitive art to be built on the Quai de Branly. The museum also presents a section devoted to the history of the Louvre, including the impressive foundations of the 13th-century keep that were uncovered during the restoration in the 1980s, and the Napoléon III apartments in the Richelieu Wing, a riot of gold, crystal, and crimson velvet, the epitome of Second Empire décor. Although the Greek and Roman, Egyptian, or indeed any of the museum's holdings warrant at least a look, the richest collection consists of its French, Italian, Dutch, German, and Spanish paintings covering the period from the Middle Ages to the early 19th century.

Some words of advice for touring the Louvre: 1. Don't even think about trying to see the museum's entire collection—or even half of it—in 1 day. Visit your favorite artworks the first time around and come back for more another day. 2. In the summer or other high-season months, buy your tickets in advance (see below); otherwise, count on at least a half hour in line waiting to purchase them. 3. Wear comfortable shoes. Check your coat as you enter, but in winter you might want to keep a pullover handy. 4. Guided tours in English are available; ask at the reception desk in the lobby. 5. When fatigue sets in, take a break in one of the museum's cafés. (If you prefer to lunch outside and come back, the tickets are valid all day, and reentry is allowed.) 6. Certain rooms are closed on a rotating basis; to find out in advance, phone or consult the Minitel or Internet site for the schedule of closings.

Museum tickets can be purchased in advance at any **FNAC** department store (including those in Belgium and Spain), ordered by phone (01.49.87.54.54), by dialing 3615 Louvre on the Minitel in France; from www.ticketweb.com in the US and Canada; or by accessing the Louvre's web site (www.louvre.fr). The buyer does not have to book for a specific date. The tickets are valid for any day. ♦ Admission; free first Sunday of the month. Museum: M, 9AM-9:45PM (limited sections open in the evening); W, 9AM-9:45PM (the full museum open in the evening); Th-Su, 9AM-6PM; closed Tuesdays. Bookstores and postcard shops: M, W-Su.

Entrance at the **Pyramid** in the **Cour Napoléon** (99 Carrousel du Louvre); the museum is bounded by Rue de l'Amiral-de-Coligny and Ave du General-Lemonnier and by Quai du Louvre and Rue de Rivoli. Recorded message in five languages (French, English, Spanish, Italian, German). 01.40.20.51.51; information desk, 01.40.20.53.17. Métro: Palais Royal–Musée du Louvre. www.louvre.fr

Within the Musée du Louvre:

COUR NAPOLÉON (NAPOLÉON COURTYARD)

Under King Philippe Auguste, this was a patch of sparsely populated farmland. Over time, it sprouted a church, charity school, meat market, menagerie for wild animals, the castle kitchens, and a street for prostitutes frequented by soldiers from the castle garrison. Napoléon III leveled the houses and paved over the courtyard in the late 19th century.

LOUVRE PYRAMID

Adding to the Louvre museum building seems to be an irresistible French pastime. The latest additions, officially opened in April 1989, were based on the designs of **I.M. Pei**. Now topping the **Cour Napoléon** is a 70.5-foot-tall glass pyramid, flanked by three smaller pyramids, a series of fountains, reflecting pools, and a lead replica of the Bernini statue of Louis XI. The largest pyramid serves as the central entrance to the museum and as an enormous skylight above the **Hall Napoléon**—a 70,000-square-foot underground cavern.

The pyramid and its underground space contain an auditorium, an area for temporary exhibitions, and the remains of the 12th-century fortress that was unearthed prior to the pyramid's controversial construction, as well as ticket offices, conference rooms, laboratories, and museum shops. Stairs and escalators lead from under the pyramid to each side of the U-shaped Louvre. Traditionalists fear this latest addition has marred the museum's grandeur with a sort of Hyatt Regency glitz. Michel Guy, cultural minister under former French president Giscard d'Estaing, has said that Pei's pyramids turn the Louvre into a "cultural drugstore that looks like an airport." However, the design has garnered fans, and, lest we forget, the **Eiffel Tower** was also first greeted with guffaws.

EXCAVATIONS

At the same time President François Mitterrand approved the **Pei** pyramid project, he also set aside close to $2 million for an immense archeological excavation of the **Louvre**'s courtyard. This ambitious project brought

70 archeologists to supervise the dig in the **Cour Napoléon** and the **Cour Carée**, where the ancient dungeons of the King Philippe Auguste fortress were exposed. More than 11 million objects were retrieved, ranging from Chinese porcelain imported during the Ming Dynasty to coins from the first century AD and an eighth-century human skeleton. Visitors may descend from the pyramid to the 12th-century dungeons and view some of the objects uncovered in the dig.

Cour Carrée (Square Courtyard)

This elegant courtyard was built, in part, during the reign of François I, with additions commissioned by Louis XIII and Louis XIV.

Richelieu Wing

Named after the famed 17th-century French cardinal and diplomat, this structure on the Rue de Rivoli side was long occupied by the Ministry of Finance. It opened in November 1993 as one of the main expansions under the Grand Louvre Project.

Le Grand Louvre

★★$$ Run by chef Yves Pinard, this elegant restaurant located under the **Louvre Pyramid** has a subdued wood-and-metal décor and features a range of well-prepared French specialties that should appeal to any taste bud: foie gras, crayfish on a spinach salad, poached fillet of sturgeon, salmon and mixed vegetables in a flaky pastry, a vegetarian dish, duck breast with orange, rack of lamb, rabbit stew, guinea fowl with chestnut puree, crème brûlée, and *Pyramide au chocolat*, a pyramid-shaped chocolate cake. ◆ M, W-Su, lunch and dinner. 01.40.20.53.41

Le Café Marly

★$$ What some lovers of the Louvre might have wished for—a quality, user-friendly cafeteria on the premises—is not what they will find here, an ersatz Italian disco replete with Venetian-red walls, gold leaf, and heavily trafficked velvet upholstered armchairs. This look draws the kind of self-consciously prettified people you sometimes bump into in airports and pray you don't have to sit next to on the plane. Restaurateurs Jean-Louis and Gilbert Coste's café is popular above all for its location in the museum's **Richelieu Wing**. Detractors would say you can find both kinds of French waiters here—snooty *and* perfunctory—and that the menu of international grazing food (peppered with the likes of *penne arrabiata* and greenbean salad) feels too much like formula. For a glass of wine or

respite from the madding crowds, the place is fine, but as far as victuals go, there is infinitely more value and variety to be had in the international food court at the underground **Carrousel du Louvre** shopping center. ◆ Daily, breakfast, lunch, tea, and dinner. 93 Rue de Rivoli (enter from the Cour Napoléon). 01.49.26.06.60

Carrousel du Louvre

This underground shopping mall is skylit by a 150-ton inverted glass pyramid and features over 35 boutiques and businesses proffering everything from Lalique crystal to miniature **Eiffel Tower** souvenirs and château rentals to 1-hour film developing. **Restorama Universal** is a huge 700-seat international food hall on the mezzanine level with a dozen or so stalls that offer modestly priced fast food of nearly every description—Mexican, Lebanese, Asian, Spanish, Italian, American, vegetarian, and, of course, French. During the shopping center's construction, architects **I.M. Pei** and **Michel Macary** uncovered a 14th-century moat built by Charles V, which has been incorporated into the design and named the **Fossé Charles V**. During the fall and spring, the mall becomes a chic circus when more than 50 fashion designers parade their ready-to-wear collections through striped tents set up here. Check at the information stand for a schedule of events. ◆ Daily. Main entrance at 99 Rue de Rivoli; also accessible from the Louvre Museum foyer. 01.43.16.47.47

Place du Carrousel

Part of the **Louvre** complex, this square was named to commemorate a *carrousel* (equestrian gala) held by King Louis XIV and his court in June 1662 to honor the birth of the king's first child. More than 15,000 spectators watched the king lead a thundering brigade of horsemen dressed as Romans, sporting golden helmets with red plumes, gold breast-plates, and red stockings. ◆ Between the Quai du Louvre and Rue de Rivoli. Métro: Palais Royal–Musée du Louvre

On Place du Carrousel:

L'Arc du Carrousel

This marble arch with pink pillars was built in 1808 by Napoléon to celebrate Austerlitz and other military victories. It was then crowned with the famous bronze horses of San Marco, plundered from Venice during one of Napoléon's military campaigns. (Originally, the horses stood in the Temple of the Sun at Corinth.) With the fall of Napoléon in 1815, Italy recovered the horses and copies were placed here. The arch can be used like a gun sight to line up the **Tuileries Fountains**, the

Egyptian **Obelisk of Luxor** in the Place de la Concorde (a half-mile to the west), the Champs-Elysées, and the **Arc de Triomphe**, more than 2 miles away.

MUSÉE DES ARTS DÉCORATIFS (MUSEUM OF DECORATIVE ARTS)

With furnishings that date from the Middle Ages through the 20th century, the Musée des Arts Décoratifs, housed in the **Rohan Wing** of the **Louvre** complex, offers collections worthy of and complementary to its neighbor's displays of European art. Lovers of medieval religious art shouldn't miss the superb collection of painted, sculpted stone and carved wood altarpieces from northern Italy, Catalonia, France, Germany, Flanders, and the Netherlands. Occupying nine rooms and a full floor, these pieces are housed in the museum's Middle Ages and Renaissance department. This section also boasts a superb collection of Renaissance tapestries, furniture, glassware, ceramics, and enamelware, and a cozy wood-paneled Gothic bedroom and a grand Renaissance reception hall. The rest of the museum, with pieces covering the early 17th century to the early 20th century, was closed for restoration at press time and is scheduled to reopen at the end of 2003. The view of the **Tuileries Gardens** from the top floor is spectacular.

MUSÉE DE LA MODE ET DU TEXTILE (FASHION AND TEXTILE MUSEUM)

Also located in the **Louvre**'s **Rohan Wing**, this museum pays homage to the capital of fashion. Selections from its 20,000 outfits, 35,000 accessories, and 100,000 fabric samples are beautifully presented by theme in exhibitions that change every year. The museum's sleek and chic collection consists of costumes dating back to the 17th century. Among the highlights of the collection are the 17th-century gloves worn by Anne of Austria, Brigitte Bardot's wedding dress (made by Jacques Esterel in 1958), a robe designed for Sarah Bernhardt, and the gown worn by the Empress Eugénie to please Napoléon III when he returned from a hard day of empire-building. There is also a library containing engravings, drawings, journals, photographs, and catalogs.

MUSÉE DE LA PUBLICITÉ (POSTER AND ADVERTISING MUSEUM)

The Musée de la Publicité, also in the **Louvre**'s **Rohan Wing**, is the first museum devoted to advertising art. It has more than 40,000 posters from the 18th century to the present and offers excellent retrospectives based on themes, artists, or brands. The museum's entire collection of posters, objects, press advertisements, and radio, TV, and cinema commercials may be consulted in the interactive media library.

All three museums are operated by the Union Central des Arts Décoratifs. ♦ Admission. Tu, Th, F, 11AM-6PM; W, 11AM-9PM; Sa-Su, 10AM-6PM. 107 Rue de Rivoli (at Ave du Général-Lemonnier). 01.44.55.57.50. Métro: Palais Royal–Musée du Louvre. www.ucad.fr for the Musée des Arts Decoratifs and Musée de la Mode et du Textile; www.museedelapub.org for the Musée de la Publicité

102 PLACE DU LOUVRE

In 52 BC, Labienus, a lieutenant of Caesar, bivouacked with his troops between the present sites of the **Louvre** and **St-Germain-l'Auxerrois** before capturing the settlement of Lutetia. ♦ Between Rues des Prêtres-St-Germain-l'Auxerrois and Perrault. Métros: Louvre–Rivoli, Pont-Neuf

103 PÂTISSERIE ST-GERMAIN-L'AUXERROIS

★★$$ Embellished with crystal chandeliers, gilded pillars, and marble tables, this elegant pastry shop and tea salon—open since 1896—makes all its sweets and ice cream in a basement factory. Try the chocolate pastries (la mousseline and le cador). ♦ Tu-Su; closed 2 weeks in August and 2 weeks in September. 2 Rue de l'Amiral-de-Coligny (at Quai du Louvre). 01.45.08.19.18. Métros: Louvre–Rivoli, Pont-Neuf

104 ST-GERMAIN-L'AUXERROIS

On St. Bartholomew's Day (24 August) in 1572, at the orders of Catherine de Médicis and Charles IX, the pealing bells of this church signaled the beginning of a brutal religious massacre. Some 3,000 Huguenots, Protestant wedding guests of Henri de Navarre and Marguerite de Valois, were slain in their beds. The 38-bell carillon in the neo-Gothic tower still rings every Wednesday afternoon, a grave reminder of the mass murder. The carillon is the only truly ancient one in Paris; all the others were melted down during the revolution.

This gargoyle-laden edifice, designed in 1220 by **Jean Gaussel**, is named for St. Germain, the bishop of Auxerre (378-448), whose students included St. Patrick of Ireland and St. Geneviève of Paris. When Louis XIV and his court moved to **Versailles**, the artists' colony he had established there took over the **Louvre**, and St-Germain-l'Auxerrois became its parish church.

Among the luminaries buried here are architects **Louis Le Vau**, **Jacques-Ange Gabriel**, and **Jacques-Germain Soufflot**; sculptor **Antoine Coysevox**; and painters **Noël Coypel**, **François Boucher**, and **Jean-Baptiste Chardin**. Every Ash Wednesday a service is held to pray for artists throughout the world who will die in the coming year. Royalists flock here annually to a Mass said for Louis XVI on the anniversary of his 21 January 1793 execution. Notice the ornately canopied and sculpted oak bench on the right side of the aisle; painter Charles Le Brun designed this red-velvet pew for Louis XIV and his family in 1682. ♦ Daily; call for a schedule of Masses in English and organ and bell recitals. 2 Pl du Louvre (at Rue des Prêtres-St-Germain-l'Auxerrois). 01.42.60.13.96. Métros: Louvre–Rivoli, Pont-Neuf

105 LA SAMARITAINE

One of the city's oldest department stores and possibly its most confusing, this emporium is named for an old Pont-Neuf water pump decorated with an image of the woman of Samaria offering Jesus a drink of water. Today the store sprawls through four grand old buildings offering everything from pop psychiatry books to kitchen sinks, all at bargain prices. Its best deal, however, is the rooftop panorama. On a pleasant summer day, walk into **Magasin II** (Store No. 2), designed by **F. Jourdan**, and ride the elevator to the ninth floor. Sip a café or *citron pressé* (lemonade) at the café, then mount the stairs and enjoy a 360-degree view of Paris. A ceramic legend locates points of interest. ♦ M-W, F-Sa; Th, 9:30AM-10PM. 19 Rue de la Monnaie (between Pl de l'Ecole and Rue de Rivoli). 01.40.41.20.20. Métros: Pont-Neuf, Châtelet, Louvre

Within La Samaritaine:

TOUPARY

★★$$ Suspended between the sky and the **Seine**, this apricot, turquoise, and electric-blue restaurant designed by **Hilton McConnico** serves such specialties as cream of tomato soup with cardamom, *daurade* (sea bream) in fennel, a different fish dish every day, and lime crepes. Try to get a window table for a panoramic view of Paris. ♦ M-Sa, lunch, tea, cocktails, and dinner until 1AM. Magasin II, fifth floor. 01.40.41.29.29

106 SLOW CLUB

Dixieland jazz is alive and well at this former ballroom, now the oldest jazz club in the city. Enjoy live Dixieland, swing, boogie-woogie, R&B, and rock 'n' roll 4 nights a week in a refreshingly unpretentious, old-fashioned atmosphere. Wednesday is the only night that there's recorded music. ♦ Cover. Tu-Sa, 10PM-3AM. No credit cards accepted. 130 Rue de Rivoli (between Rues des Bourdonnais and du Pont-Neuf). 01.42.33.84.30. Métros: Châtelet, Pont-Neuf

107 GRAND HÔTEL DE CHAMPAGNE

$$$ Small, comfortable rooms (of which there are 40; there are also 3 suites) characterize this tastefully converted 16th-century stone mansion a short walk from the Place du Châtelet, the **Louvre**, **Sainte Chapelle**, **Notre-Dame**, and the Ile de la Cité. There's no restaurant. ♦ 17 Rue Jean-Lantier (at Rue des Orfèvres). 01.42.36.60.00; fax 01.45.08.43.33. Métro: Châtelet

108 LE PETIT OPPORTUN

This little jazz club, which once featured such North American headliners as Clark Terry, Slide Hampton, and Pepper Adams, now presents French mainstream jazz groups and some Latino sounds. ♦ Cover. Shows: Tu-Sa, 10:30PM-2:30AM. No credit cards accepted. 15 Rue des Lavandières-Ste-Opportune (between Rues Jean-Lantier and des Deux-Boules). 01.42.36.01.36. Métro: Châtelet

109 HÔTEL BRITANNIQUE

$$ This peaceful hotel has much going for it: an attractive lobby that looks and feels like an intimate parlor, reasonable rates, and above all a quiet location about as close to the heart of Paris as one can get without diving into the Seine. The 40 guest rooms are comfortable, contemporary and soundproofed, and there's a generous buffet breakfast for a modest extra charge. ♦ 20 Ave Victoria (between Rue des Lavandières and Pl du Châtelet). 01.42.33.74.59; fax 01.42.33.82.65. Métro: Châtelet. mailbox@hotel-britannique.fr; www.hotel-britannique.fr

110 TOUR ST-JACQUES (ST JACQUES TOWER)

This 1522 architectural anomaly was the Gothic belfry of **St-Jacques La Boucherie**, a church that was destroyed in 1802; the tower was spared to become a factory for manufacturing lead musket balls. The tower now doubles as a weather station, appropriately enough, for at the tower's base is a statue of Blaise Pascal (1623–1662), one of France's first weather forecasters. In 1648, at the top of this tower, he used a barometer to calculate the weight of air. Cast your eyes up from outside the tower (it's closed to the public)

Restaurants/Clubs: Red | Hotels: Purple | Shops: Orange | Outdoors/Parks: Green | Sights/Culture: Blue

and you'll see meteorological equipment lurking among the gargoyles. This place also has an important religious significance: It is the starting point for the pilgrimage to Santiago de Compostela in Spain. ♦ Sq St-Jacques (at Rue de Rivoli). Métro: Châtelet

111 THÉÂTRE DU CHÂTELET

Built in 1862, this is the fourth-largest auditorium in Paris (after the **Opéra Bastille**, **Opéra Garnier**, and the **Palais des Congrès**) and the city's largest concert hall. Seating half as many people as the **Opéra Garnier**, the theater is primarily a venue for symphonies, operas, and ballets. On 21 May 1910, the New York Metropolitan Opera Company made its Paris debut here with *Aida*. Toscanini conducted, Caruso sang, and the audience, which included most of the French diplomatic corps, the Vanderbilts, and Louis Cartier (who estimated that more than $3 million worth of jewelry was worn that evening), went wild. ♦ Box office: daily. Theater: closed in August. 1 Pl du Châtelet (at Quai de la Mégisserie). 01.40.28.28.28. Métro: Châtelet

111 LE ZIMMER

$$ The interior of this café dates from 1896, but the plush look it now sports is largely the creation of designer **Jacques Garcia, who has an apparent love of red velvet and fringe. Call it Jazz Age chic, but all that fabric imbues Le Zimmer with a calm uncharacteristic of a café its size—even when families with small children are present. Hence the appeal: The trappings are positively Continental, but the atmosphere is relaxed. The café menu is on the small side, but includes a selection of amply portioned salads, seafood dishes, and heartier meat dishes. Note: One dessert here is often enough for two people. 1 Pl du Châtelet (at Quai de la Mégisserie). 01.42.36.74.03. Metro: Châtelet

112 PLACE DU CHÂTELET

Named after a fortress and prison that once stood on this site, this square is the principal crossroads of Paris, a hub of east–west and north–south traffic. The **Châtelet Fountain** in the center, flanked by sphinxes, was designed in 1808 to celebrate the triumphant Egyptian campaign of Napoléon. Below the square, five métro lines intersect, making **Châtelet–Les Halles** the world's largest underground station. ♦ Between Quai de Gesvres and Ave Victoria. Métros: Châtelet, Châtelet–Les Halles (RER)

113 QUAI DE LA MÉGISSERIE

Once a malodorous *mégisserie* (sheepskin tannery), today this spot is rife with booksellers, pet shops, fish-tackle dealers, and plant stores where mice and goldfish are sold alongside dahlias and fertilizer. The cacophony of the parakeets, turkeys, and guinea fowls whose cages clutter the pavement vies pleasantly with that of the automobile traffic nearby. If you don't fancy house pets or have a green thumb, stroll here for the splendid views of **La Conciergerie**, the towers of **Notre-Dame**, and the spire of **Sainte-Chapelle**. ♦ Between Pl du Châtelet and Rue du Pont-Neuf. Métro: Châtelet

114 THÉÂTRE DE LA VILLE DE PARIS

Formerly the **Sarah Bernhardt Theatre**, this mid–19th-century stage is now devoted to contemporary dance, jazz, and classical theater but still preserves the dressing room of the "Divine Sarah." ♦ Box office: daily. 2 Pl du Châtelet (at Quai de Gesvres). 01.42.74.22.77. Métros: Châtelet, Châtelet–Les Halles (RER)

115 PONT AU CHANGE

"Money-Changers' Bridge" was the 9th-century forerunner of an American Express office—a spot where travelers came to change foreign currency for French funds. Today this Second Empire bridge is flanked by identical state-owned theaters, both built by architect **Gabriel-Jean-Antoine Davioud** in 1862. ♦ Between Quai de la Corse and Quai de Gesvres. Métro: Châtelet

116 AVENUE VICTORIA

One of the shortest avenues in Paris doesn't commemorate any military victory but rather the royal visit of the dowager Queen of England to Paris. ♦ Between Quai de Gesvres and Rue des Lavandières-Ste-Opportune. Métro: Hôtel de Ville

117 PLACE DE L'HÔTEL-DE-VILLE

The present seat of the Paris city government, this square is where Etienne Marcel, one of the first mayors of Paris, established his city council in 1357. Marcel incited a mob to rise against the monarchy and storm the royal palace on Ile de la Cité. The next year he was killed—not by the king but by his fellow Parisians. Centered in the granite on the square is the image of a boat, the city symbol, adopted from the 13th-century coat of arms of the Boatmen's Guild. ♦ Between Quai de Gesvres and Rue de Rivoli. Métro: Hôtel de Ville

118 BAZAR DE L'HÔTEL-DE-VILLE (BHV)

Situated directly across Rue de Rivoli from the **Hôtel-de-Ville**, this is one of Paris's largest department stores. Its five floors cover a good-size city block and are replete with everything this kind of store carries, including a maze of perfume and lingerie counters on the ground floor; clothes of all kinds for men, women, and children; toys, books, and stationery; photo and video equipment; and a wide range of home furnishings, kitchenware, and appliances. But the store's most famous department is a huge hardware emporium in the basement, a do-it-yourselfer's paradise. Anyone trying to locate a hard-to-find part will invariably be directed here to BHV (pronounced "bay-aash-vay"). ◆ M-Tu, Th-Sa, 9:30AM-7PM; W, F, 9:30AM-8:30PM. 52-64 Rue de Rivoli (between Rues des Archives and du Temple). 01.42.74.90.00. Métro: Hôtel de Ville

Within BHV:

BRICOLO CAFÉ

★$ While in the hardware emporium, be sure to follow the aroma of coffee to this delightfully authentic re-creation of a *bricoleur*'s (do-it-yourselfer's) old-time home workshop, complete with rusty saws, hammers, wrenches, and tins of nails mounted on the walls, and ropes and lanterns hanging from the ceiling. You sit at beaten-up wooden tables and workbenches and peruse the quaint old advertising posters on the walls while sipping your coffee, tea, a soft drink, beer, or wine and noshing on a light breakfast or snack. ◆ M-Tu, Th-Sa, 9:30AM-7PM; W, F, 9:30AM-8:30PM

A L'OLIVIER

19 A L'OLIVIER

Founded in 1860, this shop still sells every oil imaginable, including hazelnut oil for vinaigrettes, almond-honey–oil shampoo, and apricot-nut oil for massages. Tarragon mustard and dried figs are also available. The classic bottles would be worth buying empty, and the giant pottery casks for olive oil are not to be missed. ◆ Tu-Sa. 23 Rue de Rivoli (at Rue du Pont-Louis-Philippe). 01.48.04.86.59. Métro: Hôtel de Ville

120 HÔTEL DE VILLE (CITY HALL)

Another example of late-19th–century architectural eclecticism, this building is part Renaissance palace, part Belle Epoque fantasy. Its exterior is embellished with 146 statues, among them bronze effigies of the sentries who patrolled the perimeter of the city wall during the Middle Ages. Visitors on guided tours of the state rooms are shown the splendid staircase by Philibert Delorme, murals by Puvis de Chavannes, and a lesser-known Rodin sculpture, *La République*. ◆ Tours: M, 10:30AM, departing from the information desk at 29 Rue de Rivoli; call the previous Friday to confirm time. Pl de l'Hôtel-de-Ville (between Quai de Gesvres and Rue de Rivoli). 01.42.76.40.40. Métro: Hôtel de Ville

121 LE TRUMILOU

★$ The perfect way to enjoy this authentic Parisian bistro is at a window table overlooking the Seine and **Notre-Dame**. Jean-Claude Dumond and his family prepare home-cooked food at sensible prices. Favorites include *canard aux pruneaux* (duck with prunes), lamb with white beans, sole meunière, and the ever-popular *poulet provençale* (chicken in tomato sauce with herbes de Provence). For dessert, try the *oeufs à la neige* (meringue floating in crème anglaise). ◆ Daily, lunch and dinner. Reservations recommended. 84 Quai de l'Hôtel-de-Ville (between Rues du Pont-Louis-Philippe and de Brosse). 01.42.77.63.98. Métro: Hôtel de Ville

St-Honoré

Place du Pérou 1

Ave. de Messine

Rue de la Bienfaisance

Blvd. Malesherbes

Rue de Monceau

Rue de Courcelles

Rue de Téhéran

2

Rue de Laborde

3

Blvd. Haussmann

Rue de Miromesnil

4 Rue d'Argenson Blvd. Haussmann

Rue de Berri

Rue du Faubourg-St-Honoré

Ave. M.-Herrick

5

Rue La Boétie

11

Rue Cambacérès

Rue St-Philippe-du-Roule

9

10

Ave. Percier

Ave. Delcassé

Rue Roquépine

Rue d'Artois

8

Ave. M.-Herrick

Rue du Cdt.-Rivière

6

7

18

Rue P.-Baudry

15

16

17 Rue de Penthièvre

27

1

Rue La Boétie

25 26

28 29

30

31

Rue des Saussaies

33

Rue de Ponthieu

Rue du Colisée

Ave. Franklin-D.-Roosevelt

Rue Rabelais

Place Beauvau

32

Rue Montalive

Rue du Faubourg-St-Honoré

37

56

Rue Jean-Mermoz

Ave. Matignon

Ave. Gabriel

Rue du Cirque

57

Rond-Pointe des Champs-Elysées-Marcel Dassault

Rue de l'Elysée

Ave. des Champs-Elysées

Ave. de Marigny

Ave. Ga

Rue Francois-1er

Grand Palais

Palais de la Decouverte

Ave. Dutuit

Rue Bayard

Petit Palais

Ave. Edward-Tuck

Ave. W.-Churchill

Cours Albert-1er

Cours la Reine

Rue B

N

Pont des Invalides

Pont Alexandre III

Seine

Pon Cor

km 1/8 1/4
mi 1/16 1/8

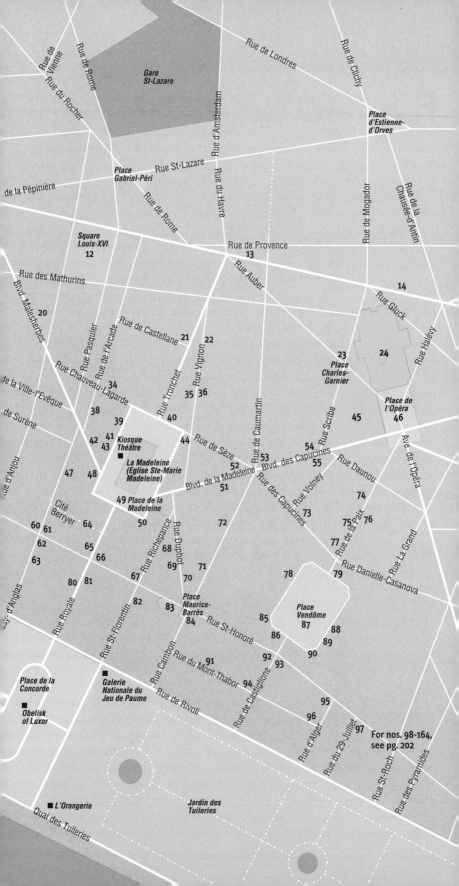

Gare St-Lazare

Rue de Vienne
Rue de Rome
Rue de Londres
Rue de Clichy
Rue du Rocher
Rue d'Amsterdam
Place d'Estienne-d'Orves
Place Gabriel-Péri
Rue St-Lazare
de la Pépinière
Rue de Rome
Rue du Havre
Rue de Mogador
Rue de la Chaussée-d'Antin
Square Louis-XVI 12
Rue de Provence 13
Rue des Mathurins
Rue Auber
Rue Gluck
14
Blvd. Malesherbes 20
Rue Pasquier
Rue de l'Arcade
Rue de Castellane
21
22
Rue Vignon
23
Place Charles-Garnier
24
Rue Halévy
34
Rue Chauveau-Lagarde
de la Ville-l'Evêque
Rue Tronchet
35 36
Rue de Caumartin
Rue Scribe
45
Place de l'Opéra 46
Ave. de l'Opéra
de Surène
38
39
40
44
Rue de Sèze
41
42 43
Kiosque Théâtre
La Madeleine (Eglise Ste-Marie Madeleine)
52
53
Blvd. des Capucines
54
55
Rue Daunou
74
47 48
51
Rue des Capucines
Rue Volney
73
75 76
Rue La Grand
Rue d'Anjou
49 Place de la Madeleine
Blvd. de la Madeleine
77
Rue de la Paix
Cité Berryer
64
50
72
78
79
Rue Danielle-Casanova
60 61
62
65
Rue Richepance
Rue Duphot
68
71
63
66
67
69
70
80 81
Place Maurice-Barrès
85
Place Vendôme 87
88
Rue Royale
82
83
84
Rue St-Honoré
86
89
Rue St-Florentin
91
92 93
90
Place de la Concorde
Galerie Nationale du Jeu de Paume
Rue Cambon
Rue du Mont-Thabor
94
Rue de Castiglione
95
Obelisk of Luxor
Rue de Rivoli
96
Rue d'Alger
Rue du 29-Juillet
97
Rue St-Roch
Rue des Pyramides

For nos. 98-164, see pg. 202

L'Orangerie
Jardin des Tuileries
Quai des Tuileries

ST-HONORÉ

Forget Fifth Avenue and Rodeo Drive. The **Faubourg St-Honoré**, named after the patron saint of pastry chefs, takes the cake as the world's most glamorous shopping district. *La plus haute* of international haute couture is here: Christian Dior, Yves Saint Laurent, Lanvin, Gucci, Hermès, Pierre Cardin, Guy Laroche, Ungaro, Courrèges, and Jean-Paul Gaultier, not to mention countless purveyors of such extravagances as diamonds, crystal, silver, mink, caviar, truffles, and Champagne.

This district includes other dazzling sights as well. Among them are a small remarkable art collection at the **Musée Jacquemart-André**; many architectural jewels including **St-Roch** (the city's finest Baroque church) and the splendid **Palais Royal** and its gardens; the city's three most important old theaters, the **Opéra Garnier**, the **Opéra Comique**, and the **Comédie Française**; several grand hotels, such as **Hôtel Le Bristol**, **Le Grand Hôtel**, and the **Hôtel Ritz**, whose name is synonymous with luxury, and the smaller (but even more chic) **hôtel costes**. Rue St-Honoré and its extension, **Rue du Faubourg St-Honoré**, are made for that favorite Parisian pastime, tasteful loitering.

Plan on visiting St-Honoré on Tuesday through Saturday, because most shops are closed on Sunday and Monday. Start with an early-bird pastry and coffee at one of the Right Bank's finest bakeries, **Boulangerie St-Philippe**, and continue down Rue du Faubourg-St-Honoré to the street's most fashionable stretch, which lies between the presidential **Palais de l'Elysée** at **Avenue de Marigny** and **Rue Royale**. Those getting a late jump on the day might consider visiting **Ma Bourgogne**, a popular neighborhood wine bar, where an elite crowd stands with a midmorning glass of Beaune. While lovers of the Italian Renaissance keep their date with Donatello, Botticelli, and Titian at the Musée Jacquemart-André, serious shoppers will head down **Embassy Row** (where the US, British, and Japanese ambassadors hang their hats) and make a mandatory stop at **Hermès**, the world-famous leather and accessories shop.

At Rue Royale, which starts at the **Place de la Concorde** and ends two short blocks later at the **Place de la Madeleine**, you will gaze on the finest in antiques, tapestries, jewelry, and silver. By midday you will have reached Place de la Madeleine. Survey the plaza and whet your appetite with truffles at **La Maison de la Truffe**, chocolate at **Marquise de Sévigné**, and cheese at **La Ferme St-Hubert**, or all of the above at **Fauchon** or **Hediard**. When you're finished with those delicacies, why not spend your life's savings on the four-star nouvelle cuisine at **Lucas Carton** or on a feast of caviar and champagne at **Caviar Kaspia**? If you're down to your last few Euros, you'll have to settle for a modest though tasty repast at **Ladurée** or **L'Ecluse**. Those feeling brash and regal by turns could knock back a shot of one of the 156 whiskeys sold at **Harry's New York Bar** and weave into **Charvet** to buy a cravat, as Edward VII was in the habit of doing not so long ago.

While your companion is changing money at **American Express**, line up for tickets inside the Opéra Garnier (also known as the **Opéra de Paris**), Charles Garnier's architectural birthday cake. If you're an antiques hound, **Le Louvre des Antiquaires**, with 240 dealers under one roof, will keep you occupied for hours. Otherwise, watch (as everyone from Louis XIV to Colette has) the sun set on the gardens of the Palais Royal, or if the shops are still open, nip over to the fashionable **Place des Victoires** for a last blast of power shopping in the upscale boutiques—**Victoire** and **Thierry Mugler**, for example.

Dinnertime already? Why not go for broke at the almost 200-year-old grande dame of gastronomy, **Le Grand Véfour**, or the century-old **Restaurant Drouant**? An evening

In the neighborhood might consist of polishing your French at the Comédie Française, catching a classical ballet or modern dance performance at the Opéra Garnier, or people-watching from the terrace of **Café de la Paix**. If you still have energy to spare, you can return to where you began the day's outing and spend the night dancing till dawn at **Keur Samba**. Glittering St-Honoré offers glamour and grandeur around the clock.

1 C.T. Loo and Co.

Located in a fantastic three-story pagoda equipped with a Chinese elevator, Michael Cardosi's Asian art gallery deals in Orientalia. Get a close look at the lacquered hardwood furniture from the Ming Dynasty and the 13th-century Nepalese sculptures. ♦ Tu, Sa; other days by appointment only; closed in August. 48 Rue de Courcelles (at Pl du Pérou). 01.45.62.53.15. Métro: St-Philippe-du-Roule

MUSÉE JACQUEMART ANDRÉ

2 Musée Jacquemart-André

Originally this late-19th-century neoclassical building—a magnificent mansion with a large reception room, winter garden, monumental staircase, and elegant private apartments—was the private residence of banker Edouard André and his artist wife, Nélie Jacquemart. The couple poured considerable amounts of money into their exquisite art collection, which now belongs to the **Institut de France**. The collection features Italian Renaissance and French 18th-century art, including works by Donatello, Botticelli, Uccello (*St. George Slaying the Dragon*), Tintoretto, Titian, Bernini, Watteau, Fragonard, and Mme. Vigée-Lebrun. It also has paintings by Rembrandt, Hals, Murillo, Van Dyck, and Reynolds, and six frescoes by Tiepolo, the only ones in France. Four of these grandiose scenes painted in 1750 illustrate the arrival of French king Henry III in Venice to visit the Doge in 1574. The Beauvais tapestries are also noteworthy. Stop in the museum's café for a light lunch (including superb salads), tea, or dessert. This lovely setting has tapestries on the walls and a ceiling painted by Tiepolo. You can go to the café without paying the museum's entrance fee. ♦ Admission, including an audio guide. Museum: daily; group tours available. Café: daily, 11:30AM-5:30PM. 158 Blvd

Haussmann (between Rues de Téhéran and de Courcelles). 01.45.62.39.94; information, 01.45.62.11.59. Métros: Miromesnil, St-Phillipe-du-Roule. www.musee-jacquemart-andre.com

Ma Bourgogne

BISTROT A VINS - RESTAURANT

3 Ma Bourgogne

★★$$ This reputable wine bar is known for such hot daily lunch specials as *oeufs en Meurette* (eggs cooked in red wine with bacon) and steak with Béarnaise sauce. Bourgogne and Beaujolais wines are featured. ♦ M-F, breakfast, lunch, and dinner; closed in July. Reservations recommended for lunch. 133 Blvd Haussmann (between Ave Percier and Rue de Courcelles). 01.45.63.50.61. Métro: Miromesnil

4 René-Gérard Saint-Ouen

Instead of clay, this sculptor uses bread dough to create shapes—elephants, chickens, half-moons, bicycles, even the **Eiffel Tower**—for any whim or occasion. If you can't bring yourself to eat these yeasty works of art, brush on some varnish and hang them in the kitchen.♦ M-Sa. 111 Blvd Haussmann (at Rue d'Argenson). 01.42.65.06.25. Métro: Miromesnil

5 Le Marcande

★★$$$ For his clientele, predominantly of business people, Chef Joël Verron prepares such dishes as *escalopes de foie gras de canard pôelées, graines de sésame, et jus de Banyuls* (sautéed foie gras in sesame seeds and Banyuls wine); *troncon de turbot rôti, purée de celeri aux amandes et jus au foie de volaille* (roast turbot with purée of celery and almonds in the juice of chicken livers); and *carré d'agneau doré au four, gratin Savoyard* (baked ribs of lamb with potato casserole). Ask for a table in the breezy dining room with a view of the charming courtyard, where alfresco eating is de rigueur in the summer. ♦ M-F, lunch and dinner; closed 2 weeks in mid-August. Reservations recommended. 52 Rue de Miromesnil (between Rue La Boétie and Blvd Haussmann). 01.42.65.19.14. Métro: Miromesnil

6 HÔTEL BRADFORD

$$$ A surprising oasis of calm and friendliness, this Best Western member hotel is wedged between the harried Champs-Elysées and Rue du Faubourg St-Honoré. The 50 rooms are spic-and-span and big enough to dance in. There's no restaurant. ♦ 10 Rue St-Philippe-du-Roule (between Rues d'Artois and du Faubourg St-Honoré). 01.45.63.20.20; fax 01.45.63.20.07. Métro: St-Philippe-du-Roule. hotel.bradford@ astotel.com; www.astotel.com

7 BOULANGERIE ST-PHILIPPE

★★$ This bakery's luncheonette (beside the crowded bread counter) features foie de veau à la vapeur (steamed veal liver), delicious house terrines, grilled meats, and wine by the glass. Order one of the éclairs, a slice of lime tart, or tarte Tatin (apple tart) for dessert and find out why the bakery is always crowded. ♦ M-F, Su, 7AM-8PM. 73 Ave Franklin-D.-Roosevelt (at Rue du Commandant-Rivière). 01.43.59.78.76. Métro: St-Philippe-du-Roule

8 ST-PHILIPPE-DU-ROULE

Before this church was completed in 1784, its parishioners prayed in the chapel of a local leprosy asylum. Designed by **Jean-François Chalgrin** (better known for his **Arc de Triomphe**), it has three aisles divided by two rows of fluted Ionic columns, a floor plan resembling that of the early Christian basilicas. ♦ 154 Rue du Faubourg St-Honoré (at Ave Myron-Herrick). Métro: St-Philippe-du-Roule

GALERIE LAMBERT ROULAND

9 GALERIE LAMBERT ROULAND

Engravings, lithographs, paintings, and sculptures are featured at this contemporary art gallery. ♦ M-Sa, 10AM-7PM. 62 Rue La Boétie (between Ave Percier and Rue de Courcelles). 01.45.63.51.52. Métros: Miromesnil, St-Philippe-du-Roule

10 SALLE GAVEAU

Opened in 1907, this is Paris's most beautiful and intimate hall for chamber music and recitals. On 26 May 1926, six young North American composers, most of them studying in Paris with famed music professor Nadia Boulanger, presented new works in a concert here. George Antheil, Theodore Chanler, Aaron Copland, Herbert Ewell, Walter Piston, and Virgil Thomson gave French music lovers their first exposure to the new vigor and self-confidence in classical composition from across the Atlantic. After years of semineglect the hall was fully restored to its original beauty and reopened in 2001. ♦ Admission. Box office: daily; closed in August. 45 Rue La Boétie (between Ave Delcassé and Rue du Faubourg St-Honoré). 01.49.53.05.07. Métro: Miromesnil

11 19 RUE LA BOÉTIE

Thirteen-year-old Henry James developed an addiction to the croissants sold across the street when he lived here between 1856 and 1857. It's still a residential building. ♦ Between Rues Cambacérès and de Miromesnil. Métro: Miromesnil

12 CHAPELLE EXPIATOIRE (EXPIATORY CHAPEL)

This memorial chapel, commissioned by Louis XVIII and designed by **Pierre Fontaine**, has become a shrine for French royalists. It was erected in 1815 on the grounds of the cemetery where, among the thousands of other victims of the revolution, Marie Antoinette, Louis XVI, and Charlotte Corday are buried. In the chapel's right apse is a statue of Louis XVI being ushered into heaven by an angel resembling Henry Essex Edgeworth, the friend who escorted the king to the guillotine. Downstairs, an altar marks the spot where Louis XVI's body was buried. ♦ W; open to groups Th by appointment. 29 Rue Pasquier (at Sq Louis-XVI). 01.42.65.35.80. Métro: St-Augustin

13 BOULEVARD HAUSSMANN

This drab expanse fronted with mammoth department stores becomes festive in December, when it's strung with Christmas lights. In 1784, 2 months after his arrival in Paris as American ambassador to France, Thomas Jefferson signed a 9-year lease on a new town house located on what is now the north side of Boulevard Haussmann. The Virginian filled it with furniture, then set about acquiring a collection of paintings, books, and engravings that would eventually adorn his beloved Monticello. History records that during his sojourn in Paris, Jefferson kept a black servant, James Hemings, whom he apprenticed to a local caterer, Combeaux, perhaps so he could take home some French culinary art along with his other acquisitions. He also started a liaison here with his deceased wife's half sister, his young mulatto slave Sally Hemings. ♦ Métros: Richelieu–Drouot, Chaussée-d'Antin-La Fayette, Havre–Caumartin, St-Augustin, Miromesnil

13 PRINTEMPS

In the late 19th century, Paris introduced the world to *grands magasins* (department stores) such as **Bon Marché** and **La Samaritaine**, and the city's shopping giants have been drawing crowds ever since. Today, two outclass the rest: **Printemps**, which opened in 1865, and **Galeries Lafayette** (see below), which opened in 1894, right next to each other on Boulevard Haussmann, and both are classified as national monuments. It was the creation of the nearby **Gare St-Lazare**, Paris's first suburban railway station, in the late 19th century that made these stores smash hits from the moment they opened. They are marvelous places to get a look at the latest in Parisian fashions and to find out the prices. All the big names are there, from agnès b. and Giorgio Armani to Yves Saint Laurent and Yohji Yamomoto. This is window shopping at its best. And if you're shopping for gifts, you're almost certain to find something for anyone in either of these stores.

Printemps underwent a serious end-of-the-century face-lift to give its hitherto rather dowdy departments a more up-to-date look. Displays are now well lit, the walls are done in pleasing pastels, the aisles have been widened for ease of navigation, and there are comfy lounges and nine eating places in its three large interconnected buildings, **Printemps de la Maison** (home furnishings), **Printemps de l'Homme** (men's fashions), and **Printemps de la Mode** (women's fashions), where fashion shows are held on Tuesdays at 10AM.

A tip to non-French shoppers: To get a card authorizing a 10% discount on many items, go to the service desk on the ground floor of the Printemps de la Maison building and present your passport. This discount is in addition to the 12% tax refund you are authorized to receive when you purchase more than 183 Euros' worth of goods in one day and take them out of the country.

For a sensational panorama of Paris, go to the ninth floor of Printemps de la Maison and have lunch or a refreshment in Groupe Flo's inexpensive self-service **La Terrasse** restaurant, which has a rooftop dining terrace. For afternoon tea, stop by **Café Flo** on the sixth floor of Printemps de la Mode beneath the vast blue stained-glass Art Nouveau cupola dating from 1923. ♦ M-W, F-Sa, 9:35AM-7PM; Th, 9:35AM-10PM. 64 Blvd Haussmann (between Rues de Caumartin and du Havre). 01.42.82.57.57. Métro: Havre-Caumartin. www.printemps.com

14 GALERIES LAFAYETTE

With its magnificent century-old Art Nouveau glass-dome cupola and its seven-story circular light well still its center of aesthetic attraction, Paris's most famous department store has gone through a thorough and dazzling renovation to prepare itself for the new century, with far more successful results than its competitor across the street. The corridors are wider, the state-of-the-art lighting is better, the décor is more chic (minimalist, but not too), and the staff is helpful, without being aggressive. Its hundreds of attractive boutiques carry every major French brand of merchandise and many prestigious international ones, including the big names in fashion. There are fashion shows every Tuesday at 11AM, and between April and October there is a second show on Fridays at 2:30PM (call ahead for reservations).

As at **Printemps**, non-French shoppers should go to the Welcome Desk on the ground floor and present their passports for a card authorizing a 10% discount, and don't forget the *detaxe* form required for the 12% tax refund non-EU (European Union) shoppers are entitled to on items worth more than 183 euros purchased on the day they leave the country.

At the vast **Lafayette Gourmet** food department, customers can sit at tasting counters sampling dozens of delicacies. The market boasts over 300 cheeses and a large wine selection. Besides the food counters here, there are seven other places to eat in the store, including a sushi bar, a **Lina's** sandwich shop, an **Angélina** tea room, and a big a self-service restaurant on the top floor called **La Terrasse** (like the one in Printemps) with a grand view of the Right Bank's rooftops. ♦ M-W, F-Sa, 9:30AM-7PM; Th, 9:30AM-9PM. 40 Blvd Haussmann (between Rues de la Chaussée-d'Antin and de Mogador). 01.42.82.34.56; 01.42.82.46.78 in English. Métro: Chaussée-d'Antin-La Fayette. www.galerieslafayette.com

Within Galeries Lafayette:

LE SPA

If you've shopped till you dropped—literally—treat yourself to an "*après* shopping" massage at this sleek day spa, which uses only Phytomer products from Brittany. 01.44.63.04.88

15 KEUR SAMBA

This nightclub uncorks around 2AM when actors, models, musicians, and diplomats of

---

every stripe and color stop by here. This black-upholstered, jumping, after-hours playpen is located near **Régine's**. ◆ Cover. Daily, midnight-7AM. 79 Rue La Boétie (between Ave Franklin-D.-Roosevelt and Rue de Ponthieu). 01.43.59.03.10. Métro: St-Philippe-du-Roule

16 DALLOYAU

Sample the *gâteau mogador* (a confection of chocolate cake and chocolate mousse with a racing stripe of raspberry jam) or the best-selling *opéra*, with layer on layer of multitextured chocolate and coffee, at this dessert shop that's been perfecting its choco-late since 1802. The Sunday-morning lines attest to the best croissants in town. ◆ Daily. 101 Rue du Faubourg St-Honoré (between Rues du Colisée and La Boétie). 01.42.99.90.00. Métro: St-Philippe-du-Roule. Also at several other locations

17 H. PICARD ET FILS

Founded in 1860, this exquisite bookstore deals in such bound treasures as Diderot's 35-volume 18th-century encyclopedia and Alexis de Tocqueville's *Democracy in America*. ◆ M-Sa; closed in August. 126 Rue du Faubourg St-Honoré (at Rue de Penthièvre). 01.43.59.28.11. Métro: St-Philippe-du-Roule

18 TROMPE-L'OEIL

On the corner of Rue de Penthièvre and Avenue Delcassé, a man gazes from his balcony at a bronze nude as two doves flutter away, casting shadows on the walls. Painted by artist **Rieti** in 1985, this trompe l'oeil enlivens an otherwise unremarkable intersec-tion. ◆ Rue de Penthièvre and Ave Delcassé. Métro: Miromesnil

19 SOFITEL WESTIN DEMEURE

$$$$ The 135 rooms and suites, as well as the public areas, of this renovated hostelry have been completely transformed by **Frédéric Méchiche**, who incorporated oak paneling, primitive trompe l'oeil paintings, and bold black-and-beige designs throughout. Rooms reflect a Regency-style elegance with modern conveniences including marble bath-

The Marquis de Lafayette, hero of the American Revolution and honorary US citizen, is buried in the Picpus Cemetery near Place de la Nation. Unlike 1,306 of the people buried there who were victims of the Terror during the French Revolution, Lafayette and a few hundred others died with their heads on. He passed away peacefully at the age of 77 in 1834. A US flag flies over the cemetery in his honor.

rooms, TV sets, CD stereos, and fax machines. Top-floor rooms afford unbeatable views of the city from their private terraces. ◆ 11 Rue d'Astorg (between Rues de la Ville l'Evêque and Roquépine). 01.53.05.05.05; fax 01.53.05.05.30. Métro: St-Augustin. hotelastor@aol.com; www.hotel-astor.net

Within Sofitel Westin Demeure:

LE RESTAURANT DE L'ASTOR

★★★$$$ Though you'll be captivated by the comings and goings of fashionable Parisians, the cuisine is worthy of your attention, too. A glass ceiling and soft yellow trompe l'oeil columns add an elegant touch to this oval dining room where the menu of chef Eric Le Cerf (a protégé of the legendary Joël Robuchon) is the star. Order such specialties as *tart friand de truffes aux oignons et lard fumée* (truffle, onion, and smoked bacon tart), roasted squab wrapped in linden leaves, and chestnut-and-truffle lobster. Desserts are tempting: Try the exceptional *crème caramélisée à la cassonade* (crème caramel with brown sugar). The wine list is limited but good. ◆ M-F, lunch and dinner. Reservations recommended. 01.53.05.05.20

20 HYATT REGENCY PARIS-MADELEINE

$$$$ The advantage of this stylish hotel is that it combines proximity to some of the most celebrated shopping districts in Paris with a discreet and relatively calm location. Located in a thoroughly renovated Haussmann-era town house, it is a short stroll away from the big department stores, Place de la Concorde, and Champs-Elysées. The hotel's 86 rooms and suites are comfortable and contemporary, an feature an abundance of cherry wood and sycamore with chrome accents. There is an immaculate fitness center replete with sauna and *hammam* as well as two restaurants; one is La Chinoiserie, under a lobby skylight designed by Gustave Eiffel and a popular brunch spot among Parisians, and the other a bistro called Café M. Personal touches also set the hotel apart, from the complimentary Hediard fruit jellies in every room to the "Concierge Tip of the Day" placed under your door each morning along with the weather forecast. Even better are the "hot tip" sheets provided by the hotel's Paris-savvy general manager, Christophe Lorvo. ◆ 24 Blvd Malesherbes (between Rue des Mathurins and Rue d'Anjou). 800.233.1234 or 01.55.27.12.34, fax 01.55.27.12.35. Métro: Madeleine or St-Augustin. Madeleine.concierge@paris.hyatt.com

21 HÔTEL OPAL

$$ For the frugal traveler, here's a property with cheerful yellow décor in the lobby, a

friendly young team at the front desk, and 36 small but neat and pleasant guest rooms with modern bathrooms. Located behind the **Madeleine** church, it's a handy place to stay if you love going to the ballet and shopping in the nearby stores. There is no restaurant. ♦ 19 Rue Tronchet (at Rue de Castellane). 01.42.65.77.97; fax 01.49.24.06.58. Métro: Madeleine. hotel_opal@club-internet.fr; www.hotels.fr/opal

22 LE ROI DU POT-AU-FEU

★★$$ For some warm consolation on a frigid evening, visit this offbeat little bistro with its quaint red-checkered tablecloths. The specialty is its namesake: *pot au feu*, a marrow-rich beef broth served with the meat and vegetables that gave up their substance to the stew. ♦ M-Sa, lunch and dinner. 34 Rue Vignon (between Rues de Sèze and Tronchet). 01.47.42.37.10. Métro: Madeleine

23 AMERICAN EXPRESS

If you did leave home without it, go no farther. Here you'll find traveler's checks, a foreign-exchange bank, tours and travel services, and the famous American Express mail pickup counter. ♦ M-Sa, 11 Rue Scribe (at Rue Auber). 01.47.77.77.58. Métro: Opéra

24 OPÉRA GARNIER (PARIS OPERA)

An opera house fit for an emperor, the pièce de résistance of Baron Haussmann's revamped Paris, and a last hurrah of Second Empire opulence, this grandiose culture palace was once the world's largest theater, with an area of nearly 3 acres and a stage vast enough to accommodate 450 performers. Designer **Charles Garnier**, a 35-year-old previously unknown architect, was selected from among a field of 171 other competitors (including the empress's favorite architect, **Eugène-Emmanuel Viollet-le-Duc**). Garnier gave the façade an unusual ornate look with friezes, winged horses, golden garlands, and busts of famous composers. He crowned his architectural extravaganza with a copper-green cupola topped by Millet's Apollo thrusting a lyre above his head. A golden bust of the architect stands on the Rue Scribe side of the theater. Garnier's orgiastic mishmash of styles (from classical to Baroque) and materials (every possible hue of marble, from green to red to blue) was less than the hit he hoped it would be. The empress, wife of Napoléon III, is said to have barked in disgust, "What is this style supposed to be? It is neither Greek nor Roman nor Louis XIV nor Louis XV!" Garnier diplomatically replied: "It is Napoléon III, Your Majesty." Second Empire advocates of family

values were in an uproar over the sensual Carrier-Belleuse lamp-bearing statues and the famous sculpted group *La Danse* by Carpeaux.

Inside, however, the effect is eminently upright, even majestic. Though Renoir loathed it, you will find a night at the opera house well worth your while, although it's mainly classical ballet and modern dance, rather than opera, that is performed here now; all grand operas take place at the **Opéra Bastille**. The gold ornaments, allegories in marble, Chagall ceilings, and the parade of Parisian society are all good for a gape. Horror fans will be interested to know that the underground grotto where Leroux's *Phantom of the Opera* lurked lies beneath the Opéra's cellars, an artificial lake that provides water for the city's fire brigade. The **Opéra Museum** in the **West Pavilion** displays opera and ballet memorabilia (such as the crown Pavlova wore when dancing in *Swan Lake* and the ballet slippers and tarot cards of Nijinsky). ♦ Admission. Box office: M-Sa. Museum: M-Sa. Pl de l'Opéra (between Rues Halévy and Auber). Reservations, 08.36.69.78.68; other inquiries, 01.40.01.17.89. Métro: Opéra. www.opera-de-paris.fr

Within the Opéra Garnier:

GRAND FOYER AND STAIRCASE

Of this apotheosis of splendor Henry James wrote: "If the world were ever reduced to the domain of a single gorgeous potentate, the foyer would do very well for his throne room." The Baroque white Carrara marble **Grand Staircase**, with its Algerian onyx balustrade, is 32 feet wide at its center. At the first landing, it divides and sweeps upward in two flights of steps to the second-floor gallery. The **Grand Foyer**, 175 feet long and decorated with mirrors and allegorical paintings, is encrusted with gilt ornamentation, and its ceiling glows with Venetian mosaics and colored marble from the island of Murano. The annual Ecole Polytechnique Ball and presidential galas take place here.

AUDITORIUM

The theater is famous for its 6-ton chandelier and five tiers of loges dressed in red velvet and gold. The ceiling is adorned with Marc Chagall's 1964 masterpiece depicting Parisian scenes and images from operas ranging from *Giselle* to *The Magic Flute*; the work is as colorful as the rest of **Garnier**'s palace yet oddly out of place. Backstage is the **Foyer de la Danse** so often painted by Edgar Degas.

Restaurants/Clubs: Red | **Hotels: Purple** | Shops: Orange | **Outdoors/Parks: Green** | Sights/Culture: Blue

PARIS MACABRE

While the most violent moments of Paris history have been in connection with political upheavals, plenty of other unsavory crises have struck at the City of Light's doorstep. Among them:

- In 843 numerous deaths were attributed to flour mixed (mistakenly, one presumes) with soil and sand.
- In 1423 and again in 1438, hungry wolves ran amok in the city, devouring an unspecified number of small children.
- On 5 January 1709, the temperature plunged to -40 degrees F. The cold wave was responsible for 30,000 deaths and many bodies did not thaw until March.
- On 1 January 1658, the Seine flooded its banks, causing the Pont-Marie to collapse and 60 people to drown.
- In 1810 a fire broke out at the Austrian Embassy, resulting in more than 100 deaths. Napoléon was there for a reception but escaped the flames; the experience led him to create a fire brigade.
- A fire at the Opera Comique on 25 May 1887 claimed 115 victims.
- When famine struck during the Prussians' siege of Paris in 1871, exotic animals from the Jardin des Plantes were slaughtered and found their way onto bistro menus around the city.
- Nearly a fifth of the buildings in Paris were damaged in the great flood of January 1910. There was no subway, gas, or electricity service, and boats ran along the Avenue Montaigne and in front of the Gare St-Lazare.
- In 1918 the German bomb "Big Bertha" struck the Eglise St-Gervais, killing 100.
- Shortly before New Year's 2000, torrential rain and winds up to 125 miles per hour battered Paris, uprooting trees, devastating the gardens of Versailles, and damaging stained glass windows at the Sainte-Chapelle.

25 CHEZ GERMAIN

★$ The models, fashion designers, and art dealers who work in the neighborhood flock to this inexpensive bistro for a quick lunch. Sample the *pastilla de pintade* (baked, glazed guinea fowl), *jarret du porc aux lentils du Puy* (ham hock with grapes), or brochette of lamb. ◆ M-F, lunch. Reservations recommended. 19 Rue Jean-Mermoz (between Rues de Ponthieu and du Faubourg St-Honoré). 01.43.59.29.24. Métro: St-Phillipe-du-Roule

26 LE MERISIER

★★$$ In keeping with this restaurant's name, which means "the wild cherry tree," owners Jean-Paul and Françoise Boyrie have paneled the dining room in cherry wood. The warm and handsome room is often filled with people from the nearby embassies, who come here for breakfast and lunch. Good choices are the *terrine à l'ancienne et sa confiture d'oignons* (duck pâté with Armagnac and onion preserves), the steak tartare, and the *pavé de rumsteck aux morilles* (steak with morel mushrooms). For dessert, the *larme au chocolat griottines* (a tear-shaped chocolate shell filled with chocolate mousse and kirsch-soaked cherries) is much acclaimed. The ambience is exceptionally relaxed and friendly. ◆ M-F, breakfast, lunch, and dinner. Reservations recommended. 28 Rue Jean-Mermoz (at Rue Rabelais). 01.42.25.36.06. Métro: St-Philippe-du-Roule

27 GALERIE BERHEIM-JEUNE

Impressionist to contemporary works, including those by such masters as Renoir, Bonnard, and Dufy, are exhibited in this art gallery. Around 1840 William Thackeray took a small pied-à-terre in the same building. ◆ Tu-Sa. 83 Rue du Faubourg St-Honoré (between Ave Matignon and Rue Jean-Mermoz). 01.42.66.60.31. Métros: Miromesnil, St-Philippe-du-Roule

28 HÔTEL LE BRISTOL

$$$$ One of the most prestigious of Paris's grand hotels, this glamorous establishment caters to the diplomats and dignitaries who conduct business down the street at the **Palais de l'Elysée**. All 185 rooms and 4 suites feature luxurious silk fabrics, antiques, Persian carpets, crystal chandeliers, and marble bathrooms, placing the hotel in a class by itself. Ulysses S. Grant was a guest here in 1877, and Sinclair Lewis stayed here in 1925, the year he won the Pulitzer prize (which he declined to accept) for his novel *Arrowsmith*. More recently, this has been Robert De Niro's home away from home while working on movies in France. Many rooms overlook the lovely private garden. A modern

fitness center, sauna, and pool are on the top floor. ♦ 112 Rue du Faubourg St-Honoré (between Pl Beauvau and Ave Matignon). 01.53.43.43.00; fax 01.53.43.43.01. Métro: Miromesnil. resa@hotel-bristol.com; www.hotel-bristol.com

Within Hôtel Le Bristol:

LE BRISTOL

★★★$$$$ The formal dining room of the hotel brings forth images of elegance with its Regency-style and wood-paneled décor. Inventive young chef Eric Frechon, the former second to Christian Constant at the **Crillon**, has received nothing but raves since taking charge here in 2000. Large macaronis stuffed with truffles, artichoke and foie gras of duck lightly sprinkled with aged Parmesan cheese, roasted Breton lobster, rack and saddle of lamb marinated in Oriental savors served with fine semolina with preserved lemon and raisins, brazed *dorade* (sea bream) with lemongrass, duck's breast with natural juices and caramelized orange-flavored turnips—these are a few samples of "cuisine of flavors, spices, and herbs" he concocts. Master dessert chef Gilles Marchal and two of the rare women to rise to the top of the overwhelmingly male profession of sommelier, Marlene Vendramelli-Pouységur and Vinnie Mazzara, are other key players on this personable young team that has garnered two prestigious Michelin stars for the restaurant. In summer the dining room opens onto the hotel's magnificent garden. Unusual for an establishment in our Big Bucks category, this restaurant draws a largely French clientele. ♦ Daily, lunch and dinner. Reservations required at least a week in advance. 01.53.43.43.40

BAR DU BRISTOL

This comfy lounge opening out onto the lobby serves breakfast and light lunch, and refreshments any time of the day. ♦ M-F, 8:30AM-2AM; Sa-Su, 10:30AM-2AM

29 LE SPHINX

Together with its sister shop, **L'Aigle Impériale** (around the corner at 3 Rue de Miromesnil; 01.42.65.27.33), this place has one of the city's largest collections of antique weapons and Napoleonic memorabilia. Along with portraits of the emperor, you'll find 19th-century French Romantic paintings, and for contrast, a stunning collection of Oriental paintings, too. ♦ M-Sa. 104 Rue du Faubourg St-Honoré (between Pl Beauvau and Ave Matignon). 01.42.65.90.96. Métro: Miromesnil

30 8 RUE DE MIROMESNIL

In May 1961, pop artist Robert Rauschenberg's first solo show was held here and received rave reviews. The building now houses several shops. ♦ Between Pl Beauvau and Rue de Penthièvre. Métro: Miromesnil

31 HÔTEL DE BEAUVAU

Le Camus de Mezières designed this mansion for Prince Charles de Beauvau, but the revolution transferred its ownership to the state. The Ministry of the Interior has resided behind its ornate iron gates since 1861. ♦ 96 Rue du Faubourg St-Honoré (at Pl Beauvau). Métro: Miromesnil

32 MURIEL

A remnant of Old Paris, this is one of the few remaining Parisian boutiques that sells only gloves. ♦ M-Sa; closed in August. 4 Rue des Saussaies (between Rue Montalivet and Pl Beauvau). 01.42.65.95.34. Métro: Miromesnil

33 AU VIEUX SAUSSAIES

This shop trades in 18th- and 19th-century silver—from sugar bowls to samovars and champagne ice buckets, specializing in gifts for weddings and christenings. Here you'll find top-name *orfèvrerie* (silverware) at lower prices than you'll see from some of the other dealers. ♦ Tu-Sa, 11-7PM. 14 Rue des Saussaies (between Rues Montalivet and de Surène). 01.42.65.32.71. Métro: Miromesnil

34 NEW HÔTEL ROBLIN

$$$ English travelers who cross the channel for a weekend of dance at the **Opéra Garnier** and luxurious take-out food from the **Place de la Madeleine** find refuge in this comfortable 78-room hotel. Its restaurant serves traditional French fare. ♦ 6 Rue Chauveau-Lagarde (between Pl de la Madeleine and Rue de l'Arcade). 01.44.71.20.80; fax 01.42.65.19.49. Métro: Madeleine. parisroblin @new_hotel.com; www.new-hotel.com

35 LA FERME ST-HUBERT

★★$$ Cheese is the focus at this rustic restaurant, and Chef Henry Voy serves the best *croque monsieur* in Paris. Other specialties include fondue, raclette, and *tartiflette au Reblochon* (melted Reblochon cheese on a gratin of potatoes with bacon). Also on the premises is a shop selling 140 different varieties of cheese; this cheese lover's heaven is especially known for its excellent Roquefort and beaufort. ♦ M-Sa, lunch and dinner. 21 Rue Vignon (between Rues de Sèze and Tronchet). 01.47.42.79.20. Métro: Madeleine

Restaurants/Clubs: Red | Hotels: Purple | Shops: Orange | Outdoors/Parks: Green | Sights/Culture: Blue

36 LA MAISON DU MIEL

Run by the Gallands family since 1908, this shop is devoted entirely to honey and products containing honey, such as soap and oil. There are sample tastings, and you can choose from a selection of various honeys in miniature jars. Don't pass up the *bruyère* (heather) honey. ♦ M-Sa. 24 Rue Vignon (between Rues de Sèze and Tronchet). 01.47.42.26.70. Métro: Madeleine

37 PALAIS DE L'ELYSÉE

The most famous address on Rue du Faubourg St-Honoré, if not in all of France, is the French version of the White House. Built in 1718 according to a design by **Armand-Claude Mollet**, the palace was purchased in 1753 by Mme. de Pompadour, Louis XV's rich and spoiled mistress, who hired architect **Jean Lassurance** to expand the building and extend the gardens to the Champs-Elysées. Expropriated during the revolution to serve as a government printing office (for the Bulletin des Lois) and dance hall, it later was known as the **Hameau Chantilly** and became a hideaway for Empress Joséphine after she was divorced by Napoléon. On 22 June 1815 Napoléon signed his second abdication here. The mansion was subsequently the site of a restaurant and fairgrounds run by an ice-cream maker named Velloni. Still later, the Duke of Wellington and Czar Alexander I stayed here. The palace has been the official residence of the French president since 1873. Except for *les Journées du Patrimoine* (National Patrimony Days) on the third Saturday and Sunday of September, the public is not admitted, but you can glimpse the dignified façade through the gateway. ♦ 55 Rue du Faubourg St-Honoré (between Rue de l'Elysée and Ave de Marigny). Métro: Miromesnil

38 HÔTEL BEAU MANOIR

$$$ Serious shoppers will appreciate this hotel's central location—down the street from the **Faubourg St-Honoré** and next to the gourmet food boutiques in the **Place de la Madeleine**. Cozily refurbished with gold-and-

red damask walls, exposed beams, marble bathrooms, and walnut cabinetry, the 32-room hostelry is part of the French Best Western Association. There's no restaurant. Next door is its less expensive sister, the **Hôtel Lido** (4 Passage de la Madeleine, 01.42.66.27.37; fax 01.42.66.61.23; lido@paris-hotels-charm.com; www.paris-hotels-charm.com). ♦ 6 Rue de l'Arcade (between Blvd Malesherbes and Rue Chauveau-Lagarde). 01.53.43.28.28; fax 01.53.43.28.88. Métro: Madeleine. bm@paris-hotels-charm.com; www.paris-hotels-charm.com

39 LA MAISON DE LA TRUFFE

★★$$$ Brooklyn delicatessens never looked like this fancy place, which specializes in black gold (fresh truffles, in season from November through February) and foie gras, caviar, smoked salmon, or any other delicacy your gourmand's heart could desire. Savor the tasty treasures at one of the 15 tables here or purchase them at the shop to enjoy on a picnic. ♦ Restaurant: Tu-Sa, lunch and dinner until 8:30 PM. M, lunch only. Shop: M-Sa, 9AM-8PM. 19 Pl de la Madeleine (between Blvd Malesherbes and Rue Chauveau-Lagarde). 01.42.65.53.22. Métro: Madeleine

39 HÉDIARD

This *épicerie* (gourmet grocery store) was founded in 1854 by Ferdinand Hédiard, who was the first to import the exotic pineapple into France. Marcel Proust once lingered here surveying Hédiard's extraordinary selection of Asian and African delicacies: spices, oils, vinegars, 30 blends of tea, freshly roasted coffee beans, baskets of rare jams and jellies and old rums. A late-20th-century renovation turned the charming Old World food shop into a modern souk. There are specialty food counters on two levels around a glass-roofed market that is a worthy rival of the more famous **Fauchon** across the square, and many food-savvy French bourgeois prefer it. In fact, the best selection of Bordeaux wines in Paris may well be here. ♦ M-Sa, 8:30AM-9PM. 21 Pl de la Madeleine (between Blvd Malesherbes and Rue Chauveau-Lagarde). Shop, 01.43.12.88.88; take-out delivery service, 01.42.65.06.16. Métro: Madeleine. Also at 126 Rue du Bac (between Rues de Sèvres and de Babylone). 01.45.44.01.98. Métro: Sèvres–Babylone

Atop Hédiard:

HÉDIARD

★★$$ Overlooking Place Madeleine, this bright, pleasant restaurant above the shop of the same name serves such tasty Provençal

According to Hemingway, Gertrude Stein characterized him and his fellow World War I veterans as "a lost generation." It was a phrase she had heard a garage manager apply to one of his mechanics who was a war veteran: "You are all a *génération perdue*." When Hemingway tried to object, she said, "Don't contradict me, Hemingway. It does no good at all. You're all a lost generation, just as the garage keeper said." Hemingway used the phrase as the epigraph for his first novel, *The Sun Also Rises*.

dishes as crusty-skinned *rouget* (red mullet) with trumpet mushrooms sautéed in olive oil and peppers stuffed with codfish paste. The dining spot buzzes with the excitement of upscale shoppers at lunch; it's more subdued in the evening. ♦ M-Sa, lunch and dinner. 01.43.12.88.99

40 MARQUISE DE SÉVIGNÉ

The ambiance in this combination tea salon–chocolate shop is as sublime as the rich hot chocolate it serves. Customers who order a coffee, tea, or hot chocolate at the little bar are entitled to a little taste of the chocolates on the spot. There are no tables. ♦ M-Sa. 32 Pl de la Madeleine (between Rues Sèze and Tronchet). 01.42.65.19.47. Métro: Madeleine

RESTAURANT & BOUTIQUE

41 CAVIAR KASPIA

★★★$$$ Besides purveying the finest in Russian and Iranian caviars, the chic little upstairs restaurant adorned in czarist turquoise and overlooking Place de la Madeleine offers vodka, aquavit, and blintzes languidly draped with smoked salmon. The shop downstairs sells all the makings for a Russian dinner. 01.42.65.33.52. ♦ Restaurant: M-Sa, lunch and dinner until 1AM. Store: M-Sa, 9AM–midnight. 17 Pl de la Madeleine (between Blvd Malesherbes and Rue Chauveau-Lagarde). 01.42.65.33.32. Métro: Madeleine

42 AU VERGER DE LA MADELEINE

Since 1936 this has remained one of Paris's finest family-operated *épiceries* (gourmet grocery stores). Jean-Pierre Legras, who features wines dating from 1789, will help you find an old Sauternes bottled in the year you were born, got married, or made your first trip to Paris. ♦ M-Sa. 4 Blvd Malesherbes (between Pl de la Madeleine and Rue de l'Arcade). 01.42.65.51.99. Métro: Madeleine

43 L'ECLUSE

★★$$ One of a chain of six wine bars selling marvelous old Bordeaux by the glass, this spot is lively, fashionable, affordable, and ideal for people-watching. ♦ Daily, lunch and dinner until 1AM. 15 Pl de la Madeleine (between Blvd Malesherbes and Rue Chauveau-Lagarde). 01.42.65.34.69. Métro: Madeleine. Also at numerous locations throughout the city

44 FAUCHON

FAUCHON

At Paris's most famous food emporium, window shopping is an aesthetic experience at all three of its stores that span the northeast corner of the Place de la Madeleine. **No. 24** sells *traiteur* (prepared) dishes that look too beautiful to eat—every exotic fruit on earth artfully arranged, along with gift baskets of pâtés, foie gras, and truffles. The store's elegant **Salon de Thé** at **No. 26** is the place to sample some of these products; it serves breakfast, lunch, salads, sandwiches, and, of course, tea and pastries; it now has an outdoor *terrasse* facing the Madeleine. **No. 28** is the *confiserie* (candy shop) and patisserie, virtually impossible to walk past without popping in for one of its amazing treats (the pear and crunchy caramel tart with almond-caramel cream, for example). Finally, at **No. 30**, there's the *épicerie* (gourmet grocery store) stocked with more than 4,500 items, including 115 choices of teas and 96 varieties of spices in its new **Boutique du Thé** and **Des Epices** on the first floor; 21 coffees, more than 100 kinds of jam, 28 mustards, and 35 varieties of honey on the ground floor; and in the basement, a magnificent wine cave with 2,500 labels of wine and spirits and a wine bar. The quality is stratospherically high, and so, for the most part, are the prices—although not for everything. There's a bottle of wine that sells for as little as 3.35 Euros. ♦ M-Sa. 24, 26, 28, and 30 Pl de la Madeleine (at Rue de Sèze). 01.47.42.60.11. Métro: Madeleine

45 LE GRAND HÔTEL INTER-CONTINENTAL

$$$$ Designed in 1861 by **Alfred Armand** and inaugurated by Empress Eugénie the following year, this 514-room property occupying a full city block in the heart of the Opéra Quartier remains one of Europe's grandest luxury hotels. Its proximity to the Opéra Garnier has long made it a favorite of visiting singers and prima ballerinas. At press time, the hotel, its bar, restaurants, café, health club, conference center, and grand ballroom are closed for a massive renovation. It is not scheduled to reopen until June 2003. ♦ 2 Rue Scribe (at Blvd des Capucines). 01.40.07.32.32; fax

---

Restaurants/Clubs: Red | Hotels: Purple | Shops: Orange | Outdoors/Parks: Green | Sights/Culture: Blue

01.42.66.12.51. Métro: Opéra. legrand@interconti.com; www.interconti.com.

Within the Grand Hôtel Inter-Continental:

LA VERRIÈRE

★★$$ Light-filled and spacious, with a glass roof and numerous plants and trees, this airy eatery serves a breakfast buffet Monday through Friday and brunch on Sunday. ♦ M-F, breakfast, lunch, and dinner; Su, brunch; closed for renovation until June 2003. 01.40.07.32.32

BAR DU GRAND HÔTEL

Tucked under the arches of the hotel is this multilevel Opéra-goers' watering hole. ♦ Daily, 11AM-1AM; closed for renovation until June 2003. Entrance at 12 Blvd des Capucines. 01.40.07.31.37

CAFÉ DE LA PAIX

★★$$ Looking like a scene painted by Renoir—brightly clothed patrons, green-and-white-striped umbrellas, dappled light—this lovely old café is classified as a historic landmark. Guy de Maupassant, Emile Zola, Sir Arthur Conan Doyle, André Gide, and Oscar Wilde frequented its large terrace on the Place de l'Opéra. Salvador Dalí enjoyed it, as did Harry Truman, Maurice Chevalier, Josephine Baker, Maria Callas, Marlene Dietrich, and General Charles de Gaulle, who ordered a take-out cold plate here on 25 August 1944—the first in liberated Paris. Tradition holds that if you sit on the terrace long enough, you will see someone you know walk by. ♦ Daily, lunch and dinner until 1AM. Entrance at 3 Pl de l'Opéra. 01.40.07.30.20

LE RESTAURANT OPÉRA

★★★$$$$ This glamorous dining spot recalls the 19th-century heyday of the **Opéra**

From the time of Napoléon, the French national government—ever leery of the revolutionary potential of the Parisian masses—had always governed the capital. But in 1975 as part of a nationwide trend toward decentralization, Parliament adopted a new constitution for the city that gave Paris the power to administer itself. The code also established the position of mayor of Paris; the mayor was to be picked by the 109 municipal counselors who were elected by universal suffrage in the city's 20 arrondissements. The central government didn't trust Paris completely, however—it kept control of the police force. Jacques Chirac, the first mayor, served from 1977 to 1995, when he was elected president of France.

Garnier, thanks to its **Charles Garnier**–inspired architectural elements, including ethereal ceiling frescoes and old gold columns and moldings. Champagne-colored table linen, Sèvres porcelain plates, and fine crystal add to the elegant ambiance. ♦ M-F, lunch and dinner; closed for renovation until June 2003. Reservations recommended. Entrance at 3 Pl de l'Opéra. 01.40.07.30.10. Métro: Opéra

46 PLACE DE L'OPÉRA

Six wide thoroughfares lined with bank headquarters, theaters, luxury boutiques, and **Le Grand Hôtel Inter-Continental** are the spokes emanating from this hub in front of the **Opéra Garnier**. It was the keystone of Baron Haussmann's massive redevelopment of the center of Paris under Napoléon III. Back when the Opéra was where one scaled the social heights, the *haut monde* and *demimonde* frequented the nearby **Café de la Paix**, **Café de Paris**, and **Café Riche**. ♦ Métro: Opéra

47 28 RUE BOISSY-D'ANGLAS

Le Boeuf sur le Toit, the famous avant-garde nightclub, was once located here. Its 10 January 1922 inaugural party was thrown by Jean Cocteau and attended by Constantin Brancusi, Pablo Picasso, and Max Beerbohm, among others. Leading the club's orchestra that night was Vance Lowry, an African-American saxophonist who was partially responsible for introducing the French to jazz and the music of George Gershwin. The club's succesor, the brasserie of the same name, is now located at 34 Rue du Colisée, between Rue du Faubourg St-Honoré and Avenue Franklin-D.-Roosevelt. 01.53.93.65.55. ♦ Between Cité Berryer and Blvd Malesherbes. Métro: Madeleine

48 LUCAS CARTON

★★★★$$$$ The nouvelle cuisine of superstar chef Alain Senderens is better (and more expensive) than ever. In fact, this is one of the Parisian capitals of nouvelle cuisine, made even more memorable by the gorgeous Majorelle Belle Epoque maple-and-sycamore woodwork in the dining room. Try the delicious foie gras in steamed cabbage, *canard Apicus* (duck roasted with honey and spices), Breton lobster with vanilla, ravioli filled with clams, and bittersweet chocolate and licorice ice cream with peppermint meringue. ♦ M, dinner; Tu-F, lunch and dinner; Sa, dinner; closed in August and 1 week at Christmas. Reservations required. 9 Pl de la Madeleine (at Blvd Malesherbes). 01.42.65.22.90. Métro: Madeleine

49 PLACE DE LA MADELEINE

Around the edges of this square, the heart of upscale noshing in Paris, are specialty shops to spoil the spoiled (see the shopping map on page 192). Amid the fumes of buses and a more or less perpetual rush hour, a lively flower market (open Tuesday through Saturday and Sunday morning) blossoms just east of the **Madeleine** church. Here, at her funeral in 1975, entertainer Josephine Baker, having already received the Légion d'Honneur and the Médaille de la Résistance, became the first North American woman to be honored with a 21-gun salute. ◆ Métro: Madeleine

On Place de la Madeleine:

PUBLIC LAVATORY

Even if nature isn't calling, look for a sign that reads *"Hommes et Dames* W.C." It will lead you underground to an elegant 1905 facility with Art Nouveau wood paneling, stained glass, and tile built by Etablissements Porcher, now one of the largest plumbing suppliers in France. ◆ At Rue Royale

LA MADELEINE (EGLISE STE-MARIE MADELEINE)

The 28 monumental steps of this church rise to meet 52 immense Corinthian columns, defining an edifice that dominates the hub of the financial district. However, the building has always been an architectural orphan. Begun as a church in 1764 under the reign of Louis XV and modeled after a Greek temple, the structure, at various times in its turbulent past, has been slated to become a bank, parliament building, theater, stock exchange, banquet hall, and yet another temple to glorify Napoléon's army (as if the **Arc de Triomphe** and the **Invalides** were not enough). In 1837 the windowless edifice, designed by **Pierre Vignon** and **Jean-Jacques Huvé**, was selected to be the capital's first railway station but was consecrated as a church dedicated to St. Mary Magdalene 5 years later.

Not a single cross adorns the pediments of this church, and its rose-marble-and-gilt interior is surprisingly sensual. The imposing bronze door portraying the Ten Commandments is by Philippe Joseph Henri Lemaire, and his gigantic *Last Judgment* on the south pediment is the largest work of its kind in the world (and it contains one of the chubbiest Christs in Europe). On the north side of the church, the inscription beneath a headless statue of St. Luke reads "On 30 May 1918, a German shell struck the church of the Madeleine and decapitated this statue." The splendid organ was played by composer Camille Saint-Saëns, and the Funeral March

of Chopin resounded here as the composer himself was laid to rest. The grandest funeral ever accorded a North American in Paris was that of Josephine Baker, held here on 15 April 1975. ◆ 01.44.51.69.00

KIOSQUE-THÉÂTRE

This kiosk sells half-price tickets to theater, dance, music hall, concert, café theater, and, occasionally, opera performances on the day of the event. ◆ Daily. No phone

50 EDOUARD BERCK

Now run by the founder's daughter, Elysabeth, this shop buys and sells stamps from all over the world; offers estimates; and sells magnifying glasses, albums, catalogs, and other tools of the hobby. It's the city's most renowned stamp dealer. ◆ M-Sa. 6 Pl de la Madeleine (between Blvd de la Madeleine and Rue Royale). 01.42.60.34.26; fax 01.42.60.68.11. Métro: Madeleine

50 BOUTIQUE MAILLE

This is the ideal place to stock up on mustard to suit all tastes—champagne or cognac, for example. The shop also sells fresh mustard, flavored vinegars, pickles, and beautifully decorated ceramic jars in which to store your favorite condiment. ◆ M-Sa. 6 Pl de la Madeleine (between Blvd de la Madeleine and Rue Royale). 01.40.15.06.00. Métro: Madeleine

50 4 PLACE DE LA MADELEINE

Alas, this is no longer the home of Durand's, the famous music publisher, where, in 1831, Liszt first met Chopin. The building now has both commercial and residential space. ◆ Between Blvd de la Madeleine and Rue Royale. Métro: Madeleine

51 CHARLES JOURDAN

In 1957, the celebrated M. Jourdan became the first cobbler to use glue instead of nails to hold his shoes together; the result was the first truly delicate feminine footwear. The most up-to-the-minute styles are still featured at this fashionable shoe boutique. ◆ M-Sa. 5 Blvd de la Madeleine (between Rues Cambon and Duphot). 01.42.61.15.89. Métro: Madeleine

52 LAVINIA

There are wine stores and there are wine emporia, and this massive new shop is definitely in the latter category. The selection of vintages here is mind-boggling—some 6,000 in all, making it an essential stop for any

---

Restaurants/Clubs: Red | Hotels: Purple | Shops: Orange | Outdoors/Parks: Green | Sights/Culture: Blue

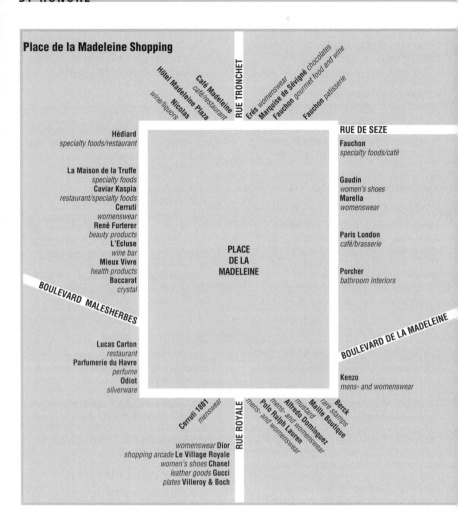

Place de la Madeleine Shopping

Hôtel Madeleine Plaza *café/restaurant*
Café Madeleine *café/restaurant*
Nicolas *wine/liquors*

RUE TRONCHET

Erès *womenswear*
Marquise de Sévigné *chocolates*
Fauchon *gourmet food and wine*
Fauchon *patisserie*

Hédiard
specialty foods/restaurant

La Maison de la Truffe
specialty foods
Caviar Kaspia
restaurant/specialty foods
Cerruti
womenswear
René Furterer
beauty products
L'Ecluse
wine bar
Mieux Vivre
health products
Baccarat
crystal

BOULEVARD MALESHERBES

Lucas Carton
restaurant
Parfumerie du Havre
perfume
Odiot
silverware

PLACE DE LA MADELEINE

RUE DE SEZE

Fauchon
specialty foods/café

Gaudin
women's shoes
Marella
womenswear

Paris London
café/brasserie

Porcher
bathroom interiors

BOULEVARD DE LA MADELEINE

Kenzo
mens- and womenswear

Berck *rare stamps*
Maille Boutique *mustard*
Alfredo Dominguez *mens- and womenswear*
Polo Ralph Lauren *mens- and womenswear*

Cerruti 1881 *menswear*

RUE ROYALE

womenswear **Dior**
shopping arcade **Le Village Royale**
women's shoes **Chanel**
leather goods **Gucci**
plates **Villeroy & Boch**

aspiring oenophile. With its abundance of rich, undulating burgundy wood spread out over three levels, the space is clearly designed to impress. All varieties are accorded clear identification, but it's the French wines, naturally, that get the most privileged place on the immense basement level. Ground level is where wines from other countries are and the second floor features a restaurant where you can sample the vintage of your choice along with a salad, cheese plate, or selection of hot dishes. ♦ M-Sa. 3-5 Blvd de la Madeleine (at Rue Cambon). 01.42.97.20.20. Métro: Madeleine. laviniafrance@lavinia.fr

53 L'OLYMPIA

Edith Piaf sang her heart out on this stage. Years later, so did a group of Brits named the Beatles, who had just launched their first world tour. Playing here is still an obligatory engagement for top pop singers. ♦ 28 Blvd des Capucines (between Rues Scribe and de Caumartin). 01.47.42.25.49. Métros: Madeleine, Opéra

54 14 BOULEVARD DES CAPUCINES

On 28 December 1895 the brothers Auguste and Louis Lumière, inventors of the cinematograph, projected their first public movie here in what was called the **Salon Indien**. This is now an office building. ♦ At Rue Scribe. Métro: Opéra

54 HÔTEL SCRIBE

$$$$ This deluxe hotel is a full-blown Second Empire confection, from the harmonious six-story Haussmann façade to the stately

Rue du Faubourg-St-Honoré Shopping

RUE DU CIRQUE
Galerie Nichido
A Fragonard
womenswear
Pierre Cardin
mens- and womenswear

AVENUE DE MARIGNY

RUE DE MIROMESNIL
Perrin *antiques*
Jean-Marie Rossi *antiques*
Ariane Dandois *antiques*

RUE DES SAUSSAIES
Caron *perfume*
Galerie de la Présidence
19th- & 20th-century art
Maude Frizon
women's shoes
Lilane Romi
womenswear
Louis Féraud
womenswear
Popoff *gallery*
Floriane
childrenswear
Marina
childrenswear
Maxim's
mens- and womenswear

RUE DE DURAS
Sotheby's *auction house*
Milady *furs*
Gemelli *jewelry*
Chopard *jewelry*
Sonia Rykiel *womenswear*
Vincent Dupontremé
womenswear
Arfan *jewelry*
Van Laack *menswear*
Roberto Cavalli
mens- and womenswear
Etro *accessories*
Pomellato *jewelry*
Gianni Versace
womenswear

RUE D'AGUESSEAU
Mont Blanc
writing supplies
Vertigo *womenswear*
Fred *jewelry*
Fratelli Rossetti
men's and women's shoes
Chloé *womenswear*

RUE DE L'ELYSEE
Frette
bed linens

Alimia
womenswear
Jean Lupu
antiques
Apostrophe
womenswear

RUE DU FAUBOURG-ST-HONORE

Map continues on right

Hervé Leger
womenswear
Lancôme
cosmetics
Valentino
womenswear
Van Cleef & Arpels
jewelry
Blancpain
watches
Gianfranco Ferre
menswear
Piaget
watches
Chanel
womenswear
TOD'S
shoes
Cartier
jewelry

RUE BOISSY-D'ANGLAS
Lanvin
Café Bleu/menswear
Sergio Rossi
shoes
Carita
hair salon
La Bagagerie
leather goods
Façonnable
menswear
Jean de Bonnot
rare books
Stephane Kelian
women's shoes and bags
Jaeger
mens- and womenswear
Elegance
womenswear
Missoni
womenswear

Comme des Garçons
Mens- and womenswear
Franck Namani
womenswear
TOD'S *shoes*
Salvatore Ferragamo
leather goods
Leonard *womenswear*
Christian Dior
womenswear/accessories

RUE D'ANJOU
Hôtel de Castiglione
Yves Saint Laurent
*womenswear/
mens formalwear*
Emmanuelle Kahn
womenswear
Aramis *menswear*
Jun Ashida
womenswear
Yves Saint Laurent
beauty products
Guy Laroche
womenswear
Givenchy
womenswear
Hermès
leather goods/scarves

Lanvin
women's boutique
La Perla
lingerie
Bottega Veneta
shoes
Camper
shoes
Iceberg *womenswear*
Loft *menswear*
PRADA
womenswear
Les Copains
womenswear
Gucci
mens- and womenswear

RUE DU FAUBOURG-ST-HONORE

Napoléon III décor in the lobby to the 217 plush, spacious rooms. The Allied forces' press corps set up headquarters here in 1944. It was the only hotel in Paris that had hot water during the bitterly cold winter of 1944–1945, and journalists who couldn't get rooms here would come to take a bath. Correspondent John Dos Passos, one of the lucky people to secure a room, wrote about the then-little-known General de Gaulle's performance at a press conference: "He has two voices, the Sorbonne voice and the *père de famille Henri Quatre, bonne soupe* kind of voice. There's more to him than we had been led to believe." ♦ 1 Rue Scribe (between Blvd des Capucines and Pl Charles-Garnier). 01.44.71.24.24; fax 01.42.65.39.97. Métro: Opéra. scribe. reservation@wanadoo.fr; www.sofitel.com

Within the Scribe:

LES MUSES

★★★$$ In the downstairs dining room decorated with big trompe l'oeil panoramas of the

Opéra district, young chef Yannick Alleno and his team at this Michelin-one-star restaurant offer flawless neoclassical cuisine. Try the chilled cream of crayfish, roasted Dublin Bay prawns, or roasted pigeon, and chocolate-and-vanilla cake with frozen crème brûlée. For a restaurant of this quality, the prices are exceptionally reasonable, especially for the prix-fixe menus available for both lunch and dinner. ◆ M-F, lunch and dinner; closed in August. Reservations recommended. 01.44.71.24.26

LE BAR
Business executives habitually gather around the elegant mahogany bar here, sipping the cocktail of the day. A pianist entertains Tuesday through Friday between 6:30PM and 9PM. A continental breakfast is served in the morning. ◆ Daily, 8AM-2AM. 01.44.71.24.24

55 MUSÉE FRAGONARD
Get a sense of what the perfume industry is all about at this museum devoted entirely to fragrance and its history. Priceless perfume-related objets d'art are also on display. There's also a shop that sells perfumes. ◆ Admission. M-Sa. 39 Blvd des Capucines (between Rues Daunou and des Capucines). 01.42.60.37.14. Métro: Opéra

56 AMERICAN AMBASSADOR'S RESIDENCE
In the 19th century the **Hôtel de Pontalba** was owned by financier and art collector Baron Edmond de Rothschild. (When the baron died in 1934 at the age of 89, he left 3,000 drawings and 43,000 postage stamps to the **Louvre**.) Subsequently, the US government had the good taste to rent the *hôtel particulier* from Baron Maurice de Rothschild to serve as the residence of the US ambassador. The 40-room, 13-bathroom building is not open to the public, but if you are invited for dinner with the ambassador, you'll see the original Oudry wood paneling and paintings by John Singer Sargent, Cézanne, and van Gogh. In one of the upstairs guest rooms is the bed where Charles Lindbergh slept after completing the first nonstop solo flight across the Atlantic on 21 May 1927. ◆ 41 Rue du Faubourg St-Honoré (between Rues Boissy-d'Anglas and de l'Elysée). Métros: Concorde, Madeleine

57 BRITISH EMBASSY
The lovely **Hôtel de Charost**, built by **Antoine Mazin** in 1723, was bought by Napoléon's sister, Pauline, who, after a tumultuous series of love affairs and marriages, became the Princess Borghese. In 1815, after Waterloo, the princess sold her **Palais Borghese** to George III of England, who turned it into his nation's embassy. Upstairs is Pauline's bed with gilded curtains descending from the talons of a Napoleonic eagle. The building is not open to the public. ◆ 39 Rue du Faubourg St-Honoré (between Rues Boissy-d'Anglas and de l'Elysée). Métros: Concorde, Madeleine

58 AU VIEUX CHINOIS
This intriguing shop specializes in Far Eastern artifacts: Chinese and Japanese ceramics, paintings, and bronzes, and sacred art from Southeast Asia. ◆ M-Sa; closed 2 weeks in August. 1 Rue d'Anjou (at Rue du Faubourg St-Honoré). 01.42.65.23.83. Métro: Concorde

59 JAPANESE EMBASSY
In 1718 **Pierre Lassurance** built this *hôtel* for Louis Blouin, confidant and premier *valet de chambre* of Louis XIV. Napoléon's sister and brother lived here, as did the king of Bavaria. It's now the Japanese ambassador's turn. ◆ 31 Rue du Faubourg St-Honoré (between Rues Boissy-d'Anglas and de l'Elysée). Métros: Concorde, Madeleine

59 33 RUE DU FAUBOURG ST-HONORÉ
Built by the architect **Grandhomme** in 1714, this house was the home of Duc Decres, who was minister of the French navy until 1820, when a bomb hidden beneath his bed dealt him a mortal wound. For 7 subsequent years, it housed the Russian Embassy, until it was sold to Nathaniel Rothschild. In 1918, the house was born anew as Cercle de l'Union Interalliée, a swank international club for businesspeople. It is not open to the public. ◆ Between Rues Boissy-d'Anglas and de l'Elysée. Métros: Concorde, Madeleine

60 HERMÈS
Started in 1837 as a saddle store by Thierry Hermès, *artisan d'élite*, this is perhaps the most celebrated leather-goods emporium in the world. Having outlasted the age of the horse and carriage, Hermès now furnishes the leather fittings for Learjets. Its bags are considered necessities, not accessories, and its gloves are unsurpassed in craftsmanship. The signature scarves are huge and come in more than 200 styles, the most popular of which is the Brides de Gala; more than a half million of these silken trifles are sold every

VEGGIE PARIS

Paris used to be a tough town for vegetarians. Not anymore! There are vegetarian restaurants in all parts of the city, numerous health food shops, and a marvelous **Marché Biologique** Sunday mornings on Boulevard Raspail between Rue de Rennes and Rue du Cherche-Midi (Métro: Sèvres–Babylone). In addition—especially since mad cow disease came along—most normal restaurants are offering vegetarian meals. For a while, Alain Passard, one of the most respected chefs in France, banished all meat from the menu at his swanky and extremely expensive restaurant, **Arpège**. Many French gourmet restaurants will prepare vegetarian meals if prospective diners phone in advance and request them. Mediterranean, Italian, Indian, and Far Eastern restaurants usually have veggie-friendly dishes available. Here are the best restaurants devoted to strictly vegetarian cuisine:

Aquarius 40 Rue de Gergovie (between Rue Raymond Losserand and Rue de l'Ouest; Métro: Pernéty), 01.45.41.36.88

Entre Ciel et Terre 5 Rue Hérold (between Rues Coquillière and Etienne-Marcel; Métros: Louvre, Châtelet–Les Halles), 01.45.08.49.84

La Ferme Opéra 55 Rue St-Roch (between Ave de l'Opéra and Rue St-Honoré; Métro: Pyramides), 01.40.20.12.12

Guen Mai 2 bis Rue de l'Abbaye (between Rues Bonaparte and Cardinale; Métro: St-Germain-des-Prés), 01.43.26.03.24

Le Grenier de Notre Dame 18 Rue de la Bûcherie (between Rues Lagrange and de l'Hôtel Colbert; Métro: St-Michel), 01.43.29.98.29

Les Quatre et Un Saveurs 72 Rue du Cardinal-Lemoine (between Rue Thouin and Pl Contrescarpé; Métro: Cardinal-Lemoine), 01.43.26.88.80

---

year. ♦ M-Sa. 24 Rue du Faubourg St-Honoré (at Rue Boissy-d'Anglas). 01.40.17.47.17. Métros: Concorde, Madeleine

Within Hermès:

MUSÉE HERMÈS

On the top floor of the store is a private museum displaying old saddles, ornamented trunks, and even Napoléon's stirrups. ♦ For admission, write in advance to Mme. de Bazelaire (Hermès, 24 Rue de Faubourg St-Honoré, Paris 75008) or call 01.40.17.48.36

JOHN LOBB

The Paris branch of the reputable London shoe- and bootmaker is located on the ground-floor rear of **Hermès**. To join the ranks of satisfied Lobb alumni, which have included Lyndon Johnson, the Shah of Iran, Gary Cooper, and the Duke of Edinburgh, stop in to be measured heel to toe. Using the measurements, one of Lobb's cobblers will fashion two wooden lasts (one for each foot) on which to model your shoes. In the nearby studio, the skins are cut and stitched, and in 1 month (first-time customers must wait a year), this labor will have produced a noble pair of handmade shoes sure to last at least a decade—and for a mere $3,000 per pair. The shop also has an entrance at 21 Rue Boissy-d'Anglas. ♦ M-Sa. 01.42.65.24.45

61 LANVIN

Shop here for women's scarves, perfumes, haute couture, and prêt-à-porter. ♦ M-Sa. 22 Rue du Faubourg St-Honoré (at Rue Boissy-d'Anglas). 01.44.71.31.73. Métros: Concorde, Madeleine

62 15 RUE DU FAUBOURG ST-HONORÉ

In 1804, Claude Rouget de l'Isle, composer of the *Marseillaise*, lived here, and after him, Felix, hairdresser to Empress Eugénie. The building now has both commercial and residential space. ♦ At Rue Boissy-d'Anglas. Métros: Concorde, Madeleine

At 15 Rue du Faubourg St-Honoré:

LANVIN

This is the place for fine men's fashion and accessories, including classic silk ties. ♦ M-Sa. 01.44.71.31.33

Within Lanvin:

CAFÉ BLEU

★★$ The café in the basement of the Lanvin boutique is a good place to fuel up with a light lunch or tea before continuing along the Faubourg St-Honoré for more power shopping.

Restaurants/Clubs: Red | Hotels: Purple | Shops: Orange | Outdoors/Parks: Green | Sights/Culture: Blue

The menu is the brainchild of chef Marcel Baudis and presents salads, foie gras, lamb stew with olives and dried fruit, fillet of red mullet in basil sauce with ratatouille, several cheeses and a velvety chocolate cake served warm. They showcase *les vins des stars* (wines of the stars)—vintages produced by actors Gérard Départieu and Pierre Richard, director Francis Coppola (a big-budget item), and other big names. ♦ M-Sa, lunch and tea. 01.44.71.32.32

62 CARITA

This lavishly decorated hair salon (whose clients have included Catherine Deneuve, Paloma Picasso, and French rocker Johnny Hallyday) has a relaxed, down-to-earth staff that sets hairstyle trends. There are separate entrances for men and women. The salon is also noted for its skin-care treatments. ♦ Tu-Sa. The boutique for buying products is open all day on Mondays. 11 Rue du Faubourg St-Honoré (between Rues Royale and Boissy-d'Anglas). 01.44.94.11.11. Métros: Concorde, Madeleine

buddha-bar

63 BUDDHA-BAR

★★$$ A two-story-high gilded Buddha presides over this spectacular bar and restaurant conveniently situated halfway between **Hermès** and the **Crillon**. Chic shoppers, models, and celebrities, including Naomi Campbell and Prince Albert of Monaco, frequent the place. Not surprisingly, the cooking is Asian—spring rolls, tempura, sashimi, Korean braised beef, and Pacific Rim fare—but the music blasted out by the DJs is unlikely to move this crowd very far on the path to Nirvana. There's a balcony bar for people who just want a drink and a gander at the *beau monde* doing its thing in the cavernous main room below. ♦ Restaurant: daily, lunch and dinner. Bar: daily, 6PM-2AM. 8 Rue Boissy d'Anglas (between Pl de la Concorde and Rue du Faubourg St-Honoré). 01.53.05.90.00. Métros: Madeleine, Concorde

64 CITÉ BERRYER

The alley, formerly an open-air market, has been classified as a historic monument. It is now a classy shopping arcade called Le Village Royale and is lined with fashion boutiques, galleries, and a pleasant coffee shop, **Florès** (01.40.17.02.19). ♦ Métro: Madeleine

65 GUCCI

A four-floor marble palazzo is filled with the trademark Gucci red and green. ♦ M-Sa. 21 Rue Royale (between Rue du Faubourg St-Honoré and Cité Berryer). 01.44.94.14.70. Métro: Madeleine

66 LADURÉE

★★★$ This turn-of-the-19th-century *salon de thé* par excellence is posh and ultra-Parisian but not snobbish. The heavenly taste of the croissants is ample reason for having breakfast here. Habitués recommend *financiers* (almond cakes), chocolate macaroons, *babas au rhum*, and *royals* (almond biscuits iced with chocolate or mocha frosting). Don't miss the painting of the rosy-cheeked cherub-turned-pastry-chef on the downstairs ceiling. The Champs-Elysées branch is open until midnight daily, perfect for those predeparture macaroon runs. ♦ Daily, breakfast, lunch, and afternoon tea. 16 Rue Royale (at Rue St-Honoré). 01.42.60.21.79. Métros: Madeleine, Concorde. Also at 75 Ave des Champs Elysées (between Rue Lincoln and Ave George-V). 01.40.75.08.75. Métros: George-V, Franklin-D.-Roosevelt), Printemps, 64 Blvd Haussmann (between Rues de Caumartin and du Havre). 01.42.82.40.10. Métro: Havre-Caumartin

67 RUE ST-HONORÉ

This ranks as one of the oldest and most historic thoroughfares in Paris. In 1622 Molière was born on this street at the corner of Rue Sauval, near Les Halles. On 6 October 1793, a tumbril traveled down Rue St-Honoré carrying a woman whose prison-shorn hair was hidden under a frumpy bonnet. Nearby, Jacques-Louis David sketched her as she passed, bequeathing to history a poignant image of Marie Antoinette, her hands tied behind her back, en route to the guillotine. Rue Royale marks the dividing line between Rue St-Honoré to the east and Rue du Faubourg St-Honoré to the west. ♦ Métros: Concorde, Madeleine, Tuileries, Pyramides, Palais Royal–Musée du Louvre, Louvre–Rivoli, Châtelet

67 AU NAIN BLEU

The Paris equivalent of FAO Schwarz sells toys luxurious enough to spoil any child. ♦ M-Sa. 406-410 Rue St-Honoré (at Rue Richepance) 01.42.60.39.01. Métros: Madeleine, Concorde

68 L'ESTAMINET GAYA

★★$$ Settle on one of the comfortable banquettes in this fine seafood bistro and order the fresh shellfish, tartare of red tuna with ginger, tuna grilled with spicy olive oil, or bouillabaisse. Meat dishes are also available. ♦ M-Sa, lunch and dinner. Reservations recommended. 17 Rue Duphot (between Rues St-Honoré and Richepance). 01.42.60.43.03. Métro: Madeleine. Also at

44 Rue du Bac (between Blvd St-Germain and Rue de l'Université). 01.45.44.73.73. Métro: Rue du Bac

69 GOUMARD

★★★$$$ Scallop carpaccio with oysters, jumbo crab salad, grilled or poached Brittany lobster, sea bass with pan-roasted vegetables, roast St-Pierre (John Dory) with baby vegetables, fig crisp, and *dôme au chocolat* (shiny dome of chocolate mousse) are some of the specialties served at this restaurant. The dining room boasts original 19th-century architectural elements, complemented by beautiful Lalique light fixtures and sculptures. ♦ M-Sa, lunch and dinner. Reservations recommended. 9 Rue Duphot (between Rues St-Honoré and Richepance). 01.42.60.36.07. Métro: Madeleine

70 HÔTEL BURGUNDY

$$$ The last pages of *Look Homeward, Angel* sprang from the fertile imagination of Thomas Wolfe while he was here in 1928. Today it is a clean, comfortable, warmly decorated hotel with 89 guest rooms, a spacious lobby, and an attractive restaurant, **Le Charles Baudelaire**, that serves traditional French fare. ♦ 8 Rue Duphot (between Rue St-Honoré and Blvd de la Madeleine). 01.42.60.34.12; fax 01.47.03.95.20. Métro: Madeleine. reservation@hotel-burgundy.net

71 29 RUE CAMBON

On his return to Paris in November 1875, young *New York Tribune* correspondent Henry James took up residence on the third floor of what is now Chanel headquarters. This is where he wrote *The American*, his first novel set in Paris. ♦ Between Rue St-Honoré and Blvd de la Madeleine. Métros: Concorde, Madeleine

72 DEMEURE CASTILLE

$$$$ The Opera Wing of this elegant hotel features 87 Venetian-style rooms, with marble, colorful damasks, and a faux patina on the walls. The 20 traditionally French guest rooms in the more intimate Rivoli Wing were decorated by designer **Jacques Grange**. Some of the accommodations have views of the Chanel ateliers, where Coco Chanel created her first haute couture designs. The hotel has sumptuous public rooms, an outstanding restaurant, and a delightful courtyard with a trompe l'oeil mural and an impressive 18th-century fountain. ♦ 33-37 Rue Cambon (between Rue St-Honoré and Blvd de la Madeleine). 01.44.58.44.58; fax 01.44.58.44.00. Métro: Madeleine.

castille_hotel@compuserve.com.fr; www.accor.fr

Within Demeure Castille:

IL CORTILE

★★★$$ Young chef Nicolas Vernier, yet another Alain Ducasse protégé, has made a great name for himself and this restaurant with the sunny northern Italian cuisine he offers here. Some of his impeccably prepared specialties include antipasti such as rabbit *porchetta* with rosemary, scallops carpaccio, and traditional Italian *charcuterie* (Parma ham, speck, bresaola, mortadella, Coppa, and pancetta, just to name a few), several varieties of pasta and risotto, swordfish with citrus juice and peppercorn, sage-flavored veal piccata with Swiss chard, and in hunting season, venison fillet with ground peppercorn and olives). For dessert, tiramisù, saffron roasted pear with honey ice cream, and any of a dozen other Italian goodies are temptations that anyone will be glad to have given into. A chic crowd from nearby fashion houses lunches either in the airy, Venetian-inspired dining room, decorated with pale blue, white, and yellow mosaics, or alfresco in the courtyard in fair weather. ♦ M-Sa, lunch and dinner. 01.44.58.45.67

73 KITTY O'SHEA'S

The most Irish of pubs in Paris serves Guinness on tap. Businesspeople headquartered around the **Opéra** congregate here. Traditional Irish stew, fish and chips, beef burgers, salads, and Kitty's cheesecake are the specialties. ♦ M-Th, Su, noon-1:30AM; F, S, noon-2AM. 10 Rue des Capucines (at Rue Volney). 01.40.15.00.30. Métros: Madeleine, Opéra

74 HÔTEL WESTMINSTER

$$$$ Fully renovated in 1997 by talented designer-architect **Pierre-Yves Rochon**, this venerable hotel is one of Paris's loveliest and most comfortable luxury establishments. It is also one of the most prestigious, just as it was when the Duke of Westminster was a regular guest here in the 1840s. The duke

liked it so much, in fact, that he authorized the hotel to use his coat of arms. Henry James and his family stayed here in 1856, when the future novelist was 12. The carriage trade continues to favor the hotel, but so do such film and theater personalities as Monica Vitti, Ute Lemper, and Michelangelo Antonioni.

The hotel's executive floor and business center also make it attractive to business travelers. The 102 guest rooms, which include 20 superb suites, are each personalized with antique furniture, lovely pastel fabrics and wallpapers, and modern marble bathrooms. The lobby exudes the atmosphere of a refined British club, and chief concierge Patrice Delamare's staff is a model of affable efficiency. The hotel boasts a fine restaurant, colorful bar, and a great location midway between **Place Vendôme** and the **Opéra**. ♦ 13 Rue de la Paix (between Rues des Capucines and Daunou). 01.42.61.57.46; fax 01.42.60.30.66. Métro: Opéra. resa.westminster@warwickhotels.com; www.warwickhotels.com

Within the Hôtel Westminster:

LE CÉLADON

★★★$$$ This delightful restaurant makes diners feel right at home, especially if they happen to live in a Regency-era mansion. Each of the three small interconnected dining rooms has warm yellow walls hung with old paintings, crystal chandeliers, and a handful of well-spaced tables. There is much celadon on display, the graceful gray-green Chinese porcelain from which the restaurant takes its name. Young chef Christophe Moisand, formerly of the **Meurice** and the **Martinez** in Cannes, quickly earned a Michelin star here with his refined array of roasted Breton sea scallops with carmelized endives, brazed line-caught bass in lettuce leaves, suckling pig fricassee with braised cabbage and truffle-laced gnocchis, stuffed squab roasted with summer savory, and other imaginative specialties. The selection of wines is outstanding, as is the service. The prix-fixe luncheon is surprisingly affordable. ♦ M-F, lunch and dinner; closed in August. Entrance at 15 Rue Daunou. 01.42.61.77.42

BAR LES CHENETS

Frequented by a neighborhood business clientele, this cozy bar specializes in champagne-based cocktails, which sounds misleadingly innocent. The bar also serves

light lunches and a very British tea in the afternoon, and there is cocktail piano between 6:30 and 9PM. Genial barman Gérard speaks six languages. ♦ Daily, 8:30AM-midnight. 01.42.61.57.46

74 ALFRED DUNHILL

The Paris branch of a famous English company, this mahogany-paneled shop sells all manner of smoking paraphernalia. Dunhill pipes made from the best French brier, with ebony mouthpieces, are among the world's finest (and most costly). And where else will you find a thuja-wood cigar box? ♦ M-Sa. 15 Rue de la Paix (between Rues des Capucines and Daunou). 01.42.61.57.58. Métro: Opéra

75 PARK HYATT VENDÔME

$$$$ In 2002 this was the new hotel Parisians couldn't stop talking about—and with good reason, because it is a knockout in every sense. Although its 188 ultraluxurious guest rooms and suites qualify it as a palace hotel, on par with the Ritz or Crillon, the hotel has a tiny entrance on the Rue de la Paix, and despite its stellar location feels like a hideaway. The most spectacular aspects of the property are the spaciousness and utter sumptuousness of the guest rooms. There are high ceilings, walk-in closets, and separate baths and showers (and guest bathrooms in the suites), with exquisitely ergonomic custom-made plumbing fixtures. Gold is the predominant color of the ravishing interiors, designed by the American **Ed Tuttle**, but the effect is never overbearing or ostentatious. Sculptural door handles, sleek bathroom amenities, and televisions that allow you to watch a staggering variety of channels via satellite are other aces in the place's favor, as is the succulent fare on offer in **Le Park** restaurant (available as room service). You can recover from sensory overload with a massage in the large, spotless spa and fitness center. The only drawback to all this is that one night might cost you what you normally fork over for a month's rent, but alas, such is the price tag for magic of this magnitude. ♦ 5 Rue de la Paix (between Rue des Capucines and Rue Daunou). 01.58.71.12.34; fax 01.58.71.12.35. Métro: Opéra. vendome@paris.hyatt.com

Ermenegildo Zegna

76 ERMENEGILDO ZEGNA

The understated high fashions for men at this sophisticated shop are made with the richest of fabrics and have an appeal that's beyond snobbery. For more than a century the Zegna family has been known for making the world's finest wools, providing the best European designers with their raw materials. ♦ M-Sa. 10 Rue de la Paix (between Rues Danielle-Casanova and Daunou). 01.42.61.67.61. Métro: Opéra

77 DUNHILL'

A few doorsteps and a couple generations away from the original Alfred Dunhill, this boutique caters to a younger but no less posh crowd who appreciate the ready-to-wear, watches and colognes for sale here. If the style still leans toward the classic, it is decidedly more contemporary than what you'll find at the grandfather store—and though the accessories include pricey lighters, there's no tobacco. ♦ M-Sa. 3-5 Rue de la Paix (at Rue des Capucines). 01.42.96.60.73. Métro: Opéra

78 HÔTEL RITZ

$$$$ If any hotel deserves to be called legendary, it is this hostelry opened by César Ritz in 1898. Millionaires, Arab princes, divas, and cinema stars have favored this ritzy establishment whose name has became a synonym for luxurious glamour. F. Scott Fitzgerald wrote a story called "The Diamond as Big as the Ritz," set big scenes in his fiction in the hotel, and downed more drinks than were good for him in the **Ritz Bar**. Marcel Proust used to arrive sporting lavender gloves and a variety of clothes that never seemed to fit him. Coco Chanel liked it so much she took up residence here. There are 440 employees (a third of whom have been here more than a quarter century) catering to the occupants of the hotel's 187 opulent rooms and suites. Sixty of these stalwarts are available for duty as private servants if your vacation just isn't a vacation without Jeeves. The prices are astronomical but, by all accounts, justified. The suites on the second floor overlooking the Place Vendôme are actually registered with the Bureau of Fine Arts. Mohammed al-Fayed bought the hotel in 1979 for $30 million and spent 10 times that amount restoring and expanding it. The hotel's legend took a turn for the tragic in 1997, however, when Princess Diana and Dodi al-Fayed left from here on their fatal flight from the paparazzi. ♦ 15 Pl Vendôme (between Rues St-Honoré and des Capucines). 01.43.16.30.30; fax 01.43.16.36.68. Métros: Opéra, Tuileries, Concorde, Madeleine. resa@ ritzparis.com; www.ritzparis.com

Within the Hôtel Ritz:

RITZ ESPADON

★★★$$$$ The culinary reputation of this lovely restaurant was made from the very start by the presence of that great turn-of-the-century chef Auguste Escoffier, whose motto was "Good cooking is the basis of true happiness." He first met César Ritz when Ritz was manager of the Grand Hotel in Monte Carlo. Escoffier's celebrated recipe for foie gras in port is still used. In 2001 Michel Roth came back to the **Ritz** after a 2-year stint at Lasserre, where he enhanced his reputation as one of France's most brilliant younger chefs. As he had previously spent 17 years at the Ritz as a protegé of longtime chef Guy Legay, this was a real homecoming, and the prodigal son has upheld the restaurant's status as one of Paris's temples of haute cuisine. Among chef Roth's noted specialties are crayfish tails dusted with powered pistachios, served with delicate frothy cream of lobster soup, with a coral cream as a starter; St-Pierre (John Dory) with tomato zabaglione cream flavored with tarragon, with a fricassee of strips of tiny artichokes and squid as a main fish course; and as a main meat course, saddle of pigeon glazed with ginger honey, stuffed and preserved pigeon legs, with soft carrots with slivers of Chinese kumquat. The crystal and silver and china are magnificent, and the army of wait staff and dining-room assistants are almost oppressively attentive. As to be expected, the wine list is nonpareil and the prices are appropriately steep. In summer, dine outside on the delightful garden patio. ♦ Daily, lunch and dinner. Reservations recommended. 01.43.16.30.80

HEMINGWAY BAR

Just off Rue Cambon is this famous little bar, which Ernest Hemingway "liberated" at the end of World War II (he was the first to arrive for a drink after the liberation of Paris). Here the legendary barman Georges served drinks to President Teddy Roosevelt, just back from an African safari. Other big-time tipplers who have imbibed here include Greta Garbo, Noël Coward, Douglas Fairbanks, Winston Churchill, J. P. Morgan, Andrew Carnegie, F. Scott Fitzgerald, and Marlene Dietrich. It's still an English-style pub, right down to its tweedy, rubicund patrons. ♦ Daily, 6:30PM-1AM. 01.43.16.33.65

VENDÔME

Lesser known than the hotel's other watering hole, this bar has a terrace for drinks or tea in the summer. ♦ Daily, 11AM-1AM. 01.43.16.33.63

Restaurants/Clubs: Red | Hotels: Purple | Shops: Orange | Outdoors/Parks: Green | Sights/Culture: Blue

Place Vendôme Shopping

RUE DES CAPUCINES	RUE DANIELLE-CASANOVA
Emporio Armani *mens- and womenswear*	**Charvet** *mens- and womenswear*
	26 Vendôme *lingerie*
	Boucheron *jewelry*
	Van Cleef & Arpels *jewelry/watches*
Alexandre Reza *jewelry*	**Mauboissin** *jewelry*
Fred *jewelry*	**Chanel** *jewelry*
Pierre Dubail *jewelry*	**Piaget** *watches*
Hôtel Ritz	**Swatch** *watches*
Cartier *jewelry*	**Chaumet** *jewelry*
Hôtel Vendôme	**Bvlgari** *jewelry*
Chopard *jewelry*	**Patek Philippe** *watches*
	Mikimoto *jewelry*
	Dior *jewelry*
	Repossi *jewelry*
	Giorgio Armani *mens- and womenswear*
	Gianmaria Buccellati *fine silver/jewelry*
	Galerie Alexander Butman
	Brioni *menswear*
	Damianil *jewelry*
	Guerlain *perfume/accessories*

PLACE VENDOME

RUE ST-HONORE	
Godiva *chocolates*	**Annick Goutal** *oils/perfume*
Gualtiero Marchesi *bar/restaurant*	**Rudophe Menudier** *shoes/accessories*
Michaela Frey *jewelry*	**Agry** *engraving*
Galerie d'Art Castiglione	**Carré des Feuillants** *restaurant*
Weedly *childrenswear/T-shirts*	**Ciro** *jewelry*
Jolly Hotel Lotti	**Jar** *perfume*
Anémone *costume jewelry*	**Ida Faerber** *jewelry*
Namani *menswear*	**Vanessa Bruno** *womenswear*
Meyrowitz *optician*	**Regent Street & B** *mens- and womenswear*
	Payot *beauty products/salon*

RUE DE CASTIGLIONE

RUE DU MONT-THABOR	
Hotel Inter-Continental	**Les Arcades** *books*
H. Stern *jewelry*	**Parfumerie Catherine** *perfume*
Casty *purses/jewelry*	**Swann Pharmacy**
	Jacqueline Perès *womenswear*
Cristal Vendôme *crystal*	**Blue Comme Bleu** *mens- and womenswear*

RUE DE RIVOLI

RITZ HEALTH CLUB

Where else can you work out alongside the likes of Tom Cruise, Madonna, Woody Allen, and any number of top models, politicians, and members of the crème de la crème of Parisian society? Staying at the **Ritz** makes you an official member, and there are flexible membership programs for others as well. Facilities include a fully equipped gymnasium, squash courts, saunas, Jacuzzis, Turkish baths, spa treatments, and the largest private pool in Paris. ♦ Daily. 01.43.16.30.60; fax 01.43.16.37.06. spa@ritzparis.com

78 11-13 PLACE VENDÔME

This is the Ministry of Justice, where, in 1848, the official measure for the meter was set in the façade. ♦ West side. Métros: Opéra, Tuileries, Concorde, Madeleine

79 CHARVET

Edward VII bought his neckties and cravats here. ♦ M-Sa; closed Monday in August. 28 Pl Vendôme (at Rue Danielle-Casanova). 01.42.60.30.70. Métros: Opéra, Madeleine

80 CHRISTOFLE

Want to make your little one's first lost baby tooth even more precious? How about encasing it in silver? Nothing is impossible for this shop, which has provided silver-plating services for more than a century. There's also a fine selection of silverware and antique gold, as well as the stunning yellow-and-blue tableware Claude Monet designed for his house at Giverny. Peek into the museum at the same address. ♦ M-Sa. 9 Rue Royale (between Pl de la Concorde and Rue du Faubourg St-Honoré). 01.55.27.99.00. Métro: Concorde

81 LACHAUME

The city's oldest and most exquisite florist has catered to haute couturiers and other well-heeled clientele (who can afford long-stemmed red roses in December) since 1845. For an instantaneous cure of the midwinter blues, gaze into the shop window at the gorgeous bunches of tulips and orchids. ♦ M-Sa; closed in August. 10 Rue Royale (between Pl de la Concorde and Rue St-Honoré). 01.42.60.59.74, 01.42.60.57.26. Métro: Concorde

82 TORAYA

★★$$ In Japanese, *toraya* means "tiger"; for Parisians, it denotes this elegant black-and-gray Japanese tea salon and pastry shop. Savor *abekawa mochi* (chunks of rice paste sugared and dusted with grilled soy powder), *kuzukiri* (noodles made from jellied arrowroot), and energizing pots of *sencha* (green tea). ♦ M-Sa, lunch and afternoon tea. 10 Rue St-Florentin (between Rues de Rivoli and St-Honoré). 01.42.60.13.00. Métro: Concorde

83 NOTRE-DAME-DE-L'ASSOMPTION

This church, built in 1676, was originally part of a convent where destitute widows and abandoned wives were given shelter; it has served as a Polish parish since 1850. The massive cupola on top has been dubbed *le sot dôme* ("the silly dome"). ♦ 263 *bis* Rue St-Honoré (at Pl Maurice-Barrès). 01.42.60.07.69. Métro: Concorde

84 CADOLLE HERMINE

Cadolle, the woman who is credited with inventing the brassiere in 1900, was the great-great-grandmother of the shop's current proprietor, Poupie Cadolle. All manner of deluxe lingerie, French beachwear, and perfume is sold here. The company also makes items to order. ♦ M-Sa. 14 Rue Cambon (between Rues du Mont-Thabor and St-Honoré). 01.42.60.94.22. Métro: Concorde

85 CARTIER

Since 1847 this jewelry store has offered the best and the brightest in French bijoux, with commensurately dazzling price tags. The 13% tourist discount on gold, however, almost brings the pretty baubles within reach. ♦ M-Sa. 7 Pl Vendôme (between Rues St-Honoré and des Capucines). 01.44.55.32.50. Métros: Tuileries, Opéra

86 3-5 PLACE VENDÔME

This was formerly the **Hôtel Bristol**. Between 1890 and 1910, whenever financier and art collector John Pierpont Morgan came to Paris, he would stay in the same corner suite in the old hotel, which was run by one of his father's butlers. The sultan of Brunei now owns it. ♦ Between Rues St-Honoré and des Capucines. Métros: Tuileries, Opéra

87 PLACE VENDÔME

Like the Place de la Concorde, Place des Victoires, and other magnificent squares, this was conceived as a setting for a royal equestrian statue. The subject was Louis XIV, and the sculptor was François Girardon. In 1685, to make way for his monument, Louis bought and demolished the Duke of Vendôme's town house and the nearby Capucines convent. **Jules Hardouin-Mansart** designed gracefully formal mauve limestone façades with Corinthian pilasters and sculpted masks that were added to the square's periphery in 1715. The Sun King, a budding real-estate shark, encouraged speculators to buy the lots behind the façades, then hire their own architects to fill in the blanks. During the revolution the heads of nine victims of the guillotine were displayed here on spikes, and for a while the Place Vendôme was known as the Place des Piques (Pike Square). On 19 June 1792 the revolutionaries lit a huge bonfire here that incinerated bundles of genealogical documents concerning the French nobility's title deeds. Needless to say, the king's gilt statue didn't survive the mob's wrath, either; it was felled in August of the same year. Today the 440-by-420-foot octagon is characterized by an aloof opulence. It is the home of the **Hôtel Ritz** and it boasts the world's greatest concentration of banks, perfumeries, and jewelers, including **Boucheron**, **Van Cleef & Arpels**, **Cartier**, **Chaumet**, **Schiaparelli**, and **Guerlain**. ♦ Between Rue St-Honoré and Rues Danielle-Casanova and des Capucines. Métros: Madeleine, Opéra, Tuileries, Concorde

On Place Vendôme:

VENDÔME COLUMN I

In place of the toppled statue of Louis XIV, Napoléon raised a 144-foot-high monument modeled on Trajan's Column in Rome. Made to commemorate Napoléon's military victories in Germany, the stone colonnade is faced with 378 spiraling sheets of bronze supplied by 1,200 cannons captured from the Austrian and Russian armies defeated at the Battle of Austerlitz in 1805. The column was originally topped with a statue of Napoléon dressed as Julius Caesar, but that was replaced by one of Henri IV in 1814. After Napoléon's defeat at Waterloo, the Bourbons commandeered the monument and mounted their symbol, the fleur-de-lis, at the top. Along came Louis-Philippe, and the fleur-de-lis was replaced with a small statue of Napoléon. But on the afternoon of 1 May 1871, the column was toppled, crashing down along Rue de la Paix and breaking into 30 pieces. Painter Gustave Courbet was blamed for masterminding this act of destruction, and when the Third Republic took power, it ordered Courbet to restore the monument at his own expense. The column was thrust up again (this time topped with a replica of the original statue), and Courbet was plunged into bankruptcy.

88 16 PLACE VENDÔME

Here Franz Anton Mesmer (1734–1815), the Austrian charlatan physician who invented mesmerism (later called hypnosis), conducted "animal magnetism" seminars wrapped in robes decorated with astrological signs. Later, in the 1930s, Obelisk Press had its office at this address. Headed by Englishman Jack Kahane, Obelisk published works that no one else would, such as Henry Miller's *Tropic of Cancer*, which appeared in 1934. It's still an office building. ♦ Between Rues St-Honoré and Danielle-Casanova. Métros: Madeleine, Opéra, Tuileries, Concorde

89 12 PLACE VENDÔME

In 1849 Frédéric Chopin, Polish composer and pianist, died here at the age of 39. It's

---

Restaurants/Clubs: Red | **Hotels: Purple** | Shops: Orange | **Outdoors/Parks: Green** | Sights/Culture: Blue

now an office building. ♦ Between Rues St-Honoré and Danielle-Casanova. Métros: Opéra, Tuileries, Concorde, Madeleine

GIORGIO ARMANI

90 GIORGIO ARMANI

This ultramodern designer boutique is set in the former Hôtel du Rhin, which became the temporary residence of Napoléon III during his 1848 presidential campaign. ♦ M-Sa. 6 Pl Vendôme (between Rues St-Honoré and Danielle-Casanova). 01.42.61.55.09. Métros: Tuileries, Concorde

91 LE SOUFFLÉ

*$$ This sedate restaurant doesn't have much in the way of atmosphere—fault the unflattering lighting—but if you've a hankering for soufflés, it is definitely your place. The puffed-up wonders are the highlights of the menu, and include both main course (with meat and vegetarian options) and dessert varieties. The raspberry-and-chocolate soufflés are standouts here. M-Sa, lunch and dinner. 36 Rue du Mont-Thabor (between Rues de Castiglione and Cambon). 01.42.60.27.19. Métro: Concorde

hôtel costes

92 HÔTEL COSTES

$$$$ In 1996 enterprising Jean-Louis Costes took over the faded old **Hôtel France et Choiseul**, transformed it into Paris's most glamorous small hotel, and made its restaurant the most sought-after canteen for fashion masters and victims. Star designer **Jacques Garcia** deserves the credit for the opulent Second Empire décor that magically combines grandeur and coziness, both in the public areas and the luxurious guest rooms. All 82 rooms are individually decorated with remarkable combinations of fabrics, fully furnished in antiques, and equipped with the most up-to-date modern conveniences, including satellite TV, a CD player, fax machine, and minibar. ♦ 239 Rue St-Honoré (between Rues de Castiglione and Cambon). 01.42.44.50.00; fax 01.42.44.50.01. Métros: Concorde, Tuileries. www.hotelcostes.com

Within hôtel costes:

COSTES

★★$$$ This ultra "in" spot for the haute couture crowd boasts more pretty faces and show-biz names than any other restaurant in Paris. The menu is Mediterranean/international: penne with tomato and basil, tomato-and-goat-cheese tart, melon with Parma ham, shrimp tempura, chicken with balsamic-dressed arugula, grilled fish or meat, or a simple club sandwich or omelette. The food is far less important than the scenery, but it's perfectly fine all the same. Eat under the white parasols in the Italianate courtyard when the weather is fine or in the plush Second Empire dining room when it's not. ♦ Daily, 7AM-2AM. 01.42.44.50.25

92 GODIVA

The world-renowned chocolatier takes its name from the 11th-century English noblewoman who sacrificed her modesty and rode naked through the streets of Coventry to plead with her husband, the earl, to reduce taxes on the townsfolk. If these exquisite bonbons had been available then, they might have made a better bribe. ♦ M-Sa. 237 Rue St-Honoré (at Rue de Castiglione). 01.42.60.44.64. Métros: Concorde, Tuileries

Alain Dutournier

93 CARRÉ DES FEUILLANTS

★★★$$$$ Alain Dutournier runs the show at this sedately elegant restaurant near Place Vendôme. His specialty is inventive southwestern French cuisine that includes starters of Jerusalem artichokes with foie gras and black truffles or marinated salmon with caviar, main courses of wood pigeon with cèpes or roasted leg of suckling lamb from the Pyrénées, and for dessert, pistachio ice cream with wild strawberries. ♦ M-F, lunch and dinner; Sa, dinner; closed in August. Reservations required. 14 Rue de Castiglione (at Rue St-Honoré). 01.42.86.82.82. Métros: Concorde, Tuileries

94 JOLLY HÔTEL LOTTI

$$$$ This 130-room luxury hotel is favored by British and Italian blue-bloods who are drawn to the large, tastefully decorated rooms, period furniture, and impeccable service. There's a restaurant on the premises. George

Orwell wrote about his experience as a *plongeur* (dishwasher) here in the 1920s in *Down and Out in Paris and London*. ♦ 7 Rue de Castiglione (between Rues du Mont-Thabor and St-Honoré). 01.42.60.37.34; fax 01.40.15.93.56. Métros: Concorde, Tuileries. hotel.lotti@wanadoo.fr

95 ROYAL SAINT-HONORÉ

$$$$ Just one block from the Tuileries Gardens, this hotel has an elegant lobby, 72 quiet rooms with marble bathrooms, and a refined air. There's a handsome bar and breakfast room with original Louis XVI woodwork that serves light snacks, but no restaurant. ♦ 221 Rue St-Honoré (at Rue d'Alger). 01.42.60.32.79; fax 01.42.60.47.44. Métro: Tuileries. rsh@hroy.com; www.hotel-royal-st-honore.com/rsh

96 4 RUE DU MONT-THABOR

In the summer of 1820, still enjoying the afterglow of the triumphant reception of "Rip Van Winkle" and "The Legend of Sleepy Hollow," 39-year-old Washington Irving moved into an apartment here. Mitigating his pleasure was Irving's powerful fear of growing old, the same problem that obsessed ol' Rip. The building is now the Hôtel Mont-Thabor. ♦ Between Rues d'Alger and de Castiglione. Métro: Tuileries

colette
styledesignartfood

97 COLETTE

The cooler-than-thou conceit of this high-profile fashion and design shop is that merchandise is displayed openly, whether on long tables or otherwise, thereby highlighting the uniqueness of each product, but unfortunately the concept consciousness comes off as 1980s-style label flashing to the *nth* degree. At fault is the sterile presentation, aggressively eclectic selection, and relentless overpricing. Many of the goods here, from the terribly trendy wristwatches, sports shoes, and shiny metal gadgets on the first floor to supposedly hip but often just plain strange clothes on the second, are remarkable only for their unattractiveness. This store has had an undeniable influence on French retailing since its opening in 1997, but not necessarily for the best. Pop in if you're curious, but an atmosphere as steeped in condescension as this may leave you screaming for Sears—or **Galeries Lafayette**. ♦ M-Sa, 10:30AM-7:30PM. 213 Rue St-Honoré (at Rue 29 Juillet). 01.55.35.33.90. Métro: Tuileries

Within Colette:

WATER-BAR COLETTE

★$$ Branding reaches orgiastic proportions i this subterranean den of refreshment, where, if so inclined, you can choose from a hundre or so varieties of still and sparkling mineral water from springs and glaciers all over the world. There's also fruit juice by Alain Milliat, tea by Mariage Frères, and sweets by Pierre Hermé. The only items on the menu to escap branding (though not overpricing) are a few light and surprisingly uninspired dishes such as gaspacho and a chicken sandwich. ♦ M-Sa, 10:30AM-7:30PM; food served 11:30AM-7PM. 01.55.35.33.93

97 MANDARINA DUCK

You may have seen a piece of Mandarina Duck luggage rolling off the carousel at the airport—it's the bag that doesn't look like everything else. This Italian company's highly creative use of synthetic materials and fabrics and dramatically different styles have earned it a loyal following among international travelers and spawned numerous impersonators. This bi-level flagship store includes all the latest luggage lines, including the "Frog" line (with strong molded plastic and featuring expandable side pockets, it's almost guaranteed not to croak), as well as a range of women's and men's clothing that, despite changing from season to season, is consistently innovative. There are two smaller stores in Paris, but you'll find the largest selection here at the flagship. Venture inside only for a look at the terrific designs. ♦ M-Sa. 219 Rue St-Honoré (at Rue du 29 Juillet). 01.42.60.76.20. Métro: Tuileries. Also at 7 Blvd de la Madeleine (between Rues Duphot and Cambon). 01.42.86.08.00. Métro: Madeleine. Also at 51 Rue Bonaparte (at Rue du Four). 01.43.26.68.38. Métro: St-Germain-des-Prés

98 HÔTEL DROUOT

The closest thing to a Sotheby's in Paris, this establishment specializes in estate sales and auctions of everything from Cartier jewels, Louis XIV furniture, and African sculpture to baskets of kitchenware and collections of rar illustrated manuscripts. On the top floor, the most valuable objets d'art are overseen by renowned auctioneers Ader Picard. Auctions take place in the afternoon starting at 2PM, but arrive early to scan the merchandise—a great experience in itself. ♦ M-Sa; occasionally on Su; closed in August. 9 Rue Drouot (a Rue Rossini). 01.48.00.20.20. Métro: Richelieu-Drouot. www.gazette-drouot.com

99 CHOPIN

$$ Amid shops selling old books, toys, and clothes in the glass-covered Passage Jouffroy

(which is classified as a historic monument), this charming hotel with salmon-colored wallpaper and green carpets offers 36 small rooms at correspondingly small rates. Some rooms have skylights. There's no restaurant. ♦ 46 Passage Jouffroy (between Blvd Montmartre and Rue de la Grange-Batelière). 01.47.70.58.10; fax 01.42.47.00.70. Métro: Rue Montmartre

00 CHARTIER

★$ This cavernous turn-of-the-19th-century soup kitchen with pinwheel fans and surly waiters offers better theater than cuisine, but it's worth a visit nevertheless. Basic, inexpensive French food—egg salad, pâté, roast chicken—is served with rough red wine. The place is always mobbed with tourists, so get here early. ♦ Daily, lunch and dinner until 9:30PM. 7 Rue du Faubourg-Montmartre (between Blvd Montmartre and Rue de la Grange-Batelière). 01.47.70.86.29. Métro: Grands Boulevards

01 MUSÉE GREVIN

The city's largest wax museum is populated with distinguished paraffin personalities, including Charles de Gaulle, Catherine Deneuve, Woody Allen, Yehudi Menuhin, Bill Clinton, Tony Blair, and Leonardo di Caprio. Children love it. ♦ Admission. Daily, 1-7PM. 10 Blvd Montmartre (between Rue du Faubourg-Montmartre and Passage Jouffroy). 01.47.70.85.05. Métro: Grands Boulevards. www.musee-grevin.com

02 8 BOULEVARD DES CAPUCINES

It was at this address in 1880, the year of his death, that 61-year-old Jacques Offenbach composed his masterpiece, *The Tales of Hoffmann*. It's now an office building. ♦ Between Rue de la Chaussée-d'Antin and Pl de l'Opéra. Métro: Opéra

03 LE GRAND CAFÉ

★★$$ This is one of the rare Parisian bistros to stay open 24 hours a day, and it has a lavish Belle Epoque décor to boot. It serves fresh shellfish platters and grilled, poached, or sautéed fish and grilled meat. Opened in 1895, this haunt of Oscar Wilde is now a lively hangout for journalists, the after-show crowd (in addition to the **Opéra Garnier**, there are several big theaters within a few blocks), graveyard-shift laborers, and anyone else out walking the streets in the wee hours. ♦ Daily, 24 hours. 4 Blvd des Capucines (between Rue de la Chaussée-d'Antin and Pl de l'Opéra). 01.43.12.19.00. Métro: Opéra

104 5 RUE DES ITALIENS

The prestigious Parisian daily newspaper *Le Monde* is headquartered here. ♦ Between Blvd des Italiens and Rue Taitbout. Métros: Quatre-Septembre, Richelieu–Drouot

105 NOURA

★★★$$ In this multilevel Lebanese restaurant complex you can enjoy all the pleasures of an ancient cuisine in a confidently 21st-century setting. Whether in the ground-level take-out section or upstairs restaurant, the food scores high marks for authenticity, from grilled meat dishes to a range of savory appetizers like *fattouche* (Lebanese vegetable salad) and *moujaddara* (creamed lentils and rice with fried-onion topping). The menu is large, and with its many vegetarian options and hot and cold starters is ideal for either a full meal or grazing. Décor throughout is high-tech chic, with subtly changing multicolored lighting, plush purple seating, and cutlery that takes sleek to new heights. ♦ Daily, lunch and dinner. 29 Blvd des Italiens (at Rue de la Michodière). 01.53.43.00.53. Métro: Opéra

106 LA TOUR DE JADE

★★$ This Vietnamese and Chinese eatery was founded by a former minister to Indochina's Emperor Bao-Dai. Sautéed mussels and curry, sautéed lamb with ginger, whole pomfret fish with hot sauce, duck with lotus seeds, and grilled prawns Vietnam style are the menu highlights. The dining room has the typical Chinese-restaurant décor—dim lighting, simple furniture, and kitschy decorative items. ♦ M-Sa, lunch and dinner; Su, dinner. 20 Rue de la Michodière (between Rue de Hanovre and Blvd des Italiens). 01.47.42.07.56. Métro: Quatre-Septembre

[Opéra **Comique**]

107 OPÉRA COMIQUE (SALLE FAVART)

The third opera house to be built on this site since 1783 (the previous two having burned down), this Italian-style horseshoe-shaped theater with four gilded balconies and 1,300 crimson seats, a true Belle Epoque gem, opened in 1898. Among operas that have premiered in the **Opéra Comique**'s various houses are Bizet's *Carmen*, Massenet's *Manon* (there are statues of those two heroines in the ornate marble lobby), Offenbach's *Tales of Hoffman*, and Debussy's *Pelléas and Mélisande*. Jérôme Savary, one of Paris's most dynamic theater directors, who took the reins in 2000, has launched a program designed to give new life to the popular repertoire of the 19th and 20th centuries, ranging from the *Revue Nègre* (the show in which Josephine Baker took Paris by storm in 1925) to Rossini, Offenbach, the French cancan, Brecht and Weill, Mistinguett, and Maurice Chevalier. The theater is popularly known as the **Salle Favart**, after Charles Simon Favart, the leading *opéra comique* impresario of the 18th century, for whom the street running along the east side of the theater is also named. ◆ Admission. Box office: M-Sa. Museum: M-Sa. 5 Rue Favart, public entrance on Pl-Boïeldieu (between Rues de Marivaux and Favart). Information: 01.42.44.45.40; reservations: 08.25.00.00.58. Métros: Richelieu–Drouot, Quatre-Septembre. www.opera-comique.com

108 CAFÉ RUNTZ

★★$$ Right across Rue Favart from the Opéra Comique, this delightful Alsacian *winstub* restored to its Belle Epoque charm by **Jacques Garcia** is the perfect spot for dinner after a show. The ambiance is warm and welcoming, and hosts Odette and Hubert Leport offer some of the most authentic Alsatian cuisine you will find this side of Strasbourg: outstanding *presskopf* (pork headcheese), *choucroute* (sauerkraut with boiled pork, bacon, and sausages), *baeckeoffe* (a stew of beef, lamb, pork, potatoes, onions, and wine), and an astute selection of Alsatian wines. ◆ M-F, lunch; Sa, dinner Oct-June; closed the month of August. Reservations recommended. 16 Rue Favart (at Rue d'Amboise). 01.42.96.69.86. Métros: Richelieu–Drouot, Quatre-Septembre

109 AUX LYONNAIS

★★$$ Alain Ducasse took the helm of this 1890 Lyonnais bistro, long patronized by **Bourse des Valeurs** traders, in 2002. Despite the shift to star management the bistro's reputation is still founded on classic Lyonnais cuisine such as roast quail, parsleyed calf's liver, and *quenelle* (poached pike dumplings). Vegetarians might have a tough time with the menu. ◆ Tu-F, lunch and dinner; Sa, dinner. Reservations recommended. 32 Rue St-Marc (between Rues de Richelieu and Favart). 01.42.96.65.04. Métro: Richelieu-Drouot

110 49 RUE VIVIENNE

On this site stood the Salle Musard, a concert hall where Tom Thumb, headliner for P.T. Barnum's show, performed in 1844. An office building stands here now. ◆ Between Rue St-Marc and Blvd Montmartre. Métros: Bourse, Richelieu–Drouot, Grands Boulevards

111 PASSAGE DES PANORAMAS

Nineteenth-century US inventor Robert Fulton painted and displayed 18 panoramas, including a portrayal of the burning of Moscow in 2 large cylindrical towers off Boulevard Montmartre. The French flocked to see the sagas, and, with his profits, Fulton bankrolled his steamboat and submarine schemes. ◆ Between Rue St-Marc and Blvd Montmartre. Métros: Bourse, Grands Boulevards

112 CLEMENTINE

★★$$ In this homey bistro named after the owner's daughter, chef Franck Langrenne prepares savory, unpretentious fare, with a handwritten menu that changes daily. Starters of homemade foie gras or salmon salad with sherry and main dishes of rabbit in lemon mustard sauce, fillet of *sandre* (a perchlike freshwater fish) with anise, and roast chicken with chèvre are some of the possible choices. As for dessert, the luscious dark chocolate fondant is always available. The service is unusually relaxed and friendly. ◆ M-F, lunch and dinner. Reservations recommended. 5 Rue St-Marc (between Rues Notre-Dame-des-Victoires and Vivienne). 01.40.41.05.65. Métros: Bourse, Grands Boulevards

113 VAUDEVILLE

★★$$ This vintage 1925 brasserie was rescued from decline and obscurity by brasserie king Jean-Paul Bucher and is now packed at lunchtime by execs from the **Bourse des Valeurs**, and at night by theater patrons. Specialties include homemade *saumon rillette* (salmon spread), foie gras, *andouillette* (tripes), grilled lobster, shellfish (year-round), and a chilled house Riesling. Dining on the sidewalk is pleasant in summer. ◆ Daily, lunch and dinner until 1AM. Reservations recommended. 29 Rue Vivienne (between Rues du Quatre-Septembre and de la Bourse). 01.40.20.04.62. Métro: Bourse

114 BOURSE DES VALEURS (STOCK EXCHANGE)

Napoléon commissioned this "Temple of Money" in 1808, and architect **Alexandre Théodore Brongniart** was inspired to adorn it with 64 massive Corinthian columns. The building's design is epic, befitting the frenzied battles that once took place on its trading floor. But in 1987, the *corbeille* (basket), as the trading area is called, was closed, and all stock trades are now done though a decentralized computer network. Nevertheless, visitors are welcome to tour the building and see the old trading floor. There are guided tours in French and English, an audiovisual program that shows how a stock market works, and a small museum of stock market memorabilia. ♦ Free. M-F, 1:15-5PM. Rue Notre-Dame-des-Victoires and Place de la Bourse. 01.40.41.62.20. Métro: Bourse

15 HOLLYWOOD SAVOY

★★$$ This stockbrokers' luncheon canteen becomes a nightclub when the **Bourse des Valeurs** goes to sleep. Waiters and waitresses join the band and the featured singer belts out creditable renditions of "Stormy Weather" and other Yankee classics. As for the cuisine, stick with the simplest items on the menu, such as the grilled fish and meat. This is no temple of the culinary arts. ♦ M-F, lunch and dinner until 1AM; Sa, dinner only. Reservations recommended. 44 Rue Notre-Dame-des-Victoires (between Rues Réaumur and Montmartre). 01.42.36.16.73. Métro: Bourse

16 6 RUE DAUNOU

Dr. Oliver Wendell Holmes (father of the famous jurist) knew this as the Hôtel d'Orient and stayed here when he made a brief trip to Paris in 1886 to meet Louis Pasteur, who had just developed the vaccine for rabies. It's now the nondescript **Hôtel Daunou**. ♦ Between Rues Louis-le-Grand and de la Paix. Métro: Opéra

17 HARRY'S NEW YORK BAR

Opened in 1911, "Sank-Roo-Doe-Noo" (the US pronunciation of the bar's address) really came into its own 2 years later, when it was purchased by a bartender named Harry MacElhone, who went on to invent the Bloody Mary. The barroom has the feel of a college fraternity hall. There are even university pennants on the wood-paneled walls. Here Princeton man F. Scott Fitzgerald stared blearily at successive scotches and watched his stories take form; George Gershwin dreamed up his great fantasy *An American in Paris*; Ernest Hemingway dodged swinging fists; Gloria Swanson glowed; Noël Coward quipped; and Jean-Paul Sartre, despite

himself, discovered both bourbon and hot dogs. In the days before each US presidential election, patrons of the bar cast mock ballots for the candidates, and results are announced on the night of the election (Paris time, before the polls on the US East Coast close). The legendary poll has an uncanny track record for predicting the winner. In the 2000 election, Bush barely nosed out Gore. There is a piano bar downstairs with music between 10PM and 2AM. ♦ Daily, 10:45AM-4AM. 5 Rue Daunou (between Rues Louis-le-Grand and de la Paix). 01.42.61.71.14. Métro: Opéra

118 RESTAURANT DROUANT

★★★$$$$ At the end of each November since 1914, 10 novelists have met here to award the Prix Goncourt, France's prestigious prize for the year's best fiction. (The prize isn't much money, but fame and fortune in the form of lucrative publishing contracts follow.) The wood-paneled **Salon Goncourt** with its round table for 10 and the magnificent staircase designed by **Emile Ruhlmann**, "the pope of Art Deco," in 1930 are the highlights of this century-old restaurant's décor. The specialties are roasted turbot, Bresse chicken in sea urchin cream, and a praline mousse and black chocolate napoleon. The dining room is popular with the elegant crowd from the **Opéra**. If you forget to make reservations, consider having a meal in the café. ♦ M-F, lunch and dinner. Reservations required. 18 Rue Gaillon (at Pl Gaillon). 01.42.65.15.16. Métro: Quatre-Septembre

119 BRENTANO'S

For the greatest hits in British and American literature, try this, one of the best and oldest English-language bookstores in Paris. ♦ M-Sa. 37 Ave de l'Opéra (between Rues Danielle-Casanova and d'Antin). 01.42.61.52.50. Métros: Opéra, Pyramides

120 ISSÉ

★★★$$$ One of the city's best (and most expensive) sushi bars also serves impeccable sashimi, grilled salmon, steaming miso soup, red caviar, delectably light tempura, and *chirashi* (raw fish on a bed of rice and served in a large bowl), the house specialty. ♦ M, Sa, dinner; Tu-F, lunch and dinner. Reservations recommended. 56 Rue Ste-Anne (at Rue Rameau). 01.42.96.67.76. Métros: Pyramides, Bourse, Quatre-Septembre

121 BRÛLERIE SAN JOSÉ

The Cahen family, owners of this tiny stand-up coffee bar, roast their own beans, and serve

---

the best cappuccino in town. At midday, neighborhood workers seeking a caffeine fix swarm here. ♦ M-F, 7AM-7PM; Sa, 9:30-6PM. 30 Rue des Petits-Champs (between Rues Chabanais and Ste-Anne). 01.42.96.69.09. Métro: Pyramides

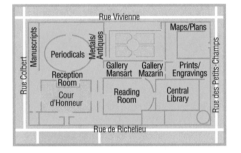

122 BIBLIOTHÈQUE NATIONALE DE FRANCE, SITE RICHELIEU (NATIONAL LIBRARY OF FRANCE, RICHELIEU)

In 1537 a copyright act was passed to ensure that a copy of every book published in France would be housed in a royal library. Although most of this amalgamation of 4.5 centuries of book and document assembly has been moved to another site of the library, this building continues to house manuscripts, engravings, photographic material, maps and plans, coins and medals, and performing arts and music materials in a building whose architectural design is as impressive as its collection.

The library came to occupy its present site in the 17th century, when Cardinal Mazarin merged two of his mansions, the **Hôtel Tubeuf** and the **Hôtel Chivry**. The collection initially included 500 pictures and art objects owned by the cardinal himself. When Colbert, finance minister to Louis XIV, moved the library to his own mansion on Rue Vivienne in 1666, the collection numbered 200,000 volumes. In 1720, the library was combined again with the original Mazarin collection.

The library received its most dramatic space in 1854, when architect **Henri Labrouste** was commissioned to design a reading room within the old courtyard of the **Palais Mazarin**. The result is the magnificent top-lit **Salle des Imprimés**, which consists of nine square vaulted bays supported by 16 cast-iron columns and a network of perforated semicircular iron arches. The room reveals a further development of ideas Labrouste first explored in the design of his **Bibliothèque Ste-Geneviève**, a landmark building that was the first monumental public edifice to freely employ iron as both a structural and a deco-

rative element. The reading room (admittance is for members and/or scholars only, althoug proof that you're an architect often works) features beautifully attenuated columns, gleaming lenslike skylights in the ceiling, and graceful curves of iron latticework. In the **Salon d'Honneur** (State Room) on the groun floor is an Houdon statue of Voltaire; the writer's heart is ensconced in the pedestal.

The library's vast book collection was transferred to the **Bibliothèque Nationale de France, Site François Mitterrand/Tolbiac** (see page 292), when it opened in 1998. What remains here is reserved for researcher and scholars; nothing is open to the public except for the third Saturday and Sunday of September every year (National Heritage Days), although tours are given to the public 1 day a month. Groups may arrange for private tours by calling ahead.

There are several public galleries and exhibition spaces in the library. The **Musée des Médailles et Antiques** features a collection vases, precious stones, jewelry, furniture, and other antique objets d'art. The **Galeries Mazarin** and **Mansart** and the **Photo Galeri Colbert** mount temporary exhibitions. ♦ Free Tour: first Tu of the month, 2:30PM. Galeries Mazarin and Mansart: open for special exhib tions only. Musée des Médailles et Antiques: M-Sa, 1-5PM; Su, noon-6PM. Galerie Colber M-Sa, noon-6:30PM. 58 Rue de Richelieu (between Rues des Petits-Champs and Colbert). 01.47.03.81.26. Métros: Bourse, Pyramides. www.bnf.fr

123 GALERIE COLBERT

Like the adjoining **Galerie Vivienne** (see below), this arcade, opened in 1826, has enjoyed a stylish renaissance. The **Bibliothèque Nationale de France**, which owns the passage, spent millions to restore the walkways, glass-roofed rotunda, faux-marble pillars, and 19th-century bronze fixtures. The gallery has two public exhibition halls featuring prints and photos, and a sma theater that hosts lunch and evening concert and there's a beautifully restored Belle Epoque brasserie, **Le Grand Colbert** (01.42.86.87.88). ♦ Free. Daily. Métros: Bourse, Pyramides

Within the Galerie Colbert:

LE GRAND COLBERT

★★★$$ One step inside the entrance of this quintessentially Parisian brasserie and the oversized potted palms, high ceilings, and theater posters tell you this is the real thing: you half expect to bump elbows with Marcel Proust on one of the banquettes. It is indeed heavily favored by Parisians, including those involved in productions in the many theaters around the nearby Palais Royale. Clustered globe lights placed strategically high cast a warm glow over a dining room that is generally bustling but rarely chaotic. Start with a lentil salad—tangy and delicious—French onion soup, or a selection of fresh oysters before moving on to the likes of chateaubriand in Béarnaise sauce, salmon with sorrel, or sole meunière. For desserts, stick to the classics, such as the house-made chocolate mousse or profiteroles. There is a good selection of reasonably priced French wines by the glass and half-bottle. Friendly service and an ample nonsmoking section come as added bonuses here. Daily, noon–1AM. Reservations recommended. Nos. 2-4 Rue Vivienne. 01.42.86.87.88

24 GALERIE VIVIENNE

From its mosaic floors to the arching glass canopy, this gussied-up gallery, established in 1823, is a most fashionable arcade. Boutiques here sell everything from high-tech jewelry and rare books to children's masks and the best brownies in Paris. ♦ Daily. Métros: Bourse, Pyramides

Within Galerie Vivienne:

SI TU VEUX

Babar, the universally loved French elephant, comes in plush, plastic, and posters at this old-fashioned toy store. There are also enough paper hats and masks to outfit any party of 6-year-olds. ♦ M-Sa. 68 Galerie Vivienne. 01.42.60.59.97. Also at 10 Rue Vavin (between Rues d'Assas and Notre-Dame-des-Champs). 01.55.42.14.14. Métro: Notre-Dame-des-Champs

JEAN-PAUL GAULTIER

Few fashion designers have the magic touch like Jean-Paul Gaultier, and happily this bi-level boutique has not escaped it. Redesigned in 2002 by **Philippe Starck**, the store is a sumptuous study in white (it previously had a darker, more industrial look) that features an abundance of oversize mirrors with gorgeous faux-gemstone frames. Not that you need a bigger-than-life reflection to look fabulous in these clothes, which are always innovative in both style and fabric and tend to be highly flattering to the wearer. The store carries the most au courant selections from the men's and women's ready-to-wear lines as well as a range of accessories (for couture fittings, women can make an appointment at the design studio next door). Though it is almost guaranteed to come with a high price tag, there may be no better souvenir of Paris than a garment from Gaultier. ♦ M-Sa. 01.42.86.05.05. Also at 44 Ave George-V (at Rue François-I). 01.44.43.00.44. Métro: George-V

LEGRAND FILLES ET FILS

For three generations, the Legrand family has run this prestigious wine shop and *épicerie* stocked with chocolate, tea, coffee, and jam. The shop is a delight, with its ceiling covered with corks and a bright red Belle Epoque façade on its Rue de Banque side. Francine Legrand, the daughter of the late Lucien, has a wide selection of *grands crus* and has a special passion for younger, undiscovered (and less expensive) wines from France's smaller vineyards in Burgundy and Bordeaux. Ask her to recommend one—she loves to chat. ♦ Tu-Sa. Other entrance around the corner at 1 Rue de la Banque (at Rue des Petits-Pères). 01.42.60.07.12

A PRIORI THÉ

★★$ US expatriate Margaret Gilbert-Hancock owns this charming tearoom and luncheon spot whose wicker chairs and tables decorated with silk flowers from Emilio Robba's shop next door spill into the Galerie Vivienne. A creative selection of quiches and salads is served, followed by divine apple crumble and brownies for dessert. Francine Legrand, whose shop (see above) is in the same arcade, chooses items for the wine list. ♦ M-Sa, breakfast, lunch, and afternoon tea; Su, brunch and afternoon tea. Nos. 35-37. 01.42.97.48.75

125 BASILIQUE NOTRE-DAME-DES-VICTOIRES

Using the plans of **Pierre Le Muet**, in 1740 architect **Jean Sylvain Cartaud** completed the Baroque church that dominates this pleasant little square. The victory it commemorates is Louis XIII's trouncing of the Protestants at La Rochelle in 1628. Inside the church are a 1702 bust of the composer Jean-Baptiste Lully, who lived down the street at 45 Rue des Petits-Champs, and an estimated 35,000 ex-voto tablets blanketing the walls. ♦ Pl des Petits-Pères (at Rue Notre-Dame-des-Victoires). Métro: Bourse

126 CHEZ GEORGES

★★$$ Handwritten menus, beveled mirrors, waitresses in black dresses, and a variety of traditional French dishes such as escargots, foie gras, steak and chips, poached haddock,

Place des Victoires Shopping

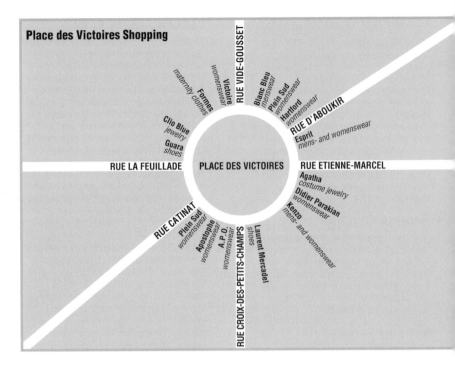

and *baba au rhum* (rum-flavored sponge cake) are hallmarks of this charming Parisian bistro. ◆ M-Sa, lunch and dinner; closed 3 weeks in August. Reservations recommended. 1 Rue du Mail (at Pl des Petits-Pères). 01.42.60.07.11. Métro: Bourse

127 AU PANETIER

Hundreds of crispy sourdough baguettes are baked daily in the wood-fired oven of M. and Mme. Cleret, whose bakery also offers an enormous variety of pastries of all sorts. ◆ M-F. 10 Pl des Petits-Pères (between Rue des Petits-Pères and Passage des Petits-Pères). 01.42.60.90.23. Métro: Bourse

128 VICTOIRE

Come here to find out what's new in the current fashion scene. This place takes pride in being the very first specialty store to discover new Paris design talent. ◆ M-Sa. Nos. 10-12 Rue d'Aboukir (at Rue Vide-Gousset). 01.42.61.09.02. Métros: Bourse, Palais Royal–Musée de Louvre

129 PLACE DES VICTOIRES

Like those at the Place Vendôme, this circle of noble mansions was designed by **Jules Hardouin-Mansart** to celebrate a triumph of Louis XIV, in this case the Treaty of Nijmegen that marked his victory over Spain, Holland, Piedmont, and Germany. Originally at its center was a gilded bronze statue (1686) portraying the king being crowned by a goddess of victory, with four bound warriors at his feet representing the conquered nations. Destroyed during the revolution, the statue was replaced in 1822 with the Astyanax Bosio equestrian version of Louis XIV that proudly rears here today. During the 19th century, the Place des Victoires fell into ruin and its buildings were converted into shops, but today it's the Right Bank's hub of avant-garde high fashion. ◆ Métros: Bourse, Palais Royal–Musée du Louvre

130 KENZO

For the young at heart: This appealing boutique, decorated with natural wood, has some of the most fanciful fashions and friendliest sales help in town. The menswear collection is downstairs, the women's wear upstairs. ◆ M-Sa. No. 3 Place des Victoires (between Rues Etienne-Marcel and Croix-des-Petits-Champs). 01.40.39.72.00. Métros: Bourse, Palais Royal–Musée du Louvre

130 CACHAREL

The design flame remains bright, thanks to th Anglo-Brazilian husband-and-wife team of Clements-Riberio, who have introduced eye-popping tartans and multicolored knitwear fo men and women, some produced in collaboration with Liberty of London. The children's collection is at 34 Rue Tronchet. ◆ M-Sa. No 5 Place des Victoires (between Rues Etienne-Marcel and Croix-des-Petits-Champs). 01.42.33.29.88. Métros: Bourse, Palais Royal–Musée du Louvre. Also at 34 Rue

Tronchet (between Rue des Mathurins and Blvd Haussmann). 01.47.42.12.61. Métro: Havre–Caumartin

131 THIERRY MUGLER

Though Thierry Mugler has numerous boutiques around Paris, this is the only one devoted entirely to menswear. On the ground floor you'll find a comprehensive selection of characteristically cool ready-to-wear and accessories. Past an achingly sleek wall-mounted light sculpture that changes colors, there's a staircase to the lower level, where you'll find formal attire and salesmen more than happy to acquaint you with it. ♦ M-Sa. 54 Rue Etienne-Marcel (between Rue d'Argout and Place des Victoires). 01.42.33.06.13. Métro: Etienne-Marcel

132 LINA'S

★★$ This airy sandwich bar with its ocher walls, blond-wood trim, and acres of windows is the perfect vantage point for spying on the chic fashion show that promenades in the vicinity of the Place des Victoires. Behind the counter, businesslike young men and women serve delicious roast beef, pastrami, and smoked-salmon sandwiches on crusty whole-grain *pain pavé* (country bread). ♦ Daily. 50 Rue Etienne-Marcel (at Rue d'Argout). 01.42.21.16.14. Métro: Sentier. Also at numerous locations throughout the city

133 FLO PRESTIGE

For those who enjoy picnicking and can afford not to bother with preparing the meal, this take-out gourmet deli offers a delectable selection of cheeses, *charcuterie*, salmon, salads, daily specials, desserts, and pastries of a quality that merits a limo for the tailgate picnic. For a setting, the nearby **Tuileries** gardens should do just fine. Or if you prefer, the shop will deliver to your hotel. ♦ Daily, until 11PM. 42 Pl du Marché-St-Honoré (at Rue du Marché-St-Honoré). 01.42.61.45.46. Métro: Pyramides. Also at numerous locations throughout the city

134 YAKITORI

★$ Try the morsels of cheese-stuffed pork, teriyaki chicken, and marinated shrimp skewered and grilled *à la japonaise*. This restaurant is perpetually crowded, but it's worth the effort to grab a seat at the counter and watch the chefs perform. ♦ M-Sa, lunch and dinner. 34 Pl du Marché-St-Honoré (between Rues du Marché-St-Honoré and Gomboust). 01.42.96.10.18. Métro: Pyramides

135 DAVÉ

★★$$ A hideout for such celebrities as George Michael and Yves Saint Laurent, this excellent Sino-Vietnamese restaurant is named after its star-struck maître d', who keeps a collection of Polaroids of his most famous customers. Scattered about the intimate dining room, which is decorated with deep red carpets and Chinese lamps, are framed photos of Catherine Deneuve, David Bowie, Serge Gainsbourg, Cher, Cameron Diaz, Leonardo di Caprio, and many others with their good-natured host. Recommended dishes include the sweet and spicy spareribs, Vietnamese rolls served with mint, and shrimp sautéed in a spicy black-bean sauce. ♦ M-F, lunch and dinner; Sa, Su, dinner. 39 Rue St-Roch (between Rues St-Honoré and Gomboust). 01.42.61.49.48. Métro: Pyramides

136 TUILERIES

$$$ Down a quiet side street, this small hotel was the mansion of Queen Marie Antoinette's principal lady-in-waiting in the 18th century. It retains much of its period charm, despite 20th-century modifications—private bathrooms, color TVs, direct-dial phones, minibars, and air conditioning—that have made its 26 rooms eminently comfortable. There's no restaurant. ♦ 10 Rue St-Hyacinthe (between Rues de la Sourdière and du Marché-St-Honoré). 01.42.61.04.17; fax 01.49.27.91.56. Métros: Pyramides, Tuileries. htuileri@aol.com

137 JUVENILES

★★$$ This lively *bistrot à vin* just down the street from the **Bibliothèque Nationale de France** is the brainchild of wine lovers Mark Williamson and Tim Johnston and is now owned and run by Tim. It's a comfortable spot for noshing on *tapenade d'aubergines, piquillos, et olives noires* (mixture of eggplant, peppers, and black olives), marinated salmon, grilled quail, and salads, or on more substantial fare, such as grilled Scottish salmon, haggis and steak, and afterward enjoying a slice of the dense, flourless chocolate cake. Wash it all down with a reasonably priced Pic Saint Loup Côteaux du Languedoc or one of the many other excellent wines from France, Spain, Italy, and Australia. ♦ M-Sa, lunch and dinner. 47 Rue de Richelieu (between Rues Villedo and des Petits-Champs). 01.42.97.46.49. Métro: Pyramides

138 MACÉO

★★★$$ It may be named after funk sax man Macéo Parker, but there's nothing funky about Mark Williamson's latest food-and-wine venture, opened two steps down the street from his wine bar in 1999. Williamson kept the rococo ceilings, large mirrors, and zinc bar left by the previous occupant, the staid old **Mer-**

Restaurants/Clubs: Red | **Hotels: Purple** | Shops: Orange | **Outdoors/Parks: Green** | Sights/Culture: Blue cure **Galant** restaurant, but made it into an elegantly modern dining space with blond-wood paneling and burgundy walls and curtainless windows to let in the light. Complementing the décor is Jean-Paul Deyries's bright, sophisticated cuisine, with a menu that changes daily, following the seasons. Pumpkin soup with oysters, carpaccio of salmon with pesto, *sandre* (a perchlike freshwater fish) in a casserole with clams and shallots, Lozère lamb roasted with rosemary and sea salt, and preserved chestnut tart with a bitter cocoa sauce or warm almond tart with chopped mangoes are but a few of the young chef's imaginative offerings. The restaurant also offers vegetarian gastronomic menus daily. The wine list is large, eclectic, and absolutely splendid, with great and intriguing wines from all over the world, but especially strong on southern France. This is the perfect place to sample the marvelous wines of Bandol or Palette, or a Châteauneuf-du-Pape from the illustrious Château de Beaucastel. ♦ M-F, lunch and dinner; Sa, dinner. Reservations recommended. 15 Rue des Petits-Champs (between Rues Vivienne and de Richelieu). 01.42.97.53.85. Métros: Bourse, Pyramides

138 HERBORISTERIE DU PALAIS-ROYAL

Herbs, oils, and lotions for needs both medicinal and pleasurable are crammed floor to ceiling in this small shop. Every potion is designed to stimulate the senses. Michel Pierre, who has coauthored a book on salutary plants, can select just the herb to remedy your ailment. Passiflore from South America promotes relaxation, eleuterocoque from Siberia increases energy, and harpagophytum from Namibia helps ease arthritis and rheumatism. ♦ M-Sa. 11 Rue des Petits-Champs (between Rues Vivienne and de Richelieu). 01.42.97.54.68. Métros: Bourse, Pyramides

139 CHEZ PAULINE

★★$$$ When tradition works this well, why change? This relaxed restaurant serves such French classics as *boeuf bourguignon*, *poularde de Bresse* (chicken from Bresse), creamed wild mushrooms with chives, warm foie gras salad, fricassee of sole and crayfish, game in season, and a variety of *plats du jour*, such as stuffed cabbage, cassoulet with preserved goose, bacon with lentils, and calf's liver. ♦ Jan-May, Sept-Dec: M-F, lunch and dinner; Sa, dinner. June-Aug: M-F, lunch and dinner. Reservations recommended. 5 Rue Villedo (between Rues de Richelieu and Ste-Anne). 01.42.96.20.70. Métro: Pyramides

140 ST-ROCH

The bullet holes in this church's façade recall one of the most significant military debuts in French history. This is the site of a fierce revo-lutionary skirmish that occurred on the steps of the church on 5 October 1795, when a Royalist mob was scattered by a then-little-known 27-year-old general named Napoléon Bonaparte. Ten days later Napoléon was appointed commander in chief of the home forces. An architectural mix-and-match, the structure is the city's finest Baroque church and is best known today for its splendid 1752 rococo organ and weekly evening concerts. Built to handle the overflow from **St-Germain-l'Auxerrois**, it was originally designed by **Jacques Lemercier**, and no less a personage than Louis XIV laid its cornerstone in 1653. But it took another century to complete. **Jules Hardouin-Mansart** was responsible for the oval **Lady Chapel**, and sculptor **René Charpentier** decorated the edifice in carved imagery. The church is dedicated to an Italian holy man who ministered to plague victims in the 14th century. Inside are memorials to playwright Corneille, philosopher Diderot, and Louis XIV's beloved gardener, André Le Nôtre, whose bust by Antoine Coysevox is to the left of the chancel. ♦ 296 Rue St-Honoré (at Rue St-Roch). 01.42.44.13.20. Métros: Pyramides, Tuileries

141 FONTAINE MOLIÈRE

The fountain, designed by **Ludovico Visconti**, was dedicated in 1773, the centennial of the playwright's death. Seurre's statue of Molière, pen in hand, is seated atop, flanked on either side by marble statues by Pradier representing light and serious comedy. ♦ Rues Molière and de Richelieu. Métro: Pyramides

142 LE POQUELIN

★★$$ Original nouvelle cuisine is served here; menu items include steamed fish with mushrooms, salmon *unilatéral* (cooked on one side), spicy chicken, and roast game. Top off your meal with a hot apple tart. The formal dining room has red theater curtains and a big portrait of Molière (né Jean-Baptiste Poquelin). Actors from the nearby **Comédie Française** dine here. ♦ M-F, lunch and dinner; Sa, dinner; closed first 3 weeks of Aug. Reservations recommended. 17 Rue Molière (between Ave de l'Opéra and Rue Thérèse). 01.42.96.22.19. Métro: Pyramides

143 LES BOUCHOLEURS

★★$$ *Boucholeurs* are the farmers who cultivate the small, finer-tasting variety of mussels featured in many of the dishes served here. These particular mussels come from a *parc à huîtres* (shellfish farm) near La Rochelle on the west coast; the bankers and stockbrokers who eat them come from the nearby **Bourse**. Try the superb *mouclade rochelaise* (small mussels in a creamy saffron-and-cognac sauce) with a bottle of Fiefs Vendéen de Pissotte. Other specialties include *moules sauce au gingembre* (mussels in a ginger sauce), *moules au curry*, and *haddock poché*. Intimate and tasteful, the small blue dining room has subtle nautical details. ♦ M-F, lunch and dinner; Sa, dinner; closed the first 2 weeks of May (or whenever the mussel season has run its course), and 2 weeks in mid-Aug. Reservations recommended. 34 Rue de Richelieu (between Pl André-Malraux and Rue des Petits-Champs). 01.42.96.06.86. Métro: Pyramides

143 MATSURI SUSHI

★$$ Customers hunker around a circular bar to snag plates of raw salmon and tuna sailing by on a conveyor belt. To tally the check, waiters simply count the dishes in front of each diner. At lunch, every fifth item is free. So is home delivery throughout the day within Paris city limits. ♦ M-F, lunch and dinner; Sa, dinner; closed in Aug. 36 Rue de Richelieu (between Pl André-Malraux and Rue des Petits-Champs). Reservations, 01.42.61.05.73; delivery, 01.40.26.12.13. Métro: Pyramides

144 L'INCROYABLE RESTAURANT

★$ What's incredible about Claude and William Breyer's eight-table restaurant hidden on a narrow cobbled passage are the generous portions and bargain prices. Traditional French dishes—*cuisses de canard confit sucrée d'oignons* (duck thighs with sugared onions), sautéed potatoes, and *clafouti* (apple, cherry, and black-currant baked custard)—are served. ♦ M, Sa, lunch; Tu-F, Su, dinner. No credit cards accepted. 26 Rue de Richelieu or 23 Rue de Montpensier (between Pl André-Malraux and Rue des Petits-Champs). 01.42.96.24.64. Métros: Palais Royal–Musée du Louvre, Pyramides

leBridgeur

144 LA BOUTIQUE DU BRIDGEUR

The only store in Paris catering strictly to bridge players, this boutique sells bridge tables, score pads, playing cards, and instruction manuals. If you write in advance, its affiliated bridge club might help find you a partner. ♦ M-Sa. 28 Rue de Richelieu (between Pl André-Malraux and Rue des Petits-Champs). 01.42.96.25.50. Métros: Palais Royal–Musée du Louvre, Pyramides

145 HÔTEL WASHINGTON OPÉRA

$$$ This hotel, once the private town house of everyone's favorite mistress (and that of Louis XV in particular), Mme. de Pompadour, would rank high on any Paris insiders' list for its excellent location near the Palais Royale and Louvre, classic look, and modern conveniences. Some of the 36 soundproofed rooms, which are all done up in blue-and-white Gustavian or red-and-cream Louis-Philippe style, have beamed ceilings, and a number of junior suites are furnished with four-poster beds. Marble bathrooms are a nice touch. ♦ 50 Rue de Richelieu (between Rues St-Honoré and des Petits-Champs). 01.42.96.68.06; fax 01.40.15.01.12. Métro: Palais Royale–Musée du Louvre. info@hotel-wo.com; www.hotel-wo.com

146 PIERRE AU PALAIS ROYAL— JEAN-PAUL ARABIAN

★★★$$$ In the shadow of the Comédie Française, this restaurant, entered through a deluxe flower shop, offers a warm immersion in the mood of France's Massif Central region. Try noted chef Jean-Paul Arabian's thinly sliced foie gras of duck, *quenelles de brochet à la crème de langoustines* (dumplings of pike with langoustine cream), crusty whole roasted duck, or pan-fried entrecôte with french fries and Béarnaise sauce. ♦ M-Sa, lunch and dinner. Reservations recommended. 10 Rue de Richelieu (between Pl André-Malraux and Rue des Petits-Champs). 01.42.96.09.17. Métros: Palais Royal–Musée du Louvre, Pyramides

146 MONTPENSIER

$$ Once the residence of a baroness who was a favorite of Louis XV, this hotel lacks the style that such a history suggests. The 43 plain rooms are of varying dimensions, and the room rates vary accordingly. There's no restaurant. ♦ 12 Rue de Richelieu (between Pl André-Malraux and Rue des Petits-Champs). 01.42.96.28.50; fax 01.42.86.02.70. Métros: Palais Royal–Musée du Louvre, Pyramides. montpensier.paris@multi-micro.com; www.multi-micro.com/montpensier.paris

147 BANQUE DE FRANCE

The mansion, which became home to the Bank of France in 1812 by order of Napoléon, was originally built for the Comte de Toulouse, the son of Louis XIV and Mlle.

Restaurants/Clubs: Red | Hotels: Purple | Shops: Orange | Outdoors/Parks: Green | Sights/Culture: Blue

de Montespan. Among its lavish treasures is a first-class work of art, *Fête à St-Cloud*, which many art historians say is the best of Fragonard's landscape paintings. That huge (7-by-10-foot) canvas hangs in the private office of the governor of the bank, so unless you have specific business with the governor you'll have to content yourself with the smaller Fragonards down the street at the **Louvre**. The building is open to the public only on the third Saturday and Sunday of September for *Les Journées du Patrimoine* (Patrimony Days). ♦ 39 Rue Croix-des-Petits-Champs (between Rues du Colonel-Driant and La Vrillière). Métro: Palais Royal–Musée du Louvre

148 GÉRARD BESSON

★★★$$$ One of Paris's finest lunch menus (which changes every 3 weeks) might begin with owner-chef Besson's *foie gras de canard* (duck-liver pâté), which may be followed by lobster with small vegetables, or wild game in season. For dessert, try the *biscuit glacé à la framboise* (a cookie topped with raspberry ice cream). The detailed wine list is strong on Bordeaux. The service is attentive, the ambiance quiet and comfortable. ♦ Tu-F, lunch and dinner; M, Sa, dinner only. Reservations recommended. 5 Rue Coq-Héron (between Rues Coquillière and du Louvre). 01.42.33.14.74. Métro: Les Halles

149 A LA CLOCHE DES HALLES

★★$ This wine bar, named after the *cloche* (bronze bell) that for decades signaled the opening and closing of Les Halles market, offers not only superb Sancerres, Morgons, and Côtes-de-Brouillys but also scrumptious plates of baked country ham, assorted regional cheeses, quiche, and homemade fruit tarts. It's crowded with local merchants, journalists, and the folks in dark suits from the **Bourse** and **Banque de France** up the street. ♦ M-Sa, breakfast, lunch, and dinner; closed 2 weeks in Aug. No credit cards accepted. 28 Rue Coquillière (at Rue Coq-Héron). 01.42.36.93.89. Métros: Les Halles, Palais Royal–Musée du Louvre

150 LA FERMETTE DU SUD-OUEST

★★$$ Jacky Mayer reigns supreme over this countrified restaurant, which is famous for

homemade *boudin* (blood sausage) with onions and sautéed potatoes; cassoulet; magnificent entrecôtes; and hearty Cahors, Buzet, and Madeiran wines. ♦ M-Sa, lunch and dinner. Reservations recommended. 31 Rue Coquillière (between Rues du Bouloi and Croix-des-Petits-Champs). 01.42.36.73.55. Métro: Palais Royal–Musée du Louvre

151 GARGANTUA

★★$$ King Kong could leave here with a full tummy—the portions are so grand, the food (lamb curry, salmon-and-spinach tarts, foie gras) so delicious, the prices so reasonable. There's a lunch counter in the rear, but this is mainly a take-out place. Pastries, *charcuterie*, wines, and salads are packed to go. The croissants and *pain au chocolat* are renowned. ♦ Daily, breakfast, lunch, and dinner. 284 Rue St-Honoré (between Rues de l'Echelle and des Pyramides). 01.42.60.52.54. Métros: Tuileries, Pyramides, Palais Royal–Musée du Louvre

152 LE CANARD ENCHAÎNÉ

France's famous left-leaning satirical weekly, celebrated for its irreverent cartoons and editorials, is based here. The paper special-izes in unearthing big political scandals and is usually first to the scene of the crime. ♦ 173 Rue St-Honoré (between Rues de l'Echelle and des Pyramides). 01.42.60.31.36. Métros: Tuileries, Pyramides, Palais Royal–Musée du Louvre

153 MANUFACTURE NATIONALE DE SÈVRES (SÈVRES PORCELAIN FACTORY)

This showroom is an outlet for the famous and venerable (ca. 1738) Sèvres porcelain factory. An exhibition of designs ranges from Louis XVI dinner plates to contemporary pieces by Louise Bourgeois. All items sold here are tax-free. ♦ M-F. 4 Pl André-Malraux (between Rue de Richelieu and Ave de l'Opéra). 01.47.03.40.20. Métro: Palais Royal–Musée du Louvre

154 PLACE ANDRÉ-MALRAUX

In 1874, this square, formerly called **Place du Théâtre Français**, was graced by a duo of elegant but simple Davioud fountains deco-rated with bronze nymphs by Carrier-Belleuse and Math Moreau. ♦ Ave de l'Opéra and Rue St-Honoré. Métro: Palais Royal–Musée du Louvre

155 COMÉDIE FRANÇAISE

In 1673, while performing in his own *Le Malade Imaginaire*, 51-year-old dramatist

Molière collapsed onstage and died as the curtain came down. (Legend has it that there were several doctors in the audience who were so enraged by the play's criticism of medicine that they would not treat its dying author.) Seven years later Louis XIV founded the **Comédie Française** with the remaining members of the playwright's troupe. Today it is France's most prestigious theatrical group, residing since the end of the 18th century in this small (only 540 seats), lovely Doric-style theater designed by **Victor Louis**. The company has survived the Bourbon monarchy, the revolution, two empires, and four republics and still plays to packed houses. After Molière, the theater's most celebrated thespian was the spirited tragic actress Sarah Bernhardt (the "Divine Sarah," born Rosine Bernard in Paris), who played roles ranging from Cleopatra to Hamlet, thereby reviving Shakespeare in France. Bernhardt was a dynamic character who was fond of saying, even in old age, "Rest? With all eternity before me?"

Today the Comédie Française is the bastion of French theater. It aims to keep classical theater alive while also staging works by the best modern playwrights, both French and foreign. A foyer-bar opens onto a gallery displaying busts of famous playwrights. The upstairs foyer is graced with a notable stone statue of Voltaire by Houdon and the leather armchair into which Molière collapsed during his last act on stage. ♦ Individual tours: third Su of each month at 10:15AM starting at the administration entrance on the Place Colette. Group tours: second and fourth Su of each month (must be reserved 3 to 4 months in advance). Box office: daily; a special window around the side of the building opens 45 minutes before the curtain to sell reduced-price tickets for the night's performance. 2 Rue de Richelieu (at Pl André-Malraux). 01.44.58.15.15. Métro: Palais Royal–Musée du Louvre

Additional theatrical performances may be seen at the **Comédie Française Studio Théâtre** (99 Rue de Rivoli; 01.44.58.98.58; Métro: Palais Royal–Musée du Louvre) at the **Carrousel du Louvre;** reservations are not accepted at this venue; tickets are sold 1 hour before each performance. Other additional performances are given at the **Comédie Française Théâtre du Vieux-Colombier** (21 Rue du Vieux-Colombier, between Rues Madame and Rennes; 01.44.39.87.00; Métro: St-Sulpice); make reservations 14 days in advance.

156 163 RUE ST-HONORÉ

On the present site of the Moroccan Tourist Office once stood the old **St-Honoré Gate,**

where Joan of Arc was wounded in the thigh by an English archer in 1429. She was hit while measuring the depth of the moat with her lance in preparation for an assault on the city. ♦ Between Rues de Rohan and de l'Echelle. Métro: Palais Royal–Musée du Louvre

157 PALAIS ROYALE–MUSEÉ DU LOUVRE MÉTRO STATION

With its two high domes of multicolored glass orbs forming a resplendent figure eight, this métro entrance, erected in 2000 to celebrate the centenary of the Paris subway, is easily the most festive in town. Artist **Jean-Michel Othoniel** used cast aluminum and some 800 glass pieces made to measure in Murano, Italy, to create his *kiosque des noctambules—*one dome representing the day, the other night. His oeuvre continues underground, with some of the orbs on display behind round recessed windows, before tapering off into a standard-issue métro corridor. Rue St-Honoré at Ave de l'Opéra

158 PALAIS ROYAL

This 6-acre enclave of flowering serenity is surrounded by, yet separate from, the urban bustle. Commissioned by Cardinal Richelieu and designed by his architect **Jacques Lemercier** in 1642, the mansion was christened **Palais Royal** when Anne of Austria temporarily lived here with her son, young Louis XIV. In 1780 the property fell into the hands of the shrewd Philippe, Duke of Orléans, who embarked on a lucrative and fancy bit of real-estate speculation. He hired architect **Victor Louis** (who built the nearby **Théâtre Français**) to design a square like Venice's Piazza San Marco, but containing a garden (700 feet by 300 feet) to be faced on three sides with elegant apartments incorporating arcades that had space for 180 shops, which the duke then sold for immense profit. (He also named the bordering streets after his three sons: Valois, Beaujolais, and Montpensier.)

Strolling through the lime-tree groves here became the fashion for French aristocrats as well as for visitors from across the Atlantic, including Thomas Jefferson and Washington Irving. The garden's elegance soon frayed, however, when the profligate Philippe became chronically broke and began renting the galleries to magicians, wax museums, circuses, and brothels. Under his dissolute management, the palace and gardens attracted the Parisian rabble, questionable dandies, and women of easy virtue; it became a raffish, depraved enclave. (As late as 1804, historians listed the presence of 11 loan sharks, 18 gambling houses, and 17 billiard halls in the palace arcades.) Marat referred to the gardens as the "nucleus of the Revolution." It was here that Charlotte Corday bought the dagger she used to kill Marat. It was also here on 13 July 1789 that Camille Desmoulins incited his fellow Parisians to take up arms. Like the **Tuileries Palace**, the Palais Royal was ransacked during the revolt of 1848; a giant bonfire was kindled in the courtyard with gilt chairs, paintings, and canopies thrown from the windows by the mob. Among the furniture destroyed was the throne on which Louis-Philippe first sat as king of France.

By the 20th century the luxurious apartments overlooking the gardens housed a number of famous residents. Poet and dramatist Jean Cocteau lived here, as did writer Colette. She resided at 9 Rue de Beaujolais and was often seen writing at her window overlooking the courtyard. Colette died as stylishly as she'd lived: suddenly and painlessly after drinking a glass of champagne.

Today the buildings of the Palais Royal house private residences and offices that are closed to the public. However, visitors may stroll through the gardens and browse among the antiques, old books, jewelry, lead soldiers, medals, and rare stamps in the arcade's curiosity shops. The garden is embellished by the fountain where the infant Louis XIV once sailed his toy boats and by two quite modern fountains resembling giant ball bearings. The larger court of the palace has been the focus of an aesthetic debate reminiscent of the one surrounding the **Louvre** transformation. minister of culture Jack Lang initiated a project (conceived by sculptor **Daniel Burennes**) that involved the planting of 280 black-and-white-striped columns of varying height, deep pools, and airport lights in the courtyard floor. In the winter of 1986 residents of the palace who objected to the scheme won a court order to halt construction on the site temporarily. The project, however, was completed the following summer. More pleasing both to residents' and visitors' eyes are the twin fountains by sculptor Pol Bury in the adjoining courtyard. Installed in 1985, these clusters of large, shiny chromium balls in basins of water budge ever so slightly just when you think they won't. ◆ Bounded by Rues de Valois and de Montpensier and by Pl du Palais-Royal and Rue de Beaujolais. Métros: Palais Royal–Musée du Louvre, Pyramides, Bourse

Within the Palais Royal:

LE GRAND VÉFOUR

★★★★$$$$ A favorite haunt since the 1760s, this glamorous restaurant that's part of the **Palais Royal** complex is named after Jean Véfour, chef to Philippe, Duke of Orléans

(who voted to send his relative Louis XVI to the guillotine and later wound up there himself). Seductively and appropriately timeworn, the gilt and wood-paneled Louis XVI-Directoire interior with the famous red-velvet banquettes is classified as a historic monument. Here Napoléon courted Joséphine, Victor Hugo romanticized, and Colette and Jean Cocteau, who lived nearby, enjoyed regular repasts. The menu offers exquisite *cuisine gastronomique* by chef Guy Martin; favorites include foie gras ravioli with truffle cream, noisettes of lamb with fennel sauce, wild duck with quince, *parmentier de queue de boeuf* (oxtail with puréed potatoes), and *galette aux endives* (endive cake). Don't miss the rare cheeses and the Burgundy wines. This is a Michelin-three-star restaurant, one of only seven in Paris. ◆ M-Th, lunch and dinner; F, lunch only: closed in Aug. Reservations required. 17 Rue de Beaujolais (between Rues de Valois and de Montpensier). 01.42.96.56.27

A LA CIVETTE
MAISON FONDÉE EN 1716

159 A LA CIVETTE

For more than 2 centuries this store has been in the forefront of tobacconists—it was the first shop in Paris to import the fine Montecristo cigar from Cuba. Shelves are cluttered with chewing tobacco, pipes, cigarillos, and stogies to delight the wheeziest connoisseur. ◆ M-Sa. 157 Rue St-Honoré (between Pl du Palais-Royal and Rue de Rohan). 01.42.96.04.99. Métro: Palais Royal–Musée du Louvre

159 HÔTEL DU LOUVRE

$$$ This modern 200-room hotel—fully renovated in 1998—is situated beside the **Palais Royal**, **Tuileries**, and **Comédie Française**, and within walking distance of the Opéra and the Louvre. It offers contemporary comforts, traditional Second Empire–style décor, and a brasserie. Request the Pissarro Suite, from which the artist painted the Place du Théâtre Français. ◆ Pl André-Malraux and Rue de Rohan 01.44.58.38.38; fax 01.44.58.38.00. Métro: Palais Royal–Musée du Louvre. hoteldulouvre@hoteldulouvre.com; www.hoteldulouvre.com

159 DELAMAIN

The window of this wonderful old bookshop displays museum-worthy items, from 18th-century hand-bound volumes on King Clovis to modern editions of Samuel Beckett. ◆ M-Sa, 10AM-7:30PM. 155 Rue St-Honoré (between Pl du Palais-Royal and Rue de Rohan). 01.42.61.48.78. Métro: Palais Royal–Musée du Louvre

160 GALERIE VÉRO-DODAT

Named after two pork butchers who were here from the start, this covered passageway was the city's first public thoroughfare to be illuminated by gas lighting. ♦ Between Rues Jean-Jacques-Rousseau and du Bouloi. Métros: Louvre–Rivoli, Palais Royal–Musée du Louvre

On Galerie Véro-Dodat:

ROBERT CAPIA

This antiques shop specializes in dolls, old photographs, and old phonograph records, including original recordings of Sarah Bernhardt and Enrico Caruso. The store is a favorite of Catherine Deneuve. ♦ M-Sa. 24-26 Galerie Véro-Dodat. 01.42.36.25.94

RESTAURANT VÉRO-DODAT

★★$$ Tasty nouvelle cuisine is served in this charming little restaurant in Paris's prettiest *galerie*, with a prix-fixe menu that offers a great range of tempting choices at prices that are more than reasonable. Fillet of poached salmon with grapefruit butter, leg of duck roasted with thyme, roast lamb with garlic, and homemade chestnut mousse cake with cream are a few of the items featured. ♦ Tu-Sa, lunch and dinner; closed in Aug. Reservations recommended. 19 Galerie Véro-Dodat. 01.45.08.92.06

L'Epi d'Or

RESTAURANT

161 L'EPI D'OR

★★$$ This humble 1950s Les Halles standby serves honest fillets of herring with warm potatoes, ham hock and lentils, *entrecôte bordelaise* (beef rib steak with Bordeaux-style brown sauce), *magret de canard de Landes aux cerises aiguës et airelles* (duck breast from Landes with sour cherries and cranberries), and unsophisticated Rhônes and Bordeaux. ♦ M-F, lunch and dinner; Sa, dinner; closed in Aug. Reservations recommended. 25 Rue Jean-Jacques-Rousseau (between Galerie Véro-Dodat and Pl des 2-Ecus). 01.42.36.38.12. Métro: Louvre-Rivoli

162 CHRISTIAN LOUBOUTIN

The specialty of this women's shoe designer is shoes with hand-sculpted heels. The heels covered in gold leaf give you a dazzling walk. ♦ M-Sa. 19 Rue Jean-Jacques-Rousseau (at Galerie Véro-Dodat). 01.42.36.05.31. Métro: Louvre–Rivoli

163 MAISON MICRO

This Greek bazaar offers produce from Hellas: vats of olives and hot peppers, burlap sacks of whole grains and flour, crates of dried fruits, and barrels of tarama. Step inside and take a whiff of the Aegean. ♦ M, 2-7PM; Tu-Sa, 10AM-12:30PM, 1:30PM-7PM. 142-144 Rue St-Honoré (between Rues du Louvre and Jean-Jacques-Rousseau). 01.42.60.53.02. Métro: Louvre–Rivoli

163 CHEZ NOUS

★$$ The city's best jock bar and restaurant is run by Gilbert Ghiraldi, an ex-rugby player. If you manage to outmaneuver the French national rugby team that huddles here, grab a table and order one of the Basque specialties. ♦ Daily, lunch and dinner. 150 Rue St-Honoré (between Rues du Louvre and Jean-Jacques-Rousseau). 01.42.61.76.28. Métro: Louvre–Rivoli

164 LE LOUVRE DES ANTIQUAIRES

An association of more than 240 antique shops encompasses three floors here. You'll find Art Deco prints, period perfume bottles, miniature 16th-century manuscripts, rare Japanese woodcuts, fin de siècle dolls and children's clothes, African tribal masks, and Thai Buddhas. In fact, one can find any old thing here except a bargain. Many of these dealers have their main antique shops (generally larger and less expensive) on the Left Bank, so take a card and pay them a visit when you're on the other side of the river. Also, before making a purchase, be sure you understand the complicated regulations concerning the removal of antiques from the country. This building was formerly the **Grand Hôtel du Louvre**, where Mark Twain stayed in 1867. It was here that Twain met the tour guide Ferguson who figures in *The Innocents Abroad* (1869). ♦ Tu-Su; closed Su in July and Aug. 2 Pl du Palais-Royal (at Rue de Rivoli). 01.42.97.27.00. Métro: Palais Royal–Musée du Louvre

---

Restaurants/Clubs: Red | Hotels: Purple | Shops: Orange | Outdoors/Parks: Green | Sights/Culture: Blue

LES HALLES, MARAIS, AND THE BASTILLE

This tour traverses three Parisian neighborhoods and a millennium of the city's history. It begins in the old Les Halles neighborhood, once the site of the great marketplace that Emile Zola called "the belly of Paris." Here you can wake up with the bustle of the marketplace and have a breakfast of coffee and croissants with local workers in cafés on the **Rue Montorgueil** shopping street, one of the surviving remnants of the old Les Halles food market. Then amble over to **St-Eustache** to admire the towering parish church of Les Halles, second only to **Notre-Dame** in size and Gothic splendor.

Emerging from St-Eustache, you'll find yourself at the **Forum des Halles**, the huge, modern, mostly underground mall that replaced "the belly" after it moved to the suburbs 3 decades ago. Here you can shop for practically anything *except* groceries in the almost 200 boutiques, catch the latest movie at one of the multiplex theaters, or swim a few laps in an Olympic-size pool. Back up on the street, stroll on to "the Beaubourg," as the **Centre Georges Pompidou** is popularly known. This huge and hugely controversial building (it looks like an oil refinery) is Paris's department store of modern culture whose **Musée National d'Art Moderne** houses one of the world's greatest collections of modern and contemporary art. Indulge in a second cup of coffee on the terrace of chic **Café Beaubourg**, a choice perch from which to watch the myriad street performers in front of the center or enjoy the grand panorama of the city from the restaurant **Georges** atop the Centre Georges Pompidou.

The **Marais** is among Paris's most historic neighborhoods, and one that happily eluded Baron Haussmann's urban renewal plans. Today a plethora of galleries, design shops, hip cafés, and bars are squeezed in between the antique aristocratic **hôtels particuliers**, or mansions, imbuing the district with a distinct vitality. Much of the Marais today is the Parisian equivalent to New York's Greenwich Village or Chelsea, particularly along the lower stretches of Rues du Temple, des Archives, and Vieille du Temple—where you'll find more gay-oriented shops and restaurants than anywhere else in the city. But while the rainbow flags fly freely, the place is only imprecisely a modern version of the Jewish ghetto that it was in medieval times, for here mothers push strollers past same-sex couples without batting an eyelash, fashion and accessory wholesalers take deliveries amid the fray, and just about everyone comes to soak up the atmosphere of narrow, twisting streets that never stop charming sophisticated strollers.

From the Beaubourg, move on to the city's most beautiful square, **Place des Vosges**, in a section of the Marais district that was once a snarl of medieval streets inhabited by rich viscounts and poor Jews. On the way, stop in at the **Musée d'Art et d'Histoire du Judaïsme**, a splendid museum of Jewish art and history. Browse the boutiques of **Rue des Francs Bourgeois** or visit the **Musée Carnavalet** (the **Historical Museum of the City of Paris**) to peruse its collection of revolution memorabilia and 18th-century shop signs, both of which are a big hit with children. Have lunch at one of the many tea salons (**Le Loir dans la Théière** is a good choice) or pick up a quick falafel or pastrami sandwich on **Rue des Rosiers**, the main artery of the old Jewish quarter, which is lined with storefront synagogues and kosher bakeries. (Remember, though, that much of the street closes on Saturday, the Jewish Sabbath.) Your dessert will be the **Musée Picasso** in the **Hôtel-Salé** on Rue de Thorigny. Now mosey down to the most beautiful square in Paris, if not the whole world, the elegant 17th-century **Place des Vosges**, home to one of Paris's best and most elegant gourmet restaurants, chef Bernard Pacaud's **Ambrosie**. (If visiting the Marais during summer, inquire about the Festival du Marais, a series of opera, chamber music, and drama performances in the district's exquisite 17th-century mansions.)

The final stop on this tour is the reinvigorated neighborhood of the **Place de la Bastille**. ere the **Opéra Bastille**, a huge silver whale of a building, looms over a neighborhood f artisans and woodworkers coexisting with trendy designer shops, art galleries, staurants, cafés, and clubs, most of which have sprung up since the Opéra Bastille pened in 1990. Once the site of the prison whose storming marked the start of the bloody rench Revolution, the Place de la Bastille is better known today for the dramas that ike place onstage in the opera house. But there is plenty to do in the area, even if you on't have opera tickets. **Bofinger, Les Grandes Marches, Le Dôme Bastille,** and **Blue lephant** are four popular dinner spots. Great dancing is afoot at the trendy **Casbah** and t Paris's most famous dance hall, **Le Balajo,** which opened in 1936 and is still kicking. omplete your Bastille rite of passage by sipping a glass of champagne at jumping **Sanz-**

Sans or a coco loco cocktail at the **Havanita Café**. More fashion-conscious night owl should check out the wee-hours scene at **Les Bains Douches** in Les Halles, a discothequ favored by movie stars, models, and other glitterati. If hunger strikes, two classic eateries **Au Pied de Cochon** and **La Tour de Montlhery**, are open around the clock. Both place are full of characters with 3AM cravings for steak and Burgundy, oysters an champagne, or the traditional Les Halles staple—a cheese-crusted bowl of onion soup.

LES HALLES

The area known as Les Halles (the marketplace) takes its name from the great wholesale food market that began here in 1100. The colorful old market operated on this site until 1969 when it moved to Rungis near **Orly Airport**, leaving behind *le trou* (the hole). This was filled 10 years later by a huge underground shopping mall called the **Forum des Halles**; the attractive 12-acre **Jardin des Halles** bordering it on the west was created in the late 1980s. As recently as a few decades ago, this whole area was a run-down garment district and slum that stretched between **St-Merri** church and the old food market. The opening of the **Forum des Halles** and the nearby **Centre Georges Pompidou** in the late 1970s brought new commercial life into the area (as well as fierce architectural controversy). Retired food merchants now share their turf with hordes of mallbound youths, street performers, panhandlers, and tourists. On the Jardin des Halles' northern perimeter are the massive church of **St-Eustache**, several old all-night restaurants serving onion soup and pig's feet, and a few bustling market streets where traditional food and kitchenware outlets have survived. Here you can still catch a bit of the flavor of Les Halles of old.

1 PORTE ST-DENIS

This imposing Roman-style triumphal arch celebrates Louis XIV's victorious battles in Flanders and the Rhineland. **François Blondel** modeled the 24-meter-high (75-foot-high) structure after the Arch of Titus in Rome; Charles Le Brun's allegorical sculptured adornments were inspired by the reliefs on Trajan's Column. South of the arch, Rue St-Denis, now the main drag of the Sentier wholesale garment district, has long been a stomping ground for women of the night. Those still practicing their ancient profession

What is the secret of the French attraction for most strangers? Why do foreign colonies flourish so easily in France? The secret is France's aloofness; they tolerate strangers and allow them to do as they please as long as they don't meddle in French national affairs or do anything to hurt their pride.

—Harlem Renaissance writer Claude McKay

here do it by day as well. Henry Miller and hi photographer friend Brassaï enjoyed prowling these streets in the 1930s. ♦ At Blvd St-Den and Rue du Faubourg-St-Denis. Métro: Strasbourg–St-Denis

2 PORTE ST-MARTIN

In 1674 **Pierre Bullet** constructed this smaller arch—only 17 meters (56 feet) high—after plans made by **François Blondel** for **Porte St-Denis**. These two triumphal arches, astride the most important routes to the nort were erected by the Sun King to announce th grandeur of the French capital to visitors, righ at the time he was tearing down the city's medieval walls that he felt were no longer needed because of his military might. ♦ Blvd St-Denis and Rue du Faubourg-St-Martin. Métro: Strasbourg–St-Denis

3 RUE DU VERTBOIS

The remains of the walls of St-Martin-des-Champs church on this street date from 1270. An inflammatory letter from Victor Hug is said to have saved the wall from demolition. ♦ Between Rues de Turbigo and Vaucanson. Métros: Temple, Arts et Métiers, Réaumur–Sébastopol

musée des arts et métiers

4 MUSÉE DES ARTS ET MÉTIERS (NATIONAL TECHNICAL MUSEUM)

Housed in buildings of the medieval St-Martin-des-Champs priory that were confis cated by the revolution in 1794, this museum was the brainchild of revolutionist Abbé Grégoire, who wanted it to serve as "a deposi tory for new and useful machines." The good abbot would be delighted to see his creation today. An 8-year, 360 million-franc (US $50 million) renovation completed in 2000—the last of the late President François Mitterrand's *Grands Travaux*—transformed the gloomy old storehouse of dusty scientific instruments and machines into a bright, airy model of the modern museum design. Of the 80,000 scientific and technical devices and 15,000 drawings in the collection, 3,000 items are on display. Among these marvels of human ingenuity are Pascal's calculating machine of 1642; Cugnot's bulky steam-powered "fire chariot," the first machine in history to move on its own power (at 2.5 mph) in 1770; Foucault's pendulum of 1855; the Laumière brothers' motion picture camera of 1895; the first plane to cross the English Channel, a Blériot, in 1909; and a Cray 2 supercomputer from 1985. The collection is divided into seven sections: scientific instruments, materials, construction, communication, energy, mechanics, and most spectacularly, transport, in the former church of the medieval priory. Pioneer flying machines float in space from the top of the lofty nave, and early automobiles are installed on ramps and scaffolds mounting the church walls. Unlike most museums in France, this one provides descriptive plaques in English as well as French, and there is an English-language audio guide. ♦ Admission. Daily, 10AM-6PM; Th, to 9:30PM. 60 Rue Réaumur (between Rues Vaucanson and St-Martin). 01.53.01.82.00. Métro: Arts et Métiers. www.musee@cnam.fr/museum/

4 ARTS ET MÉTIERS MÉTRO STATION (LINE NO. 11)

Inspired by Jules Verne's submarine *Nautilus*, this shiny copper-sheathed tube punctuated with massively bolted portholes is the most imaginative métro station in Paris. It provides an amusing foretaste of the **Musée des Arts et Métiers** for those who take the No. 11 Line to get there, and for those who don't, it's worth the price of a métro ticket just to see it. Another métro line, the No. 3, also has a stop at **Arts et Métiers**, but it is of the mundane white-bathroom-tiled variety; be careful not to confuse the two. ♦ Entrance at the intersection of Rues Réaumur, Turbigo, and Beaubourg. Métro: Arts et Métiers

5 ST-NICOLAS-DES-CHAMPS

Construction on this church began in the 12th century, and it has acquired distinguished features throughout the ages: a flamboyant Gothic façade, a Renaissance doorway, and many 17th-, 18th-, and 19th-century paintings. ♦ 254 Rue St-Martin (at Rue Cunin-Gridaine). 01.42.72.92.54. Métro: Réaumur–Sébastopol

6 ETIENNE MARCEL

*\$\$ This coolly brash eatery, another hip canteen creation from *les frères* Costes (of the hotel costes and Georges, among others) hardly needs a sign: with its '70s-style oversized thick white plastic chairs spilling onto the sidewalk along busy Rue Etienne Marcel, it would be tough to miss. The *Star Trek*–chic theme continues on the inside, with funky carpets, clear glass lighting fixtures stuffed with strange pipes, and a succession of rooms filled with more of those space-age McChairs. Such eclectic décor doubtless contributes to a uniformly overpriced menu of what is essentially international grazing fare: penne arrabiata, chicken with curried mango chutney (a dish that's served cold), and a cheeseburger for (gulp) 16 euros. Cocktails can be creative—the Lily of the Valley has vodka, sweet vermouth, and banana liqueur—but average about 10 euros apiece. At prices like these you might want to stick with a *carafe d'eau* and salad—something quick to fortify you for shopping in this increasingly trendy neighborhood. ♦ Daily, lunch and dinner. 34 Rue Etienne-Marcel (at Rue Montmartre). 01.45.08.01.03. Métro: Etienne-Marcel

7 KILIWATCH

Step into this groove station and get your fix of street cred *à la parisienne*. More like an emporium than a boutique, the store carries new merchandise in one half, and the other half is secondhand mania. All in all over 60 brands and 100 kinds of jeans are represented here. This is also a good place to pick up a hip fashion or design magazine and flyers with details of Paris club happenings. ♦ M, 2PM-7PM; Tu-Th, 11AM-7PM; F-Sa, 11AM-7:30PM. 64 Rue Tiquetonne (at Rue Montmartre). 01.42.21.17.37. Métro: Etienne-Marcel

8 ANTHONY PETO

Fancy a gray felt fedora or a dashing multicolored scarf to go with one you already own? You'll find a tasteful selection of hats and caps at this small but appealing *chapelier*, along with a small range of accessories and shirts from British designers such as Vivienne Westwood. The candycane-striped umbrellas, a throwback to the Belle Epoque, are hard to resist. ♦ M-Sa, 11AM-7PM. 56 Rue Tiquetonne (between Rues Montmartre and Montorgueil). 01.40.26.60.68. Métro: Etienne-Marcel

9 STOHRER

One of the finest and most beautiful old patisseries in Paris, opened in 1730 by a former pastry chef to Louis XV and famed for its tiny apricot, apple, and wild strawberry tarts, *pithiviers* (flaky cream-filled pastries decorated like a crown), *baba au rhum* (rum-

---

Restaurants/Clubs: Red | Hotels: Purple | Shops: Orange | Outdoors/Parks: Green | Sights/Culture: Blue

flavored sponge cake), and Viennese pastries. It also makes marvelous ice cream and fresh fruit sorbet. ♦ Daily, 7:30AM-8:30PM; closed the first 2 weeks of Aug. 51 Rue Montorgueil (between Rues Tiquetonne and Mandar). 01.42.33.38.20. Métros: Les Halles, Etienne-Marcel, Sentier

10 LA GRILLE MONTORGUEIL

★★$$ This old working-class *bougnat* (a combination café and coal depot) dating from 1904 has been restored to its original look and atmosphere by a bright and dedicated young team. Scenes in a 1937 Jean Gabin movie called *Gueule d'Amour* were shot here, and a framed shot of the star and the movie poster grace the wall above the sturdy zinc bar. Well-prepared bistro-style cuisine is served: onion soup, pickled herrings with potatoes in oil, snails, bones with marrow and sea salt, *confit de canard* (preserved duck), free-range chicken roasted with cider, grilled meat and fish. There are sidewalk tables in good weather where you can soak up the action on the lively shopping street. ♦ Daily, lunch and dinner to midnight. Reservations recommended. 50 Rue Montorgueil (at Rue Tiquetonne). 01.42.33.21.21. Métros: Les Halles, Etienne-Marcel, Sentier

10 HÔTEL VICTOIRES OPÉRA

$$$ This contemporary boutique-hotel has a great location going for it—in the heart of the Montorgueil market district and walking distance to the Louvre, Place des Victoires shopping, and Opéra. The prices are a bit steep for the neighborhood but would probably be higher in tonier parts of town. Reception staff give a friendly welcome. ♦ 56 Rue de Montorgueil (at Rue Tiquetonne). 01.42.36.41.08; fax 01.45.08.08.79. Métro: Etienne-Marcel. hotel@victoiresopera.com; www.hotelvictoiresopera.com

11 404

★★★$$ Of the scores of Moroccan restaurants in town, none is as atmospheric and festive as this longtime favorite, which looks like it came out of a page from the *Arabian Nights*. High ceilings, stone walls, and

authentic Moroccan lighting fixtures are the counterpoint to an open kitchen where bowls of exotic spices, plates of delicate pastries, and simple, time-tested cooking techniques are all on display. The most popular items on the menu are the couscous dishes and the *tajines*, stews of meat delicately blended with fruit, vegetables, and spices and served in ceramic pots. Try the chicken *tajine* with candied lemons and olives, and pair it with a bottle of Moroccan wine. At around 10PM nightly, the heady ambiance goes into overdrive as Arabic house music briefly blares and waiters clap along. You'll be so caught up in the action you'll stop wondering about the restaurant's name (which comes from a kind of 1960s Peugeot). The only real drawback here is that there is no nonsmoking section, which can make tables too close for comfort. Next door, you can enjoy the tapas. Daily, lunch and dinner; closed the last two weeks of August. Reservations recommended. ♦ 69 Rue des Gravilliers (between Rues Beaubourg and St-Martin). 01.42.74.57.81. Métro: Arts et Métiers

Within 404:

ANDY WAHLOO

This friendly place, sharing the same address as the **404**, bills itself as a "Moroccan tapas bar," but most folks simply come here for a drink—whether it's mint tea poured from impressive heights or something more potent. The windows are filled from top to bottom with packaging from mass-market Moroccan products . . . a nod to another, more famous Andy. ♦ Daily. 69 Rue des Gravilliers (between Rues Beaubourg and St-Martin). 01.42.71.20.38. Métro: Arts et Métiers

12 LE TANGO

To dance here cheek-to-cheek among Brylcreem dandies and perfumed widows is to enter a time warp that leads back to 1906, when the tango first hit Paris. A harmonious mixture of gays, lesbians, and heteros dance to calypsos, salsas, beguines—any beat but hip-hop—all night long. This club is both authentic and inexpensive. ♦ Cover. W-Sa, 11PM-dawn. 13 Rue au Maire (between Rues des Vertus and Beaubourg). 01.42.72.17.78. Métro: Arts et Métiers

13 DEHILLERIN

Half warehouse, half hardware store, this family-run kitchen emporium has been supplying the great chefs of Europe with cooking vessels and utensils since 1820. It even furnishes the French army with cast-iron frying pans, boxwood knives, spatulas, and the wire skimmers known as spiders. Mail order is available to anywhere in the world. The store also happens to be the city's

> Everything about the place struck me as being just right. I had the feeling that this was the best possible place in the world for the artist to live and work; and at the time it was. There was so much of the past and the immediate present brought together on one plane that nothing seemed left to be desired. And there was no feeling of being isolated from America.
>
> —Man Ray,
> *Self-Portrait*

leading specialist in re-tinning copper pots. Two of the staff members speak English. ♦ M-Sa. 51 Rue Jean-Jacques-Rousseau and 18-20 Rue Coquillière. 01.42.36.53.13. Métro: Les Halles

Au Pied de Cochon

14 AU PIED DE COCHON

★★$$ This nostalgic all-night eatery specializes in *fruits de mer* (chilled shellfish) and pig's feet (hence the restaurant's name), and onion soup gratinée, de rigueur in the old-time Les Halles. Local night owls still gather here at 4AM, but otherwise it's a popular spot for tourists who enjoy its lively ambiance (lively waiters included), colorful Art Nouveau–inspired main dining room, recently expanded terrace, and solid brasserie fare. If the ground floor is too boisterous, head for the more sedate dining rooms upstairs. For a Parisian version of Sunday brunch, order oysters (a dozen varieties are available) and Champagne at the bar. ♦ Daily, 24 hours. Reservations recommended. 6 Rue Coquillière (between Rues du Jour and Jean-Jacques-Rousseau). 01.40.13.77.00. Métro: Les Halles

15 AGNÈS B.

These cotton T-shirts, chic silk blouses, and skirts are comfortable and fashionable—black being the dominant tone. In her three outlets along Rue du Jour, **agnès b.** outfits today's generation. Her trademark cotton cardigans with mother-of-pearl snaps are de rigueur Parisian attire. Other shops on Rue du Jour are at **No. 2** (babies), **No. 3** (men), **No. 10** (teens), and **No. 19** (household decoration). ♦ M-Sa. 6 Rue du Jour (between Rues Rambuteau and Montmartre). 01.40.03.45.00. Métro: Les Halles

16 LE COCHON À L'OREILLE

★★$ Beautiful ceramic murals adorn this authentic turn-of-the-19th-century working-class bar-café. Butchers, foie gras wholesalers, local merchants, and paunchy men of indefinite occupation wearing blue coveralls hang out here. They come for their coffee and Calvados before dawn or to share a *pastis* (an anisette drink) at the crowded zinc bar in the afternoon. ♦ M-Sa, breakfast and lunch until 6PM. No credit cards accepted. 15 Rue Montmartre (between

Impasse St-Eustache and Rue du Jour). 01.42.36.07.56. Métro: Les Halles

17 ST-EUSTACHE

This massive amalgam of Gothic flying buttresses, rose windows, and flamboyant vaulting was built in the 16th and early 17th centuries to rival **Notre-Dame**. The incongruous neoclassical main entrance was added in the mid-18th century. Though its dimensions are enormous (346 feet long, with a 112-foot-high nave), the church is better known for its musical legacy than its architectural grandeur. Berlioz's *Te Deum* and Liszt's *Grand Mass* were first played here, and composer Jean-Philippe Rameau is buried in the church. At midnight Mass on Christmas Eve, the 8,000-pipe organ and talented church choir outshine even those of Notre-Dame. Notable treasures here are the Rubens painting *Pilgrims at Emmaus*, the Pigalle statue of the Virgin, and a colorful sculpted scene honoring the vegetable vendors forced out of Les Halles in 1969. The church is dedicated to St. Eustache, a 2nd-century Roman general who converted to Christianity when, like St. Hubert, he saw a vision of the cross poised between the antlers of a stag. (A sculpted stag's head and cross are beneath the gable in the church's Renaissance transept façade.) St. Eustache, as the story goes, was gruesomely martyred; he was roasted alive inside an immense bronze bull with his wife and children. This was once the parish church for the merchants of Les Halles and the nobility from the nearby **Louvre** and **Palais Royal**. It hosted the baptisms of Cardinal Richelieu, Jean-Baptiste Poquelin (Molière), and Mme. de Pompadour, as well as the funerals of fabulist Jean de La Fontaine, Colbert (prime minister of Louis XIV), Molière, and revolutionary orator Mirabeau. During the revolution the church was vandalized and renamed the Temple of Agriculture, doubtless in honor of its proximity to Les Halles market. ♦ Fee for tour. Daily. 2 Impasse St-Eustache (just southwest of Rue Montmartre). 01.42.36.31.05. Métro: Les Halles

18 RUE MONTORGUEIL

Paris chefs have continued to shop on this colorful market street despite the demolition of the old Les Halles markets. The market starts at Rue de Turbigo at the rear of **St-Eustache** and runs several blocks north to Rue Réaumur. Its main street, Rue Montorgueil, and all its cross streets are paved in cobblestone and are closed to traffic. The stretch between Rues Etienne

Marcel and Réaumur is especially animated, with fishmongers and fruit sellers hawking their wares, and there are fine patisseries, *boulangeries*, wine shops, bars, restaurants, and several cafés with tables outdoors in good weather. ◆ Market: Tu-Sa, 6AM-1PM, 4PM-7PM; Su, 6AM-1PM. Métros: Les Halles, Etienne-Marcel, Sentier

On Rue Montorgueil:

L'ESCARGOT MONTORGUEIL

★$$ One of the most authentic examples of 1830s décor in Paris, this restaurant has a black-and-gilt façade topped by a huge golden snail, enormous cut-glass mirrors, tulip chandeliers, and red banquettes. The old cooking allegory gracing the wall came from the dining room of actress Sarah Bernhardt. Champagne is served in carafes; escargots are served in mint, curry, Roquefort, or bourguignonne (butter, garlic, and parsley) sauce; and the customers are of the **Maxim's**, **Lasserre**, **Grand Véfour**, and **La Tour d'Argent** variety, which is not surprising, as the place is run by Mme. Saladin-Terrail, the sister of Claude Terrail, who owns **La Tour d'Argent**. Come here more for the extraordinary décor than the far-from-extraordinary cuisine. ◆ Daily, lunch and dinner. Reservations recommended. No. 38 (at Rue Mauconseil). 01.42.36.83.51

On Rue Montorgueil:

19 DUTHILLEUL & MINART

For more than a century, this store has sold uniforms and work clothes, from waiters' aprons to chefs' toques, plus an array of uniquely French occupational garb. This is a great spot for gifts, such as the popular French watchmakers' smocks. Same-day service is also available. ◆ M-Sa. 14 Rue de Turbigo (at Rue Etienne-Marcel). 01.42.33.44.36. Métro: Etienne-Marcel

20 JOE ALLEN

★$$ One of the most popular restaurants in Les Halles, this is a replica of its Manhattan namesake, right down to the old photographs on the dark brick walls. The menu, which also mirrors its US counterpart, offers spareribs, chili con carne, black-bean soup, and apple pie. ◆ Daily, lunch and dinner until 1AM. 30 Rue Pierre-Lescot (between Rues du Cygne and Etienne-Marcel). 01.42.36.70.13. Métro: Etienne-Marcel

21 LES BAINS-DOUCHES

In the 1980s architectural whiz kid **Philippe Starck** transformed these old public Turkish baths with their circa-1900 façade into the trendiest disco and restaurant in Les Halles, and it has remained so ever since. It's a favorite of Robert De Niro, Johnny Depp, and Jennifer Lopez when they're in town. The doorman is very choosy about who gets in—you'll need "*un look*" to gain entrance. What would former baths patron Marcel Proust have to say? ◆ Restaurant: daily, dinner (starting at 9PM). Disco: daily, midnight-dawn. 7 Rue du Bourg-l'Abbé (between Rue St-Martin and Blvd de Sébastopol). 01.48.87.01.80. Métro Etienne-Marcel

22 PHARAMOND

$$ This bistro is a remnant of the old Les Halles days, with 19th-century colored tiles and mosaics, handsome woodwork, and lots of mirrors, more notable these days for its quaint décor than the sadly deteriorated quality of its cuisine. ◆ M, dinner; Tu-Sa, lunch and dinner. Reservations recommended. 24 Rue de la Grande-Truanderie (between Rues Pierre-Lescot and Mondétour). 01.40.28.03.00. Métros: Les Halles, Etienne-Marcel

23 CHEZ VONG AUX HALLES

★★$$ Refined Cantonese and Szechuan dishes may be found in the company of excellent French wines at this attractive Chinese bistro. Dim sum, beef in oyster sauce, and lacquered pigeon are good choices. Be sure to ask for the less expensive prix-fixe menu. ◆ M-Sa, lunch and dinner. Reservations recommended. 10 Rue de la Grande-Truanderie (between Rues St-Denis and Pierre-Lescot). 01.40.39.99.89. Métros: Les Halles, Etienne-Marcel

24 RUE ST-DENIS

Once the route by which France's kings entered Paris to be crowned and exited to be buried in the basilica at St-Denis, this street now unfurls a lurid panoply of Parisian sleaze: peep shows, prostitutes, and such fast-food joints as **Love Burger**. ◆ Métros: Châtelet, Les Halles, Etienne-Marcel, Réaumur-Sébastopol, Strasbourg–St-Denis; RER: Châtelet–Les Halles

On Rue St-Denis:

ST-LEU–ST-GILLES

This 14th-century church is of interest less for its unimposing exterior than for its unusual interior, with its mélange of sculptures, paintings, and architectural elements from many centuries. On a street epitomizing voyeurism, the glass doors of the church appropriately provide their own peep show of medieval architecture. ♦ No. 92 (between Rues de la Grande-Truanderie and du Cygne). 01.40.26.99.75

25 ENTRÉE DES ARTISTES

This whimsical bookstore-gallery specializes in marionettes, Venetian masks, posters, postcards, and books on cinema and theater. Ask the owner to crank up the mechanical performing circus, complete with lion tamer, acrobats, and hypnotist. ♦ M-Sa. 161 Rue St-Martin (between Passage Molière and Rue aux Ours). 01.48.87.78.58. Métros: Rambuteau, Etienne-Marcel

26 AMBASSADE D'AUVERGNE

★★$$ Adorned with flickering oil lamps, a roaring fire, and cured hams dangling from heavy wood beams, this rustic restaurant serves hearty Massif Central cuisine. Specialties include *potée au choux* (stew), *aligot* (whipped potatoes, Cantal cheese, and cream), roast suckling pig, lentil cassoulet, and blood sausage with chestnuts. ♦ Daily, lunch and dinner. Reservations recommended. 22 Rue du Grenier-St-Lazare (between Rues Beaubourg and St-Martin). 01.42.72.31.22. Métro: Rambuteau

27 BOURSE DU COMMERCE (COMMERCIAL EXCHANGE)

One of the few buildings to escape the Les Halles demolition, this circular structure (built in 1887) is a graceful birthday cake of iron and glass. Not to be confused with the **Bourse des Valeurs** (the Roman temple to the north that houses the **Paris Stock Exchange**), this is where brokers in wheat, sugar, and other commodities do their trading. Beside the structure is a 101-foot classical column, topped with what appears to be a giant iron birdcage. This curiosity, called the **Horoscope Tower**, was once attached to the **Hôtel de la Reine** of Catherine de Médicis and accommodated her stargazing astrologer, Ruggieri, during the late 16th century. ♦ Reception/information: M-F; open to the public by appointment only. 2 Rue des Viarmes (at Rue Sauval). 01.55.65.55.65. Métro: Louvre–Rivoli

28 JARDIN DES HALLES

The razing of Les Halles market left 36 acres of open space, of which the western 12-acre section has been developed into an attractive tree-lined garden and children's playground in the shadow of **St-Eustache** church. Sad to say, drug dealers and their clients have gravitated here in recent years. The city of Paris has mounted a campaign to clear them out,

but if you happen to spot some suspicious-looking characters lurking about, that's probably what they are. Two escalators—one at Rue du Jour and the other to the south of the church—lead down to **Paul Chemetov**'s spacious subterranean concourse that opened in 1986 (see **Forum des Halles** on page 226). In the cobblestone plaza by **Porte St-Eustache**, be sure to note the colossal 70-ton stone head of a man with his chin in his hand. Sculpted by Henri de Miller, the statue is called *Ecoute*, presumably because it is listening to the church's beautiful organ music. ♦ Rue Rambuteau (between Rues Pierre-Lescot and du Jour). Métros: Les Halles, Châtelet

29 AU PÈRE TRANQUILLE

★$ French teenagers wearing penny loafers and fake US varsity-letter jackets crowd this late-night corner café. On a warm evening, order a kir on the terrace while you sit and watch the Les Halles parade pass by. Act III of e.e. cummings's play *Him* is set here. ♦ Daily, breakfast, lunch, and dinner until 2AM. 16 Rue Pierre-Lescot (at Rue des Précheurs). 01.45.08.00.34. Métro: Les Halles; RER: Châtelet–Les Halles

30 PASSAGE MOLIÈRE

Until recently a ramshackle spot with inexpensive tailor shops and one-room flats, this quaint 19th-century alleyway now houses art galleries, antiquarian bookshops, a small theater, and a tea salon. ♦ At 161 Rue St-Martin. Métro: Rambuteau

On Passage Molière:

GALERIE LUCETTE HERZOG

This gallery offers original prints and graphics by Alechinsky, Max Ernst, Bram Van Velde, Rassineux, Pandini, Tello, and others, along with some paintings and sculptures. ♦ W-F, 2:30-6:30PM; Sa. No. 23. 01.48.87.39.94

31 *DEFENDER OF TIME*

Inspired by the Rathaus clock in Munich, this 1-ton Jacques Monestier kinetic sculpture (1975) in oxidized brass sends a sword-brandishing warrior to do battle with a bird, crab, and dragon (representing the three elements: air, water, and earth). As every hour strikes, one of the beasts attacks, and at noon, 6PM, and 10PM, the *Defender of Time* is forced to take on all the creatures at once, always emerging victorious. A bit kitschy (as is this whole mini-shopping mall, the **Quartier de l'Horloge**), but young children love it. ♦ Rues Brantôme and Bernard-de-Clairvaux. Métro: Rambuteau

---

Restaurants/Clubs: Red | Hotels: Purple | Shops: Orange | Outdoors/Parks: Green | Sights/Culture: Blue

32 LE DUPLEX

Though true to its name the second level at this long-established watering hole away from the main Marais fray does little to create an impression of spaciousness, and though tiny and smoke-choked, its atmosphere has drawn a youthful crowd for years. And speaking of drawings, there is new artwork on the walls that supposedly changes monthly and often incorporates phallic motifs; for you to decide whether it's art or a diversionary tactic as you build up the nerve to try out your French on that dashing doctoral candidate pretending not to look your way from his perch near the tiny bar. ♦ Daily, 8PM-2AM. 25 Rue Michel-le-Comte (between Rues Beaubourg and du Temple). 01.42.72.80.86. Métro: Rambuteau

32 MONTORGUEIL

Want to feel like a movie star for the afternoon? Or simply fancy a *parenthèse de pure volupté*? Then book a beauty treatment at this day spa, located in a fabulously renovated wine storehouse hidden away in the heart of Les Halles (there's no sign; entrance is through a courtyard). One look at this space, with its high arched ceilings, exposed stone walls, and burbling artificial streams, is enough to start your chakras rebalancing, but there's more: a variety of facials using Nuxe spa products, numerous massages therapies, and revitalizing body treatments, including the *soin rêve de miel*: a nourishing, lipid-replenishing treatment for women involving, notably, copious amounts of acacia honey. There are only two treatment rooms, located on the basement level (where there is also a positively sybaritic *hammam*), but they are enormous. Upstairs is the reception area and Espace Coiffeur John Nollet, where the man who gave a certain *Amélie* her famous 'do can make your hair dreams come true. Not economically, of course. ♦ M-Sa, 10AM-7:30PM, by appointment. 32 Rue Montorgueil (between Rues Mauconseil and de Turbigo). 01.55.80.71.40. Métro: Les Halles

33 FORUM DES HALLES

Victor Baltard's 12 marvelous 19th-century iron-and-glass food halls were torn down in the early 1970s after the 800-year-old wholesale market was moved to Rungis near **Orly Airport** in 1969. In its place, **Claude Vasconi** and **Georges Pencreach** designed a four-level shopping mall. The silvery greenhouselike pavilions that form an L at the intersection of Rues Rambuteau and Pierre Lescot are just the proverbial tip of the iceberg. The three main levels are underground. This crater of consumerism is a labyrinth of 3.5 kilometers (2.2 miles) of walkways lined with more than 180 stores, dozens of snack bars and cafés, 12 restaurants, 28 cinemas, a recital hall, a multimedia center, a gymnasium, and an Olympic-size pool.

Niveau 3, the third level down, is the **Forum**'s "Main Street." It extends from Rue Pierre Lescot at the eastern end to **La Bourse du Commerce** at the west, a distance of five city blocks, and is very well lit by natural and artificial light. In the middle is an open-air plaza. On this level is the main branch of **FNAC** (01.40.41.40.00), a huge retailer of books, CDs, photos, and audio and video equipment and a popular hangout where teenagers come to buy concert tickets, peruse the latest *bandes dessinées* (hardcover comic books), and listen to the most current CDs on headsets. There are also roughly 100 boutiques for clothes, shoes, and accessories 17 eating places; **Piscine Les Halles** (01.42.36.98.44), an Olympic-size swimming pool; **Forum des Images**, a videotheque; and the 20 theaters of the **UGC Ciné Cité Les Halles** (08.92.70.00.00) complex, the largest and most technically advanced in Paris.

Be forewarned: You won't be alone here. An estimated 36 million visitors a year pass through the mall. According to a survey conducted by **McDonald's**, 80,000 pedestrians walk past its doors alone every day. To maneuver your way through this labyrinth, pick up a copy of *Le Guide du Forum des Halles de Paris*, a well-designed booklet that has a map and directory of all the establishments, at **Point d'Information** (01.44.76.96.56) on **Niveau 3** at the foot of the escalators in front of the main entrance to **FNAC**. To get there, take the escalator down from the **Porte Lescot** entrance to the **Forum**, at the corner of Rue Pierre-Lescot and Rue de la Cossonnerie.

Beneath the Forum is the **Châtelet–Les Halles** métro station. It is the world's largest underground train station, providing direct access to the métro, two RER lines (including the lines to the **Roissy–Charles-de-Gaulle** and **Orly Airports** and to **Disneyland Paris**), and various underground parking lots. ♦ 1 Rue Pierre-Lescot (at Rue Berger). Métro: Les Halles; RER: Châtelet-Les Halles

34 LE BON PÊCHEUR

$ When the adolescents at **Au Père Tranquille** grow up, they graduate to this smoky café across the street. Decorated with orange neon lights, mirrored columns, a zinc bar, and maps of Brazil on the wall, it offers salsa music on the stereo, *caipirinha* (the fiery Brazilian drink) for the thirsty, and such fare as quiche lorraine for the hungry. ♦ M-Th, Su, breakfast, lunch, and dinner until 2AM; F-Sa, breakfast, lunch, and dinner until 6AM. 12 Rue Pierre-Lescot (at Rue des Précheurs). 01.42.36.91.88. Métro: Les Halles; RER: Châtelet–Les Halles

35 RUE DE LA COSSONNERIE

Giovanni Boccaccio (1313–1375), considered one of the founders of the Italian Renaissance, was born on this 13th-century street. He was the author of *Filocolo* and the *Decameron*. ♦ RER: Châtelet–Les Halles

36 ESPACE VIT'HALLES

This popular health club, started in 1983 by French Olympic wrestler Christophe Andanson and his wife, Claudy, is one of the hottest underground (in the literal sense) singles spots in the district. Among the more than 1,000 members are **Pompidou Center** staffers flocking to aerobics classes and young **Bourse** financiers pumping iron as a respite from lusting after gold. The clean and affordable facilities include a sauna, tanning rooms, and bodybuilding equipment. Memberships are available for 1 day, 1 week, and longer. ♦ Daily. 48 Rue Rambuteau (at Rue Brantôme). 01.42.77.21.71. Métro: Rambuteau

37 GALERIE DANIEL TEMPLON

Daniel Templon helped launch conceptual art, language art, and a good deal of the "Support Surface" movement in France. His gallery is modeled after those in New York's SoHo. Among the many artists he now represents are Ross Bleckner, Eric Fischl, Raymond Hains, Sol LeWitt, Malcolm Morley, Philip Pearlstein, David Salle, Julian Schnabel, and Claude Viallat. (To gain entrance to the gallery, which does not front on the street, ring the bell and walk to the rear of the passageway; it's on the left.) ♦ M-Sa; closed in August. 30 Rue Beaubourg (between Rues Rambuteau and Michel-le-Comte). 01.42.72.14.10. Métro: Rambuteau

37 MUSÉE DE LA POUPÉE (DOLL MUSEUM)

This unusual museum is home to a private collection of over 200 porcelain-headed French dolls dating from 1860 to 1960, amassed by father and son Guido and Samy Odin. Each of the small museum's seven rooms is dedicated to an important phase of French dolldom or to themed temporary expositions often featuring dolls from other countries or dolls in regional costumes. The museum offers lectures on the history of dolls as well as doll-making classes,

and the gift shop carries a nice collection of stuffed animals, limited-edition porcelain dolls, and doll-related accessories. ♦ Admission. Museum: Tu-Su. Lectures: Th, 5:30PM, by reservation. Doll-making courses: M-Tu, by reservation. Impasse Berthaud (east of Rue Beaubourg). 01.42.72.73.11. Métro: Rambuteau

38 MUSÉE D'ART ET D'HISTOIRE DU JUDAÏSME (MUSEUM OF JEWISH ART AND HISTORY)

Located in the splendid 17th-century **Hôtel de St-Aignan**, this spacious modern museum traces the history, cultural heritage, and traditions of Jewish communities in the Middle East, North Africa, and Europe from the Middle Ages to the early 20th century through artistic expression. The museum's collection combines the holdings of the former **Museum of Jewish Art in Montmartre**, the Strauss-Rothschild collection from the **Musée National du Moyen Age** at the **Hôtel de Cluny**, and many new acquisitions from France and abroad. Among the noteworthy pieces in the permanent collection are medieval Jewish scriptures, tabernacles, silver ceremonial articles, gravestones, and sculptures; ritual objects and garments from North Africa; many old prints on the rituals and iconography of Judaism; more than 3,000 original documents relating to the Dreyfus Affair; paintings and sculptures by Soutine, Chagall, Modigliani, Lipchitz, and other Jewish modern artists who worked in France in the early 20th century; photographs of the Jewish immigrant community that lived in the Marais in the years before World War II; and an installation by Christian Boltanski evoking the history of the people who resided in the **Hôtel de St-Aignan** on the eve of the war, some of whom were deported to the death camps. The museum also mounts temporary art and photography exhibits—often on contemporary Jewish themes—and presents films, theatrical, and musical performances in the 180-seat auditorium. A research library, workshop for children, tearoom, and book and gift shop are also open to the public. ♦ Admission. M-F, 11AM-6PM; Su, 10AM-6PM. 71 Rue du Temple (between Rues Rambuteau and Michel-le-Comte). 01.53.01.86.60. Métro: Rambuteau

39 A LA TOUR DE MONTLHÉRY

★★$$ The owner, Denise, who tends *la caisse* (the cash register), serves her loyal clientele of wine merchants, advertising executives, and visiting English novelists such stick-to-the-ribs specialties as stuffed cabbage, mutton with beans, and steak with shallots. This a nice place to meet friends

---

Restaurants/Clubs: Red | Hotels: Purple | Shops: Orange | Outdoors/Parks: Green | Sights/Culture: Blue

over a bottle of Brouilly. ◆ 24 hours, M, 7AM-Sa,7AM; closed mid-July through mid-Aug. Reservations recommended. 5 Rue des Prouvaires (between Rues St-Honoré and Berger). 01.42.36.21.82. Métro: Châtelet

40 FONTAINE DES INNOCENTS

During the 16th century, Les Halles fishmongers and butchers drew their water from this fountain, which was commissioned by Henri II and designed by **Pierre Lescot** in 1547. An important relic of early Renaissance Paris, it stands on the site of what was once the overcrowded, foul-smelling **Church of the Holy Innocents** cemetery. In 1786 the church was razed and some two million skeletons were transported from the cemetery to a quarry in the Denfert-Rochereau area (14th arrondissement), which was then most appropriately renamed the **Catacombs** (see page 289). Later, during World War II, the **Catacombs** were the macabre setting for the headquarters of the French Resistance. Today, the area surrounding the fountain is the haunt of tattooed down-and-outers and indigent backpackers poring over out-of-print copies of *Europe on $30 a Day*. ◆ Sq des Innocents. Métro: Châtelet; RER: Châtelet–Les Halles

41 RUE QUINCAMPOIX

The Scottish financier John Law founded a bank on this narrow old street in 1719 after he became France's controller general, prompting a spurt of speculation in this part of the city. It later became a magnet for *les femmes de la nuit* ("women of the night"), photographed so remarkably by Brassaï in the 1930s. In recent years a rash of art galleries has sprung up here, drawn by the powerful magnet of the **Centre Georges Pompidou**. ◆ Between Rues des Lombards and aux Ours. Métros: Etienne-Marcel, Rambuteau, Châtelet; RER: Châtelet–Les Halles

On Rue Quincampoix:

46 RUE QUINCAMPOIX

The cinema and theater of the **Centre Wallonie-Bruxelles**, a Belgian cultural center, are located in this complex. Don't miss the startling entryway sculpture of an army of nudes bursting through the seams in the wall. ◆ Between Rues Aubry-le-Boucher and Rambuteau

42 GALERIE ALAIN BLONDEL

This gallery features early-20th-century works, large canvases from the 1930s, trompe l'oeil, and surrealism. ◆ Tu-Sa. 4 Rue Aubry-le-Boucher (at Rue Quincampoix). 01.42.78.66.67. Métro: Rambuteau; RER: Châtelet-Les Halles

43 PLACE GEORGES-POMPIDOU

The large inclined piazza on the west side of the **Centre Georges Pompidou** is home to an impromptu circus of folksingers, hypnotists, quick sketch artists, kerosene garglers, sword swallowers, Hare Krishnas, rowdies, acrobats, jugglers, and (be forewarned) purse snatchers and panhandlers who prey on gawking tourists. ◆ Métros: Rambuteau, Hôtel de Ville; RER: Châtelet–Les Halles

On Place Georges-Pompidou:

ATELIER BRANCUSI

Romanian-born Constantin Brancusi moved to Paris in 1904 and developed the pure, simple, and organic forms that made him one of Paris's greatest 20th-century sculptors. When he died in 1957, he willed his Left Bank atelier to France. The studio was eventually reconstructed here, with its original objects, and opened on the **Centre Georges Pompidou**'s 20th anniversary in 1997. It contains almost 140

Centre Georges Pompidou

sculptures, pedestals, sketches, and many of his photos. ♦ M, W-Su, 1PM-7PM

44 CENTRE GEORGES POMPIDOU (CENTRE NATIONAL D'ART ET DE CULTURE GEORGES POMPIDOU)

Critics took to calling the five-story jumble of glass and steel the "gasworks" and asked, "Who forgot to take the scaffolding down?" Still, this surrealistic Tinkertoy temple of modern culture is the second biggest attraction in Paris after the **Eiffel Tower** and outdraws the **Louvre**. A million people visited in 1977 during the first 7 weeks it was open, and there have been more than five million a year since. More than half of all visitors are under age 35.

Created at the behest of then-president Georges Pompidou (1911–1974) and designed by Italian **Renzo Piano** and Englishman **Richard Rogers** (whose proposal was selected from among a field of 681), the revolutionary (some say revolting) structure is home to one of the world's most important modern art museums (**Musée National d'Art Moderne/Centre de Création Industrielle**); Paris's largest public research library, with more than a half-million books (**Bibliothèque Publique d'Information**); an art workshop for children; a **Département du Développement Culturel** that puts on cinema and video arts programs in its screening rooms and dance, performance art, and lectures in theater and public spaces; and a classy sixth-floor restaurant with a four-star view.

The center also mounts several major temporary exhibits yearly. IRCAM (the **Institut de Recherche et de Coordination Acoustique/Musique**), one of the world's most advanced computer music laboratories, is part of the complex but is located in another building on the square (see page 231), as is the **Atelier Brancusi** (see above).

The high-tech design concept of the center celebrates the building's functional parts (heating ducts, ventilator shafts, stairways, and elevators) by brightly color-coding them: red for circulation of people, green for water, blue for air, yellow for electricity, white for external structure, gray for internal structure. An escalator in a Plexiglas tube snakes up the front of the complex, making the people a part of the design and offering them one of the city's best panoramic vistas, the grand sweep from Montmartre to Montparnasse, from the top floor. Pompidou, who was a patron of modern art as well as a politician, is immortalized by

Victor Vasarely in a hexagonal portrait that hangs on the ground floor. Unfortunately, innovation and popularity carry a price. The center was built with the expectation that an estimated 5,000 people would visit daily. Instead, an average of 16,600 came each day. The wear and tear was enormous—tarnished steel, peeling paint, shredded carpets, and even floors that bowed. Critics blame not just the crowds, but the design. "To put the bones and intestines outside the skin," said one, "is to invite health problems."

The center was closed in October 1997 for a massive renovation to correct these problems. It was also decided to expand the exhibition spaces and areas for cultural activities and move the administrative offices to another building. Renzo Piano and **Jean-François Bodin** were hired to plan a complete redevelopment of the interior. The center reopened on 1 January 2000.

For the latest information on the center's numerous exhibitions, film screenings, and other events, access its well-maintained web site, which is in English as well as French. ♦ Admission; entry to the museum's permanent collection is free on the first Sunday of every month. M, W-Su, 11AM-9PM. Pl Georges-Pompidou (between Pl Igor-Stravinsky and Rue St-Martin). 01.44.78.12.33. Métro: Rambuteau, Hôtel de Ville, Châtelet–Les Halles; RER: Les Halles. www.centrepompidou.fr

Within the Centre Georges Pompidou:

MUSÉE NATIONAL D'ART MODERNE/CENTRE DE CRÉATION INDUSTRIELLE (MNAM/CCI)

One of the world's largest collections of modern and contemporary paintings, sculptures, graphic art, photographs, films, new media, architecture, and design is displayed here. The period covered begins with the Fauves in the first decade of the 20th century and goes up through the Cubist, Dadaist, Surrealist, Abstract Expressionist, Pop Art, Nouveaux Réalistes, Conceptual Art, and other major movements of the century, to the museum's latest acquisitions of works by contemporary artists. The permanent collection includes important works by Matisse, Bonnard, Duchamp, Picasso, Braque, Gris, Léger, Kandinsky, Delaunay, Klee, Mondrian, Chagall, Brancusi, Calder, Giacometti, Dalí, Magritte, Miró, Balthus, De Staël, Kline,

---

Restaurants/Clubs: Red | Hotels: Purple | Shops: Orange | Outdoors/Parks: Green | Sights/Culture: Blue

Pollock, de Kooning, Newman, Kelly, Warhol, Moore, Bacon, Johns, Alechinsky, Hantaï, Beuys, Serra, and many others.

The museum owns more than 50,000 works of art, and to try to bring as many of them as possible to the public's attention, the galleries are rehung about every 6 months, with the most numerous changes being made among the most recent works. The fourth floor is devoted to the museum's contemporary collection (1960 to the present) of paintings; sculptures; graphics; photographs; film, video, and other media; architecture; and design. The fifth floor houses modern art (1900 through the 1950s) from the permanent collection. Most of the top floor (which it shares with the restaurant) is set aside for temporary exhibits. Fourth, fifth, sixth floors

Georges

★★$$ The domed brushed-aluminum dining spaces and spectacular airiness of this ultra-contemporary brasserie give it the feel of a mellow sci-fi movie set. The cuisine is in line with that of the other Costes Brothers' eateries: pleasant but undistinguished World and traditional French dishes and light fare (salads, club sandwiches, omelettes). Or you can simply have a drink. Museum-goers keep the cool, fashion model–like waitresses busy during the day, and a hip crowd takes over in the evening. The outdoor dining terrace offers an unbeatable view of the Paris cityscape by day or by night. ♦ M, W-Su, noon-2AM. Sixth floor. Direct access from the piazza by elevator noon-9PM and by escalator from Rue Rambuteau after that. 01.44.78.47.99

Bibliothèque Publique d'Information (BPI)

Occupying the second and third floors of the center, this huge general research library with more than a half-million books on its open-

Tennis went professional in 1687 when the top competitors in Paris started getting paid for playing matches.

The most strikingly original building of the 1990s in Paris was Frank Gehry's American Center headquarters. Completed in 1994, the fanciful $40 million arts center in eastern Paris's Parc de Bercy won the architect the prestigious Pritzker Prize. The American Center promptly went bankrupt, however, and the building closed almost as soon as it had opened. The French government purchased it in 1998 and at press time was remodeling it for use as a cinema center, due to open in 2003.

stack shelves attracts 12,000 users per day. Most of the books are in French, but there are many in English on practically all subjects, including a substantial collection of literary works. The collection is very strong in photography and art. The library carries 2,500 current periodicals, including 400 from the international press. It also has stereo setups for listening to its 10,000 CDs; VCRs to view its more than 2,400 documentaries; a modern language-study laboratory with inter-active audio programs; 200 CD-ROM reference disks; and 400 computer terminals for consulting catalogs, CD-ROMs, the Minitel, and the Internet. Anyone can use the library, and everything is free, except for the photo-copiers. ♦ M-F, noon-10PM; Sa-Su, 11AM-10PM. 2nd and 3rd floors. 01.44.78.12.75. www.bpi.fr

45 Rue de la Ferronnerie

Henri IV was murdered here in his carriage on 14 May 1610 as he passed along Ironmongers Row. His assassin, Ravaillac, was quartered by four horses in the Place de Grève, today called Place de l'Hôtel-de-Ville. ♦ Métro: Châtelet

On Rue de la Ferronnerie:

Papeterie Moderne

If you've got enough patience to sort through this store's marvelous hodgepodge of old Parisian signs (for streets, butcher shops, bakeries, and the like), you can take home a fine souvenir. A copy of anything in the store may be ordered; allow 10 days for pickup. ♦ M-Sa; closed 1 week in Aug. 12 Rue de la Ferronnerie. 01.42.36.21.72

46 Ducs d'Anjou

$$ This pleasant 34-room hotel sits just off the charming Place Ste-Opportune. Rooms on the courtyard are somber but comfortable. There's no restaurant. ♦ 1 Rue Ste-Opportune (at Pl Ste-Opportune). 01.42.36.92.24; fax 01.42.36.16.63. Métro: Châtelet

47 Au Diable des Lombards

★$ Cheeseburgers, rabbit terrine, and homemade ice cream are among the menu items at this trendy bistro. ♦ Daily, 9AM-1:30AM. 64 Rue des Lombards (between Rues St-Denis and Ste-Opportune). 01.42.33.81.84. Métro: Châtelet

Café Beaubourg

48 Café Beaubourg

★★$$ From the *terrasse* (terrace) of this chic yet surprisingly relaxed café, you'll have a perfect vantage on the ever-amusing comings and goings around the **Pompidou Center**. Or if the weather's inclement, move into architect **Christian de Portzamparc**'s soaring interior. Inside or out, this place offers first-rate wines and practically anything else you can think of imbibing; brunch all day; a fine selection of sandwiches, salads, grilled fish and meat, snacks, desserts; and copies of *Le Monde* and *Libération*. ♦ Su-Th, breakfast, lunch, and dinner until 12AM; F-Sa, breakfast, lunch, and dinner until 1AM. 100 Rue St-Martin (between Rue du Cloître-St-Merri and Pl Georges-Pompidou). 01.48.87.63.96. Métros: Rambuteau, Hôtel de Ville; RER: Châtelet–Les Halles

49 LES VIENNOISERIES DE ST-MEDARD

What a treat in this modish neighborhood to find an old-time bakery complete with a rosy-cheeked baker proudly displaying her fresh brioches, croissants, and tarts on the white marble counters! ♦ M, W-Su. 81 Rue St-Martin (between Rue des Lombards and Pl Edmond-Michelet). 01.42.72.84.24. Métros: Hôtel de Ville, Chatelet; RER: Châtelet–Les Halles

50 IRCAM (INSTITUT DE RECHERCHE ET DE COORDINATION ACOUSTIQUE/MUSIQUE)

One of the world's most advanced computer music centers is located in an innovative building with a brick panel façade designed by **Renzo Piano**. Toiling away in the institute's underground reaches, leading modern composer Pierre Boulez's studio of composers and electronic engineers is creating the music of the future. The building is usually not open to visitors, but you can enter the ground-floor level for information about concerts by L'Ensemble InterContemporain and the public lectures that frequently take place here. ♦ By appointment only. 1 Pl Igor-Stravinsky (between Rue du Cloitre-St-Merri and Pl Georges-Pompidou). 01.44.78.48.43. Métros: Rambuteau, Hôtel de Ville; RER: Châtelet–Les Halles. www.ircam.fr

51 FONTAINE DE STRAVINSKY

The fantastic and frivolous ballet of squirting animals, serpents, and mermaids in this lively fountain created by Niki de Saint-Phalle and Jean Tinguely makes this a great spot for an urban picnic. Several inexpensive eating places line the eastern side of the square overlooking the fountain, including a branch of the imaginative **Dame Tartine** (2 Rue Brisemiche; 01.42.77.32.22). ♦ Pl Igor-Stravinsky. Métros: Rambuteau, Hôtel de Ville; RER: Châtelet–Les Halles

52 THE STUDIO

★$ In a 17th-century cobblestone courtyard it shares with several dance studios, this Tex-Mex canteen serves margaritas, chili, *botanas* (snacks), and other Tex-Mex standards that are copious but denatured for the Franco-gringo clientele. The pleasure here is in the ambiance, especially in fair weather, when you can sit at tables in the courtyard and watch the dancers in the first-floor studios go through their paces. A traditional North American brunch is served on the weekend. ♦ M, dinner; Tu-F, lunch and dinner; Sa-Su, brunch and dinner. 41 Rue du Temple (between Rues St-Merri and Simon-le-Franc). 01.42.74.10.38. Métro: Rambuteau

53 VIEUX MARAIS

$$ In a handsome 18th-century town house a few steps from the **Centre Georges Pompidou**, this tastefully modernized 30-room hotel decorated with Chinese carpets and floral wallpaper gives guests a warm welcome and comfortable rooms with phones, TVs, air conditioning, marble bathrooms, and soundproofed windows. There's a tearoom but no restaurant. ♦ 8 Rue du Plâtre (between Rues des Archives and du Temple). 01.42.78.47.22; fax 01.42.78.34.32. Métro: Rambuteau

54 RUE DE LA VERRERIE

This narrow street, which takes its name from the 11th-century glassblowers' guild, is where Jacquemin Gringoneur once lived. He invented playing cards to amuse King Charles VI ("The Beloved"), who ruled between 1380 and 1422. ♦ Métros: Hôtel de Ville, Châtelet

54 HÔTEL ST-MERRY

$$$ You needn't be religious to get a kick out of a flying buttress over your bed, but that comes with the territory at what is the most unique hotel in Paris. It's no coincidence that the Gothic **Eglise St-Merry** is right next door—this was its presbytery in the 17th century. Stone, exposed beams, dark wood paneling, heavy wooden furniture, and wrought iron abound, making what anyplace else would have been a Gothic dream into reality. Of the hotel's dozen rooms, the top-floor suite is the most spectacular with its view of the Paris rooftops (rooms 6, 12, and 18 also have pleasant views), and room 9 has the flying buttresses. These comfortable, restful guest

rooms are as far away from cookie-cutter as you can get, and, despite modern bathrooms and amenities, easily make you forget what century this is. On top of the architectural draws, this small hotel is professionally run and the welcome is warm. Advance reservations recommended. ◆ 78 Rue de la Verrerie (at Rue St-Martin). 01.42.78.14.15; fax 01.40.29.06.82. Métros: Châtelet-Les Halles or Hôtel de Ville

55 GRIZZLI CAFÉ

★$ This midsize, bi-level café and bistro strikes a nice balance between classic and contemporary, and comes as a cozy refuge from the endless bustle of Les Halles. The street-level terrace makes for a popular spot to linger over coffee or brunch, whereas upstairs the sleek décor is better suited to evening victuals. As for the menu, you can count on a variety of competently prepared meat and fish dishes as well as a good selection of salads and a pasta dish or two. The food can be uneven but desserts are uniformly good. ◆ Daily, 9AM-2PM. 7 Rue St-Martin (between Rues des Lombards and Pernelle). 01.48.87.77.56. Métro: Châtelet or Hôtel de Ville

56 BENOIT

★★★$$$ You need not take the train to Lyon to savor blood sausage with apples and roast potatoes, crab soup, or duckling with turnips. This charming 1912 bistro with yellow mock-antique walls and red plush dining banquettes is frequented by French businesspeople who definitely know their business when it comes to good eating. ◆ Daily, lunch and dinner; closed in Aug. Reservations required; AmEx only. 20 Rue St-Martin (at Rue Pernelle). 01.42.72.25.76. Métros: Châtelet, Hotel de Ville

57 MÉRRI NEWS

Bright, well stocked with French and English titles (for 12 euros, the Sunday New York Times can be yours) and greeting cards and postcards, some of which, in deference to or celebration of the neighborhood, have a homoerotic tilt, this is the area's best newsstand/stationer's shop. ◆ M-Sa, 11AM-8PM, Su, noon-7PM. 68 Rue de la Verrerie (at Rue des Juges-Consuls). 01.44.54.04.02. Métro: Hôtel de Ville

58 LE CARRÉ

*$ Widescreen, wall-mounted plasma television screens may beam the latest fashion shows to hungry hipsters at this upscale canteen, but despite a trendy look, service is friendly and portions generous. Choose from a variety of salads, interesting fish dishes such as salmon with candied shredded cabbage, or just sip a cocktail and join your fellow diners

in the not necessarily subtle sport of people-watching. Late hours make this a neighborhood favorite. ◆ Daily, 10AM-4AM. 18 Rue du Temple (between Rues Ste-Croix de la Bretonnerie and de la Verrerie). 01.44.59.38.57. Métro: Hôtel de Ville

59 MAISON ROUGE

★$$ With its surfeit of square footage and minimalist tables packed with everyone from tourists with wailing infants to pierced, chain-smoking poseurs, this self-consciously hip grazing station feels a bit like the airport lounge of the very near future. The slick red motif is not as grating as the steep prices which range from a 10-euro plate of berries to a 16-euro plate of steamed vegetables, which can be accompanied by a 5-euro glass of milk. The bizarre menu categories include "Betty Ford suggestions"—a range of 11-euro cocktails—and Sunday "brunch chic." On the plus side, service is continuous after noon, making this a suitable place to fuel up for exploring the neighborhood's worthier attractions. ◆ Daily, noon-3AM. 13 Rue des Archives (between Rues Ste-Croix-de-la-Bretonnerie and de-la-Verrerie). 01.42.71.69.69. Métro: Hôtel de Ville

MARAIS

This district in eastern Paris has been known as the *marais* (marsh) since Roman times. It was a vast, oozy swamp on the northern branch of the Seine until the 12th century, when the marsh was drained, making it habitable for humans. Like New York's fashionable SoHo district, the Marais is now a mélange of ruin and restoration, past and present. The historically rich neighborhood possesses at least one Roman road (along Rues François-Miron and St-Antoine), what may be the city's oldest house (a 14th-century, half-timbered structure at 3 Rue Volta), and numerous twisting, huddled medieval streets.

Among those streets are three (**Rues des Rosiers, des Ecouffes**, and **Ferdinand-Duval**) that are the backbone of the celebrated Jewish quarter, formed in the 13th century when King Philippe Auguste "invited" the Jewish merchants living in front of **Notre-Dame** to move outside his new city wall.

Seven French kings resided in the Marais, starting with Charles V (1337–1380). Henri II (1519–1559) was the last; he died during a freak jousting accident when the shattered lance of Montgomery, the captain of his Scots Guards, pierced the visor of his helmet. Henri's wife, Catherine de Médicis, tried to ease her grief by having their royal **Maison des Tournelles** in the Marais demolished.

A half-century after the accident, Henri IV chose to construct the **Place Royale** on the leveled crown land in the Marais. Its name was changed in 1800 to **Place des Vosges** to honor the Vosges in eastern France, which was the first provincial department to pay its taxes after the revolution. "It's the blow of Montgomery's lance," Victor

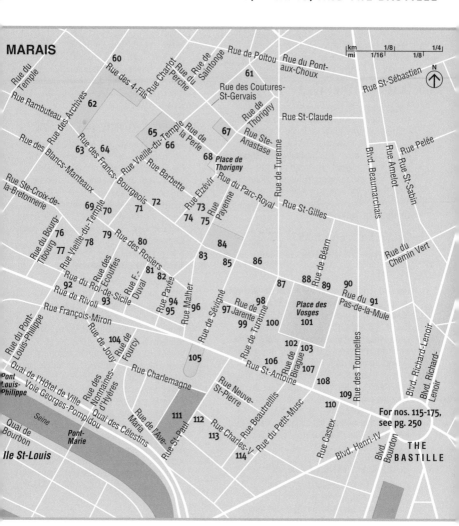

ugo later wrote, "that created the Place des Vosges."

he Marais and Place Royale (des Vosges) figured prominently in Henri IV's building boom in the 17th entury, which also included Pont-Neuf, Place Dauphine, nd Ile St-Louis. In the Marais, the king employed the eading architects of the day: **Louis Le Vau**, **François Mansart**, and **Jules Hardouin-Mansart**.

uring this era, Mademoiselle de Scudéry, Molière, Racine, adame de Lafayette, and Madame de Sévigné were xchanging witty party conversation in the great salons of e Marais that Molière parodied in his play Les Précieuses idicules. Within a century, the former swamp had become e heart of intellectual Paris. In 1630 Cardinal Richelieu, Marais resident, founded the **Académie Française** here, nd years later a 7-year-old Mozart played his first Paris oncert in the Marais. This area became an island of urban vility and sophistication, far removed from the wild boars nd party boors of Versailles.

After the revolution the elegant town houses were abandoned or carved into small factories and rooming houses. Squatters took over, and the Marais fell into a shocking state of ruin. Over the centuries, 29 of the grand hôtels particuliers were destroyed; nearly 100 remained, dilapidated and on the verge of collapse. In 1964 André Malraux, minister of culture under Charles de Gaulle, came to the rescue and designated the Marais the first historic preservation district in Paris. Within its boundaries are 1,500 architecturally important structures, making the Marais the largest historic district in France.

Many of the old buildings have been given new life, as you'll see when you visit the **Archives Nationales**, **Musée Carnavalet** (the city's historical museum), the famous **Place des Vosges**, and the **Musée Picasso**. The Marais quarter, once a juxtaposition of splendor and squalor, is almost all splendor now. On Sundays the

---

Restaurants/Clubs: Red | Hotels: Purple | Shops: Orange | Outdoors/Parks: Green | Sights/Culture: Blue

quartier is particularly animated, because unlike the rest of Paris, most of the shops here are open. Fashion victims would do well to indulge themselves in the upscale boutiques along Rue des Francs-Bourgeois.

60 RUE DES ARCHIVES

For generations, the lower section of this street bore the name **Rue où Dieu fut Bouilli** ("Street Where God Was Boiled") after the legend of the moneylender who stabbed a communion wafer with his knife, then threw it into a steaming pot, where, to his astonishment, it began to bleed. ♦ Métros: Hôtel de Ville, Rambuteau, Arts et Metiers

On Rue des Archives:

MUSÉE DE LA CHASSE ET DE LA NATURE (MUSEUM OF THE HUNT)

Housed in a portion of the **Hôtel de Guénégaud** (1654) and designed by **François Mansart**, this museum presents three floors full of hunting paraphernalia and related items, including crossbows, muskets, game trophies, whole stuffed animals, and paintings of hunting dogs and animals by the likes of Rubens and Brueghel. Among the most lavish paeans to the slaughter are the paintings of Desportes, the court artist employed by Louis XIV to portray the royal hunts at **Versailles**. ♦ Admission. M, W-Su. No. 60 (at Rue des Quatre-Fils). 01.42.72.86.43

61 GALERIE YVON LAMBERT

Works by On Kawara, LeWitt, Twombly, Schnabel, Nan Goldin, and Boltanski are showcased here. ♦ Tu-Sa. 108 Rue Vieille-du-Temple (between Rues de Coutures-St-Gervais and de Poitou). 01.42.71.09.33. Métro: St-Sébastien–Froissart

62 ARCHIVES NATIONALES/MUSÉE DE L'HISTOIRE DE FRANCE

The letters of Joan of Arc and Voltaire, the wills of Louis XIV and Napoléon I, a papyrus signed by Merovingian King Dagobert (622-638), the Edict of Nantes, the Declaration of the Rights of Man, and 6 billion other documents are stored on 175 miles of shelves in this admirable 18th-century mansion, the former **Hôtel Soubise**. Even if you have no interest in French history, the museum's fortified turrets, colonnaded courtyard (72 Corinthian columns in all), and the riot of rococo in the **Oval Salon** make a visit worthwhile. Designed by **Pierre-Alexis Delamair** for François de Rohan, the prince of Soubise, the mansion has an ornate interior (1739) that was engineered by **Germain Boffrand**, a pupil of **François Mansart**. Boffrand hired the best artists of the day, among them François

Boucher and Charles Natoire, to decorate the hotel. The archives, housed in the Hôtel Soubise since 1808, expanded into the adjacent **Hôtel de Rohan** in 1927. ♦ Admission. M-Sa. 60 Rue des Francs-Bourgeois (at Rue des Archives). 01.40.27.60.00. Métro: Rambuteau

63 CRÉDIT MUNICIPAL DE PARIS

Paris's first municipal pawnshop is still a place for hocking ("putting it on the nail," as the French say). Auctions, especially for jewelry, are frequent and well attended; check the notices posted outside. ♦ M-Th; F, 8:30AM-3:45PM. 55 Rue des Francs-Bourgeois (between Rues Vieille-du-Temple and des Archives). 01.44.61.64.00. Métro: Rambuteau

63 LE DÔME DU MARAIS

★★$$ Covered by a large glass rotunda, sumptuously adorned with scarlet walls and bronze statues, this trading house–turned-restaurant is a romantic spot for lunch or especially for dinner. Chef Pierre Lecoutre, formerly of L'Atlantide in Nantes, took over the restaurant in 1998 and has introduced imaginative dishes such as *filet de dorade grise au citron et confit de tomate* (fillet of gray dorade with lemon and preserved tomatoes), *pigeonet de pays de Racan grillé avec onions et épices* (squab grilled with onions and spices), and pheasant with endives. There is a fine list of Loire wines. ♦ M, Sa, dinner; Tu-F, lunch and dinner; closed in Aug. Reservations recommended. 53 *bis* Rue des Francs-Bourgeois (between Rues Vieille-du-Temple and des Archives). 01.42.74.54.17. Métro: Rambuteau

64 NICKEL

Is that John Malkovich emerging from a miracle manicure? Or Isseye Miyake indulging in a "love handle" body treatment? It's quite possible, though discretion is the byword at this no-attitude day spa for men, precursor to the larger Nickel in New York City. President Philippe Dumont's spa philosophy is that "men want a straightforward approach—nothing magical, just basic, clean skin care." There are only four treatment rooms here, where clients—some 40 percent of whom are not French—can choose from a range of facial treatments, massages, and other spa treatments, including epilation. Spend an afternoon here and you'll emerge just as *nickel*—that's French slang for spotless—as this spiffy blue-and-white establishment, which also has a boutique where the spa's own line of products are sold. Appointments recommended. ♦ M-Sa. 48 Rue des Francs-Bourgeois (between Rues des Archives and Vieille-du-Temple). 01.42.77.41.10. Métro: Hôtel de Ville or St-Paul

65 HÔTEL DE ROHAN

In 1705 the son of François de Rohan, prince-bishop of Strasbourg, commissioned **Pierre-Alexis Delamair** to build a mansion opposite the **Hôtel Soubise**, where his parents lived. In the courtyard to the right, above the entrance to the former stables, is one of the masterpieces of 18th-century French sculpture: Robert Le Lorrain's superb relief sculpture *The Watering of the Horses of the Sun*. The building sometimes houses temporary exhibitions. ♦ 87 Rue Vieille-du-Temple (between Rues des Francs-Bourgeois and des Quatre-Fils). Métros: Rambuteau, St-Sebastien–Froissart

66 LES PETITS MARSEILLAIS

**$$ A little beyond the central Marais fray but big on cheer and sunny Provençal flavors, this spot—owned by two friends from Marseille—is a neighborhood favorite for lunch and dinners that carry on long into the night. The strong points of the small menu are the fish dishes and pastas, though heartier fare such as lamb is usually available, too. The service is generally remarkably friendly and the clientele sociable. On the plus side, that means you may end up chatting with an artist or designer from the *quartier*; on the downside, your clothes might emerge smelling as if you've just escaped a fire at the Marlboro factory. Daily, lunch and dinner. ♦ 72 Rue Vieille-du-Temple (between Rues de la Perle and Barbette). 01.42.78.91.59. Métro: Hôtel de Ville or St-Paul

67 MUSÉE PICASSO

"Give me a museum and I'll fill it up," said Pablo Picasso, one of the 20th century's most important and prolific painters. His wish was granted posthumously here in the **Hôtel Salé**, a 17th-century building that undoubtedly would have pleased the artist, who epitomized outlaw Modernism yet preferred old houses. In the first month after it opened on 23 September 1985, this museum received 80,000 visitors. Today the mansion enshrines the artist's collection of his own works, the largest assembling of Picassos in the world: 203 paintings, 158 sculptures, 16 collages, 29 relief paintings, 88 ceramics, 30 sketch-books, more than 1,500 drawings, and numerous prints, including the *Vollard Suite*, his neoclassical etchings created in the 1920s. The museum also houses Picasso's personal art collection, including works by Matisse, Renoir, Cézanne, Braque, Balthus, and Le Douanier Rousseau.

Ironically, as late as 1945, there were only three Picassos in public collections in France, a handful far outnumbered by the many in the possession of the Museum of Modern Art in New York. But when Picasso died in 1973 with no will, France's tax collectors were quick to pounce on his estate, and in lieu of $65 million in inheritance taxes, Picasso's heirs donated a quarter of his vast personal collection to the state.

The Hôtel Salé has but a few of Picasso's masterpieces, *Still Life with Caned Chair*, *Two Women Running on Beach*, and the Neo-Classical *Pipes of Pan* among them. However, the works here are exhibited chronologically, and the collection affords an extraordinary odyssey through the artist's growth and psyche. Furthermore, revealing Picasso memorabilia are sprinkled throughout the museum: photos of Picasso at bullfights, posing on the beach with a fig leaf, hoisting a bull's skull at the beach of Golfe-Juan, playing with his children, and consorting with such friends as Jean Cocteau and Max Jacob. Also throughout the museum are portraits of the women in Picasso's life: Olga Kokhlova, the Russian dancer; Marie-Thérèse Walter, the 17-year-old earth mother; Dora Maar, the intellectual; Françoise Gilot, the painter; and his widow, Jacqueline.

Among the museum's artistic highlights are the wintry 1901 Blue Period *Self-Portrait at Age 20* in **room 1**; sketches and drawings inspired by Cézanne's geometrical style and by the primitive sculpture from Africa and New Caledonia, including sketches for *Les Demoiselles d'Avignon* in **rooms 2** and **3**; *Still Life with Cane Chair* and other works reflecting Picasso's years of Cubist inquiry (1909–1917) with Georges Braque in **room 4**; several small rooms featuring paper collages and three-dimensional paintings made of cigar-box wood, newspapers, and metal shards; the best of the 60 works in Picasso's personal art collection in **room 5**, including masterpieces by Matisse, Braque, Rousseau, and Cézanne; *La Lecture de la Lettre* and *The Pipes of Pan* from his classical period in **room 6**; and Picasso's theater and costume designs in his collaborations with Cocteau, Massine, Stravinsky, and Diaghilev in **room 6B**. Near the end of Picasso's life, his art became childlike and cartoonish. The last painting in the collection, dated 14 April 1972, is called *Young Painter*, a sketchy image of a smiling dauber. In his final years the artist confessed, "It has taken all my life to learn how to paint like a child again." Picasso's playfulness is perhaps most evident in his sculpture, which is fashioned from an amusing assortment of odds and ends. En route to the exit, descend into the museum's basement to find his sculpture collection, with originals of his celebrated monkey, goat, and skipping girl.

Restaurants/Clubs: Red | Hotels: Purple | Shops: Orange | Outdoors/Parks: Green | Sights/Culture: Blue

The Hôtel Salé was built between 1655 and 1659 by architect **Jean Bouillier** for Pierre Aubert de Fontenay, a man who got rich collecting taxes on salt for the king—hence the name *Salé*, meaning "salty." After numerous owners and uses over the following centuries (the Venetian Republic's embassy, a boys' school where Balzac studied, a science laboratory, an exhibition hall for a bronze foundry), French Minister of Culture Michel Guy took a 99-year lease on the building after Picasso's death, committed 65 million francs to its restoration, and selected **Roland Simounet**, winner of the 1977 Grand Prix for Architecture, to design the museum. Simounet's approach was to preserve the architectural integrity of the building while doubling its interior space from 9,900 to 19,800 square feet. He was highly successful on both counts, as all visitors will readily agree. ♦ Admission. April-Sept, M, W-Sa, 9:30AM-6PM; Oct-Mar, M, W-Su, 9:30AM-5:30PM. 5 Rue de Thorigny (at Rue des Coutures-St-Gervais). 01.42.71.25.21. Métros: St-Paul, St-Sébastien–Froissart

Within the Musée Picasso:

MUSEUM RESTAURANT

★$ Salads, quiche, soups, grilled salmon, and fruit tarts are served in this small, attractive tea salon. ♦ M, W-Su, breakfast, lunch, and afternoon tea. 01.42.71.25.21

68 MUSÉE DE LA SERRURE (LOCK MUSEUM)/BRICARD SHOWROOMS

Roman door knockers, medieval chastity belts, and the key of the now-destroyed **Cimetière des Innocents** may be seen in the changing exhibits of this small, quirky museum, established by the time-honored locksmithing company Bricard and housed in the **Hôtel Libéral Bruant**. (Architect Bruant built this mansion as his residence, and it is considered his most important work after the **Hôtel des Invalides** and the **Salpêtrière**

chapel.) The museum has been relegated to the building's vaulted cellar, whereas handmade replicas of some of the museum pieces, such as the lock to Marie Antoinette's **Versailles** apartments, are sold in the **Bricard Showrooms**. Here you can also examine the rich detailing and historical styles of other Bricard products. ♦ Admission. Museum: Tu-Th, 10AM-2PM, 4-5PM. Showroom: M-F, 8:30AM-12:30PM, 1:30-5:30PM. 1 Rue de l Perle (at Pl de Thorigny). Museum, 01.42.77.79.62; showroom, 01.42.77.71.68. Métros: Chemin Vert, St-Sébastien–Froissart, St-Paul

69 HÔTEL DES AMBASSADEURS DE HOLLANDE

When this Baroque mansion (built in 1660) was named, there were no Dutch ambassadors to France, and none has ever lived here. (The building did, however, belong to the chaplain of the Dutch Embassy between 1720 and 1727.) Subsequently, the hotel was rebuilt by Pierre Cottard; its most famous resident was Beaumarchais, author c *The Marriage of Figaro* and *The Barber of Seville*. The great wooden doors are embellished by what look like howling Medusas or perhaps a pair of baritones warming up. ♦ 47 Rue Vieille-du-Temple (between Rues Ste-Croix-de-la-Bretonnerie and des Blancs-Manteaux). Métro: St-Paul

70 LE COLIMACON

★★$$ A pretty stone façade, built in 1732 b **Louis Le Tellier**, graces this popular restaurant. Inside, guests dine in a romantic setting of fresh floral arrangements, candlelight, and superb service. Such specialties as foie gras and *magret de canard landais aux fruits de saison* (duck's breast with seasonal fruit) are popular favorites. There's also a good wine list. The restaurant is named for its elegant spiral staircase. ♦ M, W-Su, dinner. Reservations required. 44 Rue Vieille-du-Temple (between Rues des Rosiers and des Francs-Bourgeois). 01.48.87.12.01. Métro: St-Paul

71 A.POC

When you enter this airy white, minimalist space, you may think you've wandered into a minimalist art gallery or even an upscale dry cleaner's shop. But the petite single-color outfits strategically placed on the shop's only table will convince you that you are in designer Issey Miyake's most recent boutique A.POC, according to the master, is short for " piece of cloth"—a dress made out of a single piece of cloth that envelops the entire body—and here the customer has her own say in th design. The mother house, called simply **Isse Miyake**, is down the street at 3 Place des Vosges (between Rues de Birague and des

Francs-Bourgeois). 01.47.87.01.86. A book on Miyake's life and art is on sale for those who want to further investigate his aesthetics and methods. ◆ Tu-Sa. 47 Rue des Francs-Bourgeois (between Rues Pavée and Vieille-du-Temple). 01.44.54.07.05. Métro: St-Paul

71 A L'IMAGE DU GRENIER SUR L'EAU

Brothers Yves and Sylvain Di Maria have spent the last 2 decades assembling this remarkable collection of more than a million vintage postcards of locales from Avignon to Zaire, each one for sale. This shop, with its original tiled floors, also features French publicity photos from the 1950s and lithographs from the Art Nouveau period. ◆ M-Sa; Su, 2-7PM. 45 Rue des Francs-Bourgeois (between Rues Pavée and Hospitalières-St-Gervais). 01.42.71.02.31. Métro: St-Paul

72 RUE DES FRANCS-BOURGEOIS

Originally called **Rue des Poulies** ("Street of Spools") after a local community of weavers, this thoroughfare became known as the "Street of the Free Citizens" in the 14th century, when the local parish built an almshouse (on the site of 34-36 Rue des Francs-Bourgeois) for citizens so poor they were *francs* (free) of any obligation to the state tax jackals. Today affluent shoppers flock to the chic and unusual shops that line the street, especially on Sunday, when they are open, while most shops in Paris are closed. ◆ Métros: Rambuteau, St-Paul

72 THE FILOFAX CENTRE

Here you'll find everything to gratify your Filofax fetish. The famous pocket-size, three-ring English notebooks come in myriad styles, from black leather to rubber, and with notepaper of every hue. Also in stock are sheaves of maps, calendars, and metric conversion charts to store in your portable file cabinet, as well as a beautiful collection of handmade sterling silver pens. ◆ M-Sa. 32 Rue des Francs-Bourgeois (between Rues Elzévir and Vieille-du-Temple). 01.42.78.67.87. Métro: St-Paul

73 MUSÉE COGNACQ-JAY

This marvelously complete collection of 18th-century art was acquired by the husband-and-wife team of Louise Jay and Ernest Cognacq, who created **La Samaritaine** department stores and boasted of never having set foot in the **Louvre**. The collection was moved to the 5-story, 16th-century **Hôtel Donon**, and the works of Boucher, Tiepolo, Watteau, Fragonard, Greuze, La Tour,

Rembrandt, Gainsborough, and Reynolds are as well displayed here as they were in their old home on Boulevard des Capucines. There's also a remarkable set of perfume cases and snuffboxes as well as Meissen porcelain statuettes. ◆ Admission. Tu-Su. 8 Rue Elzévir (between Rues des Francs-Bourgeois and du Parc-Royal). 01.40.27.07.21. Métro: St-Paul

74 LUTHIER

Owner M. Brué buys, sells, makes, and restores violins, violas, bows, and old instruments at these quarters in the **Hôtel de Savourny**. ◆ W-Sa. 4 Rue Elzévir (between Rues des Francs-Bourgeois and du Parc-Royal). 01.42.77.68.42. Métro: St-Paul

75 GALLERY MAISON MANSART

The ground floor of the house **François Mansart** built for himself (and inhabited until his death in 1666) now houses Alain Thiollier's stark, high-ceilinged gallery, which exhibits contemporary works by an international group of artists every month except August. On the second floor is a chapel (with an altar inscribed to "Humanism") built by a Brazilian follower of French positivist Auguste Comte. The chapel is not open to the public, but inquire about the occasional Baroque music concerts that are held here. ◆ Tu-Sa, 3-6PM; closed in August. 5 Rue Payenne (between Rues des Francs-Bourgeois and du Parc-Royal). 01.48.87.41.03. Métro: St-Paul

76 MARIAGE FRÈRES

★★★$$ Teatime was never more toothsome than at this handsome, uniquely Parisian tea salon and boutique extraordinaire. The brothers Mariage founded their house of tea in 1854 when French incursions into the tropics were in full swing, and that colonial heritage colors the selection of teas today—which number more than 500—and overall aesthetic of the establishment. The tea itself is sold in black-and-gold-colored canisters stacked up and across the walls, but that's not all. There's also delectable array of sugars, spices, cakes, macaroons, tea-based jams (a house specialty), and high-tea paraphernalia, too. But the best way to drink in this tea frenzy is by repairing to the calm salon for brunch or afternoon tea. In addition to making your tea selection from the "tea bible" called *L'Art Français du Thé* (there's one atop every table), you can savor a selection of dishes and desserts that count fine teas among their ingredients. And the house pastries have simply got to be seen—and savored—to be believed. Because Parisians know a good thing when they taste it, reserva-

---

estaurants/Clubs: **Red** | Hotels: **Purple** | Shops: **Orange** | Outdoors/Parks: **Green** | Sights/Culture: **Blue**

tions for weekend brunch here are essential. Smoking, by the way, is not permitted at any time on the premises: it would taint the purity of the tea. ♦ 30 and 35 Rue du Bourg-Tibourg (between Rues du Roi-de-Sicile and St-Croix-de-la-Bretonnerie). 01.42.72.28.11. Métro: Hôtel de Ville. Also at 13 Rue des Grands-Augustins (at Rue de Savoie). 01.40.51.82.50. Métro: St. Michel. Also at 260 Rue du Faubourg St. Honoré (at Rue de la Neva), 01.46.22.18.54. Métro: Ternes

77 THE LIZARD LOUNGE

★$ A favorite of anglophone expats in Paris, this easy-going lounge offers three levels of involvement: On the ground-floor barroom level, you can mingle with the convivial band of regulars; from the mezzanine you can watch them mingling; and Wednesdays through Saturday nights, you can descend to the *cave* where DJs keep the dance floor in perpetual motion. The whole place was designed and built by the owners and staff (the nifty copper-walled *toilettes* on the mezzanine included), which adds to its homey feeling. American-style sandwiches, nachos, goat-cheese salad, *confit de canard*, and *plats du jour* are on the bill of fare; the Saturday and Sunday brunches offer some of the best eggs Benedict in town. In fine weather, the big doors are thrown open, and you can lunch, brunch, dine, or drink on one of the most charming streets in all of the Marais. The same team of owners also runs two similarly congenial bars in the Marais-Bastille area, **Stollys** (16 Rue Cloche-Perce, between Rues de Rivoli and du Roi de Sicile, 01.42.76.06.76) and **The Bottle Shop** (5 Rue Trousseau, between Rues du Faubourg-St-Antoine and de Charonne, 01.43.14.28.04). ♦ M-F, lunch and dinner until midnight; Sa-Su, brunch noon-4PM; bar daily 12PM-2AM; happy hour 5PM-7PM in the bar, 8PM-10PM in the cave. 18 Rue Bourg-Tibourg (between Rues du Roi-de-Sicile and Ste-Croix-de-la-Bretonnerie). 01.42.72.81.34. Métro: Hôtel de Ville

78 AU PETIT FER À CHEVAL

★$ Named after its 1903 marble-topped *fer à cheval* (horseshoe) bar, this neighborhood café offers lunchtime *plats du jour* in its back room, where one of the booths is an old

wooden métro seat. ♦ Daily, breakfast, lunch, and dinner until 2AM. 30 Rue Vieille-du-Temple (between Rues du Roi-de-Sicile and des Rosiers). 01.42.72.47.47. Métro: St-Paul

78 L'ETOILE MANQUANTE

Where Rue Vieille-du-Temple hits Rue Ste-Croix de-la-Bretonnerie is the epicenter of the gay Marais, and there is no better vantage point from which to watch the parade go by than from the terrace of this eminently likable café. In warmer weather the highly coveted outside tables go fast, but there's plenty of room in the inside, which has an atmosphere and a look all its own. Very cool, futuristic art adorns the walls and you're just as likely to s next to clubbers fueling up on cocktails and salads before taking the town as next to an off-duty baker from one of the many *boulangeries* in the area. 34 Rue Vieille-du-Temple (between Rues du Roi-de-Sicile and des Rosiers). Daily, 9AM-2PM. 01.42.72.48.34. Métro: Hôtel de Ville or St-Paul

79 RUE DES ROSIERS

Rosiers means "rosebushes" and refers to the roses that bloomed nearby within the old medieval city wall, but the fragrances wafting along this narrow, crooked street today are anything but floral. Scents of hot pastrami, steaming borscht, chopped chicken livers, an fresh matzo emanate from the kosher butcher shops, delicatessens, and bakeries that line this street, the *platzel* ("little square") of the Jewish quarter since the Middle Ages. The adjoining Rue des Ecouffes takes its name from the Lombardian pawnbrokers who were derided as *écouffes*, French for "kite," a rapacious bird. A terribly haunting reminder of the district's history was a plaque that used to hang outside an elementary school on the street. It read: "165 Jewish children from this school, deported to Germany during World Wa II, were exterminated in Nazi camps. Never forget." Down this street, the French police, in collaboration with the Nazis, marched and dragged away thousands of Jews to detention centers and, ultimately, concentration camps ♦ Métro: St-Paul

79 FINKELSZTAJN

A Jewish bakery has operated at this address since 1851, and today Sacha Finkelsztajn carries on the tradition, producing the richest cheesecake this side of Manhattan's Second Avenue. The affable baker offers newcomers a free taste of her Polish herring, chicken liver, and eggplant purée. ♦ W-Su. 27 Rue des Rosiers (between Rues des Ecouffes and Vieille du-Temple). 01.42.72.78.91. Métro: St-Paul

80 L'AS DU FALLAFEL

"The Falafel Ace" offers kosher North African, Israeli, and Middle Eastern specialties to go-

THE BEST

Richard Pestour

Director, Richard Pestour Communication

Everyone should try one of the *grands restaurants Parisiens*, such as **La Tour d'Argent** or **La Serre**, at least once.

Also try a grand brasserie like **Fouquet's**. (And ask for a *table côté club*, facing Avenue George-V, for the best celebrity-spotting.)

The restaurant **Market**, very Parisian and international, is at once trendy, beautiful, good, and full of *spectacle*. And the service is very friendly.

Lunch at the **Jardin d'Hiver** at the Hôtel Meurice.

The restaurant **La Fontaine de Mars**, for its friendly and personalized service.

Flora Danica, when you want to dine with someone chic who doesn't necessarily want to eat a lot.

Castel's. This private club (you may get in with a dinner reservation) has been around for 50 years but it's still chic.

Thiou. Chef Thiou is charming and lots of Parisian show-business people appreciate her cooking.

Le Conto on Rue Lauriston (in the 16 arrondissement). A discreet Italian restaurant where you can have lunch until 4PM—great when you don't have to work.

---

hummus, falafel sandwiches, and shawarma. ♦ M-F, Su. 34 Rue des Rosiers (between Rues Pavée and Hospitalières-St-Gervais). 01.48.87.63.60. Métro: St-Paul

81 JO GOLDENBERG

★★$$ The sweet aroma of spiced meat, the clatter of dishes, and, particularly on Sunday afternoon, the babble of strong, animated voices fill this Jewish delicatessen-restaurant. Try the *foie haché* (chopped liver), *poisson farci* (gefilte fish), Cracovian sausages, and strudel, washed down with a cold Pilsen. This famous spot was the site of a tragedy on 9 August 1982, when masked gunmen killed six customers. The PLO took credit, and the gunmen were never caught. ♦ Daily, breakfast, lunch, and dinner; closed on Yom Kippur. Reservations recommended. 7 Rue des Rosiers (at Rue Ferdinand-Duval). 01.48.87.20.16. Métro: St-Paul

82 LE LOIR DANS LA THÉIÈRE

★★$ With its flea-market furniture, sprung-out sofas, wooden tables, and raffish air, this comfortable tea salon could be in Seattle or Berkeley. The name, which translates as "Dormouse in the Teapot," recalls *Alice's Adventures in Wonderland*, as does the mural of other characters from the Lewis Carroll fantasy. Yet the light, tasty salads and fine homemade cakes and tarts are very real. ♦ M-F, lunch and afternoon tea; Sa-Su, brunch and afternoon tea. No credit cards accepted. 3 Rue des Rosiers (between Rues Pavée and Ferdinand-Duval). 01.42.72.90.61. Métro: St-Paul

82 L'ECLAIREUR

Ladies on the lookout for eclectic additions to their sartorial arsenal should check out the wares at this longstanding bi-level Marais bastion of hip. Friendly sales staff can help you navigate through the extensive selection of new designers' clothing and accessories. One section is devoted to home décor; here you can expect to be surprised by eclectic tableware, over-the-top umbrella stands, and the like. M-Sa. Rue des Rosiers (between Rues Ferdinand-Duval and Pavée). 01.48.87.10.22. Métro: St-Paul

83 RUE PAVÉE

The construction of one of the city's first *pavée* (paved) streets was a pioneer achieve-ment in the 14th century, when the city's muddy roads also served as open sewers and pigsties. ♦ Métro: St-Paul

83 BIBLIOTHÈQUE HISTORIQUE DE LA VILLE DE PARIS (HISTORICAL LIBRARY OF THE CITY OF PARIS)

Designed in 1611 by **Baptiste du Cerceau**, the Hôtel Lamoignon has housed the **Bibliothèque Historique de la Ville de Paris** since 1969 and is a mecca for French historians. The mansion was originally the property of Diane de France, the illegitimate daughter of Henri II. As the story goes, young Henri, while traveling in Italy, was in hot pursuit of the Duchess of Angoulême. When she refused to leave her house, he burned it down and had her kidnapped and taken to

---

France. Out of their tumultuous union, Diane was born. At age 7, she was legally adopted by the king and given all the rights of nobility, among them this mansion, where she lived until her death at age 82. Adorned with a colossal order of Italianate pilasters, this was the city's first private mansion. The low triangular pediment is embellished by a stag with antlers, a tribute to Diana, goddess of the hunt. On a rainy day, the library is one of the best places in Paris to read about Paris. Once in the courtyard, bear right, up the steps to the **Reading Room** door. If you manage to convince the guard you are a visiting scholar, he will give you a reader's card. Take a seat at one of the long wooden tables and gaze up at the gilded beams, one of which is ornamented with a painting of Diana and the hunt. The rest of the library is off-limits to the public. ♦ M-Sa; closed holidays and the first 2 weeks of Aug. 24 Rue Pavée (at Rue Malher). 01.44.59.29.40. Métro: St-Paul

84 HÔTEL ET MUSÉE CARNAVALET

The laughing carnival mask sculpted in stone above the Rue des Francs-Bourgeois gate of this splendid mansion is a misleading visual pun: This 16th-century building does not conceal a midway of clowns or a family of dancing bears. A truer clue to the building's contents is found in the ship (the symbol of Paris) on the gate. In 1880, the **Hôtel Carnavalet** was put into service as the **Musée Historique de la Ville de Paris (Historical Museum of the City of Paris)**, and today it vividly displays Parisian life from prehistory to the present. The building's original 1540 design is attributed to **Pierre Lescot**, who was then the architect of the **Louvre**. The *hôtel* (mansion) was spruced up in 1655 by **François Mansart**, the architect for whom the mansard roof is named. The structure's name evolved from that of an early owner, the widow of the Breton Sire de Kernevency, whose surname Parisians constantly mispronounced and permanently corrupted to its present form. In 1989 the **Musée Carnavalet** doubled its space by adding the neighboring **Hôtel Le Peletier de Saint-Fargeau**, a mansion built by **Pierre Bullet** in 1690.

The Hôtel Carnavalet presents collections on the history of Paris from the Middle Ages to just before the French Revolution, and the collections in the Hôtel Le Peletier de Saint-Fargeau (reached by a corridor on the second floor) deal with the period from the start of the French Revolution through the 20th century, and in a new wing opened in 2000, the prehistory of Paris.

The museum has something for everyone, even the most fidgety youngster. On the ground floor of the Hôtel Carnavalet is an entire roomful of old metal shop signs and 18th-century billboards dating from an age of

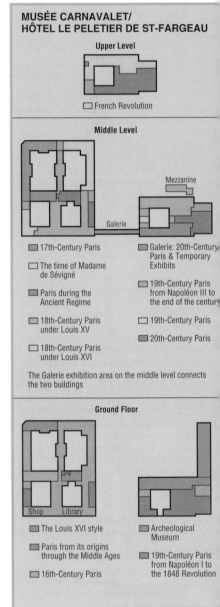

mass illiteracy. The baker advertised himself with a golden sheaf of wheat, the butcher with a suckling pig, and the locksmith with an ornate iron key. On the second floor are exhibitions of fashionable furnishings from the reigns of the last Bourbon kings (Louis XIV, Louis XV, and Louis XVI), salon murals by Jean-Honoré Fragonard and François Bouche and the apartments of Madame de Sévigné (1626–1696). This "Grande Dame of the Marais" (who was born, baptized, and marrie in the district) lived at the Hôtel Carnavalet f the last 19 years of her life. Here she entertained the greatest thinkers of the day and, in her famous *Lettres*, inscribed her witty, incisive observations on the court of Louis XIV. Her association with the royals was not forgotten by well-read revolutionary hotheads, who a century later exhumed her remains, beheaded the corpse, and triumphantly paraded through Paris with her skull.

On the top floor of the Hôtel Le Peletier de Saint-Fargeau is a lively exhibition on the French Revolution that includes the royal family's itemized laundry bill, the young dauphin's penmanship book, the rope ladder used by a political prisoner to escape from the Bastille, a model of the guillotine; a pair of drums banged by the revolutionaries, a *Who's Who* of the revolution in portraits (from crazed Marat to stern Robespierre), and the penknife Napoléon Bonaparte used during the Egyptian campaign. On the ground floor are exhibits on the empire of Napoléon I and the turbulent period in Paris history through 1848; François Gérard's lovely portrait of *Madame Récamier* is in **room no. 115**. Directly off this room is the 17th-century *orangerie* (hothouse for orange trees) of the mansion, which was transformed in the year 2000 into **Archéo 2000**, a handsome archeological museum that presents remarkable finds from digs in the 1990s in the Bercy district, Paris's earliest settlement, including Neolithic boats from 4000 to 2000 BC and other artifacts up through Gallo-Roman times. The second floor of this building covers the period from the mid-19th century through the 20th century. Here you can see Marcel Proust's famous cork-lined bedroom, complete with the bed in which he wrote most of one of the greatest literary works of all time, *A la Recherche de Temps Perdu* (*In Search of Lost Time*).

The museum also presents outstanding temporary exhibits on topics related to Paris past and present.

On your way out, catch Louis XIV, looking rather silly decked out as a Roman general with a wig. (The Antoine Coysevox courtyard statue was brought here from the Hôtel de Ville.) ♦ Admission. Tu-Su, 10AM-5:40PM. 23 Rue de Sévigné (between Rues des Francs-Bourgeois and du Parc-Royal). 01.44.59.58.58. Métros: St-Paul, Chemin Vert. www.paris-france.org/musees

85 L'ARBRE DE VIE

The size of a walk-in closet, this minuscule shop overflows with little kids' toys and handmade clothes in delightful disarray. From vintage Disney to the Smurfs (or *Strumphs*, as they're called here), mechanical robots and 1970s racing cars, the full range of dressing dolls and their clothes, puppets, marionettes, and *nounours* (teddy bears), expect to find something from your childhood, no matter what age you happen to be. ♦ Tu-Su, 11AM-7PM; M, 2-7PM. 21 Rue de Sévigné (between Rues des Francs-Bourgeois and St-Antoine). 01.48.87.05.43. Métro: St-Paul

86 LES BOURGEOISES

★★$$ Dining here on the baked St. Marcellin cheese on toast, fresh ravioli stuffed with herbed cheese, lamb stew with coriander and ginger, or such Indian specialties as chicken tandoori is like dining in the living room of owner Martine Robin's grandmother. In fact, the oil paintings, chairs, and tables all come from Robin's grandparents' antiques shop. The homemade raspberry liqueur aging in a jar by the front window is, unfortunately, purely decorative. ♦ M-Su, dinner; Tu-Su, lunch and dinner; Su, afternoon tea. Reservations recommended. 12 Rue des Francs-Bourgeois (between Rues de Turenne and de Sévigné). 01.42.72.48.30. Métros: St-Paul, Chemin Vert

87 MA BOURGOGNE

★★$$ Owned by Aimé Cougoureux, this arcade-sheltered café is where the locals go for Sunday breakfast. Specialties include sausages from Auvergne, *foie gras des Landes andouillette* (foie gras from Landes with sausages), veal tripe, and spicy steak tartare. ♦ Daily, breakfast, lunch, and dinner; closed in February and 1 week in March. No credit cards accepted. 19 Pl des Vosges (at Rue des Francs-Bourgeois). 01.42.78.44.64. Métros: Chemin Vert, Bastille, St-Paul

88 LA GUIRLANDE DE JULIE

★★$$ At his restaurant on the square, Claude Terrail, owner of the celebrated **Tour d'Argent**, presents a small, seasonally inspired menu. Start with something light, such as baked breast of duck sautéed with spices, followed by the excellent *pot au feu* or fillet of salmon with an herb crust and vegetable tagliatelle, and a bottle of wine from the **Cave de la Tour d'Argent**. Conclude with the popular warm apple tart with cinnamon and ice cream. The weekday prix-fixe lunch menu is a bargain. At night, it's à la carte. In summer, reserve a table outside beneath the brick arcade. ♦ Spring: Tu-Su; winter: W-Su, lunch and dinner until 1AM. Reservations recommended. 25 Pl des Vosges (between Rues de Béarn and des Francs-Bourgeois). 01.48.87.94.07. Métros: Chemin Vert, Bastille, St-Paul

88 21 Place des Vosges

Cardinal Richelieu (1585–1642), the French prime minister under Louis XIII and the founder of the **Académie Française**, lived here. ♦ At Rue des Francs-Bourgeois. Métros: Chemin Vert, Bastille, St-Paul

89 Pavillon de la Reine

$$$$ The most elegant hotel in the Marais, this 17th-century mansion where Catherine de Médicis once lived, discreetly distanced from the Place des Vosges by its own garden courtyard, is quietly opulent, with antique tapestries, Persian carpets, a grand fireplace, marble floors, soft leather couches, and 55 luxurious rooms and suites. There's no restaurant. ♦ 28 Pl des Vosges (at Rue de Béarn). 01.40.29.19.19; fax 01.40.29.19.20. Métros: Chemin Vert, Bastille, St-Paul. pavillon@club-internet.fr

90 André Bissonnet

Some years ago, a butcher named André Bissonnet laid down his meat cleaver, redecorated his *boucherie*, and began buying antique musical instruments and restoring them in his cold-storage room. On any given day he might be working on a 1747 viola da gamba, a 17th-century harp, a porcelain trumpet, ancient hurdy-gurdies, or a black serpent, a bizarre 18th-century horn used to accompany chanting priests. Bissonnet claims to be an accomplished player of the Breton bombardon and on request will proudly bleat out a few bars. ♦ M-Sa, 2-7PM or by appointment; closed in Aug. 6 Rue du Pas-de-la-Mule (between Rues des Tournelles and Pl des Vosges). 01.48.87.20.15. Métro: Chemin Vert

91 Joséphine Vannier

Mme. Vannier has elevated her *chocolat artisanal* to an art form. Year-round items include artist's palettes of dark chocolate with dabs of colored sugar paste as paint smears that come in three sizes, violins and other musical instruments, and a variety of birds and animals. There are seasonal creations for Valentine's Day, Easter, Halloween, Christmas, and other holidays, and surprising concoctions that spring from the *patronne*'s imagination. Even if you're not a chocolate lover, this store is always worth a browse just to see what they've come up with. ♦ Tu-Sa, 11:30AM-1:30PM and 2:45-9PM; Su, 3:30-7PM. 4 Rue du Pas-de-la-Mule (between Blvd Beaumar-

chais and Rue des Tournelles). 01.44.54.03.09. Métros: Chemin Vert, Bastille

92 Hôtel Caron de Beaumarchais

$$ Behind the brilliant blue façade of this superbly located hotel is a gem of a hostelry radiating 18th-century elegance and charm. Father and son hosts Etienne and Alain Bigeard are true gentlemen who receive guests with a natural warmth and enthusiasm. The interior is simply and tastefully decorated by Alain: The stone *cheminée* in the lobby boasts a crackling fire in the winter; the 19 guest rooms feature exposed beams, Louis XV–style fabrics, and hand-painted tile in the bathrooms; and the walls are hung with memorabilia from the comedies of playwright Pierre-Augustin Caron de Beaumarchais, the hotel's namesake, who, in 1778, wrote *The Marriage of Figaro* down the street at 47 Rue Vieille-du-Temple. Some rooms on the fifth and sixth floors have balconies looking out over the rooftops of the Marais. A continental breakfast with fresh croissants is served until noon, an unusual tradition that's appreciated by those guests who want to sleep in after taking advantage of the late-night spots in neighboring Les Halles and Bastille. There's no restaurant. ♦ 12 Rue Vieille-du-Temple (between Rues de Rivoli and du Roi-de-Sicile). 01.42.72.34.12; fax 01.42.72.34.63 Métro: St-Paul. carondebeaumarchais@ wanadoo.fr; www.carondebeaumarchais.com

93 La Tartine

★$ This is the oldest wine bar in Paris, owned since 1940 by the family of M. Bouscarel, who selects the stock of more than 60 wines himself. He buys directly from Burgundy, Bordeaux, Rhône, and Loire Valley producers, keeping the prices down and the quality up. The café is always filled with a vibrant mix of ages and personalities, happily sipping wine and munching on *tartines*, simple sandwiches on *pain Poilâne* (sourdough bread) filled with pâté, cheese, ham, or sausage. ♦ M, Th-Su, breakfast, lunch, and dinner; Tu, W, lunch and dinner. No credit cards accepted. 24 Rue de Rivoli (between Rues Ferdinand-Duval and des Ecouffes). 01.42.72.76.85. Métro: St-Paul

94 Association Culturelle Israélite Agoudas Hakehilos

The Germans blew up this synagogue, designed in 1913 by **Hector Guimard** (the architect best known for his sculptural métro entrances), during their occupation of Paris in the Second World War. Happily, the sinuous façade remains intact. It suggests an open book, perhaps the Torah. The building is closed to the public. ♦ 10 Rue Pavée (between Rues du Roi-de-Sicile and des Rosiers). Métro: St-Pau

CARAVANE

95 CARAVANE

Owner Françoise Dorget, who has a remarkable eye for fabrics, scours Morocco, India, Uzbekistan, Cambodia, and elsewhere in North Africa and the Far East for textiles and decorative items, and she sends them back to her boutique in the Marais, which has the seductive allure of an airy Manhattan loft of a wealthy person with marvelous taste. The fabrics are either sold as cloth or used to make cushions, tablecloths, napkins, place mats, or made-to-order slipcovers. Also for sale are fine ceramic bowls, small wooden chests, candle holders, Moroccan carpets, and other portable items, along with large pieces such as iron desks, beds, and a very attractive line of stretch sofas that can be shipped anywhere. Another popular item is a traditional Swiss cushion stuffed with cherry pits and shaped to fit into the small of a reclining person's back; after being heated in an oven, the cherry pits hold the heat for a very long time—an organic heating pad par excellence. ♦ Tu-Sa, 11AM-9PM. 6 Rue Pavée (between Rues du Roi-de-Sicile and Rosiers). 01.44.61.04.20. Métro: St-Paul

96 L'ECLAIREUR

Tired of cookie-cutter clothes à la Gap, guys? One of the hippest men's clothing stores in the neighborhood, and indeed Paris, awaits. Ring the bell to be gain entrance to this airy, surprisingly relaxed emporium where designer labels such as Dries van Noten, Prada Sport, and Comme des Garçons compete for your attention. Though on the pricey side, the collections are highly original and perfect either as the starting point for or accentuating an au courant wardrobe. ♦ M-Sa. 12 Rue Malher (between Rues des Rosiers and du Roi de Sicile). 01.44.54.22.11. Métro: St-Paul

97 L'OSTERIA

Though the friendliest service seems to be reserved for regulars, this tiny, signless restaurant is worth booking a table at on account of its delicious fresh pasta dishes. Among them, the gnocchi with sage butter is a standout. By contrast the salads are too small to justify their big price tags. They are tasty, though, particularly the arugula with shaved Parmesan. ♦ M-F, lunch and dinner; closed in Aug. 10 Rue

de Sévigné (between Rues St-Antoine and de Jarente). 01.42.71.37.08. Métro: St-Paul

98 JEAN-PIERRE DE CASTRO

Such antique silver and silver-plated articles as champagne buckets, candelabras, and sugar tongs are the specialties of this busy boutique. Forks and spoons are displayed by the basketful and sold by the kilogram. ♦ Tu-Sa, 10:30AM-7PM. 19 Rue de Turenne (between Rues de Jarente and des Francs-Bourgeois). 01.42.72.04.00. Métro: St-Paul

99 AUBERGE DE JARENTE

★★$ This warm, rustic restaurant serves such Basque specialties as *pipérade* (an omelette with tomatoes and peppers) and paella at modest prices. ♦ Tu-Sa, lunch and dinner; closed 2 weeks in Aug. Reservations recommended. 7 Rue de Jarente (between Rues de Turenne and de Sévigné). 01.42.77.49.35. Métro: St-Paul

99 BAR DE JARENTE

$ Though feisty Mme. Renée, a legend in the Marais, has retired, this neighborhood bar remains a fine place for coffee and a croissant in the morning or an aperitif before hitting one of the nearby restaurants. In good weather, join the locals at the outdoor tables facing the cute little Place du Marché Ste-Catherine. ♦ M-Sa, breakfast, lunch, and snacks; closed in Aug. 5 Rue de Jarente (between Rues de Turenne and de Sévigné). 01.48.87.60.93. Métro: St-Paul

99 GRAND HÔTEL JEANNE D'ARC

$$ Its grandiose name will bring a smile when you see this little hotel in the heart of the Marais. *"Mignon"* would be more like it. Here everything is cozy and quaint, from the small antiques-furnished lobby and breakfast room to the 36 guest rooms: all neat, comfortable, and charming, but some of them rather petite. But then this is an outstanding value for the price. Many North Americans like to stay here. Staff members are helpful and well informed. There's no restaurant. ♦ 3 Rue de Jarente (between Rues Turenne and de Sévigné). 01.48.87.62.11; fax 01.48.87.37.31. Métro: St-Paul. www.hoteljeannedarc.com

100 L'AMBROSIE

★★★★$$$$ One of the few Michelin-three-star restaurants in Paris, this dining spot is owned by chef Bernard Pacaud, a perfectionist whose brief bill of fare fulfills the promise of the restaurant's name—a menu fit for the gods. Some favorites have included

---

Restaurants/Clubs: Red | Hotels: Purple | Shops: Orange | Outdoors/Parks: Green | Sights/Culture: Blue

THE BEST

Wendy Lyn Whitehurst
Gourmet Consultant, Writer

Saturday-afternoon wine tastings with the owner and locals at **La Dernière Goutte** wine shop.

Walking along the Seine on a hot summer day with *pamplemousse* (grapefruit) sorbet from **Berthillon**.

Poilâne bakery for shortbread tea biscuits and flaky apple tarts.

The first-of-the-season white asparagus, figs, and melon at any outdoor market.

Lunch with friends at **Granterroirs**, a lively table d'hôte, eating at the long wooden table and buying aromatic olive oil from their gourmet market.

Walking through Paris on Christmas Eve among the lights, decorations, and animated window displays—truly magic.

Soaking up local color on the terrace of **Bistro Mazarin** with a gorgeous platter of oysters and a glass of Sancerre.

Afternoon tea at **1728**…an incredible combination of painting, sculpture, classical music, tea, and pastries under the roof of Lafayette's restored mansion.

Restaurant **Guy Savoy**, for the truffle-artichoke soup.

Wine discovery dinners at the **Bistro du Sommelier**, where the chef prepares a tasting menu paired with luscious wines from small producers.

Shopping for St-Marcellin at **Alléosse** cheese shop on the Rue Poncelet.

Tasting my way through Monsieur Linxe's newest creations at the **Maison du Chocolat**.

Ringing in the New Year with friends over a star-studded dinner of foie gras, lobster, oysters, champagne, and Sauternes!

Choosing from the large selection of spices at **Fauchon**.

The echo of my footsteps on the cobblestones up and over the rooftops, walking home after a late dinner.

John Dory braised with fennel, artichokes with foie gras, skate with sliced cabbage, *croustillant d'agneau* (rolled fillet of lamb stuffed with truffles), and the puff-pastry desserts. The dining room is discreetly romantic with subtle lighting, exquisite floral arrangements, and beautiful tapestries adorning the walls. ♦ Tu-Sa, lunch and dinner; closed 2 weeks in Feb and the month of Aug. Reservations required (at least 1 month in advance). 9 Pl des Vosges (between Rues de Birague and des Francs-Bourgeois). 01.42.78.51.45. Métros: Chemin Vert, Bastille, St-Paul

101 PLACE DES VOSGES

The oldest and most serenely beautiful square in Paris, this symmetrical ensemble of 36 matching pavilions with red-and-gold brick-and-stone façades, steep slate roofs, and dormer windows was designed in 1612 by **Clément Métezeau**. This marked the first time in Paris that an arcade was used to link houses, and balconies were employed for more than decorative purposes.

The original function of the square, commissioned by Henri IV, was to house a silk factory and its workers. The goal was to provide Marie de Médicis, his estranged queen, with lingerie cheaper than what could be imported from Genoa. Despite Henri's good intentions, his silk workers' housing project was gentrified before the last brick was laid. Into the apartments with 16-foot-high ceilings, red marble fireplaces, and parquet floors moved Riche-

lieu, Corneille, Molière, and a covey of courtiers, cavaliers, ministers, and marquises.

It remained a high-class neighborhood until the summer of 1686, when Louis XIV moved to **Versailles** and the French aristocracy followed. In the early 18th century the Marais continued to decline and eventually became the city's industrial East End. Heavy machinery was bolted to the elegant floors of the great spaces, and magnificent salons were subdivided into minuscule apartments. The neighborhood was not pulled out of its nosedive until the early 1960s, when Minister of Culture André Malraux had the **Place des Vosges** and the Marais declared a historic district. Nowadays, the Place des Vosges is frequented by knitting grandmothers, toddlers digging in the dirt, and perhaps a group of North African immigrants enjoying an impromptu soccer game beside an equestrian statue of a smirking Louis XIII. **Nos. 18** and **23** have the two best portals on the square. Also, don't miss the knockers on **nos. 4** and **17**. ♦ Between Rues de Birague and de Béarn. Métros: Bastille, St-Paul

102 ISSEY MIYAKE

Something of an art gallery for clothes, this large boutique shows the latest looks from the Japanese master. Many of these pieces are made in limited editions, whereas his **Pants Please** boutique (201 Blvd St-Germain, at Rue de Luynes; 01.45.48.10.44) sells Miyake's regular clothing lines, and **A.POC** (47 Rue des

Francs-Bourgeois, between Rues Vieille-du-Temple and Pavée; 01.44.54.07.05) sells specially cut wrap dresses. Like the other newer structures on the square, this building is a masterpiece of trompe l'oeil. The façade is made of plaster-on-wood framing, and you have to get pretty close to see that the bricks are painted on. ♦ M-Sa; closed 2 weeks in Aug. 3 Pl des Vosges (between Rues de Birague and des Francs-Bourgeois). 01.48.87.01.86. Métros: St-Paul, Bastille

102 HÔTEL DE COULANGES

The Marquise de Sévigné, whose correspondence with her daughter in Provence became one of the most famous series of letters in French literature, was born here on 6 February 1626. It's still a private residence. ♦ 1 Pl des Vosges (at Rue de Birague). Métros: St-Paul, Bastille

103 COCONNAS

★$$ Boasting a Louis XIII dining room and a sidewalk terrace overlooking the mansions and garden of the **Place des Vosges**, this casual restaurant (run by Claude Terrail of **La Tour d'Argent**) has built its reputation on serving Good King Henri's *poule-au-pot* (commemorating Henri IV's famous political promise of a chicken in every pot) and soufflé Grand Marnier. North American tourists and expatriates predominate. ♦ Spring: Tu-Su, lunch and dinner; winter: W-Su, lunch and dinner. Reservations recommended. 2 *bis* Pl des Vosges (at Rue de Birague). 01.42.78.58.16. Métros: Bastille, St-Paul

103 MUSÉE VICTOR HUGO

This museum was the French writer's home between 1833 and 1848, when Napoléon III came to power and Hugo's voluntary exile in the Channel Islands began. The museum's eclectic assortment of Hugo mementos includes the cap he wore during the 1871 Siege of Paris, his bust sculpted by Rodin, and a model of an elephant sculpture that Napoléon I proposed for Place de la Bastille. Haunting postage stamp–size pen-and-ink doodles of Rhine castles and ships at sea along with macabre sketches of witches, demons, and the hanging of John Brown show a nightmarish side to the author of *The Hunchback of Notre-Dame* (1831) and *Les Misérables* (1862). The drawings are counterbalanced by the hodgepodge of Oriental furnishings Hugo designed for the Guernsey home of Juliette Drouet, his mistress for more than a half-century. Don't leave the museum without viewing the **Place des Vosges** from one of Hugo's upstairs windows and glancing at the Nadar photo of an old

but ageless Hugo on his deathbed, 22 May 1885. ♦ Admission. Tu-Su. 6 Pl des Vosges (between Rues de Birague and du Pas-de-la-Mule). 01.42.72.10.16. Métros: Bastille, St-Paul

104 MAISON EUROPÉENNE DE LA PHOTOGRAPHIE

Opened in 1996, this cultural institution is located in a classic 18th-century town house where Parisian architect **Yves Lion** created a tasteful, contemporary interior that boasts a permanent collection of over 12,000 photographs and galleries for rotating exhibitions. Exploring the architectural diversity of the center is an adventure: The main promenade features rough stone walls; there's an elegant staircase; and vaults of the original house twist into the adjoining modern, spacious annex. Visitors are invited to participate in workshops, lectures, and conferences and to view films in the deluxe screening room. ♦ Admission. W-Su. Tours by appointment only. 5-7 Rue de Fourcy (between Rues de Jouy and François-Miron). 01.44.78.75.00. Métro: St-Paul. www.mep-fr.org

105 ST-PAUL–ST-LOUIS

Built for the Jesuits as part of their monastery in 1627, this Baroque church, with its classically ordered façade, superimposed columns, and dome, is modeled on the Gesù Church in Rome. The spacious interior is well lit and ornate with decoration and sculptures. In the transept is the painting *Christ in the Garden*, by Delacroix. ♦ Rue St-Antoine (between Rues St-Paul and du Prévôt). 01.42.72.30.32. Métro: St-Paul

106 HÔTEL DE SULLY

The most richly decorated private mansion in Paris dates from the time of Louis XIII and was designed in 1630 by architect **Androuet du Cerceau** for notorious gambler Petit Thouars, who is said to have lost his entire fortune in one night. Ten years later, the mansion was bought by the Duc de Sully, a minister to Henri IV. Today this is the site of the information office of the **Caisse Nationale des Monuments Historiques et des Sites** (Bureau of Historic Monuments

PARLEZ-VOUS FRANÇAIS?

The French take great pride in their culture and their language. If you attempt to speak their language, no matter how poorly, they will take it as a compliment. Don't be put off if they respond to you in English, however—be glad. It will be that much easier to understand one another. Here are some phrases that will enable you to start communicating *en français*. When there is both a masculine and a feminine spelling, the feminine is in parentheses. *Bon voyage!* (Have a good trip!)

Hello, Good-bye, and Other Basics

Hello/Good morning/Good afternoon ....*Bonjour*

Good evening ....*Bonsoir*

How are you? ....*Comment allez-vous?*

Good-bye..*Au revoir*

Yes...*Oui*

No ....*Non*

Please ....*S'il vous plaît*

Thank you..*Merci*

You're welcome...*Pas de quoi*

Excuse me ....*Excusez-moi* or *Pardon*

I don't speak French. ....*Je ne parle pas français.*

Do you speak English?....................*Parlez-vous anglais?*

I don't understand. ....*Je ne comprends pas.*

Do you understand? ....*Comprenez-vous?*

More slowly, please! ....*Plus lentement, s'il vous plaît.*

I don't know. ....*Je ne sais pas.*

My name is . . . .*Je m'appelle . . .*

What is your name? ....*Comment vous appelez-vous?*

miss ....*mademoiselle*

madame, ma'am ....*madame*

mister, sir ....*monsieur*

good ....*bon(ne)*

bad ....*mauvais(e)*

open ....*ouvert(e)*

closed ....*fermé(e)*

entrance ....*entrée*

exit...*sortie*

push..*poussez*

pull...*tirez*

today ....*aujourd'hui*

tomorrow ....*demain*

yesterday...*hier*

week ....*semaine*

month ....*mois*

year...*an*

Hotel Talk

I have a reservation. ....*J'ai une réservation.*

I would like to reserve . . . .*Je voudrais réserver . . .*

a double room..........*une chambre pour deux personnes*

with (private) bath ....*avec une salle de bain (privée)*

with air conditioning ....*avec la climatisatio*

Are taxes included?..

.............................*Est-ce que les taxes sont comprises*

Is breakfast included?..

......................*Est-ce que le petit déjeuner est compris*

Do you accept traveler's checks? ....*Prenez-vous chèques de voyage?*

Do you accept credit cards? ....

..................................*Prenez-vous des cartes de crédit*

Restaurant Repartee

Waiter! ....*Monsieur*

I would like . . . .*Je voudrais . .*

a menu ....*la cart*

a glass of..*un verre d*

a bottle of ....*une bouteille d*

The check, please. ....*L'addition, s'il vous plaît*

Is the service charge (tip) included? ....

................................*Est-ce que le service est compris*

I think there is an error in the bill. ....

...................*Je crois qu'il y a une erreur avec l'addition*

lunch ....*déjeune*

dinner ....*dîne*

tip ....*service, pourboir*

bread ....*pai*

butter ....*beurr*

pepper..*poivr*

salt...*se*

sugar ....*sucr*

soup ....*soup*

salad ....*salad*

vegetables ....*légume*

cheese ....*fromag*

eggs ....*oeuf*

beef ....*boeu*

chicken ....*poule*

veal ....*vea*

fish ....*poisso*

seafood ....*fruits de me*

pork ....*por*

ham..*jambo*

chop ....*côtelett*

dessert ....*desse*

As You Like It

cold ....*froid(e)*
hot ....*chaud(e)*
sweet ....*sucré(e)*
dry ....*sec (sèche)*
broiled, roasted ....*rôti(e)*
baked ....*au four*
boiled ....*bouilli(e)*
fried ....*frit(e)*
raw ....*cru(e)*
rare ....*saignant(e)*
well done ....*bien cuit(e)*
spicy ....*épicé(e)*

Thirsty No More

water ....*l'eau*
coffee ....*café, express*
coffee with steamed milk ....*café au lait*
tea ....*thé*
beer ....*bière*
rosé wine ....*vin rosé*
red wine ....*vin rouge*
white wine ....*vin blanc*
milk ....*lait*
mineral water ....*l'eau minérale*
carbonated ....*gazeuse*
not carbonated ....*non-gazeuse*
orange juice ....*jus d'orange*
ice ....*glaçons*
without ice ....*sans glaçons*

Sizing It Up

How much does this cost? ....*Combien coûte-il?*
inexpensive ....*bon marché*
expensive ....*cher (chère)*
large ....*grand(e)*
small ....*petit(e)*
long ....*long(ue)*
short ....*court(e)*
old ....*vieux (vieille)*
new ....*nouveau (nouvelle)*
used ....*d'occasion*
a little ....*un peu*
a lot ....*beaucoup*

On the Move

north ....*nord*
south ....*sud*
east ....*est*
west ....*ouest*
right ....*droite*
left ....*gauche*
highway ....*autoroute*
street ....*rue*
gas station ....*station-service*
here ....*ici*
there ....*là*
bus stop ....*l'arrêt de bus*
bus station ....*gare routière*
train station ....*gare*
subway ....*métro*
airport ....*aéroport*
road map ....*carte routière*
one-way ticket ....*aller-simple*
round-trip ticket ....*aller-retour*
first class ....*première classe*
second class ....*seconde classe* or *deuxième*
smoking ....*fumeur*
no smoking ....*non-fumeur*
Does this train go to . . . ? ....*Est-ce que ce train s'arrête à . . . ?*
Where is/are . . . ? ....*Où est . . . ?/Où sont . . . ?*
How far is it from here to . . . ? *Quelle est la distance entre ici et . . . ?*

The Bare Necessities

aspirin ....*aspirines*
adhesive bandage ....*pansement adhésif*
barbershop, beauty shop ....*coiffeur, salon de beauté*
condom ....*préservatif*
dry cleaner ....*teinturerie*
self-service laundry ....*blanchisserie*
letter ....*lettre*
post office ....*bureau de poste*
postage stamp ....*timbre*
postcard ....*carte postale*
sanitary napkins ....*serviettes hygiéniques*
shampoo ....*shampooing*
shaving cream ....*lotion à raser*
soap ....*savon*
tampons ....*tampons périodiques*
tissues ....*mouchoirs en papier*
toilet paper ....*papier hygiénique*
toothpaste ....*dentifrice*

		Numbers	
Where is the bathroom/toilets?	..........*Où est la salle de bains?/Où sont les toilettes?*	zero	....*zéro*
men's room	....*WC pour hommes*	one	....*un*
women's room	......................................*WC pour dames*	two	....*deux*
		three	....*trois*
		four	....*quatre*
Days of the Week		five	....*cinq*
Monday	....*lundi*	six	....*six*
Tuesday	....*mardi*	seven	....*sept*
Wednesday	....*mercredi*	eight	....*huit*
Thursday	....*jeudi*	nine	....*neuf*
Friday	....*vendredi*	ten	....*dix*
Saturday	....*samedi*		
Sunday	....*dimanche*		

and Sites), where you may rent any of 40 châteaux or historic mansions throughout France for private receptions, weddings, or conventions. It also houses the **Mission du Patrimoine Photographique** (Mission for Photographic Patrimony), which mounts outstanding photo exhibits. Retrospectives of Dorothea Lange, W. Eugene Smith, and Edward Curtis have been featured in recent years. At the far end of the small, well-manicured rear garden, a gateway from the *orangerie* (orange grove) opens onto the **Place des Vosges**. ♦ Garden: daily. Photo gallery: open for exhibits only. 62 Rue St-Antoine (between Rues de Birague and de Turenne). 01.44.61.21.50. Photo exhibit information, 01.42.74.47.75. Métro: St-Paul

107 HÔTEL DE LA PLACE DES VOSGES

$$ Just down the street from the **Pavillon du Roi** entrance to the famous square sits this cozy, rather than regal, 16-room hotel. There's no restaurant. ♦ 12 Rue de Birague (between Rue St-Antoine and Pl des Vosges). 01.42.72.60.46; fax 01.42.72.02.64. Métros: St-Paul, Bastille. hotel.place.des. vosges@gofornet.com

108 L'IMPASSE

★★$$ One of the best-kept secrets in the Marais can be found tucked away in a narrow alley. In this delightful old neighborhood bistro, genial Françoise Mainguy and her talented young team serve traditional bourgeois cuisine in a pleasant wood-beamed dining room. Baked goat-cheese salads; *foie gras de canard* (duck foie gras); fillet of duck

with prunes, apples, and walnuts; roasted sea scallops; and iced nougat with raspberry purée are offered here at bargain prices. Everything is homemade, even the bread. The service is warm and attentive. ♦ M-F, lunch and dinner; Sa, dinner; service to midnight. Reservations recommended. 4 Impasse Guéménée (just north of Rue St-Antoine). 01.42.72.08.45. Métro: Bastille

109 STATUE DE BEAUMARCHAIS

The 18th-century comedies of Pierre-Augustin Caron de Beaumarchais (1732–1799), *The Barber of Seville* (1775) and *The Marriage of Figaro* (1784), were transformed by Rossini and Mozart, respectively, into operas whose factotum heroes were regarded as dangerously, even revolutionarily, independent. The radical sympathies of Beaumarchais were played out in real life, too: His office was secretly running guns to American revolutionaries. In keeping with the dramatist's satiric tradition, residents of the Bastille neighborhood are constantly dressing up his statue in outrageous costumes. ♦ At Rues St-Antoine and des Tournelles. Métro: Bastille

110 TEMPLE DE STE-MARIE

This circular temple was originally the chapel of the **Convent of the Visitation**, built by **François Mansart** in 1632, and is today a Protestant church. Nicolas Fouquet, the finance minister accused of embezzlement under Louis XIV, and Henri de Sévigné, the husband of Mme. de Sévigné who was killed in a duel in 1651, are buried here. ♦ Rues St-Antoine and Castex. Métro: Bastille

111 VILLAGE ST-PAUL

This jumble of antiques shops crammed into a courtyard often becomes a lively outdoor market. It's one of the few places in Paris to shop on Sunday. ♦ M, Th-Su. Bounded by Rues St-Paul and des Jardins-St-Paul, and by Rues de l'Ave-Maria and Charlemagne. Métros: St-Paul, Sully–Morland, Pont-Marie

112 THANKSGIVING

★★$$ North Americans who long for familiar tastes can sate themselves at Judith Blysen's restaurant and shop. The store carries bottled barbecue sauce, packages of Cracker Jacks, and Pop-Tarts, whereas the restaurant features Louisiana Cajun and creole specialties. Here you can feast on Cajun popcorn shrimp, filé gumbo, and crawfish pie as appetizers; and jambalaya, crab cakes Louisiana, blackened swordfish, barbecued ribs, and red beans and rice for a main course. When Thanksgiving approaches, fresh turkey (cooked, if you call ahead), pumpkins, cranberries, and all the fixings are on hand. ♦ Restaurant: Tu-F, dinner; Sa-Su, brunch. Shop: Daily. Closed 2 weeks in Aug and 1 week in Jan. 20 Rue St-Paul (between Rues des Lions-St-Paul and Charles-V). Shop and restaurant, 01.42.77.68.29. Métros: St-Paul, Sully–Morland

112 L'ENOTECA

★★$$ The Italian food served here, beneath colorful glass lamps and wood beams, often varies in specifics but never in quality. Neighborhood residents come for *gigot d'agneau* (leg of lamb) or *soupe de coquillages* (shellfish soup). The wine bar is a pleasant place to pass the afternoon or late evening, with more than 400 Italian wines as well as Italian cheeses for nibbling. ♦ Restaurant: daily, lunch and dinner. Wine bar: noon-1AM. Reservations recommended. 25 Rue Charles-V (at Rue St-Paul). 01.42.78.91.44. Métros: St-Paul, Sully–Morland

113 ALBION

Pick up a few paperback classics in English to read at cafés and on train rides. French people who are trying to learn English buy their books here. ♦ M-Sa, 1-6:30PM; closed last 3 weeks in Aug. 13 Rue Charles-V (between Rues Beautreillis and St-Paul). 01.42.72.50.71. Métro: Sully–Morland

114 HÔTEL ST-LOUIS MARAIS

$$ A rustic 16-room hotel is all that remains of the 18th-century **Hôtel des Célestins** that belonged to the **Celestine Monastery**. Around the corner on Rue Beautreillis is the original entrance to the convent, a stone portal with a weathered wooden door. The rooms are both charming and comfortable, but the five-story hotel's landmark status prevents the owners from installing an elevator. There's no restaurant. ♦ 1 Rue Charles-V (at Rue du Petit-Musc). 01.48.87.87.04; fax 01.48.87.33.26. Métro: Sully–Morland. www.paris_hotel.tm.fr

THE BASTILLE

The area around the Bastille, rejuvenated by the building of a new opera house in 1990 and by scores of art galleries, today is often called the SoHo of Paris. But this neighborhood was not always on the cutting edge of fashion. Originally a convergence of roads leading to Paris, it became a center for jobs and industry in the 17th century when Louis XIV attracted artisans and craft guilds to the area by exempting them from taxes. A century later the working-class haven was to become the symbol of freedom when, in July 1789, a crowd of citizens seized the **Bastille** and freed its prisoners, marking the start of the French Revolution.

In the 1930s, the district was filled with *bougnats*, Auvergnat dispensaries of wine and coal. Today the *quartier* has been discovered by painters and other bohemians, and the neighborhood has undergone a mind-boggling transformation. The once seedy **Rue de Lappe**, just off the **Place de la Bastille**, is now one of the trendiest streets in Paris. Quite a change from 1944, when Somerset Maugham wrote in *The Razor's Edge* that Rue de Lappe "gave the impression of sordid lust." There are artisans' studios and ateliers and a handful of Auvergnat restaurants, side by side with oh-so-trendy bars and cafés, avant-garde art galleries, and more than one too many Tex-Mex restaurants. Upscale establishments like Jean-Paul Gaultier's headquarters on the district's main drag, Rue du Faubourg St-Antoine, have caused rents to go up and forced struggling artists and artisans to move elsewhere.

115 LE BAR À HUITRES

★★$$ Known for its fresh and reasonably priced seafood, this restaurant composes delicious platters of *coquillage* and serves fine entrées of grilled salmon and grilled lobster. The dining room, amusingly decorated by **Jacques Garcia** with thousands of seashells embedded in the walls, is well run and casual. ♦ Daily, lunch and dinner until 2AM. 33 Blvd Beaumarchais (at Rue du Pas-de-la-Mule). 01.48.87.98.92. Métros: Chemin Vert, Bastille. Also at 33 Rue St-Jacques (between Blvd St-Germain and Rue Galande). 01.44.07.27.37. Métros: Maubert–Mutualité, Cluny–La Sorbonne; 112 Blvd Montparnasse (at Blvd Raspail). 01.43.20.71.01. Métro: Vavin

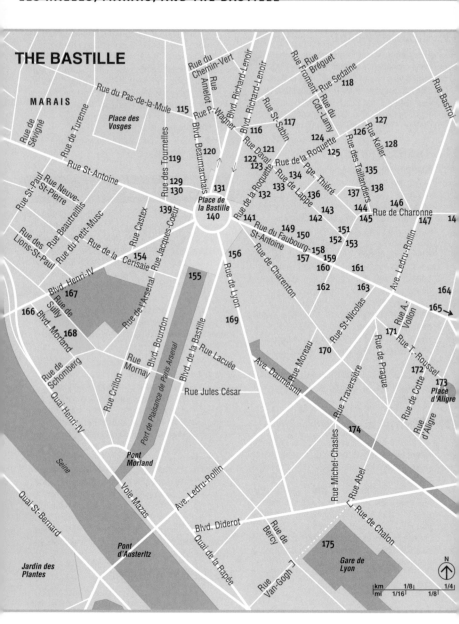

THE BASTILLE

MARAIS

Rue du Chemin-Vert
Rue du Pas-de-la-Mule 115
Rue de Turenne
Rue du Amelot
Rue P.-Wagner
Rue Richard-Lenoir
Blvd. Richard-Lenoir
Blvd. Richard-Lenoir
Rue Froment
Cdt-Lamy
Rue Bréguet
Rue Sedaine 118
Rue Basfroi
Place des Vosges
Rue de Sévigné
Rue St-Antoine
Rue des Tournelles
Blvd. Beaumarchais
Rue St-Sabin
117
127
Rue Keller
128
126
Rue St-Paul St-Pierre
Rue Neuve-St-Pierre
Rue Beautreillis
Rue du Petit-Musc
Rue de la Cerisaie
Rue Castex
Rue Jacques-Coeur
119
129
130
120
116
Rue Daval
121
122
123
124
125
Rue de la Roquette
Rue de la Pge. Thiéré
Rue des Taillandiers
135
138
137
131
132
133
134
136
Place de la Bastille
140
139
141
Rue du Faubourg-St-Antoine
142
143
144
145
146
147
Rue de Charonne
14
149
150
151
152
153
Ave. Ledru-Rollin
154
155
156
Rue de Lyon
Rue de Charenton
157
158
159
160
161
162
163
164
165 →
Rue A.-Vollon
Rue T.-Roussel
171
172
173
Place d'Aligre
Blvd. Henri-IV
167
Rue de Sully
166 Blvd. Morland
168
Rue de l'Arsenal
Blvd. Bourdon
Blvd. de la Bastille
Rue Lacuée
169
170
Rue St-Nicolas
Rue Moreau
Rue de Prague
Rue de Cotte
Rue d'Aligre
Rue de Schomberg
Rue Mornay
Rue Crillon
Port de Plaisance de Paris Arsenal
Rue Jules César
Ave. Daumesnil
Rue Traversière
Rue de la Bastille
Quai Henri-IV
Pont Morland
Voie Mazas
Ave. Ledru-Rollin
Rue Michel-Chasles
174
Rue Abel
Quai St-Bernard
Seine
Pont d'Austerlitz
Blvd. Diderot
Rue de Bercy
Rue de Chalon
175
Gare de Lyon
Jardin des Plantes
Quai de la Rapée
Rue Van-Gogh

N

km | 1/8 | 1/4
mi | 1/16 | 1/8

116 LE SEDAINE BASTILLE

Mme. and M. Rousseau's small corner bar peaks on Sunday between 10AM and 1PM when market workers escape their stalls for a quick *pastis* or rough Côte du Rhone. The floor is strewn with cigarette butts, sugar wrappers, and napkins. ♦ M-F; Su, 6AM-8PM. 18 Blvd Richard-Lenoir (at Rue Sedaine). 01.47.00.90.40. Métros: Bastille, Bréguet–Sabin

117 A LA PETITE FABRIQUE

In this little chocolate factory, you can watch the artisans ply their luscious craft in the immaculate kitchen to the rear of the shop. A Easter the boutique is packed to the gills with the traditional chocolate fish, rabbits, and chickens stuffed with small candies, and with real eggshells filled with chocolate and praline. More than 40 kinds of chocolate bars are available year-round, including praline, hazelnut, and orange fondant. Buy a bag of *orangettes* (strips of candied orange peel in chocolate) with no guilt about the calories. Taped to the counter is a magazine article hailing the benefits of chocolate as a physical stimulant, an antidepressant, a source of minerals, and a cure for broken hearts. ♦ Tu-Sa. 12 Rue St-Sabin (between Rues de la

Roquette and Sedaine). 01.48.05.82.02.
Métros: Bastille, Bréguet–Sabin

117 PAPETERIE SAINT SABIN

The two side-by-side boutiques of this elegant, modern stationery shop sell such classic French paper products as Canson Paper, colored paper from Nepal, and Oberthur agendas (which have been around more than 130 years longer than Filofax). There are also handmade sketchbooks, those wonderful Annonay notebooks and folders adorned with black blotches, and magnificent leather briefcases and carrying bags. ♦ Tu-Sa. 16 Rue St-Sabin (between Rues de la Roquette and Sedaine). 01.47.00.78.63. Métros: Bastille, Bréguet–Sabin

117 CAFÉ DE L'INDUSTRIE

★★$ Onion soup, carpaccio, entrecôte with potatoes gratin, and other simple, low-priced fare provide the sustenance, but the food here is strictly secondary. What fills the tables night after night at this quintessentially Bastille café is the ultra-easygoing, playful ambiance. Spears, anaconda skins, glamour shots of 1940s French movie starlets, and ridiculous oversize paintings grace the walls of this rambling but curiously cozy place. The attractive and refreshingly unprofessional waitresses (models, no doubt) add to the charm, as does the good recorded jazz, making the young Parisian *intello-mode* crowd that congregates here feel right at home. The owner is self-confident enough to close down on Saturday, the most popular day to dine out. This is a marvelous spot to read, write, or have a quiet conversation in the late afternoon. ♦ M-F, Su, meals served at all hours between noon and 12:30AM. 16 Rue St-Sabin (between Rues de la Roquette and Sedaine). 01.47.00.13.53. Métros: Bastille, Bréguet–Sabin

118 LIRE ENTRE LES VIGNES

★★$ "Read Between the Vines" is the English translation of this wine bar's name, and not surprisingly, its superb list of vintages is the place's distinguishing feature. But the food is good here, too. The predominantly local clientele chooses from items on the chalkboard that change daily. Foie gras, beef carpaccio, cold-cut platter, and *boudin noir* (pork blood sausage) with apples are some of the dishes you might find. Wash any of them down with a sturdy Cahors Vieilles Vignes or a lighter Monpertuis. The place is relaxed and airy, with a skylight over the main dining room, rough wooden floors, and old bottles, scales, and crockery. ♦ M-F, lunch and dinner; Sa, dinner.

38 Rue Sedaine (between Rues Popincourt and du Commandant-Lamy). 01.43.55.69.49. Métros: Bréguet–Sabin, Voltaire

119 L'ENDROIT

★★$ In French it means simply "the place," and if the implication intended is the place for good food in a winsome setting, the name is spot-on. The unusual look of the dining room, with its ocher walls tastefully adorned with artwork for sale and paper-leaf mobiles strewn from the curved wooden ceiling, hooks you quickly and keep your aesthetic sensibilities happy from start of meal to finish. There are two compelling menus to choose from, one slightly fancier and priced about a third higher than the other. From the former choose such appetizers as a tantalizing caramelized tomato tarte Tatin and main course of scallop carpaccio in pistachio oil; from the latter, filo-wrapped goat cheese with a marinated red-pepper-and-olive-oil purée and *emincé* of chicken à la vanille. Desserts are less inventive, though if you see something such as white chocolate mousse in a thyme-mango coulis on either menu, it's probably worth a go. The wine list is uncomplicated, and, adding to the fun, with many bottles, such as a light 2001 Brouilly Château de la Chaize from Beaujolais, you only pay for as much as you drink. ♦ Tu-Sa, lunch and dinner. 24 Rue des Tournelles (between Rues du Pas-de-la-Mule and de la Bastille). 01.42.72.03.07. Métro: Bastille

120 2-20 BLVD BEAUMARCHAIS

Here once stood the luxurious mansion and gardens of Caron de Beaumarchais (1732-1799), the 18th-century dramatist who wrote *The Marriage of Figaro* and who now resides in **Père-Lachaise Cemetery**. The garden was garnished with statues (including one of Voltaire), grottoes, a labyrinth, and an orchard. In 1818 his heirs sold the property to the city for less than a quarter of what Beaumarchais had invested, and it was demolished to facilitate the opening of Canal St-Martin. The buildings now have residential and commercial space. ♦ Between Pl de la Bastille and Rue Pasteur-Wagner. Métro: Bastille

121 HÔTEL DAVAL

$ Didier Gonod's friendly hotel is nothing fancy—the 23 rooms are small and simply decorated—but who could ask for more than a clean, quiet, cheap room in the heart of the lively Bastille quarter? A friendly German shepherd named Malko is in residence.

There's no restaurant. ◆ 21 Rue Daval (between Rue St-Sabin and Blvd Richard-Lenoir). 01.47.00.51.23; fax 01.40.21.80.26. Métro: Bastille. hoteldaval@wanadoo.fr

122 COUR DAMOYE

Often used as a filming location for *vieux Paris* movies, this quaint-as-can-be cobblestone *allée* running between Place de la Bastille and Rue Daval is lined with art ateliers, gift shops, an old-fashioned *brûlerie* (coffee-roasting shop), and a wine cave. The street is gated and closed to the public at night. 9AM-8PM ◆ Off Rue Daval (between Rue de la Roquette and Blvd Richard-Lenoir). Métro: Bastille

122 RELAIS DU MASSIF CENTRAL

★★$ Softly smiling and amply built Mme. Caroline Coutinho makes sure that no one leaves her restaurant hungry. Among the mainly Auvergne-inspired specialties on her amazingly complete menu are frog's legs Provençal, grilled shrimp with cognac-laced lobster sauce, *faux-filet* (beef sirloin) with Roquefort cheese, *gratin de coquilles St-Jacques* (scallops au gratin), sole meunière, and *autruche* (ostrich) with black pepper sauce. Amidst the here-today-gone-tomorrow trendiness of the Bastille, this is the real thing—which is why neighborhood workers, residents, and tourists keep coming back. ◆ M-Sa, lunch and dinner. 16 Rue Daval (between Rue de la Roquette and Blvd Richard-Lenoir). 01.47.00.46.55. Métro: Bastille

123 CAFÉ IGUANA

★$ This two-story Tex-Mex bar has a woody interior and ceiling fans and serves omelettes, chili, grilled meat, carpaccio, sandwiches, and salads. However, drinking is the main purpose of most who come here, and the cocktail list offers blue lagoons, silver bananas, white Russians, 11 types of vodka, 16 kinds of whiskey, and the darkest draft Murphy's this side of Cork. There's a tiny *non-fumeur* (nonsmoking) room upstairs. ◆ Daily, 9AM-4AM. 15 Rue de la Roquette (at Rue Daval). 01.40.21.39.99. Métro: Bastille

124 BLUE ELEPHANT

★★★$$ The Tikki Room meets Thailand in this veritable jungle of exotic flora, with a little wooden bridge, a waterfall, and young waiters in silk robes gliding among the tables serving sweet and spicy Thai specialties. Try the *tom yam khung* (spicy shrimp soup with lemon), *colvert siamois* (duck with raisins, pineapple, basil, and coconut milk), *massaman d'agneau* (a southern Muslim lamb dish in a sweet sauce), or the chicken soufflé served in banana leaves. There are Blue Elephant restaurants under the same ownership in London, Brussels, Copenhagen, and several other cities. ◆ M-F, Su, lunch and dinner; Sa, dinner. Reservations recommended. 43-45 Rue de la Roquette (between Rues du Commandant-Lamy and St-Sabin). 01.47.00.42.00. Métros: Bastille, Bréguet-Sabin

125 CITÉ DE LA ROQUETTE

Pop into this small dead-end passage for a look at the charming brick ateliers of wood-workers and violin makers, through the gate to the left of the lumberyard. This is a favorite location spot for filmmakers. ◆ Métros: Bastille, Bréguet-Sabin

126 LOUIS-PHILIPPE FOUNTAIN

This stone fountain, decorated with delicately carved fruit, acanthus leaves, shells, and lions' heads, was built in 1846 during the reign of Louis-Philippe. The now-dry fountain is off-limits to the public, closed off by iron gates (which have been adopted by locals as a bike rack). Notice the ship, the symbol of Paris, carved in the center keystone. A similar fountain was erected on the Rue de Charenton but was demolished in 1906 for the opening of the Rue de Prague. ◆ 70 Rue de la Roquette (between Rues Keller and des Taillandiers). Métros: Bastille, Bréguet-Sabin

127 THÉÂTRE DE LA BASTILLE

A red neon sign announces this theater, which, under the direction of the innovative Jean-Marie Hordé, features daring and inventive ventures in contemporary dance and theater. ◆ Box office: M-F, by phone only; 30 minutes before performances. 76 Rue de la Roquette (between Rues Basfroi and Keller). 01.43.57.42.14. Métros: Bastille, Bréguet-Sabin

128 GALERIE AKIÉ ARICCHI

Not limited by any particular style, Akié Aricchi shows the work of international painters and sculptors, both abstract and figurative. She is spontaneous and eclectic in her selection—if she likes the spirit of the artist's work, she shows it. Some of the artists she has taken to are Akiko Toriumi, Lechevallier, Tony Soulié, Helga Hommes, and Alan Simon. ◆ Tu-Sa, 3-7PM. 26 Rue Keller (between Rues de Charonne and de la Roquette). 01.40.21.64.57. Métros: Bastille, Ledru-Rollin

129 HÔTEL BASTILLE SPERIA

$$ One minute by foot from the **Place de la Bastille** and 3 minutes from the **Place des Vosges**, this bright, spotless, and tastefully decorated modern hotel should fill the bill for those who want to be in the heart of the action without going broke. All 42 rooms have good, firm beds, up-to-date bathrooms, cable

TV, and a restful pale-pink-and-gray color scheme, and there are plants everywhere. The hotel has no restaurant, but a buffet is served in the cheerful breakfast room. ♦ 1 Rue de la Bastille (at Rue des Tournelles). 01.42.72.04.01; fax 01.42.72.56.38. Métro: Bastille. speria@micronet.fr

29 BOFINGER

★★$$ Dating from 1864, this is among Paris's oldest, busiest, and most spectacularly ornate brasseries. House legend holds that it was the first in the city to pour draft beer. Specialties are *fruits de mer*, Alsatian *choucroute*, broiled lobster, Riesling and Gewürztraminer wines, and Belle Epoque splendor. Reserve well in advance to secure a table *sous la coupole*, in the gorgeous glass-domed main dining room on the ground floor, or in the upstairs room designed by the artist **Hansi**. Service can be slow on particularly busy nights. This is no place to go if you're in a hurry. ♦ Daily, lunch and dinner until 1AM. Reservations recommended. 5-7 Rue de la Bastille (between Rues Jean-Beausire and des Tournelles). 01.42.72.87.82. Métro: Bastille

30 LE PETIT BOFINGER

★$$ Spawned by **Bofinger** directly across the street in 1993, this *décontracté* (easygoing) 1940s-style bistro serves *pâté de tête* (head-cheese), *salade d'endives* with cantal cheese and walnuts, very good grilled steaks, and in winter, a steamy *pot au feu*. There is also a special children's menu, a rarity in Paris. The mosaic floors and the 1945 wall mural depicting the **Place de la Bastille** were uncovered by workers during a renovation. ♦ Daily, lunch and dinner. 6 Rue de la Bastille (between Pl de la Bastille and Rue des Tournelles). 01.42.72.05.23. Métro: Bastille

30 LE BISTROT DU DÔME BASTILLE

★★$$ This friendly seafood place features Mediterranean-style fish soup, *encornets à la plancha* (little squid grilled on an open fire), salmon tartare, *daurade en croûte de sel* (dorade baked in a crust of salt), and *bar grillé à la provençale* (grilled bass). With fish, the Mâcon Villages Domaine des deux Roches is an especially good choice from the wine

list. The quiet upstairs dining room is lovely. The famous **Le Dôme** in Montparnasse (108 Blvd Montparnasse, at Rue Delambre; 01.43.35.25.81) is this bistro's *maison mère* (parent restaurant). ♦ Daily, lunch and dinner. 2 Rue de la Bastille (at Rue des Tournelles). 01.48.04.88.44. Métro: Bastille. Also at 1 Rue Delambre (at Blvd Raspail). 01.43.35.32.00. Métro: Vavin

131 BOULEVARD RICHARD-LENOIR

One of the city's most pleasant outdoor markets is situated in the center island of this wide boulevard, between Place de la Bastille and Rue St-Sabin. Fine produce and poultry are sold: Some stalls feature organically grown fruits and vegetables; others offer roast chickens and ducks. In the fall several vendors deal in wild mushrooms. Sunday is the market's big day, when you'll find merchants earnestly hawking everything from antique furniture, cookware, and *savon* (soap) *de Marseille* to chrysanthemums, pig's feet, and Babar-the-elephant beach towels; singers and musicians entertain. ♦ Market: Th, Su, mornings. Métros: Bastille, Bréguet–Sabin

132 SUKIYAKI

★$ It's all here: standard Japanese décor, a sushi bar, and a menu featuring sashimi, sushi, sukiyaki, and Japanese barbecue that you grill at your own table. ♦ M-Sa, lunch and dinner; Su, dinner. 12 Rue de la Roquette (between Pl de la Bastille and Rue de Lappe). 01.49.23.04.98. Métro: Bastille

133 RUE DE LAPPE

Once populated with natives of the Auvergne region of France and now the main nightlife artery of the trendy Bastille, this narrow cobbled street was named in 1652 for Girard de Lappe, who owned the gardens and marshland through which the street pierced. On 23 December 1830, Louis-Philippe passed down the Rue de Lappe during a royal visit to the Faubourg, filling the residents with such enthusiasm that the following year they named the street after him. In 1848, after the February Revolution in which the "Citizen King" was overthrown, the street reverted to its original name. A dreary little passage off Rue de Lappe is still named for the rejected hero. ♦ Métros: Bastille, Ledru-Rollin

133 CHEZ TEIL

One of the few remaining Auvergnat establishments in the neighborhood, this shop sells products from the Auvergne region in central France. Take home a jar of *confit d'oie* (goose-meat confit), some *saucisson sec* (dry sausages), a tasty nut cake, or a pair of *galoches* (the Auvergnat version of clogs). ♦ Tu-Sa. 6 Rue de Lappe (between Rues de Charonne and de la Roquette). 01.47.00.41.28. Métro: Bastille

133 66 CAFÉ

$ The theme here is—you guessed it—Route 66 in the USA. The red vinyl seats, rough-hewn wood floor, and wagon wheel over the bar (which specializes in such drinks as whiskey sours, Long Island iced tea, and screwdrivers) all contribute to the all-American ambiance. US-style grub includes fried chicken, T-bone steak, cheeseburgers, apple pie, and banana splits. At night the place is jammed with boisterous young Yankees and French amateurs partaking of this slice of the American cultural pie. ♦ Restaurant: daily, 6PM-2AM. Happy hour: daily, 6-8:30PM. 8 Rue de Lappe (between Rues de Charonne and de la Roquette). 01.43.38.30.20. Métro: Bastille

134 LA PIRADA

★$ A gigantic bull's head keeps watch while Spanish-food enthusiasts drink sangria and consume tapas and paella. ♦ Daily, lunch and dinner until 2AM. 7 Rue de Lappe (between Passage Louis-Philippe and Rue de la Roquette). 01.47.00.73.61. Métro: Bastille

134 LE BALAJO

Founded in 1936 by Jo France, the *bal à Jo* (Jo's ballroom) was Paris's most popular dance hall in the heyday of the *bal musette*, frequented by Maurice Chevalier and Edith Piaf. After a long, steady decline following World War II, the place bounced back in the 1990s and is as *branché* (trendy) as ever today. Announced by a giant neon sign, the dance hall is full of people straight out of a Fellini flick dancing to Latin, swing, or rock music on the small, cramped dance floor, or relaxing on sticky red vinyl seats. A DJ spins disks on the balcony where an orchestra once played, and on the opposite wall is a zany model of a fictitious city. Tuesday, Wednesday, and Thursday nights feature salsa music; Friday and Saturday nights offer a mixed bag. Thursday and Sunday afternoons are *matinée retro* (nostalgia time), and Sunday night has tango on tap. ♦ Nights: Tu, W, Th, 10PM-5AM; F-Sa, 10:30PM-5:30AM; Su, 9PM-1AM. Afternoons: Th, 2:30PM-6:30PM; Su, 3PM-7PM. 9 Rue de Lappe (between Passage Louis-Philippe and Rue de la Roquette). 01.47.00.07.87. Métro: Bastille

134 HAVANITA CAFE

★$ Buzzing with the warmth of the Caribbean, this Cuban restaurant has well-worn leather armchairs, colorful wall and ceiling murals, and palms galore. Join the **Balajo** crowd, which arrives late for dinner, and fill up on generous portions of sautéed langoustines with fried bananas, Cuban chicken salad, and exotic fruits, accompanied by mojitos, piña coladas, coco locos, and other Cuban cocktails. Avoid heavy meals here. That's not their thing. ♦ Daily, dinner until 2AM. Happy hour: daily, 5-8PM. 11 Rue de Lappe (between Passage Louis-Philippe and Rue de la Roquette). 01.43.55.96.42. Métro: Bastille

135 LES TAILLANDIERS

★★$ The locals don't mind waiting for a table at this popular French bistro serving hearty fare at a reasonable price. Choose from such popular favorites as *petit salé* (salted pork with lentils) and *blanquette de veau* (veal in béchamel with mushrooms and rice). ♦ M-Sa lunch; Th-Sa, dinner. 22 Rue des Taillandiers (between Rues de Charonne and de la Roquette). 01.48.05.98.24. Métros: Bastille, Ledru-Rollin

136 HÔTEL LES SANS-CULOTTES

$ If you're lucky enough to land one of the 10 rooms in this charming old-fashioned inn, you're getting the best deal in the Bastille. Although small, the rooms are equipped with 21st-century comforts like showers and TV sets, and hotel guests get to have breakfast in the handsome 1900s-style **Bistrot les Sans-Culottes** downstairs (see below). ♦ 27 Rue de Lappe (between Rue de Charonne and Passage Louis-Philippe). 01.49.23.85.80; fax 01.48.05.08.56. Métro: Bastille

Within Hôtel les Sans-Culottes:

BISTROT LES SANS-CULOTTES

★★$$ Entrepreneurial young owner Ahmed Arab opened this restaurant in 1991, but the zinc bar, elegantly curved stair, ornate ceilings, wall mirrors, and other fin de siècle–style details make it look as if it's been here for at least a century. The name *sans-culottes* (without knickers) was given to the French revolutionaries, who wore the trousers of the working class rather than the knickers favored by the aristocracy. The menu, however, features both the traditional and the revolutionary: foie gras, grilled salmon with *pistou* (a creamy basil-and-garlic sauce) and saffron rice, veal kidneys with *pleurottes* (wild mushrooms), *crème brûlée pistaché*, and warm apple tart. The large outdoor terrace, the only one on the street, is the perfect vantage point from which to watch the wild parade along the Rue de Lappe. ♦ M, breakfast for hotel guests only; Tu-Su, breakfast, lunch, and dinner. 01.48.05.42.92

137 GALERIE JOUSSE SEGUIN: ESPACE GRAN DIA

Behind this red-and-yellow-painted brick façade is a collection of original-edition architects' and designers' furniture, with a particular emphasis on pieces from the 1950s. There are many works by Jean Prouvé, Alexandre Noll, and Charlotte Perriand. The building is also home to a second Galerie Jousse Seguin in which owners Patrick Jousse and Philippe Seguin have been showing a broad range of works by contemporary international artists since 1989. At opposite ends of the spectrum are Karin Kneffe's precise, realist watercolors of fruits and Thomas Grünfeld's disturbing installations of taxidermy misfits, featuring such fantastical creatures as a combination sheep–St. Bernard and a fox-pheasant-swan. Works by Serge Comte, Stephen Hepworth, and Peter Hopkins are also exhibited here. ♦ M-Sa. 5 Rue des Taillandiers (between Rue de Charonne and Passage des Taillandiers). 01.47.00.32.35. Métros: Bastille, Ledru-Rollin

138 GALERIE JORGE ALYSKEWYCZ

For the last several years this gallery's Argentinian-Ukrainian curator has dedicated his space to installations and sculptures, with the occasional painting or photography exhibit. The sculptures of Roland Cognet, Michel Roginsky, and Alejandra Riera and the conceptual installations of Arnold Schalks have been featured here. ♦ Tu-Sa, 2:30-7PM. 14 Rue des Taillandiers (between Rues de Charonne and de la Roquette). 01.48.06.59.23. Métros: Bastille, Ledru-Rollin

39 5 RUE ST-ANTOINE

This building marks the position of the **Bastille** courtyard where the angry mob gained access. A plaque at the site reads: *Ici était l'entrée de l'avant-cour de la Bastille par laquelle les assaillants pénétrèrent dans la forteresse le 14 juillet 1789* ("Here was the entrance of the forecourt of the Bastille through which the assailants penetrated the fortress the 14th of July 1789"). ♦ At Rue Jacques-Coeur. Métro: Bastille

40 PLACE DE LA BASTILLE

On 14 July 1789, 633 people stormed the **Bastille** (the French counterpart to the Tower of London), captured its ammunition depot, released its prisoners (only 7, and none political), lynched its governor, and demolished the fortress, thus sparking the French Revolution. Every year on the 14th of July, these events are celebrated in Paris with parades and dancing in the streets.

The eight-towered Bastille was built in 1370 by Provost **Hugues Aubriot** as a fortified palace for Charles V and was later transformed by Cardinal Richelieu into a holding tank where political prisoners were detained without trial. During its baleful history, the prison held Voltaire, who was imprisoned for his biting verse, as well as the notorious Marquis de Sade and the mysterious "Man in the Iron Mask." Paving stones, laid where Rue du Faubourg St-Antoine intersects the square, mark the site of the original towers. The 170-foot **Colonne de Juillet** (July Column) in the center of the square commemorates the July 1830 Revolution, which overthrew the last of the Bourbon kings. The gilded figure perched on top is not an allegory of Liberty, as many suppose, but a winged Mercury.

Half a dozen cafés and restaurants ring the spacious place, all of them with big outdoor terraces. They offer more viewing pleasure than practically any movie or stage play, just for the price of a coffee. ♦ At Rue du Faubourg St-Antoine and Blvd Beaumarchais. Métro: Bastille

141 ATELIER FRANCK BORDAS

This gallery has put out its own editions of works on paper since 1978, when the curators established an adjacent atelier where artists can create prints on the premises. Such internationally known artists as Gilles Aillaud, Jean-Paul Chambas, Jan Voss, and Robert Wilson have all exhibited in the light and airy spaces, which are perfect for viewing the original prints, artists' books, and lithographed travel cards. ♦ Tu-Sa, 2-7PM; closed in Aug. 2 Rue de la Roquette, in the Cour Février, off the Passage du Cheval-Blanc (at Rue du Faubourg St-Antoine). 01.47.00.31.61. Métro: Bastille

142 GALERIE LILIANE ET MICHEL DURAND-DESSERT

Located behind an art bookstore, this is one of the best-known galleries in Paris. Within its white lofty space is fine art in all mediums from noted artists, including Joseph Beuys, Stanley Brouwn, Yan Pei-Ming, Yves Openheim, and Gerard Garouste. ♦ Tu-Sa. 28 Rue de Lappe (between Rues de Charonne and de la Roquette). 01.48.06.92.23. Métro: Bastille

143 LA GALOCHE D'AURILLAC

★★$$ Mme. and M. Bonnet's *restaurant Auvergnat* is one of the last holdouts from the days when this neighborhood was heavily populated with craftspeople and others from the Auvergne region in central France. The

---

Restaurants/Clubs: Red | Hotels: Purple | Shops: Orange | Outdoors/Parks: Green | Sights/Culture: Blue

eatery is named for the wooden or leather clogs traditionally worn by French workers, and numerous examples of *galoches* are hung from the ceiling in neat rows. The menu features *salade du cantal* (salad with cantal cheese), lentils *à l'auvergnate* (cooked with bacon and goose fat), *confit de canard* (preserved duck breast) with apples, and sausage from Auvergne. The regional cheeses, such as cabécous, cantal, and bleu d'Auvergne, are a good excuse for another bottle of Côtes d'Auvergne or Marcillac. ♦ Tu-Sa, lunch and dinner. 41 Rue de Lappe (between Rue de Charonne and Passage Louis-Philippe). 01.47.00.77.15. Métros: Bastille, Ledru-Rollin

143 GALERIE ALAIN GUTHARC

This gallery specializes in exhibiting photographs, video, and sculpture with an emphasis on such young artists as Joël Bartoloméo and Claire Chevrier. ♦ Tu-F afternoon; Sa. 47 Rue de Lappe (between Rue de Charonne and Passage Louis-Philippe). 01.47.00.32.10. Métros: Bastille, Ledru-Rollin

144 GALERIE LAVIGNES-BASTILLE

In his large, light-bathed gallery, Jean-Pierre Lavignes displays contemporary and modern art works from all over the world that he sells *dépôt-vente* (on consignment). It's an eclectic variety of pieces, with everything from outrageous kitsch to real art (whatever that is). At the very least, it makes for an amusing foray, and with luck you may find something you like. M. Lavignes also represents noted artists Jean-Claude Meynard and Calum Fraser. ♦ M-F, 2-7PM; Sa, 11AM-12:30PM, 2-7PM. 27 Rue de Charonne (between Rue des Taillandiers and Passage Thiéré). 01.47.00.88.18; fax 01.43.55.91.32. Métros: Bastille, Ledru-Rollin

145 LA CHAISERIE DU FAUBOURG

Hundreds of chairs waiting to be repaired or retrieved by their owners are stacked *pêle-mêle* (that's French for "higgledy-piggledy") from floor to ceiling, leaving only a small passage for Gérard Decourbe to squeeze through to his desk. It's a wonder Decourbe is able to find the particular chair he is looking for, but he has a special cataloging system that makes even the Louvre's look simple. If he's not too busy, you may be able to talk him into a tour of the atelier in the **Passage de l'Homme** where chairs are repaired and manufactured. There you'll meet paint-spattered crafter Gérard Brousset, who jokes with pride that he can make old chairs look new and new chairs look old. ♦ M-Sa. 26 Rue de Charonne (between Ave Ledru-Rollin and Rue du Faubourg St-Antoine). 01.43.57.67.51. Métros: Bastille, Ledru-Rollin

145 PASSAGE L'HOMME

Take a detour into this pleasant ivy-covered passage and peek through the windows of **Ateliers d'Art** (01.47.00.81.22), where artisans keep alive the traditional craft of binding books with leather and gold leaf. ♦ 26 Rue de Charonne (between Ave Ledru-Rollin and Rue du Faubourg St-Antoine). Métro: Ledru-Rollin

146 CENTRE GAI ET LESBIEN

At the city's only gay and lesbian information center, interested folks can find information on the gay scene in Paris, including the inside scoop on restaurants, bars, and clubs. There is plenty of informational literature, a small gallery, a library of books and magazines, a bulletin board, and a small café in the corner. Numerous lesbian and gay groups hold meetings here. The friendly staff members are happy to answer questions about health concerns or gay rights issues either in person or on the phone. Free *préservatifs* (condoms) are there for the taking. ♦ M-Sa, 4-8PM. 3 Rue Keller (between Rues de Charonne and de la Roquette). 01.43.57.21.47; fax 01.43.57.27.93. Métro: Ledru-Rollin. cglparis@cglparis.org; www.cglparis.org

146 LE SOUK

★★$$ To get to Marrakech in the wink of an eye, step past the colorful bins full of spices in front of this restaurant and into its cozy dining room where amiable waiters in burnooses glide through the authentically Moorish décor. The standard couscous and *tajine* with lamb, chicken, *mechoui* (oven-baked mutton), or *merguez* (spicy North African sausage) are excellent. But for some alternate takes on the tried-and-true recipes, try the *tajine* with duck figs, and lemon or with fish and fennel, or the couscous with chicken, raisins, spiced semolina, and cinnamon. The restaurant also serves complete vegetarian meals, and there's a small but well-chosen selection of French, Algerian, and Moroccan wines. Owner Lahlu Arab is the brother of Ahmed Arab, who owns the **Bistrot les Sans-Culottes** (see page 255). ♦ Tu-F, lunch, dinner; Sa, Su, lunch. Reservations recommended. 1 Rue Keller (at Rue de Charonne). 01.49.29.05.08. Métro: Ledru-Rollin

146 PAUSE CAFÉ

★$ On a warm, sunny day, pause for a break on the terrace of this popular local hangout and have a bottle of crisp white Montlouis

Domaine Levasseur and a plate of assorted cheeses. Or try the warm goat cheese with *pain Moisan*, duck with orange, or one of the quiche-and-salad combinations. If the weather isn't obliging, take a seat by the horseshoe-shaped bar or at one of the tables in the airy dining room, which tripled its size after the café was featured in Cédric Klapish's 1996 film *Chacun Cherche son Chat*, a big hit in France. ♦ Daily, lunch and dinner until midnight; Su, brunch. 41 Rue de Charonne (at Rue Keller). 01.48.06.80.33. Métro: Ledru-Rollin

47 LE BISTROT DU PEINTRE

★★$ This corner café is an architectural jewel. It opened in 1907 as a bistro–billiard hall and retains the original Eiffel-era girders, carved wood panels, and peeling gold-leaf lettering. Have a *pastis* or some Berthillon ice cream on the terrace and luxuriate in the faded fin de siècle elegance. Traditional French bistro fare is also served. ♦ M-Sa, breakfast, lunch, and dinner until 2AM; Su, breakfast, lunch, and dinner. 116 Avenue Ledru-Rollin (at Rue de Charonne). 01.47.00.34.39. Métro: Ledru-Rollin

48 DAME JEANNE

★★$$ The two sunny little red and yellow ocher dining rooms (one of them no-smoking) in this Provençal bistro-style restaurant rarely have an empty seat—no surprise, given the high quality of Chef Francis Lévèque's cuisine and his remarkably affordable prices, for the fixed-price menus in particular. Risotto with wild mushrooms, mesclun salad, *souris d'agneau* (braised lamb shanks), *tournedos de lapin* (grilled center cut of rabbit), grilled slice of *carrelet* (fresh flounder) with crushed potatoes in olive oil, and madeleines with chocolate sauce and pear marmalade are some of his specialties. There is an excellent selection of southern French wines, also reasonably priced. Service can be a bit slow, but in a place like this, what's the hurry? ♦ Tu-Sa, lunch and dinner; closed 3 weeks from mid-Aug. Reservations recommended. 60 Rue de Charonne (between Ave Ledru-Rollin and Rue Trousseau). 01.47.00.37.40. Métro: Ledru-Rollin

49 ATELIER 33

This discreet 17th-century building was an inn before the French Revolution, and today is one of the few remaining buildings on the street that witnessed the bloody events of 1789. It is notable for its architectural details, including mansard roofs, balcony, windows, ironwork, and the wood staircase visible through the double doors in the courtyard.

Fashion designer **Henry Leparque** has renovated this historic building—now the home of his boutique and ateliers—with respect and elegance, leaving the old stone walls as a backdrop for his simple, classic men's and women's clothing. The young *créateur* helped change the Faubourg from a street of furniture-making workshops to one of fashion houses, yet his fashions are anything but trend-driven. Because his ateliers are upstairs, he is able to bring the mix-and-match concept to a new height for clients who visit the shop. They can choose their own buttons, ask for another lining in a jacket, or order a pair of gloves and a hat to go with a coat, ending up with a customized ensemble that will be ready in a week. Friendly and excitable, Leparque can easily be persuaded to give you a tour of his ateliers. Note the chairs in the dressing rooms: They once graced the winter garden of the Côte d'Azur estate of the Gould family, the heirs of the 19th-century robber baron Jay Gould. ♦ M-Sa, 10:30AM-7:30PM. 33 Rue du Faubourg St-Antoine (between Rue de Charonne and Pl de la Bastille). 01.43.40.61.63. Métro: Bastille

150 SAN SAN

★$ This Bastille bar is named after its young owners, Messrs. Sanz and Sans. The exterior is rough and raw, with exposed brick and steel beams, and the interior features a framed video screen running a continuous closed-circuit film of the bar. The eclectic menu offers such dishes as salmon steak and steak tandoori, and pear tart for dessert. ♦ Daily, breakfast, lunch, and dinner until 2AM. 49 Rue du Faubourg St-Antoine (between Rue de Charonne and Pl de la Bastille). 01.44.75.78.78. Métros: Bastille, Ledru-Rollin

151 LES PORTES

★$ Behind the rustic façade with its namesake doors, this restaurant's harried owner serves lunches of ricotta-and-tomato tarts; chicken, potato, and tarragon salad; salmon ravioli with peas and creamy fennel sauce; and such *plats du jour* as gingered salmon. At night the dining room becomes a well-populated bar. ♦ Restaurant: daily, lunch. Bar: daily, 5PM-2AM. 15 Rue de Charonne (at Rue de Lappe). 01.40.21.70.61. Métros: Bastille, Ledru-Rollin

152 CHEZ PAUL

★★$$ Although the customers are trendy, this lively 1920s-era eatery is quite unpretentious and serves such authentic bistro fare as *magret de canard* (roasted duck breast), lamb with rosemary, rabbit stuffed with goat cheese, and mint, and *La Tentation de St.*

Restaurants/Clubs: Red | **Hotels: Purple** | Shops: Orange | **Outdoors/Parks: Green** | Sights/Culture: Blue

Antoine (St. Anthony's Temptation—pig's feet, ears, snout, and tail sautéed and grilled). For dessert try the profiteroles or the *poire au vin et sa glace cannelle* (pears preserved in wine with cinnamon ice cream). ♦ Daily, lunch and dinner. Reservations recommended. 13 Rue de Charonne (at Rue de Lappe). 01.47.00.34.57. Métros: Bastille, Ledru-Rollin

152 AXIS

This boutique's humorous collection of kooky objects includes an escargot plate with snail-shaped ceramic cups, Philippe Starck's daddy longlegs juice squeezer, leg-shaped nutcrackers, and a collection of cartoon character Géteon paraphernalia. ♦ Tu-Sa; closed in Aug. 13 Rue de Charonne (at Rue de Lappe). 01.48.06.79.10. Métros: Bastille, Ledru-Rollin

153 ISABEL MARANT

One of the most successful young clothing designers to establish her base in the Bastille area, Isabel Marant describes her look as "ethnic but without the folklore"—that is, inspired by colors, shapes, and fabrics from Africa and Asia, but freely mixing raw and natural materials with the latest stretch fabrics, all with a rich, silky feel. Her clothes are elegant in silhouette, fitted close to the body, made to be worn every day and washed or cleaned easily. Besides her original boutique here, her fashions are also sold at **Galeries Lafayette**, Barneys, and other large stores and at a second boutique she has opened in St-Germain-des-Prés. ♦ M-Sa. 16 Rue de Charonne (between Rue du Faubourg St-Antoine and Ave Ledru-Rollin). 01.49.29.71.55. Métros: Bastille, Ledru-Rollin. Also at 1 Rue Jacob (at Rue de l'Echaudé). 01.47.20.77.09. Métro: Odéon

154 BAZ'ART CAFÉ

**\$\$ Here is that rare kind of place that seems to shift its function according to your mood: If you're hungry, the restaurant appeal of the Baz'Art is undeniable; if you just want to read alone with a café au lait by your side, a friendlier, more comfortable café would be hard to find. The allure comes from both a slightly off-the-beaten-path location and the décor, which couples exposed concrete walls with red velvet chairs and heavy iron chande-

liers. And the café/bistro fare doesn't disappoint, either: Try the likes of *magret de canard* with a blackberry cream sauce or goat-cheese ravioli with creamed spinach and cumin. There's a very reasonably priced selection of wines by the glass, and while many desserts are run-of-the-mill, the white chocolate mousse in a red berry coulis is seventh heaven on a plate. ♦ Daily, 9AM-2PM. 36 Blvd Henri IV (at Rue de la Cerisaie). 01.42.78.62.23. Métro: Sully Morland or Bastille

155 CANAL ST-MARTIN

Dating from 1821, this industrial canal was dug to facilitate delivery of materials to the manufacturers in the Faubourg St-Antoine quarter. It flows under Boulevard Richard-Lenoir and Place de la Bastille and comes out at Port de l'Arsenal, the pleasure-boat harbor immediately to the south of Place de la Bastille. Its northern end is at the Bassin de la Villette (northeast of Place de Stalingrad in the 19th arrondissement). Boat tours are offered between April and November by **Paris Canal** (01.42.40.96.97) and **Canauxrama** (01.42.39.15.00). The unusual cruises pass along the tree-lined canal, through more than a mile of tunnel and nine locks, and under two swinging bridges and eight footbridges between the Port de l'Arsenal and the Parc de la Villette. ♦ Métro: Bastille

156 OPÉRA BASTILLE

In the early 1980s, the French government appointed **Carlos Ott**, a Canadian-Uruguayan architect, to design what was to be the largest opera house in the world on the Place de la Bastille. The gigantesque silver-surfaced structure came under heavy criticism as soon as it went up (the building was callled the world's largest public toilet by some), but whatever its aesthetic merits, the edifice's presence sparked the renewal of the Bastille area, helping it to become the trendiest neighborhood in Paris. The facility, billed as the "people's opera house," entertains an estimated 700,000 ticket holders a year and includes an amphitheater and a stage for smaller performances. Its opening was planned for the July 1989 bicentennial of the storming of the Bastille and the French Revolution, but dissension among administrators, including the axing (figuratively, at least) of the director, and various technical problems delayed the opening of the amphitheater until March 1990, when a new production of Berlioz's *The Trojans* was premiered. Since then, all large-scale operas of the **Opéra National de Paris** have been presented here (The **Opéra Garnier**—see page 185—is now reserved mainly for dance performances.) The 2,700-seat auditorium is blandly modern in style, but the seats are comfortable, the sight lines are clear, and the acoustics are excellent. After a series of acrimonious changes of musical directors, conductor James Conlon has succeeded in establishing order, and under his magical baton, the Opéra National de Paris is now one of the world's greatest opera companies. Tours of the building are available for a small charge, but you must reserve in advance. ◆ Box office: M-Sa, 11AM-6PM. 120 Rue de Lyon (at Pl de la Bastille). 08.36.69.78.68; fax 01.44.73.13.74. Métro: Bastille. www.opera-de-paris.fr

LES GRANDES MARCHES

156 LES GRANDES MARCHES

★★$$ This large white brasserie next door to the **Opéra Bastille** began as a 17th-century inn patronized by the artisans of the working-class Faubourg St-Antoine quarter. During the days preceding the revolution, it became a meeting place for patriots. Since the Opéra Bastille was plunked down next door, it has become a canteen for opera-goers in the evening, while tourists and local business keep the place hopping at lunchtime. Thoroughly redone in 2000 by the husband-and-wife team of **Elizabeth Portzamparc** and **Christian de Portzamparc** (he also designed the **Café Beaubourg** and the **Cité de la Musique**), the sleek minimalist décor features unadorned brushed gunmetal walls, burgundy ceilings, bare wood floors, and a wide sweeping staircase to the suave upstairs dining rooms. Unlike the other brasseries Jean-Paul Boucher has acquired, **La Coupole**, **Le Boeuf sur le Toit**, and **Bofinger** among them, which look to the past for their appeal, this eatery looks to the present both in its décor and its cuisine designed by Christian Constant, one of France's most prestigious chefs. The reasonably priced three-course prix-fixe menu includes such main courses as thick-sliced veal liver, lamb roasted with garlic and thyme, and baked *suprême de sandre* (pike-perch) with hearts of endives, and fresh shellfish is always available. Tables by the front windows of the upstairs salon offer sweeping views over the **Place de la Bastille**. ◆ Daily, lunch and dinner until 1AM. Reservations required. 6 Pl de la Bastille (between Rues de Charenton and de Lyon). 01.43.42.90.32. Métro: Bastille

156 FNAC MUSIQUE BASTILLE

Your one-stop connection to the music scene carries a complete range of CDs and cassettes and a huge selection of videos and laser discs. Like all stores in the chain, this place is sleek and efficient. It features listening stations with headphones; a ticket outlet for musical, theatrical, and sports events; a photo gallery; and frequent music-related promotional events. ◆ M-Sa; W, F, 10AM-10PM. 4 Pl de la Bastille (between Rues de Charenton and de Lyon). 01.43.42.04.04. Métro: Bastille. Also at Forum des Halles, 1 Rue Pierre-Lescot (at Rue Berger). 01.40.41.40.00. Métro: Les Halles; RER: Châtelet–Les Halles

157 LA DISTILLERIE

★$$ The poem posted outside this creole restaurant promises to transport diners to the exotic world of the Antilles. Inside, the pink tablecloths, white ironwork chairs, and rum cocktails with names like *touloulou*, punch Soufrière, and *la vie en rose* will make you feel as if you've stepped into a Jean Rhys novel. Owner Elisabeth de Rozières offers such Caribbean-inspired dishes as red-snapper-and-shellfish terrine with langoustine sauce; spicy fish soup; mutton with Antillean curry sauce; shark with lime sauce; and exotic ice creams, including mango, banana, white rum, pineapple, and coconut. ◆ M-Sa, dinner until 12AM; M-Th, bar until 4AM; F, Sa, bar until 5AM. 50 Rue du Faubourg St-Antoine (between Passage du Chantier and Pl de la Bastille). 01.40.01.99.00. Métros: Bastille, Ledru-Rollin

158 VIBE STATION

Musical birds of all feathers, top DJs included, flock here for the eclectic mix of R&B, house, garage, techno, hip-hop, trip-hop, or whatever is new on tape and CD, and there's a large selection of vinyl LPs and 45s. ◆ Tu-Sa, 11:30AM-8PM; M, noon-8PM. 57 Rue du Faubourg St-Antoine (between Rue de Charonne and Place de la Bastille). 01.44.74.64.18. Métro: Bastille

159 BAR LA FONTAINE

This busy spot at the junction of Rues de Charonne and du Faubourg-St-Antoine has been a watering hole for more than 100 years. Its location makes for great people-watching, so take a sidewalk table, order a carafe of red wine, and observe the world as it strolls by. The bar is named after the 16th-century **Fontaine Trogneux** around the corner on the Rue du Faubourg St-Antoine, where two bronze lion heads spout water rather unceremoniously from their mouths into the drains below. ◆ Daily. 1 Rue de Charonne (at Rue du Faubourg St-Antoine). 01.56.98.03.30. Métros: Bastille, Ledru-Rollin

160 LIBRAIRIE L'ARBRE À LETTRES

Strong on art and philosophy, this bookstore's great collection makes you want to improve your French so you can read all the volumes. The shop is beautifully designed by **Thierry Claude**, with well-organized stacks and great lighting. ◆ M-Sa, 10AM-10PM. 62 Rue du Faubourg St-Antoine (between Passage du Chantier and Pl de la Bastille). 01.53.33.83.23. Métros: Bastille, Ledru-Rollin

161 COUR DE L'ETOILE D'OR

This courtyard, part of which is inhabited by the workshops of the Rémy furniture shop down the street, is worth a detour. Just inside the entrance, look for the trompe l'oeil window display with abundant draperies, mirrors, chairs, vases, and decorative objects. Straight ahead, you encounter another trompe l'oeil painting, this one of a woman standing at her ivy-covered balcony; through open doors you can glimpse the interior of her apartment. High up on the rear wall of the courtyard is the barely legible 1751 sundial set on a plaster wall. ◆ 75 Rue du Faubourg-St-Antoine (between Ave Ledru-Rollin and Rue de Charonne). Métro: Ledru-Rollin

162 PASSAGE DU CHANTIER

A sign at the entrance invites you to visit the artisans whose ateliers and showrooms line this passage. Look into the workshops of **Atelier Paul** (01.46.28.44.83), where reproductions of furniture from many periods are created. ◆ At 66 Rue du Faubourg St-Antoine. Métros: Bastille, Ledru-Rollin

163 RUE DU FAUBOURG ST-ANTOINE

The main artery of the old working-class Faubourg St-Antoine quarter, this street is latticed with courtyards and passages that have enticing names like Etoile d'Or, Le Bel-Air, and St-Esprit. Here carpenters' and cabinetmakers' workshops are adjacent to furniture stores, fashion houses, and funky bars and restaurants. The intersection of Rue du Faubourg-St-Antoine and Avenue Ledru-Rollin was, until 1914, a crossroads where an outdoor furniture market was located; now it is home to such chain stores as **Monoprix**

(the French version of Wal-Mart) and **Ed l'Epicier**, a no-frills grocery store. ◆ Métros: Bastille, Ledru-Rollin, Faidherbe–Chaligny, Nation

163 80 RUE DU FAUBOURG ST-ANTOINE

In a niche above the door is a statue of St. Nicholas dating from 1895. Its presence recalls the 17th-century orphanage founded by *prêtre* (priest) Antoine Barberé that once stood on Rue St-Nicholas. With his outstretcehd hands, the saint seems to be pontificating, largely unnoticed, to the steady stream of traffic below. ◆ At Rue St-Nicolas. Métro: Ledru-Rollin

At 80 Rue du Faubourg St-Antoine:

RÉMY

Here reproductions of antique furniture, chandeliers, curtains, rugs, and anything else you might need to furnish a somewhat stuffy apartment are sold by a somewhat stuffy staff of designer counselors. ◆ M-Sa. Also at 82 Rue du Faubourg-St-Antoine (at Rue St-Nicolas). 01.43.43.65.58. Métro: Ledru-Rollin. Also at 82 Rue St-Nicolas (at Rue du Faubourg St-Antoine). 01.43.43.80.72. Métro: Ledru-Rollin

164 THE BOTTLE SHOP

★★$$ Café by day, bar by night, this congenial establishment is tucked off busy Rue du Faubourg St-Antoine on a wide but lightly traveled side street, where you can eat and drink on the sidewalk terrace in fair weather. The lunch menu is eclectic: soups, lasagnas, *tartines* (open-face sandwiches), bacon-and-potato pie. At night the place becomes a neighborhood hangout with an easy mix of internationals and French twenty-somethings from the *quartier*, most of whom the staff knows by name. Weeknights are generally mellow, and the decibel level rises on Friday and Saturday nights. Happy hour draws a crowd, and exotic drink specials are offered every night. Nurse your hangover with Bloody Marys during the long Sunday brunch, which offers everything from bagels with lox to eggs Florentine to the famous English breakfast (sausages, bacon, hash browns, and muffins). ♦ Daily, 11:30AM–2AM; lunch M–Sa, noon–3:30PM; brunch Su, 11:30AM–4PM; happy hour daily, 5PM–8PM; closed 1 week in mid-Aug. 5 Rue Trousseau (between Rues de Charonne and du Faubourg St-Antoine). 01.43.14.28.04. Métro: Ledru-Rollin.

165 LE RÉSERVOIR

This great barn of a *caf-conc'* (café concert hall) is one of the most *"een"* (in) nightspots in Paris, thanks far more to its cool atmosphere, giant screens, and live music than its okay, though undistinguished, food. After-dinner concerts start every night at about 11PM and brunch concerts Sundays at 2PM. Lots of fashion models and movie stars have made this former textile warehouse their second home. ♦ M–F, 8PM–2AM; Sa, 8PM–4AM; Su, noon–5PM (brunch) and 8PM–2AM. Closed Aug 10–20. 16 Rue de la Forge-Royale (between Rues du Faubourg St-Antoine and Charles-Delescluze). 01.43.56.39.60. Métros: Ledru-Rollin, Faidherbe–Chaligny

165 CASBAH

Three bouncers at the door decide who will get into this nightclub, where everything from jeans to tuxedos is acceptable as long as you have "un look." Those who pass muster can plunge into a magnificent Casablanca atmosphere created by rich colors, dim lighting, exotic cocktails, Moroccan dishes, raï music, and incense. Don't even think of arriving before midnight. ♦ Bar: M–Sa, 9PM–dawn. Disco: W–Sa, 11PM–dawn. 18-20 Rue de la Forge-Royale (between Rues du Faubourg St-Antoine and Charles-Delescluze). 01.43.71.04.39. Métros: Ledru-Rollin, Faidherbe–Chaligny

166 PAVILLON DE L'ARSENAL

This building's heavy stone façade hides a glass-and-steel structure constructed in 1879 for Laurent-Louis Borniche, an art lover and patron, as a place to display his almost 2,000 canvases. But Borniche didn't live to see his museum realized, and after his daughter sold the building, it was used for various purposes, including workshops for **La Samaritaine** department store and archival storage for the City of Paris. Renovated in 1988 by **Bernard Reichen** and **Philippe Robert**, the building is now a fascinating museum that looks at the urban development of Paris. It also houses a center for documentation on current architectural projects and a photographic library. By presenting drawings and models of local urban design and architectural projects, the museum aims to enhance the public's understanding of the city's continual evolution. On permanent display is a model of Paris connected to a computer; at a visitor's request, a videodisc displays one of 30,000 images (of canals, monuments, green spaces, sectors under development, etc.) while a laser ray spots the corresponding locus on the model. There is also an exhibit on the successive phases of the city's construction, from the wall of Philippe Auguste to Haussmann's Paris to present-day developments. The changing exhibitions concentrate on contemporary urbanization. ♦ Free. Exhibitions: Tu–Su. Library: Tu–F, 2–6PM. 21 Blvd Morland (between Rue de Schomberg and Blvd Henri-IV). 01.42.76.33.97; Métro: Sully–Morland. www.pavillon-arsenal.com

167 GARDE RÉPUBLICAINE

This massive, rusticated stone complex houses the military barracks and horses' stables of the French National Guard. It was constructed in 1891 on the site of the garden of the former **Celestine Monastery** (founded in 1352), although all that remains today of the vast religious grounds is a stone portal on Rue Beautreillis (off Rue St-Antoine). The compound is open to the public only 2 days a year (usually in June), but you may be lucky enough to catch the uniformed gendarmes parading on horseback through the streets of Paris on public holidays. Such processions are magnificent, although some of their pomp is diminished by the humorous and necessary presence of one of the city's bright green pooper-scoopers at the end of the parade. ♦ Open to visitors 2 days a year in June. 12-28 Blvd Henri-IV (between Rues de Sully and de la Cerisaie). 01.49.96.13.13. Métro: Sully–Morland

168 BIBLIOTHÈQUE DE L'ARSENAL

Housed in the four stories of this long and slender sandstone building, constructed in 1594 as the mansion of the Grand Master of Artillery under Henri IV, is a library with an unparalleled collection of literature, illuminated manuscripts, French dramatic works, and books on literary history and the history of the theater. The archives encompass over a million printed volumes, 15,000 manuscripts, 100,000 engravings, and 300 musical works. The collection includes Louis IX's Book of Hours, Charles V's Bible, and many documents relating to the **Bastille**. To visit the fine 17th- and 18th-century salons, among them the **Salon de**

Musique with its intricate Louis XV woodwork, you must make a reservation for a group tour through the **Caisse Nationale des Monuments Historiques** (62 Rue St-Antoine, between Rues de Birague and de Turenne, 01.48.87.24.15). On the cornice of the south façade (along Boulevard Morland) is a row of eight life-size stone cannons, serving as a reminder of the original function of the building. ♦ Fee for tour. M-Sa; closed 1-15 Sept. 1 Rue de Sully (at Rue Mornay). 01.53.01.25.04. Métro: Sully–Morland

169 Dame Tartine

★★$ Airy and no-frills, this eatery appeals to students and young people in search of a reasonably priced snack, light lunch, or dinner away from the bustle of Place de la Bastille. Duck stew with orange and fresh mint and salmon with coconut milk and curry on slivers of zucchini are just a couple of the interesting combinations featured here. Every dish comes with a *tartine* (toasted bread), the restaurant's namesake. Portions are small but inexpensive, so famished diners might want to order two courses. The bland vista of the **Opéra Bastille**'s bulky midsection across the street is the only drawback. ♦ Daily, lunch and dinner. 59 Rue de Lyon (between Rue Lacuée and Pl de la Bastille). 01.44.68.96.95. Métro: Bastille. Also at 2 Rue Brisemiche (at Rue du Cloître-St-Merri). 01.42.77.32.22. Métros: Rambuteau, Hôtel de Ville

171 Le Square Trousseau

★$$ This classic Belle Epoque bistro draws lots of its regulars, from the fashion houses that have established themselves along Rue du Faubourg St-Antoine. The period décor is lovely and the ambiance chic and *décontracté* (relaxed), but the quality of the cooking is unreliable. Sometimes it's fine, other times not. The menu changes monthly, but examples of typical fare are braised leg of lamb, roast guinea fowl with green cabbage and country-style bacon, duck with prunes and white turnips, and roasted veal liver with melted lentils. The wines are first-rate but somewhat expensive. In good weather, dine alfresco under the jaunty yellow awnings at a table on the peaceful square after which the restaurant is named. ♦ Tu-Sa, lunch and dinner. 1 Rue Antoine Vollon (at Rue Théophile-Roussel). 01.43.43.06.00. Métro: Ledru-Rollin

170 China Club

★★$$ This Shanghai-chic place mixes cocktails for the gentry of the east side. The 1930s Chinese Deco atmosphere features a cozy drawing room with soft leather chairs, a 46-foot-long bar, and a restaurant where very good renditions of traditional Chinese dishes are served. The bourgeoisie from Paris's conservative west side like to come here, thinking they're living dangerously. ♦ Restaurant: daily, dinner. Bar: daily, 7PM-2AM; happy hour, 7-9PM. 50 Rue de Charenton (between Ave Ledru-Rollin and Rue Moreau). 01.43.43.82.02. Métro: Ledru-Rollin

172 Le Baron Rouge

★$ Close to the Place d'Aligre Market, this rough-and-ready wine bar named for the famed World War I German flying ace is one of the most colorful and convivial in Paris. Workers from the market, neighborhood artists, and seriously dressed business types mingle in mellow camaraderie. Wine is sold by the glass or bottle (fine vintages from Bordeaux, Bourgogne, Alsace, and the Loire) at the always-packed zinc bar, or on tap from the mountain of oak vats piled by the door for next to nothing. Platters of cheese and *charcuterie* are also available. Be forewarned: The toilet's out in the back courtyard, one of those "Turkish" models that's a hole in the floor. ♦ M, 5PM-10PM; Tu-Th, 10AM-2PM, 5PM-10PM; F, Sa, 10AM-10PM; Su, 10AM-3PM. 1 Rue Théophile-Roussel (at Rue de Cotte). 01.43.43.14.32. Métro: Ledru-Rollin

173 Place d'Aligre Market

One of the most famous and cheapest in Paris, this outdoor market has a North African flavor (undoubtedly because the majority of the merchants are of North African origin). It's always lively and crowded, with shops, stalls, and a covered market offering fabric, white rum, spices, green bananas, and secondhand goods. ♦ Tu-Sa, 8AM-1PM, 4-7PM; Su, 8AM-1PM. Rue d'Aligre and Pl d'Aligre. Métro: Ledru-Rollin

174 Viaduc des Arts

President Mitterrand's decision in the early 1980s to install the new home of the **Opéra de Paris** at the then-shabby Place de la Bastille set off a radical transformation of the long-neglected east side of Paris, a momentum that continues to this day. The most visually striking development since the completion of the **Opéra** is this former railway viaduct whose 60 stone arches have been imaginatively converted into magnificent studios for artisans.

Opened in 1994, this long row of vaulted ateliers begins near the rear of the **Opéra**

Bastille and continues seven blocks eastward along tree-lined Avenue Daumesnil to Rue de Rambouillet. All the studios have glass walls on the street, and most have dazzling display windows. For the window shopping alone, it's worth the walk. But the real fun is going inside, where you can watch highly skilled toy makers and restorers, stone sculptors, furniture restorers, weavers, flute and violin makers, embroidery workers, and other artisans ply their crafts. All have goods to sell, as do the many high-class ceramics and home decoration boutiques. These are becoming ever more numerous, unfortunately, taking over ateliers formerly occupied by artists and artisans.

Stop in at one of two large cafés in the vaults for a quick bite or drink—the chic **Viaduc Café** (41-43 Ave Daumesnil, at Rue Abel, 01.44.74.70.70) or the bustling, working-class **Au Père Tranquille** (73-75 Ave Daumesnil, at Blvd Diderot; 01.43.43.64.58). In good weather, sit outside at either place on the sprawling sidewalk terraces under the trees. Both cafés stay open until 4AM.

Pick up the free brochure on the viaduct that the City of Paris, which subsidizes the artists, distributes. Available at all the studios and at the café, the brochure has an excellent map and directory of the occupants. ♦ 9-129 Ave Daumesnil (between Rues Moreau and de Rambouillet). Métros: Bastille, Ledru-Rollin, Gare de Lyon

Atop the Viaduc des Arts:

PROMENADE PLANTÉE

Located above the **Viaduc des Arts** is this lovely promenade along the path of the old railway line that the City of Paris has developed. Planted with flower beds, flowering bushes, and trees, it extends almost 2 miles, from the start of the Viaduc all the way to the Bois de Vincennes.

175 LE TRAIN BLEU

★★★$$$ Suspended in time between here and there, this century-old dining room in the monumental **Gare de Lyon** is a train station restaurant in the grand tradition. Named for the luxurious Belle Epoque express train that once took the elite down to the Riviera, this is a traveler's dream, striking wanderlust into the hearts of even the most sedentary. The restaurant, classified as a historic monument, is characterized by vaulted ceilings; extraordinarily intricate gold-leaf moldings, friezes, and carvings; and ceiling frescoes by different artists depicting destinations from the Gare de Lyon. Images of Mont Blanc, Marseille, Monaco, Evian, Nice, Montpellier, and Algeria are enough to give even those who come here for a meal (and aren't waiting for a train) the travel bug. The restaurant's guest book has been signed by the likes of such modern-day notables as Jacques Chirac, François Mitterrand, and Serge Gainsbourg, and in the more distant past, Sarah Bernhardt, Edmond Rostand, and Salvador Dalí nourished themselves here. Upscale traditional French fare is featured. Appetizers include hot Lyonnaise sausage, *foie gras de canard*, and escargots. Some of the main courses are grilled cod with cumin-flavored ratatouille, Barbary duck with orange and coriander served with couscous and raisins, and roast leg of lamb. For dessert, try the superb apricot *clafoutis* (a soft tart made with a crepelike batter). Choose from the exceptional list of red, white, and rosé wines, but champagne might be more appropriate in this sumptuous space. The restaurant's comfortable (though smoky) lounge area is the perfect place for a drink while waiting for a train. ♦ Daily, lunch and dinner. Reservations recommended. Gare de Lyon, 20 Blvd Diderot (at Rue Diderot). 01.43.43.09.06. Métro: Gare de Lyon

MONTMARTRE

Crowned with that alabaster wedding-cake church known as **Sacré-Coeur**, Montmartre is the balcony of Paris—half dream, half nightmare. It is a tangle of contradictions: meandering country roads, seedy strip joints, early Christian sites, tourist clichés, sublime vistas, and hidden passages. The **Butte** (which is what Parisians call this sandstone height) is geographically the highest point in town (427 feet) and the traditional home of poets, singers, painters, and bohemians of all kinds.

The best day to visit Montmartre is on Tuesday, when many museums in other parts of Paris are closed, or any day when you feel like fleeing the center of the city for a few hours. Emerging from **Hector Guimard**'s Art Nouveau **Abbesses** métro station, start your tour with café au lait and brioches in one of the cafés along **Rue des Abbesses**, which is crowded with butchers, bakers, and fishmongers from the **Rue Lepic** market. Then begin the ascent to **Place du Tertre**, a 14th-century square that in summer harbors a lively crowd of street artists, outdoor restaurant waiters, and tourists. The best bets for a quick lunch here are crepes at **Le Tire Bouchon** or fish at **La Crémaillère 1900** on Place du Tertre, but for a real gourmet treat, hike on up a few block to the supremely elegant **A. Beauvilliers** restaurant. After the obligatory pilgrimage to **Sacré-Coeur**, wind down Rue Lepic past the **Moulin de la Galette** until you see the red neon signs of the Butte's other storied temple, the **Moulin Rouge.** Come back later in the evening for the cancan show or for the cabaret at the legendary **Au Lapin Agile.** Métro service ends at 12:45AM, but you'll find a taxi just down the hill on **Rue Caulaincourt**, which is filled with revelers during the wine-festival parade held in October.

The name *Montmartre* has two possible origins: the "Mount of Mercury," for the Roman temple to Mercury that once stood on the Butte, or the "Mount of Martyrs," commemorating St. Denis, the first bishop of Paris, who, along with the priest Rusticus and the deacon Eleutherius, was tortured and decapitated here by the Romans in AD 250. According to the legend, St. Denis picked up his severed head and carried it from Montmartre to another hill several kilometers to the north. A thousand years later, the **Basilique de St-Denis** was built

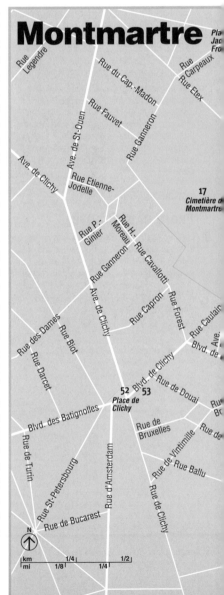

on that hill. Streets in Montmartre were named for the priest and deacon, who did not join St. Denis in the headless trek.

A lesser-known local martyr is mill owner Pierre-Charles Debray, who during the Franco-Prussian War was crucified on the blades of his Moulin de la Galette, a windmill with a garden tavern and dance hall that a half-century later would symbolize "gay Paree" in a painting by Renoir. Such artists as Renoir, van Gogh, Dufy, and Utrillo; poets Apollinaire, Max Jacob, and Jacques Prévert; and novelist Boris Vian, songwriter Aristide Bruant, and illustrator André Gill all worked in Montmartre. In the late 19th century, Toulouse-Lautrec sketched the cancan dancers at the Moulin Rouge, and in the early 1900s, Pablo Picasso, Georges Braque, and Juan Gris, working out of an abandoned piano factory nearby, gave birth to Cubism. Cabarets such as Au Lapin Agile further encouraged *la vie de bohème*, and the life was much romanticized by North Americans in Paris. Writer John Dos Passos, for instance, rhapsodized in 1918 that he wanted his

heart "to be preserved in a pitcher of *vin de Beaujolais* in the restaurant in Place du Tertre on the summit of Montmartre."

After World War I, Paris's artistic center moved to another of the city's seven hills, Montparnasse, on the Left Bank. Its nightlife, however, remained in Montmartre and grew in notoriety. Though the neighborhood is the site of what is reputedly the oldest church sanctuary in Paris (St-Pierre) and was dominated in the 12th century by an abbey run by women, today the area is best known for women (and men disguised as women) plying an older, less pious profession. Painters may once have looked for portrait models among the seamstresses and dancers in **Place Pigalle**, but seamier live sex shows, porn theaters, and peep shops took over at the end of World War II. Nevertheless, the area is generally safe, even at night.

The Butte is packed on the weekend, especially the first Saturday and the first or second Sunday of October, the dates of the local annual wine-harvest festival and the vintage-car rally, respectively. You can avoid the masses by visiting on a weekday, or just come on the weekend and join in the joie de vivre of the crowd. For those who wish to avoid the steep climb to the top, **Le Montmartrain**, a small train, departs Place Pigalle for **Sacré-Coeur** daily every half hour. (For more information, see page 278.)

1 LE PETIT CABOULOT

★★$ Slightly removed from the Montmartre tourist bustle is this busy neighborhood bistro, offering a winning combination of traditional French food and reasonable prices. Against the backdrop of vintage ad posters and an oversized curved bar, patrons dig into such favorites as crispy *confit de canard*, tradition-ally prepared fish dishes, and dessert classics such as *tarte Tatin*. There's a comfortably priced wine list. Reservations recommended. ♦ M-Sa, lunch and dinner. 6 Pl Jacques-Froment. 01.46.27.19.00. Métro: Guy-Moquet

2 LE CHÂTEAU DES SEIGNEURS DE CLIGNANCOURT

Along with **St-Pierre-de-Montmartre**, this is one of the oldest relics of this district's past. The original manor house was home to the famous porcelain manufacturer (founded in 1767) that provided Louis XVIII with plates and saucers. Regrettably, the early 16th-century house was demolished in 1861, and all that remains is its renovated turret, which now decorates the corner of a modern restau-rant. ♦ Rue du Mont-Cenis (at Rue Marcadet). Métro: Jules-Joffrin

3 LE MAQUIS

★★$$ Located at the base of Avenue Junot, this lovely little bistro features such dishes as fish soup, escargots, *brandade de morue* (Mediterranean-style purée of salted cod), and *magret de canard* (breast of duck) with

sweet-and-sour sauce, and inexpensive light prix-fixe lunches. Dine on the pretty little terrace in summer. ♦ M-Sa, lunch and dinner. 69 Rue Caulaincourt (between Rues Lamarck and Tourlaque). 01.42.59.76.07. Métro: Lamarck–Caulaincourt

4 CIMETIÈRE ST-VINCENT (ST. VINCENT CEMETERY)

Composer Arthur Honegger and painters Théophile-Alexandre Steinlen and Maurice Utrillo are buried in Paris's most intellectual cemetery. Enjoy the ivy-covered walls, a tranquil view of **Sacré-Coeur**, and (if you need to get off your feet) south-facing benches that catch the afternoon sun. The old caretaker is generally helpful but becomes cantankerous between noon and 2PM, when he is emphatically out to lunch. ♦ Daily. Rues St-Vincent and des Saules. Métro: Lamarck–Caulaincourt

5 AU LAPIN AGILE

The original **Cabaret des Assassins** was rechristened in 1880 when André Gill painted a rabbit with a red bow tie bounding from a copper kettle on the sign outside. The *lapin à Gill* (rabbit by Gill) became the *lapin agile* (nimble rabbit), and this famous cabaret turned into a stomping ground for intellectuals and artists who came for poetry readings and folk songs. (In 1985 the French government issued a five-franc stamp depicting Utrillo's oil painting of the cabaret.) A century later you can still grab a wooden stool, order a Kir, and sing along to those same old songs performed with passion and humor by a team of talented

The Best

Christophe Lorvo

General Manager, Hyatt Regency Paris-Madeleine

Market, 15 Ave Matignon: New York super-chef Jean-Georges Vongerichten's Paris restaurant, where they serve "black plates."

L'Angle du Faubourg, 195 Rue du Faubourg St-Honoré: it has cold modern décor but good southern French cuisine.

59 Poincaré, 59 Ave Poincaré: one of Alain Ducasse's restaurants.

La Cantine du Faubourg, 105 Rue du Faubourg St-Honoré: a late-night hangout for the fashion and showbiz crowd.

Le Bindi, 63 Ave Franklin Roosevelt: trendy restaurant with excellent Indian food.

Le Nirvana, 3 Rue Matignon: very good music and ambiance. For good service, ask for Nouria.

Le Pershing Hall, 49 Rue Pierre Charron: the restaurant (there is also a hotel) is a mix of trendiness and fine cuisine.

Le Man Ray, 32 Rue Marbeuf: one of the most famous bar-restaurants in the Champs-Elysées area.

---

young singers. Don't miss the 19th-century whimsy in front: a concrete fence made to look like knotty pine. No food is served. ♦ Tu-Su, 9:15PM–2AM. No credit cards accepted. 22 Rue des Saules (at Rue St-Vincent). 01.46.06.85.87. Métro: Lamarck–Caulaincourt

6 A. Beauvilliers

★★★$$$ Its name is borrowed from Antoine Beauvilliers—*officier de bouche* (literally, "officer of the mouth") to the gluttonous Count of Provence (the future Louis XVIII) and founder of the first restaurant in Paris in 1790—but this restaurant has a style all its own. **Edouard Carlier** has created one of the most elegant *salons à manger* (dining rooms) in Paris; what was once an old bakery is now three intimate Louis-Philippe–style dining rooms. One room is full of bridal bouquets, the second features 18th- and 19th-century engravings of the Montmartre windmills, and the third is a portrait gallery of Beauvilliers's contemporaries painted by Louis-Léopold Boilly and the like. All three are adorned with a profusion of bouquets that seem even more numerous when reflected in the wall mirrors and lacquered ceilings. The décor is like that of a 19th-century bourgeois boudoir. The menu changes weekly; memorable specialties have included *cul d'artichaut frais au torteau* (fresh artichoke heart filled with crabmeat), *timbale de macaroni au ris de veau au foie gras et aux morilles* (molded sweetbread macaroni with foie gras and morel mushrooms), spiced squab, and lemon pie in white rum for dessert. The wine is expensive. Be careful, or your bill will climb like Rue Lepic. ♦ M, dinner; Tu-Sa, lunch and dinner. Reservations required for dinner. 52 Rue Lamarck (between Rues du Mont-Cenis and Caulaincourt). 01.42.54.54.42. Métro: Lamarck–Caulaincourt

7 Au Poulbot Gourmet

★★$$ Innovative Jean-Paul Langevin runs a simple, cozy restaurant decorated with early Montmartre photos and original Poulbot illustrations. His specialties are *foie gras de canard* (duck liver pâté), large curried escargots stuffed with tomatoes, and a two-chocolate charlotte with pistachio sauce. ♦ M-Sa, lunch and dinner; Su, lunch except June through September. 39 Rue Lamarck (between Rues du Mont-Cenis and des Saules). 01.46.06.86.00. Métro: Lamarck–Caulaincourt

8 24 Rue du Mont-Cenis

Composer Hector Berlioz lived with his English wife in a house on this site between 1834 and 1837. The present building was built in 1925. ♦ Between Rues Becquerel and Lamarck. Métro: Lamarck–Caulaincourt

9 Villa Léandre

Down this unexpected country lane leading off Avenue Junot is a hidden village where the eccentric little houses mirror the idiosyncrasies of the people who have inhabited them (a ballerina, two successful painters, and a few genuine hermits). It's worth a quick detour. ♦ Off Ave Junot. Métro: Lamarck–Caulaincourt

10 Hameau des Artistes

Behind the gate marked *Interdit* ("No Trespassing") are footpaths leading to opulent artists' studios in structures ranging from a gray cement castle to a Tuscan villa. The gate to the "Artists' Hamlet" is open during the day; be adventurous but discreet. ♦ 11 Ave Junot (between Rue Girardon and Villa Léandre). Métro: Lamarck–Caulaincourt

---

Restaurants/Clubs: **Red** | Hotels: **Purple** | Shops: **Orange** | Outdoors/Parks: **Green** | Sights/Culture: **Blue**

GAY PARIS

If there's one major city in Europe where it's hip not to be square, it has to be Paris. It may be more bourgeois than its transatlantic counterpart, New York City, and less progressive than some of its neighbors to the north (such as Amsterdam), but Paris has a style and cosmopolitan flavor second to none. Such being the case, gays and lesbians come to the French capital from all over the world to partake of its art, architecture, cuisine, culture, and nightlife, thus contributing to the unique energy with which Paris has seduced travelers of all stripes for centuries.

Gay personalities have, of course, long been at the vanguard of French artistic and literary culture. Marcel Proust, André Gide, Jean Genet, and Jean Cocteau are some of the more prominent homosexual figures to have made their mark on the cultural landscape, without forgetting famous (or infamous) couples such as Arthur Rimbaud and Paul Verlaine, who fell in love in Paris, and esteemed expats Gertrude Stein and Alice B. Toklas. Today flamboyant captain of fashion Jean-Paul Gaultier is one of France's most adored ambassadors of *la mode*, and the die-hard socialist mayor of Paris, Bertrand Delanoë, is openly gay.

Since 1999, French gay couples (like heterosexual couples) have been able to enter into PaCs agreements, which give official recognition and certain legal benefits to couples who are somewhere between going steady and married in the social spectrum. As of mid-2003, some 65,000 PaCs had been signed.

Paris is in general a tolerant city, though—like anywhere—the occasional homophobic jerk can always pop up—like the one who stabbed the mayor in 2002 inside City Hall. Aggressive acts are least likely to happen in the Marais, the nucleus of gay life in the capital, around St-Germain-des-Prés, and other upscale sections. In the center and along the Seine almost anything goes, while the more you move away from these neigborhoods, the less inconspic-uous same-sex displays of affection become. Gay culture continues to radiate outward from the Marais, where the concentration of gay and lesbian bars, shops, and restaurants is thickest, but it exists in pockets in other parts of town as well. One of the most popular gay nightspots, for example, is Le Queen on the Champs-Elysées. Despite the ongoing ravages of AIDS (called *sida* in French) in Paris, the clubbing and even cruising scene is going strong, and if one sex club closes, another opens just as quickly. Of the latter, the biggest remains the somewhat dreary Le Dépôt (also a disco), though it has lost some of the cachet it had when it opened a few years ago. Clubs that cater to cruising (French: *la drague*) in theory provide condoms for their customers, but they are not always as available as they should be.

Many of the larger discos (including Le Queen) are still reserved for gay clubbers on certain nights of the week only, but the fact that these usually fall on the weekend tells you something about what segment of the Parisian popula-tion really knows how to party. Saturday and Sunday nights are when Le Queen (102 Ave des Champs-Elysées, between Rues de Berri and Washington; métro: George-V; 01.53.89.08.90) goes into techno overdrive, with top DJs from London and Paris; house rules Saturdays at the huge Red Light club in Montparnasse (34 Rue du Départ, between Pl du 18 Juin 1940 and Ave du Maine; métro: Montparnasse-Bienvenüe; 01.42.79.94.53); while Fridays through Sundays things get crazy on all three floors of La Loco (90 Blvd Clichy, between Rue Lepic and Cité Véron; métro: Place de Clichy; 01.53.41.88.88). On the opposite end of the musical spectrum is Le Tango at 13 Rue au Maire (between Rues des Vertus and Beaubourg; métro: Arts et Métiers; 01.42.72.17.78), where gays, lesbians, and "*hétéros cools*" dance to salsas, tangos, and '80s tunes Wednesday through Saturday from midnight to dawn. Since things can change fast in clubland, it's a good idea to either call or consult the extensive listings in the free gay weeklies such as *illico* before heading out into the night.

The best place to pick up *illico*, club flyers, and such is at one of the numerous gay bars, restaurants, or cafés in Paris. The scene is always changing, but perenially popular spots in the Marais include L'Open Café, Amnésia, Okawa, Le Cox, Mixer Bar, Le Duplex and Le Quetzal. Top lesbian spots are L'Alcântara and Unity Bar.

The English-language FACTS (Free Counseling, Treatment and Support for people touched by HIV) hotline number for HIV/AIDS support is 01.44.93.16.69. The hot line is open Mondays, Wednesdays, and Fridays, 6 to 10PM. Sida Info Service offers a 24-hour support line (in French); 0800.840.800.

The Centre Gai et Lesbien is located in the Bastille neighborhood (3 Rue Keller, between Rues de Charonne and de la Roquette; 01.43.57.21.47, www.cglparis.org; métros: Ledru-Rollin, Bastille). Its main function is to deal with questions about health concerns and gay rights issues, but it is also an attractive and easygoing gathering place where strangers will immediately feel welcome. There are bulletin boards, free brochures, and condoms galore, as well as a library and little café.

10 13 Avenue Junot

This is the former residence (1879-1946) of Francisque Poulbot, the Montmartre illustrator who drew chubby little children with cowlicks. Four of his cartoon characters frolic across the tile frieze of the house. In homage to the artist, Montmartre residents still call their children *petits poulbots*; at the corner of Norvins and Impasse du Tertre, near Place du Tertre, you will find a sign that reads *Ralentissez. Faites attention aux petits poulbots* ("Drive slowly. Watch out for the little poulbots"). This local folk hero is also credited with saving **Montmartre Vineyards** and with founding the Fraternal Association of Wooden Billiard Players. (Wooden billiards is a faddish Montmartre bar game in which winning is considered immoral—the winner always pays for the drinks.) The house is still a private residence. ♦ Between Rue Girardon and Villa Léandre. Métro: Lamarck–Caulaincourt

10 Maison Tristan Tzara

In the 1920s Viennese architect **Adolf Loos**, a pioneer of the Modern movement, was the only designer whose work reflected Dadaism. It is not surprising, then, that his "architecture without qualities" should have appealed to the Romanian Dadaist poet Tristan Tzara, who brought Loos to Paris with a commission to build this house. Set into a rising embankment, the five-story building has a rigorously symmetrical façade that is punctured by a huge double-height square terrace. The arrangement is a superb example of the Loos predilection for tensely juxtaposed, unadorned cubic forms. The interior is just as eccentrically organized. The patchwork of intersecting split-level spaces, typical of Loos's *raumplan* (room plan), provided Tzara with the sort of ironic, theatrical, and vaguely aggressive setting that befitted a Dadaist artist. This is still a private residence. ♦ 15 Ave Junot (between Rue Girardon and Villa Léandre). Métro: Lamarck–Caulaincourt

11 Square Suzanne-Buisson

This unexpected little square (named after a World War II Resistance fighter) was once the backyard of the adjoining **Château des Brouillards** (Castle of Fog), an 18th-century mansion turned dance hall. According to religious lore, St. Denis paused here to rinse his severed head. Today a statue of the forlorn-looking bishop surveys neighborhood elders playing an afternoon game of *pétanque*, a Lyonnaise sand bowling game similar to boccie. The bowling alley has stone benches for spectators, and there's no better way to learn about the old Montmartre than to eavesdrop on the conversations of these tweed-capped codgers. Admission is free (as is the gossip), and the games pick up steam around midafternoon. ♦ Bounded by Rue Girardon, Impasse Girardon, and Pl des Quatre-Frères-Casadesus. Métro: Lamarck–Caulaincourt

12 La Maison Rose

★$ Utrillo once painted a picture of this pink restaurant, and pink it has stayed—even the cutlery is rose-tinted. In the summer the tables spill onto Rue de l'Abreuvoir, and if the view doesn't make you dizzy, order foie gras with a bottle of champagne to ensure that your head spins. Such standard French fare as homemade pâté with cognac and smoked salmon is served. ♦ Daily, lunch and dinner. 2 Rue de l'Abreuvoir (at Rue des Saules). 01.42.57.66.75. Métro: Lamarck–Caulaincourt

13 Vignes de Montmartre (Montmartre Vineyards)

This is one of the last two remaining vineyards in Paris. Each year's harvest yields enough grapes for about 500 bottles of red Clos Montmartre wine. The labels are designed by Montmartre artists. The wine is nothing special, but the harvest fête, on the first or second Saturday of October, is not to be missed. Crowds line Rue Lamarck for a celebration that feels like a combination of an academic procession, the Rose Bowl Parade, and Halloween. Participants might include baton twirlers, Auvergnat farmers in wooden clogs, and the mayor's wife, who traditionally picks the first grape. The vineyards are not open to the public, but note the plaque in front on Rue St-Vincent dedicated to Poulbot, the popular cartoonist who prevented the vineyards from being sold to high-rise developers in the 1930s. ♦ Rue des Saules and St-Vincent. Métro: Lamarck–Caulaincourt

14 Musée de Montmartre

Located just behind 12 Rue Cortot (whose roll call of former tenants includes Renoir, Utrillo, and Dufy), this pleasant little museum is housed in a delightful 17th-century town house called **Le Manoir de Rose de Rosimond**. The house, which is surrounded by two charming gardens, was the country residence of Rosimond, a 17th-century actor who appeared frequently in the plays of Molière and who, like Molière, died while performing *Le Malade Imaginaire*.

The museum's eclectic collection includes caricatures by André Gill, posters and

---

Restaurants/Clubs: **Red** | Hotels: **Purple** | Shops: **Orange** | Outdoors/Parks: **Green** | Sights/Culture: **Blue**

269

THE BEST

Eric Johnson
Chef de Cuisine, Market

The emphasis on food in French culture. People are typically very knowledgeable about food here. The awareness of and interest level in food is so high—from a chef's perspective that's amazing. And food is a good example of how the city embraces culture.

Osteria, in the Marais, for the gnocchi with sage butter.

L'Astrance for the burnt-bread-crust soup.

Lao Siam, a Laotian restaurant in the Belleville neighborhood, for the garlic-roasted quail.

The steak at **L'Entrecôte** on Rue Marbeuf.

Willi's Wine Bar.

If you're in Montmartre, the restaurant **Le Moulin de la Galette**.

The selection of wines in a Parisian supermarket.

Rungis, outside Paris. It's the largest food market in Europe and practically a city of its own.

My idea of a perfect afternoon in Paris—if it's sunny—would be lunch at **Arpège** followed by a visit to the **Musée Rodin**.

If it's raining, clothes shopping in the Marais, with a stop (budget permitting) at **L'Eclaireur**, followed by a French movie.

---

drawings by Toulouse-Lautrec, stunning Clignancourt porcelain, and the piano on which Gustave Charpentier wrote his opera *Louise* in 1900.

Though it seems outlandish in Paris to visit a museum to look at a bistro, an entire 19th-century bistro complete with a scalloped zinc bar is on display here. The exhibition relates the apocryphal story that the term *bistro* originated on the Butte, where impatient Russian soldiers used to shout at Montmartre's waiters: *"Bistraou, bistraou!"* (Russian for "Get a move on!"). ◆ Admission. Tu-Su, 11AM-6PM. 12 Rue Cortot (between Rues du Mont-Cenis and des Saules). 01.46.06.61.11. Métro: Lamarck–Caulaincourt

15 L'ERMITAGE HÔTEL

$$ Those who crave an elegant yet soothing atmosphere will delight in this small hotel, housed in a three-story 1860 residence. The warm and smiling owner, Maggie Canipel, makes each guest feel right at home. The 12 breezy rooms, each lovingly decorated by Maggie, contrast with the more somber corridors. **Rooms 11** and **12** open onto a bewitching terraced garden full of chirping birds, whereas other rooms have splendid views of the city. Breakfast, served in each

guest's room, is included in the reasonable price. There's no restaurant. ◆ No credit cards accepted. 24 Rue Lamarck (between Rues du Chevalier-de-la-Barre and Becquerel). 01.42.64.79.22; fax 01.42.64.10.33. Métros: Château Rouge, Lamarck–Caulaincourt

16 LES NÉGOCIANTS

★★$ Looking for good no-frills French comfort food in an atmospheric, *très vieux* Paris setting? Among the black-and-white photographs hanging above the horseshoe-shaped zinc bar is one of Robert Doisneau, who was indeed an habitué of this neighborhood. Start with an aperitif of muscat or white wine, then order a bottle of wine and drink of it what you will—you pay according to how many markers surface on the bottle at meal's end. Fare here is heavy on *charcuterie*, from a rabbit pâté starter to a main course of old-fashioned *boeuf bourguignon*. Desserts are simple and typically include chocolate mousse as a choice. ◆ M, lunch; Tu-F, lunch and dinner. 01.46.06.15.11. 27 Rue Lambert (between Rues Labat and Nicolet). Métro: Château Rouge

17 CIMETIÈRE DE MONTMARTRE (MONTMARTRE CEMETERY)

A veritable academy of writers, composers, and painters, this is the final resting place of Stendhal, Heine, Dumas the Younger, Offenbach, Truffaut, Degas, Fragonard, and Greuze, whose eloquent headstone lauds him for having depicted "virtue, friendship, beauty, and innocence, thereby breathing soul into his paintings." Another striking memorial is the Rude bronze of a reclining Cavaignac. Composer Hector Berlioz lies between his first wife, an English actress, and his second wife, an opera singer. There is also a memorial to

---

Only about 2% of all wine sold in France is not French, and most of that comes from other Mediterranean countries like Italy and Spain.

Every man has two nations, and France is one of them.

—Benjamin Franklin

Zola, but his body now rests in the **Panthéon** (see page 62). ♦ Daily. 20 Ave Rachel (off Blvd de Clichy). 01.43.87.64.24. Métro: Blanche

18 21 RUE CAULAINCOURT

Innovative painter and graphic artist Toulouse-Lautrec spent his most productive years (1886-1897) at a studio in this building, just a stroll away from his favorite nocturnal haunts. ♦ 21 Rue Caulaincourt (at Rue Tourlaque). Métro: Blanche

19 RUE LEPIC

Montmartre's meandering old quarry road is the site of an antique-car rally held on the first or second Sunday in October (for information call 01.42.52.42.00). It starts in front of the restaurant **La Pomponnette** at 42 Rue Lepic (between Rues Girardon and Tourlaque). Portions of the hit film *Le Fabuleux Destin d'Amélie Poulain* were filmed inside no. 5 Rue Lepic, the **Café-Tabac des Deux Moulins** (at the corner of Rue Constance). Take a look inside, if you can brave the smoke: the 1950s décor is anything but ersatz. ♦ Between Blvd de Clichy and Pl Jean-Baptiste-Clément. Métro: Blanche

19 LE MOULIN DE LA GALETTE

Where once stood 14 windmills now stand only these two, le Blute-fin and le Radet, immortalized on canvas by Renoir and many others and evocative of a time when Montmartre was more farm than charm. In 1830 the Debray family, who owned the mill, started selling wine instead of milk to accompany their galettes, small loaves of brown bread, and a cabaret famous for its Sunday-afternoon public dances was born. During the Franco-Prussian War, when Montmartre was overrrun by 20,000 Prussian soldiers, Pierre-Charles Debray was crucified on one of the mills. History has also brought to the site an open-air café, music hall, television studio, and, most recently, a restaurant that was a favorite of international disco queen and Montmartre resident Dalida. The Blute-fin windmill is closed to the public, while the Radet marks the entrance to a contemporary bistro. ♦ Between Rues Girardon and Tholozé. Métro: Lamarck Caulaincourt

Within Le Moulin de la Galette:

LE MOULIN DE LA GALETTE

★★$$ The Moulin de la Galette's Radet windmill looming above the entrance to this restaurant will have you thinking of the Montmartre of yesteryear, but once you're inside, it's anything but. This stylish eatery, which

boasts a small bar and a garden terrace, opened in 2002 and replaces an Italian restaurant on the same site. The menu here is everything a contemporary bistro should be: creative but comprehensible, with prices that are uniformly on the mark. Service is friendly. For main courses try one of the fish dishes, such as steamed fresh cod with olive-oil mashed potatoes or red tuna steak served with a delectable tomato-and-sweet-onion pancake; meats include Vendée pigeon and old-fashioned fricassée of veal kidneys. The wine list is exclusively French with many bottles less than 30 euros. For a dessert to write home about, order the passion-fruit cream-filled pineapple ravioli, served with a plain-yogurt-flavored ice cream and a smattering of passion-fruit seeds. Though the dining room is not small, reservations for the terrace may be hard to come by at the last minute (with advance notice, try your luck by sending an e-mail to lemoulindelagalette@free.fr). ♦ Oct.-April: Tu-Sa, lunch and dinner. May-Sept.: Daily, lunch and dinner. 83 Rue Lepic (at Rue Girardon). 01.46.06.84.77. Métro: Lamarck–Caulaincourt

20 TERRASS HÔTEL

$$$ Built in 1912, this is the only luxury hotel in Montmartre. It has marble floors and a magnificent fireplace in the bar off the lobby; a stellar panorama that takes in the **Opéra**, **Arc de Triomphe**, and **Eiffel Tower**, and 100 sumptuous rooms. Ask to stay on the cemetery side, which in local parlance means a room with a view, unobstructed because you're overlooking the low-rise **Montmartre Cemetery**. ♦ 12-14 Rue Joseph-de-Maistre (at Rue Caulaincourt). 01.46.06.72.85; fax 01.42.52.29.11. Métros: Blanche, Place de Clichy. terrass@francenet.fr

Within the Terrass Hôtel:

LA TERRASSE

★★$$ Specialties of this cheerful modern ground-floor dining room are appetizers of flaky pastry filled with goat cheese or roasted prawns and Parmesan cheese, main courses of *sandre* (pike perch) with Provençal herbs, fillet of bass with roasted potatoes, or loin of lamb with licorice sauce, and desserts of thin hot apple tart with Calvados and vanilla ice cream or praline almond ice cream. ♦ Daily, lunch and dinner. 01.44.92.34.00

LA TERRASSE PANORAMIQUE

★★$$ On 15 April the hotel opens its seventh-floor terrace restaurant, and from then until 15 September you can dine under big white umbrellas while taking in one of the finest views there is of Paris. Featured are an array of salads, fish and meat grilled on the barbecue, and other summery fare. ◆ Daily, lunch and dinner May-Sept. Reservations required for a terrace table with a view. 01.44.92.34.01

21 54 RUE LEPIC

Vincent van Gogh and his brother Theo lived in this apartment building. ◆ Between Rues des Abbesses and Durantin. Métro: Blanche

22 RUE DE LA MIRE

Getting lost in the twisting streets of Montmartre can be done with the greatest of ease, except on this short pedestrian street. An 18th-century *mire* (trail marker) points due north. ◆ Between Rues Ravignan and Lepic. Métro: Abbesses

23 AU CLAIR DE LA LUNE

★★$$ In his cheerful restaurant with murals of **Le Moulin de la Galette** and the streets of Montmartre, talented chef Alain Kerfant presents such seasonal specialties as pheasant terrine with foie gras, fish soup with *rouille*, salmon steak simmered in Champagne, and wild hare casserole. Finish the meal with vanilla crème brûlée or chocolate profiteroles. The excellent wine list includes a 1996 Château Abbaye de Brandey Côtes de Castillon and 1997 Pouilly Fumé Domaine des Berthiers. ◆ M, dinner; Tu-Sa, lunch and dinner. 9 Rue Poulbot (between Pl du Calvaire and Rue Norvins). 01.42.58.97.03. Métro: Abbesses

24 AUBERGE DE LA BONNE FRANQUETTE

★$$ This former van Gogh studio is now an intentionally rustic restaurant-cabaret serving escargots, beef bourguignon, entrecôte, and *pâté en croûte* (pâté in a pastry crust) to Japanese, Dutch, and German bus tours. Guitarist Jacques Lescure and accordion player Chouta lead the equivalent of a nightly French hootenanny and hawk their cassettes and records at intermission. ◆ Daily, lunch and dinner. Reservations recommended. 18 Rue St-Rustique (between Rues du Mont-Cenis and des Saules). 01.42.52.02.42. Métro: Abbesses

25 LE TIRE BOUCHON CABARET

★$ If you're in the mood for a little "Maple Leaf Rag" to accompany an apricot crepe or some *cidre bouché* (bottled cider), go no farther: This *crêperie* has a jazz pianist upstairs playing the works of Fats Waller and Scott Joplin. The décor is reminiscent of an early-1960s Amsterdam jazz dive, with a vintage Coke dispenser, graffiti-scarred beams, and walls papered with posters and photos of stringy-haired musicians. ◆ Daily, afternoon snacks, dinner, and late-night snacks until 2AM. No credit cards accepted. 9 Rue Norvins (between Pl du Tertre and Rue Poulbot). 01.42.55.12.35. Métro: Abbesses

26 PLACE DU TERTRE

Part village carnival, part operetta set, this 14th-century square (*tertre* means "hillock" or "mound") is the hub of Montmartre, where busloads of tourists descend to pay homage to the Unknown Artist's awful landscapes and pathetic paintings of melancholy, wide-eyed children. In summer (when the square sprouts parasoled restaurant tables), white-aproned wait staff and hustling artists jealously guard their territories; the daily border wars make for great theater. During the Middle Ages the abbey had a scaffold here to hang anyone who disobeyed its rules, including any vineyard owner on the Butte who refused to donate a quarter of the wine he pressed to the ladies of the cloth, *les abbesses*. The tradition of exhibiting paintings in **Place du Tertre** dates from the 19th century, but unfortunately the quality of art has deteriorated over the years. Located in front of **St-Pierre-de-Montmartre**, the square is hard to miss, though you may wish you had. ◆ At Rues du Mont-Cenis and Norvins. Métro: Abbesses

27 LA CRÉMAILLÈRE 1900

★★$$ This brasserie, with an arbored garden, fin de siècle décor, and Edith Piaf's greatest hits played nightly on the piano, has a healthy neighborhood following. Seafood (fresh oysters, mussels, and sole stuffed with shrimp mousse) is the strong suit. ◆ Daily, lunch and dinner. 15 Place du Tertre. 01.46.06.58.59. Métro: Abbesses

28 LA MÈRE CATHERINE

★$$ Founded in 1793 and, as house legend has it, commandeered in 1814 by the Russians who conquered the Montmartre villagers, this is still the oldest brasserie on Place du Tertre, and the waiters swagger as if to show it. You'll find escargots, rack of lamb, and *tournedos Mère Catherine* (beef fillets cooked in port and foie gras sauce) on the menu. The dining room is adorned with Belle Epoque–reproduction mirrors and red-velvet benches, and piano and violin music from the 1920s accompanies your meal. There's also outdoor dining on the terrace. ◆ Daily, noon-12:30AM. 6 Place du Tertre. 01.46.06.32.69. Métro: Abbesses

28 LA BOHÈME DU TERTRE

★$$ No-frills traditional French cuisine—beef bourguignon, au gratin potatoes, apple tarts—is served here. ◆ Daily, 8AM-8PM; closed in January. 2 Place du Tertre. 01.46.06.51.69. Métro: Abbesses

29 Au Clairon des Chasseurs

$ In this bustling artists' café, where all the patrons seem to have sketchbooks under their arms and charcoal pencils behind their ears, painters gather by the window to case prospective clients in the square. Here you get the standard international spread: everything from pizza and *croque monsieur* (grilled ham-and-cheese sandwich) to club salads, omelettes, beef bourguignon, and spaghetti *bolognese* (with a meat sauce). Nevertheless, this café scores big points as a refuge. Ironically, the only way to escape the nagging street artists of Place du Tertre is by entering their midst; they come to this café strictly to take a break and won't pester you here. A jazz band plays Django Reinhardt–style music starting at 9PM. ♦ Daily, 7AM-3AM. 3 Place du Tertre. 01.42.62.40.08. Métro: Abbesses

30 St-Pierre-de-Montmartre

An important example of early Gothic architecture, this modest, three-aisled church was begun 16 years before **Notre-Dame** and claims to be the oldest sanctuary in Paris (two other structures, **St-Germain-des-Prés** and **St-Julien-le-Pauvre**, make similar claims). What appears to be a tiny provincial church is all that remains of the original abbey, which was founded in 1134 by King Louis VI (the Fat) and his wife, Queen Adélaide, who is buried here. The church was dedicated and consecrated by Pope Eugene III in 1147. Both Dante and St. Ignatius Loyola worshiped here.

Architecturally, the church is a composite. The vaulted choir loft definitely dates from the 12th century (notice the walls buckling beneath the weight of more than 800 years), but archeologists remain divided over whether the four capitaled columns incorporated in the church came from a Roman temple to Mercury or a Merovingian church (AD 500-751) on the site. The original church windows were shattered at the end of World War II by a bomb intended for a nearby bridge. New windows added in 1953 closely resemble in style the original Gothic stained glass; the three bronze west doors and the cemetery door depicting the Resurrection are by a contemporary Italian sculptor. Each Good Friday, the archbishop of Paris carries a crucifix up this "Mount of Martyrs" to **St-Pierre** as part of a stations-of-the-cross service.

The church's tiny cemetery is the smallest in Paris, with only 85 occupants, among whom are sculptor Pigalle, navigator Bougainville (after whom the purple flowering creeper is named), and Montmartre's first mayor, Félix Desportes. The Debray family, the original owners of the **Moulin de la Galette**, is also buried here; the family grave is easy to find—look for the miniature windmill on top. It's open only on All Saints' Day (1 November). ♦ 2 Rue du Mont-Cenis (at Rue St-Eleuthère). 01.46.06.57.63. Métro: Abbesses

31 Basilique Sacré-Coeur

Diocesan architect **Paul Abadie**'s Roman-Byzantine marble tribute, universally panned by his peers, has nevertheless become enshrined in the Tourists' Top Ten. For most people, the highlight of the church is not its design but the spectacular vista of Paris from its steps—or even better, from the dome (access through the north aisle) at dusk or dawn. The church was built as atonement for the massacre of some 58,000 citizens during the Franco-Prussian War, and within its mosaic-encrusted interior you can see priests praying for forgiveness for those war crimes 24 hours a day, a tradition that has been carried on since the church was consecrated more than a half-century ago. Begun in 1876, **Sacré-Coeur** took decades to complete; for the first 15 years of construction, pylons were sunk below grade to stabilize the foundation over the old quarry mines. The towering campanile was added in 1904 by **Lucien Magne**; one of the world's heaviest bells, the 19-ton **Savoyarde**, hangs in the belfry. From the north side of the dome you can see in the distance the green roof of the basilica built on the site where St. Denis finally put down his head. A trip to the **Basilique de St-Denis** is worthwhile (one métro ticket will get you there), if only to see the extraordinary collection of tombs where France buried its kings until the time of the revolution. (For more information, see page 297.) ♦ Admission to dome. Pl du Parvis-du-Sacré-Coeur (at Rues du Cardinal-Dubois and Azais). 01.42.51.17.02. Métros: Abbesses, Anvers

32 L'Eté en Pente Douce

★★$ This cafe and *salon de thé*, whose name means "summer on a soft slope," is hidden on a little square at the base of **Sacré-Coeur**'s sloping grassy park. Its outdoor terrace is a peaceful haven in this lively neighborhood. There's a variety of quiches and fresh pasta dishes, such daily specialties as half a duck stuffed with fruit and vegetables baked in a crust of salt, or wild boar steak with mushrooms in hunting season, and homemade apple strudel for dessert. ♦ Daily, lunch, afternoon tea, and dinner. 23 Rue Muller (at Rue Paul-Albert). 01.42.64.02.67. Métros: Château Rouge, Anvers

---

Restaurants/Clubs: Red | Hotels: Purple | Shops: Orange | Outdoors/Parks: Green | Sights/Culture: Blue

33 A LA POMPONNETTE

★★$$ Opened in 1909 and still run by the fourth generation of founder Arthur Delcroix's family, this is a veritable clubhouse for the *montmartrois* where local politicians, sports figures, and entrepreneurs gather in the congenial barroom or the dining rooms with their friends and families, ever abuzz with chatter and laughter. The walls are covered with Montmartre paintings, photos, sketches, and original prints, including ones by Poulbot. You will search in vain for anything more recent than the 1920s. But despite the restaurant's predominantly local character and clientele, outsiders need not fear the cold shoulder. This is a genuinely friendly place. Some specialties are rabbit in aspic with tarragon leaves, mackerel marinated in white wine, *magret de canard* (preserved duck breast), *filet de boeuf Chorou* (beef with wine sauce and a mousse of foie gras), and turbot with its scales replaced by slices of potato and baked in a creamed saffron sauce. The restaurant is noted for its exceptional selection of wines, by the bottle or by the glass. Closed the month of August. ◆ Tu-Sa, lunch and dinner; M, dinner. Reservations recommended. 42 Rue Lepic (between Rues Tholozé and Joseph-de-Maistre). 01.46.06.08.36. Métro: Place Blanche

34 LA VILLA DES ABBESSES

★★$$ This tea salon and restaurant offers contemporary bistro fare in a pleasant setting with comfortable chairs and intriguing art for sale on the walls. For a light lunch the salads, fresh and generously portioned, are excellent bets. Entrées include the likes of cod with coconut milk and citronella sauce, roasted red tuna steak with Chinese pepper, and steak frites. Service is swift and the place is open late, too. Daily, breakfast, lunch, and dinner (until 2AM). 61 Rue des Abbesses (at Rue Aristide-Bruant). 01.42.57.96.77. Métro: Abbesses or Blanche

35 LA MASCOTTE

★★$$ As soon as you set foot in this restaurant, you know it's the real thing. Regulars stand elbow to elbow at the brass bar feasting on platters of fresh shellfish that young owner Thierry Campion has trucked to his door daily from Brittany, washed down by cold Muscadet. Thierry's charming wife, Ghislaine, greets you as you enter the spacious Art Nouveau–style dining room where the waiters in traditional black garb with white aprons have been working for decades, and everything is *comme il faut* (as it should be)— the service, the food, and the wine. Old-fashioned crusty onion soup; Marseille-style fish soup with shredded cheese, garlic mayonnaise, and croutons; carpaccio of salmon marinated with anise and served with a cream sauce; Auvergne sausage with *aligot* (whipped mashed potatoes with garlic and cantal cheese); *fricassée de pétoncles à la provençale* (dainty scallops sautéed in wine and garlic sauce)—these are a few of the grand array of choices. Thierry loves wine and travels all over France in search of fine vintages. The result is a superb, very personal wine list coupled with the best possible advice about what goes best with your meal. ◆ Tu-Su, lunch and dinner. Reservations recommended. 52 Rue des Abbesses (between Rues Burq and Tholozé). 01.46.06.28.15. Métros: Abbesses, Place Blanche

Also at 52 Rue des Abbesses:

TRAÏT

This clean, well-lighted space is a one-stop shop for stylish stationery. The merchandise, from greeting cards and photo albums to writing implements and postcards, straddles the line between whimsical and elegant. In a neighborhood that falls prey to cliché perhaps more often than one would like, this store comes as a breath of fresh flair. ◆ Daily. 01.42.23.25.32

36 13 PLACE EMILE-GOUDEAU

On this site stood the famous old piano factory that art historians call the "Villa Médici of Modern Art." By the turn of the century this place had attracted poets Apollinaire and Max Jacob and modern painters Picasso, Braque, Gris, and Modigliani. Picasso worked here for 8 years, painting such works as *Les Demoiselles d'Avignon* (which is now in the collection of New York's Museum of Modern Art and is often cited as the first example of Cubism). This ramshackle building, which had but one water spigot to serve the 40 artists housed here, was sarcastically dubbed Bateau Lavoir after the laundry barges that used to be docked along the Seine. The original structure burned in 1970, but the city of Paris built a concrete replica and now rents studios (and provides plenty of water) to the far more prosperous, though not necessarily more talented, artists of today. There is a display window in front of the building with old photos and memorabilia of Picasso and company. ◆ At Rue Ravignan. Métro: Abbesses

36 TIMHOTEL MONTMARTRE

$$ Had this 60-room hotel been here in the 1920s, you might have asked neighbors Pablo Picasso or Georges Braque over for

THE BEST

Philippe Krenzer
General Manager, Hôtel de Crillon

Say Hello to Liza Wanklyn, wonderful manager of the **Thierry Mugler** boutique on Rue du Faubourg St-Honoré.

The fifth floor of the **Musée D'Orsay** for drinks after the "nocturne" of the museum.

Bar Henri IV, in the first arrondissement.

Bar du Petit Fer à Cheval: because it's *authentique*.

Betjeman & Barton Tea on Blvd Malesherbes.

Gardens of **Palais Royal**, and walking under the "colonnes de Burennes."

The latest place to be for shopping and nice spots: the area around Place des Victoires, Rue Etienne-Marcel, and Rue Montorgueil.

The restaurant **Murat**, Porte d'Auteuil, in the 16th arrondissement.

The last great school in Paris: **L'École des Fleurs au Crillon** (School of Flowers in the Hôtel de Crillon).

---

coffee and croissants. Today this member of a French budget hotel chain offers modern amenities (superior to those at most places in the same price range) but has the sterile atmosphere typical of chain hostelries. The charming location, however, makes up for the bland character. The upper-floor rooms on the south side have a spectacular view of the center of Paris. There's no restaurant. ◆ 11 Rue Ravignan (at Pl Emile-Goudeau). 01.42.55.74.79; fax 01.42.55.71.01. Métro: Abbesses. montmartre@timhotel.com; www.timhotel.fr

37 FONTAINE DE QUATRE-GRÂCES (FOUR GRACES FOUNTAIN)

Layered in green paint, this drinking fountain and 99 other identical ones around Paris were given to the city in the 1840s by Richard Wallace, an Englishman who collected 18th-century French art and frequently lamented that it was impossible in his beloved Paris to enjoy a glass of water in a café without paying for it. The metal drinking cup originally attached to it disappeared in the 1950s when the city adopted sanitation standards. ◆ Rue Ravignan (at Pl Emile-Goudeau). Métro: Abbesses

38 LE RESTAURANT

★★$$ Modern, minimalist décor complements owner-chef Yves Peladeau's imaginative array of original and traditional dishes: mussels sautéed in olive oil, lemon, and pepper; Basque-style fish casserole; grilled free-range chicken stuffed with preserved lemon, vegetables, and saffron; and an exquisite crème brûlée. A chic crowd dines here. ◆ Tu-F, lunch and dinner; Sa, dinner. Reservations recommended. 32 Rue Véron (at Rue Audran). 01.42.23.06.22. Métro: Abbesses

39 HÔTEL RÉGYN'S MONTMARTRE

$$ This 22-room hotel is in the heart of Montmartre, but otherwise it's nothing fancy. There's no restaurant. ◆ 18 Pl des Abbesses (at Rue des Abbesses). 01.42.54.45.21; fax 01.42.23.76.69. Métro: Abbesses. hotel@regynsmontmartre.com; www.regynsmontmartre.com

40 ABBESSES MÉTRO STATION

Named after *les abbesses*, the nuns who ran the abbey here in the Middle Ages, this métro station is the deepest in Paris—300 feet below ground level. The reason for the great depth lies in Montmartre's old gypsum mines. Gypsum, a soft stone, was burned to make the internationally famous plaster of Paris used to mold, among other things, busts of George Washington and Thomas Jefferson in the US Capitol. Over the years, the growing network of quarry tunnels beneath Montmartre turned the hill, geologically speaking, to Swiss cheese. In the 1840s the mines were closed, but not before 27 houses and several Parisians had disappeared into the void. The City of Paris is still filling Montmartre's cavities with high-pressure concrete. The métro platform was built at bedrock, precisely 285 steps below Place des Abbesses. Take the elevator and save your breath for the Montmartre summit.

The turn-of-the-19th-century exterior of the station, with its green, vinelike wrought-iron arches and amber lights, is one of the most picturesque in Paris and typifies the early Art Nouveau designs of architect **Hector Guimard**. At first, nationalistic Parisians criticized Guimard's choice of German green and suggested that he paint his métro stations *bleu, blanc, et rouge* (blue, white, and red,

---

Restaurants/Clubs: Red | Hotels: Purple | Shops: Orange | Outdoors/Parks: Green | Sights/Culture: Blue

like the French flag). His concession to chauvinism was a ship shield (the symbol of the city of Paris) in the middle of the roof, but he stubbornly held his ground on garden green. This is one of only two Guimard stations that still have their original glass roofs (the other is **Porte Dauphine** near the **Bois de Boulogne**). However, the **Abbesses** métro entrance is not original to the Butte. For decades it stood in front of the **Hôtel de Ville** (City Hall), but when Mayor Jacques Chirac gussied up the plaza in 1977, he moved Guimard's masterpiece to Montmartre. New York's Museum of Modern Art has an old Métropolitain sign and early Guimard arches similar to these. ♦ Pl des Abbesses (at Rue des Abbesses)

41 Bonjour l'Artiste

Sold here are juggling balls, batons, magic rings, trick cards, clown noses, and any other paraphernalia you might need in order to run away with the circus. ♦ M-Sa. 35 Rue des Trois-Frères (between Rue de la Vieuville and Passage des Abbesses). 01.42.51.44.53. Métro: Abbesses

42 St-Jean-de-Montmartre

Soon after its construction, this church, a Moorish grab bag of architectural tricks trimmed with what looks like turquoise Art Nouveau jewelry, was given the nickname "St-Jean-des-Briques" due to its redbrick façade. Looking amazingly contemporary for a centenarian, the 1904 church was the first in Paris built with reinforced concrete. ♦ 19-21 Rue des Abbesses (between Rues Houdon and Germain-Pilon). 01.46.06.43.96. Métro: Abbesses

43 L'Abat-Jour

Patrick Rossignol and Chantal Juan want people of all ages, professions, and lifestyles to feel comfortable in their cozy hair salon. No photographs of pouty models with trendy hairdos are displayed. The stylists will cut, shape, color, or perm your hair to suit you, using many products with natural ingredients. The salon's name means "the lamp shade,"

Of course they came to France a great many to paint pictures and naturally they could not do that at home, or to write they could not do that at home either, they could be dentists at home.

—Gertrude Stein

which refers not to any coiffure but to the business formerly located at this address, a lamp shade manufacturer. ♦ Tu-Sa. 19 Rue Yvonne-Le-Tac (between Rue des Martyrs and Pl des Abbesses). 01.42.64.39.32. Métro: Abbesses

44 Martyrium

Just off the Street of Martyrs, where St. Denis was thought to have been decapitated, is the **Chapelle des Martyres**. In the crypt of an earlier medieval sanctuary on this site, Spaniards Ignatius Loyola and Francis Xavier founded the Jesuit order of priests on 15 August 1534. ♦ M-W, F-Su. 11 Rue Yvonne-le-Tac (between Rues des Trois-Frères and des Martyrs). No phone. Métro: Abbesses

45 Gaspard de la Butte

Catherine Malaure sells her original line of colorfully patterned children's clothes in this darling little shop. You can catch a glimpse of the fabric samples and sewing machines in the backroom workshop. ♦ Daily. 10 *bis* Rue Yvonne-le-Tac (between Rues des Trois-Frères and des Martyrs). 01.42.55.99.40. Métro: Abbesses

46 Claude & Nicole

★★$ This cozy neighborhood bistro has a faithful clientele of young Montmartre residents who come for the herring fillet, *jambon persil* (ham in parsley aspic), and *blanquette de veau* (veal with béchamel sauce and mushrooms), or one of the other rotating *plats du jour*. ♦ Tu-Sa, lunch and dinner; Su, lunch. 13 Rue des Trois-Frères (between Rues Yvonne-le-Tac and de la Vieuville). 01.46.06.12.48. Métro: Abbesses

47 La Boutique des Anges

Wing your way into this shop where owners Brigitte and Patricia sell everything from heavenly inspired CDs, jewelry, and lamps to books and paper goods—all with an angelic twist. One popular item is the personal guardian angel pin (selected to correspond with your birth date) designed by local artisans. ♦ Daily. 2 *bis* Rue Yvonne-le-Tac (between Rues des Trois-Frères and des Martyrs). 01.42.57.74.38. Métro: Abbesses

48 Le Progrès

★$ Patronized by Parisians rather than tourists, this neighborhood café and bar is economical and authentic. The simple food isn't gourmet, but it is tasty, and decent wines are poured by the pitcher. There's a daily prixfixe lunch—examples include roast beef and potatoes or *rognons provençaux* (kidneys with tomatoes, olive oil, and garlic). *Charcuterie* and cheese are served all day. ♦ M-Sa, lunch and snacks until 2AM. 1 Rue Yvonne-Le-Tac (at Rue des Trois-Frères). 01.42.51.33.33. Métro: Abbesses

49 LE GASTELIER

★$ The tea salon at the foot of **Sacré-Coeur** is a perfect luncheon stop before making the final ascent up the white stairs. Try a *tarte végétarienne* and a dish of fresh mandarin-orange sorbet. Better yet, indulge in a few scoops of nougat ice cream or a plate of macaroons and then waddle over to the **Funicular** and ride up. ♦ Tu-Su, breakfast, lunch, and afternoon tea until 8PM. 1 *bis* Rue Tardieu (at Pl St-Pierre). 01.46.06.22.06. Métro: Anvers

50 FUNICULAR

The shortest, steepest métro line in Paris runs every few minutes between Place Suzanne-Valadon and the base of **Sacré-Coeur**. While fitness freaks take the stairs, the rest ride up in comfort and enjoy the view, all for the price of a normal métro ticket. ♦ Top station at Pl du Parvis-du-Sacré-Coeur; bottom station at Pl Suzanne-Valadon and Rue Foyatier. Métro: Anvers

50 RUE FOYATIER

The most photographed steps in Montmartre, all 266 of them, run from Rue Azais down to Place Suzanne-Valadon (named after Maurice Utrillo's mother, a talented painter in her own right). All hell breaks loose here at 4:30PM each day when an elementary school lets out and scores of screaming children with minia-ture leather briefcases on their backs dart across the square in search of their mothers and fathers—the local butchers, bakers, and souvenir-makers—who have come to walk them home. ♦ Between Pl Suzanne-Valadon and Rue Azais. Métro: Anvers

51 MARCHÉ ST-PIERRE

Paris's most celebrated discount fabric ware-house is the hub of the city's garment district. Pandemonium reigns over acres of tweed, bolts of polyester, and bins of last year's argyle socks in this five-story bazaar. Everyone comes here: students searching for cheap curtains, Punjabi women rummaging for sari silk, and New Wave couturiers stalking ersatz panther pelts. The costumes of the surly sales clerks range from three-piece suits to studded leather jackets and turquoise tights. The

method in this madness? Take it from the top: fifth floor, linens and sheets; fourth floor, lace curtains and duvet covers; third floor, silks, velours, and *incroyables* (exotic odds and ends); second floor, wools and polyesters; ground floor, a bit of everything. ♦ M, 1:30-6:30PM; Tu-Sa. 2 Rue Charles-Nodier (at Rue Livingstone). 01.46.06.92.25. Métro: Anvers

52 PLACE DE CLICHY

Stop by the Académie de Billard Clichy-Montmartre (84 Rue de Clichy; 01.48.78.32.85), a billiards hall set in a converted 1900 stable, and then wander down Rue d'Amsterdam, past carpet shops, used-furniture stores, and homeopathic phar-macies. ♦ At Blvds de Clichy and des Batignolles and Rue d'Amsterdam and Ave de Clichy. Métro: Place de Clichy

53 CHARLOT, LE ROI DES COQUILLAGES

★★$$$ Stop at this vivacious Art Deco–style bistro for a no-nonsense lunch of crabs, shrimps, oysters, and the like. Menu choices include bouillabaisse, *moules gratinées aux épices douces* (baked mussels with sweet spices), roasted langoustines with herbs from Provence, and grilled lobsters. Fine wines are served, including Muscadet and Chardonnay. ♦ Daily, lunch and dinner until 1AM. 81 Blvd de Clichy (between Ave de Clichy and Rue de Douai). 01.53.20.48.00. Métro: Place de Clichy

54 MOULIN ROUGE

Founded in 1889 (the year the **Eiffel Tower** was built) and still kicking after all these years, this legendary temple of the risqué proffers all the bare-breasted women, ostrich plumes, rhinestones, and multicolored lights the stage can support. The show recalls the days of the famous cancan dancers—Jane

Avril, Yvette Guilbert, Valentin le Désosse, and La Goulue, who were limned by Toulouse-Lautrec. The 60 indefatigable Doriss Girls carry on the tradition. Dinner is rather expensive and nothing to write home about, so you might want to skip it and take in the show from the bar. ♦ Cover. Show with dinner, daily, 7PM; shows only, 9PM and 11PM. Reservations recommended for dinner and show. 82 Blvd de Clichy (between Rue Lepic and Cité Véron). 01.53.09.82.82. Métro: Blanche. www.moulinrouge.com

54 CITÉ VÉRON

Don't let its shabby entrance on the boulevard deter you, because this cul-de-sac to the left of the **Moulin Rouge** is quite intriguing. Surviving family members of French writers Jacques Prévert and Boris Vian make their homes here, and you will find the highbrow **Théâtre Ouvert** (no. 4 *bis*; 01.42.55.74.40), which features the works of contemporary French playwrights; the **Boris Vian Foundation** (no. 6 *bis*; 01.46.06.73.56), which is housed in an old hunting lodge and offers exhibitions, dance, and theater classes; and an amazing warehouse-cum-boutique for used clothing, old costumes, and stage props called **Ophir** (No. 8; 01.42.64.58.40), whose doorbell you must ring to get in. Some of the best stuff collected by the owners Jacqueline and André Marcovici is not for sale (19th-century wooden carousel figures and Moulin Rouge stage props, for instance), but there's plenty more here to satisfy the most jaded of rummage-sale shoppers. Ophir is open Monday through Friday between 9AM and 1PM and afternoons and weekends by appointment only. ♦ Entrance at 92 Blvd de Clichy. Métro: Blanche

55 MUSÉE DE L'EROTISME

A touch of class amid the sleazy sex shops and strip joints of Pigalle, this attractive, modern museum of erotic art was created by three passionate collectors in 1997. More than 2,000 works are on display—sculptures, paintings, photographs, fetishes, and furnishings from Africa, Asia, Oceania, Europe, and the Americas. The two upper floors of the five-story building are devoted to temporary exhibits of works by present-day artists. ♦ Admission. Daily, 10AM-2AM. 72 Blvd de Clichy (between Rues Coustou and Lepic). 01.42.58.28.73. Métro: Pigalle

56 BRUNO

Would you like a goldfish on your ankle? Perhaps a mermaid on your chest? Bruno, one of the more popular body artists in Paris and an officer of the artisanal Order of Artistic Merit, practices safe tattooing, using only fresh needles and disposable ink cartridges. Even if you're not ready to commit to a permanent bodily souvenir of your trip, it's fun to look in the window and imagine. ♦ M-Tu, Th-Sa. 4 Rue Germain-Pilon (between Blvd de Clichy and Rue Véron). 01.42.64.35.59. Métro: Pigalle

57 RÉSIDENCE PARIS MONTMARTRE

$$ These 76 kitchen-equipped studios and apartments, located on a tranquil square with its own private garden, are rented by the night or week. The complex is operated by the Pierre & Vacances group. ♦ 10 Pl Charles-Dullin (at Rue des Trois-Frères). 01.42.57.14.55; fax 01.42.54.48.87. Métros: Anvers, Pigalle. www.pierre-vacances.fr/location

58 THÉÂTRE DE L'ATELIER

When this charming theater was first built in 1822 on this cobblestoned square (named in 1957 after actor Charles Dullin), it was known for the Stefan Zweig adaptation of Ben Jonson's *Volpone* and for *L'Opéra Bouffe*, which critics called the best stage performances outside Paris (Montmartre was not yet part of the city proper). Under directors Laura Pels and Juliette Meeus, this theater is truly Parisian, and there isn't a bad red-velvet seat in the house. ♦ Box office: M-Sa, 11AM-7PM. 1 Pl Charles-Dullin (at Rue d'Orsel). 01.46.06.49.24. Métro: Anvers

59 PLACE PIGALLE

Nineteenth-century sculptor Jean-Baptiste Pigalle's celebrated rendering of the Virgin Mary is displayed in **St-Sulpice Church**, but his name became synonymous with porn theaters, sex shops, and prostitutes by being associated with this square. Known as "Pig Alley" to World War II GIs who came stalking the professional wildlife, **Place Pigalle** has lost many of its hookers to Rue St-Denis and the **Bois de Boulogne**; these days transvestites predominate. **Le Montmartrain** (06.08.26.38.38) is a small white tourist train that takes visitors on a circuit of the Butte de Montmartre with a stop at **Sacré-Coeur**. It departs from the Place Pigalle métro entrance on the center island of Boulevard de Clichy daily every half hour between 10AM and 7 or 8PM (depending on the weather) between Easter and October; daily, every 30 minutes between 10:30AM and 5PM the rest of the year. ♦ At Blvd de Clichy. Métro: Pigalle

60 LE DIVAN DU MONDE

Starting as a Second Empire dance hall, this space has undergone a dozen deaths and rebirths: as a brasserie, a late-19th-century bohemian music hall called Le Divan Japonais (there's a famous poster by Toulouse-Lautrec), a turn-of-the-19th-century strip joint, a comedy theater, a cabaret, and various other incarnations, before expiring as a porno movie theater. After closing for several years, this phoenixlike institution rose once again from its ashes in 1994 as Paris's most imaginative club for live performances of World, other contemporary music (jazz, soul, fashion), and soirées of techno, rap, and rock with top DJs. It was an instant hit with the Parisian public and continues to be so, both for its music and its laid-back atmosphere. There are shows most nights and tea dances for children the first Sunday of every month and for adults on the remaining Sundays. For schedules and reservations, contact the box office or consult local listings. ♦ Box office: M-F, 11AM-7PM. 75 Rue des Martyrs (between Blvd de Clichy and Rue des Abbesses). 01.44.92.77.66. Métro: Pigalle

61 L'ORIENTAL

★★$ Moroccan specialties are served at this intimate restaurant where décor is accented with touches of marble and mirrors. Thoughtful preparation is the key here: Choose from among such dishes as *bistilla au poulet* (puff pastry filled with chicken, almonds, and mint), *tchakchouka* (a zesty mixture of scrambled eggs, onions, peppers, and spices), or prawn and saffron *tajine* (stew). ♦ M-Sa, lunch and dinner; closed in August. Reservations required. 76 Rue des Martyrs (between Blvd de Rochechouart and Rue d'Orsel). 01.42.64.39.80. Métro: Pigalle

62 LA FOURMI

★$ A decrepit old zinc-bar bistro slightly spruced up and furnished with tables and chairs scrounged from here and there, this is one of the key hangouts for plugged-in Paris youth. Here they learn where underground concerts and other cool events are taking place or simply sit around and smoke, drink (the beer is quite cheap), and talk. If the dense cloud of cigarette smoke doesn't bother you, this is as good a spot as you'll find to encounter today's generation on its home turf. Surprisingly enough, the food (salads, sandwiches, and a *plat du jour*) is not bad at all. ♦ Daily, 8:30AM-2AM. 74 Rue des Martyrs (corner of Blvd de Rochechouart). 01.42.64.70.35. Métro: Pigalle

63 CARLTON'S

$$$ Surprise, surprise—there's a comfortable, well-appointed modern hotel offering 103 peaceful rooms amid the strip joints and kung fu cinemas of Pigalle. Have a drink on the rooftop terrace, which offers a spectacular 360-degree panorama of Paris, with **Sacré-**

Coeur right up on the hill. There's no restaurant, but there's a large Belle Epoque breakfast room and a neat modern bar in the lobby. ♦ 55 Blvd de Rochechouart (at Rue Lallier). 01.42.81.91.00; fax 01.42.81.97.04. Métro: Pigalle. carltons@club-internet.fr; www.montmartrenet.com

64 CARAVELLE

$$ This hotel has 31 comfortable but minimally decorated rooms. Ask for one in back and avoid the traffic noise. There's no restaurant. ♦ 68 Rue des Martyrs (between Ave Trudaine and Blvd de Rochechouart). 01.48.78.43.31; fax 01.40.23.98.72. Métro: Pigalle. hotel-caravelle@wanadoo.fr

65 MUSÉE DE LA VIE ROMANTIQUE (MUSEUM OF THE ROMANTIC PERIOD)

Painter Ary Scheffer was one of the most successful artists of the Romantic period, and his charming home and studios in La Nouvelle Athènes, a neighborhood popular with artists, writers, and musicians between the 1820s and the mid-19th century, became a prime gathering place for a group that included nearby residents Delacroix, Géricault, George Sand, Chopin, and Liszt, and visitors Turgenev, Rossini, and Charles Dickens at Scheffer's open house every Friday in his studios and garden. Besides the museum's paintings by Scheffer, the favorite portraitist of Louis-Philippe and his circle, a large part of its collection is devoted to writer George Sand (née Aurore Dupin), including a lovely portrait of her by Auguste Charpentier, furniture and art objects from her homes, and a remarkable selection of that romantic lady's jewelry. The museum also puts on excellent temporary exhibitions. The greenhouse tea salon and its wisteria-shaded garden are open between May and October. ♦ Tu–Su, 10AM-5:40 PM. ♦ Admission. 16 Rue Chaptal (between Rues Blanche and Fontaine). 01.48.74.95.38. Métros: St-Georges, Blanche, Pigalle

66 L'ANNEXE

★$$ This lively bistro wallpapered with cancan scenes is only a quick stroll from the glitter of Pigalle. Try the *suprême de pintade* (breast of guinea fowl) cooked in cider, grilled salmon with dill, grilled lamb chops, or, if you have the stomach for it, *andouillette grillé* (grilled tripe sausage). ♦ M-F, lunch and dinner; closed in August. 15 Rue Chaptal (at Rue Henner). 01.48.74.65.52. Métro: St-Georges

---

Restaurants/Clubs: Red | Hotels: Purple | Shops: Orange | Outdoors/Parks: Green | Sights/Culture: Blue

Additional Highlights

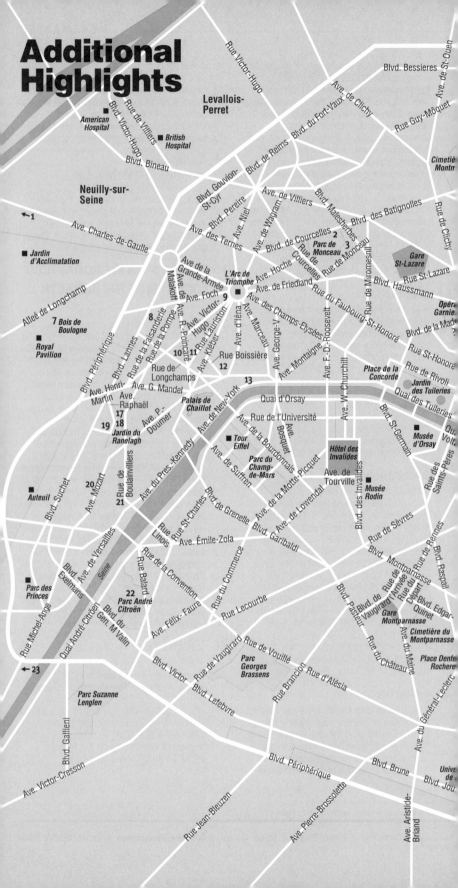

Rue Victor-Hugo

Levallois-Perret

Blvd. Bessieres

Ave. de St-Ouen

Ave. de Clichy

Rue Guy-Môquet

American Hospital

Blvd. Victor-Hugo

Rue de Villiers

British Hospital

Blvd. du Fort-Vaux

Blvd. de Reims

Rue de Clichy

Cimetiè Montn

Blvd. Bineau

Neuilly-sur-Seine

← 1

Ave. Charles-de-Gaulle

Blvd. Gouvion-St-Cyr

Blvd. Pereire

Ave. Niel

Ave. des Ternes

Ave. de Villiers

Blvd. de Courcelles

Blvd. Malesherbes

Blvd. des Batignolles

Rue de Clichy

Jardin d'Acclimatation

Ave. de la Grande-Armée

Ave. de Wagram

2 **Parc de Monceau** 3

Rue de Courcelles

Rue de Monceau

Gare St-Lazare

Rue St-Lazare

Allée de Longchamp

Ave. de Malakoff

R.-Poincaré

L'Arc de Triomphe

Ave. Hoche

Ave. de Friedland

Rue de Miromesnil

Blvd. Haussmann

7 **Bois de Boulogne**

8

Ave. de la Falaisanderie

Ave. Victor-Hugo

9

Ave. d'Iéna

Ave. des Champs-Élysées

Rue du Faubourg-St-Honoré

Opér Garnie

Blvd. de la Mad

Blvd. Périphérique

Blvd. Lannes

Rue de la Pompe

Ave. Lauriston

Ave. Kléber

Ave. Marceau

Ave. George-V

Ave. F.-D.-Roosevelt

Rue St-Honoré

Royal Pavilion

10

11

Rue Boissière

Ave. Montaigne

Place de la Concorde

Rue de Rivoli

12

13

Ave. W.-Churchill

Jardin des Tuileries

Rue de Longchamps

Quai d'Orsay

Quai des Tuileries

Ave. Henri-Martin

Ave. G. Mandel

Palais de Chaillot

Ave. de New-York

Rue de l'Université

Blvd. St-Germain

Qu Volt

Ave. Raphaël

Ave. P.-Doumer

Ave. de la Bourdonnais

Ave. Bosquet

Musée d'Orsay

17

18

Tour Eiffel

Hôtel des Invalides

Rue des Saints-Pères

19

Jardin du Ranelagh

Ave. de Suffren

Parc du Champ-de-Mars

Ave. de la Motte-Picquet

Ave. de Tourville

Musée Rodin

Rue de Rennes

Auteuil

20

Rue de Boulainvilliers

Ave. du Pres.-Kennedy

Ave. de la Bourdonnais

Ave. de Lowendal

Blvd. des Invalides

Rue de Sèvres

Blvd. Suchet

Ave. Mozart

21

Rue St-Charles

Blvd. de Grenelle

Blvd. Garibaldi

Blvd. Montparnasse

Blvd. Raspail

Rue Linois

Ave. Émile-Zola

Rue de Vaugirard

Rue du

Blvd. Edgar-Quinet

Blvd. Exelmans

Ave. de Versailles

Seine

Rue Balard

Rue de la Convention

Rue du Commerce

Rue Lecourbe

Blvd. Pasteur

Rue de Vaugirard

Rue d'Arrivée

Gare Montparnasse

Cimetière du Montparnasse

Parc des Princes

22 **Parc André Citroën**

Quai André-Citroën

Blvd. du Gen. M Valin

Ave. Félix- Faure

Ave. du Maine

Place Denfe Rochere

Rue Michel-Ange

Blvd. Victor

Blvd. Lefebvre

Rue de Vaugirard

Rue de Vouillé

Parc Georges Brassens

Rue d'Alésia

Rue du Château

Ave. du Général-Leclerc

← 23

Parc Suzanne Lenglen

Blvd. Gallieni

Blvd. Périphérique

Blvd. Brune

Unive de Blvd. Jou

Ave. Victor-Cresson

Rue Jean-Bleuzen

Blvd. Pierre-Brossolette

Ave. Aristide-Briand

ADDITIONAL HIGHLIGHTS

There are some wonderful spots in Paris that are not in the areas covered elsewhere in this book. This chapter features Paris's other highlights, which include something for everyone: eerie catacombs; pleasant parks, including the well-known **Monceau** and **Bois de Boulogne**; the famous **Cimetière du Père-Lachaise**, the burial place of generations of writers, musicians, and artists, from Chopin to Jim Morrison; the controversial **Bibliothèque Nationale François Mitterrand**; and a variety of interesting museums, including the high-tech **La Villette** science museum, several fine art collections, and museums devoted to the lives and works of such notables as singer **Edith Piaf** and architect **Le Corbusier**.

1 GRANDE ARCHE DE LA DÉFENSE

The axis that starts with the **Carrousel Arch** in front of the **Louvre** and runs westward through the **Tuileries Gardens** to the **Obelisk of Luxor**, then down the Champs-Elysées to the **Arc de Triomphe**, has been extended westward with this 300,000-ton white Carrara marble monument in La Défense district. Designed by **Johan Otto von Spreck-elsen**, who won an international competition for the commission, the arch is actually a hollow cube built on 12 pillars set 99 feet into the ground. The building houses the Ministry of Planning and Development, the Foundation for the Rights of Man, headquarters for several cultural foundations, and private offices. Inaugurated in July 1989 as part of the 200th anniversary of the French Revolution, the building brings monumental dazzle to the sterile high-rise jungle that has become Paris's business district. ♦ 1 Parvis de la Défense (just west of Pl de la Défense). Métro: Grande Arche de la Défense

2 PARC DE MONCEAU

This small and quirky park dates from 1778, when Philippe-Egalité, the Duke of Orléans, commissioned painter **Carmontel** to design a private garden on the Monceau Plain, then outside the city limits. Carmontel created a whimsical landscape full of architectural follies: a pyramid, a pagoda, a Roman temple, windmills, and artfully placed ruins. The park changed hands a few times after the revolution, and by 1862 it had been revamped by **Alphand**, an engineer under Baron Haussmann. Alphand gave the landscape the picturesque English garden–inspired elements still evident today. Of particular interest are the **Naumachie**, an oval basin with a colonnade said to have come from the unfinished mausoleum of Henri II at **St-Denis**, and the round **Barrière**

Monceau, one of the many *barrières* (tollhouses) built along the old city wall (now destroyed) in 1784 by **Claude-Nicholas Ledoux**. Although Ledoux's commission called for 55 such tollhouses, historians are unsure how many were actually built; only 4 still stand. ♦ Blvd de Courcelles (between Blvd Malesherbes and Ave de Vigny); also accessible from Aves Velasquez, Ruysdaël, and Van-Dyck. Métro: Monceau

3 MUSÉE CERNUSCHI

An exquisite collection of ancient Chinese art is housed in the tastefully modernized Belle Epoque mansion built by financier Henri Cernuschi. The museum also puts on outstanding temporary exhibits. It is by the east gate of the **Parc de Monceau**. ♦ Admission. Tu-Su. 7 Ave Velasquez (between Blvd Malesherbes and Parc de Monceau). 01.45.63.50.75. Métro: Villiers

3 MUSÉE NISSIM DE CAMONDO

Around the corner from the Museé Cernuschi, this elegant early-20th-century *hôtel particulier* overlooking the Parc Monceau is preserved just as the family of the Count Moïse de Camondo lived in it, amidst the finest in late 18th-century French furniture, Savonnerie carpets and Beauvais tapestries, Sèvres porcelain, and works of art, including paintings by Guardi, Hubert Robert, and Mme. Vigée-Lebrun. Camondo, a prominent banker for the Ottoman Turks, died in World War I, and the rest of his family perished in Nazi concentration camps. Admission. ♦ W-Su, 10AM-5PM. 63 Rue de Monceau (between Blvd Malesherbes and Ave Ruysdaël). 01.53.89.06.40; Métro: Villiers. www.ucad.fr

6 PARC DES BUTTES-CHAUMONT

If you're tired of the crowds in the **Luxembourg Gardens** and need a break from the all-too-French symmetry of the **Tuileries**, do as the French do: Buy some ripe Brie, a baguette, and a hearty *vin de pays*, and head for this urban wilderness in northeastern Paris. The unusual park was built in 1867 by Baron Haussmann, who also laid out the sewers and the city's grand boulevards for Napoléon III. Before Haussmann, **Buttes-Chaumont** was a city dump. In what must be the most inspired use of landfill in history, a then-new material—concrete—was used to form natural-looking cliffs, ravines, rivers, and an artificial lake. There's even a grotto and waterfall that have been restored. Buttes-Chaumont's island, set in the lake, is capped with a classical colonnaded temple and commands one of the city's most striking views of Montmartre and **Sacré-Coeur**. Visitors not inclined to mountaineering may prefer sipping a *citron pressé* (lemonade) on the terrace of the **Pavillon du Lac**, which serves tea and light lunches and is located on the park's west side. ◆ Daily. Bounded by Rues de Crimée, Manin, and Botzaris. Métros: Buttes-Chaumont, Botzaris

4 RUE DE PARADIS

This shabby little street is the domain of the finest French and European tableware outlets. Nearly 50 shops selling porcelain, silver, earthenware, crystal, and glass are crowded along its three blocks. All the most elegant brands of tableware may be found here at prices that are 30% to 50% lower than in the US. ◆ Between Rues du Faubourg St-Denis and du Faubourg-Poissonnière. Métros: Château d'Eau, Poissonnière

On Rue de Paradis:

MUSÉE BACCARAT

A glittering collection of Baccarat crystal is displayed here. Some of the pieces were used by heads of state, including the Queen of Siam and King Louis Philippe. Also on view are the Baccarat glasses commissioned for Henry Ford II's yacht and Franklin Roosevelt's White House. The most dazzling pieces are the two 1-ton, 79-light candelabras ordered by Czar Nicholas II for his St. Petersburg palace. Baccarat crystal is sold here as well. ◆ Free; fee for group tours. M-Sa. 30 *bis* Rue de Paradis (between Rues du Faubourg St-Denis and d'Hauteville). 01.47.70.64.30

5 PARC DE LA VILLETTE

The old slaughterhouse district, a 136-acre site in northeastern Paris, was transformed in the mid-1980s into a huge complex of parks and buildings devoted to science, technology, music, and other cultural and entertainment events. A series of 26 bright red "follies"—whimsical structures designed by architect **Bernard Tschumi**—are laid out in a grid

pattern throughout the park. They serve a variety of functions, including a café, weathervane, children's play area, and belvedere. In late June and early July the **Villette Jazz Festival** is held in **La Grande Halle de la Villette** and the **Cité de la Musique**, and from mid-July to mid-August, **Cinema en Plein Air**, a free outdoor festival of classic films, is held on many evenings, as are several dance concerts. For information on events at the **Parc de la Villette**, contact the Paris Office de Tourisme (08.36.68.31.12; www.paris-touristoffice.com) or La Villette's phone or web site. 6AM-1AM. ◆ Bounded by Blvd Sérurier and Canal St-Denis and by Ave Jean-Jaurès and Blvd Macdonald. There are Centres d'Acceuil (orientation centers) at the Porte de Pantin and Porte de la Villette entrances. 01.40.03.75.75. Métros: Porte de Pantin, Porte de la Villette. www.la-villette.com

Within Parc de la Villette:

CITÉ DES SCIENCES ET DE L'INDUSTRIE

La Villette's centerpiece is a vast $600 million gray granite, glass, and dark steel museum and exhibition building converted from a huge 19th-century slaughterhouse by French architect **Adrien Fainsilber** and opened in 1986. It has become one of Paris's most popular attractions, with more than 3.5 million visitors per year. Unlike more traditional museums, the **Cité des Sciences et de l'Industrie** is very much a hands-on experience, with lots of interactive exhibits and participatory attractions providing fun and knowledge for visitors of all ages.

The core permanent exhibition is **Explora**, and new temporary exhibitions are presented throughout the year, many of them translated into English. Explora is organized into three sectors, each offering 200 to 300 presentations. The **South Gallery** takes you through major activities of contemporary industrial society—aeronautics, the automobile, the conquest of extreme environments in space (where you can experience weightlessness), and the ocean—and the relationship of societies to the planet in exhibits on energy, the environment, and the greenhouse, garden of the future. The **North Gallery**, the most interactive of the sectors, has exhibits on the mental and sensory mechanisms of humans and their technical ramifications—expression and behavior, mathematics, sounds, images, and computer science. The **North Balcony** and **Mezzanine** deal with fundamental questions that human beings ask about themselves in life and health,

---

Restaurants/Clubs: Red | Hotels: Purple | Shops: Orange | Outdoors/Parks: Green | Sights/Culture: Blue

medicine, biology, light games, rocks and volcanoes, and stars and galaxies.

In the building there are also an excellent **planetarium** to take you on exciting trips to the edge of the universe; an **aquarium** with 200 species of Mediterranean fish, shellfish, and mollusks; **La Cité des Enfants** with interactive exhibits geared to 3- to 5-year-olds and to 5- to 12-year-olds; and **La Mediathèque**, which houses more than 300,000 books on science, 3,000 videodiscs, and a large conference center. In back of the building you will find a full-scale submarine, the **Argonaute**, next to the gigantic silver sphere of **La Géode** (see below). ♦ Admission. Tu-Sa, 10AM-6PM; Su, 10AM-7PM. 30 Ave Corentin-Cariou (at Blvd Macdonald). 01.40.05.80.00 (information); 01.40.05.12.12 (reservations). Métro: Porte de la Villette. www.cite-sciences.fr

LA GÉODE

The most popular attraction is **La Géode**, a polished-steel sphere, 117 feet in diameter, where Omnimax films are projected on a gigantic 180-degree screen (wider than the human field of vision), to thrilling effect. The theater sits directly in back of the **Cité des Sciences et de l'Industrie**. ♦ Admission. Tu-Su, hourly, 10AM-9PM. Reservations recommended, especially during school vacations. 30 Ave Corentin-Cariou (at Blvd Macdonald). Reservations and information: 01.40.05.12.12. Métro: Porte de la Villette

CITÉ DE LA MUSIQUE

Opened in 1995, this complex is **Parc de la Villette**'s newest attraction. Architect **Christian de Portzamparc**'s monumental ensemble of buildings is arranged along a glass-roofed interior street and includes two concert halls, an opera house, and a museum. The schedule of high-quality programs includes dance performances, operas, and concerts of classical and contemporary music from around the world. The **Conservatoire National de Musique et de Danse** (National Conservatory of Music and Dance), where students often give free recitals, is based here, as is the **Ensemble InterContemporain**, a research and educational institution devoted to late-20th-century music. The five-story **Musée de la Musique** displays a collection of over 4,500 music-related items, including 16th-century Venetian lutes; the 19th-century instruments of Adolphe Sax, inventor of the saxophone; five Stradivarius violins; and Frank Zappa's modular E-Mu synthesizer. ♦ Admission. Box office: Tu-Sa, noon-6PM; Su, 10AM-6PM. Museum: Tu-Su. 211 Ave Jean-Jaurès (between Blvd Sérurier and Rue Adolphe-Mille). 01.44.84.45.45 (information); 01.44.84.44.84 (reservations). Métro: Porte de Pantin. www.cite-musique.fr

LA GRANDE HALLE DE LA VILLETTE

A fine example of 19th-century cast-iron-and-glass construction, this huge pavilion built in 1867 for cattle trading has been converted into a multifunction venue for music festivals, trade fairs, and other large-scale exhibitions, with a capacity of more than 15,000 people. ♦ Place de la Fontaine aux Lions, facing 211 Ave Jean-Jaurès (between Blvd Sérurier and Rue Adolphe-Mille). Information and reservations 01.40.03.75.75. Métro: Porte de Pantin.

7 BOIS DE BOULOGNE

Stretching along the western flank of Paris and occupying more than 2,200 acres, this is the city's ultimate playground. The Merovingians hunted wild boar and wolves in the *bois* in the 6th century, it was enclosed by Henri II in 1556, and in the 17th century Jean-Baptiste Colbert transformed the land into royal hunting grounds. After Napoléon III gave the forest to the City of Paris in 1852, **Baron Haussmann** remodeled the landscape; using London's Hyde Park as his guide, he built many of the lakes, restaurants, racetracks, and paths that are here today. Haussmann designed the park so it would be entered from Avenue Foch, which he also designed and which leads grandly down to the Porte Dauphine. Once in the park, you can choose from a seemingly infinite variety of activities and attractions. The most notable include the **Bagatelle** (01.40.67.97.00), a magical 50-acre park with an 18th-century villa built by the then-future king, Charles X, a rose garden with 8,000 bushes of 700 varieties, and a grand iris garden; the **Jardin d'Acclimatation** (01.40.67.90.82), an amusement park for children with a miniature zoo; the **Auteuil** steeplechase racecourse (01.40.71.47.47) and the **Longchamp** flats track (01.44.30.75.00); the **Shakespeare Garden** (01.42.27.39.54), where the bard's works and classic French plays are performed in an open-air theater in summer; **Les Serres d'Auteuil** (01.40.71.74.00), a magnificent 19th-century greenhouse complex where concerts are given in May and June; and **Le Pré Catelan**, another flower and tree garden that shelters a luxurious café-restaurant of the same name (see below). There are numerous sports facilities, including the **Roland Garros Stadium** (01.47.43.48.00), where the French Open tennis tournament is held. Bicycles can be rented opposite the main entrance to the **Jardin d'Acclimatation** (at the Carrefour des Sablons) and near the **Royal Pavilion** (at the Carrefour du Bout-des-Lacs) daily May through September and on Saturday and Sunday the rest of the year. As did the Bois de Vincennes, the forest lost thousands of trees in the devastating windstorm of December 1999, and its effects will be visible for many years to come. ♦

Métros: Porte d'Auteuil, Porte Dauphine, Porte Maillot

In the Bois de Boulogne:

Le Pré Catelan

★★★★$$$ Elegant, romantic, and authentically *Proustien* (you can easily imagine Swann and Odette meeting here), this gorgeous Belle Epoque restaurant in the middle of the park features terrace dining in the summer. Some specialties include small crab cooked in its shell with fine aromatic jelly, scallops cooked in their shells with cider and served with crushed roasted walnuts, sea bass meunière with preserved lemon marmalade, spit-roasted shoulder of lamb, and for dessert, a remarkable casserole of preserved carrot and caramel served with spice cake. The restaurant boasts two Michelin stars. ♦ Tu-Sa, lunch and dinner; Su, lunch, May-Oct. Reservations required. Route de Suresnes (at Allée de la Reine). 01.44.14.41.14. Métro: Porte Dauphine

8 Musée de la Contrefaçon (Forgeries Museum)

It is not unusual to see the great ladies of Parisian society stopping by this one-room museum in the elegant 16th arrondissement to compare a new handbag or a Cartier watch to the near-perfect forgeries on display. The museum is a veritable capitalist's cabinet of curiosities, where *authentique* products are exhibited surrounded by bogus imitations from Japan, Korea, Italy, Morocco, Taiwan, and elsewhere. Note the ingenious copies of Louis Vuitton luggage, which wear counterfeit tags guaranteeing they are genuine Vuitton. A short visit here is enough to cast doubt forever on that little shop near the hotel selling Dior key chains, Omega watches, bottles of Benedictine, flacons of Chanel No. 5, and magnums of Cordon Rouge champagne at bargain-basement prices. ♦ Admission. M-Th, 2-5PM; F, 9PM-noon. 16 Rue de la Faisanderie (between Rue Cothenet and Pl du Paraguay). 01.56.26.14.00. Métro: Porte Dauphine

9 Musée Dapper

Set in the heart of an elegant residential area, this handsome museum specializes in the arts of Sub-Saharan Africa and of African diasporas in the Caribbean, Latin America, and the United States. Since opening in its previous location nearby 1986, the museum has mounted consistently superb exhibitions based on the arts of particular cultures (Dogon, Fang, Tshokwe, Luba) or on large artistic and cultural themes. And since it moved into its spacious new quarters in December 2000, its program now includes music, dance, and theatrical presentations in its modern auditorium. The Dapper Foundation also sponsors lectures by world-renowned experts in the field and publishes magnificent books on African art, including the catalogs of its exhibitions. ♦ Daily, 11AM-7PM. Admission; free the last Wednesday of each month. 35 Rue Paul Valéry (between Aves Victor-Hugo and Foch). 01.45.00.01.50. Métro: Ménilmontant

10 59 Poincaré

★★★$$$ The former Parisian flagship restaurant of multi-Michelin-starred chef Alain Ducasse remains under the master's control despite his relocation in 2000 to the **Plaza Athénée**. The handsome Belle Epoque *hôtel particulier* has a sleek, contemporary dining area on the ground floor, with lots of onyx and white marble and polished metal and glass, whereas the upstairs rooms are cozy, with wood paneling, bookcases, and loose-fitting slipcovers of pearl-gray cotton over the chairs and banquettes. The menu is divided into four elements—vegetables, lobster, lamb, and fruit (no beef, because of mad cow disease)—with each element prepared by Ducasse's culinary team in a variety of renditions. Like all great chefs, Ducasse considers the quality of the basic ingredients as the key to fine cuisine. So, portrayed in huge color photos in the dining rooms are the lobstermen, the shepherds, and the suppliers of the fruit and the vegetables who are the restaurant's esteemed *fournisseurs*. The quality of the products, impeccable preparation and service, and an impressive collection of wines make this quite a dining experience. ♦ M-F, lunch and dinner. Reservations required. 59 Ave Raymond-Poincaré (between Rue St-Didier and Pl Victor-Hugo). 01.47.27.59.59. Métro: Victor Hugo

10 Le Parc

$$$$ Located in the well-to-do 16th arrondissement, across the river from the **Eiffel Tower**, this aristocratic hotel is as noble and cozy as an English manor. The 116 sumptuous rooms and suites were decorated by leading British designer Nina Campbell, and the furniture was commissioned from Viscount Linley, the nephew of Her Majesty the Queen. The public areas, including the cozy lobby bar, are decorated in the style of an English gentlemen's club. **59 Poincaré** (see above) is the canteen for the hotel, along with **Les Jardins du 59 Poincaré** in the summer (see below). ♦ 55-57 Ave Raymond-Poincaré (between Rue St-Didier and Pl Victor-Hugo). 01.44.05.66.66; fax

---

Restaurants/Clubs: Red | Hotels: Purple | Shops: Orange | Outdoors/Parks: Green | Sights/Culture: Blue

01.44.05.66.00. Métro: Victor-Hugo. le-parc@compuserve.com; www.sofitel.com.

Within Le Parc:

LES JARDINS DU 59 POINCARÉ

★★★$$$ In summer **59 Poincaré** (see page 285) spreads out beneath chestnut trees in the hotel's verdant garden courtyard, where you can sample a range of dishes from all over the world in a more laid-back atmosphere than inside. But be sure to book early. *Le tout Paris* loves this place. ♦ Daily, lunch and dinner, 15 May-15 Sept. Reservations required. 01.44.05.66.10

11 HÔTEL TROCADÉRO DOKHAN'S

$$$$ Hidden away in the ritzy 16th arrondissement, this small hotel (just 41 rooms and 4 suites) is the kind of pied-à-terre everyone who has ever dreamed about Paris dreams about.

Intense but understated luxury, not unlike what you might find in a posh London town house, is the name of the game, and indeed French decorator **Frédéric Méchiche** drew on the neoclassical stylings of 18th century English architect Robert Adam for his design (but an elevator decorated like a vintage steamer trunk is an original twist). Guest rooms, while not particularly large, are thoroughly sumptuous, from the choice of fabrics right down to the sparkling marble bathrooms. Most Parisian of all are the suites, on the top floor under mansarded eaves. There is no restaurant in the hotel, but the intimate lobby features a popular champagne bar. Another plus, one floor is all nonsmoking. ♦ 116 Rue Lauriston (at Ave Raymond Poincaré). 01.53.65.66.99; fax 01.53.65.66.68. Métro: Boissière or Trocadéro. hotel.trocadero.dokhans@wanadoo.fr

12 MUSÉE GUIMET

Reopened in 2001 after 5 years of top-to-bottom renovation, the "new" **Guimet** presents a dazzling selection of 3,000 of the 45,000 objects of ancient Asian art in its collection in bright, airy galleries in which each of the civilizations represented has a room of its own. The museum is rich in Hindu and Buddhist art from the Indian subcontinent and areas where the two religions spread in Afghanistan, Nepal, Tibet, and Southeast Asia, and in Khmer sculpture and paintings and sculptures and ceramics from China, Korea, and Japan.

Though this is a national museum—officially the **Musée National des Arts Asiatiques** (National Museum of Asiatic Arts)—the Guimet's collection came into being as the result of not French national efforts but of those of inspired French private collectors who scoured Asia for art treasures in the late 19th and early 20th centuries. The most important of these was Lyon industrialist Emile Guimet, who built the museum for his own collection in 1889 and gradually absorbed other collections over his 29 years at the helm. Since the French government's acquisition of the museum in 1928, it has transferred most of its Asiatic art holdings from the **Louvre** and other national museums to the Guimet. The museum also puts on major temporary exhibitions. ♦ Admission. M, W-Su. 6 Pl d'Iéna (at Ave d'Iéna). 01.56.52.53.00. Métro: Iéna. www.museeguimet.fr

13 MUSÉE D'ART MODERNE DE LA VILLE DE PARIS (MUSEUM OF MODERN ART OF THE CITY OF PARIS)

The City of Paris's rich modern art collection is housed in the **Palais de Tokyo**, a large Art Deco pavilion built for the **1937 Exposition Universelle**. The exhibits have a distinctly Parisian flavor—they are mainly paintings, drawings, graphics, sculptures, and photographs by 20th-century artists who have lived and worked here. Fauvism (Matisse, Derain, Vlaminck), Cubism (Braque, Gris, Picasso, Léger), Surrealism (De Chirico, Picabia, Brauner), the so-called School of Paris, Abstraction, *Nouveau Realisme*, and conceptual art are all well represented.

Recent acquisitions include works by Simon Hantaï, Magdalena Abakanaowicz, Tony Stoll, and Louise Bourgeois and photographs by Marc Riboud and Willy Ronis. Of the approximately 200 works the museum has on permanent display, the most spectacular are the monumental paintings by Matisse (two panels of *La Danse*), Sonia and Robert Delaunay, and Raoul Dufy (including his amazing 6,095-square-foot *La Fée Electricité* the world's largest painting). ♦ Free. Admission for special exhibitions only. Tu-Su. 11 Ave du Président-Wilson (between Rues Gaston and de la Manutention). 01.53.67.40.00. Métros: Alma-Marceau, Iéna. www.cofrase.com/artforum/mamparis

15 MUSÉE EDITH PIAF

In a tiny museum filling two rooms of a private apartment near her grave in the **Père-Lachaise Cemetery**, the renowned French chanteuse lives on through the adoration of her fans, who come to look at her dressing gown, shoes, birth certificate, autographed letters, photographs, and portraits of her lovers. Recordings of the "little sparrow" play softly in the background, and the museum's devoted curator Bernard Marchois is always present to recount the final days of the great entertainer's life. ♦ M-W, 1PM-6PM, Th, 9AM-noon, by appointment only. Closed Sept and June. 5 Rue Crespin-du-Gast (between Passage de Ménilmontant and Rue Oberkampf). 01.43.55.52.72. Métro: Ménil-montant

14 HÔTEL JACQUES DE MOLAY

$$ Thanks to its upbeat décor and warm service, this small hotel would be a wonderful place to drop anchor even if didn't boast a prime location in the upper Marais. Virtually at its doorstep is the charming Square du Temple, a pocket-size park with a duck pond and waterfall; the Rue de Bretagne, a lively market street; and contemporary art galleries galore. The hotel takes its name from the grand master of the medieval order of the Templars, who once had their fortresslike headquarters in the neighborhood. Mme. Langlois makes guests at home in the lobby, spacious but cozy with its wood beams and exposed stone walls. The 23 modern, cheer-fully decorated guest rooms are spread out among four floors, each with its own color scheme. Breakfast, whether taken in your room or from a buffet set up in the lobby, is reasonably priced. ♦ 94 Rue des Archives (at Rue de Bretagne). 01.42.72.68.22; fax 01.42.72.00.41. Métro: Arts et Métiers, Temple. hotelmolay@wanadoo.fr; www. hotelmolay.com

15 MÉNILMONTANT

When the **Bastille** became a hip area in the late 1980s and rising rents drove artists out, many of them moved to this working-class neighborhood just to the north. But in the 1990s it was déjà vu—especially after the opening of the phenomenally successful **Café Charbon** in 1995—when the young and the artistic flocked here, followed soon by the *bobos* (bourgeois bohemians), and all of a sudden Ménilmontant was the most happening *quartier* in Paris. Dozens of quirky bars, cafés, restaurants, and clubs now line Rue Oberkampf and its side streets, there are art galleries and imaginative boutiques galore, and a vibrant ambiance reigns in this Paris equivalent of New York's East Village. To explore the area, start at métro station Parmentier and walk up the hill on Rue Oberkampf, the main drag. The best thing is simply to *flâner*, stroll freely and observe, but here are some lively establishments you might like to check out: **Mécano-Bar** at 99 Rue Oberkampf, an old mechanic's workshop

converted into a funky bar; **Les Couleurs** at 117 Rue St-Maur, a bar so cool it doesn't even have a sign outside; **Café Charbon**, a beautiful fin de siècle dance hall at 109 Rue Oberkampf, still delightful in spite of its stardom; **Cithéa** at 114 Rue Oberkampf, one of the best clubs for live music in town; and **Le Robinet Mélangeur**, a jolly, bright-colored little bar at 123 Blvd de Ménilmontant. For visitors who have the impression that Paris is nothing but a fossilized museum-city, a stroll through this neighborhood is the perfect antidote. The grande dame has plenty of life in her yet. ♦ Rue Oberkampf (between Ave de la République and Blvd de Ménilmontant). Métros: Parmentier, Ménilmontant

16 CIMETIÈRE DU PÈRE-LACHAISE (PÈRE-LACHAISE CEMETERY)

🅟 Named after Louis XIV's confessor, Father La Chaise, and designed by **Alexandre Théodore Brongniart**, this is the largest and most elite cemetery in Paris. The remains of France's most famous lovers, Abélard and Héloïse, keep company with those of Molière, Balzac, and painters Corot, Daumier, David, Pissarro, Modigliani, and Seurat. Also buried here are 19th-century photographer Nadar; city-shaping Baron Haussmann; Jane Avril and Yvette Guilbert, two cancan dancers who modeled for Toulouse-Lautrec; Fulgence Bien-venue, who built the Paris métro; and Ferdinand de Lesseps, who designed the Suez Canal.

In remembrance of things past, a single red rose may grace the black marble slab marking Marcel Proust's grave, and singer Edith Piaf's unremarkable resting place is always surrounded with flowers. Music lovers might also search out the graves of Callas, Bizet, or Poulenc. Chopin's body is buried here (his heart is interred in Warsaw), as are the remains of Eugène Delacroix, Prosper Mérimée, and Alfred de Musset, who, like Chopin, loved George Sand, the great female luminary of 19th-century French literature. Literati, as well as gays and lesbians, flock to Oscar Wilde's tomb, a stylish sphinx sculpted by Sir Jacob Epstein in 1909, and leftists make the pilgrimage to the grave of Laura Marx, daughter of Karl. Sarah Bernhardt lies here, as does Jim Morrison, the Doors' lead singer who died in Paris in 1971. Lovers Gertrude Stein and Alice B. Toklas are together in death as they were in life. One side of their gravestone memorializes Gertrude; the other, Alice.

A monument to deported World War II Resis-tance fighters in the cemetery's southeast corner is right near the **Federalists' Wall**, where the last 147 survivors of the Paris Commune insurgency were shot by

---

government forces on 28 May 1871. They were buried on this spot in a common grave that has been a place of pilgrimge for left-wing sympathizers ever since.

This lush 108-acre sanctuary in eastern Paris is a museum of French history, but it's as much a park as a cemetery. Parisians by the hundreds come here to picnic, harvest escargots off the tombs, or neck on the benches. Chopin's tomb is used for posting love letters, and legend holds that women who kiss or rub the statue of Victor Noir, a French journalist (1848-1870) killed by Pierre Bonaparte, will marry within a year. If you're lucky, you may encounter Vincent de Langlade, who has spent his life studying this most famous of graveyards; he is the author of a dozen books on the necropolis. If you can't find him, pick up the detailed map available for sale at the cemetery's entrance and set out on your own celebrity search. ♦ Daily. Blvd de Ménilmontant (between Rue du Repos and Pl Auguste-Métivier). Métro: Père-Lachaise

17 BON

$$ This restaurant was launched by one-man design universe **Philippe Starck, and it shows: from the array of glamorous candelabras to the signature distorted mirrors and bowls of green apples, there is lot going on here before you even sit down. On the way to your table you can stop for drink at the comfortably contemporary bar or pop into the discreet boutique where you can buy everything from organic couscous to CD remixes, all signé Starck. Handsome wait staff happily answer any questions about the menu, which though has gone through drastic metamorphoses in the past now has a southwestern French bent. ♦ Daily, lunch and dinner. 25 Rue de la Pompe (between Rues J.-Richepin and G.-Naudad). 01.40.72.70.00. Métro: La Muette

18 JARDIN DU RANELAGH

Directly across Avenue Raphaël from the **Musée Marmottan** are these sumptuous English-style gardens, home to one of the last hand-cranked merry-go-rounds in Europe. Children in ruffled dresses or seersucker suits hold on for dear life with one hand while wielding red sticks in the other, trying to hook the elusive brass ring. ♦ Ave Raphaël (between Ave Ingres and Blvd Suchet). Métro: La Muette

19 MUSÉE MARMOTTAN-MONET

The 16th arrondissement in Paris, which stretches from the **Arc de Triomphe** down between the **Bois de Boulogne** and the Seine, is a haven for the Proustian bourgeoisie. Out-of-town shoppers know this quarter as a place to buy old table linens, fine chocolates, and designer silk dresses, and others know it as the location of Omar Sharif's private gambling club. The best-kept secret of the select 16th, however, is the 19th-century Passy town house that contains this museum, which features more than 100 original paintings, pastels, and drawings by Monet, including the 1873 painting *Impression: Solei Levant*, the source of the term *Impressionism*, and breathtaking lily pond–inspired abstractions. This treasure trove of the artist's work from Giverny is relatively deserted, except when busloads of Japanese tourists descend.

After you take a good look at the 300 illuminated medieval manuscripts on the ground floor, skip the two floors devoted mainly to the cold First Empire furniture and Flemish tapestries, and head straight for the basement. Here amidst the joyous splashes and swirls of poppies, tulips, irises, and apple blossoms, you'll experience the essential spirit of Monet's Giverny work. The exhibition culminates in a circular gallery with the artist's notebooks and palette in the center and 16 of his water lily canvases on the walls. Stand in the middle of the room and pivot around to behold Monet's magical pond as it changed with the sun's daily round. (In summer you can visit the actual pond and gardens at Monet's Normandy home in Giverny. For more information, see "Day Trips" on page 296.) The museum also has fine works by Renoir, Sisley, Caillebotte, and other Impressionist colleagues. Berthe Morisot is particularly well represented, thanks to a large collection of her paintings donated by her heirs, which also includes one of the powerful portraits of her painted by her brother-in-law Edouard Manet. ♦ Admission. Tu-Su, 10AM-5PM. 2 Rue Louis Boilly (at Ave Raphaël). 01.44.96.50.33; 01.42.24.07.02 (recorded message). Métro: La Muette. www.marmottan.com

20 FOUNDATION LE CORBUSIER

Charles-Edouard Jeanneret, better known as Le Corbusier (1887-1965), was the Swiss architect who helped revolutionize today's urban environment with his passion for cubist forms. Within Paris and its suburbs stand 15 of his modular buildings, including the apartment house in which he lived in 1933 (24 Rue Nungesser-et-Coli); a **Salvation Army** headquarters (12 Rue Cantagrel) built in 1933 of glass, brick, and exposed concrete; and the famous **Swiss Dormitory** and **Brazilian Pavilion** (constructed in 1932 and 1959, respectively) at the Cité Universitaire (19-21 Blvd Jourdan). The headquarters and research library of the Foundation Le Corbusier are housed in **Villa Jeanneret**; the adjoining **Villa La Roche**, also designed by the architect in 1923, contains a sparse collection of Le Corbusier's own painting, sculpture, and furniture design and is open to the public. ♦ Admission. M-F; closed in Aug. 8-10 Sq du

Docteur-Blanche (off Rue du Docteur-Blanche, between Rues Raffet and Henri-Heine). 01.42.88.41.53. Métro: Jasmin

21 CASTEL BÉRANGER

French architect **Hector Guimard** established his reputation in 1898 as the country's premier Art Nouveau designer with this seven-story apartment building, which sits along a quiet residential street in the 16th arrondissement. Guimard's quasi-organic expressionism is seen here in its full glory, particularly in the curvilinear floral details of his ironwork, faïence, and carved-wood elements, which prefigure the architect's more purely sculptural métro entrances of 1900. The private building contains 36 apartments, no 2 alike. ◆ 14-16 Rue La Fontaine (at Hameau Béranger). Métro: Jasmin

22 PARC ANDRÉ CITROËN

When the offices of automobile manufacturer André Citroën moved outside the city in the 1980s, an expanse of land the size of 50 football fields was left free in the quiet 15th arrondissement. The city transformed half this area into public grounds, now the only park in Paris where sitting on the grass is not forbidden. Landscape designers **Alan Provost** and **Gilles Clément** have made water a dominant feature here: Shallow pools border the park, and waterfalls tumble from small stone structures. The park's north side has six small gardens, each with a different theme and dominant color. The red garden, for example, contains cherry and apple trees. ◆ Daily, 7:30AM-10PM, May-Aug; 7:30AM-7PM the rest of the year. Entrance at 25 Rue Leblanc (between Rue St-Charles and Quai André-Citroën). 01.45.57.13.35. Métros: Balard, Javel–André Citroën; RER: Blvd Victor

23 JARDINS ALBERT KAHN

Turn-of-the-19th-century banker and idealist Albert Kahn envisioned a society in which there would be a crossbreeding of cultures; these enchanting gardens, in which 360 species of plants from around the world thrive in one place, are the horticultural embodiment of his sociological ideas. Here you'll find an English garden, French flower beds, a rose garden, and a meticulous Japanese garden with a wooden teahouse. This Eden has been a sanctuary of meditation for such notables as Colette, Einstein, Ferdinand Foch, Edouard Herriot, and Arthur Honegger. When your stomach's needs transcend those of your spirit, go to the **Palmarium**, a glass-and-iron rotunda where sandwiches and pastries are served. Kahn also had an interest in photography that was furthered by his friendship with cinematography inventor Louis Lumière. Between 1910 and 1920, Kahn sent documentary photographers all over the world to compose his Archives de la Planète. More than 72,000 photographs and in excess of a half-million feet of film are housed in the **Musée Albert Kahn**, on the grounds of the gardens. ◆ Admission. Tu-Su. Reservations required for tea ceremonies; call the museum. 14 Rue du Port (between Rue des Abondances and Quai du 4-Septembre), Boulogne-Billancourt. Museum: 01.46.04.52.80. Métro: Boulogne–Pont de St-Cloud. www.museealbertkahn@cg92.fr

24 CATACOMBS

The **Catacombs** began as a network of quarries that extended for miles beneath Paris. In 1785, several million skeletons were transported to these quarries from the over-crowded **Innocents Cemetery** near Les Halles. Here the skulls, femurs, and tibias of 30 generations of Parisians were stacked in a neat but rather macabre fashion. Carved near the entrance is an ominous medieval sign: "Stop. Beyond Here Is the Empire of Death." Apparently the warning deterred the occupying Nazis, because they never discovered that the secret headquarters of the French Resistance was literally under their feet. The dark reaches of the catacombs then housed radios capable of reaching London, as well as a telephone switching system handling Resistance communications for hundreds of miles around.

Today visitors can explore the Catacombs and view the skeletal inhabitants as part of an hour-long tour. Bring along a flashlight and a sweater, be prepared for a lot of steps, and be sure to stay close to the group. In 1793 a Parisian took a wrong turn from his own wine cellar, got lost in the Catacomb tunnels, and was not discovered until 9 years later, by which time he was mummified.

Before or after descending into the Catacombs, pause to admire the splendid bronze *Lion of Belfort* by sculptor Frédéric-Auguste Bartholdi of Statue of Liberty fame, which commemorates one of the few French successes of the Franco-Prussian War, Colonel Denfert-Rochereau's defense of Belfort. ◆ Admission. Tu-F, 2-4PM; Sa-Su, 9-11 AM, 2-4PM. 1 Pl Denfert-Rochereau (at Ave du Général-Leclerc). 01.43.22.47.63. Métro: Denfert-Rochereau

---

CyberParis

The French rushed into the Internet Age at an escargot's pace, but in the last few years they've finally brought themselves up to speed. For Internauts seeking information about Paris, there are vast amounts of it now on the World Wide Web, in both French and English. And people traveling to Paris without their computers will be relieved to know that there are now plenty of web cafés and other spots around town where they can get online.

Good Spots for Internet Access

· **@cidnet Cybercafé** (15 Rue Daval, between Blvd Richard-Lenoir and Rue St-Sabin; métro: Bastille; 01.43.38.32.58; www.cyber@acidnet.fr): An ultra-laid-back net café a few steps from Place de la Bastille with nine PCs, two Macs, snacks and refreshments, and a lounge area with comfy chairs. Open M-Sa, 10AM-9PM.

· **Café Orbital** (13 Rue de Médicis, between Rue de Vaugirard and Place Edmond-Rostand; RER: Luxembourg; 01.43.25.76.77; www.cafeorbital.com): A cozy but rather expensive Internet café by the Luxembourg Gardens. Open daily to 10PM.

· **Clicktown** (15 Rue de Rome, between Rue de Stockholm and Pl Gabriel-Péri, opposite the Gare St-Lazare; Métro: St-Lazare; 01.53.42.63.42; www.clicktown.fr): 320 cutting-edge computers; open 24 hours daily; modest rates, especially in off-hours.

· **CyberCube** is a chain of four highly professional computer and multimedia shops with all the latest word processing, graphics, audio/video, and printing software and hardware, expensive for ordinary personal use of the Internet. Its locations are 12 Rue Daval (between Blvd Richard-Lenoir and Rue de la Roquette; métro: Bastille; 01.49.29.67.67), 5 Rue Mignon (between Rue Serpente and Blvd St-Germain; métros: Odéon, St-Michel; 01.53.10.30.50), 3 Rue Molière (between Ave de l'Opéra and Rue Thèrese; métros: Louvre, Pyramide; 01.40.20.10.50), 9 Rue d'Odessa (between Rue de Départ and Blvd Edgar-Quinet; métro: Montparnasse; 01.56.80.08.08). Web site www.cybercube.fr. Open M-Sa, 10AM-10PM.

· **Cyberport** (Forum des Images, Place Carrée, Nouveau Forum des Halles, at Porte St-Eustache; métro: Les Halles; 01.44.76.63.12; www.forumdesimages.net): The Ville de Paris's up-to-date multimedia center. Open 1-9PM; closed Mondays.

· **easyEverything**: 37 Blvd de Sébastopol (between Rues Berger and Réaumur; métro: Chatêlet-Les Halles) and 6 Rue de la Harpe (between Rues de la Huchette and St-Severin; métro: St-Michel); 01.40.41.09.10; www.easyeverything.com/france. Huge, bright, contemporary Kafkaesque in ambiance, with more than computers in each facility. Open 24 hours a day, 7 days a week.

· **Netk@fe** (32 Rue Monsieur-le-Prince, between Rues Racine and Vaugirard; métro: Odéon; 01.56.24.18.55; www.momi.fr): A relaxed, well-equipped Internet café with 11 setups, US and French keyboards, webcam, scanners, both color and black-and-white printing, and some of the best rates in town. Open daily to midnight.

· **Le Rendez-Vous Toyota** (79 Ave des Champs-Elysées, at Rue Lincoln; 01.56.89.29.79; www.lrv.toyota.fr): The Toyota dealership's top-floor café offers 15 free minutes on the Internet. Open M-Th to 9PM, F-Sa to midnight.

· **Web Bar** (32 Rue de Picardie, between Rues Perée and Dupetit-Thouars; métro: République; 01.42.72.66.55; www.webbar.fr): The coolest Internet café in town, with art shows and music. Open daily to 2AM.

· **Wyniwyp** (8 Rue Pierre-au-Lard, corner of Rue du Renard; Métro: Rambuteau, Hôtel de Ville; 0800.944.475; www.wyniwyp.net): Owing to its small size and modern look, this cyber spot is refreshingly calm; other advantages are the latest computers, friendly welcome, and attractive rates. Open daily 10AM-10PM.

Useful Web Sites (English or Bilingual)

· *Bonjour Paris*'s site (www.bparis.com) features well-written articles by experienced American journalists in Paris, a bulletin board, and a chat line.

· *Living in France* magazine's guide (www.parisfranceguide.com) is useful both for visitors and people planning to move to Paris. It offers formidable lists of phone numbers and addresses of English-language contacts in Paris, including doctors and dentists, in-depth features related to the needs of English-speaking people who are planning a long stay in the city, cultural and practical pointers for visitors with varied interests, useful and timely travel information, and classified ads.

The **Paris Office de Tourisme**'s huge web site (www.paris-touristoffice.com) offers lots of valuable facts about the city. There is a list of hundreds of hyperlinked web sites of hotels; apartment rental agencies; restaurants; monuments and museums; music, theater, cinema, and sports venues; attractions for children; and airlines companies and travel services. Also, there are several search engines.

Paris Free Voice's (www.parisvoice.com) film, theater, and restaurant reviews, monthly cultural listings, journalistic pieces about the city, and want ads are featured here.

Time Out's (www.timeout.com) reviews and listings are a helpful source of up-to-date information.

Useful Web Sites (Mainly in French)

Musée du Louvre (www.louvre.fr)

Musée d'Orsay (www.musee-orsay.fr)

Centre Georges Pompidou (www.centrepompidou.fr)

Château de Versailles (www.chateauversailles.fr)

Parc de La Villette (www.la-villette.com)

Bibliothèque Nationale de France (National Library; www.bnf.fr)

Le Monde (newspaper; www.lemonde.com)

Libération (newspaper; (www.liberation.com)

Pariscope (www.pariscope.fr) features weekly listings for movies; theater; opera; and jazz, pop, and classical concerts.

Télérama magazine (www.telerama.com) offers its reviews and schedules of movies, plays, operas, art exhibits, and TV shows.

Weather satellite photos and forecasts are available from the **French National Meteorological Service** (www.meteo.fr/temps).

The **Paris public transport system** (www.ratp.fr) site shows how to get from point A to point B, with maps and instructions in French and English.

The **French national railway** (www.sncf.fr) site has train schedules and allows you to make reservations and purchase tickets.

France Télécom (www.pagesjaunes.fr) has both yellow pages and white pages for the whole country. Also here is an interesting search engine for streets that gives the name, address, and phone number of every business on the street. Click on *plan*, and a detailed view of the surrounding neighborhood appears. Click on photos to visualize the establishment.

Internet Access Numbers in France

AOL: 08.36.06.13.10

CompuServe: 08.36.06.13.19

Microsoft Network: 08.36.01.93.01

25 BIBLIOTHÈQUE NATIONALE DE FRANCE, SITE FRANÇOIS MITTERRAND/TOLBIAC (NATIONAL LIBRARY OF FRANCE, FRANÇOIS MITTERRAND/TOLBIAC)

The **Bibliothèque Nationale**'s vast collection of 11 million books was moved from its former home on Rue Richelieu (see page 208) to this ultramodern building that includes four seven-story glass towers in which the books are stored. The controversial structures, designed by architect **Dominique Perrault**, are L-shaped—like open books—and are connected to the reading rooms by an 8-kilometer (5-mile) rail system to transport the books. The reading rooms are located in the two long sections of the building that parallel the river. The **Haut-de-Jardin** (Upper Garden) chambers, open to the general public, have 1,600 seats, 180,000 volumes on open shelves, 2,500 periodicals, 10,000 reels of microfilm, 340,000 microfiches, 100,000 digitized images, and a huge audiovisual collection. The public can also order books from the stacks either on the spot or 1 day in advance. A research area on the **Rez-de-Jardin** (Garden Level) is open only to scholars by special arrangement. There is a large woodland park the size of the **Palais Royal**'s garden in the center of the complex, but it is for visual effect only, not open to the public. The complex was inaugurated in December 1996 and fully opened in October 1998. Popularly known as the "TGB" (for *très grande bibliothèque*), it certainly merits its nickname. Unlike the other parts of the Bibliothèque Nationale, which are free, this one charges a modest daily or yearly fee. ◆ Fee. Tu-Sa, 10AM-8PM; Su, noon-7PM; closed 2 weeks between the first and third Monday in Sept. and national holidays. 11 Quai François-Mauriac (between Rues de Tolbiac and Emile-Durkheim). 01.53.79.59.59. Métros: Bibliothèque François Mitterrand, Quai de la Gare. www.bnf.fr

25 LE BATOFAR

This big red ex-lighthouse boat once braved the storms of the Irish Sea but is now seeing more peaceful, though perhaps no less noisy, duty at its mooring in the Seine in front of the TGB as a venue for live performances by techno, electric jazz, rap, and other up-to-date musical groups and DJ-guided soirees. There's an old London double-decker bus to take you home in the wee hours. ◆ M-Th, Su, 9PM-2AM; F-Sa, 9PM-4AM; Su, noon-5PM (brunch) and 8PM-2AM. Closed 10-20 Aug. Quai François-Mauriac (in front of the Biblio-thèque Nationale). 01.56.29.10.00. Métro: Quai de la Gare

25 LA GINGUETTE PIRATE

Another trendy musical boat moored at the same quay, this magnificent Chinese ocean-going junk offers live funk, rock, reggae, jazz, pop, and electro-pop evenings at even more modest prices than those of the **Batofar**. ◆ Tu-Sa, 6PM-2AM; Su, 4-11PM. Quai François-Mauriac (in front of the Bibliothèque Nationale). 01.56.29.10.20. Métro: Quai de la Gare

26 BOIS DE VINCENNES

Only slightly smaller than the **Bois de Boulogne**, this large park on the eastern edge of Paris is the city's second main recreation area. Like the Bois de Boulogne, this is a former royal hunting ground; it was given to the city by Napoléon III in 1860. Sadly, the ferocious windstorm that struck France in December 1999 destroyed 70,000 of the park's 180,000 trees, and despite the replanting that started almost immediately, the evidence of this devastation will be visible for many years. The major attraction here is the **Château de Vincennes**, a stern medieval fortress that has served variously as a royal residence, prison, porcelain factory, and arsenal. King Henry V of England died here in 1422. The *bois* (woods) that extends to the south of the château contains the 80-acre **Parc Floral de Paris** (01.43.43.92.95), where first-rate jazz concerts are held on weekends in summer; **Daumesnil Lake**, where rowboats and bicycles are available for rent; the **Kagyu Dzong Buddhist Center** (01.40.04.98.06), which boasts the largest sculpture of the Buddha in Europe; the **Hippodrome de Vincennes** (01.49.77.17.17), a trotters' racecourse; and the **Zoological Park**, Bois de Vincennes. The zoo, with 550 mammals, including giant pandas Yen-Yen and Lili, and more than 700 birds, provides a welcome contrast to the **Menagerie** at the **Jardin des Plantes**—here the animals live in surroundings similar to their natural habitats. ◆ Admission for château. Daily. Château, 01.48.08.31.20; zoological park, 01.44.75.20.00. Métros: Porte Dorée, Porte de Charenton; RER: Vincennes

27 PARC MONTSOURIS

Prior to the 19th century, this park was an abandoned granite quarry stubbled with windmills, and when Baron Haussmann got his hands on it, he turned it into a charming English-style park, with rustic winding paths, a waterfall, and an artificial lake. At the turn of the 19th century, the 50-acre swath of green was a refuge for the artists and literati of nearby Montparnasse; Henri Rousseau and Georges Braque lived near here; Hemingway came often. Today, joggers run the park's 1-mile perimeter, matrons feed the swans, and brass bands play marches in the band shell. ♦ 20 Rue Gazan (between Blvd Jourdan and Ave Reille). RER: Cité Universitaire

Within Parc Montsouris:

LE PAVILLON DE MONTSOURIS

★★$$ The outdoor terrace of this Belle Epoque glass-and-iron restaurant has accommodated a great many famous customers, including Lenin, Trotsky, and Sartre, whereas Mata Hari preferred the relative seclusion of the upstairs dining room. The carpaccio of *lotte* (monkfish) and duck fillets roasted in honey and spices are good choices here, and the desserts are exceptionally good. The wines are quite expensive, unfortunately, and outdoor tables are hard to come by in the summer without a reservation. ♦ Daily, lunch and dinner. Reserve at least a week in advance for an outdoor table in the summer. 01.45.88.38.52

1 HONFLEUR AND DEAUVILLE

Normandy, with its rugged coast, is the country of Camembert, Calvados, apple orchards, and brick-and-beam-crossed plaster houses topped by steep shingled gables. **Honfleur** is one of the coast's most solidly Norman and picturesque harbors; Samuel de Champlain departed from here in 1608 to found Québec. Don't miss the Saturday-morning market bustling around the old wooden Ste-Catherine church. The old port section of Honfleur has many seafood eateries, most notably **L'Assiette Gourmande** (02.31.89.24.88), and just outside of town lies **La Ferme St-Siméon** (Rue Adolphe-Marais (02.31.81.78.00), one of Normandy's finest restaurants.

Farther west along the coast is **Deauville**, the summer playground of Europe's social elite. Known for its casinos, private mansions,

racetracks, and a film festival each fall, Deauville has a broad boardwalk and sandy stretch of beach that is a mere 2-hour train ride from the center of Paris. ◆ Trains leave frequently from Paris's Gare St-Lazare. Drivers should exit Normandy autoroute A13 at Beuzeville. Deauville is 200 km (124 miles) from Paris.

1 D-DAY BEACHES

Before arriving at the D-Day beaches, you pass Dives-sur-Mer, the site from which William the Conqueror embarked in 1066 to vanquish England. It was an important moment in history but further from memory than the events of 6 June 1944. Just to the west, in Bénouville, is the Pegasus Bridge, the first spot taken by the Allies in Normandy. Farther on, the D-Day beaches begin, each with its own museum, its own monuments, and its own stories to tell. The most

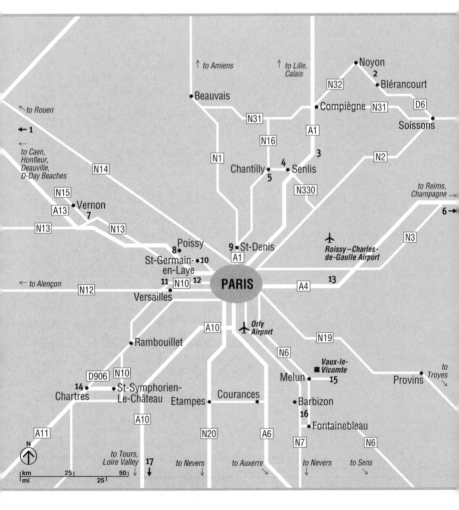

heartrending sight is the US cemetery at **Omaha Beach**, 16 km (10 miles) east of Pointe du Hoc, where 9,000 of the 23,000 North Americans killed in the Normandy operations are buried. Even if you have come to experience modern history and the sorrows of the victors, it is worth visiting Bayeux to see the magnificent 231-foot-long Bayeux Tapestry (1076) depicting William's conquests and the Norman invasion of England—a good meditation on the regularity of war. The tapestry is located in the **Centre Guillaume le Conquérant** (13 bis Rue de Nesmond, off Rue Larcher, 02.31.51.25.50), which is open daily. The **Bayeaux Office de Tourisme** is at Pont St-Jean (02.31.51.28.28; www.mairie-bayeux.fr). Two important museums devoted to the Normandy campaign are the **Musée de la Bataille de Normandie** in Bayeux (02.31.51.46.90) and the **Musée du Débarquement Arromanches** in Arromanches (02.31.22.34.31; www. normandy1944.com). ♦ Bayeux is 261 km (163 miles) northwest of Paris, reached by autoroute A13 to Caen and N13 to Bayeux.

2 MUSÉE NATIONAL DE LA COOPÉRATION FRANCO-AMÉRICAINE

Created by Anne Morgan, J.P.'s youngest daughter, who led a major civilian war relief and postwar recovery operation in this area during and after World War I, the museum was built in the ruins of a 17th-century château by **Salomon de Brosse**, architect of the **Luxembourg Palace** in Paris. In 1989 it was renovated for France's bicentennial by Frenchman **Yves Lion** and Canadian **Alan Levitt**. Exhibits include hundreds of historic World War I photographs and war memorabilia and a collection of graceful late-19th- and 20th-century paintings, drawings, and sculptures on loan from the **Musée d'Orsay**. Represented here are Whistler, Calder, and Childe Hassam, as well as French artists who worked in the US. The handsome modern gardens were designed by American **Mark Rudkin**. ♦ Admission for museum. Museum: M, W-Su. Gardens: daily. 03.23.39.60.16. Métros: Château de Blérancourt, Blérancourt. www.culture.fr

3 PARC ASTÉRIX

For an amusement-park experience that's both culturally keyed-in and close to Paris, make the journey to the Val d'Oise, home of this Gallic fantasyland based on Albert Uderzo's comic-book characters Astérix and Obélix, the pair known far and wide for their fictional forays against the Romans of ancient Gaul. There are admirably re-created

medieval, ancient Greek, and Parisian villages, lots of live-action shows, and a host of first-rate rides that rival Disneyland's for thrill value. Among them are Tonnerre de Zeus (Zeus's Thunder), the largest wooden roller coaster in Europe, and Goudurix, a double-looping coaster on which riders are turned upside down seven times at speeds reaching 75 kilometers (47 miles) per hour. On the slower but spookier side, there's Transdemonium, a family ghost train, but like most everything else at the park, the attraction has a humorous tilt. ♦ Admission. Open April-October; call ahead or check web site for opening days and hours as they vary according to holiday and seasonal schedules. Drive north on autoroute A1, 30 km (18 miles) to the Parc Astérix exit (between exits 7 and 8), or take the RER B3 train to Roissy Charles de Gaulle I; from there a CIF bus has service to the park. 03.44.62.34.44; www.parcasterix.com

4 SENLIS

This entire town is classified as a historical monument. It is girdled by 23-foot-high, 13-foot-thick Roman walls that are punctuated by watchtowers and pierced by massive gates. The town's cathedral is older than **Notre-Dame-de-Paris** or **Chartres** and lofts a lacy spire considered the most beautiful in France. After visiting the cathedral, tour the ruins of the royal castle, the 28 towers of the Gallo-Roman wall, and the thousand-seat Roman amphitheater just outside of town. The streets of Senlis, such as the Rue du Châtel and Rue de la Treille, are winding, stone-paved canyonways dark with history. The best bet for exploring them is to follow the small arrows that indicate a walking route through town. ♦ Take the train from the Gare du Nord station, or follow autoroute N17 or A1, 48 km (30 miles) northeast of Paris.

5 CHÂTEAU DE CHANTILLY

In 1671, Louis de Bourbon entertained King Louis XIV in his newly completed gardens at this château in the town of Chantilly. On that occasion, Vatel, the most famous chef in France, failed to deliver the fish course on time and, rather than live with the shame, promptly took his own life. Such is the tradition of excellence here.

Rising like a mirage from a moat in the midst of a dense beech forest, the château, which now houses the **Musée Condé**, is an artful conglomeration of the best of 16th-, 18th-, and 19th-century French architecture. During the revolution, the original château, built in the early 15th century, was razed, stone by stone, by vengeful mobs. The Duc d'Aumale,

---

Restaurants/Clubs: Red | Hotels: Purple | Shops: Orange | Outdoors/Parks: Green | Sights/Culture: Blue

who was responsible for the subsequent reconstruction in 1844, showed his fine eclectic taste in other areas as well: His art collection of medieval miniatures and French, Flemish, and Italian paintings is now on display in the Musée Condé. Each June the famous Prix de Diane horse race is run at a track on the edge of the palace grounds, and the **Grandes Ecuries**, Chantilly's extensive stables, are in use today as part of the **Musée Vivant du Cheval** (Living Museum of the Horse). The dressage exhibitions are great entertainment for children. ♦ Admission. M, W-Su. Trains leave from the Gare du Nord station. **Paris Vision** and **Cityrama** (see "Orientation" chapter) offer seasonal half-day trips on Sunday. If traveling by car, take highway N16 48 km (30 miles) north of Paris. Musée Condé, 03.44.57.08.00; Musée Vivant du Cheval, 03.44.57.40.40

6 CHAMPAGNE

The Champagne region is a realm of flowing hills dotted with vineyards, medieval stone towns, and châteaux. Its capital, Reims, was the coronation site of French kings, beginning with Clovis in 496. The cathedral here is stunning and definitely worth a stop. Epernay, the region's second city, is the home of Moët et Chandon, the giant among an estimated 145 Champagne producers in the region. Most of the largest producers offer tours, which usually culminate in some free sampling and (be forewarned) a persuasive sales pitch once your resistance is down. Five minutes north of Epernay is one of Champagne's best restaurants—the **Royal Champagne** in Champillon (Rte N2051; 03.26.52.87.11). In Reims, **Boyer "Les Crayères"** (64 Blvd Henri-Vasnier, at Ave du Général-Giraud; 03.26.82.80.80) is one of France's most outstanding restaurants, with three Michelin stars. For information, contact Reims's **Office de Tourisme** (12 Blvd du Général-Leclerc; 03.26.77.45.00). ♦ Take a train to Reims from the Gare de l'Est or drive east 143 km (89 miles) on autoroute A4.

MUSÉE D'ART AMÉRICAIN
GIVERNY

7 MUSÉE CLAUDE MONET, GIVERNY

Anyone who's seen the beloved Claude Monet water-lily paintings knows what this place looks like. Monet's Normandy house and gardens have been well tended and restored, looking much as they did when the Impressionist painter lived here between 1883 and 1926. After the **Académie des Beaux-Arts** moved Monet's paintings to the **Musée Marmottan-Monet** (see page 288) in Paris in 1966, **La Maison de Claude Monet** in Giverny was neglected. Grass grew in the studio and a staircase caved in. But a renovation that was begun in 1977 and funded in part by Lila Acheson Wallace has awakened its former charms. Unfortunately, this is no secret, so on the weekend and in warm weather, tourists swarm over the 4-acre property. Spring, when the early flowers are blooming and before the foreign tide hits France, is the best time to visit this horticultural-artistic shrine. Autumn, when you'll be able to see all the colors of the great painter's palette but with fewer distractions, is another good time. There are no paintings by Monet here, but two unexpected pleasures are to be found: Monet's collection of Japanese prints on display in the house and the reproductions of the blue-and-yellow plates and cups designed by Monet, reproductions of which are on sale in the gift shop. ♦ Admission. Tu-Su, 10AM-6PM; open 1 April through the end of Oct. 48 km (30 miles) northwest of Paris. Trains leave from Gare St-Lazare in the direction of Rouen. Get off at Vernon, which is about 4 miles from Giverny, and take a bus or taxi. **Cityrama** and **Paris Vision** (see "Orientation" chapter) offer seasonal tours. Drivers should exit the Normandy autoroute N13 at Bonnières. 02.32.51.28.21. www.foundation-monet.com

7 MUSÉE D'ART AMÉRICAIN GIVERNY

A few minutes' stroll from Monet's house, this tastefully designed museum was inspired by the colony of American Impressionists who gathered around the master in the late 19th and early 20th centuries. It was created by industrialist Daniel J. Terra in 1992 and is a sister institution of the Terra Museum of American Art in Chicago. The collection includes more than 1,000 works by talented but little-known painters of the Giverny art colony, along with works by more famous compatriots who worked in France, including Samuel F. B. Morse (the future inventor of the telegraph), James A. M. Whistler, John Singer Sargent, Winslow Homer, and Mary Cassat. A selection of these artists' work is always on display. The museum also mounts two major temporary exhibitions on a wide range of American art themes and several smaller ones during the season. There are concerts, lectures, and art workshops. Note the attractive modern gardens designed by **Mark Rudkin**. Lunch beneath wisteria-laden trellises on the terrace of the museum's very good restaurant in fine weather. ♦ Admission. Tu-Su; open 1 Apr through the end of Nov. 99 Rue Claude Monet, Giverny. 02.32.51.94.65. www.maag.org

8 VILLA SAVOYE

More than 70 years after its conception, this structure continues to be a striking evocation of modernist architectural purity. The last of several houses built in and around Paris in the 1920s by **Le Corbusier**, this "machine for living" synthesized many of the radical ideas the great Swiss architect espoused in his book *Vers une Architecture*. Le Corbusier wished to build a new type of bourgeois suburban villa, one that would reflect the precise, controlled rationalism made possible by modern technology. The result is an independent domestic mechanism separated from the landscape, which, in this case, it barely even touches. The villa is essentially an L-shaped series of rooms laid into a square tray that is elevated on slender *pilotis* (columns). As you travel on a continuous internal ramp into the building, you experience various light-filled spaces that eventually dissolve into the open air of the rooftop solarium. The strip windows, glass walls, flat roofs, cubic forms, and grid of columns were revolutionary at the time but now are familiar components of the International Style that Le Corbusier helped establish. (For more information on Le Corbusier, see **Foundation Le Corbusier** on page 288.) ◆ Admission. M, W-Su. 82 Chemin de Villiers, Poissy. RER: Poissy. By car, take autoroute N13; the villa is 24 km (15 miles) northwest of Paris. 01.39.65.01.06

9 BASILIQUE DE ST-DENIS

Around AD 250, St. Denis, the first Christian evangelist to come to Paris, was beheaded by the Romans. Legend has it that he picked up his head and carried it from Montmartre several kilometers north until, finally, he fell and was buried by a peasant woman. Whatever the facts, the grave of St. Denis became a place of pilgrimage. By the 12th century, pilgrims were so numerous that many were actually trampled to death in the stampede to the saint's shrine. Abbot Suger (1081-1151) decreed that a new church, large and full of light, be constructed on the site. The result was the first Gothic edifice in the world and one of the lesser-known treasures of Paris. The basilica became the starting place for the Crusades and the burial place of three dynasties of French royalty. Most macabre are the tombs of Marie de Médicis and Henri IV, who are depicted twice in marble. On the tops of their tombs are sculptures of the two in their finest Renaissance collars and jewels; below, their skeletons are shown being eaten away by worms. Badly neglected after the revolution, the structure has been restored and is now a repository of exquisite funerary sculpture. The soaring nave glows with a rainbow of light from the stained-glass windows, illuminated most brightly on winter mornings. ◆ Admission to tombs. Take métro line 13 to the Basilique de St-Denis stop. If traveling by car, take autoroute A1; the basilica is less than 3 km (2 miles) north of Porte de la Chapelle. 01.48.09.83.54. www. monuments.fr

10 CHÂTEAU DE ST-GERMAIN-EN-LAYE

For Louis XIV, this fortress in the town of St-Germain-en-Laye meant security. Born and bred in St-Germain, he later took refuge here during the popular uprising in 1648-1653 known as the Fronde. Built in 1122 around a château that guarded the western flank of Paris, **St-Germain-en-Laye** contains an earlier version of Paris's **Sainte-Chapelle** (though it has long been without its glass), also designed by architect **Pierre de Montreuil**. Today the château also houses the **Musée des Antiquités Nationales**. The château's gardens were designed by the industrious **André Le Nôtre** before he was whisked away to landscape **Versailles**. In one corner of the gardens is the **Pavillon Henri IV** (21 Rue Thiers; 01.39.10.15.15), where Louis XIV was born and Alexandre Dumas wrote *The Three Musketeers*. Since 1830 this building has also been a restaurant-hotel and a good place to lunch overlooking the Seine. ◆ Admission. M, W-Su. Pl du Général-de-Gaulle, St-Germain-en-Laye. 13.01.39.10.13.00. www.culture.fr. There is a bus (no. 158) from the Grande Arche de la Défense métro station. RER: St-Germain-en-Laye

11 CHÂTEAU DE VERSAILLES

What can you say about the palace that has everything? On a royal whim, Louis XIV transformed a small hunting lodge bordering a marsh into the most lavish statement of monarchic privilege that has ever existed. Owing to just such excesses, the monarchy has long since fallen, but **Versailles** has not. Since 1978 the French government has spent over $19 million on the restoration of this palace, concentrating on 50 rooms in the more private family apartments. The **Hall of Mirrors**, designed by **Jules Hardouin-Mansart**, may well be the most dazzling room ever built, and it offers a grand view of the gardens. Unfortunately, all that splendor can be numbing: One grand hall soon begins to resemble the next. To get the most from a visit, read up on the palace's history beforehand and reserve plenty of time for loitering. Indeed, some visitors prefer to spend the entire day just wandering in the 250 acres of gardens.

Restaurants/Clubs: Red | Hotels: Purple | Shops: Orange | Outdoors/Parks: Green | Sights/Culture: Blue

Designed by the incomparable **André Le Nôtre**, the gardens are too big to be crowded and too varied to bore. The air smells of damp earth and the place is as quiet as Eden, but the precise geometry and balance of the designs betray the fact that nature, along with everything else, was forced to bow before the Sun King. The famous fountains, **Grandes Eaux**, splash Sunday at 3:30PM on, May through September. The **Neptune Basin** floodlight-and-fireworks show is held four times a year; find out when—it's worth the trip. There are rowboats for rent on the Grand Canal and bicycles for rent on the Allée St-Antoine by the start of the Grand Canal. If you are traveling with small children, don't miss the **Hameau** (the Hamlet), a cute little mock farm village on a duck pond built for Marie Antoinette so that she and her ladies-in-waiting could play at being peasant girls; there is a delightful zoo with farm animals. ♦ Admission to château. Château: Tu-Su, 9AM-5PM. Gardens: daily. **Paris Vision** and **Cityrama** (see "Orientation" chapter) offer various tours. If traveling by RER, take the C line from the Invalides or St-Michel stations and get off at the Versailles-RG station. Or take the métro to Pont-de-Sèvres and transfer to bus 171. Trains leave from Gare Montparnasse. Cars should follow autoroute N10, 24 km (15 miles) southwest of Paris. Information, 01.30.83.78.00; reservations, 01.30.83.77.88. www.chateauversailles.fr

At the Château de Versailles:

L'Académie du Spectacle Equestre

Once Versailles was home to 5,000 horses, including 600 cream-colored, blue-eyed Lusitano stallions that formed the private collection of Louis XIV. They were kept in the **Grand Ecurie**, a grandiose *manège*, opposite the palace gates on the **Place d'Armes** (across from what is today the tour-bus parking lot), and formed an integral part of the king's *carrousels*, elaborate equestrian galas. With the advent of the French Revolution, the renowned riding school here fell into disuse, but the tradition was reborn in 2003 with a complete overhaul of the stables and establishment of an elite riding school run by

Bartabas, of internationally acclaimed Zingaro Equestrian Theater fame. Both developments make the site worth a visit. Architect **Patrick Bouchain** had 15 globe-shaped chandeliers, covered in crystal leaves, suspended from the ceiling of the Grand Ecurie, and the seating, though made entirely of pine, is surprisingly futuristic. Best of all, visitors can see *les écuyers*, or riding students—none of whom is older than 26—do dressage and drills on Lusitano horses that Bartabas donated to Versailles. It is possible to walk through the stables after each hour-long show. ♦ Admission. Tu-F, 9AM-1PM; Sa-Su, 11AM-3PM. 01.39.02.07.14

12 Parc de St-Cloud

For true escapists, this 1,100-acre park, lying just outside of Paris and landscaped by **André Le Nôtre**, is a little dream come true: a province of leafy woods that is a world apart from the urban bustle and a delight for children. For just a few francs, you can rent a tandem bicycle and take a romantic ride by the park's 17th-century fountains. The haunting **memorial to the Lafayette Escadrille**, the American volunteer fighter squadron in the French air force during World War I, is in the western reach of the park, and eight of these American pilots who died for France are entombed there. ♦ Rte N185, St-Cloud and into the park. Métro: Boulogne-Pont de St-Cloud

13 Disneyland Paris

With its 100 millionth visitor in 2001 and more than 12 million visitors arriving each year, this all-American institution in Paris has long put its disappointing start behind it. Opened in 1992, the 4,806-acre resort and amusement park in Marne-la-Vallée only 32 km (20 miles) east of central Paris, offers a **Magic Kingdom** theme park similar to those in California, Florida, and Japan, as well as 6 hotels, 29 restaurants, a campground, golf course, and office, retail, and residential space. Originally called **Euro Disneyland**, the $2.5 billion property announced its first quarterly profit in the summer of 1995, and profit has steadily increased since then. Besides adopting a new name, the amusement park has introduced more than a dozen new attractions in recent years in an effort to boost attendance; among them is **Space Mountain**, a Jules Verne–inspired roller coaster that reaches the speed of 47 miles per hour—20%

Approximately 1.6 million motor vehicles enter Paris every day from the suburbs.

Disneyland Paris greeted its 100 millionth visitor on 10 January 2001, nearly 9 years after it opened amid howls from intellectuals denouncing it as a "cultural Chernobyl" and a symbol of American bad taste.

faster than any other Disney ride. **Honey, I Shrunk the Audience**, a three-dimensional theatrical experience, has become one of the park's most popular attractions, as has **Indiana Jones and the Temple of Peril: Backwards!**, a white-knuckle roller coaster in the heart of a lush jungle. There are also lots of parades and shows, such as "Disney's Toon Circus." Like its counterparts, the amusement park is divided into five major "lands": **Adventureland**, **Discoveryland**, **Fantasyland**, **Frontierland**, and **Main Street, USA**. And, like the US parks, there tend to be lines at the ticket windows and for the rides inside. The park recently introduced the FastPass system, however—a free service available at five major attractions that allows you to book specific times for those rides, and this helps speed things up nicely. A new Walt Disney Studios theme park adjoins Disneyland Paris. ♦ Admission. Hours vary according to day and season; call ahead, or even better, check the web site for hours, prices, and travel details. Drive east on autoroute A4, 32 km (20 miles), or take the RER A4 train to Marne-la-Vallée/Chessy. 01.60.30.60.30 or 01.60.30.60.23. www.disneylandparis.com

14 CHARTRES

The cathedral at Chartres must be among the most spiritual places in the world. Though the town has changed dramatically since the building of the cathedral, you can still see the signature spire cutting into the sky above the wheat fields, a sight that for medieval pilgrims meant they had reached one of five primary holy places to be visited on the path to heaven. Carved in the cathedral's celebrated portals and glowing in its stained-glass windows, Bible stories unfold with an overwhelming panoply of symbols and images. This imagery is brilliantly interpreted by Malcolm Miller—an English scholar who has devoted decades to research and writing on the cathedral—during his morning and afternoon tours. Before or after the tour, spend some time alone sitting in a pew and absorb the majesty of the cathedral. The 12th- and 13th-century stained-glass windows (the finest in France) are so brilliant that in medieval times peasants believed they were made of ground-up gems. Modern science disproves this notion, but no one has explained how medieval glassmakers at Chartres created such beauty.

After touring the cathedral, stroll around the old town and along the banks of the Eure River. Or explore the area on two wheels— there are bicycles for rent at Place Pierre-Semard. If you are interested in 20th-century

folk art, visit **Picassiette's House** (20 Rue du Repos; 02.37.34.10.78), an extraordinary complex of rooms, chapels, and gardens constructed entirely from broken glass by a cemetery worker; it is open between Easter and All Saints' Day; there's an admission charge. Picassiette's House is a 30-minute walk or a 5-minute taxi ride from the cathedral and is open only a few hours a week; inquire about the schedule at the tourist office in the Place de la Cathédrale (02.37.18.26.26) before you set out. Stay overnight at **Château d'Esclimont** (02.37.31.15.15), a gorgeous 16th-century castle 25 km (16 miles) from Chartres in St-Symphorien-le-Château, near Ablis. ♦ 100 km (62 miles) from Paris. Trains leave from the Gare Montparnasse; **Paris Vision** and **Cityrama** (see "Orientation" chapter) offer half-day trips.

15 VAUX-LE-VICOMTE

When Nicolas Fouquet, superintendent of finances for Louis XIV, threw a housewarming party in July 1661 to celebrate the completion of this château, he spared no expense. Molière's troupe was there to perform; the guests ate from solid-gold plates; and horses, jewels, and swords were the party favors. But this excess was not generous enough. Because he neglected to offer the château itself to the seethingly jealous king, Fouquet was thrown in prison on trumped-up charges. Louis then commandeered the architects and artisans who had built the château and put them to work on what was to be the royal palace at **Versailles**. Today, Fouquet's château—58 km (36 miles) southeast of Paris—is the largest private property in France. It's beautifully restored and generally uncrowded, and the gardens, which cover more than 125 acres, are simply stunning. Candlelight concerts of Baroque music are given on Thursday and Saturday evenings between May and mid-October. ♦ Admission. Daily Apr through 11 Nov; hours are irregular the rest of the year; for information, call 01.64.14.41.90. Rte D215 (just east of Rte N36), 5 km (3 miles) from Melun. www.vauxlevicomte.com

16 CHÂTEAU DE FONTAINEBLEAU AND BARBIZON

Newly returned from ignominious imprisonment in Spain, French King François I (who reigned between 1515 and 1547) was determined to recoup his dignity by creating a new court that would dazzle the world. He chose an old hunting lodge in the forest of Fontainebleau as its site and commanded the services of scores of Italian artists and craftsmen, who, the artist Vasari wrote, turned it into a "new Rome." Keep in mind that the château is the size of an entire town; to tour it even casually requires at least a couple of hours. And that doesn't count a tour of the **Fontainebleau Forest**, a magnificent 96-square-mile expanse of towering trees and dramatic promontories where you can ride, climb rocks, or simply walk. At one edge of the forest is the hamlet of **Barbizon**, once the hub of the pre-Impressionist movement of painting. Rousseau, Millet, Daubigny, and Corot painted here, and many of their houses and studios have been lovingly restored and opened to the public. ♦ Admission. M, W-Su. **Paris Vision** and **Cityrama** (see "Orientation" chapter) offer day-trip tours. Trains run from the Gare de Lyon station to the Fontainebleau station, where there is a bus to the palace. 66 km (41 miles) southeast of Paris. 01.60.71.50.70

17 LOIRE VALLEY

The Loire Valley would be a perfect destination for a day trip were it not for the profusion of magnificent châteaux: Two weeks spent in the valley would only begin to do it justice. Throughout the centuries, French nobles have chosen to build their country houses along this calm river with lush banks. Visit as many châteaux as you can—**Chambord, Chenonceau, Cheverny, Chinon, Loches**, and **Villandry** are particularly beautiful. But take your time, because each château warrants at least a morning of contemplation. Save your afternoons for wine tasting. For information about this region, contact **Comités Régionaux de Tourisme, Pays de Loire** (2 Rue de la Loire, 44200 Nantes; 02.40.48.24.20; www.cr-pays-de-la-loire.fr), or **Centre-Val de Loire** (9 Rue St-Pierre-Lentin, 45041 Orléans Cedex, 02.38.79.95.00, www.loirevalleytourism.com). ♦ 184 km (115 miles) from Paris to Blois; 230 km (143 miles) to Tours. Take the train to Blois or Tours and from there catch a bus to Chambord or Cheverny (two buses M, W, and F). **Paris Vision** and **Cityrama** (see "Orientation" chapter) offer day tours to Cheverny, Chenonceau, and Chambord.

300 BC   A tribe called the Parisii lives in a small settlement known as **Lutetia** on what is the modern-day **Ile de la Cité**. These early hunters and fishers are well organized; they circulate their own gold coins.

52 BC   After a fierce resistance effort during which most of their settlement is destroyed, the Parisii are conquered by the Romans. Lutetia is rebuilt and spreads out to the left bank of the **Seine**. Roman prefects rule from a compound on the site of the **Palais de la Cité**, the place from which future French kings will govern.

AD 100   Trade and fishing are the main commercial activities of Lutetia. Boatmen play a central role in government and in the thriving economy of the young town. A coat of arms bearing the likeness of a boat and representing the Boatmen's Guild becomes the official symbol of Lutetia. A similar coat of arms remains the official seal of modern Paris.

250   St. Denis (or Dionysius) leads a Christian mission to the city and establishes a community near the Seine. Twenty years later, Denis, the first bishop of what will become Paris, is killed at **Montmartre** (Martyr's Mount, or Mount of Mercury).

276   Lutetia continues to grow beyond the confines of the original settlement on Ile de la Cité, but the outlying parts of the city are vulnerable to attack by barbarians. A raid destroys the Left Bank settlements and forces the villagers to retreat to the island, where they build a fortified wall.

300   Lutetia becomes known as Paris.

450   Attila the Hun and his armies rampage through Europe and come close to taking Paris but are turned back at Orléans. The prayers of a 27-year-old nun named Geneviève are credited with halting the Huns' advance on Paris. She later becomes the female patron saint of Paris.

452   King Childebert builds a church in an open pasture on the outskirts of Paris. In later centuries, the church is repeatedly destroyed by invaders and rebuilt. The final building, erected in 1163, is named **St-Germain-des-Prés** after St. Germanus, an early bishop of the city.

476   An invading tribe of Franks, under the leadership of King Clovis, captures Paris from the Gauls, marking the end of Roman rule over Paris and the founding of France. Clovis and the Franks convert to Christianity.

508   King Clovis makes Paris the capital of his kingdom of Franks, settling in the Palais de la Cité. Thus begins the Merovingian dynasty, which will rule until the eighth century.

751   The first of the Carolingian kings assumes the French throne. The dynasty is named for Charlemagne, who went on to rule the entire Western world as head of the Holy Roman Empire. Charlemagne subsequently makes Aix-la-Chapelle (Aachen) his foremost city, and Paris declines.

885   Paris in the Middle Ages is under constant attack by roaming tribes, most notably the Normans. After decades of invasions and sieges, the Normans are defeated by Count Eudes, who is later crowned king of France.

987   Hugh Capet, a Parisian nobleman, becomes king of France and moves the throne back to Paris.

1050   King Henri I, grandson of Hugh Capet, appoints a representative called the *prévôt de Paris* (provost of Paris) to function as mayor of the city and maintain order.

1100   A marketplace in **Les Halles** appears for the first time. A permanent market is built about 80 years later and survives in the same location until 1969.

1135   The **Basilique de St-Denis** is built on the outskirts of Paris in the new Gothic style.

1163   Pope Alexander III lays the foundation stone for the cathedral of **Notre-Dame**, based on a design sketched out by Bishop Maurice de Sully. The work takes 2 centuries to complete.

1171   An ancient, loosely organized association of river merchants and fishers is formally chartered as a guild by King Louis VII. The guild receives monopoly rights to river trade, and its coat of arms is adopted by Paris as the city's official seal. The guild becomes immensely powerful.

1180   King Philip II begins an extensive building program in Paris. A 30-foot-high city wall is built and, within it, the Louvre fortress is constructed.

1190   King Philip II leaves Paris to lead a crusade. In his absence, he leaves the Boatmen's Guild, not the provost, in charge of Paris.

1215 The **University of Paris** is founded.

1220 The crown cedes to the Boatmen's Guild all tariff-collection rights, another sign of the growing power of the guilds. Paris is now clearly divided into three separate entities. The government is located on the Ile de la Cité, the **Rive Gauche** (Left Bank) is dominated by university and academic life, and the **Rive Droite** (Right Bank) is home to most commercial activity.

1239 King Louis IX purchases sacred Christian relics—including the crown of thorns and pieces of the cross—from the emperor of Constantinople and later builds the Gothic **Sainte-Chapelle** (Holy Chapel) to house them.

1253 The **Sorbonne** is founded. The world-famous university begins as lodgings for a handful of theology students. It expands quickly and, by the late 13th century, is headquarters for the University of Paris and has more than 15,000 students. (Except for a period shortly after the revolution, it has remained open continuously to the present.)

1260 Louis IX appoints the Boatmen's Guild to administer the affairs of the city. The power of the guild is beginning to threaten that of the king.

1300 The earliest surviving house in Paris is built.

1337 As France sinks into the drawn-out campaigns of the Hundred Years' War, building and expansion in Paris come to a virtual standstill.

1348 The plague, also called the Black Death, rages throughout Europe. Paris is hit particularly hard; thousands die.

1357 Etienne Marcel, leader of the Boatmen's Guild and an early mayor of Paris, leads a revolt against the young King Charles V. The king moves the royal residence to the **Marais** district. Marcel establishes a city council at the **Place de l'Hôtel-de-Ville**, site of the present seat of Paris city government. Marcel later allies himself with the British and is subsequently killed by a mob.

1364 Restored to power after the death of Marcel, King Charles V builds a new city wall around Paris.

1370 Wary of an uprising and threats against his rule by the powerful guilds, Charles V has his provost build a fortified palace called the **Bastille**. The eight-towered palace is later converted into a prison and becomes a symbol of corruption and abuse of power.

1413 Construction begins on **Pont Notre-Dame**.

1420 English armies under Henry V capture France. John Plantagenet, Duke of Bedford, is appointed regent of France. France is under British rule.

1429 Joan of Arc leads an attack on Paris in an effort to win back and liberate the city. She is wounded in the unsuccessful siege.

1431 King Henry VI of England dispenses with the regency and has himself crowned king of France in Notre-Dame Cathedral.

1437 Charles VII leads a counterattack against the British and succeeds in recapturing Paris.

1453 With the Hundred Years' War finally over, Paris can begin rebuilding after years of neglect. Recovery is slow but steady.

1510 The **Hôtel de Cluny**, originally built in 1330 but largely destroyed during the invasions, wars, and revolutions that followed, is rebuilt. (It now houses the **Musée de Cluny**.)

1527 King François I tears down most of the original structures of the **Louvre**.

1529 The prestigious **Collège de France** is founded by King François I.

1534 Ignatius Loyola and some of his followers take the vows that lead to the founding of the religious order called the Society of Jesus, whose members are known as Jesuits.

1537 A law is passed to ensure that at least one copy of every book published in France is kept in a royal library. The **Bibliothèque Nationale de France** (National Library of France) is founded.

1546 François I reestablishes Paris as the seat of royalty and commissions the building of a new Italian Renaissance palace on the grounds of the Louvre.

1559 Henri II dies of wounds received in a jousting tournament. His widow, Catherine de Médicis, has the **Maison des Tournelles** in the Marais demolished and commissions a new palace at the **Tuileries**.

1564 The **Palais des Tuileries** is completed. Designed by Philibert Delorme, it connects the two corner pavilions of the Louvre and takes its name from the *tuile* (tile) factories that had previously stood on the site. (It is razed in 1882-1884.)

1572 Charles IX orders the assassination of 3,000 Huguenots on St. Bartholomew's Day.

1578 Work starts on the **Pont-Neuf**.

1594 Henri IV converts to Catholicism, settles in Paris, and continues building and expanding the Louvre and Tuileries palaces.

1605 Henri IV commissions a new palace in the Marais district.

1610 While waiting to move into his new palace, Henri IV is killed, becoming the only king to die within the Louvre.

1612 Under Louis XIII the Marais district becomes fashionable with the aristocracy.

1616 Marie de Médicis, Henri IV's widow, orders the construction of an avenue called the **Cours la Reine** (Queen's Way).

1627 The development of **Ile St-Louis** begins.

1631 The **Palais du Luxembourg** is built for Marie de Médicis; she never actually occupies the structure.

1632 Cardinal Richelieu commissions the **Palais Cardinal** (now the **Palais Royal**).

1635 The **Institut de France**, home of the prestigious **Académie Française**, is founded.

1666 Landscaper André Le Nôtre creates a wide, tree-lined avenue dubbed the **Grand Cours**. It is later renamed the **Avenue des Champs-Elysées**.

1672 Louis XIV transfers the court to Versailles. Most of the aristocracy follows.

1676 The **Hôtel des Invalides** is founded by Louis XIV to shelter several thousand veterans, most destitute.

1685 The **Place Vendôme** is built as a setting for a monument to Louis XIV. During the revolution, the monument is destroyed and the heads of victims of the guillotine are displayed on spikes, giving it the temporary name **Place des Piques** (Pike Square).

1718 The **Palais de l'Elysée** is built. Since 1873, it has been the official residence of the French president.

1728 The **Palais Bourbon** is constructed by the duchess of Bourbon, one of Louis XIV's daughters. Today it houses the Assemblée Nationale, the lower house of the French Parliament.

1744 Louis XV vows to build a temple dedicated to St. Geneviève if he recovers from an illness. He does recover and builds the **Panthéon**, which later becomes a necropolis for France's distinguished atheists, among them Voltaire, Rousseau, and Hugo.

1755 Louis XV commissions a large square beside the Seine as the site for an equestrian statue of himself. The resulting 21-acre **Place de la Concorde** is the largest square in Paris.

1786 The remains of the dead from the **Cimetière des Innocents** are moved to the **Catacombs**.

1789 A mob storms the Bastille prison on 14 July, captures the ammunition depot, releases the half-dozen prisoners kept there, kills the warden, and destroys the fortress. The French Revolution has begun.

1792 The **Comédie Française**, France's most prestigious theater troupe, moves into a new theater at the **Palais Royal**.

1793 A bloodthirsty mob takes over Paris and conducts a massacre of former government officials. Louis XVI is guillotined in the Place de la Concorde. During the next 13 months the Reign of Terror kills thousands, most executed at the guillotine.

1804 Napoléon crowns himself emperor in a ceremony at Notre-Dame.

1806 On Napoléon's orders, work commences on the **Arc de Triomphe**. The structure is not completed until 1836, well after Napoléon's downfall.

1841 The church of **Ste-Marie Madeleine**, better known as **La Madeleine**, is consecrated.

1848 The revolutionary fervor spreading throughout Europe is especially strong in Paris. The monarchy is overthrown once and for all.

1850 Baron Haussmann begins a series of public works projects and restorations that over the next 2 decades completely transform Paris.

1860 The City of Paris expands its boundaries by annexing outlying villages, including Montmartre.

1870 The Franco-Prussian War brings an end to a period of growth and prosperity. The population starves during the Siege of Paris, and the Paris Commune is suppressed. The Palais des Tuileries and the Hôtel de Ville are virtually destroyed.

1875 The **Opéra Garnier**, also known as the **Paris Opéra**, opens. Designed by Charles

Garnier, the opulent Second Empire structure is for a time the largest theater in the world.

1876   Work commences on the **Basilique du Sacré-Coeur** in Montmartre. Construction will take decades.

1889   Amidst considerable controversy and opposition, the **Tour Eiffel** (Eiffel Tower), designed by Gustave Eiffel, is built for the Exposition Universelle (International Exhibition). It later becomes the most widely recognized symbol of Paris.

1900   The first underground railway line in Paris (the métro) opens. The **Grand Palais**, **Petit Palais**, and **Pont Alexandre III** are built for the Exposition Universelle. The city enjoys a period of commercial and artistic growth known as the Belle Epoque.

1914   During World War I, Paris is saved from a German invasion by the Battle of the Marne.

1920   **Montparnasse** replaces Montmartre as the center of artistic life in the city.

1937   The **Palais de Chaillot** is built for another Exposition Universelle. The structure houses four museums, two theaters, a library, and a restaurant.

1940   In the early days of World War II, the city is bombed. But France falls quickly and occupation rather than destruction follows.

1944   Paris is liberated by the Allies. General Charles de Gaulle leads a victory parade down the Champs-Elysées.

1950   Existentialism is in full bloom, and its major proponents, Jean-Paul Sartre and Albert Camus, are the intellectual stars of Europe. Paris is once again a center of intellectual fervor.

1962   **The Mémorial de la Déportation** (Deportation Memorial) opens, commemorating the thousands of French, mostly Jews, who died during the Holocaust.

1968   Student demonstrations in the **Latin Quarter** and violent labor disputes throughout the city threaten to topple the government.

1977   Much like the Eiffel Tower of the last century, the **Centre Georges Pompidou** opens to a critical outcry. It quickly becomes the most popular tourist destination in Paris.

1985   The **Musée Picasso** opens and becomes an immediate hit.

1986   The **Musée d'Orsay**, a showcase for 19th-century art and culture, is unveiled.

1988   The renovation of the Les Halles district is completed.

1989   As the bicentennial of the fall of the Bastille is celebrated, a new addition to the Louvre is greeted with tremendous criticism. Designed by American architect I. M. Pei, the project includes a 70.5-foot glass pyramid. Again, the critics are silenced by enormous crowds of visitors.

1992   The inaugural performance is held at the new **Opéra Bastille**. The huge new opera house revitalizes the Bastille area.

1995   Socialist President François Mitterrand's 14-year term comes to an end. Conservative leader Jacques Chirac, former mayor of Paris, is elected president of the republic.

1996   President Jacques Chirac declares the banning of nuclear tests in the South Pacific.

Writer Marguerite Duras dies at age 81. Author of more than 70 books, she is most famous for *The Lover*.

1997   After dissolution of the Assemblée Nationale by President Jacques Chirac, the Socialist Party obtains the majority vote, and Lionel Jospin is named prime minister.

Europepride 97, a gay and lesbian rights landmark event, takes place in Paris.

Diana, Princess of Wales, is killed in a car accident near the Ritz.

1998   The French national football (soccer) team wins the World Cup at the Stade de France in the northern suburbs.

High school students stage massive nationwide demonstrations to protest overcrowding and poor funding of schools.

1999   Along with 10 other members of the European Community, France adopts the euro as its official currency.

2000   The French National soccer team wins the European Cup.

2001   In the municipal elections in March, Paris elects its first Socialist mayor, Bertrand Delanoë.

INDEX

RESTAURANTS

Only restaurants with star ratings are listed below. All restaurants are listed alphabetically in the main (preceding) index. Always call in advance to ensure a restaurant has not closed, changed its hours, or booked its tables for a private party. The restaurant price ratings are based on the average cost of an entrée for one person, excluding tax and tip.

★★★★	An Extraordinary Experience
★★★	Excellent
★★	Very Good
★	Good

$$$$	Big Bucks ($120 and up)
$$$	Expensive ($70–$120)
$$	Reasonable ($25–$70)
$	The Price Is Right (less than $25)

★★★★

Arpège $$$$ **135**
Guy Savoy $$$$ **141**
L'Ambrosie $$$$ **243**
La Tour d'Argent $$$$ **54**
Le Cinq $$$$ **153**
Le Grand Véfour $$$$ **216**
Le Jules Verne $$$$ **122**
Le Pré Catelan $$$ **285**
Lucas Carton $$$$ **190**
Pierre Gagnaire $$$$ **145**
Restaurant Plaza Athénée $$$$ **160**
Taillevent $$$$ **142**

★★★

A. Beauvilliers $$$ **267**
Angélina $$ **159**
Atelier Maître Albert $$ **47**

HOTELS

The hotels listed below are grouped according to their price ratings; they are also listed in the main index. The hotel price ratings reflect the base price of a standard room for two people for one night during the peak season.

$$$$	Big Bucks ($300 and up)
$$$	Expensive ($150–$300)
$$	Reasonable ($75–$150)
$	The Price Is Right (less than $75)

$$$$

$$$

REDITS

ter and Researcher
the Ninth Edition

hony Lechtman

torial Director

vin Tan

ket Design

n-Yee Lai

ign Director

h Carlson-Stanisic

ign Supervisor

ola Ferguson

Map Designer

Patricia Keelin

Associate Director of Production

Dianne Pinkowitz

Senior Production Editor

Mareike Paessler

The publisher and authors assume no legal responsiblity for the completeness or accuracy of the contents of this book nor any legal responsibility for the appreciation or depreciation in the value of any premises, commercial or otherwise, by reason of inclusion in or exclusion from this book. All contents are based on information available at the time of publication. Some of the maps are diagrammatic and may be selective of street inclusion.

ACCESS® PRESS does not solicit individuals, organizations, or businesses for inclusion in our books, nor do we accept payment for inclusion. We welcome, however, information from our readers, including comments, criticisms, and suggestions for new listings. Send all correspondence to: ACCESS® PRESS, 10 East 53rd Street, New York, NY 10022.

PRINTED IN HONG KONG

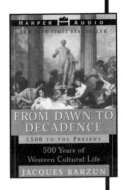